As expounded by the
Gnani Purush "Dada Bhagwan"

# Pratikraman

## The Key that resolves all conflicts

Originally Compiled in Gujarati by :

## Dr. Niruben Amin

**Publisher :** **Mr. Ajit C. Patel**
**Mahavideh Foundation**
Tri-Mandir, Simandhar City,
Ahmedabad-Kalol Highway, Adalaj,
Dist.-Gandhinagar-382421,
Gujarat, India.
**Tel. :** +91 79 39830100, 23974100
**E-Mail :** info@dadabhagwan.org

©      : All Rights Reserved Mr. Deepakbhai Desai
Tri-Mandir, Simandhar City, Adalaj-382421
Dist.-Gandhinagar-, Gujarat, India.

**Edition** : 2000 copies,      June 2010

**Price**     : Ultimate Humality
(leads to Universal oneness) and
Awareness of "I Don't Know Anything"

**MRP** ₹ 150 )

**Printer**   : Mahavideh Foundation (Printing Division),
Basement, Parshwanath Chambers,
Nr. RBI, Usmanpura,
Ahmedabad-380014
Gujarat, India.
Tel. : +91 79 27542964 / 30004823

# Trimantra

## The Three Mantras that Destroy All Obstacles in Life
*(Recite this mantra five times every morning and night)*

### Namo Vitaragaya
I bow to the One who is absolutely free from all attachment and abhorrence

### Namo Arihantanam
I bow to the living One who has annihilated all internal enemies of anger, pride, deceit and greed

### Namo Siddhanam
I bow to the Ones who have attained the state of total and final liberation

### Namo Aayariyanam
I bow to the Self-realized masters who impart knowledge of liberation to others

### Namo Uvazzayanam
I bow to those who have received the Knowledge of the Self and are helping others attain the same

### Namo Loye Savva Sahunam
I bow to all saints everywhere who have received the Knowledge of the Self

### Eso Pancha Namukkaro
These five salutations

### Savva Pavappanasano
Destroy all demerit karma

### Mangalanam cha Savvesim
Of all that is auspicious

### Padhamam Havai Mangalam
This is the highest

### Om Namo Bhagavate Vasudevaya
I bow to all who have attained the absolute Self in human form

### Om Namah Shivaya
I bow to all human beings who have become instruments for salvation of the world

### Jai Sat Chit Anand
Awareness of the Eternal is Bliss

\*\*\*\*\*

# Note About This Translation

The Gnani Purush Ambalal M. Patel, also commonly known as Dadashri or Dada, had said that it would be impossible to translate his satsangs and the knowledge about the Science of Self-Realization verbatim into English because some of the meanings would be lost in the process. Therefore, in order to understand precisely the science of Akram Vignan and Self-Realization He stressed the importance of learning Gujarati.

Dadashri did however grant his blessings to translate his words into English and other languages so that spiritual seekers could benefit to a certain degree and later progress through their own efforts.

This is a humble attempt to present to the world, the essence of His Knowledge. This is not a literal translation but great care has been taken to preserve His original words and the essence of His message. For certain Gujarati words, several English words or even sentences are needed to convey the exact meaning; hence, many Gujarati words have been retained within the English text for better reading flow. At the first encounter, the Gujarati word will be italicized followed by an immediate explanation of its meaning in brackets. Thereafter the Gujarati word will be used in the text that follows. This serves as a two-fold benefit: firstly ease of translation and reading and secondly it will make the reader more familiar with the Gujarati words critical for a deeper understanding of this science. A glossary of all the Gujarati words is provided at the back of the book. For additional glossary, visit our website at :

**www.dadabhagwan.org**

Many people have worked diligently towards achieving this goal and we thank them all. Please note that any errors encountered in this translation are entirely those of the translators.

*****

4

# Introduction to The Gnani

One June evening, in 1958 at around six o'clock, Ambalal Muljibhai Patel, a family man, and a contractor by profession, was sitting on a bench on the busy platform number three at Surat's train station. Surat is a city in south Gujarat, a western state in India. What happened within the next forty-eight minutes was phenomenal. Spontaneous Self-Realization occurred within Ambalal M. Patel. During this event, his ego completely melted and from that moment onwards, he became completely detached from all of Ambalal's thoughts, speech, and actions. He became the Lord's living instrument for the salvation of humankind, through the path of knowledge. He called this Lord, 'Dada Bhagwan.' To everyone he met, he would say, "This Lord, Dada Bhagwan is fully manifested within me. He also resides within all living beings. The difference is that within me He is completely expressed and in you, he has yet to manifest."

Who are we? What is God? Who runs this world? What is karma? What is liberation? Etc. All the world's spiritual questions were answered during this event. Thus, nature offered absolute vision to the world through the medium of Shree Ambalal Muljibhai Patel.

Ambalal was born in Tarasali, a suburb of Baroda and was later raised in Bhadran, Gujarat. His wife's name was Hiraba. Although he was a contractor by profession, his life at home and his interactions with everyone around him were exemplary, even prior to his Self-Realization. After becoming Self-Realized and attaining the state of a Gnani, (The Awakened One, Jnani in Hindi), his body became a 'public charitable trust.'

Throughout his entire life, he lived by the principle that there should not be any commerce in religion, and in all commerce, there must be religion. He also never took money from anyone for his own use. He used the profits from his business to take his devotees for pilgrimages to various parts of India.

5

His words became the foundation for the new, direct, and step-less path to Self-Realization called Akram Vignan. Through his divine original scientific experiment (The Gnan Vidhi), he imparted this knowledge to others within two hours. Thousands have received his grace through this process and thousands continue to do so even now. 'Akram' means without steps; an elevator path or a shortcut, whereas 'Kram' means an orderly, step-by-step spiritual path. Akram is now recognized as a direct shortcut to the bliss of the Self.

## Who is Dada Bhagwan?

When he explained to others who 'Dada Bhagwan' is, he would say :

"What you see here is not 'Dada Bhagwan'. What you see is 'A. M. Patel.' I am a Gnani Purush and 'He' that is manifested within me, is 'Dada Bhagwan'. He is the Lord within. He is within you and everyone else. He has not yet manifested within you, whereas within me he is fully manifested. I myself am not a Bhagwan. I too bow down to Dada Bhagwan within me."

## Current link for attaining the knowledge of Self-Realization (Atma Gnan)

"I am personally going to impart siddhis (special spiritual powers) to a few people. After I leave, will there not be a need for them? People of future generations will need this path, will they not?"
~ Dadashri

Param Pujya Dadashri used to go from town to town, and country to country, to give satsang and impart the knowledge of the Self as well as knowledge of harmonious worldly interaction to all who came to see him. During his final days, in the fall of 1987, he gave his blessing to Dr. Niruben Amin and bestowed his special siddhis upon her, to continue his work. "You will have to become a mother to this whole world, Niruben" He told her as he blessed her. There was no doubt in Dadashri's mind that Niruben was destined to be just that. She had served him with utmost devotion day and night for over twenty years. Dadashri in turn had molded her and prepared her to take on this monumental task.

From the time of Pujya Dadashri's mortal departure on January 2 1988 to her own mortal departure on March 19th 2006, Pujya Niruma as she lovingly came to be called by thousands remained true to her promise to Dadashri to carry on his mission of the world's salvation. She became Dadashri's representative of Akram Vignan and became instrumental in spreading the knowledge of Akram Vignan throughout the world. She also became an exemplary of pure and unconditional love. Thousands of people from all walks of life and from all over the world have attained Self-Realization through her and are established in the experience of the pure Soul, while carrying out their worldly duties and obligations. They experience freedom here and now, while living their daily life.

The link of Akram Gnanis now continues with the current spiritual master Pujya Deepakbhai Desai whom Pujya Dadashri had also graced with special siddhis to continue to teach the world about Atma Gnan and Akram Vignan. He was further molded and trained by Pujya Niruma who blessed him to conduct Gnan Vidhi in 2003. Dadashri had said that Deepakbhai will become the decorum that will add splendor to the Lord's reign. Pujya Deepakbhai, in keeping with Dada's and Niruma's tradition travels extensively within India and abroad, giving satsangs and imparting the knowledge of the Self to all who come seeking.

Powerful words in scriptures help the seeker in increasing his desire for liberation. The knowledge of the Self is the final goal of all one's seeking. Without the knowledge of the Self there is no liberation. This knowledge of the Self (Atma Gnan) does not exist in books. It exists in the heart of a Gnani. Hence, the knowledge of the Self can only be acquired by meeting a Gnani. Through the scientific approach of Akram Vignan, even today one can attain Atma Gnan, but it can only occur by meeting a living Atma Gnani and receiving the Atma Gnan. Only a lit candle can light another candle.

7

# EDITORIAL

Should there not be some unfailing remedy for those who are sincerely trying to move forward along the path of liberation? There should be some remedy to successfully remove all *kashays* (internal anger, pride, deceit, greed, attachment and abhorrence) that hinder people every moment of their lives. How is one to remove the gross and subtle conflict from his life? How do we prevent ourselves from being hurt or hurting others? How can we shelter ourselves from the *kashays* that bombard us? How do we stop them from recurring?

Many of us have faithfully adhered to religious rituals. We have surrendered ourselves to strict penance, fasting, meditation and other such austerities, only to discover that we still make mistakes through our mind, our speech and our conduct. Why have we not found inner peace? What should we do when we realize our faults and how should we get rid of them? There should be some method through which we can eliminate *kashays* from our lives and progress spiritually towards liberation. Surely there should be a way to live happily with peace and love. What spiritual knowledge have the *Vitarag* Lords (the supreme enlightened Beings) bestowed upon the world? What is true religion? Is there any assurance that one can be absolved for the sins he commits? And if there *is* such a method, why is it not evident?

One can attain an abundance of knowledge from scriptures, but why can he not incorporate it into his daily life? Ascetics and spiritual teachers continue to preach, but where do they fall short in getting the desired results? Practically every religion mandates stringent rituals and austerities, yet why does the aspirant not achieve any results? Why do his *kashays* not decrease or his sins erase? Does the liability for all this not fall upon the heads of religion? This statement is not made with any malice, but with compassion. There should be some way to eliminate our

8

problems. What have the Gnanis and the *Tirthankars* said about one's progress from the state of ignorance to the attainment of Absolute Knowledge (*Keval Gnan*)? How can we be liberated from the bondage of our past karma, and the bondage created through our inherent attachment and abhorrence (*raag-dwesh*)?

It is said that the path of liberation is for the brave and not for cowards, but where should this valor be used to expedite liberation? Is it possible for a person with a lot of bad karma to attain good karma?

How can you suppress the fires of suffering that torment you throughout your life? How can a man cope with a domineering wife, difficult children and his financial worries that overshadow his peace, day and night?

How can one recover from incessant *kashays* that exist between a guru and a disciple? When a person expends his mind, speech and body by committing adultery or cheating others out of their wealth, where else but in hell or lower life forms can he expect to take birth in his next life? And if one has done so, how can he become free from the consequences of his actions? How can one remain cautious so as to not fall prey to such acts? What are the answers to such questions that have agonized people for time immemorial?

Every human makes mistakes against his will. People become trapped in their own mistakes and suffer incessantly due to their earnest desire to be free of such mistakes, find inner happiness and progress towards their liberation.

The *Tirthankars* and the Gnanis have given this world the only weapon to combat such suffering, and that weapon is the spiritual science of *alochana* (confession of one's mistakes), *pratikraman* (asking for forgiveness), and *pratyakhyan* (firm resolve and determination never to repeat the mistake). Infinite beings have achieved the wealth of liberation with this weapon by destroying the very root from which a vast tree of hatred and abhorrence grows. Gnani Purush, Dada Bhagwan, through his *Keval Gnan* (Absolute Enlightenment) expounded in his spoken words the science of *pratikraman*, precisely as it is. His spoken words are to be found in this book, along with many other books; words which will prove invaluable to the aspirant of truth and liberation.

The speech of the Gnani is dependent upon the individual that he is addressing. The answers the Gnani gives are aimed to bring about a solution for a specific problem for an individual in front of him. Therefore, at times these spoken words, when compiled in book form, may appear contradictory. For instance, for the inner satisfaction of one individual the Gnani may say, '*Pratikraman* is awareness and *atikraman* is discharge (of karma).' But for the individual with heightened inner awareness, the Gnani may say, '*Atikraman* is discharge, and so is *pratikraman*. Discharge has to be destroyed by discharge.' Both the answers are correct as a solution for the particular individual concerned, but they are relatively contradictory because of the difference in predicaments of each individual concerned. In short, the reader is asked to understand the subtleties of the Gnani.

With this in mind, we beseech the reader's forgiveness for any apparent flaws in this compilation. It is our sincere hope that the reader attains the inner essence of the Gnani's words.

**- Dr. Niruben Amin**

# PREFACE

*Please note that Pujya Dr. Niruben Amin wrote the entire preface of the Pratikraman Book in poetry form in couplets. The translation of this in English is devoid of the rhyming words in many places. Here is the message of the preface is preserved as a preference over the rhyming words.*

# PART 1

## PRATIKRAMAN

Unity of mind speech and body, is the worthy goal of life;
When that is broken, Akram Vignani's pratikraman is the solution in life!

Dada shows the proper method of doing pratikraman;
Connect directly with the Soul of the other, with 'Dada Bhagwan' as the witness!

Announce the faults in your heart, ask for forgiveness, repent heartily;
Decide that 'I won't repeat it', then the faults are cleansed simply!

Doing good karma is religion, doing bad karma is non-religion;
Beyond religion and non-religion, lies Self-religion!

Good karma gives credit and this brings the result as happiness;
Bad karma gives debit and this brings the result as unhappiness!

When 'credit-debit' is zero, Self-bliss prevails;
The first two increase worldly entanglements, the third brings Liberation!

With the 'Lord within—Dada Bhagwan' as witness, repentance is done heartily;
This science becomes effective, for every ailment there is a remedy!

While eating-drinking, bathing-walking, speaking-laughing;
If no one is hurt, these natural interactions are called 'kraman'!

All that cause hurt to others through attachment-abhorrence, are atikraman;
To turn back from these is known as the process of pratikraman!

Anger-pride-deceit and greed, all are nothing but atikraman;
They all go away instantly, when for them you do pratikraman!

Atikraman through attachment-abhorrence affects both;
By doing pratikraman for them, the effect is resolved in both!

A stained cloth and its washer, there is trouble for both;
Kraman affects no one and everyone acts in natural mode!

Every embodied Soul routinely projects endlessly;
Mere hearing of communal riots, third world war is imagined!

Innumerable fractions exist in one second where one does endless atikramans;
Atikraman creates worldly life and it comes to the end by pratikraman!

If the insulter is seen as wrongdoer, that is atikraman;
If speech was harsh, act was wrong, that too is atikraman!

If the children are beaten, that is atikraman;
Feeling, 'why did he swear at me?' is also atikraman!

If anyone feels hurt by you, it is atikraman;
Remember Dada there, and do instant pratikraman!

No intent is there at all in your heart to hurt the other person;
Yet you are instrumental in the hurt, hence Dada gave this great discourse!

If one is hurt with or without your knowledge, this is atikraman;
If his face doesn't show but mind was disturbed, this too is atikraman!

Any embodied Soul hurt through mind-speech-body;
Instantly, heartily and certainly, do its' pratikraman properly!

What decreases karma's load is religion and what increases it is non-religion;
No new karma is bound by doing pratikraman and that is supreme religion!

Ask for energy to advance higher, pray heartily;
Pray to Gnani, Self, guru, God's idol or a deity!

Shout out for forgiveness for the purpose of cleansing faults;
Small faults will be gone and Samayik will dissolve the knots!

How can there be freedom from sinful karma of endless times?
This happens when one inscribes Gnani's knowledge to heart!

If this is not available, find what is revealed in the scriptures;
Revealed creates intellect-wisdom that annuls sinful karma!

12

A strong desire to annul sinful karma and to do pratikraman;
Shall free one from weight of sins of endless lives!

Injustice in personal or business, what is its' penance?
Decide in front of God-'I don't ever want to do it again'!

Innate self's mistakes from previous life hurt at present;
Get bliss of Freedom when, with equanimity you accept!

Endure with gratitude, all the pains that others give;
Doing Dada-given pratikraman, puzzles you shall leave!

Scientific method of Jains, of recall-repentance-resolve;
Other religions too, give top priority to similar resolve!

Perfection and thoroughness, imparts this Vitarag Science;
Takes practical religion to top, and grants religious contemplation!

Helping climb upward steps, pratikraman grants absolute contemplation;
Tirthankar Lords convey perfect religion of the Self and of worldly interaction!

Dadashri explains the essence of recall-repentance-resolve;
In front of Gnani or Guru, admit the faults of the self!

Free of fear and with decisive mind; hand over charge to guru;
And awaken easily again when you do pratikraman given by guru!

To be free from karma, paramount weapon is pratikraman;
Progress without guru by doing Dada-given pratikraman!

Excess pain is in chanting-penance-fasting; meditation and yoga;
Only pratikraman is savior, it shall definitely give you moksha!

Repentance frees from sins, gives a sacred-state;
Repent repeatedly in front of God and ask for forgiveness!

Repentance done by a person is always from the heart and natural;
'Pratikraman frees from karma' is the law that is natural!

To heartily ask for pardon of faults is the way to freedom;
Even if not heartily done, it preserves goodness for the self!

If you have to drink alcohol, apologize with decision of wanting to quit;
One day it shall be quit, is the scientific exactness!

This is 'Akram Vignan'; it has got to give result;
Moksha in two hours, hear Gnani's Gnan -Agna!

Subtle pain inflicted to someone, that too is called atikraman;
You may be aware or not, instantly do pratikraman!

That which is done voluntarily is where one can 'do' purusharth -self effort;
That which is done due to pressure of forces is mandatory and is karma effect!

Doing is mandatory; like-dislike is voluntary;
Facing insult is mandatory; pratikraman is voluntary!

Ignorant one has free will to do repentance and resolve;
When stealing-killing pleases; a huge tuber of sin is formed!

Sensualist's thoughtful pratikraman results in celibacy;
Purity from hearty pratikraman then rests on Dada!

Pratikraman and Trimantra done together certainly give the result;
Prayer to great Gods and freedom from sinful karma is the result!

Endless pratikramans have shown no result yet, why?
Not one was with 'shoot-on-sight' knowledge, that's why!

Pratikraman done in morning and evening, but mechanically;
Pratikraman without repentance, pratikraman it can't be!

What was memorized is spoken daily, just like a record;
Not finding the real culprit, he hurts the person in front!

Not a single mistake is absolved, whole life he did;
Pratikraman like a parrot; Mahavir's path it can't be!

Pratikraman in Maagdhi language isn't understood very well;Ascetics and
saints say, 'I did' and raise the egoism as well!

Mahavir's so called followers 'perverse and insensitive', without exception;
Believe that Self resides in rituals; leaving no space for complaint!

Disciples of middle twenty-two Tirthankars, proficient they were;
Alert at every moment each day, they did pratikraman everywhere!

If you ask the meaning of daily pratikraman, they know it not;
Annual pratikraman of Samvatsari, sins will not wash!

14

On Paryushan, see whole year's sins, feel the heartache;
You feel like dying that day, alas! How people were hurt!

Did you ever have these feelings, or simply got dressed and jeweled up;
Like going to a wedding on the Paryushan day, formal and smug!

'Forgive my bad actions'-to those they like, no remorse for all others;
You've ruined Vitarag Gods' reputation; this isn't Mahavir's religion!

In true Vitarag religion, five hundred pratikramans are done daily;
It is done 'shoot-on-sight' and with repentance nightly and daily!

This is Mahavir's reign and 'Gnani' is ornamental to the reign;
In Kali-Kaal, Kramic path stagnant; Akram moksha unveiled through 'Us'!

With instant-cash pratikraman, adverse mediation vanishes;
Where Akram Gnani has manifested, 'Godly state' is attained with ease!

Pratikraman's purpose is fulfilled, be it credit karma or freedom;
Whether done in ignorance or knowledge, it is the main support!

Self-knowledge is freedom-path and not pratikraman alone;
Pratikraman after Self-awareness starts You on to Liberation!

After the illusion-I am Chandulal- is gone, bondage of karma stops;
With the illusion, pratikraman is for recurrent cycles of dirtying and cleansing!

Pratikraman is recommended, do it 'shoot-on-sight';
If you can't do that- next is- do it morning and night!

Can't do this, do it fortnightly, or every four months;
Once a year if nothing else, if no mother aunt will do!

Even aunt isn't real in this Kali-Kaal, she is like a hired one;
Where's moksha? Where's religion? It is only the egoism's illusion!

Doer or helper, pratikraman should be done proper;
Created are decorative words, intents are forgotten!

Atikraman is at every step, yet the remedy is pratikraman;
In the realm of the Vitarag there is no secret or corruption!

You do pratikraman for the dead and not for the living;
Bhaav-pratikramans are true; wrong are those with words and rituals!

Those won't have proper result, its' true value is illusory;
Believed as Self's benefit; its' a loss and not a victory!

To recite like a parrot is effect-dravya pratikraman;
'It shouldn't be so' intent- is called as bhaav-pratikraman!

If chain of life after life mistakes isn't broken, it isn't 'Samvatsari' of Mahavir;
They're ineffective pratikramans and they disgrace Lord Mahavir!

Please forgive me readers but my heart is getting filled;
I do pratikraman for the strong words that were scribed!

Action with 'I am the doer' casts more veils of illusion, eludes liberation;
Chanting in AM and PM he drinks the ointment, meant to be applied!

Vows of Kramic path to eat no root vegetables or at night;
Taken without understanding, vows won't help in Liberation!

Vows can be taken for only faults whose pratikraman was done;
Explanation of proper pratikraman, Akram Vignan has done!

To cleanse the blemish, ascetics apply soap on the table;
Followers scrub the floor; world laughs at this!

They take vows to renounce and slowly they can quit it;
But vow to renounce what is quit, how can one deal with such understanding?

For all atikramans done through acts, pratikraman must be done in Kramic;
In Akram Path, body is separate from the Self; no action will touch!

Credit and debit karma get cleansed by doing pratikraman;
For moksha, both types of karma are renounced and the Self is acquired!

Without awareness, pratikraman 'shoot-on-sight' can't be done;
After 'Gnani' awakens the Self, the kite string stays in hand!

Pratikraman in ignorant state binds less sins;
After Self-vision, with awareness, it is done in the true form!

Wash and wear clothes daily, write account book daily;
When pratikraman done yearly then; why not wash clothes yearly?

Gnani too, after scolding someone, does pratikraman right away;
This is just natural evidence and here, no one's fault is at play!

16

And yet He says 'is' to what 'is'; and 'isn't' to what 'isn't';
How can a true Gnani say to what 'is' as what 'isn't'?

In the Vision the world is flawless but the speech finds the faults;
Gnani Himself does pratikraman for pain caused by truth!

Fault is seen because of fault in the self; purify your vision there;
Or else, kashays will arise, when you fight for relative truth!

Accepted by plaintiff and defendant, is the speech of Vitarags;
Call it open Saraswati; their ego-less words are accepted by all!

Talk that doesn't include pure Soul is false, that's for sure;
Pratikraman for 'I am Chandu', a measure of true understanding for sure!

Forcing the medicine on patient, the doctor may appear harsh;
Ailment may get cured or not, do pratikraman for being harsh!

'Dada' is doctor of religion; He swings the whip at the ascetics;
Elegance of Gnani's silence, flows as compassion towards the wrong!

Having missed non-violent speech, Gnani does pratikraman;
Faulty it is in speech, flawless in His vision!

Tirthankars' speech is always accepted by all totally and completely;
Fourteenth moon is 'Akram Gnani', difference in opinion and speech!

Faulty was the perverse vision; 'Dada' charged such a speech;
Flawless is today's vision and yet flows out such a speech!

Guru says, 'I am untouched' but is exposed when called a 'fool';
He is touched and he reacts, is that religion a gymnast's pool?

Vows-chants-penance and discipline in practice give worldly rewards;
They are not needed for liberation; there, only pratikraman works!

Ascetics should routinely ask for forgiveness an hour a day;
It's true religion even if it is done in mind and not in person!

True religions are only two, Pratikraman and absence of kashays;
Rest is not necessary, world hasn't followed 'this' core-religion!

When you follow Gnani's words, you'll reach liberation-gate;
Go ahead, Dada is responsible for you, don't miss at any rate!

Insistence is great atikraman, it has ruined the country;
It has poisoned internally; this hatred must be ousted!

They command in Kramic path, don't steal, lie, or do wrong;
Scriptures shout to follow non-violence, truth, non-theft!

Scriptures people have put away with frown on their face;
Scriptures don't bring change in life, why should one attach 'this' trouble?

'I want to do it but can't', one should never sing this song;
Say, 'why not' firmly and decide repeatedly to perform!

Stealing-lying happened but do pratikraman for that;
Behavior can never change so, understanding you can change!

All the world's religions are on 'I am the body';
Only Akram Vignan is free of 'I am the body'!

'I want to give up' or 'I can't give up', both are states of doership;
Are you able to empty your bowels at will? What is the limit of your ability?

If you want to act with doership, ask for energy for sure;
Dada's 'Nine Kalams' change causes, the effect does not!

You are infinite energy; 'energy-less' how can you ever say?
Pratikraman is also the self-effort that is done in illusory state!

Even saints-devotees in the country are unaware in the spiritual song;
They say 'I did' to 'It happens' and say 'do what I say' to the 'top'!

If you do something wrong, correct it by doing pratikraman;
It's called illusory self-effort; become a non-doer if you want to be eternal!

You are not the doer of anything; You are only the Knower;
Knower and doer are different, so the action in this life cannot change!

Know the wrong one as wrong; change 'his' opinion;
That verily is the religion of true effort; 'see' and 'know' and make 'him' decide!

'I can't do, brother, I can't'; you should never say this;
Soul's nature is, you become what You envision!

This matter is very subtle, you can't resolve without understanding;
Only Gnani can differentiate the realm of the Self and the non-Self!

To reform a boy thief, you can't punish or beat him up;
He'll form wrong tuber and opinion to steal will strengthen!

Asking for energy from Dada, 'I won't steal in this lifetime';
Dada will give shelter and pure love; his heart will change!

If you've stolen, ask for energy; ask for specific energy;
Remedy is change of opinion, absolute humility to God!

'Gnani' has all the remedies and his diagnosis is accurate;
'Dada Bhagwan' is the scientist; expose to Him your ailments!

Ask for energy and you shall get it one day, don't doubt;
Hence He gave Nine Kalams filled with secret of Vignan!

In Akram, don't see conduct, dispose it all with Gnan;
New adverse internal meditation ceases, old ones are 'seen' and cleared!

Spirituality means purifying of chit, impure chit binds karma;
Not hurting any embodied Soul, this pure interaction is religion!

No new karma shall bind the mahatmas of this Akram way;
They clear old karmas and follow five Agnas all day!

When facing sticky karmas, dissolve them with pratikraman;
One life to go with this knowledge that guarantees no new karma!

Do pratikraman as soon as atikraman or attack happens;
Valiance here is wonderful! One enjoys the Absolute Self!

'Kraman' created prakruti and Atikraman has expanded it;
Pratikraman diminishes it and Akram Gnan has explained it!

Don't have a single bad feeling for a thief or a prostitute;
They don't wish to do bad but are trapped in circumstances!

An ignorant person sees others' faults, his own faults he can never see;
How can he judge when he is the criminal, the lawyer and the judge!

Even the ignorant person does pratikraman up to a certain degree;
Some proficient and vigilant people have repented and released faults!

After becoming pure Soul, is pratikraman worth doing for him?
In Akram, he has to do this because the other person does get hurt!

Despite doing pratikraman if the other person doesn't forgive;
Have no impact of this, You shall get freedom from faults!

Opponents of Atikraman make their presence known through pratikraman;
Disagree with faults and get freedom from faulty nature!

All faults are to be settled and they are not 'My' intents;
Pratikraman isn't necessary here if one can remain that aware!

All the worldly interactions without atikraman are naturally settled;
Pratikraman for atikraman will dispose both the inner and the outer!

True pratikraman is the one that when done reduces faults;
How can there be liberation if there is no reduction in faults?

Pratikraman cleanses and there is no malice in others then;
No divisive difference of minds and intact are the relations with them!

Mind becomes pure and clean as proof of cleansing of sins;
Happiness is evident on the face, and light as a feather you feel!

'Chandu, it is your mistake' when someone says this to you;
Tell Chandu, 'Chandu, your mistake maybe there', hence the rebuke'!

The boss should never see the under-hand's faults;
With police, judge or wife, why does he remain so meek?

Delay in doing pratikraman, do pratikraman for that too;
Mind wanders during Arati or Vidhi, for this inertia too!

To err is human nature, the way to be free from this err;
Only the Gnani shows it, 'Do pratikraman, O, lucky one'!

Cause of fault is interference of the self; others have no concern;
The one who pays heed, stops the faults and binds no karma!

Akram Gnan manifests pragnya; pratikraman is automatic;
His state is free from abhorrence, like God, who has no egoism!

'No hurt' is Lord Mahavir's word, do pratikraman for 'hurting';
You should get resolution or disposal; this life isn't for fighting!

No such vision of faults is with Kramic path Gnani;
Look at the awareness of the one on Akram path; pratikraman is at every step!

Pratikraman is not needed if good qualities are seen in others;
Good behavior with them is the only inner intent of ours!

Egoism supports self's faults and takes the side of the self;
Even the great sages are seen wedded to the egoism!

When the prices go up in business and customer is unhappy;
Don't risk Self-realization; see the doer to be the 'Vyavasthit'!

How has Dada placed us in Akram state while doing all our karma?
'Vyavasthit' controls this life and yet pratikraman frees from karma!

Look at Akram's ultimate principle, it follows not the intellect;
It answers from all angles and brings the fool on the path!

If the black-marketer of this time understands 'Vyavasthit';
Pratikraman is his solution and dissolution of prakruti follows!

If the ignorant one charges interest, he will become a cruel person;
Self-realized one will do pratikraman here and clean this stain!

Doing creditor's pratikraman, sends him positive effect;
Doing raag-dwesh or fighting binds 'extra items'!

Faults of getting angry, stealing, dishonesty and immorality;
Scolding and objecting; pratikraman cleans this slate!

When dismissed by the boss, if he stays in pure Soul;
Even a death sentence won't bind; the judge is simply doing the job!

Due to senseless egoism, one allows a scorpion to bite;
'Gnani' will do its' pratikraman and put it aside!

On seeing someone aversion arises, understand that it is the enmity from
the past;
You should do pratikraman for it and get freed from dislike or hatred!

Clashes between husband and wife, and the in-laws are unsettled account;
Do their pratikraman as well; they are the connections of the relative self!

This world is a place to pay off accounts of karma;
'Akram' says do pratikraman to be free from karma!

Pratikraman improves relations and additional loss won't be there;
Echoes from others will arise or else India-Pakistan like war will be there!

When there is insult or loss of faith, cleansing removes the faults;
Cleansing must be done repeatedly like separating milk and salt!

If others are hurt you should know it right away;
Hurting words changes expression and smile will go away!

Giving pain makes you insolvent, if you terrorize, intimidate;
If you broke heart or hated, he will return the wrath as a snake!

Fight between in-laws causes hurt, attacks or suicide;
Do deep and prolonged pratikraman with self-criticism!

Gnani says 'I cause pain occasionally and unintentionally;
Exception though this is, here, pratikraman I do specially!

Give protection, so he doesn't fall, I consider his thoughts;
Handle his 'Vyavasthit' and stop him before he falls!

One makes a mistake, asks forgiveness, repeats same mistake;
Explain him with love, forgive him and have good thoughts!

Others go on making mistakes and are never aware of this fault;
No repentance or forgiveness, hence the loss of love and respect!

They should be opposed and to tolerate them is senseless;
Make them aware of it and forgive them with pure heart!

And yet if nothing happens, then finally you should tolerate;
Or else, mind will be spoiled, say 'that's how it is' and tolerate!

If someone is hurt by me and then he doesn't come near me;
End this with pratikraman, I complete the account of karma!

Is there anything wrong if one lets go because of egoism?
Gnani says it is wrong, there's charge of being instrumental!

Yet, if he stiffens up, resolution 'pending'; you shouldn't oppose him;
Keep on doing pratikramans, some day inner burning will subside!

After prolonged altercation do collective pratikraman;
'Dada Bhagwan, I am diligently doing its' pratikraman!'

Collision in the world is the account of the worldly interactions;
Pratikraman repairs the mind, not to break it, is Gnan-essence!

Relative self's conflict, pratikraman ends its origin;
When conflicts end, liberation happens in three lifetimes!

If he multiplies, you divide with the same number;
Thus avoiding conflict and clash is benefit of Akram!

Conflicts of speech and body are called gross forms;
Others know not- are of mind and called subtle forms!

Someone is seen attacking; 'Vyavasthit' arises in mind;
Still if his fault is seen; in subtler level mistake you've slipped!

If you strongly decide that no one is at fault here;
Yet if fault is seen, it is the subtler form of conflict!

Engrossment with file number one is the subtlest conflict;
Awaken, do pratikraman, it's the eminent way to be free!

Vibrations of pratikraman will reach other person instantly;
Karma binding of atikraman happens when ego and intellect join!

Seed of raag-dwesh result in like-dislike type circumstances;
Single remedy of pratikraman will destroy the root of raag-dwesh!

Different types of thoughts about pride, envy or doubt may come;
Do instant pratikraman, or else it reaches other person before too long!

Doubt that 'a robber will rob me' makes a happy person unhappy;
You're owner of universe, can morning dew extinguish a volcano?

What is the reason for fear? You consider yourself as temporary;
Fear vanishes with the understanding – vision of 'I am the eternal Self'!

Repentance burns the faults like a string that burns to ashes;
In next life, uprooting of these faults, a simple touch causes!

After attaining Self-realization, even pratikraman is an effect;
Slash the faults by pratikraman, remaining as the pure one, the dirt is cleansed!

Atikraman in eating-drinking brings on body's ailment;
Atikraman is innate nature and pratikraman is self-effort!

Ask for Gnani's forgiveness if you break the laws of eating;
If you don't endorse addiction, then one day you'll be quitting!

If you don't do pratikraman, the parmanus will stick again;
Addiction will return in next life, opinion supporting it will make it stick!

If discharge is not known-seen and pratikraman is not done;
Mind will continue to form since the opinions aren't gone!

After Self-state, do purusharth of the Self, Liberation surely you'll get;
But in following Agna, doing pratikraman, there may be defect!

Dada sometimes drank tea but first He did its' Pratyakhyan;
Otherwise tea will stay with you, Gnani remains forever alert!

Pain happens to the body, simply 'see' and 'know' it as separate;
Non-violent intent and separation, is absence of arta and raudra dhyan

Atikraman binds karma and not bound through conduct;
Pain never touches 'Ambalal' for a moment, due to 'Vignan'!

Adverse meditation arta and raudra, harass every moment;
Arta results in animal state and raudra sends one to hell!

Worry of future is artadhyan, and one hurts the self;
Bullet of worry doesn't hurt others, even his wife isn't aware!

Causing pain to others, giving pain even in thoughts;
Raudradhyan it is called cause others get its' effect!

Change the meditation of arta and raudra when it happens;
'It is the result of my karma', see others as just the evidentiary nimit!

To see the world as flawless is known as dharmadhyan;
Cleaning with pratikraman, Gnani counts it as dharmadhyan!

Repenting done once turns raudra to arta meditation;
Pratikraman again for it, arta becomes dharma contemplation!

You have become pure Soul; non-Self complex does arta-raudra dhyan;
non-Self complex does pratikraman, that's when it is dharmadhyan!

Pure Soul's is shukla meditation, non-Self complex's dharmadhyan;
In the end thus parmanus are made absolutely pure!

Arta-raudra meditation never happens in Akram Gnan;
Inside shukla, outside dharma; because ego is lifeless!

Faults that happen now since their pratikraman wasn't done;
One can get freedom from them if proper pratikraman is done!

Knowing the fault is dharmadhyan, meditation as the Self is shukladhyan;
Inner 'Absolute', outer 'dharma'- know it as state of one more life!

On Akram path, one can go as far as this State;
If inner and outer are 'Absolute', moksha happens in the same life!

'Guests show up at late night'; on seeing them there is strife in mind;
'Why did the deadbeats show up now'-words promptly flash in mind!

Yet, to their face he says, 'Welcome, will you take some tea?'
The guests will ask for Khichdi, vegetables or for some curry!

Wife gets upset, husband asks, 'When are they leaving?'
Wife says, 'How do I know? Your friends, your habits!'

Tradition states 'Guest is God'; yet there is arta-raudra dhyan;
For this, pratikraman is necessary, or else, he digs a mine of loss!

Self-realized person's intents don't change by doing pratikraman;
He gets rid of faults forever by doing pratyakhyan and pratikraman!

The fault remains pending if pratikraman is not done;
Increase one-two lives, or to Liberation if instantly done!

If a person is openly angry, today from karma he is free;
If angry in his mind, he will bind karma for the next life!

Do pratikraman for abhorrence, because attack is committed;
Attachment is discharge karma; Gnani explains this thoroughly!

However, if one isn't alert and Agna he didn't follow;
Do pratikraman for attachment as well or he will fall!

If there is inner link or violent intent, it is called kashay;
If they are absent, it isn't kashay, there's only discharge!

Yet, if others get hurt from your discharge kashay;
Doing pratikraman is proper according to Tirthankars!

Kashays may be heavy, they're relative's property after all;
'Seer' is not burned there; Gnan gives him protection!

Discharge faults are lifeless after Self-realization state;
Their karma are not heavy, Gnani jokes about the faults!

Heartily pratikraman ends the faults in short effort;
Repeated pratikraman, by law, frees one from bondage!

Wholesome pratikraman is acceptable when there're multiple faults;
'Dada, I am doing wholesome, please accept it as the total for all'!

If no courage for face to face, ask forgiveness in the mind;
Do face to face with a noble person; others will abuse it otherwise!

Before going to Liberation, exhaust the subtle body;
Do collective pratikraman and you will be free finally!

It is called self-effort when one does pratikraman for faults;
State of valiance is being the Knower of the one who knows!

Anger kashay that is bound for infinite lives is like a crack in a boulder;
Business of repeating lives continues if there's no pratikraman!

Anger that one didn't repent for is like a crack in the ground;
It persists since pratikraman-pratyakhyan were not done for that!

Fifth step of spirituality is wholesome pratikraman-pratyakhyan;
By doing them one arrives at the sixth which is called pratyakhyan!

Faults cause millions of veils; do as many pratikramans;
Because collectively done in past, veils continue to hinder!

Pratyakhyani veils are like a line drawn in the sand;
Burnt out kashays are like a line that is drawn in water!

When karma of kashay unfolds and affects the self within;
There is suffering of pain; they're called pratyakhyani kashays!

When karma of kashay unfolds and do not affect the self;
Bliss prevails within; they're called ash-like kashays!

At the fourth step is Self-realization; fifth is one of no-resolve;
Sixth is with resolve where file is thick in worldly life!

At the sixth step, external conduct is not accounted;
At seventh sobriety manifests and eight is one of 'never-before'!

When sexuality-tuber and attachment with woman is gone;
One crosses the ninth and thus to the tenth he goes!

When parmanu of anger-pride-deceit-greed do not exist at all;
There's total void of these kashays; one achieves the state of God!

In discharge karma, even one parmanu of kashay isn't seen;
Dada has seen Absolute Self, experience-state one achieves!

Preaching while kashays are there, one goes to hell, alas!
Big difference in punishment if a lawyer commits a crime!

An ignorant person should not go on stage and preach;
'I am learning'; others listen to the words and learn!

After becoming pure Soul he knows 'vyavasthit' as the doer;
Instant pratikraman is done, Self-realized is only the Knower!

No one's fault is seen and freedom from all attachments prevails;
While all worldly acts are done, this is the way of Akram Vignan!

Where there is absence of anger, it is Lord Mahavir's forgiveness!!
Not a thing to be given, is the valiant person's natural forgiveness!

Where one is in Knower-Seer state, kashays are totally absent;
Mistake in Knower-Seer state, rule of kashays will be in front!

Go on doing pratikraman, sticky karma will be lighter;
Result of pouring lead in the ears, Mahavir had to suffer!

Wherever violence was done, mosquitoes or bedbugs were killed;
Place their Souls before you and repent, then you will be freed!!

Always keep the inner intent to save all living beings;
They may be saved or not, you will be saved from the risks!

Spray chemicals in the farm or cut the grass or tender shoots;
Repent for doing this even if you have to do it again!

Pray to God everyday heartily for about ten minutes;
From whence befall upon me; business involving violence!

If intent is for total non-violence, karma's account won't bind;
Pratikraman frees from revenge, violence, attachment-abhorrence!

Freedom from all kinds of enmity is attained with pratikraman;
The other person may free you or not, now 'he is' responsible!

Do pratikraman for old faults and those faults are then disposed off;
When there's no new karma drawn, where's the question of the bond?

Past is gone forever and your future is in 'Vyavasthit's' hands;
Remain in present all the time and hold on to 'Gnani's' talks!

What do you do if fireworks blast off? Let the big ones go off;
Do pratikraman for bomb-like attacks; their impact will fizzle off!

If atikraman gets started while you do pratikraman;
Wash it patiently; you'll never run out of this 'soap'!

It is improper to form even a single wrong thought about the enemy;
He is under the realm of unfolding karma; and one who is alert will be free!

Lord Parshvanath had to pay off enmity's debt over ten life times;
Enmity is disposed with equanimity with awareness of Akram Vignan!

Pure Soul has manifested, now, do Self-effort valiance;
Uproot spiritual blockades and opinions, and do their pratikraman!

Relative self forms opinions; direct light of the Self uproots them;
Call the opinions as incorrect and do divisions to uproot them!

Opinions are effective and cause others to have dislike for you;
That inevitably gives result by keeping you away from the Self!

Getting what you like or dislike depends on credit or debit karma;
See Self in the evidentiary nimits; pudgal is alien, under the realm of the non-Self!

Pratikraman frees from opinions, there's no approval in action;
Circumstances made him a thief; in your heart hold no accusation!

Freedom from opinions, is freedom from the root of faults;
Your previous protection of faults is why they had carried on!

Freedom from opinions means, parmanus have purified;
They don't bind anymore and thus get pure; if they bind karma, they
become mixed!

Pudgal's parmanus say, 'you had become greedy for us;
You've become pure Soul now, so you have to now purify us!'

By doing pratikraman, you will be the opponent of opinions;
You'll see the relative as flawless and you'll see the real as pure!

In the morning, say five times, 'I will not be involved in sexuality;'
Say this with same level of focused awareness as when counting money!

Bondage of karma these days may send one to animal from human state;
From five senses to one sense, beware now and reach Liberation state!

Now you have Akram Gnan, uproot all the veils;
Be alert at every moment and finally be done with sexuality!

Own fault is not seen, there's intoxication of sexuality all day;
Sexuality's blockade is great; never it allows freedom any day!

Sexual thought upon seeing, know the secret of this event;
Illusory attachment filled in past life, brings on the circumstance says our
Gnan!

The mind shows phases then according to charged moha;
Do repeated pratikraman, it will uproot sexuality's tuber!

Continue cleansing the impurities with remorse till the end;
Cleansing shall exhaust them; clear and distinct Self-experience is next!

Sexuality's seed, once sown, shall take form, then end;
Cleansing before it takes root will make it insignificant!

Only if both have sexual fever, should they take the medicine;
To exert pressure or to beg for it is considered as forgery!

Sexuality's inner blockade is reason for wandering life after life;
Change opinion of pleasure in sex, pratikraman is the remedy!

Vow to have one wife in this time is the boon for celibacy;
If for another woman, you don't spend the mind uselessly!

The ascetics will not see a woman's face, there, who is at fault?
Whose womb were you born from? Find it out and kill that fault!

Mind's restlessness ends, celibacy contains the mind;
Self-realization conquers the world, not just the mind!

Gnani's energyful words and your strong resolve;
You can be in brahmacharya, whether married or not!

With Akram-Gnan, if one succeeds in celibacy;
He'll be king of kings and the world will bow to him!

Win over sexuality, be alert, do pratikraman at every moment;
Stick to vows, do Samayik; these purify mind, speech and body!

The result of illicit sexuality is the attainment of animal state;
Pratikraman and strong resolve, freedom from it you can get!

Caught up in greed or temptation, keep on doing pratikraman;
Only strong obedience of Agna will break this veil!

Every act of Dada is for our Gnan advancement;
Cut off the relative self; now prevail in Self-Gnan!

At final boundary of Atikraman, Vasudevas and Prativasudevas;
Suffer in the seventh hell, others aren't capable to reach there!

To improve the spoiled game; don't spoil intent anywhere;
Do pratikraman for the spoiled; that's how 'eternal' you'll get!

Telling a lie is karma's result; intent there, is karma-bondage;
Hence, do repentance here and your opinions you will change!

After the opinion about lying is gone, you are not responsible at all;
Lying then is karma-result; remember that it too will give result!

In relative religion, one 'has to do' pratikraman for the wrong;
'Knower-Seer' in real religion, pratikraman 'happens' for the wrong!

Whole life, do one thing only, see what 'Chandu' is doing;
Dispose off good and bad, evacuate shop, do no new filling!

If your speech causes pain to others, do pratikraman instantly;
Decide to be in Agna, know speech is of the non-Self's and under its' realm!

You make a suggestion and show different opinion;
Lying for the Self, know it as the great truth!

Dada has declared to the world that worldly interaction is mandatory;
'Vyavasthit' controls interactions but pratikraman is voluntary!

Ask for forgiveness in every way, in person or with soft eyes;
If the other person hurts you, stop bowing down to him!

In suggesting, your purpose is pure but the others get hurt;
Do pratikraman for 'not knowing how to say it properly'!

Others should feel no pain; such should be your speech;
Interactions should be dramatic; or else you have to clean!

For making fun, jest, 'joke'; one has to do pratikraman;
Otherwise, Gnani's speech, His 'tape-record' is less clear!

When an intelligent person makes fun of the less intelligent;
It is misuse of the light and ends up as punishment of the self!

If something wrong comes out in speech or in one's inner intent;
Others tape this instantly, doing pratikraman here is correct!

By doing pratikraman, your speech will improve in this lifetime;
Dada's speech became acceptable to all, after his interactions purified!

Instead of feeling remorse keep heightened awareness;
Veils that obstruct on the way, remove them with pratikraman!

'This' Satsang's poison is better than the nectar of outside world interaction;
Here, quarrel or fight; yet there's Liberation, by doing huge pratikraman!

If you can't come near Dada, feel the regret and do pratikraman at that time;
Flush out the worries and raag-dwesh and remember Dada all the time!

If an ant is swept away in urine, Dada does pratikraman;
Reading of a book without performing due rites; that is a mistake!

Even though helpful for all, if two people were made to separate;
Benevolence for the ignorant, yet you have to do its' pratikraman!

If pratikraman does not happen, it is prakruti's fault;
It isn't obstruction karma; keep intent of 'seeing' with heightened energy!

31

To cleanse sticky karma use the soap according to the stickiness;
Exert extra energy then there will be a strong Knower-Seer state!

For the burden of old mistakes, no choice but to wash them off;
Do pratikraman, clean relative-self; it's Dada's only treatment!

Sit down for one hour daily to do sticky file's pratikraman;
He'll be milder, he'll turn around and there'll be definite change!

Resolution after repentance, is the best form of purification;
Decision that 'I won't do it again' is God Mahavir given resolution!

You've to only form inner intent to dispose with equanimity;
Whether the disposal may occur or not, that is nature's authority!

Sticky karmas of file number one are disposed off just by 'seeing';
No need for pratikraman there, Akram Gnan's remedy is simple!

Only the guilty one commits a crime, a judge shouldn't take responsibility;
Chandulal makes the mistakes and pratikraman is also his responsibility!

After attaining Akram Gnan, when does the reservoir get empty?
After eleven to fourteen years, then, no more kashay remain!

Interference happens rarely, death likewise is a rare event;
'Future' is not under vyavasthit, 'what has happened' is vyavasthit!

When horrible karma unfold, if Gnan of 'vyavasthit' is present;
If You 'see' what is happening, then, pratikraman is not required!

Call it true pratikraman that 'speaks up' on the third day;
Attraction towards us, even Dada Himself will lay!

Pratikraman done for the dead reaches the immortal Soul within;
Our puzzles are solved, when we think- 'no one ever dies'!

In opposition through speech and body against anyone;
Total energy won't manifest even if the mind is antagonistic!

See thoughts in mind, keep them separate and they will be gone;
If someone was hurt by thoughts, pratikraman for it must be done!

If your inner intent is bad for the other or his for yourself;
Don't look for the reason why; go to the path of pratikraman!

Vitarag you will be, when with a clean mind, you go through what you don't like;
Do pratikraman when it spoils and ask here for the energy to purify!

At bedtime, check the account of pure Soul and do the clearance;
See the world as flawless and go to sleep after doing pratikraman!

Wrong thought for Gnani or Tirthankar; cleanse it off instantly;
Ask for forgiveness again and again and 'see' the intellect's coquetry!

Cleanse off the pain you caused in temples by doing pratikraman;
Those karma will rise to give result, there is no other deterrent!

Focusing on old faults, 'seeing' them will destroy the veils;
They are in memory for removal; therefore do instant pratikraman!

Pratikramans were not done: hence they come in memory,
Pratyakhyans were not done; hence they come as desire!

Faults come to memory again and again, cleanse them again and again;
Remove them like layers of an onion, they will be uprooted in the end!

If it is in memory, do pratikraman if in desire, do pratyakhyan;
Past-projected happiness causes desire; surrender this false pride!

Phone and keep other's pure Soul in front, see your own faults;
To repent and ask for pardon is Akram's short pratikraman!

Mistakes made in past life give result in this life;
Proper pratikraman for them gives immense bliss!

If one hour a day is spent for the purpose of doing pratikraman;
You get chance to balance account with relatives and neighbors!

This will burn off faults and the film will be easily seen here;
Disposal is attained thus and freedom from bonds will be there!

'That's what I did', says Dada, cleared with each and everyone;
'I' did not rest while there was unhappiness in mind of anyone!

Get success with Akram, such an easy path won't be there again;
Give up this habit of temptation, awaken, only half-life remains!

Do only that which Gnani shows, don't follow your own patterns;
If you do, the result is unpredictable and that is called swachhand!

Doing pratikraman ends all enmity in this life itself;
It is Lord Mahavir's principle and nothing's beyond that!

If both do for each other, their faults will come to an end faster;
Half the work will end it and then other issues can be addressed!

After committing one crime, a series of crimes will start;
Corruption, adultery, will take one to an animal state!

Call it proper pratikraman, one that's done at every moment;
Faults of whole life are seen-known and cleanly balanced!

Akram's unparalleled pratikraman is rewarding established truth;
One sees the link from childhood to present as in a video film!

Feel free and light as a feather, cleanse from gross to the subtlest;
Finally find root cause of faults and experience bliss that is different!

Once pratikraman starts, it may not stop for a longtime;
Like a pulley unwinding after a rope has gone through it!

While doing pratikraman of life, one isn't in Liberation or worldly state;
Direct light of Soul shows the deepest faults and manifests energy of Self!

Inner self is totally nonfunctional, only pragnya is functional;
Breaks the layers one by one, results in ending birth and death!

While doing pratikraman, there is no effect whatsoever on the Self;
Raag-dwesh's approval is why the fault was created in the inner-self!

When link of pratikraman continues and Self's experience occurs;
Complete Knower-Seer state manifests and the bliss is more and more!

If a fault is acknowledged, consider it gone there and then;
Seeing family as faultless, consider it true pratikraman!

When is the other person truly at fault? If Self is the doer;
But Self is non-doer and all acts are just discharge karma!

If any embodied Soul is seen guilty, you haven't achieved purity;
This is sense organ based knowledge, with pratikraman clean impurity!

In conviction, world is innocent, when does it become an experience?
When surrounded by bugs and snakes, you see their innocence!

Gnani's conviction and actions prevail in seeing the world as faultless;
He does pratikraman for missing Self-focus, preserves the state of alertness!

Once a year in Aurangabad, 'Dada' arranged sacred ceremony;
Ask each other's forgiveness to clear endless lives' animosity!

He invoked great protection to help clean everyone's karma;
They fell to each other's feet, cried openly and felt lighter!

Enmity with dharma colleague formed over many a lifetimes;
Do pratikraman for that, get freed and hold Gnani's Agna at heart!

Confession with Gnani done in person or in writing;
Gnani has to free him because at heart he has oneness!

When secret faults are confessed, Gnani's sacred ritual cleanses them;
You do pratikraman-repentance and read the confession for a month!

Where purity of heart is there, one feels unity with everyone;
In exposing a major fault; the mind feels Gnani's splendor!

God's grace befalls upon you as a result of the confession;
Confession is always secret here; Gnani has no deception!

If you hide the faults from Gnani, the faults will become double;
Freedom will be difficult and the awareness will be much veiled!

Confession can be done to a Guru or to 'Dada' within you;
If inner Dada can't be seen, pray to 'this' One in particular!

Odd are sexuality's faults now, enmity with daughter, brother, sister;
In satsang or with colleagues; beware, there's still time to cleanse them!

Just as a wife doesn't forget her husband even for a moment;
Same with pratikraman will solve infinite mistakes!

Bombarding of short pratikraman, take forgiveness from the pure Soul;
Repentance of, 'I won't do it again' is sufficient in short version!

If the enmity is deeper, you have to do proper pratikraman;
Then the enmity will end and bring end to new atikraman!

35

In the further depths of pratikraman, past life can also be seen;
If discharge karmas are simple, layers can be thoroughly pierced!

When faults are 'wholesale', hundreds of them with one person;
Do wholesome pratikramans and follow that with the resolves!

Faults that were committed knowingly must be cleansed individually;
Wholesome pratikraman clears those that were done unknowingly!

Collectively clear certain sexuality's innumerable mistakes;
Then one reaches the goal; otherwise, one wanders places!

While getting married, he dressed up and showed off immensely;
He has to do pratikraman now if he didn't think it as temporary!

Slipping from Self-intent to self-intent, engrossed in Chandu;
One who follows the five Agnas can never slip to Chandu!

Self never gets engrossed in the intents of the relative self;
Self 'knows' engrossment, what gets engrossed is the ego!

Even in dream, proper pratikraman can be done;
Do it after waking up, crime can be admitted any time!

'Sorry' is not pratikraman but it is a good thing to say;
Making mind free of attacks, it calms the other!

After attaining shukladhyan, pratikraman in 'Kramic' is poison;
Pratikraman is Akram's medicine to be taken by file one!

'Self' is not to do pratikraman but makes 'file one' do it;
Energy of manifested Pragnya shows faults and warns you!

After getting Akram Gnan, 'self' becomes 'pure Soul';
Rest is 'Vyavasthit', only 'see' the 'file one' now on!

Go on 'seeing' what 'Chandu' is doing, nothing else is to be done;
If you missed 'seeing', there, pratikraman is the thing to be done!

All circumstances arise as a result of Self's extra result;
Pratikraman will purify them and cause them to disperse!

The Scientist of the Absolute has no need for doing pratikraman;
Remedy is for those burnt by interference in the natural process!

Gnani's speech may appear contrary but depends on the questioner;
The fever from cold is the same, one gets quinine other gets metacine!

Pudgal does atikraman and pudgal runs the world;
Becoming charged through 'I am this', parmanus become pur-gal-fill-empty!

'I am doing' pratikraman, is puran-charge;
The 'non-Self' is doing pratikraman, is galan-discharge!

Pratikraman is done by pudgal, it asks for pure Soul's pardon;
Soul hands over the phone to pudgal and gets pudgal's pardon!

Direct light of Self makes you do own pudgal's pratikraman;
When harm is done to others, do their pudgals' pratikraman!

Ask for forgiveness from pure Soul for faults of own pudgal;
Pratikraman towards the relative self will clear all the faults!

You are the Knower of faults and the doer is quite different;
Knower state won't last long, so pratikraman you perform!

This packing called 'Chandu', make it God;
As long as there is the reflection, climbing is Your path!

Atikraman and pratikraman are done by the ego;
Pragnya, the direct energy of Self, warns against the faults!

Hurt to his ego is verily the stain on your self;
Beyond your control it is, pratikraman washes it!

Listen to the Vitarag, there's nothing to be done;
Bondage is in 'doing', be it religion or not religion!

Knowing world as flawless in the gross level is not enough;
Knowing it at the subtlest level will bring it in one's conduct!

Gnani does pratikraman even before fault happens;
Erasing after writing, Gnani's awareness is eternal!

Only the subtler and the subtlest faults have remained in Gnani;
World hears and praises Him yet there is fault in the eyes of the natural law!

Dada 'sees' everyone's faults yet 'sees' the Self in all;
Therefore, He never reproaches, 'seeing' unfolding karma as it is!

In pilgrimage, mahatmas fight and yet do pratikraman in the evening;
Ask for each other's forgiveness, look at Akram-astonishing!

Decide to follow Agna, yet if you missed it someplace;
Do instant pratikraman, your marks will be a full hundred!

The One installed and still in Agna is the absolute Self, does pratikraman
for missing;
Don't apply intellect to Agna; you get hell-state for this swing!

When getting insulting words, see unfolding karma and pure Self;
See pure while remaining in pure, pure focus is religion of the Self!

Essential for Liberation is the Self-Gnan and nothing else;
Pratikraman is one remedy and it may not be needed for everyone!

In Akram one has been told 'to do'; when awareness is dim;
For Liberation, Akram has placed, Agna-pratikraman's team!

Doing harm is the result and one's intent here is the cause;
Doing these pratikramans in Akram will uproot the cause!

If Dada calls you foolish, this atikraman makes you blissful;
This atikraman is an exception; everyone finds it very helpful!

Chandu's acts are discharge karma, 'seeing' them gives experience;
Pratikraman is not required there, the vision of the Self will end them!

Parmanus tainted in the past, pratikraman will not purify;
Only the part where others were pained, pratikraman will purify!

Parmanus get purified by staying in the Knower-Seer state;
Doership is atikraman state and non-doership gives him free state!

'I am not the doer of anything at all' is in one's awareness all the time;
No need for pratikraman there, everyone can't be in this state all the time!

Akram Science made you 'jump' straight from 'K.G.' to 'Ph. D.';
To make up for the middle standards, pratikraman is the stairs unseen!

Akram Vignan is the complete and functional established truth;
There is nothing to be done here; Aho! Aho! It is so beneficent!

After giving Self-knowledge, Dada gave us complete Science;
Enlightening all different tracks connected with the Self in the center!

Rarely though it may look controversial, it's never so with Gnani;
Generator's energy is distributed to 'A. C.' or 'Heater' as necessary!

Hence, there is no controversy; it is the way in which one uses electricity;
Please read keeping this in mind; to the well informed is our request
with humility!

# PART 2

## UNDERSTANDING SAMAYIK

## DEFINITION OF SAMAYIK

*Samayik is to Be the Self and 'see' the self.*

There is difference in Akram's pratikraman and samayik;
Pratikraman for atikraman; cleanses the house of inner Self!

Awareness of, 'I am pure Soul'; remaining in Five Agnas;
Natural spontaneous state as this; that is samayik!

Knowing state prevails in samayik; every moment in the present;
If applied awareness does not always prevail; in samayik it will!

Samayik of Akram will dissolve the nature of mind, body and speech;
Aura of samayik prevails all day for the Self-realized!

For what little one was told 'to do'; defective goods did one bring;
No other solution to be rid of it; nothing's achieved without worthiness!

Traditional definition of Samayik is to drive away the thoughts;
To try and stabilize the mind but ineffective are these efforts!

Mind is not steady and he keeps looking at the clock;
He also makes small talks as he listens to discourse!

After deciding for Samayik, he gets few moments of freedom;
He does what the mind likes, scandal, slander, and deception!

Samayiks done in houses of worship are a sight to see;
Teachers need to wake up, followers need to improve!

Once the mind becomes slippery, how can you contain it?
You decide not to think about your shop, yet you'll think it!

Reading a book during Samayik is actually a form of study;
Focus placed elsewhere, is not the correct method to do it!

Oh! Puniyaa Shravak's samayik, no one can do like it;
Ascetics, teachers, saints, sect-leaders struggle there!

You did the act of Samayik, did you ever do intent samayik?
Intents are driven away and only acts have remained in Kramic!

Instead of doing such samayik, have equanimity in life;
At home with husband, children, in-laws and relatives!

What is the use of doing an awkward and tense samayik?
If the mind can't remain steady, it isn't worth two cents!

Mahavir's scale applies here and those on His path are accepted;
It is not a lawless reign here and falsehood shall not be tolerated!

Removal of arta and raudra dhyan is the essence of Jain religion;
If they aren't removed, it is Jain by birth only and a waste of life!

Samayik without a subservient mind yields no spiritual gain;
Is driving away cats and dogs a samayik or a disgrace?

Karma through mind is samrambha; karma through speech is samaarambha;
Know the three-fold bondage: karma through body is arambha!

'What is broken in the house?' asks the man while doing Samayik;
'Your Soul has broken'-says Dada; he has ashamed Lord Mahavir!

The one whose arta-raudra dhyan have totally stopped;
Is always in samayik; the Lord has already authenticated this fact!

While doing samayik, the big boss visits the 'public house of pleasure';
Or he calculates money in business; just see how wrong his leisure is!

Useless samayik is where the inner and outer self, prevail as separate;
Lord Mahavir will not accept it, a dual mode is not allowed there!

Gnan Vidhi is such a 'samayik' that one cannot do by himself;
Therefore, Dada always tells us to be there again and again!

The goal of continuous awareness, 'I am pure Soul' is samayik;
Remaining within five Agnas all day, the work gets done!

Seeing pure Soul in everyone for one hour nonstop;
Puniyaa Shravak's samayik, it's the highest pure applied awareness!

Forgetting the world while remaining in pure applied awareness is Samayik;
Inauspicious attention gives lower life state and that is a false samayik!

True meaning of samayik is, it won't allow any adverse intent;
Even when insulted or beaten up, he won't change his inner intent!

In true samayik, he becomes Shraman-like follower of the Lord;
Attaining a state of equanimity, he is the true lover of Mahavir!

In Akram path, mahatmas are taught about samayik;
No need for lotus position, it may lock up the knee!

First do pure-Soul-Vidhi, be steady in the Self-state;
For every part of the inner self- antahkaran, Be the 'Seer' and the 'Knower'!

Separating as the Self, 'see' everything that's happening within;
See the film for forty-eight minutes and a fountain of bliss sprouts!

In Akram, samayik is necessary, especially for sharpening focused awareness;
The one in such pure focused awareness, becomes free from all mistakes!

A thought comes, sexual vision arises, say, 'Not mine' and separate;
In samayik, one can quickly and easily dissolve knot of sexuality!

In Akram, samayik or pratikraman are not just overt rituals;
It is pragnya's Knowledge in action, and the Self's original energy!

Samayik strengthens the mind, increases the ability to Be the Self;
It dissolves all tubers and gives clear experience of bliss as the Self!

Sexuality, kashays, attachments and faults are seen in samayik;
Seeing as the Self, dissolves them and all impurities get cleared up!

Various phases of past faults are dug up in detail and are seen;
Once there is the Self's Presence; all faults get exposed and seen!

As such, if one attempts to recall, he won't remember anything;
With Self-state in samayik, he can 'see' faults by the second!

41

Seeing faults in samayik, 'see' them again and again to the end;
This results in conduct as the Self, it's commission is the empire's wealth!

To start, do samayik for eight minutes, later, for forty-eight;
Dhyan-meditation can't last longer, don't cut short for a minute!

During samayik, if the mind wanders, why should you get frightened?
Mind is to be Known, You are the Knower; is there effect in the home
from outside riots?

Mind is used in the 'vyavahar' samayik; Self does the Self samayik;
Vyavahar results in credit-karma, nirgranth – tuber-free from the Self!

In Akram, samayik and pratikraman are done at the same time;
Knowing-seeing and cleansing is when one perfects the practice!

Sexuality's force is excessive these days; samayik purifies the disease;
Violence, pride, greed, deceit, anger- will then leave with ease!

For awareness of separation, Dada recommends samayik;
Those who practice will have experience same as a Gnani!

O, pure Soul Lord, You are separate, Chandu is separate;
O, pure Soul Lord, You are real, Chandu is relative,

O, pure Soul Lord, You are permanent, Chandu is temporary;
Ask for energy that is lacking, wherever it is felt necessary!

Mirror-samayik is unique; it is a wonderful research of Gnani;
'See' him 'completely' separate; unleash the torrent of correction!

'You did such and such faults'- show him a lot;
If done by a hired hand, this samayik will have no effect!

In 'reproach samayik', heavily rebuke your relative self;
Go to terrace and tell him off, you are the boss and servant too!

As the body-complex, by nature, gets older and older;
Do samayik from the start; remaining weakness remove later on!

'Can't do, Can't do'-is the topic of samayik;
'Did it, Did it'- breaks the obstruction, by doing samayik!

'Seeing' the 'Seer' separate, happens in Akram samayik;
'pure Soul' lights the Self-and the non-Self, absolute Self lights both!

Soul verily is samayik, when that remains all time;
Gnani says, 'Do samayik to cleanse the faults of past time'!

After granting awareness of the Self, gives five Agnas to follow;
Do 'Pratikraman-samayik', if you miss any Agna, dear fellow!

This samayik-pratikraman erected forever by Dada Bhagwan;
Serves to eternalize the message of Lord Mahavir Bhagwan!

## - Dr. Niruben Amin

# CONTENTS
## PART 1 - PRATIKRAMAN

### [1] The True Nature of Pratikraman

### [2] Every Religion Supports Pratikraman

## [7] Business Transactions Become Pure

## [8] Freedom from the Chains of Life-After-Life Accounts

## [9] Pratikraman in Varying Situations

## [10] When Conflicts Arise

## [14] Release from Bondage of Inner Enemies

## [15] On The Path of Cause Ahimsa

## [16] Revenge of Enmity is Unbearable

## [17] Removing the Root Cause of Opinions

## [18] He Who Conquers Sexuality is the Emperor of the World

## [19] The Problem of Compulsive Lying

## [20] Awareness When Words are Flowing in Speech...

## [21] Faults of Prakruti Will Depart This Way...

## [22] Solution for Sticky Files

## [23] When the Mind Becomes Turbulent

## [24] Gnan Rescues Those Drowning in the River of Worldly Life after Life

## [25] Understanding the Principles of Pratikraman

## PART-2  UNDERSTANDING SAMAYIK

\*\*\*\*\*

# Special notes to readers

◆ The word **Self**, with 'S', refers to the awakened Soul, which is different from the worldly soul (non-awakened self), written with 's'. The term **Shuddhatma** (pure Soul) is used by the Gnani Purush for the awakened Self, after the Gnan Vidhi. Similarly, any word in the middle of a sentence, with capitalized first letter, or in inverted comas at the beginning of the sentence, refers to the awakened Self. This is an important distinction for the correct understanding of the difference between the awakened Self and the non-awakened self.

◆ **Seeker** - refers to a questioner who has not attained Dada's Gnan, so all Dadashri's answers under that are in response to them.

Otherwise:

**Questioner** - refers to those who have attained Dada's Gnan of the Akram Path.

◆ Wherever the name **'Chandubhai'** is mentioned, the reader should substitute his or her name.

◆ Numbers in parenthesis i.e. refer to the page number in the original book in Gujarati from which text was translated.

*****

# PRATIKRAMAN

## PART ONE

## [1]

## The True Nature of Pratikraman

### Worth Doing in Life

**Seeker:** What is the most important thing a human being should do in this life?

**Dadashri:** To speak and act exactly according to the thoughts in his mind. If you want to speak pleasant words, but there are negative thoughts in the mind, then you should do *pratikraman* (three step process of reversal from aggression through thoughts, speech and actions. These are recall of mistake, repentance and asking for forgiveness, and asking for energies not to repeat the mistake with firm determination). Who shall be your witness to the *pratikraman*? You should do *pratikraman* with 'Dada Bhagwan' as your witness. This person that you see in front of you is not Dada Bhagwan. This person is A.M. Patel of Bhadran (a town in Gujarat, India). 'Dada Bhagwan' is the fully enlightened One within. He is the Lord of the universe that is manifest within this body. *Pratikraman* should be done in His name, as follows:

'Dear Dada Bhagwan, this mind has had negative thoughts for which I ask your forgiveness. Please forgive me!'

I too do *pratikraman* with Him as the witness.

**Seeker:** So then what is our duty in this worldly life (*sansar*)?

**Dadashri:** You have to see how this worldly life is unfolding by being a witness (*sakshi bhaav*). And if the ego arises, you have to ask for forgiveness from the Lord. Any place where the ego of 'I am the doer' arises, you have to ask for forgiveness. Do you ask for forgiveness?

**Questioner:** Yes.

**Dadashri:** Whose forgiveness do you ask? Do you ask for God's forgiveness?

**Questioner:** Yes.

**Dadashri:** You should ask for God's forgiveness. That is the only solution, because if you ask for forgiveness, you will be forgiven.

If you make a mistake, then you should say, 'Dear Lord! I have no desire to make a mistake, and yet it occurs, so please forgive me.'

**Questioner:** Many times I used to have this question as to why we worship the Lord, and why are we asking for forgiveness from Him.

**Dadashri:** We are asking for forgiveness for the mistakes that were committed to the world. The one who has not committed a mistake, why does he have to ask for forgiveness?

## The Absolute Self is Beyond Karma

**Seeker:** In order to reach *Parmatma* (fully enlightened One), if we put aside religion and carry out only good actions, can we reach Him?

**Dadashri:** No, attaining the state of the absolute Self and karma have nothing to do with each other. If you do good deeds, you are doing *dharma*, nothing else. When you do bad deeds, you are doing *adharma*. If you do good deeds, people will say that you are a good person.

Doing good deeds is called *dharma* and doing bad deeds is called *adharma* and to transcend *dharma* and *adharma* (good deeds and bad deeds) is called *Atma-dharma* – the religion of the Self. If you do good deeds, you get credit and so you have to come back to enjoy that credit. When you do bad deeds, you create a debit and for that you have to suffer the debit in the next life. Where there is neither credit nor debit, the Self is attained. Where there is not even a dollar's worth of credit or a debit, there the Self is attained.

## Purity Through Repentance

**Seeker:** Having come into the worldly life, karma is inevitable. What should we do if we knowingly or unknowingly create wrong karma?

**Dadashri:** If that occurs, there is a remedy for it. Once a wrong karma – anything that hurts others through thoughts, speech or action – occurs, repentance should follow immediately. Repentance should be done wholeheartedly and with sincerity. Even after repentance, should it occur again there is no need to worry; just repent again. You are not aware of the science behind all this, so you may feel that despite your repentance, the wrong karma does not stop. Why it does not stop is also a science in itself. You should simply carry on repenting. If you repent for the wrong karma wholeheartedly, all of it will be washed away. If you hurt someone, then you should absolutely repent.

**Seeker:** When we carry out our normal daily activities of the body, do we have to repent for it?

**Dadashri:** Yes of course! Until you become Self-realized, if you fail to repent, you will continue to bind more karma.

Repentance will loosen the entangled knots of karma. If not, the result of the wrongful action you bind will be so horrendous that you may even forfeit human birth in your next life. And if you manage to attain human life again, it will be full of suffering and misery. You will be deprived of food and respect, and you will suffer constant insults. That is why repentance along with other rituals becomes necessary. This is called *paroksha bhakti* – indirect worship. Indirect worship is necessary until one attains Self-realization.

Now who should be a witness to your repentance? It should be done in the presence of the God you believe in, whether it is Lord Krishna, Dada Bhagwan or any other God. There is a cure for everything in this world. First the cure is born, and then the problem or affliction arises.

Today, the cure for all the diseases that have emerged in the world has already arisen. There is already a medicinal plant growing, and then later the disease arises. Therefore, the world is very exact. You have to go for the cure and solution. The cure is already there!

## Kraman, Atikraman, Pratikraman

Why has the world come into existence? It is due to *atikraman* (aggression towards other living beings through thoughts, speech and action). *Kraman* (neutral actions; actions that do not have any good or bad implications) alone does not cause any problems. For example, if you go to a restaurant and break two dishes, and leave after paying for them, then it is not considered *atikraman* and, therefore, *pratikraman* is not necessary. But if you tell the manager that his waiter has broken them, then that is *atikraman*. *Pratikraman* has to be done for the *atikraman* that was done. Everything else is just *kraman* anyway. Natural and spontaneous talk is *kraman*, and there is no problem with that. However, *atikraman* occurs in this inevitably. Therefore, do *pratikraman* for it.                          (Gujarati Book Page-4)

**Seeker:** How does one know that *atikraman* has occurred?

**Dadashri:** You will know and so will the other person. You will know it from the expression on his face and you will be affected too. It will affect you both. That is why *pratikraman* should be done.

If a policeman tries to stop you and you do not stop; that is considered *atikraman* and for that you have to do *pratikraman*. Otherwise, you will have to go to court.

When we eat, it is not considered *atikraman*. Is having your hair cut considered *atikraman*?

**Questioner:** No.

**Dadashri:** Is shaving *atikraman*?

**Questioner:** No.

**Dadashri:** When you brush your teeth in the morning, is that *atikraman*?

**Questioner:** No, not even that.

**Dadashri:** Anger, pride, deceit and greed are all considered *atikraman*, so if you do *pratikraman*, they will leave. If you do *pratikraman* immediately after *atikraman*, the anger, pride, deceit and greed will disappear.

## Endless Projections Due to Jolts of Ignorance

Every living being (*jiva*) is 'projecting' (planning, intention, *bhaav*), not due to its natural disposition but due to external forces. And we should continue doing *pratikraman*. This occurs due to the force of ignorance (*agnan* – ignorance of the Self) due to circumstances. We should keep doing *pratikraman*.

There is not only one type of projection; there are endless kinds. Whenever one encounters anything, he will not refrain from projecting (doing *bhaav*). If one is on a bridge he will say, 'Why did they construct this bridge so high?' He will question that. Hey! What concern is it of yours? Are you married to the bridge? The moment he embarks upon the bridge, he starts this foolishness. The bridge is meant for getting across. There is no other concern with it and yet what does he do? 'Why did they have to build this bridge so high?' Do people say such things or not?

**Seeker:** Yes, they do, and in just five minutes, five thousand phases arise.

**Dadashri:** You say five thousand, but five minutes means three hundred seconds. Then there are endless *samaya* (the smallest indivisible time unit) in that second. Therefore, so many phases can arise in a second. This is how one continues to do endless *atikraman*.

The worldly life has arisen by *atikraman* and is destroyed by *pratikraman*.

## The Real Meaning of Pratikraman

**Questioner:** If something unpleasant is occurring, and if I tolerate it, is that what you call *pratikraman*?                    (6)

**Dadashri:** No, you should not 'tolerate' but you should do *pratikraman*.

**Questioner:** So what is *pratikraman*?

**Dadashri:** If a person insults you, you should understand who the real culprit is behind the insult. Is it the one who insults or is it the one who feels insulted? This should be determined first. You should understand that the person who insults you is not at fault, not even to the slightest degree. He is merely a *nimit* (someone instrumental in the process) and it is due to the unfolding of your very own karma that the two of you are brought together. The fault is your own and you should do *pratikraman* if any negative feelings arise towards him. If you feel that he is worthless or deceitful, you have to do *pratikraman*. You do not have to do *pratikraman* if you have no ill feelings towards him or if you feel obligated to him for being instrumental in the discharge of your karma.

If anyone insults you, it is due to your very own *karmic* account and you should see the other person as a *nimit*. Even when your pocket gets picked, the pickpocket is a *nimit* who is settling your own *karmic* account. Generally, people blame the *nimit* and that is the cause of all conflicts.

## Walking in the Wrong Direction is Atikraman

In your daily worldly interactions when you do something, you will know that you did something wrong against such and such a person, won't you? The worldly interactions you carry out are *kraman*. *Kraman* means worldly interactions (*vyavahar*). Now if you have a misunderstanding with someone, you will realize that you used harsh words towards the other person or that you behaved wrongly towards him. Will you not know that? All that is called *atikraman*.

*Atikraman* is to walk in the wrong direction, and to walk back the same distance in the right direction is *pratikraman*.

## It is Erased Immediately in This Way

Where there is conflict, there is no *pratikraman* and where there is *pratikraman*, there is no conflict.

Give to others what you would like to receive yourself and for that, you will bind merit karma (*punya*). A person cannot take one word of insult and yet he hurls five insults towards others. It is a grave liability to give to others what you do not like yourself. It should not be so. And if someone uses curse words towards you, it is in accordance with natural justice. Do not ask him why he is doing so. You should accept it as a credit in your *karmic* account.

**Seeker:** What occurs if we go to collect money that is owed to us?

**Dadashri:** He will give you two more insults. And if you ask him why he gave you only two insults, why not three, four or even one, he will tell you, 'You think I have nothing better to do?' Therefore, everything is in accordance to the natural justice. So deposit it in your *karmic* account. You should not retaliate in return, but if you do, then do *pratikraman*.

You have no right to physically punish your child. You only have the right to explain things to him. If you spank your child and fail to do *pratikraman*, you will bind negative karma. *Pratikraman* is necessary here. The spanking is due to the wrong nature of the *prakruti* (the mind, speech and body complex being the relative-self). It is *kashays* (inner weaknesses of anger, pride, deceit and greed) which lead to the spanking, but if you remember my words, 'Do *pratikraman*,' after you have spanked him, and if you do *pratikraman*, you will immediately erase the mistake. It is possible to erase it immediately.

## Who is Exempt from Doing Pratikraman?

**Dadashri:** How many *pratikramans* do you do?

**Questioner:** Not even one.

**Dadashri:** So then how many *atikramans* do you do? Wherever there is *atikraman*, you always have to do *pratikraman*. There is no need for *pratikraman* if there is no *atikraman*. 'I am Chandubhai' is *atikraman*. However, for the sake of worldly interactions, this is pardoned. But does anyone get hurt because of you? If not, then there is no *atikraman*. If during the course of your day you hurt anyone, this is *atikraman* for which you should do *pratikraman*.                              (8)

This is the science of the *vitarags*, the fully enlightened Ones. *Atikraman* takes you to a birth in the lower life forms, while *pratikraman* will take you into a higher life form. Only *pratikraman* will help you until you attain final liberation.

Who does not need to do *pratikraman*? The one who does no *atikraman*.

## Recognizing Atikraman

**Questioner:** We have no intention of hurting anyone and yet we become instrumental (*nimit*) in hurting people. So is it necessary to form an opinion that we have to do *pratikraman* for the *atikraman* we do?

**Dadashri:** If something you said or your action hurt someone, you are considered to have done *atikraman*. You have to do *pratikraman* for that. You have erred by doing *atikraman* and, therefore, you will bind karma.

**Questioner:** If the other person is just a *nimit*, then why should he feel hurt? Then what is the need for *pratikraman*?

**Dadashri:** You have to do *pratikraman* if he is hurt by you. It is not considered *atikraman* if he is not hurt by you. Therefore, you do *pratikraman* only if *atikraman* occurs.

All this eating, drinking, talking, etc., is *kraman*. *Kraman* is going on the whole day long. Getting up early, getting up late is all *kraman*.

If someone was to get up right now and start swearing at someone, you will all think, 'Why did he have to do *atikraman* when everything was going on smoothly?' That is called *atikraman*. When you hurt someone's feelings, that *atikraman* may be spontaneous and natural, yet you have to do *pratikraman* for it. Even if you do not utter a word through your mouth but your mind becomes negative towards him, then too you have to do *pratikraman*. *Pratikraman* means to ask for forgiveness in a way you understand. You understand that you did wrong and you have to decide not to do it again. You should vow not to do that again. If it still occurs again, if you repeat the mistake again, then you should repent again. As soon as you become aware of the mistake, you should repent and that much of your mistake will be destroyed. In the end everything will gradually come to an end.

How can you consider it a *dharma* (religion; rightful action) when it cannot destroy karma which creates further bondage? When can new karma stop? They can stop with *pratikraman*.

## Asking for Energies to Rise Higher

**Questioner:** How and from whom should we ask for energies to rise higher within?

**Dadashri:** You can ask for the energies from your own *Shuddhatma* (pure Soul) or from the Gnani Purush. And those who are not Self-realized should ask for energies from their guru or from whatever God they believe in. You should make a list of all wrong you see within and ask for the energy to overcome them. Through faith, or with Gnan (enlightened knowledge), decide what is definitely wrong and then do *pratikraman* for it; ask for the *shakti* (energy) from the Gnani Purush that it should not be so. Then the mistakes will go away.

Large tubers of mistakes can be dissolved with *samayik* (to Be the Self and to 'see' the self) while other minor mistakes can be removed with prayer (*pratikraman*). Mistakes that have arisen in absence of prayer or *pratikraman* can be removed through prayer. All this *atikraman* has arisen due to ignorance of the Self. *Paudgalik shakti* (energies of the physical matter, energies of the non-Self) can be overcome through prayer (*pratikraman*). It is easy to slip down and difficult to climb up because *paudgalik shakti* is involved in slipping.

## Settlement of All Karma with the Gnan of the Gnani Purush

**Seeker:** There are all kinds of karmas (acts through thoughts, speech and body) one has to do in worldly interactions, many of which are considered bad or demerit (*paap*) karma. (Demerit karma, sin, is that which hurts others and as a consequence brings suffering to the self. Merit karma is that which helps others and as a consequence brings pleasure to the self.) How can we be saved from these demerit karmas?(10)

**Dadashri:** Whatever knowledge about demerit karma one has, that much knowledge will help him. If you want to go to the railway station, and you have the directions to go there, then that knowledge will help you get there. How can you be saved from demerit karma? With whatever knowledge you have about it…but that knowledge does not lie in any books or with anyone else except a Gnani. Elsewhere, you will find worldly knowledge. Only a Gnani Purush has the *nischay-gnan* (knowledge of the Self). *Nischay-gnan* is not to be found in any book. It is hidden in the heart of a Gnani Purush. You will find a solution when you hear *nischay-gnan*; when you hear it live in His speech.

Books contain worldly knowledge; it, too, can give you a lot of solutions. The intellect (*buddhi* – knowledge through the medium of the ego) increases with worldly knowledge. Intellect-based knowledge (*matignan*) will increase. *Matignan* increases with scriptural or literate knowledge received through 'hearing' (*shrutgnan*), and thus comes a solution as to how to become free from demerit karma (*paap*). Otherwise, there is no other solution. And the other thing is one's own inner intent (*bhaavna*). One can be free if he does *pratikraman*. But what should that *pratikraman* be? It should be 'shoot-on-sight' *pratikraman*, meaning it should be instant *pratikraman*. If *pratikraman* is done the instant a wrongful act occurs through thoughts, speech or acts, then you will have the solution.

# Repentance for Unjust Worldly Interactions

**Seeker:** When I see injustice in daily life interactions and in business, the mind becomes upset. So what should I do when that affects the way I interact with people? How should I repent if there is any injustice on my part?

**Dadashri:** In the repentance there should be *alochana* (recall and confession of mistakes), *pratikraman* (repentance and asking for forgiveness), and *pratyakhyan* (resolve never to repeat the mistake and asking for the energies for this). This should be done in the presence of whichever God you believe in. Which God do you believe in?

**Seeker:** Lord Shiva.

**Dadashri:** Yes, so Lord Shiva should be your witness when you repent. You should do *alochana* which is to confess or admit that you erred with such and such a person. You should repent repeatedly. If you err, you should repent. In doing so, the mistake will decrease. Injustice will occur even though you may not wish to. This is due to the faults of the non-Self complex (*prakruti*). This fault of the non-Self complex is from the past life, not of the current life. Today you want to improve but because of your past life mistakes (cause), these faults continue to occur in this life (effect) and they will not leave without harassing you. For this you should continuously do *alochana*, *pratikraman* and *pratyakhyan*.

**Seeker:** What is the solution when I have to tolerate a lot of things?

**Dadashri:** You should tolerate without complaining. Tolerate with equanimity, without cursing the other person in your mind and with the understanding that he has released you from the bondage of your previous karma, and thank him sincerely for doing so. You should feel obliged to him. No one suffers without a reason. Your suffering is the result of your own past demerit karma.

**Questioner:** Please write this '*alochana, pratikraman, pratyakhyan*' down for me. Help me get the confirmation from the Gnani Purush so that I can start doing *alochana, pratikraman* and *pratyakhyan*.

**Dadashri:** Yes, of course, you will have to do that! That you will learn here.

## Oh! Pratikraman Even for That!

**Questioner:** Is *pratikraman* to be done only for seeing faults in others?

**Dadashri:** Not just for that, but also for telling lies or for doing something wrong. *Pratikraman* should be done if any transgression through thoughts, speech or acts is committed towards any living being. *Pratikraman* should also be done for violating any of the five *mahavrats* (the five supreme vows are *ahimsa*/non-violence; *satya*/truth; *achaurya*/non-theft; *aparigraha*/non-acquisitiveness and *brahmacharya*/celibacy).

**Questioner:** Why should I do *pratikraman* when the doer of the wrong is separate ('Chandulal')?

**Dadashri:** The Self is not doing *pratikraman* but the Self is making the one who makes the mistake (the relative self) do *pratikraman*. Pure Soul (*Shuddhatma*) does not do *pratikraman*.

*****

# [2]

# Every Religion Supports Pratikraman

## The Highest Relative Religion

The highest and most profound element of the Jain religion is *alochana, pratikraman* and *pratyakhyan*. It is actually in other religions too, but what is it like there? There people ask for an overall general forgiveness. It exists in Islam, Christianity and other religions. The custom of asking for forgiveness has been going on everywhere, but the method shown by the *vitarag* Lords, the one of doing *alochana, pratikraman, pratyakhyan* in the presence of the guru, is very scientific. It gives instant results. (13)

In the other, by asking for forgiveness, one reduces the demerit karma (*paap*), that is all; whereas with this *pratikraman*, demerit karmas are eliminated completely.

The Lord (all enlightened Ones) has said that true relative religion is that of *alochana, pratikraman* and *pratyakhyan*. And these, too, have to be done instantly; they will not work if left pending. If you hurt someone, keep a mental note of it and then after doing *alochana*, do cash *pratikraman* and *pratyakhyan*. This is what the Lord calls relative and real (*vyavahar* and *nischay*) *pratikraman*. But who will be able to do this?

This instant, 'shoot-on-sight' *pratikraman* is only possible for the one who is Self-realized, and he is, therefore, able to see his own faults. However, if a person who has not attained Self-realization also were to apply the principle of *alochana*, *pratikraman* and *pratyakhyan* in his daily life, it would still be beneficial for him even though he does not understand it. Self-realization will eventually come in front of him.

The one whose *alochana, pratikraman* and *pratyakhyan* are sincere will attain the Self for sure.

**Seeker:** Give me some solution, a vow or some form of repentance whereby, if I commit a demerit karma, I can attain purity and become free from it.

**Dadashri:** 'We' - the Gnani Purush and the fully enlightened One within - give you all that here. 'We' give you all the cures; all kinds of medicine. 'We' give you *alochana, pratikraman pratyakhyan*; 'we' give you everything.

## Pratikraman Means to Turn Back from Demerit Karma

**Dadashri:** What is the meaning of *pratikraman*? Do you know?

**Seeker:** No.

**Dadashri:** Tell me the way you understand it.

**Seeker:** It is to turn back from demerit karma *(paap)*.

**Dadashri:** To turn back from demerit karma! What wonderful justice the Lord has given, that to turn back from demerit karma is called *pratikraman*. But the demerit karmas still continue. Why is that?

**Seeker:** You are the only one to explain that. One is *alochana*, the second is *pratikraman* and the third is *pratyakhyan*; I do not understand these three words completely.

**Dadashri:** *Pratyakhyan* means 'I am letting go of that thing today, I am giving it up.' That is the intent behind it. If you want to give up something, then you have to do *pratyakhyan*.

**Seeker:** *Pratikraman* would be to repent. Is *pratyakhyan* to resolve never to repeat the mistake?

**Dadashri:** Yes, repentance is called *pratikraman*. Once *pratikraman* is done, the *atikraman* will not occur again. To vow, 'I will never do that again. I promise not to repeat the mistake again,' is called *pratyakhyan*. When you do *pratyakhyan* in this way in your mind, one layer of karma will be shed. Now if the same *atikraman* should occur again, it is because of another layer of karma so you should not be worried; you should just continue doing *pratikraman*.

**Seeker:** I should ask for forgiveness in my mind.

**Dadashri:** Yes, you have to ask for forgiveness.

## Alochana

**Seeker:** What is *alochana*?

**Dadashri:** *Alochana* is to confess your misdeed exactly the way it occurred to your guru or to the Gnani. What do they call that in the court?

**Seeker:** To make a confession.

**Dadashri:** Yes, you should tell your guru or the Gnani Purush everything exactly as it occurred, without fear. You should not be afraid of what the guru will say; to be afraid, means he may even hit you! But you should confess everything to him without any fear. Then the guru will tell you to do *pratikraman*. So what do you have to do *pratikraman* for? The amount of *pratikraman* one needs to do depends on the amount of *atikraman* one did. *Atikraman* includes deeds that are unacceptable by society and the world – deeds that are condemned and anything that hurts others. If any of this applies, *pratikraman* is necessary.

**Seeker:** After doing *alochana* and *pratikraman*, should one not be aware that the mistake does not occur again?

**Dadashri:** That mistake will never occur again. True *pratikraman* is one where that mistake will never occur again, or it will gradually come to an end.

When you say that having done *pratikraman*, the mistake occurs again, that is referring to the kind of *pratikraman* that is done in the worldly life; it is a *laukik pratikraman*. *Laukik* means that it rewards you with a worldly life. When he does *pratikraman*, at least for the duration of that time he is not doing *adharma* (wrong karma through thought, speech and actions) and he binds merit karma (*punya*).

What is real *pratikraman*? It should be 'shoot-on-sight' *pratikraman*. Do they not have a rule of 'shoot-on-sight' during mass riots? That is how *pratikraman* should be.        (16)

The guru had said to do *pratikraman*, but after doing *pratikraman*, *pratyakhyan* should be done too. One should do *pratyakhyan* by recalling the guru's face and do *pratyakhyan* thus; 'I will not make the mistake again.' *Pratyakhyan* of your mistake means, 'I will not do it again.' Hence, all the three, *alochana*, *pratikraman* and *pratyakhyan*, should be done together.

**Seeker:** And should one maintain awareness that it does not occur again?

**Dadashri:** Constant awareness! Awareness does not mean for half an hour but it should be constant for twenty-four hours. Constantly! These people, after attaining Gnan from me, maintain constant awareness. They have not slept, lost awareness, for even a second.

If anyone who is not Self-realized has awareness and does *pratikraman*, then his wrong actions will decrease by that much and he will bind new merit karma (*punya*). As long as one has *darshan mohaniya* (right belief deluding karma or ignorance of the Self), one will continue to bind karma.

*Alochana* is always there with *pratikraman*. And *pratikraman* is the greatest spiritual weapon. So if you catch on to *pratikraman dharma*, meaning you practice *pratikraman*, then you will be fine even if you do not have a guru. Therefore, if you learn just this much from Dada, it is more than enough. This encompasses everything. Ask for forgiveness from 'Dada' whenever you do something wrong. You will become free from that misdeed. Is this difficult? Is Dada asking you to fast (as penance) for your wrong deeds? If Dada were to tell everyone to fast, people will feel that Dada starves them, but does Dada do that?

When someone insults you and you are affected by his actions, but you feel that it is a consequence of your own mistake and you continue to do *pratikraman*, then that is the Lord's greatest Gnan. That verily will take you to liberation (*moksha*). If you abide by just one word or one sentence of 'ours,' it will take you to *moksha*. What will you do with anything else?

## There is Atikraman As Long As There is Belief of Doership

**Dadashri:** You have to understand who binds karma. What is your name?

**Seeker:** My name is 'Chandulal.'

**Dadashri:** Then the one who says, 'I am Chandulal' is the one that binds karma. Then even when you go to sleep, karmas are being bound throughout the night. What is the reason behind this? This is because 'I am Chandulal' is false assertion (*aropit bhaav*). You are really the pure Soul but you say you are 'Chandulal' [*reader should insert his or her name here*] and so you are in violation of the truth. In reality, you are not 'Chandulal,' and yet you claim that you are. 'I am Chandulal' is a false assertion and, with this belief, you are continuously charging karma. With your conviction of 'I am Chandulal' comes a series of other wrong beliefs such as, 'I am her husband; his uncle; her father; their boss; etc.' Even in your sleep you bind karma. There is no way to avoid karma bondage during sleep but if you purify your ego - 'I am Chandulal,' then you will bind less karma.

Even after the ego becomes somewhat clean, you will still have to perform some rituals. If your daughter-in-law breaks something expensive and you shout at her, 'You have no sense,' you will have to do *pratikraman* for hurting her feelings. The hurt you cause is *atikraman* and if you do *pratikraman* immediately, the karma will be erased or it will become lighter.

(18)

Whenever you do *atikraman*, if you hurt someone in any way, you should erase it with *pratikraman*. It should be a 'shoot-on-sight' (instantaneous) *pratikraman* and not the kind that is done only once a year. Only then will it lighten this burden of suffering. If you conduct yourself according to the ways prescribed by the *Vitarags*, your suffering will depart.

## This is How You Do Pratikraman

That which has become automatic is called *atikraman* and *pratikraman* is what you will have to learn. *Atikraman* is automatically learned and done. If you want to shove or push someone, you do not have to learn to do it. You have learned that by observing others. Now, if you do *atikraman*, you have to do *pratikraman*. Generally, when people are sitting around talking, there is no need to do *pratikraman*. But if there is any pushing or shoving or making fun at the expense of another human being, that is *atikraman* and for that one should do *pratikraman*.

**Seeker:** How does one do *pratikraman*?

**Dadashri:** If you have attained Self-realization, you will have awareness of the Self within the other person. It is precisely the Self within that person that you should address. Otherwise, you can direct your *pratikraman* towards God by saying, 'O Lord! I repent for my mistake. I ask for your forgiveness and resolve never to repeat it.' That is *pratikraman*. If something wrong occurs, would you not recognize it right away?

**Seeker:** Yes.

**Dadashri:** If you do *pratikraman* for that, it will get washed away.

**Seeker:** Does it really get washed away?

**Dadashri:** Yes, yes of course it will! After *pratikraman*, the fault will not remain. Even a massive karma will become like a burned rope that appears intact but will disintegrate into ashes upon the slightest touch.

**Seeker:** And how should I repent? Should it be done outwardly so that it is visible to others or should it be done from within, in the mind?

**Dadashri:** In the mind! You should remember Dadaji, apologize for your mistake and resolve never to repeat it. In doing so, the pain will be erased and the mistake destroyed. If you fail to do this, your mistakes will accumulate. I have given you a weapon; this *pratikraman* is the greatest weapon. To become free from the ties of the worldly life, it is the only greatest weapon. The worldly life has arisen due to *atikraman* and *pratikraman* will bring it to an end. That is all there is. *Atikraman* is wrongdoing; when you recognize that, you should do 'shoot-on-sight' *pratikraman*. The moment you see the mistake, shoot it down.

This *pratikraman* is the only path where a person can see his own faults and is able to shoot them down. In doing so, all one's mistakes come to an end.

## Repenting is Never Insincere

**Dadashri:** How many such *pratikramans* do you do?

**Seeker:** If I hurt anyone, I repent immediately.

**Dadashri:** Repenting is the suffering you experience. It is not considered *pratikraman*. Still, it is a good thing.

**Seeker:** If I repent after a bad deed, how can I be freed from that? Then a person will just keep on doing it, won't he?

**Dadashri:** I will show you a way for all that.

**Seeker:** On the one hand, you commit aggression and on the other, you repent. It is a never-ending thing.

**Dadashri:** It is not like that. If a person does bad karma (deed) and he repents, his repentance can never be insincere. When he repents, that repentance is sincere and with that, a layer of karma is removed. An onion still appears whole even though one layer is gone. Another layer will be removed the next time. Repentance never goes to waste. Every religion calls for repentance. Even Christianity tells one to repent.          (20)

## The Correct and Complete Path

**Seeker:** So can our demerit karma (*paap*) be removed through repentance?

**Dadashri:** Demerit karma is removed only with that. There is no other way.

**Seeker:** So one keeps asking for forgiveness and then he keeps repeating the bad deed (*paap*)?

**Dadashri:** You are free to keep asking for forgiveness. You have to keep on asking for forgiveness. Yes! This is the path of one hundred percent attainment! Without asking for forgiveness, there is no freedom from this world. All mistakes are erased with *pratikraman*.

**Seeker:** Bad karmas are erased by doing *pratikraman*. What is the science behind that?

**Dadashri:** Demerit karma is created through *atikraman* and it is destroyed with *pratikraman*. Demerit karma is destroyed by turning back.

**Seeker:** So where does the law of karma apply? If we destroy demerit karma with *pratikraman*, then the law of karma no longer applies, does it?

**Dadashri:** This verily is the law of karma. Asking for forgiveness is itself the applied law of karma. (Karma is caused by intent of aggression and destroyed by intent of *pratikraman*.)

**Seeker:** Then everyone will continue to do wrong and then ask for forgiveness.

**Dadashri:** Yes, you can continue doing wrong and continue asking for forgiveness; that is what the Lord has said.

**Seeker:** But one has to ask for forgiveness with a sincere heart, right?

**Dadashri:** A person who asks for forgiveness does so with his heart. It will even suffice to apologize insincerely, as long as the apology is made.

**Seeker:** Then it will just become a habit.

**Dadashri:** Even if it does become a habit, it is fine as long as one asks for forgiveness. If he doesn't, then he is in serious trouble. What is the meaning of asking for forgiveness? That is called *pratikraman*. And what is a wrongdoing called? It is called *atikraman*.

What is the law of karma? You have to do *pratikraman* for any *atikraman* you do. Do you understand that?

**Seeker:** Yes.

**Dadashri:** So ask for forgiveness without fail. Do not listen to this over-wise person! If someone is doing wrong and is asking for forgiveness, let him do so. 'This is the complete law.'

If someone is drinking brandy and asking to be forgiven, I would tell him to keep asking for forgiveness. Continue asking for forgiveness and continue to drink, but make a firm resolution that now you want to quit this habit. Sincerely resolve this in your mind. Then you may continue to drink and keep asking for forgiveness. One day the addiction will come to an end. I give you this absolute guarantee through my Science.

This is a Science! It is bound to grow and proliferate, yielding immediate results.

'This is the cash bank of divine solution.' This is the only 'cash bank.' Such a bank has not appeared in the last million years! It offers liberation within just two hours. I am ready to grant you whatever you ask of me.

## 'We' Have Come To Give Happiness

If someone feels the hurt to the slightest extent, it is called *atikraman*. It may not be evident externally but he may be hurt internally (*garbhit*). Such internalized hurt and pain may not be evident but it does not mean that he is not hurt. One should not cause such internal pain and hurt. I have not hurt anybody to the slightest extent in this life. However, if it occurred, I would ask for forgiveness. We have not come here to give pain to others; we have come here to give happiness. (22)

## Free Will Versus Destiny

**Dadashri:** Have 'we' come here of our free will (*marajiyat*), or was it mandatory (*farajiyat*)?

**Questioner:** Free will.

**Dadashri:** No. It was mandatory and written in fate, and

what is of your free will? A shove from this man was also mandatory, and whether you do *pratikraman* or not is your free will.

If a man gives a donation of 5000 rupees because the city mayor pressures him to give, he will receive credit for it 'here' (in this life) but nothing over 'there' (the next life). Whereas if someone gives a donation of his own free will, then he will reap the rewards for it in the next life. That was of his free will.

What is free will? This, the current life, is all mandatory. All external actions carried out are mandatory, but the inner intent with which they are carried out is free will. When someone slaps you, it is mandatory and repentance within is an improvement of free will. Spoiling of inner intent in the process – is also free will.

If a bad deed has occurred and you repent a lot, if you repent heavily, then that mistake is erased. But you need someone to help you become free from that.

## Pratikraman and Pratyakhyan Are One's Free Will

Now you should not have the desire to take fruits from someone else's orchard. If you want some fruit, then ask for it. 'We,' too, used to steal anis seed from people's farms when 'we' were young – about twelve or thirteen years old. But later, a lot of repenting cleared it all up.

In the *Kramic* path (the step by step path to liberation), only the inner intent (*bhaav*) of doing *pratikraman* and *pratyakhyan* are under one's control.

Effect (*dravya*) is not under anyone's control. Only the inner intent (*bhaav*) is under your control. Therefore, repent for any wrongdoing. 'Our' *dravya*, i.e., the Gnani's effect, is good and so is the inner intent. Your effect is associated with *swachhand* (actions guided by one's belief that, 'I am Chandulal') and, therefore, repentance is necessary.

Do you think the Lord would interfere in such matters? He is just the Knower-Seer and in eternal bliss. He Sees and Knows everything. Do you think He inspires one in all this? When the tuber (inner complex of karma effect) of stealing sprouts within, one will have thoughts of stealing. If that tuber is large, he will have many thoughts and he may even go ahead and steal. He will also tell you how cleverly he went about stealing. When he does that, he nourishes that tuber. With nourishment, new seeds continue to be planted and the tuber of stealing grows bigger. Say there is another thief and even though he steals, it bothers him, 'What I am doing is wrong, but what else can I do? I have to feed my family.' He steals but he repents sincerely and, in doing so, his tuber of stealing does not get nourishment. And for his next life, he plants the 'seeds' of not stealing and, consequently, he will not steal in his next life.

## Repent Heartily

Nature forgives a man who repents after he steals. When he repents, nature does not count it as an offence or sin. People, on the other hand, will punish him and he will have to suffer the consequences of his actions in this life.

**Questioner:** But that is what everyone believes – that it is wrong to tell a lie, to eat meat, to misbehave and yet people do all those things. Why is that?

**Dadashri:** If a person was to repent heartily, his faults would eventually disappear. But people speak superficially. Although you may commit a terrible mistake, if you sincerely repent for it, it will not occur again. If it occurs again, it does not matter as long as you continue to repent.

**Questioner:** So is it possible for a man to improve? (24)

**Dadashri:** Yes, very much so. But there has to be someone to improve him. An M.D. or an F.R.C.S. doctor will not work there. You need an improver and not an entangler.

If a mistake occurs even after a lot of repenting, one will feel, 'Why does this occur even after repenting so much?' Actually, with sincere repentance, the mistakes will definitely go away.

*Pratikraman* brings about a state of lightness. The moment one makes that mistake again, the repenting starts.

When do the effects of karma caused in past life (*sanskar*) change? Either when you repent day and night, or when you attain our Gnan.

Repenting is no ordinary thing. Repentance should occur.

**Questioner:** What if one does all kinds of bad and negative things all day long and then repents at night?

**Dadashri:** Yes, provided he repents heartily.

**Questioner:** What if he repents and makes the same mistakes again the next day?

**Dadashri:** Yes, if he repents heartily then his work will be done.

**Questioner:** The repentance that occurs, is it because of the planning (intent; *bhaav*) from the past life?

**Dadashri:** Repentance occurs because of the knowledge (*gnan*) in this life.

**Questioner:** What should we do if we have done some negative things in life and we feel bad about them, but there is no repenting?

**Dadashri:** The fact that you feel bad about it is repentance itself, is it not? You can never feel bad about anything without the 'heat' of it. Can one feel bad from the coolness of a situation? This 'heat' itself is the 'feeling bad about it.' Feeling bad is more than enough. But do you say that you will not do it again?

**Questioner:** Yes, I do.

**Dadashri:** Make a list of things that you repent and bring it to me so I will know at which 'station' the 'car is stuck'; then we can send a car there. When repentance occurs, then realize that you are starting to turn back from *atikraman* or *aggression*.

If a person repents any of his actions, that person will one day become pure (*shuddha*); that is certain.

## Beginning from Repenting to Pratikraman

Generally, when people make apologies, that is not considered *pratikraman*. It is comparable to ordinarily saying 'sorry' and 'thank-you.' There is nothing significant in that. The importance is of *alochana*, *pratikraman* and *pratyakhyan*. *Alochana*, *pratikraman* and *pratyakhyan* are necessary in the worldly life and on the path to *moksha*.

**Questioner:** If I go to the temple on Sundays and confess all my wrongdoings, then will I be forgiven for the demerit karma (deeds) that I have done? (26)

**Dadashri:** If demerit karma can be washed away like that, then there would be no such thing as health and illness. Then there would be no pain or misery, would there? But there exists endless misery. The reason for asking for forgiveness is that when you do so, you destroy the root of your demerit karma (*paap*) so that it will not sprout again, but you still have to suffer its fruit, regardless, do you not?

**Questioner:** There are some roots which sprout again.

**Dadashri:** If the root has not been destroyed properly, it will sprout again. No matter how much of the root has been destroyed, the fruit has to be suffered. Even Lord Krishna was struck by an arrow. There is no way out. I too have to suffer!

In every religion – Christian, Muslim, Hindu – there is the principle of asking for forgiveness, but it varies with each religion. In every religion, it begins with repentance, whereas here we have *pratikraman*.

The whole world runs on the basis of ego, 'I am Chandulal' (*vikalp*). It is proper that the Muslims cover their ears and loudly recite their prayers, and what do the Christians do? Have you ever been in a church? Why, what objection do you have? When you dress appropriately and go, no one will question you, will they? On Sunday, they will ask for forgiveness for all their wrongdoings of the past six days. They keep repenting.

It is only our people who do not repent. And those that do, do so once every twelve months! On that day, they go out and buy new clothes to wear!

**Questioner:** Is mental repenting the same thing as *pratikraman*?

**Dadashri:** Do it the way you have been told to do it. If the other person is hurt if you gave him a slap, then do *pratikraman* by admitting your mistake, repenting for it and making a decision not to slap him again. Do it that way. Or else if you have scolded him, then admit to hurting him by scolding him, and that you will not scold him again.

## That is Dharmadhyan

**Seeker:** Can you please explain this *pratikraman*, this repentance of demerit karma (*paap*)?

**Dadashri:** What is *pratikraman*? It is when a mistake occurs, you 'shoot it on sight'; that is called *pratikraman*. You do that once a year, don't you?

**Seeker:** I do not really know how to do *pratikraman*.

But I do *bhaav-pratikraman* (intent *pratikraman*).

**Dadashri:** What kind of *bhaav-pratikraman* do you do?

**Seeker:** If I feel I made a mistake, then I repent for it with the Soul as the witness.

**Dadashri:** Is that so! How many times a day does this occur?

**Seeker:** Four or five times. I do it at night.

**Dadashri:** That much of your actions go towards *dharmadhyan* (absence of adverse internal meditation). If you are doing what you have just said, then it goes into *dharmadhyan*.

**Seeker:** How do I repent for any wrongdoing (*paap*)? Is the method that I use the right one?

**Dadashri:** Whatever it may be, it is not complete, but some *dharmadhyan* occurs with that. What is of importance is your intent.

**Seeker:** But should I do it or not?                (28)

**Dadashri:** Whatever you are doing at the moment is fine, but learn the new way that I teach you. But for now, whatever you are doing is fine.

**Seeker:** The poet, Kalapi, has said:

*'Yes, repentance; the pure abundant stream is flowing from the heaven.*
*By jumping in it, the sinner becomes virtuous.'*

What do you have to say about that?

**Dadashri:** That is for the sinners at the gross and superficial level. That is for wrong actions at the gross level and to repent for them.

**Seeker:** Is there awareness of the Self in that?

**Dadashri:** No. There is no awareness of the Self in it; there is worldly awareness. A straightforward (*sarad*) person will not like all this wrongdoing and, therefore, he repents. People of every religion will repent just the way you do.

**Seeker:** That will bring purity in worldly interactions, will it not?

**Dadashri:** No, *pratikraman* is necessary for that.

## Nine Kalams, the Highest Pratikraman

**Questioner:** Is there any other solution for getting rid of wrongdoing (*paap*), other than repenting?

**Dadashri:** There is no other solution, other than repenting, to get rid of any hurt caused through thoughts, speech and acts (*paap*). What is all this wrong doing (*paap*)? What do we consider as *paap*? Right now we are all sitting here and there is no problem with that. Then if someone says, 'Why do you come late?' that is called *atikraman*. When you say anything that anyone does not like, it is considered *atikraman*.

The Lord has said to do *pratikraman* for such *atikraman*. So what do you have to do *pratikraman* for? Repent for that which others do not like and that which hurts them. You don't have to do it for that which they like.

You have to repent for that. Do you do that?

**Questioner:** Yes.

**Dadashri:** Do you do *pratikraman* in the name of Dada Bhagwan or not?

**Questioner:** That book you gave us! I do it from that. I do the Nine Kalams (The nine highest intents/*bhaavna* for the one on the path of liberation).

**Dadashri:** You do that, don't you? That is *pratikraman*. The greatest *pratikraman* lies in the Nine Kalams of Dada Bhagwan. That *pratikraman* is such that it can lead to the salvation of the whole world.

**Questioner:** Is it true that no matter what wrongdoing (*paap*) is in the vessel of repentance, it...

**Dadashri:** It will become lighter due to repentance.

**Questioner:** Does it not burn to ashes?

**Dadashri:** It will be burned completely. Many such *paap* will be burned; they will come to an end. The 'soap' of repentance is such that it will apply to all kinds of 'clothes.'

**Questioner:** And when it is done in Your presence, what will remain?

**Dadashri:** You will be blessed. Therefore, there is no other 'soap' as the 'soap' of repentance in this world.

## Repentance Reduces Karmic Liability of Karma

**Questioner:** The best way to destroy *paap* is through repentance. That is a wonderful thing. That is what the great saints have said in the Puranas (ancient Hindu scriptures). Is it possible for a killer to be forgiven if he repents after killing someone?                                            (30)

**Dadashri:** If he takes pleasure in the killing, then if his sentence, karma effect, were to be for a year, it would become three years. And when he regrets and repents his actions, his one year sentence would be reduced to six months. The karma liability of any wrong actions will increase threefold if you take pleasure in it. But if you repent for them, your liability will be reduced. And if you rejoice after doing a good deed, then others will get increased benefit.

# Trimantras Are Scientific

**Questioner:** New demerit karma (*paap*) may not be bound due to *pratikraman*, but one still has to suffer the effects of his past karma, does he not?

**Dadashri:** You are right when you say that new karmas are not bound when you do *pratikraman* and the effects of past karma have to be suffered. And to reduce that suffering, I have shown you another way, and that is to recite all the three *mantras* (Trimantra) together. When you recite all the three *mantras* together, your suffering will be reduced. If a man is tired of carrying a very heavy load on his head, when he suddenly sees something which draws his attention, he forgets his misery. In spite of the load, his misery feels lighter. That is how it is with this Trimantra. You will feel less of a load. Therefore, this Trimantra is a helpful thing. Did you ever recite the Trimantra before? Even for one day? Recite it more and everything will become lighter and it will get rid of any fear you may have.

**Questioner:** If we look at it scientifically, if a person does wrong or makes a mistake, he should be punished accordingly. So then how can the Trimantra destroy the punishment of that wrong deed?

**Dadashri:** What are these *mantras*? When we recite them, we are doing *bhakti* (worshipping) of these Purush (those who are enlightened). Which Purush? We are doing *bhakti* of the world's greatest Purush (Five categories of enlightened ones). How much energy arises in such devotion!

**Questioner:** You have a great deal of their *bhakti*; you have praised them a lot; you have received vibrations from them, but demerit karmas (*paap*) still remain pending, do they not?

**Dadashri:** By doing their *bhakti*, by doing their *kirtan-bhakti* (chanting worship), all demerit karma is burned to ashes. Do you want to destroy your demerit karma? I will do that for you within an hour!

Demerit karma cannot be cut with a knife. It cannot be cut into slices. It has to be destroyed to ashes (destroyed by Gnan in the Gnan Vidhi).

**Questioner:** Even the Catholic Priests say, 'Come to us and confess and all your sins will be destroyed.'

**Dadashri:** Is it easy to make a confession? Are you able to make a confession? Confessions are done in the dark. The person who confesses does not show his face. He will only go to confession at night.

Whereas here, with me, forty thousand men and women have confessed everything to me. Many young ladies have made confessions to me. They confess everything. They gave me their confessions in writing. When the confessions are done openly, will the *paap* not be destroyed?!! It is not so easy to confess.

**Questioner:** So this *pratikraman* and confession, they are both the same thing, are they not?                        (32)

**Dadashri:** No, they cannot be the same. *Pratikraman* is to keep washing off after an *atikraman* (aggression through thoughts, speech or action) occurs, and when new 'stains' occur, one has to keep washing them off. And confession of one's sins or wrong action is a different thing.

**Questioner:** What is the difference between *pratikraman* and repentance (*prashchyataap*)?

**Dadashri:** *Prashchyataap* is repentance and is general in its application and for a number of faults but not specific to any particular fault. Christians do a general confession of their faults every Sunday. *Pratikraman*, on the other hand, is specific to a fault. The one who commits the *atikraman* does *pratikraman*. *Pratikraman* is done instantly; it is done the moment *atikraman* takes place. 'Shoot-on-sight' *pratikraman* should be done so that that particular fault is erased.

**Questioner:** What do they mean when they say to censure the self? What is that?

**Dadashri:** That means to accept your mistake, ask for forgiveness, to repent; all that is censuring. Now the Self is not to be censured. *Pratishthit atma* (the relative self) has to be censured.

## Pratikraman Destroys Wandering of Life after Life

Without *pratikraman*, there is no path to liberation. The path where there is no *pratikraman* is a wrong path. If the Jains were to do real *pratikraman*, their tubers of inner anger, pride, deceit, greed (*kashays*) would wither away and become lost, and would be gone in their next life. Who do 'we' call 'a Jain'? It is the one who does *pratikraman* the moment anger-pride-deceit-greed occurs; it is the one who practices the Lord's Agna (special directive). *Tirthankars* have left this *pratikraman* for people to follow because humans will not refrain from making mistakes. The celestials make mistakes, the humans make mistakes. The entire *chaturgati* (the four worlds of existence within which the soul migrates) makes mistakes. They do not refrain from making mistakes. What is the solution for destroying those mistakes? The answer is '*alochana, pratikraman* and *pratyakhyan.*'

What is the basis of the world's existence? Fault of transgression (*atikraman dosh*) is the cause of its existence. Those who do *pratikraman* and *pratyakhyan* daily are considered *sadhus* (those who live and strive for only the state of the Self), *upadhyayas* (those who have attained Self-realization and help others attain it) and *acharyas* (Self-realized masters). The world is not likely to let anyone go to *moksha*. It will hook you and pull you back in it, in every way that it can. And that is why, when you do *pratikraman*, the hook is freed. That is why the Lord has given all the three components of *alochana-pratikraman-pratyakhyan*, in one word. There is no other way. Now when can one do *pratikraman*? It is when one has the awareness of the Self. That awareness arises after attaining Gnan from the Gnani Purush.

*Alochana*, *pratikraman* and *pratyakhyan* combined are the essence of Lord Mahavir's teachings. And in this path of *Akram Vignan*, the Gnani Purush is the essence of all teaching. You should simply understand that the Gnani's Agnas (directives given by the Gnani) is your religion as well as penance. But alas! From time immemorial, people have had a tendency to interfere and not follow instructions.

*****

# [3]

## These Are Not Lord Mahavir's Pratikramans

## That is the Essence of Religion

If it is real *pratikraman*, then *pratikraman* and *pratyakhyan* is the essence of the entire scriptures of the Jain religion.

**Seeker:** This is very scientific.

**Dadashri:** Yes, it is very scientific. Repentance is in all religions but the scientific part is *pratikraman* and *pratyakhyan*! They are scientific; the method itself is scientific and anger, pride, deceit and greed will decrease. One does have control over his anger, pride, deceit and greed but, generally, people do not want to reduce them.                                  (34)

Everywhere, it begins with repenting (*prashchyataap*). Yes, the Christians start with repentance. Even the Muslims have repentance. People say, 'We are repenting for everything we have done.' Here 'we' have given it in the form of *pratikraman*; 'we' tell you to do *pratikraman* whenever *atikraman* occurs. *Atikraman* means that you went beyond what is acceptable in worldly interactions and so you have to do *pratikraman* for it.

**Seeker:** Sometimes there is interference (*dakho-dakhal*) because there is a lot of sensitivity; what should one do to stop that from occurring?

**Dadashri:** Do *pratikraman* and repent and have an inner intent, 'This should not occur and this should occur.' The one who has learned the Nine Kalams of Dadashri is blessed.

## Cash Pratikraman is Shoot-on-Sight

Otherwise, the Lord has said to continue doing *pratikraman*.

**Seeker:** For endless lifetimes, one has been doing *pratikraman* but he has not attained liberation.

**Dadashri:** That is because his *pratikraman* has not been real. Liberation is possible only when true *pratikraman* and true *pratyakhyan* are done. *Pratikraman* should be 'shoot-on-sight.' Now if I happen to utter even one negative word, there should be instant *pratikraman* within; it should be done right away, in the moment. Here nothing should remain pending; it is not acceptable. This *pratikraman* cannot be allowed to sit stagnant. That is why there has to be 'shoot-on-sight' *pratikraman*. What kind of *pratikraman* do you do? Is it the 'instant cash' of 'shoot-on-sight' *pratikraman* or do you let them stagnate?

**Seeker:** For what circumstances and how should one do the 'cash-shoot-on-sight' *pratikraman*?

**Dadashri:** Have you ever done 'cash-*pratikraman*'?

**Seeker:** No. I have not. But I do read *pratikraman* every day.

## Pratikraman without Repentance

**Dadashri:** Do you recite the Navkar Mantra?

**Seeker:** Yes, I do recite the Navkar Mantra....

**Dadashri:** And you still have worries?

**Seeker:** I do four to five *samayiks* (*samayik* of Jain tradition is different from the one prescribed by Dadashri) every day.                                                                          (36)

**Dadashri:** Wow! You do four to five *samayiks*?

**Seeker:** And I do *pratikraman* both morning and night.

**Dadashri:** *Pratikraman* means to repent. What does one have to repent for?

**Seeker:** I am not really able to repent. I just keep doing the rituals.

**Dadashri:** *Pratikraman* is to retrace one's steps. *Pratikraman* means to repent for the anger and wrong actions you have done.

**Seeker:** We cram all the *sutras* (concise statement that usually requires a commentary for understanding) that are written in it.

**Dadashri:** What is the point of cramming it? Even a radio memorizes, does it not? This radio keeps talking the whole day long, every day.

## Crude and Hollow Pratikramans

**Seeker:** All these activities....

**Dadashri:** Now why are you attacking someone else? You do not attack the real culprit but you attack some third person. You attack whoever is a handy target. Why do you not catch the main culprit?

**Seeker:** The main culprit is not anyone on the outside, is it? One, himself, is the main culprit, is he not?

**Dadashri:** This is not *pratikraman* for sure. This *pratikraman* is in a crude form, and then to wait for a year and to claim, 'We have done all our *pratikraman*,' is even cruder.

What is considered real *pratikraman*? If one were to do *pratikraman* for twelve months, then all his mistakes will be reduced. Whereas all these people have been doing *pratikraman* all their lives; these ascetics (*sadhus*), these monks (*sanyasis*) who are sixty, seventy, eighty years old and not a single mistake of theirs has diminished. On the contrary, they have increased!

## Parrot-like Pratikramans Are Useless

**Questioner:** How much truth is there in the Jain sectarian *pratikraman* and *samayik*?

**Dadashri:** None whatsoever. Doing *pratikraman* in the Maagdhi language (language spoken during the time of Lord Mahavir 2500 years ago) is like a parrot repeating, 'Ram...Ram' (the Lord's name). Is the parrot going to go to *moksha* by simply repeating, 'Ram, Ram?' When we do *pratikraman* in the Maagdhi language, our state is like that of the parrot.

**Questioner:** In the sectarian *pratikraman*, one has to do that, Dada, does he not?

**Dadashri:** No, no. Why should you follow someone who is on the wrong path? Are you a parrot? Our birth is that of a human being. Anyone that does anything without understanding is like a parrot. What am I telling you here? First understand, and then sing with me. This human birth is for the purpose of understanding. *Maharaj* (Jain guru) keeps reciting in the Maagdhi language; neither the *maharaj* nor his followers understand any of it. Each one of them a parrot! Ram...Ram!

They do *pratikraman* but what is their *pratikraman* like? The doer of *pratikraman* does not know anything; and the one that makes them do it does not know anything either, as to what it is all about. Have you done such *pratikraman*? You did? You cannot understand it, right?

What can we consider as real *pratikraman*? It is that which decreases your faults. How can it be called *pratikraman* if your faults increase? The Lord did not say for us to do it this way. The Lord has said to do *pratikraman* in a language that can be understood. Do *pratikraman* in your own language; otherwise you will not reap any benefits from it. The Jain *pratikraman* rituals are being done in the Maagdhi language. Now what good does it do for people who do not even understand Gujarati to be doing *pratikraman* in Maagdhi? Even the *sadhus* and *acharyas* do not understand it themselves, which explains why their own faults do not decrease. Such is the state of things of today.

The Lord has instructed that only the Navkar Mantra be recited in the Maagdhi language and that, too, with complete understanding. Only the Navkar Mantra was worth retaining in the Maagdhi language because they are the Lord's words. But before doing *pratikraman*, first you should understand the true meaning of *pratikraman*; you should understand that you are doing *pratikraman* and for whom? It is being done because someone insulted you or you insulted someone else.        (38)

*Pratikraman* means to bring about the end of the inner enemies of anger, pride, deceit and greed.

## Is This Religion?

**Questioner:** How does one purify the ego in the *Kramic* path?

**Dadashri:** It is like removing dirt with soap; like removing one type of dirt with dirt. (Soap has its own impurities; it is like removing one type of dirt with dirt). You have to take support of both *pratikraman* and *pratyakhyan*. The ego is purified when you take constant support of the two, otherwise the ego cannot be purified.

That is why anger, pride, deceit and greed have increased. The disciples of the middle twenty-two *Tirthankars* (that is $2^{nd}$ *Tirthankar* to the $23^{rd}$ *Tirthankar*) were deep thinkers and they used to do *pratikraman* and *pratyakhyan* every moment. The disciples of Lord Mahavir are obstinate (*vaanka*) and unaware (*jada*) and even in twelve months they would not do proper *pratikraman*. Once a year they will say, '*Michhami dukkadam* (forgive my transgressions).'

Can you call this *dharma* religion? If you call this *dharma*, what will you call *adharma* (lack of religion)? This *adharma* you call *dharma* and you believe it to be *dharma* too. People will point out mistakes in others and tell them they are doing wrong. If someone is being deceitful with them, they will accuse that person of doing *adharma*. If someone is being shrewd, they will accuse him of doing *adharma*. But they have no clue if we were to ask them to define what *dharma* is. Because he is alive, he can see other people's mistakes easily.

If I were to go sit in the *upashraya* (meditation hall) the *maharaj* (priest) will see five-ten faults in me right away; 'Why does he need to keep hair on his head? Why does he have to comb his hair? Why does he wear a ring on his finger? Why does he wear a garland?' He will find all mistakes because his vision has become spoiled. His is a state worthy of compassion. You would know that if you were to instigate him a little. If someone were to instigate *mahatmas* (Self-realized ones in *Akram Vignan*), they may get agitated at first but Gnan will take over later and calm things down, whereas such a *maharaj* will not calm down. If he is afraid of saying it aloud, he continues to have negative speech within, so when some one provokes him, he will explode with anger.

## Afterwards, There Will Be the Obstinate and the Unaware

Scripture writers have written that the disciples of Lord Mahavir can be considered obstinate and unaware (*vaanka* and *jada*) and Lord Rushabhdev's disciples were naïve and unaware (*bhoda* and *jada*). That is the only difference. There are no exceptions; except for one or two, they are all the same. Disciples of both these *Tirthankars* do not understand *pratikraman*. That is why the Lord had told them to do *pratikraman*. This fact is documented in the scriptures.

If the disciples of the first *Tirthankar* Lord Rushabhdev were told to do obeisance, they would to do so until dawn.

Each one of them would be five thousand to ten thousand feet tall. Their nose would be two hundred feet long! But they would do exactly whatever they were told. They would do it from morning until night. If the Lord forgot to tell them to stop, they would not stop.

And if Lord Mahavir were to tell his disciples to do *samayik* for an hour and if after three minutes the Lord leaves to go out, they would keep looking at the hourglass.

Lord Mahavir recognized what his followers were like. They were not alert thinkers (*vichakshan*). The disciples of the middle twenty-two *Tirthankars* were alert thinkers. What is the meaning of *vichakshan* in Gujarati?

**Questioner:** Very clever and shrewd; like a fox.   (40)

**Dadashri:** No. Hey, you! You took the wrong meaning of it by referring to a fox! *Vichakshan* means to think from every moment to moment (*kshana* to *kshana*) – as to what is occurring. 'What occurred here? That was wrong!' And they immediately did *pratikraman*. They did not have to be told to do *pratikraman*. *Pratikraman* was done automatically. They did *pratikraman* the moment a fault occurred. Alert thinking (*vichakshan*) means they recognized that they made a mistake the moment it occurred. They recognized that the words that came out while they were speaking with another person, were harsh and, therefore, they did *pratikraman* right away. Or if you and I had a quarrel, if I had a negative thought towards you, then I would do *pratikraman* right away at that time, 'shoot-on-sight' *pratikraman*. Only then will that mistake be erased, otherwise it will not, will it? Is it possible to remember the mistake if you wait twelve months to do *pratikraman*?

So the disciples of the middle twenty-two *Tirthankars* were very good. They would instantly do *pratikraman*, on the spot, if they said anything negative. Only these disciples of Lord

Mahavir keep it pending, 'I will do *padakmanu* (Jain ritual of doing *pratikraman*) when *paryushan* (once a year Jain ritual of doing *pratikraman*) comes.' Then, when that time comes, they go and say, '*Michhami dukkadam.*'

Now who understands what this means? They do not even understand what the term '*padakmanu*—slang term for *pratikraman*' means. Now what do you do with that? There was a seventy-year-old Jain sitting amongst a few of us. I wanted to help him and so I said to him, 'They do not understand *padakmanu* and they say they do *padakmanu*.' I called out to one old man, 'Sir, come here.' He asked, 'What is it?' I asked him, 'Where did you go?' He told me, 'I went and did *padakmanu*.' So I asked him, 'What is *padakmanu*?' He said, 'I have been doing it for forty years, but I do not know what it means. Tomorrow I will ask the *maharaj*.' God bless! Is that Lord Mahavir's fortune or someone else's? What luck that all this goes on! 'I will go and ask the *maharaj*!' Now how can one tackle all this?!

Do you do *padakmanu* or not?

**Seeker:** Yes, I do, only once a year. That day I ask for forgiveness for the whole year.

**Dadashri:** Is that it? Then is it all resolved that day?

You have been doing it for forty years! Should you not ask? If you do something, should you not ask, 'Sir, what is all this? Why am I doing it?' Is there not a need to ask this? Who is going to tell you off if you ask?

When these people do *pratikraman* once a year, they wear new clothes. What is *pratikraman* for? Is it for getting married or what? To do *pratikraman* means one has to repent so much. Why does one need to wear new clothes for that? Are they getting married? In addition, they do early morning *pratikraman* (*rayshi*), and late evening *pratikraman* (*devshi*).

By the evening, they don't even remember what they ate in the morning, so how are they going to do *pratikraman* in this way?

What is the definition of the *vitarag dharma* – religion as prescribed by the Omniscients? Jain *dharma* is to be found everywhere but not the *vitarag dharma*. How can you call one a Jain when he does *pratikraman* just once a year? Nevertheless, there is no problem with doing once a year *pratikraman* (*samvatsari pratikraman*). It is better to do it once a year than not at all.

## Michhami Dukkadam

**Questioner:** What is '*michhami dukkadam*'?

**Dadashri:** *Michhami dukkadam* is a word of the Ardhamaagdhi language (language spoken during the time of Lord Mahavir). By *michhami dukkadam* one is trying to say, '*Mithya me dushkrutam*' meaning, 'May my bad deeds (*dushkrut*) become fruitless (*mithya*).'

But nothing like that occurs in simply saying it; you have to do *pratikraman* for that. Saying '*michhami dukkadam*' without the understanding means it all goes to waste. All the effort goes to waste. *Michhami dukkadam* means whatever wrong actions that have occurred, may they become null and void.                                                                        (42)

**Questioner:** Should we do *pratikraman* for our job?

**Dadashri:** No. You should not worry about the work you are doing. This *pratikraman* is for all kinds of things, not just for wrong actions (*dushkrut*). Therefore, there is no need to worry. *Dushkrut* means that there is direct violence (*himsa*) involved. Did you understand that? It does not suit Jains to have bugs infest the grains in their grocery business. Yet, if that occurs, then they should repent for it, should they not? 'Dear Lord, why did this have to occur to me?' He should not be pleased about it, should he? His opinion should be to the contrary, should it not?

## Gnani Promotes the Vitarag Religion

People drink medicine that was meant only for external use and then they accuse the doctor of being incompetent. They will complain that the doctor did this or that and that he did not give them the right medicine, and that is why their son did not get better. Hey, you! How can your son heal when he drank the medicine meant for topical use? Would he not die from it? Topical medicine can be poisonous if ingested, can it not? Similarly, people have ingested the medicine that was meant for 'external use only' and thus they belittle the Jain religion.

How elevated is the *Vitarag* path and just look at how many divisions there are in it today! Some smart Alec came along and created a division and pulled away. Hey, you! You may have created a separate division, and you may find people who will praise you, but do you know who bears the ultimate liability? And it is all because you created the division, is it not?

Why did you start a separate 'cooking stove'? All the cooking was to be done on one stove, so why did you start another? Egotistic people will always create divisions.

Even here, with Dada's family and subsequent followers, after two to five generations, there will be divisions of all kinds. There will be 'revisionists.' I have cautioned everyone right now. I have cautioned them against becoming 'revisionists.' This is a science. Keep it alive. It will let you achieve your goal.

Lord Mahavir said it himself, 'My disciples will be obstinate (*vaanka*) and unaware (*jada*)'; that is always the rule, not just for this *chovisi* (succession of twenty-four *Tirthankars* in the third and fourth era of each of the time cycles) but for all the *chovisis*.

Is the Jain religion at fault here? It is because of the current time cycle. Now this fifth era of the time cycle is always like it is. In every fifth era, there is an existence of a Gnani Purush. Otherwise, what would become of this world and the spiritual realm of the final *Tirthankar*? It will become a jungle. Therefore, there is always a presence of support of this kind or another. Once the support is there, things continue. The spiritual realm will shine. It will shine a lot.

The current spiritual realm is not 'ours.' 'We' are considered a decorative ornament of the current reign. What need do 'we' have for a realm? Why would 'we' take on the problem? This is considered Lord Mahavir's realm. A realm is befitting for a *Tirthankar* but not for 'us.' 'We' simply give support to it.

This Gnan of 'ours' is simply the same *Vignan* (science of Self-realization). But it has arisen for people who have become entangled in nooks and crannies. At the moment, many people have become stuck in the little nooks. Not only the crooked nooks, but within that nook many little paths are going in all directions; so one cannot be easily found in it. So it is not easy to make Gnan reach these people in these deep pockets.

How straightforward is the Gnan of the Lord! This straight line and that straight line! It has north, north-west, south, and south-west, etc., but with exact approach and direction. Whereas with these nooks, there are nooks within the nooks within the nooks, and one goes around in circles and comes back to the same place again. That is why this traditional *Kramic* path has become useless. That is why this *Akram Vignan* has manifested.

*Akram* means there is no such thing as progressing one step at a time. One does not have to do anything in this path. In the presence of the Gnani Purush, all your demerit karma can be destroyed; that is how much energy there is in this Gnani. There is energy of all kinds here and yet the Gnani Purush does not want to become the owner of that realm. Why would he become the owner? Owners have misery. No one, except a *Tirthankar*, can become an owner. *Tirthankars* do not have a sense of ownership. They are the natural owners of everything. What would 'we' want any of that for? 'We' are simply a *nimit* (instrumental in delivering the science of *Akram* to the world). After 'our' work is done, 'we' will move on.

If one's conduct is in accord with the awareness that existed during the times of the middle twenty-two *Tirthankars*, then he would be considered a God. 'Chandulal' (the relative self) cannot refrain from doing *raudradhyan* (adverse meditation that hurts the self and others) and *artadhyan* (adverse meditation that hurts only the self), but because he does *pratikraman* for it, he is considered to have come back into *dharmadhyan* (absence of adverse meditation). (44)

The one whose *pratikraman* becomes 'cash' *pratikraman* (instant *pratikraman*) from all aspects is considered to have reached the state of God. Such a one is one who does not experience any further *raudradhyan* or *artadhyan*; such a one does not bind much karma. Even if he does, it is of no significance as long as he does *pratikraman*; it will all be erased. That is the kind of 'state' I have given you. I have given you 'the state of Godhood' in the palm of your hand. It is up to You to get Your work done. I will move ahead having done 'my' Work.

## Words That Have Flowed Through Compassion

The disciples of the twenty-two *Tirthankars* were all people who did 'shoot-on-sight' *pratikraman*. They had so much awareness that the instant they made a mistake, they became aware of it. Now the disciples of the twenty-fourth *Tirthankar* Lord Mahavir and the first *Tirthankar* Lord Rushabhdev are different. Those of Lord Rushabhdev are unaware (*jada*) and naïve (*bhoda*) and those of Lord Mahavir are cunning and crooked (*jada* and *vaanka*). '*Vank jadaya pachhima*—Afterwards they will be crooked and unaware.' Now is this not what Lord Mahavir has said Himself? But if we ask the ascetics (*sadhus, monks*), 'Has the Lord said this?' they will say, 'Of course the Lord has said that.' But they do not include themselves in it; they do not feel it applies to them. They will say, 'People have become like that,' but everyone says the same thing so it is not applicable to anyone, is it? No one takes the blame. So then go back to Lord Mahavir, and start all over again!

Although 'we' make such statements, 'we' have already done *pratikraman* before speaking in this manner. However, you should not speak such things. Although 'we' speak so harshly and point out mistakes, 'we' speak out of compassion and 'we' see everyone as flawless (*nirdosh*). Someone has to make the world understand all this. People need to be explained the truth and the reality exactly as it is.

But one thing is for sure: during the times of the middle twenty-two *Tirthankars*, people were very good at doing *pratikraman*. Therefore, they did not fall on the wrong track and thus they made good progress. That is very good.

**Questioner:** The *pratikraman* they did, was it like the one we do, the 'shoot-on-sight' kind? Please explain this in detail.

**Dadashri:** Yes, the 'shoot-on-sight' kind. But that was not the path to *moksha*. By doing this *pratikraman*, it helped them in their worldly life; it helped to attain a better life form in their subsequent life. It gave them a good life and helped keep away misery and obstacles in life. They would not bind enmity and revenge. Therefore, it was a path of worldly happiness. And those who wanted to go to *moksha*; it helped them on their path to *moksha*. It helped them in both ways.

And look at this *pratikraman*, this *padakmanu*. The *maharaj* speaks *padakmanu* and the rest listen. And then people talk amongst themselves. If we ask them the meaning of *padakmanu*, they will reply that it has to do with doing *pratikraman*, but not a single mistake gets cleansed. If, despite using soap and clean water, the stain on the cloth does not go away, is it because one used the wrong soap, or was there something wrong with the water, or is the one doing the washing at fault? Not even a single mistake is reduced. Why is that? One does so many *pratikramans* every day; you are aware of that, are you not? Have you gone to a *maharaj* to do *pratikraman*?

**Questioner:** Yes, I have.                                    (46)

**Dadashri:** Despite doing *padakmanu*, why has not a single mistake been erased? It is because the *pratikraman* is done in the Maagdhi language. Even when a parrot says, 'Ram has come...Ram has gone...' even when the parrot speaks of *moksha*, etc., what good does it do for us? So to take the Lord's name like a parrot is the same as doing *pratikraman* without the understanding.

Mistakes can only be cleansed if *pratikraman* is done with the understanding. That is why I told the *maharaj* to conduct *pratikraman* in Gujarati. Only if people understand it will they realize that they are doing *pratikraman*, and that previously they did not do it correctly. Should there not be a benefit of doing *pratikraman*?

## One Attains According to the Goal

**Questioner:** You said that during the time of the middle twenty-two *Tirthankars*, people used to do 'shoot-on-sight' *pratikraman*, they were aware from moment to moment, and they used to do *pratikraman* for both worldly happiness and *moksha*.

**Dadashri:** No, not for that kind of happiness. Many did it to attain liberation, many had other intents and for some it was happiness. With this *pratikraman*, whatever one's intent was, he derived the benefits accordingly.

**Questioner:** But what I am saying is that only liberation can be the intent behind *pratikraman*. How can the path of worldly happiness be applicable to *pratikraman*?

**Dadashri:** The meaning of *pratikraman* is, 'I am asking for forgiveness for my wrong actions of today,' and so that wrong action is erased and one binds merit karma (*punya*). Once merit karma is bound, one is compelled to enjoy its fruit.

**Questioner:** But the same is applicable in the path of *moksha*, is it not? So that is *pratikraman* and so is this one?

**Dadashri:** Everyone's intentions are different. Everyone's intentions and goals are different.

**Questioner:** But *pratikraman* has to do with one's mistakes. Whatever mistakes or wrong actions take place, one has to do *pratikraman*. So to cleanse the mistakes means to go to *moksha*?

**Dadashri:** No, it is not like that.

**Questioner:** How is it? Please explain to me that by doing one kind of *pratikraman* we bind merit karma and...

**Dadashri:** The *pratikraman* we have here (in the path of *Akram Vignan*) is for the intention of attaining *moksha*. But the *pratikraman* that takes place in the worldly life is for erasing mistakes connected with the worldly life; they are done for the purpose of attaining worldly happiness. Whatever their intent is behind doing *pratikraman*, the merit karma caused will bring that goal.

**Questioner:** That is correct. I am trying to understand that you have talked about two types of *pratikraman*, in which the result of one *pratikraman*...

**Dadashri:** Not two types of *pratikraman*; there is only one type of *pratikraman*.

**Questioner:** Yes, but whatever one's goal is, in that there are two types of goals, correct? One is the goal of *moksha*...

**Dadashri:** Not two types of goals, there are many types of goals. The goals vary with each individual.

**Questioner:** Now the goal of the worldly happiness that is there, does that mean that one attains *dharmadhyan* (absence of adverse internal meditation) with *pratikraman*, and not *shukladhyan* (meditation as the Self)?

**Dadashri:** There is no connection between *pratikraman* and *shukladhyan*. There is no connection between *shukladhyan* and the worldly life. With us here, because we have *Akram Vignan* (where the Self is attained in directly two hours), there is *shukladhyan*. Otherwise, we cannot even utter the word '*shukladhyan.*'

**Questioner:** So how does one do that *pratikraman*? Say, for example, I want to do *pratikraman*, I want happiness in my worldly life; how should I do *pratikraman* for that? What kind of goal should I have? Meaning having decided the goal, how should I carry out the *pratikraman*?

**Dadashri:** No, no. When one does *pratikraman*, then the mistake that had occurred within is washed off.          (48)

**Questioner:** Once it is erased, it is erased for good?

**Dadashri:** That is why one binds merit karma (*punya*).

**Questioner:** Yes, so similarly in the path of *moksha*, one also binds *punya*, right?

**Dadashri:** No.

**Questioner:** So how am I to understand that?

**Dadashri:** In the path of *moksha*, we are doing *pratikraman* in order to become free.

**Questioner:** But that is for becoming free, and the other kind?

**Dadashri:** In the other *pratikraman*, there is no connection with becoming free.

**Questioner:** But if he has decided in his mind that, 'I want...'

**Dadashri:** No, but he does *pratikraman* as, 'I am Chandulal.'

**Questioner:** So one is Self-realized (*gnani*) and the other is *agnani* (one who does not have Self-realization)?

**Dadashri:** That is it.

**Questioner:** That is the difference. Yes, then it is correct. So when the person without Self-realization (*agnani*) does *pratikraman*, he binds *punya* – merit karma.

**Dadashri:** Whatever an *agnani* does, he will bind either merit karma (*punya*) or demerit karma (*paap*). There is nothing else. There can never be the path of liberation there.

**Questioner:** Yes, that is correct.

## Will Pratikraman Yield Fruits?

**Questioner:** Even *Akram Vignan* helps us attain the state similar to that of the twenty-two *Tirthankars*, does it not?

**Dadashri:** It will not bring you into that high a state but this *Akram Vignan* will give you the fruit of *moksha*! The other will not give you *moksha*. That is the difference.

**Questioner:** Which one?

**Dadashri:** This *Akram Vignan* will give you *moksha*. But the *pratikraman* of *Kramic* path cannot give *moksha*, there is only the awareness and, therefore, one will bind merit karma for *moksha*. The other only brings awareness.

**Questioner:** But they were under the shelter of the *Tirthankar* Lord, were they not?

**Dadashri:** Those who took the shelter of the *Tirthankar* Lords attained *moksha*. All other people bind merit karma.

**Questioner:** But does *pratikraman* not open the path of liberation for one?

**Dadashri:** No.

**Questioner:** Why is that? Was that not applicable in that time era?

**Dadashri:** *Pratikraman* is not the path of liberation.

**Questioner:** But the intent behind it will bring one on this path, will it not?

**Dadashri:** *Atmagnan*–the knowledge of the Self is the path to *moksha*. *Pratikraman* will lead to the path of *moksha* after one attains *Atmagnan* (Self-realization). After that, every *sadhana* (efforts of activity necessary to achieve or accomplish a goal) will lead to the path of *moksha*.

**Questioner:** So will that *pratikraman* become the cause for him to attain *Atmagnan*?

**Dadashri:** No, they do *pratikraman* for their past actions and they do new *atikraman* due to their illusion or ignorance of the Self (*moha*). The *moha* has not ended! The *moha* continues, does it not? *Darshan moha* ('I am Chandulal') means to do *pratikraman* for past wrong actions and destroy them and create new ones. One binds *punya* (merit karma) when he does *pratikraman*.                                                    (50)

**Questioner:** That means that the layers of his mistakes become thinner, do they not?

**Dadashri:** The mistakes themselves are destroyed.

**Questioner:** So what other mistakes are created for him?

**Dadashri:** All kinds. *Darshan moha* means that new mistakes continue to arise and *pratikraman* gets rid of them.

**Questioner:** So *pratikraman* keeps one in *dharmadhyan* (absence of adverse internal meditation)?

**Dadashri:** How can all of it be *dharmadhyan*? *Shukladhyan* is never there, so how can *dharmadhyan* be there?

**Questioner:** Is doing *pratikraman* not considered *dharmadhyan*?

**Dadashri:** That *pratikraman* (of *Akram Vignan*, after Self-realization) is of a different kind.

**Questioner:** What is that?

**Dadashri:** The *pratikraman* of *Akram Vignan* destroys whatever *moha* (illusion) there is. In doing that *pratikraman*, that particular *moha* will not arise again, whereas *darshan mohaniya* (the karma of illusory attachment, which is there due to 'I am Chandulal'), which exists in the ignorant state, will give rise to another *moha*. And *pratikraman* will once again destroy it. With *darshan mohaniya*, *moha* will arise again. *Pratikraman* will again destroy it. It will keep going on in this way.

**Questioner:** The activities that reduce *moha*, are you calling that the same thing as reducing mistakes?

**Dadashri:** As many subatomic particles (*parmanus*) as there are in this world, there are that many mistakes. Those mistakes will be settled with this *pratikraman*.

Worldly people (those who do not have Self-realization) do *pratikraman*; if some have awareness, and they do both morning *pratikraman* (*rayshi*) and evening *pratikraman* (*devshi*), they will reduce their mistakes by that much. However, as long as *darshan mohaniya* prevails, there can never be liberation; the mistakes will continue to arise. However many *pratikraman* one does, he will erase that many mistakes.

**Questioner:** Please give us an example of that. During the time of the twenty-two *Tirthankars*, what mistakes were created and how did one do *pratikraman*?

**Dadashri:** Exactly in the same manner as we do over here. Whatever mistakes one made, it was done in the same manner. Just as we do *pratikraman* for the mistakes we see, that is how they did it.

**Questioner:** If a person stole something or said something wrong, then he would feel that he did wrong and that he ought not to do so.

**Dadashri:** Yes, and so he will not say the wrong thing again.

**Questioner:** So his new karma bondage was one of, 'I should say the right things,' is that it?

**Dadashri:** That will occur again.

**Questioner:** So the entire procedure is changed in this manner?

**Dadashri:** Yes. There is *darshan mohaniya*! So it occurs this time round. For the next life, the bondage will be just like that.

**Questioner:** So the 'negative speaking' comes to an end and the charging is that of 'speaking positively'?

**Dadashri:** It will be corrected only in this very life. In the next life, if he meets the wrong kind of people, he will learn to speak negatively again.

**Questioner:** So by doing *pratikraman*, the old mistake is gone?

**Dadashri:** Yes, it is gone.                                    (52)

**Questioner:** Then You said that as long as *darshan mohaniya* (karma) prevails, one binds new karma. He makes new mistakes for sure.

**Dadashri:** The new mistakes will continue for sure.

**Questioner:** The fruit of which he will bear in his next life. Whatever negative comments he made, he erased that much but he continues to make new mistakes.

**Dadashri:** Yes, but the mistake of speaking negatively is gone in this life. And so he will not speak negatively in this life. But in his next life, if he meets people who give him a different understanding, then he will develop the habit again. Everything continues to grow because of *darshan moha*.

**Questioner:** But how did he get rid of that mistake? Was it because he did *pratikraman* at the time?

**Dadashri:** Based on the scriptures, 'This is wrong, this should not be so,' that is what he will say. 'I am doing *pratikraman*, *pratyakhyan*, and I will not speak this way again,' that is what he decides. So that entire mistake is cleansed and that much time he spends for his Self. In that, there is nothing of the physical self and so he binds *punya* – merit karma.

Have you ever seen an elephant? Do you know what the elephant does after it takes a bath?

**Questioner:** It is called *gajsnanvatta*! It throws dirt all over its body again.

**Dadashri:** Then it washes it off again. Therefore, as long as there is *darshan mohaniya,* '*gajsnanvatta*' will continue.

**Questioner:** A mistake occurs as you say, and so one does *pratikraman* for it in this life – and so he becomes fault-free (*nirdosh* – without fault). So then why would he make mistakes again in his next life?

**Dadashri:** He will do it without fail. As *darshan mohaniya* continues, depending upon the circumstances he encounters, he will act accordingly.

**Questioner:** So the main point You are making is that one only becomes fault-free (*nirdosh*) if he does *pratikraman* after attaining *Atmagnan* (Self-realization). And, thereafter, he is not likely to repeat his mistakes in any life to come.

**Dadashri:** For countless past lives, one leaves stealing behind… but in his next life if he has parents who steal, then he will become a thief again. What will the one with *darshan moha* not do?

**Questioner:** Then does the *pratyakhyan* (vow never to repeat the mistake) he did, not bear any fruit?

**Dadashri:** No. That is only applicable for that particular life, not after that. Thereafter, he encounters new circumstances and he does all kinds of things.

It is here (in the path of *Akram Vignan*) that *pratikraman* has been useful for us. Because there is no more 'income' (no new causes of karma), we can get rid of the pending stock. Your *darshan moha* is gone; the 'income' has stopped. Would that be the case if the 'income' were still flowing in? So for others the 'income' still continues in full force. They have more income than 'expense,' i.e., they bind more karma than they discharge. How much income is there for them? However much imagination (*kalpana*) they have, their karma bondage is equivalent.

## This is How History Was Created

**Questioner:** Why have Jains been asked to do *samvatsari* (annual holy day when Jains repent for all their wrongdoings through the year)? What is the history behind it?

**Dadashri:** Do *pratikraman* in whichever manner you can. That is what it is. The Lord has said to 'sweep' every day; 'For the liabilities and faults created in the night, do it in the morning as well as at night, do it twice a day.' The first thing He said was to do 'shoot-on-sight' *pratikraman*.

So one will ask, 'Sir, do I have to carry a 'gun' with me all the time?' The answer is, 'Use the 'gun' in the morning for wrong actions of the night and in the night for wrong actions of the day.' Then out of the thousands of people, two came up and said, 'Sir, what should we do? We are not able to do it at night or in the morning.' So the Lord told them to do *pakshik pratikraman* (fortnightly *pratikraman*). For those who could not do that either, the Lord said, 'Do it quarterly.' The Lord has to show some way of doing it, does He not? Eventually, the Lord had to go as far as to say, 'At least do *samvatsari* (annual) *pratikraman*.' Do it on the day of *samvatsari*, at least. Do a collective *pratikraman* and say, 'I am asking for forgiveness from everyone.'

Therefore, in this day and age, forget about the 'shoot-on-sight' *pratikraman*; people cannot even manage to do *pratikraman* at the end of the day, once a week or even once a month. That is why it is done once a year, and that even without the understanding. They wear new clothes and make a fashion parade out of it. Therefore, no one actually does true *pratikraman* and that is why the faults keep increasing. One can only call it *pratikraman* if the faults decrease.

The world continues to exist because of *atikraman* and it will end with *pratikraman*.                                        (54)

## What if the Guidance is Crooked?

**Seeker:** Dada, we are doing this *pratikraman*.

**Dadashri:** Do you know how to do *pratikraman*? That is all fine. This is like placing a jewel in the palm of a child. *Pratikraman* can only be done, truly, after one understands it having attained Self-realization. In order to do *pratikraman*, you have to have the one who makes one do *pratikraman* (the Self) and the doer (non-Self) of *pratikraman*. You need it all together. Who is the one making you do *pratikraman*?

**Seeker:** The *maharaj* makes us do *pratikraman*. I do not understand what *pratikraman* is, but in it he says this male doll and female doll are married, they did this and that; all that is demerit karma and for that they make us do '*michhami dukkadam*' *pratikraman*.

**Dadashri:** No, there is no demerit karma taking place in what the *maharaj* is telling you. They have free time on their hands and because they have not become enlightened (*samkit*), their minds have become ruined and they have ruined the minds of others.

Now even to speak this way is wrong because Krupadudev Shrimad Rajchandra (Gnani of the *Kramic* path) has said that if a person is doing that and you tell him he is wrong, then he will stop doing even that much *pratikraman*. Therefore, do not say anything.

That is why *pratikraman* has been ruined – because it has come to this level. Even as it is, it is acceptable. One cannot get rid of it altogether. You have to make do with whatever there is. Things will improve out of this. The time is improving it.

## There is No Need for Ornaments There

**Seeker:** Is there a particular technique of doing *pratikraman*?

**Dadashri:** If you do not know anything else, ask for forgiveness: 'Dear Dada, with you as my witness, I do not understand this one way or another.' There is no need for a technique here. What is your intent?

Clever people will then take the goal and make it 'ornamental'-elaborate. And when they do that, people get scared that they do not understand anything and they cannot do it. Hey, you! The heck with it! Just ask for forgiveness. Say, 'Dear Lord, I do not understand it but I have made a mistake and, with you as my witness, I ask for forgiveness.' Should there be anything 'ornamental' here?

## Atikraman at Every Step

You may earn a 'dime' or 'two' in a year with the kind of *pratikraman* (*Kramic*) you are doing. Whereas when you do the real *pratikraman*, you will earn a 'dollar' for every hour of every day for three hundred, sixty-five days of the year!

Do you understand what real *pratikraman* is? We do *kraman* (normal actions) in the worldly life. *Kraman* means, 'Dear Mom, give me some food to eat.' The mother will give you food to eat. There is no problem there. But when you say, 'Mom, you made this curry very salty!' then that is considered *atikraman*. And whenever you do *atikraman*, you have to do *pratikraman* for it. There is no need to do *pratikraman* if you do not do any *atikraman*. Do people do *atikraman*?

**Questioner:** *Atikraman* occurs automatically.          (56)

**Dadashri:** The Lord has told us to do *pratikraman* whenever we do *atikraman*. There is no problem if you do not do *atikraman*. There is no need for *pratikraman* if you give me salty curry and I eat it.

**Questioner:** *Atikraman* occurs at every step.

**Dadashri:** Then as long as *atikraman* occurs, you will

not attain a human birth again. Be cautious. This is not the rule of some wishy washy person; this is the rule of the *vitarag* Lords. Bribery will not work here. Yes, everyone here knows that. Falsehood will not work here.

**Questioner:** Is there a way for it?

**Dadashri:** If ever this lady (Self-realized person sitting next to Dada) sitting here has a thought about you like, 'Why did this person have to come here and crowd everything?' She may get a thought like that but she will not allow you to notice it. She will keep a smiling face, all the while doing *pratikraman* within. To have a negative thought is *atikraman*. She does five hundred or so *pratikraman* a day. There is nothing but mistakes and yet people have no awareness of it.

## Instant Pratikraman is Needed

**Seeker:** If we do *pratikraman* for any wrongdoing when any karma is discharging, we still have to suffer some effect of that karma, do we not?

**Dadashri:** Who has to?

**Seeker:** We do.

**Dadashri:** Because *atikraman* occurs, *pratikraman* follows. But You cannot do these *pratikraman*. Even the monks (*sadhus*) and ascetics, do not know how to do them; the 'shoot-on-sight' *pratikramans* have to be done the instant a mistake is made.

**Seeker:** We do the *pratikraman* of *rayshi* (at morning) and *devshi* (at night).

**Dadashri:** Those *pratikramans* will not work. What should *pratikraman* be like? One should be able to recognize one's mistakes the moment they occur and, therefore, *pratikraman* should be instant. Despite doing these *rayshi* and *devshi pratikraman*, you have been wandering around in vain for infinite lives.

In the old days, people did 'shoot-on-sight' *pratikraman*. People cannot do that nowadays, so they recall all the mistakes of the whole day and do their *pratikraman* at night. That is called *devshi pratikraman*. And recalling all the mistakes of the night and doing *pratikraman* for them in the morning is called *rayshi pratikraman*.

## Pratikraman Can Never Be Ritual

If a person of the current time cycle wants to know *dharma* (religion), what 'we' teach him is that there is no problem if he happens to say something wrong, there is no problem even if he said something wrong in his mind, but he has to do *pratikraman* for it and vow that he will not do it again. 'We' teach people to do *pratikraman*.

**Seeker:** So then the *pratikraman* we do morning and night; are they wrong?

**Dadashri:** You are doing *pratikraman* of a corpse; you are not doing it for the living. If you do *pratikraman* like a corpse, then you will bind merit karma.

**Seeker:** Does that mean that whenever we do something wrong, we should do *pratikraman*?

**Dadashri:** *Pratikraman* should always be done 'shoot-on-sight'. It should never be left pending.                    (58)

**Seeker:** A living being (*jiva*) is constantly binding karma, so should he be constantly doing *pratikraman*?

**Dadashri:** Of course, he has to.

Many *mahatmas* should be doing up to 500 *pratikramans* daily. How many would this Niruben be doing? For the past eight years, she does 500 to a thousand *pratikramans* a day.

**Questioner:** That is all *bhaav-pratikraman* (*pratikraman* of inner intent, at the causal level). It is not possible to do that many *kriya-pratikraman* (*pratikraman* through ritual, at the effect level), is it?

**Dadashri:** No, there can never be *pratikraman* in *kriya* (action, discharge; effect). For *pratikraman*, you have to have *bhaav-pratikraman*; *pratikraman* is an internal process. There is no action-oriented *pratikraman*. *Kriya-pratikraman* is a corpse, a corpse! In *bhaav-pratikraman*, time is not wasted in wrong places or unworthy matters and *samayik* is done. The benefit one gets of *samayik* is that the mind remains good.

**Questioner:** Is that *nirjara* (*karmic* discharge) or not?

**Dadashri:** *Nirjara* is constantly occurring. *Nirjara* is going on for every living being but your inner intent (*bhaav*) that you want to do *pratikraman* is good. Because that inner intent is good, the *karmic* discharge (*nirjara*) will also be good. But *pratikraman* has to be the 'shoot-on-sight' kind.

All these people here (*mahatmas*) do fifty to a hundred *pratikramans* a day. Nothing can ever be achieved without *pratikraman*. And the *pratikraman* practiced elsewhere is *dravya-pratikraman* (it is being done in discharging effect); you need *bhaav-pratikraman* (*pratikraman* done through intent at the causal level, so effective results are obtained).

**Questioner:** So we need *bhaav* (inner intent) along with *dravya* (effect; discharge)?

**Dadashri:** Yes, but only *dravya* occurs. There is no *bhaav* in it. This is because it is very difficult for the human beings of the *dushamkaal* (the current era where there is lack of unity of mind-body-speech) to maintain the *bhaav* (purity in intent). Such *bhaav* arises only with the grace and blessings of a Gnani Purush. Otherwise it will not.

**Questioner:** Please explain what *dravya-pratikraman* is and what *bhaav- pratikraman* is.

**Dadashri:** Speak with inner intention, 'This should not be so.' That is called *bhaav-pratikraman*. In *dravya-pratikraman*, you actually have to utter each and every word. However many words that are written for the ritual, you have to speak each word. That is *dravya-pratikraman*.

## Did You Do the Real Pratikraman?

The Lord has said that if you understand the language of this *pratikraman* (Maagdhi language), then do *pratikraman* in this way. The Lord has not interfered in this. He further said that if one does not understand it, then explain *pratikraman* to him in the language he understands.

**Questioner:** According to Lord Mahavir, it is said that ultimately, even if you do *samvatsari* (annual) *pratikraman*, you will not have any problems.

**Dadashri:** No, He has not said anything like that. And this *pratikraman* was not there at all. *Pratikraman* during the time of Lord Mahavir was not like it is today. These *pratikramans* of today started after the Lord's departure.

*Pratikraman* should be there for sure. Furthermore, it should be in one's own language. Without *alochana*, *pratikraman* and *pratyakhyan*, there is no *moksha* for anyone.

If a person has learned eating by making loud belching sounds (ritual of reciting words without understanding *pratikraman*), does that mean that your hunger is satisfied?

**Questioner:** No, it will only be satisfied if we put something in our own stomach.                                    (60)

**Dadashri:** Why? We took a plate and we put food on it and we belched!

**Questioner:** Yes, but the food did not go in our stomach; it remained on the outside.

**Dadashri:** So with these *pratikramans*, if the Lord were here, he would put everyone in prison. You fool! Is this what you do? *Pratikraman* means to ask for forgiveness for one mistake and to purify that mistake. If there is one stain, you clean that stain until it is gone. You make that spot as clean as it was before; that is called *pratikraman*. Today we see nothing but stained cloths.

Here, one has not done *pratikraman* for even a single mistake and, on the contrary, he has accumulated warehouses of mistakes.

Why has Niruben's conduct and thinking become so elevated? The answer is because every day she does five hundred or so *pratikraman* whereas these people haven't done even one.

## Rayshi-Devshi Pratikraman

*Pratikraman* means to reduce fault. If the fault is not decreasing, then one is not doing real *pratikraman* but he is doing *atikraman*. On the contrary, he is increasing his faults. Instead, these two Kutchhi brothers, Rayshi and Devshi, are preferable (Kutch is the western part of Gujarat where names of men end with 'shi').

**Questioner:** '*Rayshi-devshi*' is some living being,' is just a figment of imagination according to Krupadudev.

**Dadashri:** But people understand that this is '*rayshi*' and that is '*devshi*,' do they not? So then this is Devshi's brother. So a man sat down to do *pratikraman* in Kutch. He did *pratikraman* of Rayshi. So another person hears that many people do *pratikraman* of Devshi, some do it of Rayshi; so then why don't they do *pratikraman* for our Khetshi? Are there not names like Rayshi and Devshi?

Now the *pratikraman* that they do, there is no energy in it. They do it without understanding.

And how do they do it? They do it in the Maagdhi language. They do not understand even a word of it. What do you accomplish by saying, 'Pardon me, pardon me,' in English when you yourself don't understand English?

Having done so many *pratikramans*, if they had done just one real *pratikraman*! Instead, had they been explained to in Gujarati, to do *pratikraman* in this way, they would realize, 'I have wronged this person and that is why I am doing *pratikraman* for it.' But people do not understand it at all and they let all the faults accumulate for a year. Or they do *rayshi-devshi* (nightly and daytime) *pratikraman*.

Then that other person will say, 'I did *Premshi pratikraman*!' He thinks that, 'The other person did it in his name so I will do it in my name!'

Here, people have ingested medicine meant for external use. So, now ingest medicine that was meant to be ingested, and rub the medicine that was meant to be rubbed. If one realizes his own mistakes, then he can become the absolute Self – *Parmatma*.

There is always a veil that occurs in any act of 'doership.' Once the veil appears, it conceals the mistake; he will never be able to see his mistake. His mistake will only become visible when the veil is destroyed. Only the Gnani Purush can destroy the veils; one can never do it on his own. The Gnani Purush will fracture and cast off all veils of ignorance.

Ordinarily, one cannot remember all that occurred during the day. People forget. So they cannot afford *rayshi-devshi* (nightly and daytime). People are unaware, are they not?

It is like this: Those who do *rayshi* and *devshi pratikraman*, the Lord rewards with a quarter because they made the effort. It should take him two hours to do both, right? Therefore, one earns a quarter for his effort. A quarter for one *samayik* and so would he not get two quarters for two? And our *mahatmas* do up to hundred *pratikraman* a day for which they earn a hundred thousand dollars. (Note: The concept of money and the amount is used only as an analogy for understanding).

## Lifeless Pratikraman

What should it really be like? What was *pratikraman* like five hundred years ago? One would ask the *maharaj*, 'How should I do 'shoot-on-sight' *pratikraman*? In my business, I give them less betel nut for their money. When they come to buy pure salt, I give them impure salt. When they come to buy oil, I give them adulterated oil. I cheat when I weigh things. How should I do *pratikraman*?' So the *maharaj* tells him to do *devshi pratikraman*. Recall the entire day's mistakes and do *pratikraman*. Do *pratikraman* for giving less betel nut to Lallu. I gave bad salt to such and such, so I am doing *pratikraman* for that. I gave contaminated oil to this person, for that I am doing *pratikraman*. I am doing *pratikraman* for all the conflict I caused in the shop. So the *maharaj* tells him to do it at night as *devshi pratikraman*. The debt is still pending in the *karmic* book. In doing *rayshi* and *devshi pratikraman*, the Kutchhis turned them into people's names. Rayshi, Karamshi, Devshi....!

*Rayshi* means doing *pratikraman* for mistakes made in the night. In doing so, people turned it into names of people, so then what is left? Five hundred years ago, this *pratikraman* was somewhat alive. In the current times, they are worshipping this *pratikraman* after it has died. Let go of it, you fool! Let go of the dead *pratikraman*! But then one would say, 'No, this is how we have to worship it! This verily is *pratikraman*. Everyone is welcome to come there.' You fool, why are you worshipping dead *pratikraman*?

What kind of fools are you people?! The Lord had predicted this right from the beginning. He knew everything; he knew how people were going to turn out.

## The Renunciation Necessary for Liberation

And in the *Kramic* path, people do *pratyakhyan* but they do not do *pratikraman*. They take *pacchkhan* from the Lord, but they do not understand *pratikraman* at all. They do not even understand *pratyakhyan*. They take *pacchkhan* of not eating potatoes and things like that. They take *pacchkhan* of not eating green vegetables. Those *pacchkhan* are not for going to *moksha*. *Pacchkhan* for *moksha* are different. *Pacchkhan* is to say you will never repeat the mistake for which you do *pratikraman*. We do *pratikraman* for going to *moksha*. You will not find such a *pratikraman* anywhere else. *Pratikraman* that liberates has never arisen before. True *pratikraman* does not exist in the *Kramic* path. There is not a single person at the moment that is doing real *pratikraman*.                (62)

People do collective *pratikraman*, one *pratikraman* for all mistakes. The *maharaj* recites the text written in the Maagdhi language and others just continue listening. So they tell you to rub the 'soap,' but *where* do I rub the soap? On my garment or on the table? Those *pratikramans* all go to waste.

When the *maharaj* makes them do *pratikraman*, he keeps rubbing the soap on the table and people keep rubbing it on the floor and the tile. No one has done *pratikraman*. They have taken *pacchkhan*, but what kind of *pacchkhan*? Their *pacchkhan* are, 'I will not eat green vegetables. I will not eat potatoes. I will not eat root vegetables. I will not eat at night.' Vow of not eating at night is *pacchkhan* to them. This *pacchkhan* and the path to *moksha* have nothing to do with each other. *Pacchkhan* is for the worldly path. In doing that, his next life will improve and he will have many worldly comforts.

Our *pratyakhyan* (vowing not to repeat the mistake) is for whatever we do *pratikraman* for; that verily is our *pacchkhan*. The fact that it occurs again is natural. The layers of an 'onion' keep on coming; that does not mean that whatever you did (*pratikraman* and *pratyakhyan*) was wrong. When you take *pacchkhan* and the mistake is repeated, what do you understand from that? There is no connection between *pacchkhan* and the mistakes that occur. One thinks that mistakes should end just because he did *pacchkhan*. It is like the hundreds and thousands of layers of an onion and so, until all the layers are gone, the fault will keep recurring. How is the poor man to understand this?!

How is one to understand what the past is like and what the next life is going to be like?                                    (64)

One has to do *pratyakhyan* for the mistakes he makes. If one does not do anything wrong, then why should he have to do *pratyakhyan*?

**Questioner:** Then what is *pratikraman* for?

**Dadashri:** *Pratikraman* is for any wrongdoing, *alochana* is for any wrongdoing and *pratyakhyan* is for any wrongdoing.

Today, all these *sadhus* and *sadhvis* (monks and nuns) tell me, 'You are not doing *pratyakhyan*. You are not taking *pacchkhan*.' Hey, you! *Pacchkhan* is to be made where there is acquisitiveness (*grahan*). When one does not acquire, what *pacchkhan* (vow of fasting of certain food) should he take?

Therefore, the *sadhus* and *sadhvis* (male and female monks or ascetics) do not do *pacchkhan* at all. They consider renouncing as *pacchkhan*. Renunciation is not *pacchkhan*. *Pacchkhan* is for that which has not been renounced. Then it will result as renunciation (*tyaag*).

Do you not understand what one has to take *pacchkhan* of?

**Questioner:** Is it of something that one has attained (*grahan*)?

**Dadashri:** You have to take *pacchkhan* of something that you have yet to renounce. Those people consider what they have renounced as *pacchkhan*; 'We have taken *pacchkhan*,' they will say.

A vow (*vrat*) is that which becomes one's natural state of conduct (*vartey*). For 'us,' all these *vrats* are a natural state of conduct. The vows of non-violence (*ahimsa*), telling the truth (*satya*), non-stealing (*achaurya*), celibacy (*brahmacharya*) and non-acquisitiveness (*aparigraha*) have become a natural conduct in 'us.' There is not an ounce of *parigraha* in 'us.' So a vow cannot be wishy washy.

Hence, in the path of *Akram*, there are no such things as rules, principles and vows; all that is applicable in the worldly path. All these rules of vows, *japas* (chanting), penance, meditation, principles and rules, etc., are found in the worldly path.

The worldly path means to accumulate *punya* (merit karma).

The Lord has shown us two paths. One is that of merit karma and the other is the path of *moksha*. What does the path of *moksha* mean? It is the path of *alochana*, *pratikraman* and *pratyakhyan*, and the one who abides by these three will go to *moksha*, without fail.

**Questioner:** The merit karma one builds will bring favorable circumstances in his next life, is that not so?

**Dadashri:** The merit karma he accumulates will be helpful to him in his next life. What else can they do?

## No Iriyapathiki Pratikraman in Akram Vignan

In the *Kramic* path, there is *iriyapathiki kriya* (walking with extreme caution so as not to hurt any living being), starting from the first *gunasthanak* (qualities evident in the relative from progressively higher levels of spirituality) to the twelfth *gunasthanak*. What is *iriyapathiki kriya*? As long as the ego is present, there is *iriyapathiki kriya*. Therefore, there is no more *iriyapathiki kriya* once the state of *kshayak-samkit* is attained (Permanent conviction of the right belief, 'I am pure Soul'). After *kshayak-samkit*, the ego no longer remains and thus there cannot be any *iriyapathiki kriya*.

*Iriyapathiki* action (*pratikraman*) means to do *alochana*, *pratikraman* and *pratyakhyan* for any wrongdoing that occurs when one goes out and does things as 'Chandubhai.'

After one's ego is gone, there is no such thing as 'action' for him. There is action as long as the ego is present. The *Kramic* path means that the ego is present until the end; until one attains final liberation. There is no ego in this *Akram* path, it there?

Did you understand some of it?                          (66)

**Questioner:** Yes, then we have to do *pratikraman*.

**Dadashri:** 'You' do not have to do *iriyapathiki pratikraman*. You do that in the *Kramic* path. If in this *Akram* path you do the *pratikraman*, then it would prove that you are the owner of the body.

**Questioner:** That is right.

**Dadashri:** What occurs when 'You—the awakened one in *Akram*' become the doer?

**Questioner:** It means that it is being done with the understanding that, 'I am the body.'

**Dadashri:** That proves it.

**Questioner:** With that proof, everything becomes

contradictory.

**Dadashri:** So if 'You' wish to do it, then 'You' (the awakened Self) have to tell 'Chandubhai' (non-Self), 'Go ahead and do *pratikraman*.' You have to 'do' it this way. Do *pratikraman* for the major things. Do not get stuck with very subtle matters, because if you try to enter into subtle matters, you will miss the major ones. Will they not be left out?

**Questioner:** Yes, they will.

## Compassion for the Pratikraman of Tradition

It is like this. We were told to do *pratikraman* in a language the *antahkaran* (inner working components of the mind, intellect, *chit* and the ego) would understand. We don't have to criticize anything that these other people are doing. Whatever they are doing, it is good. At least they have a good intent behind it.

I am not blaming any ascetic or priests (*sadhu* or *acharya*) for it. What can anyone do if no one understands this?

They have a sincere intent of wanting to follow the Agnas of Lord Mahavir. At least they are ready to abide by the Lord's Agnas and whatever understanding they have of them. That is what we have to consider. If they do not have the understanding, the main thing is that their intent is good, and out of one hundred, eighty-eight of them are ready to follow it for sure. So how can we call that path wrong? But the eighty-eight people cannot see a single fault of theirs. And they brag saying, 'Yes, I only have a little anger,' but they will not admit that they make mistakes.

In India, there is no one who can make the statement, 'I experience *moksha* (liberation),' because if you were to provoke him a little, there would be an instant counter-attacking reaction. The moment you provoke him, he will show his fangs! Whereas here, if someone were to give a *mahatma* two slaps, he would not react or retaliate and if for some reason there is retaliation, he would do *pratikraman*. Elsewhere, there is no *pratikraman* or anything of the sort.

## With Pratikraman, There is No Remainder

One can only go to *moksha* if his accounts of credit (merit karma), as well as debit (demerit karma), are closed. If there is any credit left over, one will have to take another birth. If there is any debit left over, one will have to take another birth.

**Questioner:** Is the remainder that of karma or of one's *bhaav* (one's inner intent)?

**Dadashri:** Who is the mother of karma? *Bhaav* is. As long as the mother is there, the children will be there too.

**Questioner:** Is *pratikraman* for the purpose of bringing both credit and debit to zero – without a remainder?

**Dadashri:** Yes, *pratikraman* is for both, but one will forget about the credit part. That is why you have to keep on doing *pratikraman* for the credit.

## The Path of Lord Mahavir

But this is how everything has continued up until now and it has become very old; it is 2500 years old. When something becomes very old, it will become like that, will it not? It is good that they even do it once a year, is it not? What kind of *pratikraman* do you do?                                    (68)

**Questioner:** The 'shoot-on-sight' *pratikraman*.

**Dadashri:** That kind of *pratikraman* is needed and in order to do this kind of *pratikraman*, one has to have awareness of the Self (*jagruti*). Otherwise, how can one do them without awareness? When one does not even realize that a mistake has even occurred, he will forget in a very short time, will he not? If such awareness is not there, *pratikraman* will not occur. That is why 'we' bring people into the state of awareness. They are in constant awareness and so they can do the 'shoot-on-sight' *pratikraman*. If a man loses his grip on the string of his kite, what is the point of shouting and complaining when his kite takes a nosedive?

**Questioner:** He cannot do anything once he loses the grip.

**Dadashri:** Such is the state of all humans today. So when 'we' help by putting the string back in your hands, then if it takes a nosedive, all you have to do is pull on the string and it will come back under control. Until then, the situation is not in your hands at all.

When is one considered to have attained the path of Lord Mahavir? It is when one can see hundreds of his faults and does hundreds of *pratikramans* every day. The knowledge of the Self is way beyond that. But here, one reads four books (scriptures) and then walks around with the intoxication (*keyf*) of 'having attained the Self.' He has not attained even a drop of the knowledge of the Self! When knowledge does not progress, intoxication increases. Because of intoxication, one's *gnan-avaran* and *darshan-avaran karma* cease to be removed. (*Gnan-avaran* karma is knowledge-covering karma. *Darshan-avaran* is vision-covering karma.)

## Pratikraman in the Ignorant State

**Questioner:** How should one do real *pratikraman*?

**Dadashri:** Real *pratikramans* are only of value when I give you the right vision, because without attaining the awareness of the Self (*jagruti*), it is not possible for anyone to do *pratikraman*. And such awareness cannot be attained without 'us' giving you Gnan (knowledge of the Self). You will have constant awareness when 'we' give you Gnan. Otherwise, if I tell you about *pratikraman* and explain it to you, you will still forget it by tomorrow.

Now, when you cannot remember it as it occurs, how are you going to remember it in the evening? How is one going to remember his mistakes by the evening when he is confused and worried the whole day? There is no awareness at all. Unconsciousness! One walks around in absolute ignorance. One has no awareness of 'Who am I?' so how can he see his faults? He would be blessed if he could.

**Questioner:** But can someone who has not taken Gnan do *pratikraman*? If we explain the process of *pratikraman* to those people who have not taken the Gnan, would they benefit from it?

**Dadashri:** No, there will not be any awareness, will there? Awareness arises because demerit karmas (*paap*) are destroyed with Gnan and when this awareness arises, everything - all mistakes, remains in awareness (*khyal*).

**Questioner:** Therefore, this solution of *pratikraman* cannot be given to everyone.

**Dadashri:** It cannot be done, can it? It will not help others. But you should tell them to at least do whatever little they can. Whatever little one does, one will benefit from it. But one will not be able to maintain awareness. How can awareness remain? But ultimately, he will benefit if he knows about *pratikraman*. But how can one benefit when he does not even know this cure?

Therefore, these people do *Paryushan* once a year because they do not have awareness. (*Paryushan* is the most important Jain religious observance of the year. This is a time of intensive study, reflection and purification). There is no awareness whatsoever. (70)

**Questioner:** Did you ever do *samayik*?

**Dadashri:** 'We' used to do only *pratikraman*. 'We' did *pratikraman* all the time.

**Questioner:** I am talking about before you attained Self-realization.

**Dadashri:** In those days, it was not like it is today.

Even before Gnan, 'we' used to do *pratikraman*, but what kind? It was *pratikraman* inclusive of repentance for 'this is a wrong karma that is being bound.' But those cannot be regarded as true *pratikramans*. True *pratikraman* began after Gnan.

## Real Pratikraman Through Right Vision

**Questioner:** How can one do pure *pratikraman*? How can we do real *pratikraman*?

**Dadashri:** True *pratikraman* begins after Self-realization. Once the enlightened vision (*samkit*) is attained, the right vision (*drashti*), the vision as the Self (*Atmadrashti*) arises; only then will you be able to do real *pratikraman*. Until then, one can still decrease his faults with *pratikraman*. If one does not have this enlightened vision but still does *pratikraman* for his mistakes and repents for them, he will bind lesser demerit karma. In doing *pratikraman* and repenting, karma may even get destroyed altogether!

Why do we quickly remove tea or coffee stains form our clothes?

**Questioner:** To remove the stain.

**Dadashri:** Likewise, you should immediately wash away internal stains the moment they occur. These people here immediately wash away their internal stains. The moment something occurs, the moment any *kashays* (anger, pride, deceit and greed) arises within, they immediately wash them away until it becomes spotless and meticulous within. Here you do it only once a year. On that day, people soak their clothes!

'Our' *pratikraman* is called 'shoot-on-sight' *pratikraman*. What you are doing is not called *pratikraman* because not a single piece of clothing of yours becomes clean, whereas here in our path, all our clothes have become clean and spotless. *Pratikraman* is that where all the stains (*atikraman*) are removed and the clothes become immaculate.

You have to wash each item of clothing every day. Whereas over there, they gather one year's worth of washing and they wash all of them on that one day. They accumulate a year's worth of dirty laundry and then attempt to wash it all at once. That is not acceptable with the Lord. These people soak their clothes in steaming water once a year, don't they? Here each clothing item needs to be washed separately with great care. When you manage to wash at least five hundred a day, you will make progress.

However many faults you are able to see within, that many faults will decrease. What is the reason that you are not able to see these faults? It is because of that much weakness-unawareness. Is it because you have become free from your faults that you are not able to see them?

The Lord has emphasized the need to do *pratikraman* daily, but people only do it once a year during *Paryushan*. The Lord said that a true merchant is the one who keeps an account in his record book for the entire day, tallying his ledger in the evening. If he were to log everything just once a year, how would he manage to remember all his accounts and set his books straight? The Lord has stressed the importance of keeping a logbook for the entire day, as a true merchant would. If an entry is made incorrectly, that is if a misdeed occurs, it should be erased with *pratikraman*.

*****

# [4]
# How Amazing is the Awareness of the Gnani Purush

## Flawless Vision and Yet Harsh Speech

Everyone in this world is flawless; without faults (*nirdosh*) and yet look how 'our' speech comes out. 'We' have seen everyone as *nirdosh*; no one is at fault (*doshit* – one who has faults). To 'us,' no one appears at fault; 'we' see no one at fault, but the speech says so. 'We' see no one as being at fault whatsoever, so how can 'we' speak in this manner? Is it necessary for 'us' to speak in this way? 'We' cannot speak this way about anyone and that is why *pratikraman* immediately follows. This occurs because 'we' fall short by four degrees (360° is absolute enlightenment, Dadashri is at 356°) and, therefore, 'we' should do *pratikraman*.

Although 'we' interfere deliberately and use stern words, according to nature, it is a mistake on 'our' part, is it not? And for that, 'we' make him (A. M. Patel) do *pratikraman*. There is *pratikraman* for each mistake. However, when 'we' scold people, 'we' know how to do it without hurting them.

**Questioner:** Is *pratikraman* necessary even if the scolding is done with good intentions? (72)

**Dadashri:** You bind merit karma (*punya*) with good intentions. If you do not have Gnan and you get angry with him, even then you will bind merit karma; because it depends on your intention. Everything in the world is bound according to one's intention.

'We' cannot say something 'is' when 'it is not' and 'we' cannot say 'it is not' when 'it is'; and that is why some people feel hurt by what 'we' say. If 'we' were to say something exists when it does not, you will be deluded; and if 'we' speak the way we do, people feel slighted and question, 'Why does he speak that way?' Therefore, every day 'we' have to do *pratikraman* for all the people we have to speak about in this way! No matter what, no one should be hurt. If a person says there is a ghost in the banyan tree, and I tell him there is no such thing as a ghost in the banyan tree, that person will feel hurt and so, in turn, I have to do *pratikraman*. *Pratikraman* has to be done always without fail! 'We' have not come here to hurt anyone. 'We' have come to make people happy, but 'we' cannot give happiness to both the *gnanis* (Self-realized) and the *agnanis* (non-Self-realized). Therefore, we have to do *pratikraman* for the other side.

**Questioner:** Many times there is ignorance (*agnan*), but it manifests in Gnan's clothing.

**Dadashri:** If ignorance arises, it will not last long, not even for a second. And here, it will not last at all. That is because... what is 'our' Knowledge (Gnan) like? It is the Knowledge of demarcation; demarcation between Knowledge and ignorance and so it will not work here at all.

Then if he is hurt, 'we' have to do *pratikraman* for it. 'We' have to turn things around as much as 'we' can by telling him, 'Dear brother, I am doing *pratikraman* if I did anything wrong.'

You cannot hurt any human being at all. You may have a misunderstanding with him, but as far as he is concerned, his opinion is based on his understanding, is it not? You may feel that he does not understand, but according to him, he believes he understands so how can we hurt him?

## Then There is No Pratikraman

**Questioner:** Now, if we continue to understand that the

other person is acting in accordance to the unfolding of his karma, then there is no reason to do *pratikraman*, is there?

**Dadashri:** That is a good state, is it not? But *pratikraman* is only necessary if you had a negative inner intent (*bhaav*) towards him.

**Questioner:** And if a negative *bhaav* towards him did not arise, then I don't need to, right?

**Dadashri:** No.                                                                    (74)

**Questioner:** We do not consider him as being in the wrong at all.

**Dadashri:** Then you do not have to.

The whole world is flawless (*nirdosh*). Not even for a moment has any living being (*jiva*) become at fault (*doshit*). The fault (*dosh*) you see in others is due to a fault in your own self. And it is because you see the other person at fault that *kashay* occurs; otherwise there would be no *kashay*.

So the fact that you see a person at fault is definitely the wrong vision. It is like a blind person running into another blind person. When a blind man bumps into something, should you not realize that he is blind and that is why he is bumping into things? What is the reason for bumping and clashing so much? It is because he cannot see.

Otherwise, there is no one *doshit* (at fault) in this world. *Kashays* remain because of the faults one sees.

## Truth-Untruth is Relative

**Questioner:** Why should one do *pratikraman* if what he says is true?

**Dadashri:** This so called truth is itself untrue. Whatever truth there is, it is all untrue. Which point do you consider to be the truth? I will show you that it is not the truth.

**Questioner:** When we speak the truth, when we tell the other person something openly and he feels bad, then why should we do *pratikraman* for it?

**Dadashri:** No one can tell the truth. No one has yet been born in India who can tell the truth. How can one tell the truth? That truth is according to one's own understanding, but it is wrong according to the other's understanding.

I do not see anyone *doshit* (at fault). This speech that comes out is always associated with *pratikraman*. 'This should not be so' – that is the opinion 'we' have, and it is separate from the speech. How do 'we' see? 'We' see them flawless (*nirdosh*) but why does the speech come out as it does? There should not be any *avarnavaad* – to not say as it is. 'We' should remain silent (*maun*). Now if 'we' remain silent, you will not realize what occurred, and that too cannot be called the truth. This cannot be the truth.

## Except for Shuddhatma, Everything is Untrue

**Questioner:** What should I do if the other person takes it wrong through his understanding?

**Dadashri:** All of these so called truths that you come across are relative truths; they are false. They are right according to the way of the world, but if you want to go to *moksha*, then they are all wrong. *Pratikraman* should be done for each and every thing. You should do *pratikraman* even for saying, 'I am a spiritual teacher (*acharya*),' because this is a wrong belief. In reality you are pure Self.

Therefore, everything is all wrong. Do you understand this?

**Questioner:** Yes, I do indeed.

**Dadashri:** Everything is false. Because people do not understand, they say, 'I am telling the truth.' Hey, you! If it were the truth indeed, then it would not offend anyone.

## What is the Definition of True Speech?

When I speak here, is there anyone who is ready to speak against what I say? Is there ever any dispute? Do they all not continue to listen when I speak? They do not dispute it, do they? That is the truth. That speech is the truth and it is Goddess Saraswati (Goddess of speech). Any speech that creates dispute is wrong, exactly wrong!

Otherwise, one would say, 'Shut up. You have no sense.' So that person is wrong, so is the one doing the talking and so are the others listening. The listeners may not say anything but they are all wrong too.                                        (76)

**Questioner:** But the unfolding of our karma is such that the other person believes us as being wrong. Even though what we say is the truth, completely correct. We tell him, 'I did not do it,' but he still insists, 'No. You only did this!' so is that the unfolding of our own karma? That is why he sees us as wrong, is it not?

**Dadashri:** It is never the truth. No man can tell the truth; it is always untrue. The truth is that which the other person accepts. Otherwise, it is the truth according to one's own understanding. People will not accept as truth what you believe to be the truth.

So the Lord declared who speaks the truth; it is one with *vitarag* speech! What is *vitarag* speech? It is speech that will be accepted by the speaker and the listener. It is speech that is with the intent of hurting no one. Otherwise, all speeches are associated with attachment-abhorrence (*raag-dwesh*). They are lies, cunning falsehood and worthy of being thrown in jail! Can there be any truth in it? Speech with attachment cannot be the truth. Do you think that there can be any truth in that? When 'we' scold anyone here, their soul will accept it. There is no dispute here. Has there been any dispute here? Some person may have fallen short in understanding, but there is never a dispute here. No one has ever contradicted Dada's word, because it is pure talk of the Self; it is Saraswati (Goddess of speech) herself! It is *deshna* – speech of the Omniscient One.

Can one call speech with attachment-abhorrence the truth?

**Questioner:** No, we cannot.

**Dadashri:** Then what you say, is that the truth?

**Questioner:** But is it not considered the worldly truth?

**Dadashri:** That which is the worldly truth is the untruth from the real (*nischay*) view.

Worldly truth means if it is acceptable to the other person, then it is the truth (*satya*), and if it does not fit, then it is untrue (*asatya*). Worldly truth means in reality, it is not the truth.

**Questioner:** If we believe it to be the truth but it is not acceptable to the other person...

**Dadashri:** That is all wrong. It is all wrong. If it is unacceptable, then it is all wrong. 'We,' too, say that if someone does not understand what 'we' are saying, 'we' do not fault him. 'We' see that as 'our' fault; 'Where are 'we' at fault that he did not understand 'us'?' He should understand what 'we' are saying. 'We' do not fault him for not understanding what 'we' are saying; 'we' consider that as a fault on 'our' part. 'We' should know how to make him understand. Therefore, the other person is never at fault. It is a grave mistake to see the other person as being at fault. 'We' have never considered others as being at fault – never!

It is simply that when someone asks 'us,' 'we' are obligated to answer and 'we' have to do *pratikraman* for it. Truth (*satya*) is that which is always spoken with *pratikraman*.

If there is no *pratikraman*, then that truth is not the truth at all. The truth of this world is not the truth in *nischay* from the real viewpoint.

## That Current Flows from the Stream of Compassion

'We' immediately apply the 'medicine' (*pratikraman*) and then 'we' remain *vitarag*. 'We' do not have any *raag-dwesh* (attachment-abhorrence). 'We' are ready to apply the medicine. However, if by any chance a slight dislike (*abhaav*) occurs towards someone, which usually never occurs, but in case it should, then 'we' have the medicine of *pratikraman* which 'we' apply immediately. There is an instant medicine of *pratikraman*, is there not?

It is in this life that I speak this way about the priests (*maharaj*). I speak about everyone who is doing wrong in every religious path in the world. As if I am the King of all the religions! That is how I speak about people! As if it is only my concern. But what concern is it of 'ours'? I am just one of the men! And I should not speak in this manner, but people should become free from all this (ignorance). So by speaking this way, I have invited demerit karma! In due time, if there are any demerit karmas that have to be suffered; only then will I have to suffer them. Otherwise, I have not created any other kind of demerit karma and there are no other demerit karmas that I have created for myself.                                                            (78)

The rule is that you can talk to anyone about Gnan. But if that person is not capable of accepting it, or if he is a little slow, then you have to present it slowly. You have to become *vitarag*. But behind all this 'we' have compassion towards people such that, 'These people, having come this far, should gain something. They have so much 'fever' and yet they are not taking the medicine! The medicine is ready!' But this (approach) is not considered as per rules and hence *pratikraman* has to be done. If there is any undue exchange, then you have to do *pratikraman*. The Lord has called this '*pratikraman* of compassion.'

## Flawless Vision Yet Flawed Speech

Now all these things that 'we' have to say like, 'This is not proper'; having spoken that way means 'I' stepped out of *syadvaad* (that which is accepting of and acceptable to all) speech. Yet it has to be said in order to put people on the right path. But what does the Lord say? He says that this is proper and so is that. A thief stealing is right and it is also right when a person's pocket is picked. The Lord is *vitarag*; he would not meddle in this, whereas 'we' meddle in everything. This task of meddling has fallen upon 'us.'

**Questioner:** But that, too, is to remove all these 'diseases' from us, is it not?

**Dadashri:** Yes. It is to get people ready for liberation. The intent behind this is good. This intent of 'ours' is for other people; it is not for our self.

And along with that, it is 'our' conviction (*pratiti*) that no one is at fault. In 'our' conviction everyone is flawless (*nirdosh*). That conviction has completely changed and, therefore, 'we' speak this way knowing and believing that everyone is *nirdosh*.

**Questioner:** Do you say it with the understanding that one is flawless (*nirdosh*)?

**Dadashri:** Yes.

**Questioner:** Then why do you have to do *pratikraman*?

**Dadashri:** But I should not say those things, not even a word. How can anyone even speak such negative words? The other person is not here and is not being hurt. And you do not have any problem in believing that, as far as Dada is concerned, those people are flawless (*nirdosh*). Then why did Dada speak such harsh words? That is why I have to do *pratikraman*. There should be no harsh words.

**Questioner:** You always remain detached (*vitarag*), even when you are saying something, so why do you have to do *pratikraman*?

**Dadashri:** Because there is separation, 'I' (the Self) do not have to say it. It is to the one within, the one who says everything, that one has to do the *pratikraman*, and I tell him, 'Go ahead and do *pratikraman*.' And 'You' have the same. 'You' do not have to do the *pratikraman*. 'You' (the Self) have to tell 'Chandubhai' (the non-Self) to do it. 'You' do not have to do *pratikraman*; the one who did *atikraman* (wrong doing), has to do the *pratikraman*.

**Questioner:** How is the *pratikraman* for that mistake?

**Dadashri:** *Pratikraman* has to be done afterwards. The mistake is never about Gnan. 'We' may have been harsh towards someone who was going against *syadvaad* (acceptable of all and to all). Harshness would not occur when there is *syadvaad* in speech. This is *syadvaad* but not absolute *syadvaad*, is it? Therefore, when *Keval Gnan* occurs, there will be absolute *syadvaad*.

## Absolute Vision Shows Mistakes

'Our' Gnan is non-contradictory and the speech is not absolutely *syadvaad* (acceptable of all and to all). Someone may get hurt in the process of speaking. Whereas this is not so with *Tirthankars'* speech; nobody will get hurt from their speech. A *Tirthankar's* speech is absolutely *syadvaad*. They speak without scolding anybody. They speak similarly, however, without hurting anyone.

**Questioner:** Your *syadvaad* speech is not absolute

because someone gets hurt. Even then, that *darshan* (vision) is absolute, is it not that the mistake occurred in unfolding of *syadvaad*?(80)

**Dadashri:** Yes, *darshan* is complete. There is no problem in *darshan* (enlightened vision). Gnan - experience of the Self as the absolute Self, is there too, but Gnan is short by four degrees. Therefore, it is not *syadvaad*. 'We' have absolute *darshan*. Everything immediately will come in *darshan*. I can know the mistake right away. I can instantly know even the subtlest mistake. It will take a long time for you to see such mistakes. You currently 'see' the gross mistakes. You see only the overt mistakes that you are able to see. That is why 'we' say that it is our fault, yet no one can see 'our' fault. We can see our own fault.

**Questioner:** So You see all faults that have occurred with reference to *syadvaad*?

**Dadashri:** We can see all such faults that occurred in *syadvaad-anekant* (*anekant:* All-inclusive, impartial and acceptance of all viewpoints). Now our speech is heading towards absolute *syadvaad*. When the speech becomes absolute *syadvaad*, then *Keval Gnan* (absolute knowledge) is attained. We have *darshan*; that is the only reason we know that this is a mistake. It is 'full,' absolute *darshan*. That is why I told everybody that I am giving you *Keval Darshan* (absolute vision).

'We' have to do *pratikraman*. Words keep coming out of 'our' mouth. See how mandatory this is! Is it ever appropriate to speak this way about religious masters (*acharyas*)? For that matter, one should not speak this way about anyone. 'We' know that everyone in this world is *nirdosh* (flawless). So then is it right to talk about anyone?

**Questioner:** No, it is not.

**Dadashri:** And yet that is the very kind of speech that comes out, but 'our' *pratikraman* immediately continues along with that speech. See what kind of a world this is!

'Our' opinion behind what 'we' say is different. What kind of a world is this? When 'we' speak, our opinion behind it is, 'This is not how it is. This is wrong. This should not be so.' But look how this world runs. 'We' remain in the awareness of how this world runs.

As 'we' speak, there is also the awareness along with it that, 'It should not be this way,' because 'we' have seen the whole world as *nirdosh* (flawless). Why has that not come into our experience (*anubhav*)? It is because of this meddling speech.

**Questioner:** Although there is meddling, Your awareness is constant and very high.

**Dadashri:** No, but although the awareness is there, until this kind of speech ends, the absolute state cannot be attained. How forceful this speech comes out!

Now when was this speech created? It was when 'we' had not seen the world as *nirdosh* (flawless). 'He is at fault in this manner. Why is he doing it this way? It should not be like this. How can the Jain religion be like this? Etc.' Therefore, whatever was stored (in ignorance in the past life; before Gnan) is what is being discharged today. Those opinions are being discharged today. And today 'we' are no longer in agreement with those opinions.

## Pratikramans of the Gnani Purush

Have you done your *pratikraman*? Make sure you do *pratikraman*; otherwise, it will not become clean. Do *alochana*, *pratikraman* and *pratyakhyan* every day in the presence of Dada.

**Questioner:** It is not our intention to say anything negative about the other person, so then should we do *pratikraman*? We are only speaking the truth, are we not?                    (82)

**Dadashri:** It is like this: the instant 'we' utter a word, there is simultaneous *pratikraman* being done with fervor.

**Questioner:** But when you tell the truth about something, then why is *pratikraman* necessary?

**Dadashri:** No, I still have to do *pratikraman*. Why did I see someone's fault? Why did I see his fault even though he is flawless? Why did I criticize him despite this? Any truth that hurts others is not considered truth and should not be uttered. If uttered, this truth becomes a fault. It represents violence.

'We' do instant *pratikraman*. 'We' have seen all the *sadhus* and *acharyas* as *nirdosh* (flawless). To 'us,' no one is at fault (*doshit*); even though 'we' say otherwise, to 'us,' no one is *doshit*. But because 'we' speak to the contrary, there is always instant *pratikraman* behind it. This is the result of the lack of four degrees necessary for *Keval Gnan* (absolute enlightenment). Otherwise, 'we' experience complete *vitaragata* (total absence of attachment and abhorrence).

And you will have to do a lot of *pratikraman*. Even though 'we' speak, 'our' awareness prevails, whereas you cannot speak this way at all. You have to have the awareness. You can never speak this way.

**Questioner:** What occurs if we do not do *pratikraman*? Will we be liable for the wrongdoing?

**Dadashri:** They will file a 'claim' against you. They would have filed hundreds of claims against 'us' in the *karmic* court. What occurs if you do not settle those claims? They will remain pending. Hence those claims will remain pending until you do *pratikraman*.

## After Self-Realization, Unaffected and Pure as a Lily

**Questioner:** One can remain like the water lily

(*jadkamadvat*) after attaining this Gnan. (Not a single speck of dirt from the pond or a drop of water touches the pure lily flower).

**Dadashri:** Yes, one remains as the 'lily.' This path itself is one of the water lily. For how many years were you able to remain that way? How many years has it been since you took Gnan?

**Questioner:** It will be a year.

**Dadashri:** So what state will you be in after ten years? When so much energy of Gnan is evident in just the first year, then what will it be like after ten years? And elsewhere, worldly people claim; those who have gone to the Himalayas (the hermits and ascetics) claim that they live like the water lily. But really they are not able to do so. It is all talk; all imagination! Webs of imaginations! If they claim that, then if one of them is passing by and you tell me that they live like the 'water lily,' I would call out and say to him, '*Maharaj*, you do not have any sense.' Then you will quickly discover that water lily! You can never say that to any *maharaj*. It is wrong to insult someone unnecessarily, so then I would give him two hundred and one rupees. If he is not appeased with the two hundred and one rupees, what would I tell him? I would tell him, 'Forgive me, my mind is a little off. I had a fight with my brother.' He then would agree and say, 'Yes, his mind is like that.' He will even put his hand on 'our' head and bless 'us.'

Is it so easy to fool these 'tops' (Dadashri has said that every human is like a 'top.' A top is a toy that is wound with a string, and when flung on the ground it spins. Human beings are like tops. They 'wind' causes of karma in their past life and then, in the current life, they 'spin' from the effect of these karmas). They are nothing but tops! How can these 'tops' win against someone who knows how to lose (the Gnani)? How high can the 'tops' fight against the one who has mastered the art of losing?

Who are we calling 'tops'? We are not referring to people. Lord Krishna has said that it is the *prakruti* (the mind-speech-body complex; the relative self, the non-Self) that forces one to 'dance and spin' and he does, but then he claims 'I danced!' That is what we call as 'top.' Whatever Lord Krishna referred to as a 'top' is what we are calling a 'top.' The word to describe this phenomenon is a 'top.' No one else will use the word 'top (*bhammarado*).'

Who would say such things that offend people? I can say them because I know how to do *pratikraman*. Not only will I say it, but I will also take the medicine for it (do *pratikraman*). But the world should be rid of all the wrong things. The wrong support and encouragement that was given to the wrong teachers should not be there. Then is there a problem if one does *pratikraman*? At least such support and encouragement will go away.                                                          (84)

If we tell someone, 'You have no sense,' is his state of water lily (*jadkamadvat*) not likely to go away? The water (*jad*) will fly away and so will the lily (*kamad*)! Now what do people say? Why don't we test him for a month? Hey, you! You cannot do that; you will go mad in doing that.

So right away you have to test the rupee coin; you have to tap it to see whether it is real or fake (meaning you have to test the guru right away, before accepting him, to see whether or not he has *kashays* in him). You will know right away. Then you have to spend two hundred rupees after him! That is when you have to tell him that your mind is a little crazy; that will appease him because he thinks that otherwise a good (sane) person will never say such things, and that this man talks this way because he is a little crazy. He knows how to evaluate justice! But at least you got your answer, did you not? What we wanted is not here because here whatever equanimity there was, went out of the window! So then you will no longer stop to sit at that shop, will you? So is there a problem in doing that?

No one else will teach you to test in this manner. What do people generally feel? They will think, 'What if someone was to do that to me?' Whereas I am happy if someone were to test me. If by doing so they become wise, then it is good. But without testing, how long will you keep the fake rupee in your home? If you were to spend that fake rupee, you will not get even a piece of *jalebi*!

## This is All There is to the Path of Moksha

The way to liberation is through *alochana* (recall and confession of wrong action), *pratikraman* (asking for forgiveness) and *pratyakhyan* (taking a vow never to repeat the mistake and asking for energies for this). What do our *mahatmas* (Self-realized in *Akram Vignan*) do? They do *alochana*, *pratikraman* and *pratyakhyan* throughout the day. If you were to ask them to do rituals and practice austerities, such as fasting and external penance, they will tell you that they have no need for such austerities because they have peace within; they have no worries and they are content. They remain constantly at peace with themselves and free from all woes and anxieties, undeterred by the external world. So why would they want to complicate their lives by introducing chaos in the form of fasting, etc.? People who are confused do all those complicated penances and other rituals. People who do rituals enjoy doing them and need to do them. That is why I say that penance is for those who derive pleasure from it. Those who have a passion for the worldly life should do penance.

**Questioner:** People believe that in doing penance, karmas are being discharged (*nirjara*).

**Dadashri:** That will never occur. What kind of penance brings about discharge of karma? Internal penance. It is not the penance that is visible to the eye and heard by the ears. That is all external penance. Only internal penance (*adeetha tapa* – invisible penance), can lead to discharge of karma. That is the kind of penance these *mahatmas* 'do.' Any penance which is visible to others, known to others, will result in merit karma (*punya*). Penance that is not visible externally will lead to liberation.

So people will think that we (in the path of *Akram*) do not follow any rules (*niyam*) or take any vows (*vrat*). Vows and rules are not for the path to *moksha* in *Akram Vignan*. They are necessary for those who want to wander around in the worldly life. Those who want to go to *moksha* should quickly get on the train of *alochana*, *pratikraman* and *pratyakhyan*. You have to do that twenty-four hours a day and nothing else.

## Ask for Forgiveness for All the Kashays

What should these *sadhvijis* (Jain nuns) do? They know that *kashays* (anger, pride, deceit and greed) occur throughout the day, so what should they do? Every evening, they should recall the day's events during which they experienced even the slightest *kashay* with anyone. For each and every incident where such a *kashay* arose, they should do *pratikraman* and *pratyakhyan* for forty-eight minutes. If they do this, then they are on the path of liberation.

But these poor people do no such thing, so what can be done? If they were to understand the path to *moksha*, they would be on it, but first they need to understand it thus. (86)

**Questioner:** Until they can confess and repent on a one-on-one basis, they will still harbor a grudge from within. So they need to ask for forgiveness in person, don't they?

**Dadashri:** There is no need to ask for anyone's forgiveness directly. The Lord has forbidden this. You can only ask someone for forgiveness, directly, if that person is well meaning and noble. However, if you do that with a weak (*kashay-laden*) person, he or she will only throw it back in your face. The weak person will become weaker. The entire world is weak and unless the person whose forgiveness you seek is good-natured, you should not attempt to apologize to that person personally. A weak person will always retaliate by saying, 'See, I knew all along that you were wrong, but you did not understand. Now you realize that you were wrong.' Hey! You do not realize that you are the one at fault and you are the wretched one in need of improvement. She has improved and is improving. He would not know this. The poor man has no awareness, does he? It is a different matter if one has even little awareness. But he has no awareness, not even a little.

## No Moksha through Rituals

The path to *moksha* is *alochana*, *pratikraman* and *pratyakhyan*. That itself is the path of *moksha*. First you should admit your mistakes. Then you should repent because it was the wrong thing to do, and then you should make a firm decision that you will not do it again. That is what our path to *moksha* is.

The path to liberation does not have any rituals or anything like that. Rituals are only present in the worldly life. It is for those who want material and physical comforts. For them, rituals are appropriate; however, they are not needed for liberation. What is the path of liberation? It is of *alochana*, *pratikraman* and *pratyakhyan*. Continue doing this. This is our path to *moksha* in which no rituals are necessary.

Did you understand rituals (*kriyakand*)? What is that for? It is for material comforts; therefore, the Lord (Lord within) had said that whoever wants to enjoy material comforts can practice penance – and through this, you will attain relative worldly happiness, you will attain the comforts of the celestial world. You will attain worldly happiness, but if you do not want this temporary worldly happiness then we have this path of *moksha* (*mokshamarg*). And then some people may complain about, how come there is no ritualistic activity in the path of *Akram* Liberation. Our path is not of rituals, we do not have a business. And if they lie, or speak negatively, then do not see it as their fault. They speak because of their karma coming into effect. And you, too, speak on the basis of the unfolding karma effect. However, You are to remain the Knower of the fact that it is a lie, and that is being the Self (the *purusharth*).

There is the Purush (Self) and the *prakruti* (non-Self). You (the Self) should have the awareness of what the *prakruti* (the non-Self) is doing. The day the *prakruti* ceases to do anything will be the day you will have attained the 360° of *Keval Gnan*. Thereafter, there will be no conduct of violence (*himsak vartan*), no hurtful speech (*himsak vani*) and no hurtful thoughts (*himsak manan*).

*Alochana-pratikraman-pratyakhyan* verily is the path to *moksha*. This is what I have done for countless lives. For so many lives I have done *alochana*, *pratikraman* and *pratyakhyan* and these efforts have brought me thus far.

That is why the *Tirthankar* Lord has said that after infinite lives have gone, even after attaining transient and changing right belief about the Self (*vyavahar samkit, upsham samkit*), thereafter comes a period of time wherein there is *ardhapudgal paravartan* (when the soul is left with 50% of its transmigration cycle). So tell me, how many lifetimes have been reduced? Even coming into the state of *ardhapudgal* one has shed so many lives.

**Questioner:** One comes within the limit.

**Dadashri:** Yes, he comes into the limit and from there he will grow. The Lord had twenty-seven lives after he attained right belief (*samkit*). But everything has come into a limit. That is what the Lord said.                                              (88)

## Dharma of Only Two Things

There are two *dharmas* – doctrines of rightful duty, religion. One is to not engage in any *kashays* (anger, pride, deceit and greed) and the other is to do *pratikraman*. If *kashays* occur as a result of your past karma, you should do *pratikraman*. That is *dharma* (duty or religion) and nothing else. Unfortunately, it is precisely these very two things that people have eliminated.

If you say something hurtful to anyone, you should do *pratikraman*. He in turn should also do *pratikraman*. What *pratikraman* should he do? His *pratikraman* should be, 'I must have erred somewhere in the past which is why this person has been given the occasion to insult me.' He should do *pratikraman* for his previous life's karma and you should do *pratikraman* for the present. Doing up to five hundred such *pratikraman* a day will bring liberation.

Now, such *dharmadhyan* (absence of adverse internal meditation) and these kinds of *pratikramans* are not to be found anywhere. So what is one to do? Ultimately, one still has to suffer everything, crying. So why not do it with a smile?

If you do just this much, then even if you do not seek any other religion, you will not have any problems. It is more than enough if you do just this much, and for that I give you My blessings and a guarantee. I am placing my hand on your head and assure you, 'Go! As far as *moksha* is concerned, I will give you My full support all the way to the end!' I will be with you the entire way, giving you My full support. All that is required of you is your readiness. If you were to apply any of this in your daily life, it is enough.

## Obstinacy of Viewpoint is Atikraman

The world has arisen out of *atikraman*, and *pratikraman* will bring an end to it. That is the law of nature. This *pratikraman* is no longer to be found in the scriptures and that is why it has all stopped. The *pratikraman* that people talk about is simply an inanimate ritual (*jada kriya*) which does not destroy even a single mistake. And yet they speak about destroying mistakes. Nothing is achieved by simply reciting rituals.

**Questioner:** *Matagraha* (obstinacy of viewpoint) is considered *atikraman*, is it not?

**Dadashri:** *Matagraha* is the greatest *atikraman*. India is dying from this poison. Presently it is the deadliest poison. Every person has created so much of this poison.

## In Essence, 'We' Are Lord Mahavir's

**Questioner:** You have so many Jain words and terminology in your speech.

**Dadashri:** All that is manifested is Gnan; the words automatically flow. But ultimately 'we' are Lord Mahavir's! 'We' do not like anything else. 'We' do not like any one else's talks. 'We' are ready to accept scientific facts. Lord Mahavir's talks are all scientific. 'We,' too, are considered scientific.

What special directive (Agna) has Lord Mahavir given for this *dushamkaal* (current era of the time cycle of lack of unity in thoughts, speech and acts)? He has asked that one should follow the Agnas and when this is missed then one should do *pratikraman*.

*****

# [5]

## The Way of Akram Vignan

### New and Precise Religion through Akram Vignan

What is the current *dharma* (religion) like now? Everything is encompassed in a positive ego. All the scriptures say, 'Practice kindness. Speak only the truth. Do not steal,' etc. Hey, you! Is one able to do all that? That is why they have put the religious books away on the shelves. What did people do? They felt it was not possible to follow what the books dictated and so they were of no use to them. They were not able to practice kindness. They could not speak the truth. These books say the same things over and over again. That is why people put away the books on a shelf. (90)

What do the scriptures say? They say, 'Do not steal, do not lie, do not deceive.' So what can we do? Tell us what else can we do if we cannot do that? What can we do if we have to go somewhere and they do not give us a ticket and we are forced to buy it on the black market? But these scriptures tell us not to do such things. Then we have no choice but jump in the lake!

The world is trying to turn around the result (effect). Now how can effects be changed when people themselves have changed? In the past, when there were a very small percentage of people who had changed, it was appropriate to say, 'Change your conduct. Purify your conduct!' But what can one do when ninety-five percent of today's conduct is bad? What can you do when all conduct is bankrupt today? So 'we' have made a new discovery. And truly people consider 'discharge' (effect) as 'charge' (cause). That 'we' got rid of by telling people it is meaningless to believe an effect to be the cause.

Conduct has nothing to do with religion. If you believe, 'I am the doer of conduct,' then you give rise to new conduct all over again. Therefore, it will give rise to religion, but you will not attain purity (the Self). There will not be any purity (*shuddhata*) in 'discharge,' the effect, the conduct. The good (*shubha*) and the bad (*ashubha*) will continue but the pure (*shuddha*) will never be attained.

Therefore, give people knowledge (*gnan*) that is compatible with the times. If you make a statement on the loud speakers that there is plenty of grain supply in our country, and that in the past one could buy grains at 12 cents per pound and that one can buy grain again at 12 cents per pound, people will tell you not to say such things. They will tell you to speak according to the times. All these religious scriptures are not in tune with the times and are thus incompatible with the current era.

## Ask for the Energy and the Strength to do Pratikraman

What does our Science of *Akram* say? If I were to ask a person, 'Have you been stealing for long?' he would reply, 'Yes.' If we ask with love and kindness, he will admit everything. Then if asked, 'How much and for how many years have you been stealing?' He would reply, 'I have been doing it for a couple of years.' Then 'we' tell him, 'There is no problem if you steal.' I place my hand on his head and with love I tell him, 'But continue doing *pratikraman*.' What do we teach him?

**Questioner:** Do this much *pratikraman*.

**Dadashri:** He may ask, 'How?' and I would show him the way to do it. So he gets some consolation and he will feel, 'Oh, ho ho! People are generally contemptuous towards me but this man is giving me love!'

Whatever *pratikraman* he does, it wipes off the entire *karmic* consequences (creating 'cause karma') of stealing! His opinion has changed. Today, his opinion is not accepting what he is doing; his opinion (*bhaav*) is not supporting it. 'Not his opinion!' You, Sir, do you understand this?

So what am I saying? I do not have any problem with your stealing. If there is a young man fifteen, or so, years of age, and he has stolen a few times, and if you were to tell him, 'There is no problem with what you have done, but now you should do this one thing so that you will not incur any *karmic* liability,' he will ask you, 'What should I do?' Then you should teach him to recall Dada Bhagwan, or whichever God he believes in, and with Him as the witness, repent for his actions. Teach him to do *pratikraman* in his God's name by saying, 'It is wrong to steal and I will never steal again.'

Having taught him this, what will his parents say? They will say, 'He stole again!' Hey, you! Even if he steals again, tell him to do *pratikraman* again, teach him again what to say. I know what occurs when one speaks in this manner. He should continue this *pratikraman* even if he continues to steal. Only I understand what occurs when one says and does such *pratikraman*. There is no other way.

So the science of *Akram Vignan* teaches us that whatever has been ruined will not improve (effect cannot be changed or improved), but you can improve things in this manner through change in cause.                                              (92)

Now in the *Kramic* path there is no such way to improve a person. There one will say, 'Do whatever it takes to improve him.' Hey, you! He will not improve. It is *prakruti* (the formed non-Self complex). If there is too much salt in the soup, you can remove it by one process or another. There are all kinds of solutions for improving the soup. But this (*pratikraman* and repentance) is the solution for that. Many people have benefited from this solution.

'Your past stealing is not a problem, but instead of doing it that way, do it this way.' When you say this to him, he will feel you are not harping on his mistakes and his ego will not be hurt. The other approach will hurt his ego.

I have seen a father hit his son because he was stealing, and the son made a vow from within to get even with his father when he grew up. Hey, you! In trying to stop him from stealing, you created an enemy within him! You cannot hit him. Threatening people is never the solution to improving them. Once in a while it is fine to show sternness in your eyes, but if the child is rebellious, you cannot do even that.

Therefore, this tells you where and how you should conduct yourself; where you need to use not only discretion (*vivek*), but right discretion. Such right discretion, which is beneficial for all, is nowhere to be found and yet they tell you to use right discretion (*sadvivek*).

## Disease Cannot Be Cured Without Medicine

So when someone tells me, 'What should I do, I have started a business of stealing?' I will tell him, 'You can do it; I do not have any problems with that. But these are the consequences of stealing. If you can handle such a liability, then go ahead and do it. I do not have any objection.' So then he will ask me, 'Sir, how have you obliged me in this? The responsibility will ultimately be mine anyway.' I will tell him, 'As per my role in this, I will tell you, do *pratikraman* in 'Dada's name, or Lord Mahavir's name. Say the following, 'Dear Lord, I do not want to do this but I have to. I ask for your forgiveness for that'.'

Keep asking for forgiveness in this way even while you continue doing what you are doing. Do not do it willingly and deliberately. Whenever you have the desire that, 'I do not want to steal anymore,' then you can stop it. You do want to stop stealing, don't you? Yet, if there is a push from within and you have to steal, then ask for forgiveness. That is all! You do not have to do anything else.

You cannot tell a thief, 'Stop that business from tomorrow.' You will not achieve anything by saying that. Nothing will work, will it? You can never tell him, 'Stop this or stop that.' 'We' never tell anyone to stop doing something. In the current time cycle of the fifth *ara* (era), telling anyone to stop doing something is not appropriate. Nor is it appropriate to tell anyone, 'Do this.' That is because one is not able to let go of anything even if he wants to. Yes, and on the other hand, they will complain, 'I want to but I am not able to do it. I want to fast but I cannot.'

Hey, you! Why do you keep saying this over and over again? Instead, why don't you ask the Lord for forgiveness? 'Dear Lord. I want to fast but I am not able to, and for that I ask for your forgiveness.' But instead, he keeps saying he cannot do it. You should never say, 'I cannot do it. I cannot do it.' Is there some law that says that you have to say this? It is a type of ego. If you can't do it, there is no need for you to keep saying it over and over. Why does one complain like that? He is showing his ego.

This science seems very new and strange to people. It is something they have never heard of, never seen before, never known before! What have they been telling us so far? They have said, 'Stop all the bad deeds and do good deeds.' One does not have the capacity to stop anything nor create anything and yet they uselessly keep saying, 'Do this.' Then that person will say, 'I am not able to do it. I want to speak the truth, but I cannot.' Therefore, 'we' came up with a new science. 'Dear brother, you do not have a problem speaking a lie, do you? You can handle that, can you not? So when you speak a lie, do this;

do *pratikraman* for it in this manner. There is no problem if you steal, but if you do, then do *pratikraman* for it.' Whereas what do those other people say? They say, 'No, stop stealing.' How can he stop that? If someone is constipated, he will need laxatives and if someone has diarrhea, he will need some other type of medicine. Is this world such that it can continue as it is? (94)

A father may think, 'My son can stop stealing if he wants to.' Hey, you! Why don't you go ahead and stop your own mistakes! Stop all your mistakes. Even the guru says, 'Stop this and stop that.' *Maharaj*, why don't you quit sniffing the tobacco spice powder yourself? Why don't you stop your anger?

Should You not tell 'Chandubhai' (non-Self) to stop getting angry?

**Questioner:** Yes.

**Dadashri:** He has to do *pratikraman* if he does not stop. What does he have to do?

**Questioner:** *Pratikraman*, Dada.

**Dadashri:** How many *pratikramans* does he have to do?

**Questioner:** Many, almost a thousand a day.

**Dadashri:** So if he does *pratikraman* in this way, he is free.

**Questioner:** The entire intent (*bhaav*) changes with *pratikraman*.

**Dadashri:** Inner intent changes. The whole path changes. And one cannot achieve anything by forcing children to change. That is a wrong approach.

**Questioner:** People who do not understand this will claim that Dada tells people to steal.

**Dadashri:** Yes, they will present that argument. They do

not understand this, do they? Whenever they do, it will help them. What can they do when they do not understand? That is because this is very difficult to understand. One needs a very sharp intellect (*buddhi*) to understand this.

**Questioner:** You are telling a thief that he can steal but that he should keep the awareness that what he is doing is wrong. He should repent for his actions, and he should do *pratikraman* for it. That really gets a lot accomplished.

**Dadashri:** It will work wonders.

**Questioner:** Eventually, he will feel that he does not want to steal.

**Dadashri:** All these traditional punishments for teaching people a lesson do not work. But this one approach of *Akram* science is very different; it works.

## Every Relative Worldly Religion is Dehadhyasi

That is why 'we' say that all the religions of the world are of the path of *dehadhyas* (the belief 'I am this body'). They increase *dehadhyas*, whereas ours is without *dehadhyas*. Every religion says, 'You are the doer of penance. You are the doer of renunciation. You are the one doing the penance. You are not doing penance.' Even when they tell you, 'You are not doing penance,' it is the same as attributing 'doership' upon you. In this manner, they accept 'doership' and even in making the statement, 'I cannot do penance,' one accepts 'doership.' Any path that accepts or believes in 'doership' is the path of *dehadhyas*. In *Akram*, we do not accept 'doership.' Nowhere in any books of *Akram Vignan* will you find the term, 'Do this or do that.'

No one ever opposes or questions this. If they did, they would find the answer that, 'There is no one in this world that has the independent energy or power to even go to the toilet!' If someone were to question 'us,' we would explain to him,

'This is how it is. So why do you needlessly keep badgering people?' You are taking people on the wrong path by telling them, 'I do this, I do penance, I renounce. So you should renounce too. You should do the same. Stop eating potatoes.' Why are you unnecessarily hounding people? So, things that needed to be done have been set aside and they make people do things that ought not to be done. They, themselves, cannot do the things they are not supposed to! It is all a sheer waste of time and energy. What needs to be done is something completely different. What one needs to do is to ask for energy (*shakti*). Everything that is occurring right now is because of the *shakti* that was previously asked for.

**Questioner:** Whatever we did in our previous lifetime has come as an effect in this life, has it not?          (96)

**Dadashri:** Yes, everything has come into effect. Therefore, ask for the energy and strength in the form of a cause (the effect of which will come later). And when you ask for the energy and strength by reciting the Nine Kalams (nine deep inner intents asking for energies), those Nine Kalams are the essence of all the scriptures combined. That is all you have to do. What does one need to do in this world? One needs to do only this much; ask for *shakti* (energy) if he wants to do anything with the sense of doership.

**Questioner:** Is it simply a matter of asking for the energy?

**Dadashri:** Yes, because not everyone goes to *moksha*, do they? But if you want to 'do' anything, then do just this much: ask for *shakti*.

**Questioner:** This is applicable to only those who have not attained Gnan, right?

**Dadashri:** Yes, this is applicable to only them. This is for the worldly people because at the moment, the path they are on is completely wrong and they will never succeed in their endeavors.

**Questioner:** I had talked to people but they do not understand how good and logical Dada's science is. They are not even ready to understand that much.

**Dadashri:** That is what I am saying. They are not ready to understand this. They do not want to go deep into this. This is something new and contrary to what they believe, understand, do and accept; and they are afraid of it.

**Questioner:** They believe this is wrong because it is contrary to what the world believes.

**Dadashri:** Yes.

**Questioner:** And the other thing is that they feel, 'Should I let go of what I have done all my life?'

**Dadashri:** Yes, 'Will all that I did go to waste?'! They will have to get rid of that fear, will they not?

**Questioner:** That is the main point.

**Dadashri:** The Guru Maharaj will say, 'There is lot of misery, but we will put up with the way it (the traditional path) has been going on.' So I tell them, 'Hey, you! You can make do with it but why don't you let your disciples change?' So to that he will say, 'No. I will be alone. What will I do?' That is how it is.

This disease of wrong belief (*mithyatva*) has spread; nature is responsible for spreading this disease. And it is also nature that will turn it around. 'We' are just the instrument (the *nimit*) in all this.

There was no essence or substance in the old path and that is why this new one has come about. The one without substance was believed to be the one with substance.

That is why Krupadudev Shrimad Rajchandra has said, 'I have created an opportunity for you to lose everything. An opportunity of losing everything has come.'                    (98)

## You Must Never Say, 'I Cannot Do It'

All the books talk only about worldly interactions, don't they? 'Do it this way, do it that way, be kind, have patience, keep equanimity.' What else can one do besides all that? And none of it is in his control. Nothing is in your control and they tell you to do something new, 'Do this, do that.' What is the meaning of that?

**Questioner:** It will create confusion.

**Dadashri:** That has already occurred. People will think, 'I am not able to do this,' and they start believing it too. It is fine if only confusion occurs but one ends up believing, 'I cannot do it.' So then he begins to become relatively inanimate (*jada*, tree-like), 'I cannot do it, I cannot do it this way, I want to but I cannot.' Hey, you! Who taught you all that? Do not say things like that! Do people say this?

**Questioner:** Yes, they do.

**Dadashri:** Because religious teachers (*updeshaks*) have brainwashed people into believing that they have to do all that. The Lord would never talk this way. Would Lord Mahavir ever speak this way? The Lord who spoke the entire scripture, would such a Lord say things like this? But these teachers of today speak in this way. 'Practice celibacy!' they tell you. Hey, you! Are you able to practice it yourself? Then why are you telling me to? A real *sadhu* (Self-realized being who is unmarried) can do so, and the other is the *go-putra* (bull). These two kinds of beings can practice celibacy. The celibacy of a true *sadhu* is considered true celibacy. And the celibacy that the bull practices is considered forced celibacy (*parvash*).

Really, none of these poor people are at fault (*doshit*). In 'My' Gnan, they are flawless (*nirdosh*) for sure; nevertheless, I still have to speak this way for the sake of worldly interactions. Otherwise, the facts will never be known.

These people make statements like, 'Don't steal. Don't be cunning. Don't tell lies.' You cannot make such statements; you cannot make such baseless statements. Is this how you talk? Entire India is devastated and ruined. You have brought it to its very end.

'I want to do it but I can't' – if one's karma effect unfolds to the contrary, what can anyone do about it? The Lord has said for us to be the Self (*swaroop*) and know the unfolding karma effect (*udayakarma*); He did not tell us to 'do' anything. He only told us to 'know.' Instead, people are complaining, 'I tried to do it but I could not. I am trying but I am not able to. I really want to do but I can't.' Hey, you! But why do you keep 'singing' about it without any purpose? Do you know what the self turns into with continued projection that is envisioned (*chintavan*) of 'I want to do it, but I cannot'? It will turn into a stone. And here, one is merely trying to perform acts and yet he says over and over again, 'I can't do it. I can't do it.' How many people say this?

**Questioner:** Everyone, almost everyone.

**Dadashri:** And when one says, 'I cannot do it,' he, the Soul, becomes like whatever he envisions (*chintavey*). So when he says, 'I can't do it. I can't do it,' he becomes inanimate, lifeless (*jada*). So in speaking this way, these people will have to become *jada*. But these poor people do not realize their liability when they say such things and that is why they say it. I am telling everyone not to say it: 'Hey, you! You cannot say 'I can't do it'!' One should never say it. You are full of infinite energy (*anant shakti*). When we explain this to a person, thereafter he will say, 'I am full of infinite energy.' Otherwise, up until now he kept saying, 'I cannot do it.' What? Your infinite energy has gone away?

**Questioner:** No.

**Dadashri:** What is this Gnan saying? 'Give me energy

(*shakti*).' It does not say, 'Do this. Do that.' Those who tell people, 'Do this…do that,' are at fault of leading people on the wrong path. Is, 'Do this,' to be found anywhere in this Gnan?

**Questioner:** There is nothing of the sort. It says, 'Give me the energy.'

**Dadashri:** But here they say, 'Do this...do this.' Hey, you! What should I do? You have done it and so have we. Nothing came out of it. And here we are saying, 'Dear Dada Bhagwan, Please give me the energy!' That is enough!

For so many millions of years, billion years, people of India have spoken spiritual language (*adhyatma vani*), but what is the definition of spiritual language?

Here people affirm, 'I did,' for that which 'happens' on its own.

**Questioner:** Why is there this increased *artadhyan* (adverse internal mediation confined to the self) in people today? (100)

**Dadashri:** All the misery today is due to that only. Every form of misery has arisen due to this. If it were to be openly declared to people that this portion is due to 'it occurs,' and that portion is under your will, then a significant amount of these miseries would be alleviated.

Now what do you have to do in all this? The answer is to improve whatever goes bad. You have to improve it with inner intent (*bhaav*). When something goes wrong, give your support to turn it around and be useful. That is all you have to do. Improve (with *pratikraman*) whatever goes bad.

Therefore, 'it occurs' (everything just occurs automatically and precisely as it should). If I suddenly insult someone, it is something that 'just occurred.' Then I improve it from within by saying, 'It was wrong and I repent for the actions. I am asking for forgiveness and I will not do it again.' That is called 'improving' the situation. That is called relative spiritual effort (*bhrant-purusharth*); illusory spiritual effort.

Real spiritual effort is nowhere to be found in the world, but this here is called illusory spiritual effort. The one who does wrong is the one who admits he did wrong, and he is the one who repents his actions.

Otherwise, the world has not even 'touched' the real *dharma* - religion of the Self. No one has understood even a word of it. They believe that whatever is occurring is absolutely correct.

But there people say, 'He does not listen to me. He does not obey me!' Hey you! How will he listen and obey? Does anyone ever listen to anyone else? The other person has done everything. You have done everything. If you tell someone to do something and he does as you say, then you will get adjusted to the idea of, 'He listens to me and does what I tell him.' In reality, however, even he does not ever listen. All these things are things that have already occurred. The rehearsal for it has already been done and that is why 'we' call it *vyavasthit*. Why is that? Because it has already taken place. What is the point of looking at it? That which has already occurred is what we call '*vyavasthit*.'

One has to understand this but people keep talking about '*dharma*–religion.' These are good people; they are all important people, and no one can deny that. But what do you call 'a religion'? What do you consider *sat dharma*–true religion? They all sing the same old tune; has anyone said anything new? Should one not gain some benefit out of it? Should some change not be evident? We have done all this (in our past lives). It is like milling milled flour and in the process you blow away some of the flour.

Man is not capable of 'doing' anything. It is not his nature (*swabhav*) to do anything. The doer is another realm and authority (*parsatta*). These living beings are simply 'knowers'. Therefore, You should only know, and once you know that this Knowership is only Yours, then the faith you had on the wrong things will disappear. Your opinions will change. What kind of changes? Your opinion, 'It is good to tell lies,' will change. There is no higher *purusharth* than the one which gets rid of such opinions. This is an intense message, which requires profound thinking.

**Questioner:** Yes, but the entire talk is logical.

**Dadashri:** Yes. It is logical. It is worthy of deep thinking and what do people say? 'We know it all, but we cannot do it.' So what can be done about 'I can't do it'? What did he say?

**Questioner:** 'I am not able to do anything.'          (102)

**Dadashri:** This statement of 'I cannot do anything' is a grave liability. What liability? The answer is that even in the state of illusion (absence of Self-realization), because there is a presence of the self (the relative *atma*) within, one becomes whatever one says. One becomes what he envisions (*chintavan*). One becomes what one contemplates (*manan*). Therefore, one will be born either as an animal or a stone; a form which is not able to do anything. So people are not aware of the consequences of saying such things. Have you ever heard people say, 'I cannot do anything'?

**Questioner:** Yes.

**Dadashri:** You should never say, 'I cannot do it.' Besides, it is not even that. In actuality there is nothing to be done. Even the simple act of emptying your bowels is not in your hands, so how is it possible for you to do anything else? No such man has yet been born who has even the slightest energy to do anything. You are to simply know (*janavoo*) and make a firm resolution (*nischay*) to remain as the Knower, the Self. That is all You have to do. Once you understand my words, Your work will be done. This is not a simple thing to grasp.

Do you understand this? Is it not better to 'know' than to 'do'? Is it easy to do anything right away?

**Questioner:** I understand what you are saying, but surely some things still need to be done having understood all this? Just as we do not possess the power to do anything, do we not also lack the power (*satta*) to know?

**Dadashri:** No. You have the power 'to know.' 'To do' is not in your power. This is very subtle, but it will be enough if you understand just this much.

## Change the Opinion

A young boy has turned into a thief and he would steal at every opportunity. He even steals from guests who come to his house. Hey, you! He stole from the guests even when it left them with no money for their fares to return home. What were the poor guests to do? How could the guest ask for it back? And he could not say anything to the host because if he did, the host would beat the young boy. So then the guest has to borrow some money from someone to return home. What could he do? That young boy stole his money. Now what lesson should we teach this boy? We should tell him to ask Dada Bhagwan (the Lord within) to give him the energy not to steal in this life.

People may question what good it does to ask for the energies or strength on the one hand and still he continues to steal. Let him steal. Is he asking for the energies or not? Yes, he does keep asking for the energies. Only then I know how this medicine is working within him. How can you know how this medicine works?

**Questioner:** It is true that he has no idea what this medicine is doing. And, therefore, he does not know the benefits in asking for energy.

**Dadashri:** What is the intent behind asking for energy? First of all, the boy is asking for the energy to stop stealing. So firstly he has changed his opinion about stealing to, 'It is wrong to steal. It is good not to steal.' When he asks for this energy, he arrives at the opinion of 'stealing is wrong.' The greatest achievement is that his opinion has changed. From the moment his opinion changes, he ceases to be the offender.

Secondly, because he is asking for energy from the Lord within, the absolute state of humility (*param vinayata*) arises within him. When he earnestly and sincerely says, 'Oh Lord, grant me the energy to...,' the Lord within will immediately give him the energy. The Lord has no choice. He will grant it to everyone. (But) One has to ask. That is why I am telling you, 'Keep asking.' You never ask for anything; you never have.

Do you understand why you should ask for energy?

**Questioner:** This is a very scientific solution. His opinion changes and he asks for the right thing.                          (104)

**Dadashri:** And he asks for the energy. To say, 'Give me,' is not any ordinary thing. The Lord will be pleased and will tell you 'Here, take it!'

In addition to this, his opinion changes. You cannot force or intimidate him into changing his opinion. That will only reinforce his opinion, 'I will steal.' Hey, you! You cannot give this 'medicine' by force or intimidation. Bring him to Dada for the medicine. Dada will seat him on His lap and make him wise. You need someone who is familiar with the medicine, don't you?

It is not easy to change an opinion. But it can be done stealthily in this manner. If you were to keep telling him that stealing is wrong, then he will think that you are needlessly harping on him and he will not change, whereas this method of 'ours' is scientific.

His biggest opinion has changed, but now he says, 'That

opinion of mine has changed but now, my Lord, give me the energy. Now I need Your energy. My opinion has already changed.'

**Questioner:** And the giver of more is sitting here, so it is worth asking.

**Dadashri:** Yes, I am ready to give whatever you ask. I can make you like Me within an hour. That is the guarantee and assurance I have given, have I not? I have been giving this guarantee for so many years; 'I can make you like Me but you have to be ready.'

The Gnani Purush can show you all the cures. I can diagnose the disease and also give you the cure. All you have to do is ask Him, 'What is the truth? This is how I have understood it.' So then He can immediately show you, and by pushing that 'button', the cure will start.

**Questioner:** Should I do *pratikraman vidhi*, or not, when I become aware of a mistake?

**Dadashri:** There is no problem. If you made a big mistake then tell Dada, 'Dada, I ask for your forgiveness. Please give me the energy again.' Ask Dada for the energy; for whatever your misdeed or weakness you are asking to be forgiven, ask for the energy to overcome that weakness. Ask Dada for the energies; don't use your own. Otherwise, you will run out of it. If you ask for the energy and use it, it will not deplete but it will increase. How much stock can you have in your shop?

You should ask Dada for the energy, and the energy in everything; 'Dada, give me the energy.' In everything you do, ask Dada for the energy. If you fail to do *pratikraman*, you should ask for the energy to do *pratikraman* in the proper way. Take all the energy by asking. 'We' have as much energies as you need.

## Ask for Energy and Accomplish Your Work

I told one man that the Nine Kalams that I have given you

encompass everything. Nothing has been left out. Read them daily. He told me he cannot do so. I told him, 'I am not telling you to do anything.' Why are you telling me, 'I cannot do them?' All you have to do is say, 'Dear Dada Bhagwan, give me the energy.' That is all I am telling you to do, I am telling you to ask. He then told me, 'I will enjoy doing that!' All these other people tell you to 'do' things.

'Dearest Dada Bhagwan! Give me the infinite inner energy not to hurt, cause someone to hurt, nor instigate anyone to hurt the foundation of any religion, even to the slightest extent.'

'Give me the infinite inner energy not to hurt, even to the slightest extent, the foundation of any religion and to conduct my thoughts, speech and action in a manner that is accepted by all.'
(106)

Religion means any three people waving around a staff (*danduko*); when there is a gathering of three, it is called *gachha* (sect). When three *sadhus* (ascetics) sit down together, and one of them puts a stake into the ground and then they sit and convene, that is considered as a *gachha* has begun. The Lord has said that it is not a *gachha* when there is a single person. That is why Krupadudev Shrimad Rajchandra has said,

'*Gachha-maat ni jeh kalpana, tey nahi sadvyavahar.*'
'Sectarian views and self-guided whims are not right worldly interactions.'

Therefore, all this needs to be reconstructed. All new materials are coming in and the old walls and foundation need to be removed. Plaster made out of pieces of bricks and sand will be removed and replaced with the foundation of R.C.C. (reinforced concrete cement). The foundation of religion should be very strong.

That other man told me, 'It is not going to occur, so I am not going to do it.' I told him to ask for the energy. He asked me, 'Who will give me that energy?' I told him, 'I will give you the energy. I am ready to give whatever energy you ask for.' What can I do if you don't know how to ask? Then I, myself, have to teach everyone how to ask for the energy. Do I not have to teach that? Am I not teaching all this? Is this all not what I have taught; why don't you recite one of the Kalams?

**Questioner:** 'Dearest Dada Bhagwan! Give me the infinite inner energy not to hurt, cause someone to hurt, nor instigate anyone to hurt the ego of any living being, even to the slightest extent.'

'Give me the infinite inner energy not to hurt the ego of any living being and to conduct my thoughts, speech and action in a manner that is acceptable by all.'

**Dadashri:** So, after one understands this, he will say, 'I can do this much; this encompasses everything.'

He tells me, 'How can I do it when it cannot be accomplished?' I asked him, 'Is this a thing to be 'done'? You are not to 'do' it. You should not do anything. Leisurely eat two extra *rotlis* (*chapaatis*) daily, but every day ask for this energy.' So then he tells me, 'I like what you are saying.'

**Questioner:** At first, there is a suspicion whether or not we will receive the energies we are asking for.

**Dadashri:** That is the very suspicion that starts to get dispelled with this method of asking for energy. Now are you asking for energies?

## 'See' and 'Know' Just as You Would a Movie

**Questioner:** When we ask for energies in these Nine Kalams; when we say, 'Let me not do, nor cause others to do, nor instigate others into doing it,' does that mean we are asking for energy so that such things do not occur in the future, or is it to wash off all that we have done in the past?

**Dadashri:** That gets washed off and at the same time the energy arises. The energy (*shakti*) is already there, but it manifests because the mistakes (*kashays*) get washed off. The energy is there already but it has to manifest. That is why we are asking for Dada's grace, 'May our *kashay* be washed off so that the energy can manifest.'

Complete energy is there but it remains unmanifested. Why is it not completely manifest? It is because one has interest and attraction for the worldly things and interactions. Nevertheless, it has decreased significantly since attaining this Gnan, has it not?

**Questioner:** Yes.                                        (108)

**Dadashri:** As this intensity of interest in the non-Self decreases, the energies will manifest. You are not to avoid it, reject it with scorn (*tiraskar*). To like it means to forget one's Self, to forget one's energies and to become engrossed and involved with it, to become the mind and the body (*tanmayakar*). Eat and drink but do not become *tanmayakar*. When you go to see a movie and in the movie, if there is a good looking woman or a good looking man, do you go and hug them? And if someone is beating up someone, do you scream at him and ask him why he is doing it? Do you say, 'Don't hit him'? You understand that you just have to 'see' and not say anything.

How many years has it been since you saw a movie? You used to see them back then, didn't you? You did not ask, 'Why are you hitting him?' did you? Yes! There you have to only 'see.'

The movie does not tell you, 'Carry me with you'! It tells you to just see and leave. What can the poor movie do if you take it the wrong way? The movie does not tell you, 'Take me home with you.' What occurs when one goes around with a 'layer of sticky glue' (one has *raag-dwesh* within) on him? You have to wash that glue off before you go there. If you go there plastered in glue, then whatever is there, the moment you touch it, will stick to you!

So once that energy arises within, the inner energies will manifest and, thereafter, that energy (*shakti*) verily will do all the work. You will not have to do anything. If you try to do anything, your egoism will increase. You will feel, 'I am trying to do it but it does not occur.' 'It is not occurring' – that is what you will end up with. So ask for that energy. These Nine Kalams encompass *pratikraman* of the entire world. Do it properly. 'We' will show you but then 'we' have to go back to 'our' 'home' no?

**Questioner:** In doing *pratikraman* of '*dosho*' (wrongdoing; mistakes), if we recite the Nine Kalams one after another every day, is there energy in it?

**Dadashri:** Reciting the Nine Kalams is different and doing *pratikraman* for mistakes is different. You should do *pratikraman* for your wrongdoing, every day.

**Questioner:** The Nine Kalams you have given us is for the purpose of purification (*shuddhata*) of thoughts, speech and actions?

**Dadashri:** No, no! There is no need whatsoever for such purity (*shuddhata*) in the path of *Akram Vignan*. These Nine Kalams have been given to you so that you may become free from all the *karmic* accounts (*hisaabs*) which have bound you with others over countless past lives; they are for cleaning up your 'account books'!

**Questioner:** These 'accounts' are accounts of thoughts, speech and actions?

**Dadashri:** No, thought-speech-action is a different thing. In the *Kramic* path, whatever one's conduct is today, if it is being done with full pleasure, will and endorsement, then the seed (cause of *karmic* effect) will be sown, and the result (fruit-effect) will unfold in the next life and continue. But if the person does not have any discipline, then there is no question for him; he is not on any path. And there is no need for conduct or anything else in the *Akram* path. In the *Akram* path, *artadhyan* (adverse internal meditation that hurts the self) and *raudradhyan* (adverse internal meditation that hurts the self and others) should cease completely.

**Questioner:** That means that this question does not even arise for the one who takes Gnan in the *Akram* path because for him thought, speech and action are in the form of discharge (effect).

**Dadashri:** Thought, speech and action are indeed in the form of discharge, so then what connection can there be?

## The Magnificent Nine Kalams

These Nine Kalams liberate one from his *roonanubandha* (bondage created due to attachment-abhorrence in the previous life) with others over endless previous lifetimes. It is *pratikraman*; it is the highest *pratikraman*. It is a tremendously powerful *pratikraman*.

**Questioner:** Our inner intent is exactly the same as what the Nine Kalams say. We have the same intent, same wishes and the same opinion as the Nine Kalams.

**Dadashri:** When you recite the Nine Kalams, all your mistakes, until now, loosen up. The 'fruit' of this is inevitable. The effects of your past mistakes will present like a burned rope. The moment you touch it, it will disintegrate into ashes.

*****

# [6]
# The Thorns Vanish and the Blossoms Remain

## Purity of Chit Verily is the Spiritual Accomplishment

**Questioner:** How can karma be purified (*shuddhi*)?

**Dadashri:** Purity of karma occurs by purifying the *chit*. When the *chit* (inner complex of knowledge and vision) becomes pure, so will the karma. Karma becomes impure (*ashuddha*) because the *chit* is impure; once the *chit* becomes pure (*shuddha*), so will karma.                              (111)

**Questioner:** Will all the karmas become pure? Will whatever karma that one does become pure?

**Dadashri:** Karma will become pure after the *chit* becomes pure. When the *chit* is impure (*ashuddha*), karma becomes impure. When the *chit* is auspicious and beneficial to others (*shubha*), then karma is virtuous. When *chit* is bad, inauspicious-hurtful to others (*ashubha*), karma is bad. So everything depends on the *chit*! So it is the *chit* that has to be 'repaired.' People say, 'I have to purify my *chit*.' Therefore, spirituality (*adhyatma*) in this world is for the very purpose of purifying the *chit*. Therefore the *chit* needs to be purified.

*****

The *chit* becomes impure when one steals and, by repenting, the very same *chit* becomes pure again. Impurity of the *chit* remains in the world because of failure to repent. And that is why all impure deeds (actions; karma) continue. People do not repent even when they know they have done something wrong. Even when they know they have done something wrong they say, 'Everyone does it!'

So one loses the awareness that his *chit* is becoming impure.

**Questioner:** How can I purify worldly interaction (*vyavahar*)?

**Dadashri:** If one maintains purity of *chit* in his worldly interactions such that, 'I don't want to deceive this man,' then his worldly interactions have become pure. Then, if deception does occur, then the worldly interactions become impure. Hence, if one conducts himself with ethics and discipline, remains fair and honest, then purity will be maintained in his worldly interactions.

Honesty is the best policy and dishonesty is the best foolishness.

For purity in worldly interaction, if you interact with others without hurting anyone, then that is considered purity of worldly interactions. Do not hurt anyone, even in the slightest, and if anyone hurts you, suffer it, but under no circumstances should you hurt anyone.

**Questioner:** Can we become free if we do *pratikraman* for our karma (actions)?

**Dadashri:** Almost everything will come to an end with *pratikraman*; some karma may still remain. All these karmas are bound by *atikraman* (transgression through mind, speech and action). With whatever interest and degree of intensity (*rasa*) the *atikraman* was bound, its effect will have to be suffered with equal and matching intensity (*rasa*). Even if *pratikraman* is being done, the intensity of the effect will have to be suffered. The effect of interest taken (in the cause during the charging) will remain because he took interest, did he not? The greatest liability is that of *atikraman*. There is no problem with the day-to-day functions of life where no one is hurt. The effect of *pratikraman* is that it stops bondage of new karma. The old karma will have to be suffered.

## After the Doership is Gone

**Questioner:** After attaining Gnan, our 'doership' has gone away. So does that mean our new body complex (*pudgal*), ceases to be formed?

**Dadashri:** Bondage of new karma stops when doership, 'I am doing this (*kartabhav*),' goes away.

**Questioner:** So then what is the solution to discharge the remaining old karma?

**Dadashri:** No, that will occur automatically. If you remain in the Five Agnas (special directives given by Dadashri after Self-realization in Gnan Vidhi) that you have been given, then the old karma will be settled with equanimity, without binding any new ones.

**Questioner:** But if we have bound heavy karma, should we bring an end to it by suffering through it slowly?

**Dadashri:** No. You have to keep doing *pratikraman* for it. A very heavy and sticky karma requires more *pratikraman*. If you feel that it is a sticky karma, then if you do *pratikraman* and *pratyakhyan*, it will wash off. It will not go away completely because this knowledge you have been given is *ekavtari* Gnan – one more life remains before attaining *moksha*.

**Questioner:** What if there is no awareness when *atikraman* occurs?

**Dadashri:** So, the *pratikraman* does not occur, is that it?

**Questioner:** Later, when I become aware, I do *pratikraman*.

**Dadashri:** So if you doze off once, it does not mean you bind karma because of that. When do you bind karma? It is when you believe, 'I am Chandulal.' The result of dozing is that karma effect remains pending; it remains incomplete. So the effect will come later on again. The effect of dozing (lack of awakened awareness) will come. No karma should be left incomplete. If you doze off, lose awareness, there will be consequences to that. It will not be the same as the effect of 'doership,' but there will be the effect of a karma that is pending and it will remain so until it is settled with equanimity.

## Only the Pratikraman Remains

**Questioner:** So, Dada, the only thing that remains is *pratikraman*, right?

**Dadashri:** Only *pratikraman*, and that, too, only if *atikraman* occurs. Really, *atikraman* does not occur all day long; everything runs smoothly. If there is some dispute over a certain dish on the dining table, then that is *atikraman*. Now this *atikraman* is not a mistake of today; it is from the past life. It is a *charitra mohaniya* (discharging illusory conduct). Today, we do not like it at all, but it occurs all the same, does it not?

*Charitra moha* – The conduct of the non-Self that remains after the Self has separated. It is, as Dadashri says, 'Discharge *moha*.' The awakened one within is free from the illusion and hence it is called *charitra moha*, discharge *moha*, as opposed to the illusion of the worldly being whose *moha* is called *darshan moha* because he believes that he is 'Chandulal' and that it is happening to him.

## Atikraman and Aakraman

*Pratikraman* must be done for both – *atikraman* (aggression in thoughts, speech and acts) and *aakraman* (attacking nature.) *Aakraman* must not exist in us. *Aakraman* means attacking nature. *Aakraman* means one would constantly attack every single interaction, even every word. If attack occurs in every word, such attacking nature is called *aakraman*. (114)

What is the difference between *atikraman* and *aakraman*?

**Questioner:** Does *aakraman* mean direct attack?

**Dadashri:** Yes. That is it; attack. To assault, *aakraman*! And what is *kraman*? Simple conversations and talk in daily life where no one gets hurt is *kraman*. If you were to joke or make fun of someone, he may not react externally because he is weak, but if he feels the hurt inside, then it is an *atikraman*. I make fun of everybody, but how is it? It is harmless and innocuous and it is done to remove his weaknesses and make him stronger. There is some fun involved, but he also makes progress at the same time. This kind of joking and fun does not hurt anyone.

It is natural for *atikraman* to occur and to do *pratikraman* is our *purusharth* (spiritual effort).

**Questioner:** It has become a habit for people to do *pratikraman* for their *atikraman*. It is a kind of an opinion one develops that '*atikraman* has occurred' and, therefore, he feels that *atikraman* occurred. But really, it may not have occurred at all, is that not possible?

**Dadashri:** But one will immediately recognize *atikraman*. Would you not know from within that you spoke harsh words? Is there not a difference between vomiting and rinsing your mouth?

**Questioner:** There is.

**Dadashri:** You will know all that. If you experience suffering (*dukh*) even to the slightest extent; then 'know' that *atikraman* has occurred here.

**Questioner:** There is another word '*parakram*.' What is *parakram*?

**Dadashri:** That which is above *kram-akram* is *parakram* (extraordinary spiritual effort). For now, at least do *pratikraman*. *Parakram* will come when it does. It is a very big 'station' and it is very long. If you wait for it, then you will miss out on this *Akram*.

For the time being, do *pratikraman*. As yet, you still have to do *pratikraman* for the *aakraman*, so how are you going to be able to do *parakram*?

**Questioner:** But there is a need to do *parakram* against *aakraman*, is there not?

**Dadashri:** You have to do *pratikraman* against the *aakraman*. *Parakram* is beyond the two, *kram* and *akram*. Where did you 'steal' this word '*parakram*' from?

**Questioner:** I read it in Aptavani Six.

**Dadashri:** Is that so! We have a very good tool of *pratikraman*. You have to do *pratikraman* for your obstinacy (*aadayee*). There is tremendous energy in *pratikraman*. You do not enlist the 'army of *pratikraman*,' do you? If you did, then you would win. Can a whole army win or not?

## Kraman Creates and Atikraman Proliferates Prakruti

**Questioner:** Actually, *pratikraman* is important in every way, is it not? Because whether a person understands or not, whether he can see his mistakes or not, whether he has knowledge of what to do or not, *pratikraman* will automatically bring about a solution, will it not?          (116)

**Dadashri:** All this has arisen because of *atikraman*, and if one wants to go to his own 'country' (domain of the Self), then he has to do *pratikraman*. Is that not easy? Is it easy or is it difficult?

**Questioner:** It is very easy.

**Dadashri:** All this has arisen due to *atikraman* and it will stop with *pratikraman*.

**Questioner:** The entire *prakruti* (the complex of thoughts, speech and action, the non-Self) has arisen out of *atikraman*, has it not?

**Dadashri:** *Prakruti* has arisen out of doership in normal action (*kraman*) and through *atikraman* it has proliferated.

**Questioner:** The entire *prakruti* proliferates with *atikraman*.

**Dadashri:** The proliferation decreases with *pratikraman* and as a result, one will become aware.

**Questioner:** The *prakruti* proliferates with *atikraman*, then after that comes *aakraman*; that is what you call it, right? What occurs with *aakraman*? Are *atikraman* and *aakraman* through attack?

**Dadashri:** That is *atikraman*, is it not?

**Questioner:** It is heavier than *atikraman*, is it not?

**Dadashri:** No, this is all the same. Little *aakraman* and big *aakraman*; it all falls under *aakraman*, and that is called *atikraman*.

**Questioner:** Whether it is a little or big *aakraman*, is it all *atikraman*?

**Dadashri:** Yes.

## No One is Wrong in This World!

**Dadashri:** But he asked a good question. A question has to be asked and understood scientifically in order to have a solution. Otherwise, there will be no solutions.

What I am saying is, say you go to do *darshan* of someone but when you get there you feel, 'I expected this person to be a Gnani but he is a phony!' Now the fact that you went there is karma effect (*prarabdha*) but the negative thought that arose, 'Oh no! How did I end up coming to this worthless person?' is your negative *purusharth*. You will have to suffer the effect of this negative *purusharth*. It is natural to have that thought but what should you do right away? Instead, you should immediately erase the negative thought with a positive one with, 'Oh no! Why did I make such a mistake?' You should immediately erase the negative thought with a positive one.

**Questioner:** Should one ask for forgiveness?

**Dadashri:** Yes, you should ask for forgiveness in the mind. You should do *pratikraman*.

**Questioner:** I am asking for forgiveness for any wrongdoing, committed knowingly or unknowingly, through my mind, speech and action.

**Dadashri:** Remember to do *pratikraman* in the name of Lord Mahavir or whichever God you believe in. Recall Dada and do *pratikraman*. When you do your *pratikraman*, your *bhaav* (inner intent) should be, 'Regardless of what the other person is like, why did I have to behave so negatively?' There is no accountability on your part in saying someone is good when he is good, but there is a liability in calling someone bad when he is good, and there is also liability in calling a bad person, bad; tremendous liability. Because, in reality, he is never bad; it is his *prarabdha* (karma effect) that makes him appear bad. What do we mean by *prarabdha*? It is his circumstances that have made him bad, so how can we blame him?

Did you understand that? This is a very subtle and profound talk. You will not find this in the scriptures, nor will you hear it from any ascetic (*sadhu*).

If you understand, in short, what *purusharth* (spiritual effort; cause is) and what *prarabdha* (karma effect) is, then you will be on the right track. You should not spoil your inner intent (*bhaav*) and if it does get spoiled, then there is nothing wrong if you immediately correct it.                                    (118)

If a group of women is passing by and one of the people you are with makes a comment, 'Look at that prostitute! What is she doing here?' and based on his comment, you also start to believe her to be a prostitute, then you will incur a tremendous liability. She is saying, 'Circumstances have forced me to be this way; in all that, why are you committing a fault? I am already suffering my karma effect, but why are you creating a fault all over again (cause karma)?' Why should you take on a liability on her account? She has not become a prostitute of her own will. No living being likes to be or become bad. It is circumstances that initially drive a person to do things, but later it becomes a habit. Nevertheless, initially, it was circumstances that drove her to do so.

## It Cannot Be Done through the Intellect (Buddhi)

**Questioner:** Mistakes like that occur everywhere during one's entire life, do they not?

**Dadashri:** No, a mistake will occur, but if you know that as a mistake, and become a true judge (not partial to file number one), then You will be able to see that you made a mistake. So then you have to remove the stain of that mistake by doing *pratikraman*.

**Questioner:** But we have to do that through the intellect (*buddhi*), don't we?

**Dadashri:** No, not through the intellect (*buddhi*). It is done with the light of knowledge (*Gnan prakash*) that 'we' give you. The *buddhi* will not let you see your mistake, will it? The intellect (*buddhi*) is the lawyer, so it will not allow you to see the mistake at all.

**Questioner:** After attaining Gnan, when one becomes *antaratma* (awakened pure Self; *Shuddhatma*), do faults then begin to decrease?

**Dadashri:** One will begin to 'see' the mistakes and the mistakes will decrease. His vision will turn towards his own faults. As long as one is an embodied self (*jivatma*), as long as one is a *moodhatma* (not awakened to the Self), one will know how to see other's faults. If you ask him about his own faults, he will tell you he has only two or three and that otherwise he has no faults, but the other person is full of faults!

## Pratikraman for Those Who Are Not Self-realized

**Questioner:** Is *pratikraman* only for those who have taken Gnan or is it also for those who have not taken Gnan?

**Dadashri:** It is like this; *pratikraman* is there even for those who have not taken Gnan; the same word is applicable for all. It is simply a term, but how can those who have not taken Gnan have awareness? How can they do *pratikraman* without the awareness of the Self?

In which time cycle did such awareness exist? After Lord Rushabhdev, the disciples of all the twenty-two *Tirthankars* used to be very aware. They constantly did 'shoot-on-sight' *pratikraman*.

Such awareness only arises when 'we' give Gnan, otherwise, the awareness can never be there. Otherwise, people are asleep (spiritually) with open eyes; that is what the scripture says.

**Questioner:** Can people who are not Self-realized only see certain kinds of faults?

**Dadashri:** That is all; only that much. You simply have to tell them to learn to ask for forgiveness for their mistakes.

Whatever faults they are able to see, they should ask for forgiveness. They should never protect their mistake, or say there is nothing wrong with it, otherwise the mistake doubles. If you do something wrong, ask for forgiveness.          (120)

**Questioner:** How should those who are not Self-realized do *pratikraman* when they see their own faults?

**Dadashri:** There are some people who, despite not having this knowledge, are very aware of their faults. They understand what *pratikraman* is and they do it. Others are not included in this, but we still need to explain to them the meaning of *pratikraman* and tell them to repent for their mistakes.

## Is Pratikraman Necessary After Self-realization?

**Questioner:** Dada, I still do not understand why we have to do *pratikraman* after attaining the state of the Self? There is no need, is there?

**Dadashri:** No, there is also no problem if you do.

**Questioner:** I do not have a problem with doing it, but how should I do it? I am either 'Chandulal' or I am pure Soul – *Shuddhatma.*

**Dadashri:** 'You – the Self' are not to do the *pratikraman.* The Self does not have to do *pratikraman.* 'You,' as a neighbor of 'Chandubhai,' have to tell him, 'Chandubhai, why are you doing such *atikraman*?'

**Questioner:** But, Dada, why should I go anywhere near the 'neighbor'?

**Dadashri:** The neighbor is the result of your own past mistakes (from your past life). It is your unsettled crime (liability, nature's court).

I will tell you something; listen to what I tell you. Say a young man goes to downtown Ahmadabad and goes on a spending spree and creates a two thousand rupees debt. Now from today onwards, he decides that he does not want to create a debt of even a dime, and he follows through with it. He does not spend any more money and hands over his paycheck to his father. Nevertheless, he still has to pay off his old debt, doesn't he? Why does he have to pay the past debt even when he decides not to get into debt anymore? In the same manner, this 'Chandulal' is the result of mistakes of the past life. His account is written in the *karmic* book of cause and effect; you will have to resolve it, won't you?

**Questioner:** So after attaining Gnan, does one not have to do any *pratikraman*?

**Dadashri:** There is no problem if you do not. It is not mandatory to do this.

**Questioner:** I do not have any problem with doing it; I am not even opposed to it. I just want to understand this; I just have this question.

**Dadashri:** What happens in the process of *pratikraman*? It is when the Self puts pressure on the 'relative' self. *Atikraman* is the process whereby the 'real - the awakened Self' becomes suppressed. When the karma is an *atikraman*, and one becomes interested in it, then it causes damage again. Therefore, until you accept that which is wrong as wrong, you are liable for it. Therefore, *pratikraman* is very necessary.

**Questioner:** I still cannot understand it.

**Dadashri:** If your action hurts your father, it is considered *atikraman* on your part. Now, the hurt that you caused your father, do you have to encourage that action or discourage it? What should you do to 'Chandulal'?

**Questioner:** I believe I should not do anything that would hurt him whatsoever.

**Dadashri:** No, that will occur. *Atikraman* occurs automatically. What is *atikraman*? It is that which happens on its own. No one ever wants to do *atikraman*.

**Questioner:** But that is fine, if it is done deliberately.

**Dadashri:** No one will do it deliberately. It is not possible to do so, even if one wants to.                                    (122)

**Questioner:** Then, Dada, how can we say that one has done *atikraman*?

**Dadashri:** If you say harsh words to your father, if you had a verbal 'boxing,' will you do *pratikraman* or not? If you do not do *pratikraman*, then it means that you are siding with the *atikraman*, but if you do *pratikraman*, then who are you siding with? With *pratikraman*.

**Questioner:** I do not have such a *bhaav* (inner intent) of doing *atikraman*.

**Dadashri:** Your inner intent is not so, but even then you are on the side of *atikraman*. If you do not have any intent of opposing it, *atikraman*, then you are on the side of *atikraman*. Therefore, do *pratikraman* and that will mean that you do not side with the *atikraman*.

If you step on someone's foot, should you or should you not say you are sorry?

**Questioner:** We should say it. That is true.

**Dadashri:** That itself is *pratikraman*. There is no other thing.

**Questioner:** Yes, in that sense, but not otherwise, right?

**Dadashri:** That is what I refer to as *pratikraman*. It is like when we say we are sorry. It is just like saying 'sorry.' 'We' call that *pratikraman*.

**Questioner:** What if the other person does not forgive me for my *atikraman*, despite my *pratikraman*?

**Dadashri:** Do not be concerned about the other person. Don't worry about others forgiving you. The nature of aggression (*atikraman*) in you should go away. You should become an opponent of *atikraman*. That is how it should be.

**Questioner:** What if the other person continues to feel hurt?

**Dadashri:** Do not be concerned about the other person. Be firm in your conviction that you are an adversary of *atikraman*. It is not your wish to do *atikraman* but if it occurs, you should feel remorse and your intent should be that you do not want it to happen again.

**Questioner:** I now have the courage to say 'sorry' to the other person. I will do *pratikraman* if any *atikraman* occurs.

**Dadashri:** Not a single person is yet born on this earth who has the ability to do even a hair's worth (the slightest) of work.

**Questioner:** How can it be acceptable if a person intentionally does *atikraman*, when both the parties are destroying each other off? Then is it possible to become free by doing *pratikraman*?

**Dadashri:** What else can you do? This is all a process to turn back from ignorance (*bhranti* – wrong belief; illusion). It is not worth delving deep into this. Our concern is just with what works.

Here, 'we' have not left anything unanswered. All you have to do is to follow the Agnas. Sometimes, if you have to ask, go ahead and ask. But do not 'dissect' too much; do not try to analyze anything, otherwise you will 'lose it'! The *buddhi* will take over and you will be led astray by it. This is nothing but mischief of the *buddhi*.

This Gnan is such that one does not have to ask even a word of question; all the solutions are given.

## Short Pratikraman

**Questioner:** What if I don't know how to do a lengthy *pratikraman*? I cannot do *pratikraman* very fast, but if I make a mistake and feel that I should not have talked the way I did, is that considered *pratikraman*?                                    (124)

**Dadashri:** Yes, that is *pratikraman*. That is all it needs to be. Your current opinion is this and so you can wash it off in this manner.

Now that is not the exact *pratikraman*, but you removed yourself away from that old opinion, did you not?

**Questioner:** Then what is correct? Can I do it in short like that?

**Dadashri:** There is nothing wrong with that. If you do not do it as shown, it is fine because in that situation that is *pratikraman* all the same. But if 'we' give this answer to every situation, then people will do it haphazardly. There is no problem if that occurs under certain circumstances; it will do. That is *pratikraman* all the same. To have the opinion of, 'This should not be so,' is *pratikraman* for sure, because you changed your opinion, did you not? One way or another, your opinion has to be changed.

## Do Not Oppose Pratikraman

*Pratikraman* is to be done in order to get rid of that opinion of yours. It is to be done to show that you no longer endorse that opinion and that now you are opposing it. *Pratikraman* is to be done to show your opposition towards any aggression. Do you understand?

**Questioner:** Do we have to do *pratikraman* to show that we oppose the *atikraman* that occurred?

**Dadashri:** Yes, and that we do not wish to do the same again. We do *pratikraman* to remove these tendencies from our nature. If we don't do *pratikraman*, it means that was our wish.

**Questioner:** But for us (*mahatmas*), all such intents are being settled, discharging (*nikaali*), are they not?

**Dadashri:** Yes, it is all discharge *bhaav*, but if you (the self) want to keep that as part of your nature; there is nothing wrong with it.

**Questioner:** If it is all just discharging (an effect of karma), then why should I do *pratikraman*?

**Dadashri:** Everything is a discharge; everything! *Pratikraman* is only for *atikraman* that occurs; it is not for anything else. If you do not do *pratikraman*, your relative nature (*swabhav*) will never change. It will remain as it is. Do you understand?

Unless you show your opposition to it, it will always stay with you. If you happen to get angry, you do *pratikraman* because you do not wish to support your anger. If you fail to do *pratikraman*, it would mean that you are in favor of your anger. This is how you free yourself of your faults. This allows you to shed your karma. There should be a means through which you can defy, oppose, the anger.

Do you want to keep anger as a part of you or do you want to be rid of it?

**Questioner:** I want to get rid of it.

**Dadashri:** If you want to get rid of it, then you should do *pratikraman* for it. Only then can you maintain that you are opposed to your anger. Otherwise, it would be the same as supporting it.

**Questioner:** Whatever was meant to occur, did occur.

Whether we do *pratikraman* for it or not; it would not make any difference, would it?

**Dadashri:** You can get by with that, but if you want great benefit, then you should do this *pratikraman*. Do you want to do what will just work or do you want to do more?

**Questioner:** It is not the question of doing it or not. I am simply asking scientifically.                                              (126)

**Dadashri:** Everything is a discharge for sure, but wherever *atikraman* takes place, you should think upon it. Otherwise, it will remain as part of your nature. You are against *atikraman*; this much should be decided upon. You should make the decision that you are not in agreement with it.

**Questioner:** If we have already decided that we are not in agreement with it, then *pratikraman* has to be done only in our minds, right?

**Dadashri:** Yes, only in your mind. Everything has to be done internally, in your mind only. You do not have to say anything aloud. If you are opposed to it, you may not do *pratikraman* but if you say, 'I do not like it,' even then it is more than enough. Then you have become free from it. You should not get stuck in those problems.

**Questioner:** When we do *pratikraman*, does that mean we are resorting to the *Kramic* path, a bit?

**Dadashri:** This is not to enter the *Kramic* path. We are in opposition to such a nature of *atikraman*. Until we decide this, such a nature will remain with us. That is how subtle this talk is. You will be blessed if you understand it. If you happen to swear at someone, it is not a problem, but should you not at least oppose the action of swearing?

**Questioner:** We may do the *pratikraman*, but the other person is bound to bind more karma, is he not?

**Dadashri:** That is not your lookout (concern). You have to say it in your mind (silent *pratikraman*) and so you are free.

## The Exact Definition of 'Settlement of Karma'

**Questioner:** If there is an incident where even before any *atikraman* occurs, if we have the awareness of, 'This is a discharge; this *bhaav* (inner intent) is not mine,' is that not *pratikraman*?

**Dadashri:** Everyone cannot maintain such awareness like you. Not everyone can maintain the awareness of, 'This *bhaav* is not mine.' So it is better to teach this simple thing of *pratikraman* to most people.

**Questioner:** When the *pratikraman* is done, the Self does not accept it as its own *bhaav*, does it?

**Dadashri:** No, it is true what he says, that we are only doing *pratikraman* to show that this is not our *bhaav*. Other people do not have the awareness of 'These *bhaavs* (feelings of repent and aggression) are not mine,' do they?

Settling a file with equanimity and the absence of the slightest *atikraman* is all a discharge (*nikaal*) in worldly interaction. *Atikraman* should not occur; but if it does, then you have to do *pratikraman*. Then it counts as a discharging worldly interaction (*nirjara* of karma).

### The Doer of Atikraman Does Pratikraman

After 'we' give Gnan, one begins to see all his own faults. Until then, he sees other's faults and not his own. If he wants to, he will find a hundred faults in someone else. He will see only two or three of his most obvious ones but he will not be able to see his other faults. Now that Gnan has been nurtured and has grown into a good size plant, you will immediately begin to see all your faults. What do you see every day? Do you see your own faults or those of others?

**Questioner:** Only my own.

**Dadashri:** So if you can see your faults, and if they are big, then do *pratikraman* for them. You have to do *pratikraman* even if they are small. The one who makes the mistake has to do *pratikraman*. Therefore, 'Chandulal' has to do *pratikraman*. 'You' (the Self) do not have to do anything. 'You' have to tell 'Chandulal' to do the *pratikraman*. And all other faults, the ones that are light, go away merely by 'seeing' them. But the faults can only go away when you can 'see' them. When all faults go away, then one becomes flawless (*nirdosh*).

You will not see a single fault of anyone in this world, even if he were to hit you. That is the kind of vision (*drashti*) I have given you. Do you see any fault?

**Questioner:** I see my own fault.                              (128)

**Dadashri:** And if you see someone else's fault, do you do *pratikraman* immediately?

**Questioner:** Yes, Dada.

**Dadashri:** You will not have any attacking inner intent or thought (*aakraman*) towards anyone. You will never even have an attacking thought when someone swears at you, hits you or causes you harm. And yet the whole world, the ascetics and the monks (*sadhus* and *sanyasis*), they will all attack with, 'What is it... What did you say... I will do this, I will do that to you!'

Whereas these people (those who have taken Gnan) will not even think about attacking. That is called '*Gnani bhakta*' – worshipper of Gnani. *Gnani bhakta* means he has become free.

## Real Pratikraman is That Which Decreases Faults

What does *pratikraman* mean? It means to become lighter and feel freer. It means that the person will feel very uneasy within if he were to repeat the same mistake. People in general keep multiplying their faults.

Have you witnessed a real *pratikraman* where your fault has gone or decreased?

**Questioner:** Only here. Nowhere else.

**Dadashri:** *Alochana, pratikraman* and *pratyakhyan*, is the only tool for the path of *moksha*. There is no other tool in this world. The other fact is that this tool will become very effective after receiving the Gnan from the Gnani Purush. Thereafter this tool of *alochana, pratikraman* and *pratyakhyan* will be helpful.

If *pratikraman* is done before attaining Gnan, then the faults will become weak. But the level of *pratikraman* needed will not remain; one needs awareness for that.

After taking Gnan, you will be able to know that a mistake (*dosh*) has occurred. Only then will you be able to do *pratikraman*. Until then, *pratikraman* cannot take place. After taking this Gnan, an awakened awareness (*jagruti*) will prevail whereby you will be able to tell right away that *atikraman* has taken place; you will come to know this right away. Once you know you made a mistake, you will do *pratikraman* right away. This process will continue to take place systematically. Once *pratikraman* takes place, those mistakes get erased. Once the mistakes are erased, the other person will not feel any negativity or aversion towards you. Otherwise, when you meet the other person again, there will be a sense of separation with him. Does such a separation (*bheda*) not occur when that happens?

**Questioner:** Yes.

**Dadashri:** Even at your workplace, when *atikraman* occurs with someone and you do *pratikraman* for it, his mind will become one with you; otherwise it will not.

## Signs of Washing Off the Mistakes

**Questioner:** How am I to wash away my *paap* (demerit karma; wrong actions) karma now?

**Dadashri:** For each stain (demerit, *paap* karma) you should do *pratikraman*. If any stain is stubborn, then it will need to be washed over and over again.

**Questioner:** How can I tell whether the stain is gone or not?

**Dadashri:** You will know when your mind becomes clean from within. Your face will glow. There will be a natural smile on the face. Can you not tell? How can you not? How can you not tell where the problem is? And even if the 'stain' (*paap*) has not gone, there is no problem. You just keep on doing *pratikraman*. Keep scrubbing away with the soap of *pratikraman*. Do you understand what *paap* is?

**Questioner:** Is it *paap* when one does not follow Dada's Agnas?

**Dadashri:** No, it is not like that - that is not *paap*. *Paap* (demerit karma, sin) is when you hurt anyone; whether it is a tree, a human, an animal or any living being. To pluck leaves from a tree unnecessarily is a *paap*; the tree also feels pain.

By not following the Agnas, you will be the one to sustain a loss, whereas *paap* hurts others. It is a *paap* when you hurt others, therefore, you should not inflict even the slightest pain on others.                                                                    (130)

**Questioner:** If a man acts according to his nature, does he bind merit or demerit karma?

**Dadashri:** He will bind demerit karma if he hurts anyone. He is doing it based on his nature, but he should understand that he is hurting others and that is why he should ask for forgiveness; his *pratikraman* should be, 'I have a bad nature, and that is why I have hurt you and for that, I ask for your forgiveness.'

When you do *pratikraman*, your clothes will become clean. Why leave dirt on your clothes when Dada has given you such a simple solution? Why not use it and get your clothes radiantly clean?

## There is No Suffering Where There is No Mistake

Whenever you hurt someone even slightly, you should know (*janavoo*) that the mistake is yours. When the state of internal harmony within is disturbed, you will understand that the mistake is yours. The other person's mistake is evident because he is suffering, but you became instrumental (*nimit*) in the process; you told him off, so the mistake is yours too. Why does Dada not have any suffering?

Dada does not have any suffering because he no longer has any mistakes. So if someone is hurt by your actions, you should immediately do *pratikraman* and erase that mistake. Also if someone else commits a mistake because of you, you have to do *pratikraman*.

Awareness should prevail at every step of the way. We have *kashays* of anger, pride, deceit and greed within us. They will make us make mistakes and create an account of *karmic* debt. But against that, we should credit the *karmic* account immediately and clear it by asking for forgiveness. We cannot keep this business pending. This *pratikraman* is considered a cash business.

**Questioner:** The mistakes we make now are from the past life, are they not?

**Dadashri:** These mistakes are due verily to the demerit karma (*paap*) of the past life. But generally, people do not destroy the old ones and continue to increase new ones. In order to break the cycle of mistake, one has to 'see' the mistake and call it a mistake. You cannot protect the mistake. 'This' is considered the 'Gnani's 'key.' It can open any 'lock.'

Then, when one destroys his own mistakes, his work will be done. Or it can occur if a Gnani Purush helps him achieve that. The Gnani Purush can save you. If you tell the Gnani, 'Please save me,' then he will. He does not expect a fee for doing it. Besides, how much value can you put on something that is invaluable? This is considered priceless; it is very precious so there can never be a price for it.

Mistakes are bound to occur; they are inevitable. New mistakes will continue to occur. You will continue to 'see' them. When you see them, you should do *pratikraman* for them. You should repent for them and do *pratyakhyan* – vow not to do it again and ask for energies for this. That is called 'shoot-on-sight.' It means that the moment the mistake occurs it is instantly washed away. What is your wish, to wash away your mistakes the moment they occur or wash them off once a year?

## Ineffective Pratikramans

**Questioner:** I never got much out of doing *pratikraman* as it is prescribed in the *Kramic* path, but when I do the *pratikraman* as shown in *Akram Vignan*, I feel as light as a flower.                                                                          (132)

**Dadashri:** But those *pratikramans* that you did were of the *Kramic* path, and were done without any understanding. *Pratikraman* means the faults should decrease right away. *Pratikraman* means to backtrack whatever distance you have traveled in the wrong direction. But in doing *pratikraman* without the understanding, people have not only failed to backtrack the path they walked on, but they are stuck in the same place. On the contrary, they are going further in the wrong direction! So how can that be called *pratikraman*?

## Pratikraman for Mistakes of Past Lives

**Questioner:** Does *atikraman* occur when there is some pending *karmic* account from the past life?

**Dadashri:** Yes, that is when it occurs.

**Questioner:** So when we do *pratikraman*, does that *pratikraman* wash away the demerit karma from all my past lives?

**Dadashri:** We are breaking that *karmic* account. That is why our people do 'shoot-on-sight' *pratikraman*. That is why our faults are uprooted immediately.

## Pratikraman of Bigger Faults

**Questioner:** If I see a major mistake in myself, how should I do *pratikraman* for it?

**Dadashri:** The process of *pratikraman* is mainly in words, but in the end it is all cumbersome wording. Instead, if you do not know how, then you should say, 'Dear Dada Bhagwan (or the Lord you believe in), I have made this mistake, I became excessively upset with this gentleman and so I am asking for forgiveness. I repent doing that and I will not do it again.' Even if you say this much, it will be more than enough.

Otherwise, there is a hassle of verbiage. They use big words; it takes long to recite them, so how is anyone to make any headway? Instead, you can say this; it is short. The intent of the *pratikraman* is more important than the words.

## Effective Pratikraman

Even when the other person is at fault, you should ask for forgiveness.

**Questioner:** What if everyone were to ask for forgiveness for their mistakes, in front of everyone, in the presence of Dada?

**Dadashri:** That is a kind of a beginning. It does not wash off the mistake. You should do *pratikraman* in such a way that the other person will come and talk to you. For the time being, start it in My presence.

Whenever inner conflict (*gooncha*) is likely to occur, you will inevitably remember Dada and there will be no more internal conflict. 'We' are telling you not to create a new conflict, but in the event it does occur, then do *pratikraman* for it. Now you know right away what to do should conflict occur. Elsewhere, people are tired of listening to the same old preaching of, 'Be truthful, be kind, do not steal,' etc.

Do not sleep on your conflict. If you have any conflict within, you should clear it before falling asleep. If you cannot clear this conflict, you should simply do *pratikraman*. You should ask for forgiveness because you are the one feeling disturbed. In this way, you will succeed in finding a solution; otherwise, these mistakes will continue to occur. Forgiveness is the greatest scripture.

## Bestial Ego and Humane Ego

When you scold someone, do you have the awareness (*khyal*) of how you would feel if someone scolded you? You should keep this in mind before you scold anyone.      (134)

To think about the other person and to put yourself in his shoes, and then do the work, is the mark of a human ego. To think of only yourself and to be inconsiderate when interacting with others and to push people around – what is that called?

**Questioner:** That is a bestial ego.

**Dadashri:** Have you done that before? Ever?

**Questioner:** What should we do if such circumstances arise after attaining Gnan?

**Dadashri:** After becoming a gnani, Gnan remains separate.

Nothing will occur to the One who knows how to remain separate. If 'One' remains separate and continues to 'see' all the drama, then there is no problem. And even if the mixture occurs, and he becomes 'one' with it, it is not the old 'Chandulal.' And even if it does not remain separate, that file will return for the 'signature' (to be settled with equanimity). That file will come back again because you have not 'signed off' on it (it has not been discharged correctly, settled with equanimity). But ultimately, only You (the awakened one in *Akram Vignan*) will have to bring it to an end. Do you understand what I have said so far?

**Questioner:** Yes, Dada!

**Dadashri:** The paper will come back to you if it has not been signed. Then you will have to 'see' it, read it and settle it with equanimity and then You will be free.

Now in what circumstances will this not occur? It is when the karma is so very dense and sticky that you will become unaware (*ajagrut*) and make mistakes. At such a time, you should repent. And repentance occurs after the mistakes, does it not? Repentance will 'loosen it' and so when it comes back the next time, it will be weak enough where you will be able to settle it with equanimity.

'You' should say, 'Chandubhai, go ahead and repent. Why did you do the *atikraman*?' What is Dada's rule? You have done *atikraman*, so do *pratikraman*; that is all! Is this not according to the rule?

Our science is within the natural law from every aspect. It is the exact science.

The entire knowledge of the *Kramic* path was given by the Lord through *Keval Gnan* and has come into the level of imagination (*kalpana*). And even this *Akram* Gnan of Ours has been conveyed through *Keval Gnan*, but it is something that is out of one's capacity to imagine. You can find contradictions in the other path, but not here.

## Applaud the One Who Shows Your Mistake

If someone showed you your mistake, would you thank him and applaud him?

**Questioner:** That all depends on one's ego.

**Dadashri:** Hey, you! God only knows! There is no telling what the fool will say! But why not step back and think for a moment, 'What would I do if that were to happen to me?'

**Questioner:** In this matter, I would grab on to it and tell him he did the right thing.

**Dadashri:** No, no, no. Because one can never see one's mistake as it is. Only in certain matters will you be able to realize your mistake. In other matters one will not be able to 'see' it as it is and that is why he will only say the wrong thing.

'Chandubhai' is the one who makes mistakes. If someone says, 'You have made a mistake,' then at that very same time, You should say, 'Chandubhai, you must have made a mistake, and that is why this person is pointing it out. If that was not the case, is anyone likely to say anything? People in general would not say anything without a reason, so there must be some mistake somewhere. So why should you have any objection if someone points out your mistake? So, dear 'Chandubhai,' you must have made a mistake somewhere and that is why he is telling you, so ask for forgiveness.' And if 'Chandubhai' hurts anyone, you have to tell him, 'Do *pratikraman*, dear man! Because we want to go to *moksha* and we can no longer afford to do as we please.'

## Do Not See Mistakes of Those Who Depend On You

**Questioner:** I see mistakes of others, I see my own

mistakes, so should I just keep 'seeing' those mistakes? What else do I need to do?                              (136)

**Dadashri:** When you see your own mistakes, you can share with some people, but not with certain people. And when you see other's mistakes, deal with them by doing *pratikraman*. These are the three ways you deal with them. You can either do *pratikraman* if you see the mistake, and settle it, or if you do not do *pratikraman*; then who can you show their mistakes? You may show the mistakes of policemen, magistrates, those in a superior position than you; their mistakes. But all those who work under you, those who are dependant (*ashrit*) on you, you should not show them their mistakes. Did you understand?

## Tell 'Chandubhai' to Do Pratikraman Instantly

Everyone is full of mistakes. So there will be all kinds of mistakes made, will there not? No one, without exception, is free from mistakes. To point out mistakes in others is the work of a fool. Do you like to point out other's mistakes?

**Questioner:** To 'see' a mistake of anyone is a mistake and when it occurs, am I to do *pratikraman* for it?

**Dadashri:** When 'he - file one' sees mistakes of others, he should stop right there and tell 'Chandubhai' (the non-Self), 'Oh, ho ho, do you still see mistakes of others? Do *pratikraman* for that.' Doing this is considered as having seen your own mistake. If you do this fifty times a day or so, that is more than enough.

You have no right whatsoever to see mistakes of others. If you do, you should do *pratikraman*. 'Chandulal' is adept at seeing mistakes in others. It is nothing new. This habit is not easy to break, but through *pratikraman* it will eventually cease. When he sees mistakes in others, You should immediately make him do *pratikraman*, which is 'shoot-on-sight' *pratikraman*.

## Nischay Here Means to Follow This and Not That

**Questioner:** I am not yet able to do the kind of *pratikraman* that is called for.

**Dadashri:** You should make a firm resolution (*nischay*) for whatever you want to do.

**Questioner:** To do the '*nischay*' involves the ego of 'doership,' does it not? What is that? Can you please explain?

**Dadashri:** That is merely use of words, just to say it.

**Questioner:** Many of the *mahatmas* are under the impression that they do not have to do a thing, including making *nischay* (firm resolution).

**Dadashri:** No, if they were to ask me, I would ask them how they can make that resolution (*nischay*) without the ego. That *nischay* is a decision. It means that when you undertake something, you do it in a certain way and not the other way. We cannot say that it is a wrong belief, can we? But we can get the idea across through the medium of words, otherwise they would not understand, would they? And yet, this reaches them.

## Can Pratikraman Be Done Later?

**Questioner:** I am unable to do 'shoot-on-sight' *pratikraman* when I am under stress, and sometimes it is not until the evening that I realize that I have made a mistake. Can those mistakes be erased even though *pratikraman* is done much later? Would that still resolve everything?

**Dadashri:** Yes, even if it occurs later on, you should do *pratikraman*. If you do something wrong, you should do *pratikraman*.

**Questioner:** After attaining Self-realization, when *atikraman* occurs, *alochana*, *pratikraman* and *pratyakhyan* do not happen right away.

**Dadashri:** Why does it not?                                    (138)

**Questioner:** It does not occur right away.

**Dadashri:** If it does not take place right away then do it after a couple of hours or even at night. You can also do *pratikraman* after a week for all the mistakes committed throughout the week. Just do them collectively.

**Questioner:** But it should be done immediately, right?

**Dadashri:** There is nothing better than immediate *pratikraman*. Most of our *mahatmas* do 'shoot-on-sight' *pratikraman*.

## Pratikraman for Lack of Awareness

**Questioner:** Sometimes, even while I think of Dada or do *arati* (devotional singing accompanied with burning oil wicks), my mind wanders and I begin to sing something entirely different, but eventually I do come back to the present.

**Dadashri:** When that occurs, you should do *pratikraman*. There is no problem when thoughts arise if You are able to 'see' that 'Chandulal' is having these thoughts, and if you can 'see' that then You and 'Chandulal' are separate. But such awareness is a little dim at that time.

**Questioner:** There is no awareness at all during that time.

**Dadashri:** Then you should do *pratikraman* for the loss of awareness by saying, 'Dada Bhagwan, please forgive me for this lack of attention and awareness.'

**Questioner:** Sometimes I realize much later that I have to do *pratikraman* for certain people.

**Dadashri:** But you do eventually remember, don't you? You need to spend more time in *satsang* and ask about everything in detail. This is a science and it requires your understanding. You need to ask questions.

You do have the good intention to do *pratikraman* and yet you are not able to, right?

**Questioner:** Yes, I do wish to, for sure.

**Dadashri:** Yes. You do not have the practice yet. You have to have the practice first. You have to first practice for the first, two, three or four days.

If the doctor tells you not to eat with your right hand today, you will still end up using it when you start eating.

**Questioner:** If I have constant awareness, then it occurs naturally and spontaneously.

**Dadashri:** Yes, it is possible for all this to occur naturally and spontaneously. One does not have to do anything. That is why I will do that for you.

**Questioner:** I still like doing *pratikraman*; I enjoy it and feel good. But I should be able to see my mistakes the way I am supposed to, am I not? That does not occur.

**Dadashri:** You will be able to see them now. It takes some time. You will be able see them when they become lighter. Right now it is all dense but it will become lighter with *pratikraman*.

It is not easy to see your own mistakes. 'We' illuminate everything for you, but you should have the intent that you want to see your mistakes; then you will be able to. It is like when you sit down to dinner, you have to make the effort to raise your hand to the dinner plate. The food is not likely to enter your mouth, without your effort, is it? There should be some effort on your part.

It is natural for humans to err, but how can they become

absolutely free (*vimukta*) from that? Only the Gnani Purush can show you the way, through *pratikraman*.          (140)

## The Gnan Within You Cautions You

**Questioner:** Sometimes, I feel that a mistake is occurring but the other person may not even be aware of it; can that be possible?

**Dadashri:** Yes, I see everyone's mistakes and yet they have no idea of their mistakes.

**Questioner:** Not like that. I feel that I have erred towards you but you do not even feel that I have done anything wrong. So then what happens to the repenting that I do?

**Dadashri:** Yes, you become free when you repent when you have done something wrong. What is it to you whether the other person is aware or not?

**Questioner:** I thought, 'Did I do something wrong?'

**Dadashri:** Yes, what can you do if his 'post office' is closed? Your post office is open, is it not? If you have stamped it the wrong way, then you have to correct it and stamp it the right way.

**Questioner:** Or is it the intellect (*buddhi*) that looks for mistakes and continues to interfere every now and then?

**Dadashri:** What interference does it do?

**Questioner:** It tells me, 'You have erred; you should not have done that.'

**Dadashri:** Hmm! Then it is saying the right thing, is it not? But where will you find someone to alert you this way?

**Questioner:** But, Dada, perhaps that mistake may not have occurred, even then.

**Dadashri:** No, it is not that the mistake may not have

occurred; it will say that only if the mistake has occurred. It is cautioning you from within. Who in this world will caution you? No one else will come to caution you. The Gnan that has been placed within you is cautioning you. It will constantly caution you!

## The One Whose Abhorrence is Gone is A God

*Pratikraman* is occurring naturally and spontaneously from within. People ask if this is true. I tell them that I have placed a special 'machine' inside them which starts the process. Everything is ready as long as you are earnest about it.

**Questioner:** That is true, Dada. *Pratikraman* is occurring naturally. Furthermore, this science is such that there is no more abhorrence (*dwesh*).

**Dadashri:** Yes, abhorrence will not occur.

**Questioner:** That is a wonder, Dada!

**Dadashri:** That is what you call '*Khuda*' (Muslim word for God; divine). The one who does not have any abhorrence is called '*Khuda*.'

## Never Say the Negative

**Questioner:** This person is saying, 'Someone like me cannot do *pratikraman* – what is that?

**Dadashri:** He does not realize that it is, indeed, occurring within him, but when he says that he cannot do it, the machinery and the process come to a halt. Whatever your 'prayers,' so will be your worship. They will continue to take place from within; they will start after a while.

**Questioner:** I do not like it when I hurt someone, but that is as far as it goes. It does not go any further from that. *Pratikraman* does not occur.                          (142)

**Dadashri:** The 'machinery' within us works according to

our instructions. If you say you cannot do something, then you
will not be able to do it. If you tell yourself you are tired of doing
*pratikraman*, then the 'machinery' will also become sluggish. It
is 'Chandubhai' who is doing the *pratikraman* and he is the one
who is supposed to do it. All You have to do is keep driving him
on to do *pratikraman* and, before you know it, he will be doing
five hundred or more *pratikraman* a day.

This science can destroy every mistake completely. It can
make one a *vitarag* – absolutely free from all attachment. Once
you decide that you want to do *pratikraman*, *pratikraman* will
occur. When you say, 'I cannot do it (*pratikraman*),' then that
will be the case. You should never say it does not occur. It
definitely will. Why will it not?

## Pratikraman Every Night

Do you want to get rid of *pratikraman*? How is it
possible? That is the main thing; that is the ticket to *moksha*.

**Questioner:** On the contrary, one needs to 'see' how
more *pratikramans* occur.

**Dadashri:** Yes. That will occur with awareness. You should
do it every day. You should do *pratikraman* the whole day 'on
the moment' (instantly). If you cannot do them on the spot, then
recall all the mistakes of the day at night, and do *pratikraman*
for them all; do *alochana*, *pratikraman* and *pratyakhyan*.

In your *alochana*, tell Dada Bhagwan, 'This is what
happens. Now, this should not happen, but it still does. I repent
for it and I am making a *nischay* (firm determination) that I will
not do it again.'

**Questioner:** Whatever takes place during the day, from
morning till night, I take 'Chandulal' to task – 'what wrong and
right did you do?' I make him tally up the entire account in the
night.

**Dadashri:** Whenever possible, try to do 'shoot-on-sight' *pratikraman* as soon as the mistake is made. If you fail to do so, do *pratikraman* collectively in the evening. In the latter, however, you might forget a few of your mistakes. Who is going to take care of those? Therefore, your business is to do 'shoot-on-sight' *pratikraman*.

## Closure and Settlement is Non-Violence

**Questioner:** Complete awareness is to be maintained for the mistakes. You have to get after them.

**Dadashri:** These mistakes need to be brought to an end. They have to be settled.

**Questioner:** When we do *pratikraman* for mistakes, the process that occurs within settles the mistake once and for all (*nivedo*). Instead of the word 'shoot,' is the word *nivedo* more appropriate?

**Dadashri:** The word 'shoot' is for fun. It gives one valor; when a person hears the word 'shoot,' he feels heroic, does he not?

**Questioner:** The process of *pratikraman* brings an end to the mistake; is the final settlement due to a mutually satisfactory solution (*samadhan*)?

**Dadashri:** Once a satisfactory solution has been attained, there is no need to 'shoot' or do anything of the sort. What does our science say? It says, 'You have hit the other guy, so do *pratikraman*.' What does the Lord say? He says, 'Bring about a closure (*nivedo*) and settle (*nikaal*) everything. As far as possible, do not fight; this birth is not meant for fighting.' The Lord has not permitted even writing the word '*maar*' (to hit, to hurt). He said, 'Do not write the word '*maar*'.' The word '*maar*' is the starting point of *himsa* (violence) from within.

## Pratikraman Changes Dhyan

**Questioner:** Does 'shoot-on-sight' *pratikraman* represent a change in one's meditation (*dhyan*)?          (144)

**Dadashri:** Yes, that is indeed a change in one's *dhyan*.

**Questioner:** When one 'shoots,' he destroys the *pudgal* (the non-Self complex that arises and dissipates) and that is meddling with what was to be in *vyavasthit*. So then what will his next life be like?

**Dadashri:** It will be just the same. Whatever kind of link there is, that link will be the same.

**Questioner:** When one 'shoots' the *atikraman* and turns things around; will his life have the same longevity or will it be shorter?

**Dadashri:** There is no effect on the lifespan. All the circumstantial evidences would come together and his life would end. The 'spinning top' would stop spinning.

How are things with you?

**Questioner:** I can see five hundred to a thousand mistakes.

**Dadashri:** Just look! Every day he can see five hundred mistakes! If someone were to publish this in a newspaper, people would come to do his *darshan* and pay respects. Otherwise, is anyone able to see his own mistakes? They cannot see even five mistakes! There are so many prominent *acharyas* (spiritual masters) but even they cannot see five or so of their own mistakes.

How many of your own mistakes can you see now?

**Questioner:** Numerous.

**Dadashri:** What more! Even if just one mistake is seen, one can be considered a God! So what occurs when one can see all of them?

**Questioner:** Dada, I can see mistakes very frequently.

**Dadashri:** Yes. You will see them at every second, and you have to do *pratikraman* for each of them.

## Such Clarity is Not To Be Found in the Kramic Path

From the moment 'shoot-on-sight' *pratikraman* occurs, one is considered a gnani. The gnanis of the *Kramic* path do 'shoot-on-sight' *pratikraman*, but they do not have such magnificent progress.

## Clear Judgment

**Questioner:** We do *pratikraman* for the mistakes, but what should we do if the other person has such qualities (*guna*)? Should we do *pratikraman* for that?

**Dadashri:** You do not have to do anything; your interaction towards that person will only be good through intent (*bhaav*); by your inner intent. You don't have to do anything for that.

If the karma is very sticky and there is a tuber (*gaanth*) of it, one is bound to make mistakes. But with repentance it loosens up to the extent that in the next life, one will be able to wash it off with ease. The mistake will remain even after *pratikraman*, but to what extent? In the next life it will appear like a tuber, but it will disintegrate with a mere touch. In doing *pratikraman* you get the energy; you get a 'refund'! So if *pratikraman* is being done, it can be washed off. One should be able to see his mistake; 'What kind of a mistake occurred?' He should be able to see it 'on the moment.' One should have at least that much judgment (decision). It should be a clear judgment. Only then will it work.

## Sleeping With the Ego

The moment you begin to see your own mistakes, know

that your ticket for liberation has arrived. Generally, people, including prominent monks and religious teachers, cannot see their own mistakes. Inability to see one's own mistakes is the greatest of all shortcomings. This Science is such that it gives you an unbiased judgment by uncovering and disclosing all your mistakes. It uncovers them after they occur, but it uncovers them, does it not? Whatever happened has happened. That is different. If a train is moving at a fast speed, it can cause damage, can it not? But that is when you become aware, do you not?

No one else can know. None of these monks (*sadhus*), recluse (*sanyasis*), spiritual teachers (*acharyas*), etc., know anything. They cannot tell when mistakes occur and they do not do 'shoot-on-sight' *pratikraman*. At times, they may realize that a little mistake has occurred.

If the mistake is immense, then they will know that, 'This is wrong.' But then, if someone comes and tells them, '*Maharaj*, why did you do that to your disciple?' Then despite knowing that he has made a mistake, he will speak to the contrary, 'You have no idea what that disciple of mine is like. That is exactly how he needs to be treated!' That is what he will say. On the contrary, he will say just the opposite. Where there is a hill, he will dig a hole. Do people do this in order to protect their ego?

**Questioner:** Yes.

**Dadashri:** He will do anything to protect his ego. All these famous monks or ascetics (*sadhus, acharyas*), everyone will do that because the ego has to be protected, right? Otherwise, who will he sleep with? He may not have a wife, but he likes to sleep with his ego, does he not? Therefore, that will be the first thing he will protect.

*****

## [7]
## Business Transactions Become Pure

## Dadashri Has Made Mahatmas Free From All Liabilities

**Questioner:** When we hurt someone mentally, it is considered an unjust act. If we are running a business, the merchandise is the same, but to make a greater profit, we increase the price. By doing that, we hurt the customers. Is that harmful to us?                                                                    (147)

**Dadashri:** If you increase the price, they will feel hurt. There is no problem if you do not increase the price. In all this, the pain (*dukh*) will arise if you do it as a doer. But if You understand *vyavasthit*, then the responsibility is not Yours at all. Understand and accept that *vyavasthit* is the doer. In reality, the responsibility is not Yours. I have placed You at such a stage that it ceases to be Your responsibility. Therefore, I have placed you in a state whereby You do not bind karma (create new cause) despite carrying out your karma (discharging the effect of past karma).

Despite this, if your desire is, 'Even though I have been placed in a state of 'non-doership,' I am still able to 'do' everything,' and thus you become the doer, then there will be bondage of karma! This is only for those to whom I give Gnan; everyone else is in a state of 'doership' anyway. If one understands my Gnan and abides by the Five Agnas, then he will attain closure and settlement.

**Questioner:** I am not the 'doer' but by taking part in that karma, other people are hurt by my karma.

**Dadashri:** But 'who' is this 'I'? Is it 'Chandubhai' or the *Shuddhatma*?

**Questioner:** 'Chandubhai.'

**Dadashri:** You are *Shuddhatma*, are you not?

**Questioner:** Yes.

**Dadashri:** Then 'Chandubhai' is the doer. What does that have to do with You? 'Chandubhai' is separate and You are separate.

**Questioner:** 'Chandubhai' becomes a doer and he becomes *tanmayakar* (become the body and the mind). That is when I know that the other person is hurt.

**Dadashri:** Then You have to tell 'Chandubhai', 'Ask for forgiveness. Why did you hurt him?' But You do not have to ask for forgiveness. The one who does *atikraman* has to do *pratikraman*. If 'Chandubhai' does the *atikraman*, then You have to make him do *pratikraman*.

**Questioner:** If I have a *sari* business and my competitors raise their prices by five rupees, and I do the same, is that wrong business practice? Does that affect me or not?

**Dadashri:** But who is the 'doer' there?

**Questioner:** 'Chandubhai,' the *sari* seller.

**Dadashri:** 'You' are a *Shuddhatma* (the Self), and so You are not responsible for what 'Chandubhai' says or does.

And by any other means, if You feel someone has been hurt, then tell 'Chandubhai', 'You have done *atikraman*, so do *pratikraman*.' But I have not left behind any responsibility for You at all. I have removed Your responsibility and liability.

**Questioner:** If You set 'Chandubhai' free in that manner, then he is likely to do anything on a whim!

**Dadashri:** No. That is why I have given you *vyavasthit*. You cannot change anything at all in this current life. The life in which I am giving you *vyavasthit*, that *vyavasthit* cannot be changed at all. This is why I am setting You free. I can see all this in my Gnan, so that is why I do not need to reprimand you for any of your karma effects. I do not question you, 'Why did you do that?' This is not meant for another life, but for this life; 'You are not at all responsible!' I have gone to that extent!

## This is the Magnificence of Akram Vignan

This is a science. It gives instant freedom. Once you understand this science, you will find incontrovertible clarification (*tado*); you will continue to find clarification wherever you want. Where you cannot find a clarification, there is not a science. You should be able to find the solution if you are looking for one. There should never be any contradictions. That is called an established, incontrovertible principle that delivers the ultimate (*siddhant*). Hundreds of years can pass but it can never have any contradictions; that is defined as a *siddhant*. This *Akram Vignan* rises above all intellects (*buddhi*). Great minds of Bombay have come, but it did not submit to their *buddhi* because this Gnan transcends *buddhi*. Intellect is limited, whereas there is no limit to Gnan.

## Should One Charge Interest or Not?

**Questioner:** Can one charge interest on money he loans to others?

**Dadashri:** If 'Chandulal' wants to charge interest, let him do so, but tell him he will have to do *pratikraman* for it.

**Questioner:** Why should *pratikraman* be done? Is charging interest *atikraman*?

**Dadashri:** Because *atikraman* has been done. When do you consider charging interest an *atikraman*? When the interest is such that it hurts the other person, it is considered *atikraman*. (150)

**Questioner:** In the scriptures, it says not to charge interest, what kind of calculation is that?

**Dadashri:** They have said 'no' to charging interest because in doing so, a human being becomes like a butcher. That is why they have said no to interest. It is harmful, that is why. There is no problem if one can remain noble and charitable while doing it.

Ideal worldly interaction (*vyavahar*) is one that makes sure no one gets hurt by you. And if someone does get hurt, then do *pratikraman* immediately. We cannot interact with people in the way they interact with us. This 'give and take' of money in the world is a normal custom; that is not what we are referring to as '*vyavahar*.' You have to make sure that you do not hurt anyone, and do *pratikraman* if you do. That is call ideal *vyavahar* (worldly interaction).

## Do Pratikraman of the Debt Collector

If you have loaned someone money and he is not returning it, your *pratikraman* will affect him positively and he will be inspired to return your money. Generally, people create havoc and curse their creditors who demand payment from them. Would this not create a negative effect? On the contrary, people make matters worse. The entire world is effective and that is why you have to do *pratikraman*.

**Questioner:** If we do *pratikraman* for the one who has loaned us money, will he not continue to demand it back from us?

**Dadashri:** It is not a question of whether he will demand the return of it or not. The important thing here is to not allow attachment or abhorrence (*raag-dwesh*) to occur. The debt may continue.

## Pratikraman for Black Marketeering

**Questioner:** These days there are so many taxes that there is no choice but to 'steal.' Otherwise, we cannot balance everything out financially in big businesses. When everyone asks for bribes, we have to 'steal' for that money, do we not?

**Dadashri:** You steal, but do you or do you not repent doing so? It will become lighter if you repent.

**Questioner:** Then what should one do in such circumstances?

**Dadashri:** When you know you are doing wrong, then repent heartily and sincerely. One should feel a sense of 'burning' from within (*khed*); only then can he be free. Today, if you have bought goods on the black market, then you have to sell them on the black market. So then tell 'Chandubhai' to do *pratikraman*. Yes, before (Gnan) you did not do any *pratikraman*, and that is why you filled ponds and ponds of karma. Now when you do *pratikraman*, you will be able to clean it. Who is instrumental (*nimit*) in greed? That one has to do *pratikraman*. If you sell iron on the black market, tell 'Chandulal,' 'There is no problem in selling this way; it is under the control of *vyavasthit*, but now do *pratikraman* for it and make sure that you do not do it again.'

**Questioner:** There are many places where people are starving and, on the other hand, I am making money on the 'black'. How can that be settled with equanimity?

**Dadashri:** Whatever he is doing, it is correct. Whatever the *prakruti* (non-Self complex) does, it verily is an effect of (past life) causes. But we can know and understand that whatever is occurring is not right, so then we have to tell 'Chandulal,' 'Don't do this, and ask for forgiveness and say that you will not do it again.' He will ask for forgiveness but he will do the same thing again because it has become woven into his *prakruti*, has it not? But then 'You' have to keep on cleaning afterwards.

## Pratikraman for Stealing

**Dadashri:** Do you get irritated with people?

**Questioner:** I get irritated when I see mistakes in people at home.

**Dadashri:** 'Chandulal' gets irritated, does he not? (152)

**Questioner:** Yes, 'Chandulal,' of course!

**Dadashri:** And what about 'You'? Do 'You' not get irritated?

**Questioner:** He is the one that gets irritated and he is also the one that suffers.

**Dadashri:** The one who gets irritated is bound to suffer, so then how much of a loss did You incur?

**Questioner:** A huge loss.

**Dadashri:** Is that so? You do not get the *bhaav* (inner intent) of hurting others, do you? You do not have *bhaav* to deprive others of money and other things, do you?

**Questioner:** No, I do not.

**Dadashri:** Do you feel like stealing from others?

**Questioner:** Stealing from others, how?

**Dadashri:** When you weigh the goods you sell, you put down greater weight than what you give.

**Questioner:** That happens on and off.

**Dadashri:** Even now? Do you do *pratikraman* later on?

**Questioner:** Sometimes I do, sometimes I do not.

**Dadashri:** Should you not pay attention? Instead of one hundred kilos, you charge for one hundred and one kilos, is that not stealing one kilo?

**Questioner:** What occurs if I do *pratikraman* for that?

**Dadashri:** It means You are not of that opinion. Today, that is not Your opinion. Today *pratikraman* is occurring with a great force, but You are not in agreement with the stealing. Today do you have the opinion of stealing?

**Questioner:** Absolutely not.

**Dadashri:** Therefore, when you do *pratikraman*, it shows that that is not Your opinion today. It occurs due to forces of the past.

**Questioner:** Will the effect of this karma change in the next life?

**Dadashri:** No. It is considered gone in this life, is it not? People of the world (those without Gnan) have the opinion of stealing and further solidify it by saying that it (stealing) is necessary. Whereas what do you feel?

**Questioner:** 'This should not be so.'

**Dadashri:** Therefore, you are headed north while others are going south. Here You are seeing the past nature of 'Chandulal.' How horrible it was, based on his actions of today! What was his past nature like?

**Questioner:** Extremely horrible! What should I do when I continue to see mistakes even after doing *pratikraman*?

**Dadashri:** You have to keep doing *pratikraman* over and over again. Otherwise, do collective *pratikraman* for all the mistakes. If You continuously see mistakes for fifteen minutes, then do collective *pratikraman* for those mistakes.

People say, 'We will adulterate the goods and then ask God to forgive us.' Now there is no one out there to forgive you. You (the relative self) have to ask for forgiveness and 'You' (the real Self) have to forgive.

## Lots and Lots of Pratikraman for Unethical Conduct

If a person tells me, 'I don't care about religion but I want worldly happiness,' then I would tell him, 'Be honest and ethical.' I would not tell him to go to the temple. I would tell him that giving to others is a Godly quality. To not take away something that belongs to others is a human quality. To be ethical and honest in this manner is the highest religion. Dishonesty is the best foolishness. 'Just because I am not able to be honest, does that mean I have to jump in a lake? My Dada has taught me to do *pratikraman* whenever I am dishonest.' Your next life will become pure. Know and accept dishonesty as dishonesty and repent for it. The one that repents is honest for sure.

One gives for charity, one earns money through dishonest means; it is all there. A solution is shown for that. If one has made money unethically, then what should one tell 'Chandulal' at night? Tell him, 'Keep doing *pratikraman* over and over,' and ask him, 'Why did you make money unethically? So now do *pratikraman*.' Make him do 400 to 500 *pratikramans* a day. 'You' do not have to do them. Make 'Chandulal' do them. The one who does *atikraman*, make him do the *pratikraman*.

(154)

If you have a disagreement with your partner, then you will immediately realize that you have said more than you should have and so you should immediately do *pratikraman*. Our *pratikraman* should be like 'cash payment'; it cannot be left pending. Just as we have cash in the bank, the payment they make is also in the form of cash.

## How Can the Obstacles Be Stopped?

If a man goes to his boss for his permission and the boss refuses, he will begin to have negative thoughts about his boss; 'My boss is worthless. He is like this…he is like that!' Now he does not realize the consequences of his negative thinking. So if he turns his negative inner intent (*bhaav*) around by doing *pratikraman*; that is what 'we' call awareness.

I will explain to you how obstacles in life come about. If you call a person that works for you an idiot, it becomes an obstacle for your own common sense. Now tell me – this is how obstacles are created, and everyone in the worldly life has fallen into this trap and their human life goes to waste. You have no right to tell anyone they have no sense. If you do this, that person may retort by calling you an idiot and create an obstacle for himself. Similarly, if you call someone unworthy, you are creating an obstacle for your own self worth. Now tell me, how can this world be saved from such obstacles? If you do *pratikraman* immediately, then you will be able to wash away these obstacles before they become impossible to remove.

## Pratikraman for Scolding Your Workers

**Questioner:** In my work, in order to accomplish certain deadlines, I have insulted and mistreated many people.

**Dadashri:** You should do *pratikraman* for them all. When you mistreated them, you were only fulfilling your duty. You did not do it for yourself, therefore, your intention was not bad.

**Questioner:** In that sense, I was a very bad person; many would have been hurt by me.

**Dadashri:** For that, you have to do a collective *pratikraman* that, 'Owing to my strict nature, for whatever mistakes I have made, I am asking for forgiveness.' You do not have to do it individually.

**Questioner:** I have to do collective *pratikraman*?

**Dadashri:** Yes, you have to say that, 'Owing to my strict nature, and in the process of doing my official duty of the Government, whoever has been hurt by my conduct, I ask for forgiveness.' You should say that every day.

## You May Scold But...

**Questioner:** When a boss scolds an employee, the employee will feel hurt, will he not? If an employee does something wrong, does the boss not have a right to scold him?

**Dadashri:** Scolding carries a great responsibility. You should scold in a way that it does not 'burn' your hands and that the employee does not get hurt. Generally, people do not stop to consider this and they start scolding. Whatever is going to occur to the one being scolded will be, but the one doing the scolding carries a grave liability. He becomes trapped. (156)

**Questioner:** He has a responsibility as a boss, so he has to take steps to meet his obligations. So what can he do? He has no choice but to do it, right?

**Dadashri:** No, he can do that, but find a way so that it will not hurt the other person.

**Questioner:** What other way can he find? If the worker is not doing his job, he has to be told off, does he not?

**Dadashri:** But when you scold him, do you weigh your scolding or not? Can scolding be weighed before it is given? Can you scold him worth a quarter pound? No? So how can you do that?

**Questioner:** It is done without 'weighing,' but it is understood that certain steps will be taken if one does not do his work. All these rules are agreed upon.

**Dadashri:** There is no problem in taking steps within the rule on paper, but your scolding is done through your mouth. So when you do that, do you 'weigh' your scolding or do you do it without weighing it?

**Questioner:** But, Dada, if he does not do the work he has been assigned and the task remains unfinished, should I not scold him?

**Dadashri:** Yes, you have to scold him.

**Questioner:** Sometimes the scolding has to be done, or else I have to let him go; I have to dismiss him from work. Then I feel bad that his children will go hungry.

**Dadashri:** But it is like this. You have to warn him that, 'I will have to dismiss you, so make sure that you do your work carefully.'

**Questioner:** We warn him, we give it to him in writing that he is not doing his job, that his work is not satisfactory and that he will be fired. We give him all that in writing.

**Dadashri:** What after that?

**Questioner:** After that, we have to let him go if he does not improve. Then when we let him go, his poor children come here to my home crying. We feel hurt and they feel hurt.

**Dadashri:** If you want to stop feeling hurt, then you should let go. Finish the work yourself.

**Questioner:** If I do not take these steps, then I get scolded by upper management.

**Dadashri:** Take those steps, but do it with the awareness of, 'I am *Shuddhatma* and 'Chandubhai' is now taking all the steps.' There is no problem in that. The entire 'Chandubhai' is a discharge. Therefore, 'You' are not liable for 'Chandubhai' taking the steps. 'You' have to tell 'Chandubhai' that as far as possible, don't take those steps, try not to take any such steps. Despite that, if it occurs then that is correct.

**Questioner:** What you are saying is true. We took the steps by remaining separate but having taken those steps, that man feels hurt. Is there anything else besides *pratikraman* that I can do?

**Dadashri:** Just *pratikraman*. There is nothing else you can do.

## Repent for Being the Nimit

**Questioner:** At work, if a man working under me makes mistakes, I have to reprimand him. I have to do that because that is the position I hold at work.

**Dadashri:** No, but when that occurs, You should make 'Chandubhai' do *pratikraman*. After it occurs, repent for the fact that you had to do what you ought not to. Through your being a *nimit* (instrument), the other person is hurt and so you have to repent in the following manner: 'How come I had to do that? Why did I have to be the *nimit* (instrument)? I should not become a *nimit* like this.' But you are in a position that you have no choice but to do that. You have to do what you have to.                                               (158)

## The One at Fault Has To Be Penalized

**Questioner:** I am a P.A. (personal assistant) of D.S.P. (District Superintendent of Police). I have to fire a lot of people, for which I feel bad. Is there a *karmic* bondage in that?

**Dadashri:** Does it sometimes happen that you send a note to those higher up to fire a man, and yet he does not get fired? Does that occur or not?

**Questioner:** Yes, that occurs.

**Dadashri:** Hence this firing is a routine for you (part of your job). And your inner intent is that you do not want to fire him. Then there is no liability of bondage for you. It is like this: whatever the extent of one's mistake, his punishment will be fitting – that is the rule. That is not something one can stop. Hence you should maintain the inner intent that this man should not be hurt. However, you should continue to do your routine job.

## Responsibility Ends With a Change in the Inner Intent

If Gnan is given to a person that administers capital punishment, who has to hang someone, but his inner intent is not in accordance with what he does, then he is not liable for any bondage. And the one who has inner intent that the person deserves to be hung, then there is *karmic* bondage for him even if he does not do the hanging. Hence the inner intent (*bhaav*) is the main thing. If it is not one's inner intent but he sends someone to prison, he can still bind *punya* (merit karma). That is how the world is. One has to be prudent about his inner intent.

## Meet Your Obligation While Staying as the Self

**Questioner:** If we report someone's crime, do we or do we not incur a *karmic* liability?

**Dadashri:** No, nothing will occur.

**Questioner:** If a worker under me does not perform and I bring it to my manager's attention, will I bind karma?

**Dadashri:** No, you will not.

**Questioner:** And if I do not bring it to my manager's attention, then our management will be ruined.

**Dadashri:** That is why you have to bring it to your boss's attention. But do it politely. And you should explain everything to him. You cannot speak to the man arrogantly.

**Questioner:** How is that done in the worldly life?

**Dadashri:** You just have to maintain such a *bhaav* (inner intent) and then whatever occurs after that is correct. You should maintain your inner intent and it is necessary to explain things to him. No matter how many times you have to explain to him, it is correct. And it is also correct if you do not say anything to explain it to him.

**Questioner:** If someone is being obstinate and I do not have the authority to punish him, but I report him to my boss so that he will be punished, now the boss punishes him but I am the one who reported him to the boss. So I became the *nimit*, did I not?

**Dadashri:** No, that is not Your *bhaav*. 'Chandubhai' does that, does he not? So what should You do? You should continue 'seeing' what 'Chandubhai' does. The world will go on. Do not worry at all about that. Have the inner intent that no living being be hurt. Then go about your business, whatever it may be. Do not interfere in it. Do not have any doubts. 'You' should remain as the Self. However, you have to meet your obligations, do you not?

## Ultimately, Pratikraman as the Solution

Up until now, you had been trapped but you have learned the art of escape, have you not? What do people generally say? 'If the scorpion is going to bite, let it.' Hey, you! But do you have the energy to allow it to bite you? They will say, 'In the absence of such energy, the one who allows the scorpion to bite him is a gnani.' Hey, you! If you don't have the energy (*shakti*), put aside the scorpion. Whether it is a scorpion or some other poisonous critter, just put it aside. Yes, but do not harm it.

**Questioner:** Are there such gnanis that will let the scorpion bite them?

**Dadashri:** That is what people say, that if one is a gnani then he should let the scorpion bite him.

**Questioner:** That is an ego, is it not?

**Dadashri:** It is all an ego.

**Questioner:** So if the scorpion cannot be plucked off, should we pull it in a way that it is not killed?

**Dadashri:** Yes, but despite that, if it dies, then do *pratikraman*. That is the solution for it.

**Questioner:** The intention is not to kill it.

**Dadashri:** That is not the intention but what should you do if it does die? Should there not be a solution for that? And to begin with, one does not have the energy to let it bite and then he goes around creating a big deal. Instead, why not exercise caution; there are all kinds of solutions. We have the entire science of *Akram* with us.

**Questioner:** This is all very practical, Dada.

**Dadashri:** Yes, it is practical!

\*\*\*\*\*

**[8]**

# Freedom from the Chains of Life-After-Life Accounts

## How to Be Free From Past and Future Life Accounts?

**Questioner:** What should we do to be free from the relations of previous lives (past life accounts; *roonanubandha*) that are now in front of us?

**Dadashri:** If you are forced to live with someone you do not like, then on the outside you should continue your worldly relationship with that person – and from within you should do *pratikraman* in his name. The suffering for you in this life is the effect of your *atikraman* in your past life. What were the causes behind your suffering today? In your previous life you did *atikraman* against that person and, as a result, in this life you have to suffer the consequences. If you do *pratikraman* now in the presence of whichever God you worship, you will erase your mistakes. Repeated *pratikramans* will wipe off the many mistakes that have been caused in these sticky (*cheekani*) relationships.

(162)

If a man dislikes his wife, he will see many mistakes in her and will harp on her negative points. This constant faultfinding leads to scorn (*tiraskar*). The scorn leads to fear. He will experience fear in certain interactions with her and when he sees her, he feels a sense of suffocation and uneasiness. We all tend to be afraid of those or that which we dislike intensely. All this is a result of scorn. In order to break free from this feeling of contempt, one has to keep asking for forgiveness. Even though the other person may not be aware of it, you have to continue asking for forgiveness from within.

## Pratikraman of the Relatives and the Dear Ones

Life is nothing but a drama. Is it appropriate to assume that people playing the role of your wife and children in a play are yours to take home with you? In your daily interactions, it is acceptable to say, 'This is my son, Shatayu,' when you are introducing him to someone, but you should say it as you would in a drama. The reason you have to do *pratikraman* is because you have believed all these relatives to be real. You should do *pratikraman* because all along you have acted as if they really are your children and your wife. If you did not have this belief, then *pratikraman* would not be necessary. With this belief comes attachment and abhorrence and with *pratikraman* you are liberated. Dada shows you how to do *alochana*, *pratikraman* and *pratyakhyan* to liberate you.

**Questioner:** Sometimes I feel bad that he has taken Gnan, and I have Gnan, so then why should such problems continue?

**Dadashri:** It is all unfolding of karma (*udayakarma*) in which you have to do *pratikraman*. You are bound to be pushed around by the unfolding karma. You will not be able to avoid the pressure of the unfolding karma. It is not his wish that he hurts you, and yet he will be pushed by the unfolding karma. One has no choice but to suffer one's karma!

**Questioner:** I feel like I want to do good for him, but I end up spoiling everything and then I end up being the one who gets blamed.

**Dadashri:** But what problem do you have with that? Whatever occurs is correct. The one who wants to do good should not be afraid. And the one who wants to do bad will not achieve anything, no matter how cautious he is. You should make up your mind that you want to do good.

**Questioner:** I used to have a lot of fear before, but not anymore.

**Dadashri:** There is no need to talk like this. If he leaves here feeling bad, he will return the next day feeling good. You should do *pratikraman*.

These are all relative relationships; they are not real. If there is no *pratikraman* then the relationship will tear apart. What does *pratikraman* mean? It means to mend. If you keep mending even as the other person keeps tearing, the cloth will last longer. But what would occur if the other person is tearing and you do the same? (164)

**Questioner:** My husband lives separate from me; he has also taken the children with him. This has occurred because it should be my karma, right?

**Dadashri:** Of course, what else? Nothing new outside of karma effect occurs. This has happened because of failure to do *pratikraman*. Things turn around by doing *pratikraman*.

## Pay Off the Accounts with the Checkbook of Pratikraman

The whole world is a *karmic* debt (*hisaab*) and in order to settle that *karmic* debt, we have the tool of *alochana-pratikraman-pratyakhyan*, whereas the others in the world do not have any tool to settle this debt with. Are you settling some of your debt now? All you have to do is settle the accounts, do you not? What else do you have to do?

No one has the independent power to harass or hurt another person and no one has the independent power to tolerate. Each person is merely a 'puppet' going about his business on the stage of the worldly life. With *pratikraman*, these 'puppets' learn to live in peace and harmony. No matter how insane the other person may be, he will come to his senses through your *pratikraman*.

## Do Not Suffer Two Losses

Gnan means not to incur two losses. And even if you incur one loss, if you do *pratikraman*, you will only have one loss. One should not incur two losses (first loss is effect in this life, second loss is the loss/effect that has to be suffered in the next life through causes of attachment–abhorrence created in this life).

**Questioner:** But I will be forgiven if I do *pratikraman*, will I not?

**Dadashri:** One does *pratikraman* for one's mistake of hurting anyone through thought, speech and acts (*dosh*). There is no need to do *pratikraman* if you have not made a mistake. That account is settled. And if nothing has occurred, then there is no problem. As you continue to do *pratikraman*, everything will start becoming smoother in the interaction with that individual. The relationship with that person will be absolutely clear.

If you do not get along with a certain person, if you were to do *pratikraman* all day long for several days for that person, you will be able to get along with him and he will come seeking your company. All conflict is because of one's *atikraman* (mistakes).

And none of these wise (!) people do *pratikraman*. Do you think they do *pratikraman*? One will say, 'Why should I do *pratikraman* when it is his mistake?' If you ask the other person, he will say, 'He is at mistake; why should I do *pratikraman*?' Well so be it, let them 'bomb' each other like India and Pakistan!

## The World Echoes Your Own Projections

**Questioner:** If a person is harming me in some way, should I continue to simply 'know' and 'see' what is taking place by understanding that it is my unfolding karma, or should

I do *pratikraman* for it at night or should I meet with that person and do direct *pratikraman*?

**Dadashri:** In such an event, what would someone who does not have Self-realization (*agnani*) resort to? He would fight, curse, shout insults, etc; this is what an *agnani* will do.(166)

**Questioner:** Yes.

**Dadashri:** He may curse and swear, but that will not stop the harm. He has brought such an account (karma) with him and so that is bound to occur. But when he retaliates, he creates a new account (karma) for the coming life. He perpetuates the account. That is not what we do here in *Akram Vignan*; we simply have to 'see' and 'know' what is happening. The underlying foundation of this awareness is, 'The harm the other person is doing is the result of my own past karma.' Just like when the step-well (*vaav*) echoes back 'thief' if you first say 'thief' in it; can you then claim that the water well is harming you? No, it is the effect of your own action coming back to you. Because the echo comes back to you right away, you can know that it is the result of your own doing. Otherwise, one does not recognize it. Therefore, there is no need to do *pratikraman* in this case of the other person harming you at all. You have to do *pratikraman* if you are the one causing the harm. We do not have to do *pratikraman* if he is causing the harm. You just keep 'seeing.'

If someone does us good, that is the result of our own doing and if he causes us harm, that too is the result of our own doing. Worldly people (those who do not have Gnan) react differently in both situations. They have attachment towards the one doing good and abhorrence towards the one doing harm. Both are the results of attachment and abhorrence (in the previous life). No one does good or bad; it is simply the echo of your own doing. There is nothing else. How can anything come from outside this?

## Pratikraman Also for Those Who Insult You

**Questioner:** Sometimes I feel unappreciated and disheartened. I feel that no matter how much I do for that person, he keeps insulting me.

**Dadashri:** You should do his *pratikraman*. This is the way of the world. There are so many different kinds of people who will hold you back from your liberation.

**Questioner:** Why should I do that *pratikraman*?

**Dadashri:** *Pratikraman* should be done because in your unfolding karma effect, he has to bind a new karma. That is why I am doing *pratikraman* and I will never make such a mistake again where I become instrumental (*nimit*) in another person binding karma.

The world will not let anyone become liberated. The bondage of this life is such that only *pratikraman* can release you. For this reason, Lord Mahavir has given us *alochana*, *pratikraman* and *pratyakhyan* in just one word, '*pratikraman*.' There is no other way out. When is one able to do *pratikraman* correctly? It is when he attains the knowledge of the Self from the Gnani Purush. With this knowledge, awareness (*jagruti*) arises and this awareness will allow you to do *pratikraman* and be released from the burden of *karmic* liability.

You should do *pratikraman* so you become free of liabilities.

## This is How You Regain Trust

**Questioner:** How can I restore the trust I had for someone who has betrayed me?

**Dadashri:** You should repent for all the times you have harbored negative thoughts about him. Whatever bad thoughts you had for him after you lost trust in him, you have to repent for them. Only then will things be settled. That is why *pratikraman* is so necessary.

## Why Repeated Pratikramans?

**Questioner:** All these expert ladies have come together and they are being deceitful towards each other. Then they immediately do *pratikraman* by open confession to each other. The deceit occurs but they immediately recognize that they have done wrong. However, this gentleman says that we should not let such mistakes occur at all.

**Dadashri:** No, that will not work. (Dada addressing the man) Have you brought a new rule here? Here it is a 'no-law law.' The law here (with *Akram Vignan*) is that there are no laws whatsoever!                                              (168)

**Questioner:** If one does true *pratikraman*, then that mistake should not occur again.

**Dadashri:** No, you cannot say that. There are some mistakes that have fifty to a hundred layers.

**Questioner:** Is there not some kind of a strong *pratikraman* which can destroy all the layers in one go?

**Dadashri:** No, that cannot occur.

**Questioner:** Dada, why don't You 'do' *Akram pratikraman*?

**Dadashri:** You cannot eat with both your hands. You have to eat with just one hand. Everything is good in proportion. If you have had a fever that lasts a few days, will taking a whole bottle of medicine in one shot work?

**Questioner:** No, it will not work.

**Dadashri:** On the contrary, it will make it worse. Everything is good if it is in proportion. Then it will work.

## The Method for Removing Salt from Milk

Everything will be solved through the grace of 'Dada.' You know that the milk is going to go bad and that you will not be able to make tea with it in the morning, so then you will use your technique to remove the salt from the milk. Whatever salt you put in the milk (whatever *atikraman* that occurred unintentionally), you should look for ways to remove it. Our science is such that it will get rid of everything. Then later you have to apply cream and bandages in order to fix the wound (the damage). You have to stop the bleeding first. Then if it still goes in the wrong direction, then would you not know that it has not settled down?

**Questioner:** Yes, I would.

**Dadashri:** Then you have to let go of it. Thereafter, all you have to do is keep patching it up. Then he will not bleed. And someday he will invite you to his home. And you should go. Then if the bleeding occurs again, you will be able to address it (do *pratikraman* appropriately) in a timely fashion.

**Questioner:** This is what occurs. In trying to 'operate (improve)' on the other person, twenty-five other complications arise.

**Dadashri:** Yes, that has occurred. So you need to exercise caution when you are dealing with such situations. That is called discretion (*vivek*). Even when you give something real to someone, you should do so with discretion. You cannot give it after slapping him. Even if you are 'feeding' someone 'real food,' you cannot do it after you have 'slapped' him, because here, in this work, everyone has a vote. If this were to take place in a village, you could get away with it. Those people (simple and sincere people) do things 'heartily' and so whatever you do would work, whereas here (with city people) you will not get away with it. Nothing fits in the city.

**Questioner:** That is correct.

**Dadashri:** There, you can get away with everything because people approach everything heartily. So you have to take into consideration where things are likely to go wrong and proceed.

## You Should Know the Method

**Questioner:** I am talking about the problem that when one's belief is destroyed, his ego feels hurt.

**Dadashri:** If you do not know how to break his belief and if he feels hurt, then you should not even try.

I only break people's belief, such that, 'No, You are not 'Chandubhai.' 'Chandubhai' is not your real Self.' In this way, his greatest belief from countless past lives begins to fracture and collapse further. There should be 'exactness.' Otherwise, it will hurt him a lot.

I destroy the belief about God. Therefore, if I tell him that 'there is no God,' then it would be a disaster. Then I should be able to explain and make him understand from which perspective there is God and from which perspective there is not. That should all be there, and I should also explain to him for whom there is a God and for whom there is not. I would explain to him in every way without hurting him even in the slightest. None of 'our' 'weapons' hurt. You should especially know how to use your weapon so that the other person does not get hurt. Your weapon may hurt you but you should make sure it does not hurt him.

**Questioner:** That is true.    (170)

**Dadashri:** That is called an 'operation.' If there is some weakness within, then you should get rid of it. New forgiveness should be procured from the other person. The other person should not be hurt at all; life should be lived with this goal in mind.

We have not come here to inflict pain on anyone. Should anything occur, may we give happiness. That is our goal. No one should get hurt. Therefore, it is due to our lack of understanding that the other person gets hurt. Furthermore, the sense that 'the mistake is his' must not be there within you. When the term 'by his mistake' arises in the slightest, know that he is only the complex of mistakes. It is you who have taken up the task of improving him. So then improve him without hurting him.

## Where Dislike Occurs the Moment You Set Eyes on That Person

**Questioner:** Sometimes dislike occurs the moment we set eyes on a person, the moment we see his behavior.

**Dadashri:** That is because you have an old habit and that habit will not refrain from pushing you. You still get influenced by it. But you should apply our Gnan to it, should you not? The habit is from the past and so it will continue to arise, but if you keep applying our Gnan to it, it will gradually become still. The old habits have to come to an end, don't they?

**Questioner:** My question is, why does it occur only for certain people? Is it due to some contemptuous tendencies that arise or something like that?

**Dadashri:** It will only come if there is a *karmic* debt from the past, right? But today it is of no consequence. Today we are looking at his *Shuddhatma* (the Self). That day you had a dislike for his external packing – the relative self. The interactions were at the 'packing' level – the relative level. Today you have nothing to do with that packing. He has to face the consequences of his packing. Before, you used to believe that he is 'Chandulal' and that is why you had scorn towards him.

**Questioner:** That is based on an opinion, is it not?

**Dadashri:** The dislike is an effect of all the prior opinions you have formed. By doing *pratikraman* for it, you can change it around. You have to say that he is a very nice man, then he will appear nice to you.

**Questioner:** Should I do *pratikraman* or *pratyakhyan* for that opinion?

**Dadashri:** You have to do *pratikraman*. If you had a bad opinion about someone, you have to change that opinion now, to a good one, by saying that he is a good man. That which appeared as 'bad' to you, when you call it 'good' the change will take place. He appears 'bad' to you today because of your past opinions. Truly, no one is ever bad. Tell this to your mind. The opinions are formed by the mind. That stock is with the mind. Whatever opinions 'we' give, 'we' wash them all away.

**Questioner:** What is the tool to wash them off?

**Dadashri:** *Pratikraman*. If one has attained this *Akram* science, which means he has attained the separation between the Self and the non-Self, then he will not bind any karma. Yes, but if he does not do *pratikraman* for his opinions, then its effect will remain in the mind of the other person and, therefore, his negativity towards you will continue. No new karma will be bound if you maintain a clean inner intent, and if you do *pratikraman*, even the effect of past karma will go away. To divide by seven that which you had multiplied by seven is called *purusharth* (spiritual effort).

Therefore, the shadow of your mind falls upon his mind. See the effect of the shadow of my mind falling upon others. Even a fool becomes smart. If you have in your mind, 'I do not like Chandu,' then dislike for 'Chandu' starts the moment he comes, the snapshot (vibrations) of which reaches him. That snapshot (vibration) reaching him will tell him what is going on in your mind. The effects in your mind will entangle the other person. He will not know exactly what is going on but it will entangle him. Therefore, you should destroy such opinions. You should wash off all your opinions, and then you are free. Then your mind will change.

Many people's speech has been completely spoiled, and that too is because of opinions. Hence, the problem lies with the opinions one has stored. There is no problem with opinions that have not been stored.

**Questioner:** But are we not liable for the scorn we experience today?

**Dadashri:** No, you are not liable; when you 'see' and 'know' then you are not liable. When you become aware of the fact that, 'When this person comes along, I feel scorn towards him and when that person comes along, I feel happy within,' then it is more than enough.

**Questioner:** Should one do *pratikraman* then?

**Dadashri:** You should do *pratikraman* if the other person feels hurt. Thoughts will come and go; you do not have to do *pratikraman* for that. For that you have to have in your mind that 'this should not be so.' That is more than enough if you say that. You need *pratikraman* when someone gets hurt by your anger or negativity.

**Questioner:** So I do not have to do *pratikraman* for having such thoughts?

**Dadashri:** All that will continue to take place. It took no time when it went in and it takes no time to come out.

*****

## Pratikraman in Varying Situations

### The Reaction of Hurt in the Other Person

**Questioner:** How can I tell if the other person is hurt?

**Dadashri:** You will immediately see it on his face. The sparkle in his eyes will have disappeared and his face will appear gloomy. Of course, you will be able to tell whether or not he has been affected. It will be all too obvious.

**Questioner:** Yes. (174)

**Dadashri:** Man definitely has the ability to know what has occurred to the other person.

**Questioner:** But some people are so good at hiding their true feelings that you cannot tell by their expressions.

**Dadashri:** Even then you will know that you have said some hurtful things, and that it is bound to hurt him. For that you should do *pratikraman*. If you said something hurtful, will you not know if you hurt him?

**Questioner:** Yes, I would know it.

**Dadashri:** You are not doing *pratikraman* for him. You are actually doing it to change your previous opinions. What is *pratikraman*? It reverses your past opinions. By doing *pratikraman*, the effect your words may have had on him is erased. Just keep in mind that you want to settle your interaction with him with equanimity and, as a result, his mind will also improve. If, however, you are determined to only get it your own way, his mind will react in the same way with as much hostility.

**Questioner:** Does that mean that we have to continue doing *pratikraman* and will all our habits go away gradually?

**Dadashri:** Everything goes away with *pratikraman*.

**Questioner:** The stronger the inner intent (*bhaav*) is behind the *pratikraman*, that much...

**Dadashri:** No, it has to be done with true heart (heartily); whether you know the words or not, that is not important – it has to be done heartily.

## Bankruptcy of Prakruti

**Dadashri:** For some people, if someone interferes in their business, they only feel satisfied when they say things like, 'You have no sense, you do this and you do that,' etc. Then they sleep soundly at night.

**Questioner:** Why does that happen?

**Dadashri:** It is a kind of ego that takes pleasure in, 'I let him have it!' You used to do the same, did you not?

**Questioner:** But I did lots of *pratikraman* of all those people.

**Dadashri:** That is why everything is resolved.

**Questioner:** Why does he not do *pratikraman*?

**Dadashri:** *Pratikramans* have not commenced for him at all!

**Questioner:** Why not?                                                    (176)

**Dadashri:** He is still in the bankrupt state. His debt has not reduced at all, has it?

**Questioner:** What debt? What kind of debt?

**Dadashri:** He is bankrupt (spiritually). *Pratikraman* was possible for you. His bankruptcy is of the ultimate kind; his is first in line to file such a bankruptcy, and so he can afford not to do *pratikraman* (!)

**Questioner:** Then a time comes when, if a person can see his own mistakes – when he makes a mistake, he will not rest until he does *pratikraman*?

**Dadashri:** It will take a long time for him to reach that state; there is still a very heavy *karmic* debt. He has not refrained from hurting anyone that comes across him. He has hurt whomever he met.

**Questioner:** So does one become 'bankrupt' when he hurts people?

**Dadashri:** Then what else? Bankruptcy is inevitable.

**Questioner:** What kind of actions lead to bankruptcy?

**Dadashri:** Acts such as these; where one hurts others. He has not left anyone out, not even the parents. There has been an association with rogues and thugs in the past lives. So many lives have been spent doing just this, so he is only bound to be like that, and only continue to like that, is he not?

**Questioner:** Not anymore.

**Dadashri:** So many karmas were bound. Have you seen his height? The body is full of knots… the more the karma, the smaller the body; it is compressed.

**Questioner:** So what is the solution now? What else can he do if he cannot do *pratikraman*?

**Dadashri:** If he does it for a short time, he will slowly make headway.

**Questioner:** Except for *pratikraman*, there is no other solution at all.

**Dadashri:** It may not be effective now, but if he continues to do it, it will gradually become effective.

**Questioner:** It will finally occur one day.

**Dadashri:** The speed to bring it to a conclusion is also the same.

**Questioner:** If this has been the case from a very young age, does that mean that he had made those *bhaavs* (inner intents) in his past life?

**Dadashri:** He made those *bhaavs* in the past life. To show off, he made the *bhaav* of, 'I will bully everyone...I will put fear in them...I will do this...I will do that...'

**Questioner:** What a grave wrongdoing it is to intimidate and scare people, isn't it?

**Dadashri:** He will realize that when the time comes. You realize that when someone intimidates you and what liability they are incurring. But wouldn't you realize it if you are doing the same?

## Pratikraman for Abuse in Close Relationship

**Questioner:** I do not want to do anything to hurt him and yet I end up doing so. Give me such a blessing that not a single atom (*parmanu*; subatomic particle) of mine gets excited.

**Dadashri:** Today we will give you that blessing. You just have to keep on asking for forgiveness. You tormented him a lot in your past life.

**Questioner:** It occurs a lot. This is my big (*karmic*) tuber.

**Dadashri:** Yes. You have to do something, do you not? Keep asking for his forgiveness, any free time you get, ask for his forgiveness and do his *pratikraman*, in short. You have done *atikraman* against him, hence you have to do *pratikraman*;

have you abused him a lot?

**Questioner:** I am doing a lot of *pratikraman* in his name.

**Dadashri:** Yes, do it daily: 'I am asking for his forgiveness' and 'Dear Dada Bhagwan, grant me the energies not to hurt or abuse him.' Keep on asking for this and 'we' do grant that, if you ask for it.                                                    (178)

**Questioner:** I will ask for it every day.

**Dadashri:** Good.

**Questioner:** If I have hurt anyone in the slightest and I get a free moment and do his *pratikraman*, will that do?

**Dadashri:** You have to do that at the time. You have no desire to hurt anyone anymore, do you?

**Questioner:** Sometimes I do end up hurting others.

**Dadashri:** What do you do when that occurs?

**Questioner:** *Pratikraman.*

**Dadashri:** If you do *pratikraman*, your case will not go to the court of Nature. Settle it by saying, 'Sir, I ask for your forgiveness.'

## Karma Destroyed through Repenting

**Questioner:** What is it called when, after treating someone with contempt, you are repentant?

**Dadashri:** If you are repentant, you will break the habit of being contemptuous. However, if you feel no repentance and on the contrary feel good about yourself and your deeds, that is a sign of going downwards to lower life forms. You must have repentance after doing something wrong.

**Questioner:** What should I do to be free if I have hurt someone so badly that he is seriously depressed?

**Dadashri:** Do *pratikraman*. And if you happen to meet that person again, then you should tell him, 'I am stupid. This is a serious mistake of mine, please forgive me.' His wounds will heal when you say this.

## Solution for the Effects of Contempt of Past Life

**Questioner:** What should we do in order not to suffer the effects of contemptuous behavior towards others in the past?

**Dadashri:** For acts of contempt there is no other solution but repeated *pratikramans*. You have to keep on doing *pratikraman* until that person comes around. And if you occur to meet him face to face, then you should speak to him nicely and ask for forgiveness directly. Tell him, 'I have made a very big mistake. I am a complete fool. I have no sense.' When you discredit yourself, the other person feels better, his hurt will lessen and his wounds will heal.

'We' can 'see' the effect of contempt from previous lives; therefore, I am telling you not to be contemptuous towards anyone. Do not mistreat people. If you treat your workers with contempt, they will take revenge in their next life. They may even become a snake and bite you out of enmity. Contempt will never free you from its grip. Only *pratikraman* can save you.

## Can Such Serious Demerit Karma Be Washed Away?

**Questioner:** If we have made someone miserable beyond words and have hurt him so deeply that we cannot remove his pain, will we bind karma even if we do *pratikraman*?

**Dadashri:** You should continue to do *pratikraman* in his name. Do *pratikraman* with the same intensity as the intensity of pain you caused him.

**Questioner:** A mother-in-law says something to her

daughter-in-law and the daughter-in-law commits suicide as a result. Will the daughter-in-law attain peace if the mother-in-law does *pratikraman* afterwards? (180)

**Dadashri:** We have to continue doing *pratikraman*; we are not liable for anything else.

**Questioner:** What if the person is living?

**Dadashri:** After doing *pratikramans*, you have to tell him, 'I have no sense. Please forgive me.' You should say that and he will be pleased. The other person becomes happy when you show him that you have less sense. If you say this even after breaking his arm, he will not worry about his broken arm. He will be happy. This is because the breaking of his arm had already been decided (it was in his karma), but you became the *nimit*. And so it occurred through your *nimit* (you as the *nimit*). So that karma became settled. The account became settled through a credit and a debit.

## The Knower of the Kashays and Lack of Kashays

**Questioner:** Bad feelings, intents, arise but I immediately recognize that I made a mistake.

**Dadashri:** That is why I tell you that all wrong and bad *bhaav* is discharge. Do you understand that? And it does not charge or bind karma. For such intentions, one immediately knows, 'It should not be this way…it should not be so.' Otherwise, to become involved with the wrong intentions (*asaiyam*) is called 'giving in to *kashays*.' But are you not able to remain separate from the bad intents (bad *bhaav*)?

**Questioner:** Yes, yes.

**Dadashri:** Now, bad *bhaav* is effective (it is an effect and its causes were previously created). Even if you try to stop them, you will not succeed, but if 'Chandulal' were scolding someone, from within You would know it should not be that way. Why is that? Why does that occur? It is because even if 'Chandulal' is doing the action, You are the Knower. You will even know what is going on within; You are the Knower of both these. You are the Knower of both: the absence of kashay reaction (saiyam parinam) and presence of kashay reaction (asaiyam parinam). That is You (the Self). Do You experience that?

**Questioner:** Yes.

**Dadashri:** Yes. Just keep 'seeing' this circumstance, the drama unfolding.

## Unaffected Even While Giving the Sentence of Hanging

One judge asked me, 'Sir, now that you have given me Gnan, should I or should I not impose a death penalty?' So I asked him, 'If you don't impose the death penalty then what will you do?' He replied, 'But I will become liable for demerit karma (paap).' I asked him, 'Have I made you the 'pure Self' or 'Chandulal'?' He replied, 'You made me the pure Self.' So I told him, 'Then you are not responsible for whatever 'Chandulal' does. And if you want the responsibility, then you are 'Chandulal.' If you want to share the liability, then 'we' don't have any objection. But you should not become a partner in this.'

I then showed him a way to resolve this by saying, 'Oh, Dada Bhagwan, why do I have to deal with such an unpleasant task?' and do pratikraman for it. I taught him to do pratikraman in this manner and fulfill his work for the government according to the laws.

## Pratikraman Frees You from All Liabilities

**Questioner:** Would not belief and conviction that one becomes free of all liability after doing pratikraman give him a license towards indiscriminate and self-guided behavior (swachhand), regardless of the welfare of the other?

**Dadashri:** No, you don't have to look at it that way. It is true about *pratikraman*. The importance is given to *pratikraman*. You are free from your responsibility when you do *pratikraman*. Once you do *pratikraman*, you are home free regardless of the state of the other person.

**Questioner:** When I apologize directly to the one who works under me, you would not believe how it goes to his head.

(182)

**Dadashri:** There is not need to say anything to him. When you inadvertently say something hurtful, do you not repent it? When you repent your actions, you are doing *pratikraman*. Then you are not responsible at all. That is why 'we' have said that we will take on your responsibility, because if you do this much, then the responsibility is no longer yours. After that, 'we' know how to defend that. You are within the law of Nature if you do this much. And then 'we' know how to deal with whatever occurs. Do you understand that? We can handle it. But at least do what 'we' tell you to; then it is more than enough.

If a person becomes so depressed that he feels like committing suicide because of what you said to him; if you find yourself in that state, then you should continue doing *pratikraman* for half and hour to an hour that, 'Why did I have to get in such a situation? I became a *nimit* (instrument) for this?' Then the responsibility is no longer yours. So do not be afraid. If you abide by what 'we' say up to this point, then 'we' will take the responsibility of it with the 'higher courts.' 'We' will take care of any dispute that arises thereafter. But you have to go as far as this; it is more than enough. Deal with whatever is in your *karmic* debt (*hisaab*); do not dwell too deeply into it.

## The Protective Fence of the Gnani Purush

Very rarely do 'we' end up hurting a person even though 'we' do not wish to. Now generally, this does not occur, but it happens towards a rare person. In the last twenty years or so,

I may have hurt two or three people. That too, only if one is a *nimit*. Afterwards, 'we' do his *pratikraman* and build a 'fence' around him so that he does not fall down. However high 'we' have taken him, he should not fall from that level. 'We' give him all the support and build protection around him. We will never let him fall. Even if he is insolent towards 'us,' or swears at us, 'we' would never let him fall. That poor man does not have the understanding. He speaks in a state of complete ignorance. We do not have a problem with that. If 'we' let him fall, then it was wrong for 'us' to elevate him in the first place.

'We' are with principle. We would go as far as diverting the course of a road in order to protect a newly planted tree, but we would not harm the tree. We have principles we follow so we would never allow anyone to fall. He will remain in the very same place he was in. 'We' will turn all his thoughts around. Here, sitting at home, 'we' change all these thoughts around. 'We' put in extra effort in that area. 'We' have to make the special effort. 'We' do not have to make extra effort for you all; but for him 'we' have to put in a lot of effort. 'We' have to catch all his thoughts and 'we' have to exert effort such that his thoughts do not go past that point. Such cases are very rare; not all the cases are like this.

**Questioner:** What is all this about creating a fence around him? What does he need that for?

**Dadashri:** 'We' have to catch hold of his *antahkaran* (inner mechanism of mind-intellect-*chit*-ego). 'We' have to take his *vyavasthit* in 'our' hands.

**Questioner:** How is that?

**Dadashri:** 'We' take charge of all that, otherwise, he will fall, will he not?

## God Does Not Forgive or Punish

**Questioner:** Whatever *pratikraman* we do, we do

because we did *atikraman*. So if we have hurt the other person because of our *atikraman*, is that why we do *pratikraman*?

**Dadashri:** Yes, for that very reason. There is no other reason. Now 'You', the Self do not have anything to do with him anymore. Now You no longer have any worldly dealings with him. All You have to do is make sure that he (the relative self) does not hurt anyone. You have to tell whoever the culprit is to do *pratikraman*. The *Shuddhatma* has nothing to clean. All that has been done.

**Questioner:** But will we not do such *atikraman* again? (184)

**Dadashri:** It is not that it will not occur again... but *atikraman* is a discharge (effect of past causes), so it will be there. Only those that are there will come out. The question of whether '*atikraman* should occur or not' does not even arise. Whenever You feel that *atikraman* has occurred, then make him do *pratikraman*. If no *atikraman* is taking place, then you have to simply continue 'seeing' the discharge, nothing else.

**Questioner:** I have a relative who makes so many mistakes, so many blunders, that even God would not forgive him. And then he asks me to forgive him; he keeps on saying, 'I made a mistake. I made a mistake.' So what should a man do?

**Dadashri:** Man has to grant forgiveness, God cannot grant forgiveness. God has a weakness. (!) Humans are shrewd. Because eventually God (nature) will take complete revenge, then forgiveness will be granted. God is going to punish him for sure. You do not want to take revenge. You will forgive him; therefore say, 'May everything work out well for you.'

## The Problem of Recurrent Mistakes

**Questioner:** Someone does something that hurts me and then he asks for forgiveness; I forgive him. I forgive him internally even when he does not ask for forgiveness. What should I do if he keeps doing the same thing over and over again?

**Dadashri:** Try as best as you can to explain to him in a loving, gentle manner. There is no other solution (*upaya*) for it and you do not have any authority and power (*satta*) over the matter. You have no choice other than to forgive him. If you do not, then you will end up doing so after some more suffering. There is no other solution. You have to make him understand and make him see his mistakes. If he changes his internal intent and recognizes that it is wrong for him to hurt you, your work is done.

If he changes his inner intent to that he does not want to make the same mistake, and it still occurs, that is a different matter. If a man decides that he does not want to make any more mistakes and ends up making them, then it is a different matter. But if he says he wants to keep on doing it, then there is no end to it. That means he is on the wrong track. But after deciding he does not want to make mistakes again, if he repents his mistakes, then there is no problem if that mistake occurs again. Even when he decides he is not going to repeat it and he repents it, then if the mistake occurs again, he should repent again.

What is the reason for this? This is because there are many layers to a mistake, like those of an onion. A layer will go away by repenting, but another layer will surface. So the onion will look the same. It will all come to an end when all the layers go away; it will not occur until then. One has made countless mistakes for countless lives.

## Maintain Your Love Despite Their Mistakes

**Questioner:** What if he is not even aware that he is making mistakes, and continues doing so? What if he does not even repent?

**Dadashri:** Then it is meaningless, is it not? It is meaningless when he is not even aware. You should oppose his negative behavior. You should make him aware. The position opposing is to make him aware.

**Questioner:** If he keeps repeating the mistake every step of the way, then I lose the love and respect for him.

**Dadashri:** What else can you do? If possible, do not lose love for him, because what else can there be in this time cycle of *Kaliyug* (period of difficulties due to lack of unity in thoughts, speech and acts)? These relationships are relative (temporary); what else can there be? You, on the contrary, will ruin things for yourself if you take away that love. What do you do when you are not aware of things? So keep it like that.          (186)

What good does it do you to know that your son stole some money when you sent him to buy vegetables? You have to accept him the way he is. Can you throw him out? Can you find another son? You won't find another one, will you?

**Questioner:** What assurance do we have that another will not be worse?

**Dadashri:** Yes. Ask everything today and get your work done.

## Accept the Other Person

**Questioner:** So what should we do about a person like that? He keeps making mistakes but he does not repent making them. What can we do when he does not even realize this much?

**Dadashri:** You should not kill yourself. What else can you do? Killing the body means committing suicide. Then there is the killing of the mind. When the mind is killed, one loses interest in the worldly life. You should not do that; because of that, you would lose interest in your children and everyone else. You should not do that; you should tolerate it and accept it. The worldly life means to accept it any way you can and somehow pass your life. Right now it is the reign of *Kaliyug*, what can one do in it? There is no safe side anywhere. Consider this the safe side and go to sleep. Sincerity and morality are gone forever. Therefore, take this Gnan; then you can be happy forever. You will have no obstacles like these. Oh! It will be wonderful.

## Inadequate Pratikraman is Due to Lack of Awareness

**Questioner:** If someone does not come here anymore because I have upset him, and then egotistically I say, 'I have done my *pratikraman*. Now what can I do if he does not come anymore?' What about that?

**Dadashri:** But that is all wrong. In a way, it did occur because of you, through you as a *nimit*, did it not? So you should do whatever you can. Then, if nothing occurs, so be it. If it does not occur, that does not mean that you have to destroy yourself.

**Questioner:** That is right. But here we are talking about one's inner understanding, what a person should have in his understanding. I have done my *pratikraman*; I do not have any negative feelings towards him. If one shoots the bullet, then he can do this much (*pratikraman*) and it is easy for him to erase it all, but the one who got 'shot by his bullet' is still hurting, is he not?

**Dadashri:** But he must be hurting so much that he does not come here to do *darshan*. He should be feeling, 'I met this useless person, so that is why I can't go there.' That is why you have to settle the matter with equanimity, don't you?

**Questioner:** The other thing is that how can I know that the *pratikraman* I have done has been effective and that I no longer have any opinions about him? How can I know that my opinions about him have been wiped off one hundred percent?

**Dadashri:** But even so, he continues to hurt and harbor an opinion about you.

**Questioner:** Yes, it has not gone away for him and some of mine (opinions) still remain within; sometimes I feel how sensitive he is to take the little I said so seriously. Even this little thought occurs to me, so that much weakness remains in getting rid of the opinions.

**Dadashri:** Even if the opinion remains within, you would not know of it.

**Questioner:** That is true, I cannot know. This is very subtle. So is it better to do his *pratikraman* for our safe side?

**Dadashri:** Such cases are very rare in this world. Therefore, turn it around. Just look: he does not even come anymore.

## Even Though You Are the Non-doer, Others Get Hurt

When our *mahatmas* talk about doing something, they are saying it in discharge *bhaav* (effect of intent from his past life). It is like when an actor says, 'I am going to kill you,' in a play; when he says this, he is not liable for violence (*himsa*).

**Questioner:** I remain as the non-doer but whatever karma 'Chandubhai' does, some people around him get hurt and they believe that I verily am the one who has caused the hurt. So when I am affected by that, what should I do?

**Dadashri:** I have already told you that if 'Chandubhai' does *atikraman* against anyone, if he hurts anyone, then You have to tell 'Chandubhai', 'Do *pratikraman* in the name of that person.' If there is no *atikraman*, then nothing needs to be done.

*****

## [10]

## When Conflicts Arise

### Unsettled Accounts of Past Life

**Questioner:** Conflict occurs only with those with whom we have a *karmic* connection (*roonanubandha*), right? Conflicts will not occur with others, will they?                    (189)

**Dadashri:** Conflict occurs only with those with whom we have past life accounts (*hisaab*).

**Questioner:** I do not have conflict with anyone anymore. I am able to make sure of that everywhere else, but with her, although the conflict has reduced significantly, every six to eight months I am not able to do inner penance (*aantarik tapa*); I end up saying things to her.

**Dadashri:** There is no problem with that. You have no choice but to settle that. She has to discharge her karma, you have to discharge your karma, and that is precisely where the conflict occurs. So you cannot attribute the mistake to just one person; both are at mistake for sure. One may be forty percent at mistake, or sixty percent, or thirty percent, etc. Nevertheless, both the parties are at mistake to some degree.

**Questioner:** Then we are able to come to a closure (*samadhan*) on the issue within two to five minutes.

**Dadashri:** That will occur.

**Questioner:** Now if, at that time, I am able to do *parakram* (extraordinary spiritual effort) and settle that circumstance with equanimity, there would be bliss (*anand*). But as of now, I am not able to do that.

**Dadashri:** So here you have to gradually maintain awareness and do it. As you spend time with Me, those changes will come. If just one word of mine falls on your ears, then that very one word will continue to do the work.

## The Purusharth of Conversation with 'Chandubhai'

**Questioner:** We have a saying, 'One lives to be a hundred if he defies death once.' In this manner, how wonderful would it be if we can gain control over our *kashays* (inner anger-pride-deceit-greed) when they arise. How much would we have conquered!

**Dadashri:** It is like this: what do you mean by 'control'? It means You can do it whenever you wish. If You can find Your Gnan, Be in Your Gnan, then these wretched things (*kashays*) will remain in control for sure; Gnan verily will do all the work.

Hence the best solution for that is to talk to 'Chandubhai', 'How are you 'Chandubhai'? What is going on? Why did you hurt her?' Talking to him in this way is verily the solution. What should you say?

**Questioner:** That I should constantly talk with him and keep telling him, 'This is not a good thing you are doing. Why do you miss this key opportunity and enter into *kashay*?'

**Dadashri:** That is what You have to say. You can tell him everything. And if he still misses the opportunity, you can tell him again and make him do *pratikraman*. *Pratyakhyan* should also be done. Otherwise, he is likely to believe that whatever he did was right.

## Forced Expression of Unpleasant Karma

When you do *pratikraman*, your opinion is gone in regards

to 'this is right and that is wrong'; that opinion of yours is broken.

**Questioner:** *Mahatmas'* opinions have been destroyed, but when there is unfolding of karma, they get shaken up. What this gentleman said few minutes ago was unbecoming of him and beyond his nature.

**Dadashri:** Yes, you realized that it came out beyond his nature, did you not? There is so much force in karma unfolding that even if one does not wish to say anything, he will end up saying it. So then there is increased repentance about it and you question why it occurred. The answer is that there is a grave disease within, so let it come out. And for that, today find some quiet time and keep repenting for five hours or so.

What do you have to say (to 'Chandulal') in your repentance? 'Where do you have to go? What problems do you have? And if problems do occur, then 'whatever occurs is correct.' Just let go. If you hang on to it, then you will take a beating.'

Did the *prakruti* you thought you did not have, come out?

**Questioner:** He, file one, has never done this before. I do not even know why he did it!

**Dadashri:** That is the very thing You have to 'see.' It was time for the other person's disease to come out, and it was time for yours to come out, and that is why everything came together.

**Questioner:** This is the unfolding of his karma; he is not the one saying this.

**Dadashri:** Yes, it is not Him, the Self; it is the unfolding karma that is working very forcefully. You should ask him whether it was his intention (*bhaavna*) to speak this way and he will tell you, 'No, that was not my wish and yet it occurred.' And so it came out; it has been washed away purified. 'Clear cut!' It is like this, the mind has to be cleared.

## Collective Pratikraman

**Questioner:** Do we need to do *pratikraman* more often or would it suffice to do it just once for karma created during a prolonged period of conflict where there was an exchange of a lot of words?

**Dadashri:** Do as many individual *pratikraman* as you can, and then do collective *pratikraman*. If too many *pratikramans* accumulate, do them all at once: 'Dear Dada Bhagwan, I am doing a cumulative *pratikraman* for the mistakes I have committed.' Then it will be all over.

## Conflicts Are Natural But Grudge and Separation Are Not

**Questioner:** This discussion about the ego is very good. It is applicable to situations at home, in any organizations or institutions. Even when doing Dada's work, there is conflict between egos; it is applicable there, too. We need closure, satisfactory resolution (*samadhan*), there too, do we not? (192)

**Dadashri:** Yes, you will need a closure, will you not? The one with Gnan will attain closure, but what closure can the one without Gnan take? A separation will start to occur there; the mind will start to create a separation with him. Here the mind will not create any separation.

**Questioner:** But, Dada, one should not get into conflict, should one?

**Dadashri:** Getting into conflict is part of one's nature. That is what one has brought with him from his past life. It will not occur if he did not bring it with him. Therefore, You have to understand that he has a habit of doing so. That is what You have to 'Know.' Then it will not affect You, because the habit is of the one who has the habit, and You are the Self. Then it will get discharged. The problem arises when You get stuck there (ego). However, conflict will occur. It is not possible to not have conflict. You only have to make sure that you do not drift apart due to the conflict. Conflict will occur without fail; it will occur between husband and wife too, and yet they remain together, do they not? That will occur. That is why 'we' have not put any pressure on anyone that 'you cannot get into conflict.'

**Questioner:** A *taanto* (continued grudge linked to a conflict) should not remain in that.

**Dadashri:** A *taanto* does not remain at all. Anyone who says, 'A *taanto* remains for me,' that, too, is not a *taanto* (applicable to only those who have Self-realization).

**Questioner:** But should we not have a strong continued intent (*bhaav*) that conflict must not occur?

**Dadashri:** Yes, you should. That is all you have to do. You have to keep doing *pratikraman* for that and maintain such inner intent. If it occurs again, then do *pratikraman* again because one layer goes away for sure, then another layer will go. They are with layers, are they not? Whenever I had a conflict, I used to make a mental note of it and tell myself that, 'Today I learned something new. I got good knowledge today!' With conflict you will not slip; it will constantly keep You in awareness. It is a 'vitamin' for the *Atma* (the Self). That is why there is no problem with conflict. But do not separate after having a conflict. Therein lies your *purusharth* (spiritual effort). If you find that the mind is separating from the other person, then do *pratikraman* and settle everything down. How is it that 'we' get along with everyone here? Do 'we' or do 'we' not get along with you? That is how it is. Conflict arises due to words. I have to speak a lot and yet I do not have any conflict with you, do I?

One man tells me, 'I am very rebellious. It is only here in your *satsang* that people allow me to come. Otherwise, they do not allow me to attend anywhere else.' I told him, "We' have a place for everyone here, rebel or not.' Rebel if you want to, but attain your Self. By rebelling he may curse a few people; what else is he going to do? He may say, 'You have no sense. You are like this or you are like that.' He is going to curse the non-Self complex (*pudgal*), is he not? Can anyone curse the Self?

Conflict will occur. Do pots and pans not make noise when we bang them together? It is *pudgal's* (non-Self) nature to get into conflict, but that too only if there is such a *karmic* stock within. If there is no such stock within, there will be no conflict. 'We' too used to have conflict. But after attaining Gnan, there has not been any conflict because our Gnan is experiential (*anubhav*) Gnan. What is more, 'we' have come here having settled everything through this Gnan. 'We' have thought everything through, whereas you still have to settle everything. You are sitting in *moksha*, having constructed the third floor, but you still have to construct the first floor, do you not? Now you will have to construct (work) backwards, having sat on the third floor.

And for the traditional way to *moksha*, people just walked away after digging the foundation, leaving behind their cement bowls, spades, hoes and all their tools. If there is no inner peace, why would one bother? First 'we' give you peace and then you can take care of the rest below. That is why 'we' brought out this *Akram* science. Not *Kram* (step-by-step), but *Akram* (step-less)!                                    (194)

## Guarantee of Liberation in Three More Lives

If a person does not have any conflict, I guarantee that he will attain *moksha* (ultimate liberation) in only three lifetimes. If conflict occurs, you should do *pratikraman*. Conflict occurs between two *pudgals* (effective complexes of thoughts, speech and acts) and these conflicts can be dissolved with *pratikraman*.

If the other person is 'multiplying' then you should be 'dividing' so that there will be no remainder (no more balance on account). To blame the other person by thinking, 'He did this to me and he did that to me,' is a mistake in itself. If, while walking, you bump into a wall, why don't you blame the wall? Why do we refer to trees as inanimate (*jada*)? All those that hurt you are green trees. Do you fight with a cow if it treads on your foot? That is how it is in the case of all human beings. How does the Gnani Purush forgive everyone? He understands that 'these poor people do not understand; they are like the trees.' And those who understand do not have to be told anything; they will do *pratikraman* immediately.

Non-violence (*Ahimsa*) is not such that it can be understood completely. It is very difficult to understand completely. Instead, it is better to catch on to a principle of, 'I will never get into any conflict.' What occurs then? Then the energies (*shakti*) within will remain intact and continue to increase day by day. Then you do not incur the loss of energy through conflict.

However, if conflicts do occur, then if you do *pratikraman* afterwards, it will be erased. You have to understand this much – 'Here in these situations, conflicts occur and so I have to do *pratikraman*, otherwise, there is a tremendous liability.' For sure, you will go to *moksha* because of this Gnan, but conflict will create problems for you and delay Your *moksha*.

There is no problem if you have negative thoughts towards this wall because it is a one-sided loss, whereas even a single negative thought towards a living being carries a grave liability. That is a two-sided loss. But if you do *pratikraman* after that, then all the losses will be washed away. Therefore, do *pratikraman* wherever conflict arises so that conflict comes to an end.

## Mistakes: Gross, Subtle, Subtler and Subtlest

**Questioner:** You gave us an example of gross (*sthool*)

conflict about bumping into a pole, thereafter of subtle (*sookshma*), subtler (*sookshmatar*) and the subtlest (*sookshmatam*) forms of conflict. What is a subtle (*sookshma*) conflict?

**Dadashri:** The conflict that you have with your father is subtle conflict.

**Questioner:** Like what?

**Dadashri:** Do you hit each other?

**Questioner:** No.

**Dadashri:** That is subtle conflict.

**Questioner:** Does subtle mean through the mind? Do verbal conflicts also come under subtle?

**Dadashri:** No, verbal conflict falls under gross conflict. Those the other person is not aware of, those the other person cannot see, are subtle conflict.

**Questioner:** How can we avoid such subtle conflict?

**Dadashri:** First, you should tackle the gross conflict, then the subtle, then the subtler and finally the subtlest conflict.

**Questioner:** What is an example of a subtler (*sookshmatar*) conflict?

**Dadashri:** *Sookshmatar* conflict applies only to those who are Self-realized. If you slap somebody and this other person here remains in his awareness as being the pure Soul, and is aware that the slap is being given by *vyavasthit*, he sees all that. But despite this, if he happens to see even a slightest mistake in you, then that would be considered subtler conflict.          (196)

**Questioner:** Please explain that to me again. I did not understand it completely.

**Dadashri:** For you who have taken this Gnan of the Self, to see mistakes in others is an example of subtler conflict.

**Questioner:** So when I look at mistakes of someone else, it is subtler conflict?

**Dadashri:** No, not like that! You have arrived at a decision that people are flawless (*nirdosh*); they are without mistakes but, despite this, if you happen to see mistakes in someone, that is subtler conflict. You should be able to see those mistakes of yours (You should be able to see that you (file one) are seeing mistakes) because he is a pure Self and the mistake is separate.

**Questioner:** Who is the one that sees the mistake?

**Dadashri:** The seer of the mistake ('Chandulal,' the intellect).

**Questioner:** But that is not the mind seeing the mistake. That phenomenon is not in the mental layer.

**Dadashri:** Whatever layer it is in; it sees the mistake.

**Questioner:** So is all that the mental conflict that we have talked about?

**Dadashri:** All that belongs to subtle (*sookshma*) conflict.

**Questioner:** So what is the difference between the two?

**Dadashri:** This all goes beyond the realm of the mind.

**Questioner:** The mental conflict and those mistakes...

**Dadashri:** They are not mental; they are not of the mind.

**Questioner:** Does that mean when there is a subtler conflict occurring, a subtle conflict is also present?

**Dadashri:** You do not have to be concerned about that. Subtle is different. The subtler is different. The subtler is the ultimate stage.

**Questioner:** It was mentioned once during *satsang* that when we become engrossed with the relative self ('Chandulal'), it is considered as the subtlest (*sookshmatam*) mistake.

**Dadashri:** Yes, that is the subtlest mistake. Such a mistake should be avoided. It occurs inadvertently, right? But do you eventually come to realize that mistake?

**Questioner:** Despite the prayer of, 'Besides the experience of the Self, I do not want any temporary, worldly thing,' 'Chandubhai' becomes engrossed on and off. Is that not a subtler mistake?

**Dadashri:** No, that is called *sookshmatam* - subtlest.

**Questioner:** There is one desire (*bhaavna*) that I have and that is, except for the element of pure Soul (*Shuddhatma*) and Dada's five Agnas, I have no desire for anything else.

**Dadashri:** This is the main thing for everyone. So what everyone has to do is gradually become aware of that.

**Questioner:** I can see that I violated the third Agna, I violated the second Agna, and so on; I can literally see all that.

**Dadashri:** Yes, you will actually 'see' that; that is correct.

**Questioner:** Is that violation considered as conflict?

**Dadashri:** You will have to check that file again.

**Questioner:** You talked about the subtler conflict being one where in our opinion the other person is *nirdosh* (flawless), but even then, we see them at fault (*doshit*). Is that why we get into conflict with him?

**Dadashri:** When you see him as *doshit*, that mistake applies to you, does it not?

**Questioner:** I get engrossed (*tanmayakar*) for a fraction of the time and then I come back.

**Dadashri:** You come back.

**Questioner:** Is there any other remedy available or is *pratikraman* the only cure for this?

**Dadashri:** There is no other weapon.

**Questioner:** Yes.

**Dadashri:** These Nine Kalams of ours are *pratikraman* too. There is no other weapon. There is no other instrument in this world except *pratikraman*. It is the greatest weapon because the world has come into existence due to *atikraman*.

**Questioner:** But, Dada, *pratikramans* occur very fast, at the same moment.

**Dadashri:** Yes, it occurs at the same moment.

**Questioner:** That is amazing, Dada!

**Dadashri:** That is amazing for sure.

**Questioner:** Dada's grace is tremendous!

**Dadashri:** Yes, it is tremendous. Only that, it is scientific!

## What? Is That Not an Ego?

**Questioner:** It is a wonderful thing. Each and every sentence – 'Whatever happens is justice,' 'Fault is of the sufferer' – are all divine sentences. And the *pratikramans* we do in the presence of Dada, their vibrations do reach the other person.

**Dadashri:** Yes, that is true. Vibrations do reach immediately and give fruit (results). We become assured that, 'It appears there has been an effect.' All the vibrations will reach them.

**Questioner:** But, Dada, when we have to do *pratikraman*, is that not our ego?

**Dadashri:** No. 'You' the pure Self, do not have to do *pratikraman*. It is 'Chandulal' who is at mistake and, therefore, he is the one who should do *pratikraman*. The pure Self is simply the Knower and has never erred. And that is why the Self does not have to do it. This worldly life has come into existence only because of *atikraman*. Who does *atikraman*? The ego and the intellect get together and do *atikraman*.

*****

## [11]
## Purusharth Against Bad Qualities of Prakruti

### Attachment to Abhorrence and Abhorrence to Attachment

**Questioner:** If someone bears a grudge with me without any reason, or has abhorrence (*dwesh*) towards me, or is being deceitful with me without any reason, does that mean that in some previous life I had attachment (*raag*) for him?

**Dadashri:** Yes. You have created a *karmic* account (*hisaab*) and this is its reaction. (200)

**Questioner:** So what kind of an account is that? Is it one of attachment (*raag*) or is it one of abhorrence (*dwesh*)?

**Dadashri:** Deceit (*kapat*) falls under attachment (*raag*); and ego and anger fall under abhorrence (*dwesh*). Deceit and greed (*lobh*) go into attachment (*raag*). Desire for greed (*lobh*) goes into attachment. Do you understand what I am saying?

**Questioner:** Yes, I do.

**Dadashri:** Which kind of attachment is this? It is greed (*lobh*) and deceit (*kapat*). And pride (*maan*) and anger (*krodh*) go into abhorrence (*dwesh*). Therefore, if someone is being deceitful, that is attachment (*raag*). Anyone one has attachment for will resort to deceit.

Not a single lifetime has gone by without *raag* (attachment). Until one attains Self-realization, one continues to do attachment and abhorrence (*raag* and *dwesh*); there is no third thing at all.

**Questioner:** Dada, abhorrence results from attachment, does it not?

**Dadashri:** Yes, it is the result of attachment. When you become overly attached to someone, you will experience abhorrence towards him. Anything that is done in excess will lead to an initial dislike and then abhorrence. When anything exceeds its limit, one starts disliking it. Excess dislike is abhorrence. Do you understand?

**Questioner:** Yes, I understand.

**Dadashri:** You should understand that whatever you encounter are reactions meant for you, or effects of your past causes. When you greet someone with respect and at that time you feel that he has a sour face, then you should understand that it is a reaction to your own past causes (*raag*). So then what should you do? You should do *pratikraman*. There is no other solution in this world. How do people who do not have Self-realization react? They will respond by sulking in return, perpetuating the cycle of attachment-abhorrence. Now that we have become the pure Self, someway or other we need to accept our own mistake and bring an end to it. Even as Gnani Purush 'we' accept all the mistakes and be done with that case.

## Pride for the Welfare of Others

**Questioner:** But, Dada, if one has too many *parmanus* (subatomic particles) of pride (*maan*), is that not harmful?

**Dadashri:** Which kind?

**Questioner:** If we have a pride like, 'Let me do good for this man. Let me do something useful for him.'

**Dadashri:** No, there is nothing that is harmful in that. The harm is for the one who is contemptuous and has scorn towards others.

What do you consider as harmful pride? It is pride which

is in excess; pride which is contemptuous towards others. But, otherwise, there is no problem with the approach of, 'I want to do something good for others.'

**Questioner:** When I analyze it, I feel I have a deep-seated desire for respect and a good image of myself. It is not to take advantage of others but to do good for others. (202)

**Dadashri:** This pride that you are talking about is what has brought you here (to the Gnani Purush). If you did not have such pride within you, you would be somewhere else right now.

**Questioner:** Because, where a temple of Simandhar Swami is concerned, I feel that I want to compete for it.

**Dadashri:** You will not find that kind of talk in this world anywhere. That is the greatest thing.

What is considered pride? If I tell you something that is likely to hurt someone and the same is then in our conduct, that is considered pride.

But this temple part will make people very happy. For the one who gets up in the morning and has *bhaav* (love) towards the Lord (Simandhar Swami), Dada has complete *bhaav* for him. Therefore, this is a very good thing. This kind of thing does not occur. Then whether the temple gets built or not, it is of no consequence. But it is a very good thing to have such an elevated *bhaav*. Do you understand everything?

**Questioner:** Yes. That *bhaavna* (desire, intent in discharge) is constantly there that, 'I want to do something...I want to do something.' And no matter how much I do, I feel that I have not accomplished anything.

**Dadashri:** Yes, You will feel that way. It is as if your hunger is never satisfied! That is a great thing. Only one who has brought forth great merit karma (very *punyashadi*), this person attains such a desire!

## Subatomic Particles of Jealousy

**Questioner:** What can I do to stop jealousy?

**Dadashri:** There are two ways to deal with that. One is to repent when he experiences such feelings. The other is to realize that jealousy is the result, or effect, from your previous life, and it just occurs. You, the Self, are not being jealous. Feelings of jealousy are *parmanus* (subatomic particles) brought over from the past life. If You do not accept them, if You do not become engrossed (*tanmayakar*) with them, they will go away. It is best if you do *pratikraman* when jealousy arises.

## Pratikraman Frees You from the Poison of Suspicion

**Questioner:** I do not want to be suspicious about anyone, but despite this, if it occurs, how can I become free from it?

**Dadashri:** If that occurs, you have to invoke the pure Self of that person and ask for forgiveness. You should do *pratikraman* for that. These doubts and suspicions arise because of mistakes you made in your previous lifetime.

**Questioner:** Whatever we have to suffer due to unfolding of our karma (*udayakarma*), does it decrease if we do *pratikraman*?

**Dadashri:** It will decrease. And 'You' do not have to suffer it. 'You' have to tell 'Chandubhai' to do *pratikraman*, then it will go down. However much *pratikraman* you do, it will decrease by that much. Then there will not be anymore problems.

It is due to unfolding of karma that everyone has come together. Neither the *gnani* nor an *agnani* (non-Self-realized) person can change it. So why should one incur two losses?

**Questioner:** You said it right, Dada; that this world has been this way from the beginning.

**Dadashri:** There is nothing more to this. It appears

otherwise because it has been covered up. And then suspicion is the venom that kills. So if suspicion arises, do not let it and do *pratikraman*. When you reach a state where you will no longer have to do any *pratikraman*, that will be the state where no one will ever have any doubts or suspicions about you. You will attain a suspicion-free (*nihshank*) state.

The moment you have the slightest bad thought about anyone, wash it away immediately with *pratikraman*. If these thoughts are allowed to linger even a short while, they will reach the other person and proliferate. They can grow in a matter of hours and continue for days. You should not allow your vibrations to flow in this way.

**Questioner:** What should we do for that?          (204)

**Dadashri:** You should immediately erase them with *pratikraman*. If you cannot do *pratikraman*, then recall Dada, or whichever God you believe in, and say it in short, 'This thought that I am having is not right and it is not mine.'

If you are walking alone at night and fear arises that you might get mugged, or if in a forest a thought arises about encountering a tiger, you should do *pratikraman* for this. The moment suspicion (*shanka*) arises it will ruin everything. Do not let suspicion arise. Do not allow yourself to become suspicious of any living being. Suspicion brings nothing but suffering.

The moment you have suspicion you should make 'Chandulal' do *pratikraman*. You are the Lord of this universe so how can suspicion come to You? Suspicion may arise because we are human beings, but you should do instant *pratikraman* for this mistake.

Do *pratikraman* for anyone about whom a suspicion arises, otherwise this suspicion will eat you up alive.

**Questioner:** Does suspicion fall under *karmic* knots or

tubers (*granthi*)? Does it come under a negative trait of *prakruti*?

**Dadashri:** It goes into neither. It is much more than both. It is very destructive or hurtful to the relative self (*atmaghat*). It is a kind of an ego. To have suspicion means to have serious mistrust, starting from mild, doubt-related uneasiness, to suspicion; these are all attributes that are harmful to the self (*atmaghati*). There is not a single benefit in it. It continues to cause tremendous harm. That is why 'we' have told you not to have any suspicion. So do not have any suspicion, and if it arises, and even if it may seem so, and even if it is well founded, you will not gain anything from it.

It is a kind of an ego. Do you understand what I am saying?

**Questioner:** Is *pratikraman* the solution for suspicion? When suspicion arises, should I do *pratikraman* immediately?

**Dadashri:** Yes, you should do *pratikraman* for whoever suspicion arises.

**Questioner:** So that is the only solution for it, is it not?

**Dadashri:** Yes, that is the only solution; otherwise suspicion will eat you up alive.

**Questioner:** Whenever any suspicion arises, it is better to clear it off so that it can be resolved.

**Dadashri:** If you have suspicion about anything, you should look into it and then come home and go to sleep. And ultimately all this inquiry will have to be stopped.

## Root Cause of Fear

**Questioner:** Fear (*bhaya*), self preservation instinct (*bhaya sangnya*), what are these? How do they arise? How do they charge and discharge?

**Dadashri:** One experiences fear to whatever degree he

believes himself to be temporary.

**Questioner:** I did not understand what you mean about one believing himself to be temporary.

**Dadashri:** 'I am Chandubhai' is a temporary state and, when one believes he is 'Chandubhai,' then he will be subject to fear. 'I am *Shuddhatma* – the pure Soul, nothing at all can happen to Me, I am eternal'; with this awareness, what is there to fear?

**Questioner:** Then there is no fear.                              (206)

**Dadashri:** The experience of 'temporary' applies to non-Indians to a greater degree as compared to Indians. This is because of the belief of doership. 'I am the doer and these actions are of my own doing.' So here (in Indians) there is less fear. Non-Indians fly away like startled birds!

## Suspicion and Fear

**Questioner:** Is there a connection between fear and suspicion?

**Dadashri:** Suspicion gives rise to fear and fear creates suspicion. They are both like cause and effect. One should not have any suspicions at all. Do not be suspicious about anything. Do not be suspicious about whether your son or your daughter is going off on the wrong track. Make an effort to improve this.

**Questioner:** But suspicion occurs from moment to moment.

**Dadashri:** Suspicion is the same as killing your own self. Do not ever have suspicions.

**Questioner:** But why does suspicion arise? The question is not about 'doing' it; it simply occurs every moment for me.

**Dadashri:** Because it occurs you have to say, 'This suspicion is not mine, this is not mine'; the moment it occurs you have to say this.

The Self is beyond suspicion and our *mahatmas* are in that state. This world is rotting away because of suspicion. Suspicion is demise of the world. One is going to die someday but why does he not have suspicion over that? Is he not going to die someday?

**Questioner:** One definitely knows that he is going to die.

**Dadashri:** But why does he not have suspicion over that? If he starts to have suspicion about his death, he immediately removes it. The moment he has suspicion, he gets rid of it. He feels very afraid. That is why it has to be removed. You have to pluck it out and throw it away. The moment it sprouts, you have to uproot it and throw it away.

## Pratikraman Destroys Karma by Seventy-five Percent

When one repents for any of his actions (karma), the effect - consequence of that is destroyed by seventy-five percent. Then when that karma unfolds, the effect will be very weak, like that of a cindered rope. The shape of the rope will remain intact but the moment you touch it, it will disintegrate. No action goes unrewarded. By doing *pratikraman*, that rope will be burned but its shape and design will remain intact. So what do you have to do in your next life? If you just touch it the cinders will blow away. In your next life, all you will have to do is shake off the ashes.

## In the Path of Akram Vignan, All Actions are Lifeless

No action, once carried out will go away. But after attaining this Gnan, after separating the Self, all actions become near dead; dying (they will not create a new charge). They are all *nischetan kriya* – non-living actions; actions that do not have the support of the Self. Hence You are no longer responsible for them.

This is the science of *Akram*. There is no science despite living a complete worldly life, being completely immersed in illusory attractions (*moha*), one attains *moksha*. Such is this science, *Akram Vignan*.

What does attaining *moksha* mean? In the *Kramic* path, the traditional step-by-step path, one climbs higher as he reduces his *moha*. And on that path even the gnanis will have worries. They are happy from within but on the outside they have worries. Here, 'we' do not have any external or internal worries at all. In this world it is not possible to have a worry-free life anywhere. This is only due to the glory of this *Akram Vignan*; thousands of people enjoy that state!

## Pratikramans Begin to Decrease

**Dadashri:** Do you have to do *pratikraman* now?

**Questioner:** We have to do *pratikraman* for sure, do we not?

**Dadashri:** Have they decreased now? There are not as many as before, are there?

**Questioner:** There are fewer now, but I do have to do them.

**Dadashri:** *Alochana, pratikraman* and *pratyakhyan* is the only tool to attain *moksha*; there is no other. Karma will continue to occur even if you do not want it to.

**Questioner:** Karmas come and get stuck in our throat!

**Dadashri:** Yes, they will. That is the rule of karma. You will know that *atikraman* has occurred. If you are not able to settle with equanimity, *atikraman* will occur. What do you do when you do *atikraman*?

**Questioner:** I do *pratikraman*.

**Dadashri:** Good, in that sense you are very shrewd. You are as shrewd on the inside as you are on the outside. You are so shrewd that you have made sure that you do not bind any karma. That is very good. It is good to be shrewd in this matter. In the worldly life, in the absence of Self-realization, shrewd people are hurting themselves, whereas here if a person is shrewd then it is good.

## Destroy Effect with Effect

**Questioner:** The *pratikraman* that we do, we do only because of our karma, right? *Pratikraman* that we do is not in our control. Is doing *pratikraman* not an effect of our past karma?

**Dadashri:** *Pratikraman* is verily an effect. But we have to destroy effect with effect and clear it, wash it off immediately. You should say, 'Chandulal, wash it off. Why did you do that?' There is no problem with karmas that do not hurt anyone. You can eat everything and enjoy yourself. Even eat *karela* (bitter gourds)! Put some jaggery (raw, unrefined sugar) in it, but eat them, because the body also needs bitter juices; so eat *karela* even if you have to put jaggery in them.

## Pratikraman is Purusharth

No one should be hurt in the slightest. There is no end to the hurt one inflicts on others unknowingly. Work with others without hurting them. If you have to delegate work to them, do so without hurting them. That is called *kraman* (neutral actions; actions that do not hurt anyone). But when does anything become *atikraman*? Say you are in a hurry and one of your workers has gone for his tea break, so when he returns you start shouting at him, 'Where did you go? You are useless, what took you so long,' etc; that is *atikraman*. That *atikraman* occurs naturally, even when you have no desire for it to occur.

It is natural for *atikraman* to occur, but to do *pratikraman* is spiritual effort (*purusharth*). It erases your wrongdoings through thoughts, speech and acts. *Pratikraman* removes any stain caused by *atikraman*.

*****

# [12]
## Defeating Addictions with Gnan

### Settle Them with Equanimity

If the soup is too spicy, you start complaining, 'You ruined the soup,' etc., then You realize that you made a mistake in behaving the way you did. You did not deal with that 'file' with equanimity. What does settling the file with equanimity mean? Take less of that soup and do whatever you have to in order to bring about a resolution. Otherwise, you will have to do *pratikraman*. Are you able to see your mistakes right away?

(210)

**Questioner:** I can see them right away.

### Even Physical Diseases Go Away with Pratikraman

**Dadashri:** Our Gnan tells us to do *pratikraman*. Even eating too little is *atikraman*, because it will make you hungry at an odd time. Eating too much is also *atikraman*. Therefore, remain within normality.

Whatever physical diseases one has, all of them have been caused by *atikraman*. They will all go away with *pratikraman*.

**Questioner:** How would one do *pratikraman*?

**Dadashri:** You have to find the nature of the disease. You have to find with which *nimit* the disease arises. You have to search deep into your relationships with each of those. Whichever relationships come to mind, those very relationships were excessive and those are the files. There is no problem with those you do not remember.

There is also a problem if someone serves you too much food and forces it on you. What do you do if someone serves you too much?

**Questioner:** We have to tell them no, otherwise we will suffer after eating all that.

**Dadashri:** You have to put your hands together and plead with them; do whatever it takes. This is how everything is in the world. It is difficult to achieve normality.

## Pratikraman for Breaking the Discipline

You should make a list of all that did not happen according to your goal and then do *pratikraman* for that just before bedtime. That is more than enough.

**Questioner:** Dada, even now, sometimes I end up eating a little more than I should. But I do *pratikraman* for it.

**Dadashri:** There is no problem with that.

**Questioner:** This is how I do *pratikraman*: 'Dear Dada Bhagwan! I ask for forgiveness for breaking the discipline I have taken with You, Dada.' Is it acceptable to do it this way?

**Dadashri:** So You are hanging on to the discipline (*niyam*) and the body (*pudgal*) is breaking the discipline. It is sure that because You are doing the *satsang*, You are hanging on to the vow. You want to abide by the Agna.

**Questioner:** Yes.

## Drank Tea after Doing Pratyakhyan

**Questioner:** I am addicted to the bad habit of smoking. What should I do?

**Dadashri:** Maintain from within that smoking is wrong; it is harmful. Furthermore, when someone points out your mistake, never defend or protect the act of smoking in any manner. If you do, it will only serve to reinforce and protect your addiction. Admit that you have a weakness and that it is a bad habit. Only then will a time come when you will be able to break yourself away from this addiction. If you do not, then this addiction will stay with you. Are you trying to let go of it?

**Questioner:** I am trying, but without success.     (212)

**Dadashri:** No, you should not make any attempts. What you should do is not protect your addiction. If someone tells you, 'Why don't you stop smoking?' and you respond by, 'No, there is no need to stop smoking,' then that is the protection of your addiction. In the presence of criticism, when your addiction has a chance of dissolving, you defend it by saying, 'No, there is nothing wrong with smoking.' So what happens then? It will not go away. So always maintain the belief that it is wrong to smoke, then one day it will go away.

**Questioner:** What if I simply keep 'seeing' the discharge that is occurring and not do *pratikraman* for it? Will that then increase or decrease?

**Dadashri:** It will not increase. In not doing *pratikraman*, you will see those same *parmanus* again in your next life.

**Questioner:** But what if we do not increase anything new and simply keep 'seeing' the discharge?

**Dadashri:** There is no need to do *pratikraman* at all. One hundred percent there is no need for it! The reason I have put forth *pratikraman* is that otherwise you will not be free of your opinions. The moment you do *pratikraman*, you are opposing that opinion. That is not your opinion anymore; otherwise, it will remain pending. There is no need for *pratikraman* in this science. It is solely for this reason you have been given *pratikraman*, otherwise, that opinion of, 'There is no problem,' will still remain.

Scripture writers have taken an objection to this and are questioning why 'we' have put *pratikraman* in *Akram Vignan*. But what they do not realize is that this is the *Akram* path. And people's opinions will remain unwashed. One may drink alcohol but if he does not do *pratikraman* for it, his opinion (that it is acceptable to drink alcohol) will remain.

'We,' too, do *pratikraman*. One should be free from all opinions. It is not acceptable for any opinion to linger on.

Therefore, scientifically it is not necessary, but technically you do need it.

**Questioner:** Besides, what harm is there in it? What is the harm in doing *pratikraman*?

**Dadashri:** It is not a question of harm.

**Questioner:** Then what?

**Dadashri:** The issue is not about harm or no harm. That is not why *pratikraman* has been given. It has been placed for 'exactness.'

One should never say, 'What harm is there?' When can you make such a statement? You can say this in an average business interaction.

If a man does *pratikraman*, he attains the highest of his spiritual goals. Technically, *pratikraman* is required but, scientifically, it is not necessary.

**Questioner:** Scientifically? How is it unnecessary, scientifically?

**Dadashri:** Scientifically, it is all a discharge and, therefore, where is the need for *pratikraman* at all? This is because You are separate and he (Chandulal) is separate. Such level of energy (of *vitaragata*) is lacking in people (*mahatmas*) and, therefore, if *pratikraman* is not done, the old opinion will remain. And is it not a fact that when you do *pratikraman*, You are separate form that opinion? Is that not an accomplished fact?

The residual, the mind that does not get discharged is based on the residual opinions. This is because the mind has been formed through opinions. After careful clearing of these opinions, if some remain, their results will unfold in the future; will they not? But it will not be like the old times (past lives) when one had a strong opinion that we realize from now that if it (opinion-filled mind) is like this now, what will it be like in the future.                    (214)

**Questioner:** So that means that 'Chandulal' and 'Chandulal's' *parmanus* are discharge (effect). So if he does not do *pratikraman*, that many *parmanus* will remain pending for discharge.

**Dadashri:** Your mind will harass you that much. How do you feel when you have taken some alcohol (there is a lack of clarity)?

**Questioner:** So do they remain in the form of causes for the next life?

**Dadashri:** Yes. The mind is formed because of opinions and when an opinion remains, that much of the mind still remains.

**Questioner:** But, Dada, what about everything that occurred before Gnan?

**Dadashri:** There is no question of that at all. Most of it has gone away because of the Gnan, and whatever is left will discharge in the next life without any problems.

**Questioner:** So, does some of it still remain after Gnan?

**Dadashri:** Yes, it will remain, but you have to resolve

your problems yourself. If you don't do *pratikraman*, if you are lazy in this aspect, that much will remain. Should you not do the *purusharth*? Is it acceptable not to do *purusharth* after becoming a Purush (Self-realized)?

'You' have nothing to do with any actions of 'Chandubhai.' But You have to keep an eye on 'Chandubhai.' You have to see what he is doing, how many cigarettes he smokes, and tell him to do *pratikraman* if he does *atikraman*. You have a right to do *kraman* (normal action); you do not have a right to do *atikraman* (actions that hurt others or the self).

I do not have any objection to your addiction, but you should do *pratikraman* for it. Confess to God that it is wrong for you to drink and that you are sincerely sorry for it, and ask for the energy to not drink again. Do this much for your own sake, Dear.

In this matter, people generally make things worse by raising objections and criticizing the addict. They don't realize that they are making things worse. They are hurting the situation more than helping it. What have I said to you? No matter how grave a mistake you have made, do *pratikraman* for it in this manner. What does *pratikraman* mean?

**Questioner:** *Pratikraman* means that I end up doing things due to my *prakruti*, but I repent those actions, and I want to become free from them. Is that *pratikraman*?

**Dadashri:** Yes. But you repent doing it. But what does *pratikraman* mean? You are going against your opinion that you want to drink alcohol. If you become free of that opinion then drinking alcohol will not be a part of your next life. You can never let go of *pratikraman*. Do you understand? These sentences have been written in such a way that they will help you become free from everything.

**Questioner:** This morning, Dada, you said that before

drinking tea you do *pratyakhyan* (making the decision of 'I will never do it again,' and asking for the energy for this).

**Dadashri:** Yes!

**Questioner:** Since we were on the subject, I had to mention this.

**Dadashri:** 'I' (the Self) do not drink tea, but sometimes circumstances lead me (A. M. Patel) to do so. These circumstances are out of my control and so I am forced to drink tea. But when A. M. Patel drinks tea, he does not drink without first doing *pratyakhyan*, otherwise, the one who likes tea will continue to do so. *Pratyakhyan* is like smearing oil, then pouring colored water over it. Yes, we use the 'oil of *pratyakhyan*,' then, even if one pours green colored water over it, it will not stick. So I drink tea after doing *pratyakhyan*.

This is worth understanding. Do *pratyakhyan* whenever you do anything, even if it does not hurt others. *Pratikraman* should be done whenever *atikraman* has occurred. Drinking tea is not considered *atikraman*. You are compelled to drink tea, but that is not considered *atikraman*; but if you do not do *pratyakhyan*, then a little of it will 'stick' to you. From now on remember to do *pratyakhyan*.

**Questioner:** Yes, definitely.                                         (216)

**Dadashri:** When you go out for a drive in your car, apply the 'oil' (do *pratyakhyan*) – 'I have no choice but to do this but I vow not to do it again'; this is the 'oil' that 'I' apply when I have to travel.

**Questioner:** I had to eat potatoes and onions in his home.

**Dadashri:** Do *pratikraman* for that. If you do *pratikraman*, it will be fine. One should do as circumstances dictate.

## During Physical Ailments

**Questioner:** I do *pratikraman* when I hurt someone, but when I am suffering from some physical ailments, do I have to do *pratikraman* for that?

**Dadashri:** 'You' have to continue 'seeing' it. You also have to 'see' the one becoming engrossed in the physical pain. You have to continue to suffer it (*bhogavavanoo*) and continue to 'see' (*jovanoo*) the suffering. *Veda* means to 'know.' *Veda* means to suffer. The Gnanis are in the state starting from suffering (*bhogavavanoo*) to the state of 'Knowing' (*janavoo*).

**Questioner:** When the pain is intense, the non-Self complex (*pudgal*) becomes very uncomfortable.

**Dadashri:** Yes. Every one will notice that, but you have to make sure that you do not hurt anyone. Sometimes, if you say something that hurts the other person, then You have to tell 'Chandubhai' to do the *pratikraman.*

**Questioner:** That *pratikraman* is done properly. But during any physical pain, the mind goes through a lot of changes in *bhaavs* (inner intents). I can say that there is *artadhyan* and *raudradhyan* during that time.

**Dadashri:** This Gnan is such that it will never cause *artadhyan* or *raudradhyan*. But whatever *artadhyan* or *raudradhyan* that do occur, occur on the external part, and so it truly does not touch You. How do we define *artadhyan* and *raudradhyan*? It is when one has violent intent (*himsak bhaav*), but I do not see that in you.

**Questioner:** When *ashata-vedaniya karma* (karma which brings pain) unfolds, I have no choice but suffer them. While suffering it, if I even say, 'I am going to die, I am going to die. I have not done anything wrong, so why is this suffering unfolding for me?' Then what kind of intent should one keep during such situations?

**Dadashri:** 'I am separate from this suffering'; such affirmation will lighten the pain. And if you say, 'This is happening to me,' then the load will feel heavier.

**Questioner:** The anxiety he experiences because of pain, is it with *artadhyan* or *raudradhyan*?

**Dadashri:** It is with *artadhyan*. It is not a question of *dhyan*. If one is in Gnan, then it is the non-Self that suffers the pain. You have to know who is suffering the pain and maintain awareness of who You are. Then You have to tell 'Chandubhai', 'Chandubhai, you go ahead and suffer it. Only you have to suffer it. You have to suffer the effect of your own causes.' If You can remain separate in all that, You will benefit from the separation. Otherwise, if you say, 'I am suffering a lot,' then you will suffer it many fold over.

**Questioner:** Everything you have said applies to the *mahatmas*. But the rest of the people who are suffering, do they suffer with *artadhyan*?

**Dadashri:** There is only *artadhyan* there; the result is pain and suffering. Such result of suffering as the self is *artadhyan*.

**Questioner:** Then he continues to get irritated with others. That is *raudradhyan*, is it not?

**Dadashri:** Then there is *raudradhyan*. In this flawless (*nirdosh*) world, no one should appear to be a *doshit* (one at fault). The world is completely *nirdosh*. Therefore, whatever you see is due to the mistake in your own vision.

**Questioner:** Is *vedaniya karma* (karma that brings physical suffering) bound by *atichar* (transgression of code of conduct; doing something in excess) or *atikraman*?

**Dadashri:** It is bound by *atikraman*.

Very rarely do 'we' have physical suffering. There was an entire month after the car accident when it seemed that this light was going to extinguish.

**Questioner:** Nothing like that is going to happen, Dada!

**Dadashri:** No, not like that. But did Hiraba (Dada's wife) not pass away? Would the same not befall this body? What kind of karma was it that brought the suffering (*vedaniya*)?

**Questioner:** The karma of suffering (*ashata-vedaniya*).

**Dadashri:** People assume that 'we' have suffering, but *vedaniya* (suffering) does not touch 'us.' It does not touch the *Tirthankars* either. 'We' felt no sorrow when Hiraba passed away. 'We' are not affected by anything. People think that 'we' have suffering, but suffering has not touched us for the last twenty years. That is precisely the Science that 'we' have given you. So if you fall short because of your weakness, then that is your loss. If you understand this Science, you will not face any suffering. Do you fall short on some days? For a few minutes?

**Questioner:** No.

**Dadashri:** Then that is good.

**Questioner:** Dada Bhagwan is not affected by the *vedaniya* karma, but it affects Ambalalbhai, does it not?

**Dadashri:** No. Neither one of them are affected. That is the energy of this Science. One would go insane if it affected him. It is because of ignorance of the Self that suffering occurs. If there is understanding, then it would not even touch this file number one ('Chandulal'; the relative self). It will not affect anyone. Whatever suffering there is, is due to lack of understanding. How could there be any suffering once this Gnan is understood? In the presence of Gnan, there is no suffering of pain or enjoying pleasure.

*****

## [13]

# Liberation from Artadhyan and Raudradhyan

## The Meaning of Artadhyan

**Questioner:** *Artadhyan* and *raudradhyan* are constantly occurring. Can you please explain the two clearly?     (220)

**Dadashri:** *Artadhyan* involves only you. It occurs when you suffer silently without anyone's knowledge; you suffer from within, but you do not hurt anyone else. And *raudradhyan* is when you hurt others.

A person who does not have Self-realization and has the belief, 'I am 'Chandulal'- [*insert your name*]' will have worries like, 'What will become of me or what will occur if such and such happens to me?' He will worry about his daughter's marriage even when she is five! Does he think his daughter is going to get married because of him? Besides, she will get married when she is 24 or 30, not at the age of five! When he worries in this way, that is called *artadhyan*.

To have negative thoughts about yourself; or worry whether or not your life will run smoothly; or if you fall sick, to have worries about dying; is all *artadhyan*.

**Questioner:** What about thinking or worrying about the future?

**Dadashri:** It is considered *artadhyan*. Even that is considered *artadhyan* in the absence of Self-realization. What will occur tomorrow? There is a letter from the Internal Revenue Service (government tax department). What will the I.R.S. do?

In thinking about the future, if one experiences fear, then *artadhyan* has occurred for sure.

In *artadhyan*, one continues to worry about himself, 'What will happen if this occurs? What will happen if that occurs?' He will continue to have fear of this kind.

## Raudradhyan Hurts the Self and Others

When you imagine that the other person has hurt you, that is *raudradhyan*.

When you have a thought because of another person (*nimit*), the thought of harming him… all that is *raudradhyan*. Say, for example, a cloth merchant cheats his customers by stretching the material when he measures it; the moment he thinks about cheating his customers, he is in *raudradhyan*.

**Questioner:** When others are hurt because of us, is that *raudradhyan*?

**Dadashri:** Yes, whether one gets hurt or not. But if you tell him he is worthless, he is deceitful, he is a thief; that is all *raudradhyan*.

Actually, there is no one at fault (*doshit*) in this world. It is through our misunderstanding that the other person appears at fault.

**Questioner:** I experience *raudradhyan*. I see mistakes in others. How does my doing that hurt the other person? If I see him as the culprit, how does he feel hurt in that? If the person I see at fault is unaware of it, how is that *raudradhyan*?

**Dadashri:** It will have an effect and thus it is called *raudradhyan*. Why would he not have an affect? You may think that he does not know. He will be affected somewhere without fail. He will not even know.                                        (222)

## Dharmadhyan from Artadhyan-Raudradhyan

**Questioner:** Many times it occurs that I get deeper and

deeper into *artadhyan* and *raudradhyan* and still I am not aware of it. So how can I become aware about this?

**Dadashri:** When one feels hurt (*dukh*), is that not *artadhyan*? And in *raudradhyan* there is increased suffering; that suffering is more like a burning pain. All of it, *artadhyan* and *raudradhyan*, are hurtful to man. It is nothing but *ashata-vedaniya* (the karma of suffering).

**Questioner:** That occurs every moment. What do I have to do to be free from all that?

**Dadashri:** Keep 'seeing' that 'in reality, no one is at fault (*doshit*) at all. I see it that way because of the unfolding of my own karma. But truly it is not that way.' Therefore, if he appears at fault (*doshit*), this vision will show him as flawless (*nirdosh*), and keep doing *pratikraman*.

If you have a negative or bad thought about anyone, you should come to the conclusion that, 'It is the unfolding of my own karma, and how is that poor man to be blamed?' In doing this, he will cease to appear at fault (*doshit*) to you. And that is considered *dharmadhyan* (absence of *artadhyan-raudradhyan*). So, where *raudradhyan* was going to take place, you turned it into *dharmadhyan*. And that will give you great inner bliss. 'He appears at fault only due to the unfolding of my own karma. He is just a *nimit* (evidentiary doer).'

Currently, the other person is never truly at fault; he is simply a *nimit* (instrumental evidence) in the unfolding of your own karma.

## Our Own Kashays Are Our Enemies

Do *nimits* ever come to you?

**Questioner:** Sometimes.

**Dadashri:** Yes. That person is simply a *nimit*. He is not the actual doer. If a thief picks your pocket, he is a *nimit*. He is not really at fault. Our *kashays* (anger-pride-deceit-greed) are the real culprits.

Your *kashays* are your own inner enemies. There are no other enemies on the outside. And those inner enemies are what are killing you; nothing on the outside is hurting you.

## Repenting Changes the Dhyan

If a person has committed severe *raudradhyan*, he can turn it into *artadhyan* by doing *pratikraman*. If two people are at fault of the same kind of *raudradhyan*, where they both have expressed a desire to kill someone, their inner state for violence is *raudradhyan*. If one of them goes home and sincerely repents for having such a destructive *bhaav*, his *raudradhyan* will become *artadhyan*, while the other will continue his *raudradhyan*.

Through repentance, *raudradhyan* can be changed to *artadhyan*. With repentance, one is diverted from a birth in hell to a birth in the animal kingdom. With further intense repentance, one can turn *raudradhyan* into *dharmadhyan*. With initial repentance, *raudradhyan* turns into *artadhyan* and with repeated repentance it becomes *dharmadhyan*. Actions and events may not change, but changes are taking place from within.

The minute you turn your back on *raudradhyan*, by repenting, changes will occur. But if you take pleasure in it and insist, 'No, that man needs to be punished. I am correct in thinking that way,' then that will take you all the way to the lowest form of life (*nigod*). Coming back into the human form will be very difficult. So beware; to take pleasure in *raudradhyan* will make you regress back to the lowest life form.

So never do *raudradhyan* and if it occurs, then repent for it. Also, never do *artadhyan*, and if it occurs then repent for it.

(224)

If *artadhyan* takes place and you repent for it, the Lord has said that he will give you credit for that as *dharmadhyan*. Did the Lord (the Lord within) say anything wrong by this? Do you think that the Lord is wise or is he crazy?

**Questioner:** Where will we go by calling him crazy? The Lord is always wise.

## Pratikraman Converts Artadhyan to Dharmadhyan

**Dadashri:** Repent in the name of Dada. That will change it into *dharmadhyan*. Do at least what you know. Repent when *raudradhyan* (pain and hurt caused to others) occurs and also when *artadhyan* (pain to the self) occurs. It is not possible for one to do *dharmadhyan* in this era of the time cycle. Therefore, start a factory of converting *artadhyan* and *raudradhyan* into *dharmadhyan*. It is not possible for one to know how to do *dharmadhyan* directly, because even when he is doing *darshan* of the Lord, his *dhyan* is on his shoes that he left at the door. So the Lord himself says, 'When he is doing my *darshan*, he is also doing *darshan* of his shoes, so what can I do?'

Therefore, *dharmadhyan* is not possible in this time era. So what does Dada say? He says to repent for all the *artadhyan* that occurs, and doing that will give you the benefit of *dharmadhyan*. And without *dharmadhyan*, it is not possible to become free form this body complex (*pudgal*). This *pudgal* can never attain *shukladhyan* ('I am *Shuddhatma*-'; the state of the Self).

Therefore, there is nothing wrong if *artadhyan* occurs; it can be changed to *dharmadhyan*.

You should ask, 'Hey! Chandulal, why do you keep doing *artadhyan*? Now repent for the *artadhyan* you have done. Do *pratikraman*.' So it changes into *dharmadhyan*.

**Questioner:** When 'we' remain separate as the Self and make 'Chandulal' do *pratikraman*, what is it called?

**Dadashri:** You are the pure Self now, but should this *pudgal*, the non-Self complex, not also attain liberation? This *pudgal*, which is a complex of thoughts, speech and acts, should be such that it does not hurt anyone. If you do not make it do *pratikraman*, it will not be free from mistakes. So if you do not keep this *pudgal* in *dharmadhyan*, there is no liberation, because the *pudgal* cannot attain the state of *shukladhyan* (the state of the Self). So that is why you should keep it engaged in *dharmadhyan*. You should make it do repeated *pratikramans*. *Pratikraman* should be done as many times as *artadhyan* occurs.

*Artadhyan* occurs because of ignorance from your past life and for that you should do *pratikraman*. *Artadhyan* is an effect.

## One Never Loses Shukladhyan in Akram Vignan

**Questioner:** One comes into *artadhyan* and *raudradhyan* by falling from *shukladhyan*; is that why one has to do *pratikraman*?

**Dadashri:** That is all true, but in reality You (the Self) do not have to do *pratikraman*. *Shukladhyan* never goes away. You have to work with the circumstances. If You (the Self) were to do *pratikraman*, then *shukladhyan* would go away, would it not?

**Questioner:** If *raudradhyan* and *artadhyan* occur in discharge, then one has to do 'on the moment' (shoot-on-sight) *pratikraman*.

**Dadashri:** *Artadhyan* and *raudradhyan* should not remain pending in the *karmic* account.

And You, too, are in the state of *shukladhyan* and

*dharmadhyan*, but you simply have to do *pratikraman*, that is all. You will not attain as many worldly benefits as 'we' do, but You too are enjoying the same state as 'we' are in, are You not?

*Raudradhyan* and all that will happen; it occurs naturally, but it should be followed by instant *pratikraman*.     (226)

## Whoever Comes Here is Trapped

'You' do not have to do anything, do you? You have become a *Shuddhatma*. You have to tell 'Chandubhai' to do the *pratikraman*. Why did you do *atikraman*? What do You have to say? You have to say, 'You did the *atikraman*, so do *pratikraman*.' You do not have to do *pratikraman* if you give a donation to someone, because *dharmadhyan* is also included in this science.

*Pratikraman* is to be done for *atikraman*. This science is not just *shukladhyan*. It is not possible for one to go straight to *moksha*. It is possible for him to become *ekavtari* (just one life more before *moksha*). Some can become *beyavtari* (two lives before *moksha*) and some can become *tranavtari* (three lives before *moksha*), and if someone is 'greedy' (in wanting to enjoy the worldly life), he will complete fifteen lives before going to *moksha*. He will say, 'I will not be coming back, so let me do all the *atikraman* I can!'

My business partner was such that I used to ask him, 'Are you going to complete the full fifteen lives?' and he in turn would ask me, 'Is that what you think?' I told him, 'Yes. You are not coming back so why don't you complete your greed of fifteen lives right here?' However, there will not be more than fifteen lives.

If one is too greedy there will not be more than fifteen lifetimes, will there? He has now come inside the limit. Therefore, if one has desire for worldly happiness and he wants to enjoy the worldly life for another five–six thousand more lifetimes, then he should not meet Dada. And if he does meet Dada, he should not take Gnan. Once you meet Him and take Gnan, you will not be able to get out of it, even if you so desire. You will have to go to *moksha*. One would never find such a fool who does not want *moksha*, once he understands all this. However, I have to forewarn you. Then if you say, 'Please free me from these fifteen lives,' you will not be able to be free, because this is the stamp (visa guarantee) of the Gnani. No one can erase it and no one can cancel it.

Gnani means someone with a 'license.' He has the license of the entire world. The celestial beings (*devlokas*) come to listen to this science. This *satsang* is considered a gathering of *paramhansa* (the One who separates the Self from the non-Self) where there is no discussion other than that of the Soul and the Supreme Soul. There are no worldly discussions here and it (gathering) is with *dharmadhyan*. Ours is *Akram* (step-less), is it not?

## Mahatmas Do Not Have Artadhyan or Raudradhyan

*Artadhyan* and *raudradhyan* are causes for a birth in the lower life (*tiryanch*) forms.

**Questioner:** I do not want to do *artadhyan* and *raudradhyan* at all and yet they occur.

**Dadashri:** What I am saying is that I do not have a problem if they occur. Why don't you do *pratikraman* for it? 'We' have never raised any objection as to, 'Why did you do it?' Just do *pratikraman*. 'We' do not wish to get rid of anyone. 'We' do not have any negativity here; there is only positivity here. 'We' are not here to ruin anyone. Tell them (*artadhyan* and *raudradhyan*) they can stay and that you will do *pratikraman*. And so they will leave on their own.

Our Gnan is such that *artadhyan* and *raudradhyan* do

not occur; it does not allow *artadhyan* and *raudradhyan* to occur. And whatever *artadhyan* and *raudradhyan* you see is not Your *dhyan*; it is simply a suffocation of sorts. Truly they can never occur! There is no *artadhyan* or *raudradhyan* if there is *Atmagnan*. And where there is a presence of *artadhyan* and *raudradhyan*, there is no *Atmagnan* there. There can be no contradiction in this matter.

There is *dharmadhyan* in the physical self and *shukladhyan* in the Self. But when that suffocation comes, you think that *artadhyan* and *raudradhyan* are occurring. And this is why You have to say, 'Why did you do *atikraman*? So now do *pratikraman*!'                                                (228)

There can never be *artadhyan* and *raudradhyan* where there is *Atmagnan*. With *artadhyan* and *raudradhyan* one will never be able to attain the Self. Now whatever *artadhyan* and *raudradhyan* there seems to be is merely suffocation. Who can have *artadhyan* and *raudradhyan*? The answer is, it occurs to the living ego, 'I am Chandulal.' I have taken that living ego away, leaving behind only the lifeless ego (discharging ego). That discharging ego does not experience any *artadhyan* or *raudradhyan*. That which is dead cannot move nor do anything anew.

Therefore, there is nothing complicated, just understand it. There is nothing to it if you understand what I am saying.

The Gnan I have given to you is such that it keeps working on its own. Understand it completely in detail. And if you still do not understand it, then do *pratikraman* repeatedly. That is why those who do not understand it have been asked to do *pratikraman*. Nothing at all happens to the one who understands *Akram Vignan*. Whatever occurs, it is happening only to the external self (the non-Self), and one feels in the mind that it is happening to him. Truly, it is all happening to the external part (the non-Self).

**Questioner:** So is this all an illusion?

**Dadashri:** No. It is not an illusion. All this suffocation is bound to arise. This happens when there is a lot of interference (*dakho*) of karma. What occurs if there is a dust storm here? You will not be able to see beyond it, will you?

**Questioner:** So they are all veils?

**Dadashri:** These are all *mohaniya karma* (karma of illusory attraction). Whatever karmas were filled, they come out as they dissipate.

Now You have to get your work done! Keep doing *pratikraman*. That is the only solution and cure for such karma. You (the Self) have nothing to do with it and, therefore, *mahatmas* do not have any *artadhyan*. The *Atma* does not have *artadhyan* and *raudradhyan*. Our *mahatmas* do not experience any *artadhyan* and *raudradhyan* at all because they are *Shuddhatma*. They are not the name or the form.

**Questioner:** What should we do if the results of previous *artadhyan* and *raudradhyan* come into effect now?

**Dadashri:** That is exactly what will come forth, will it not? But now you can let go of them through Gnan. In those days, you could not let go because you did not have Gnan. Now You can become free from them because of Gnan. That is why you have to do *pratikraman*. You did not do *pratikraman* in those days. You have incurred *apratikraman* mistakes (mistakes of not doing *pratikraman*). The entire world has arisen as a consequence of this very mistake. Freedom begins from the moment one starts to do *pratikraman*.

## When Does One Bind Karma After Gnan?

**Questioner:** After taking Gnan, if *artadhyan* and *raudradhyan* occur, knowingly or unknowingly, and at that moment, if the *mahatma* repents and does *pratikraman*, then will he bind new karma?

**Dadashri:** You will not bind any karma if you do *pratikraman*. Do you do *pratikraman* every time?

**Questioner:** I immediately do *pratikraman*.

**Dadashri:** And are you 'Chandulal' or are you 'Shuddhatma'?

**Questioner:** I am *Shuddhatma*.

**Dadashri:** Then there is no problem. There is no problem if you do *pratikraman*.

**Questioner:** If I became *nimit* of *raudradhyan* and did not do *pratikraman*, and the entanglement remains, then did I bind karma?

**Dadashri:** When is karma bound? It gets bound when *darshan* (the knowledge of being the Soul) changes. When *darshan* changes, or when the faith is shaken up; otherwise, you will not bind any karma. Nothing will happen to the one whose conviction of being the pure Soul does not falter.        (230)

**Questioner:** So there is no time limit, is there? The Limit, such as the karma, will be bound within a certain time?

**Dadashri:** When does karma get bound? When the conviction (*pratiti*, 'I am pure Soul') becomes shaken up and unsteady. What occurs when you mix salt and sugar together?

**Questioner:** Everything changes.

**Dadashri:** Then all the karma will be bound. So let sugar be sugar and let salt be salt. Therefore, conviction must not be tainted or spoiled. No stain must ever fall on the conviction (I am pure Soul).

## Adverse Meditation is an Effect; Wash It Off with Pratikraman

**Dadashri:** Now *artadhyan* and *raudradhyan* cannot

occur anymore, can they?

**Questioner:** No, they do not happen anymore. They have stopped since the last ten days.

**Dadashri:** When will it occur again?

**Questioner:** When I see mistakes in others?

**Dadashri:** Do *pratikraman* when he (Chandulal) sees mistakes. *Artadhyan* and *raudradhyan* do not occur now that You are not the doer. And if he (Chandulal) sees mistakes in someone, that is *dravya* (effect of past life karma); it is not *bhaav* (cause). It is considered *artadhyan* and *raudradhyan* when there is presence of *bhaav*. This is just the *dravya* – the effect. Therefore, he will end up saying things that were already filled within.

**Questioner:** Is it considered *artadhyan* or *raudradhyan* when he sees mistakes of others?

**Dadashri:** Yes. He (Chandulal) will see mistakes in others if that is the kind of baggage he has brought with him from his previous life. The Self is flawless and does not see mistake in others. He (Chandulal) should do *pratikraman* when he sees mistakes in others. That is all he has to do. Everything he does in this life is a discharge of the *karmic* baggage he has brought with him from his previous life.

The Lord has called it *dravya* (effect). He said that it is the baggage of past life karma (*bharelo maal*) within him that is discharging. When You say that baggage of past life karma is coming out, the other person will immediately understand.

In the scriptural language it is called *dravya-parinam* (effect-result). And the other, the cause of karma, they call *bhaav-parinam* (cause).

Now, how is a person to know all such subtleties? And

if one tries to teach this to others, he will make mistakes. Instead, it is better to have our own simple, colloquial language that a person can understand right away. This is all baggage that was filled, which is coming out now.

**Questioner:** What happens is that often I talk negatively about someone who is not present; I call him names, I think he is worthless, and at the same time, I think I am something, I am right, I am never at fault, I have not made any mistake. So when such *artadhyan* and *raudradhyan* are occurring continuously, what should I do to maintain awareness so that I can remain separate from all that?

**Dadashri:** That may happen. That is when You realize that awareness does not remain. So whatever occurs during the daytime, decide in the evening that You want to do *pratikraman* from nine to eleven.

**Questioner:** That is right; *pratikraman* is the solution.

**Dadashri:** Yes, do *pratikraman* at night for anyone you meet on the road, in your vicinity, etc.

**Questioner:** Whomever I meet.

**Dadashri:** Whether you met him or not, just do *pratikraman* for all of them for an hour or two. You don't realize how much energy it will generate and You will also experience tremendous bliss!

**Questioner:** I understand it. So ultimately, in my free time I should do *pratikraman*.                        (232)

**Dadashri:** Remember them all and do *pratikraman*.

## Exactness of the Pratikraman Vidhi of Dadashri

**Questioner:** When we do *pratikraman* for *artadhyan*, what does that fall under?

**Dadashri:** It does not fall under anything. The stain that occurred with *artadhyan* gets washed off with *pratikraman*.

**Questioner:** And what about doing *pratikraman* for *raudradhyan*?

**Dadashri:** You have to do that *pratikraman* for the other person.

**Questioner:** But here it is, printed in this book, that it turns into *dharmadhyan*.

**Dadashri:** Yes. It will definitely go into *dharmadhyan*, if you do *pratikraman* for *raudradhyan*, because you stopped the *raudradhyan*.

**Questioner:** So then where does the *pratikraman* for *artadhyan* go?

**Dadashri:** It is not like that. It is not written like that. It is different in the books. Stopping *raudradhyan* is *dharmadhyan*. Is that not what is written in the book?

**Questioner:** And what about *artadhyan*?

**Dadashri:** That which stops *raudradhyan* is *dharmadhyan*, and that which stops *artadhyan* is also *dharmadhyan*. Yes, both.

**Questioner:** And if one repents?

**Dadashri:** Then when he repents he washes off his mistakes.

**Questioner:** Sometimes in *satsang* you say that to have control in situations where *artadhyan* and *raudradhyan* are likely to occur; that is called *dharmadhyan*.

**Dadashri:** The way that *dharmadhyan* remains 'in control' is by maintaining the awareness that, 'All this is the unfolding of my own karma. The other person is simply a *nimit*'; that is what we call *dharmadhyan*.

**Questioner:** Yes, but only if it remains in control, right?

**Dadashri:** You have to do *pratikraman* once you shoot a 'bullet.'

**Questioner:** Does *pratikraman* for *raudradhyan* lead directly to *dharmadhyan*?

**Dadashri:** No, not like that. It is like this; everything is based on exact words. There is a difference between *pratikraman* and repentance. To do *pratikraman* correctly is to remain as the pure Self and make 'Chandulal' do *pratikraman*.

You (the Self) have to simply check, that is all. You have to see that there is no interference from anyone or anything (traditional ritualistic words of *pratikraman*) when you are doing the *pratikraman vidhi* (the orderly way of reciting the specific *pratikraman*). Are 'My' words (Dadashri's words of *pratikraman vidhi*) in it, or not? That is all You have to 'see.' There is no need for you to see mistakes in others.

**Questioner:** It is not an issue of seeing mistakes, but we need to know it exactly, don't we?

**Dadashri:** No, each and every word in this *vidhi* is correct! No one at all has the right to cross out or negate any of it in the future!

## Exact Pratikraman

**Questioner:** I was not talking about negating them, it's just that two or three sentences all came together...

**Dadashri:** No, if for some reason someone were to bring the entire book here, then I can tell you what was said under what circumstances...we need to make the 'before' and 'after' connection. We need to put it in context. If you just pull out a sentence from the middle, then we would not be able to give a proper meaning to it.

**Questioner:** No, no, in Aptavani Two, page number 109 (in Gujarati version; English page 127), it is written that repentance in *raudradhyan* results in *artadhyan* and exact *pratikraman* in *raudradhyan* leads to *dharmadhyan*.                    (234)

**Dadashri:** From the whole sentence that has been spoken, all you have to do is make sure there is no meddling from others. Tell me if there is any meddling from others (not of *Akram Vignan*). Another thing is, do not try to do a comparative analysis. Whether it means this or that depends on circumstances. Do you understand that?

*Yathartha* ('as it should be') means that the Gnani Purush can say the sentence exactly as it should be; no one else can do that.

**Questioner:** Please explain this *yathartha* ('as it should be') to me.

**Dadashri:** *Yathartha* means that it should be exactly as it is. Generally, a person would not understand it that way, would he? Some spiritually elevated people may understand it. It is possible for you to do exact *pratikraman* if you understand it.

**Questioner:** Up until now, I understood it this way: that if I think about doing something wrong to another person, I block it and that, to me, is *dharmadhyan*. 'This person hurt me,' so I will immediately react to that by thinking I want to do this or that to him. But then I feel that that is not my task. I used to believe this to be *dharmadhyan*.

**Dadashri:** Yes. That is considered *dharmadhyan*. It is *dharmadhyan* because it stops *artadhyan* and *raudradhyan* from taking place. That is cash *dharmadhyan*, instantly available, just like cash money.

But it is a very big accomplishment to be able to do this exact (*yathartha*) *pratikraman*. Otherwise, that other *pratikraman* is a different thing.

**Questioner:** Dada, once it got printed in a book, it all went into a common language.

**Dadashri:** Yes. But it reaches the one who is true and sincere, does it not? Who would understand it exactly?

**Questioner:** I thought about it and came to the conclusion that exact (*yathartha*) *pratikraman* is one in which there is no doership.

**Dadashri:** Yes, there is absolutely no doership after attaining Gnan, but exact (*yathartha*) means that it should be done exactly as it is.

**Questioner:** Gnanis do not have to do any *pratikraman*, do they?

**Dadashri:** These *Akram Vignanis* (those who have Self-realization via *Akram* Gnan Vidhi) do have to do them.

**Questioner:** No, but it is the exact (*yathartha*) *pratikraman*, is it not?

**Dadashri:** Exact *pratikramans* are done by those who live with us. There are some *mahatmas* (like Niruben) who can do the exact *pratikraman*. Others can do that too. You too can do it like them. There is no problem if you do not understand it exactly, but I do know that you are capable of doing them exactly (*yathartha*). The word '*yathartha*' (exact) is itself a very heavy word. It means 'as it should be.'

## Dharmadhyan in Relative, Shukladhyan in Real

Let me tell you what this Science of ours says. Right now

there are only two types of unfolding discharge taking place –
either a good intent (*bhaav*) or a bad intent (*bhaav*).

**Questioner:** Yes.

**Dadashri:** Then look at that discharge and You will 'see'
your fault; the one whose fault it is will see his fault. He will see
it as good, if it is good. But You have to 'see' your own faults,
and nothing else.

This spiritual effort (*purusharth*) will make a difference in
your coming life. But that is not what 'we' are saying. What
'we' are saying is that you have become *Shuddhatma* (pure
Soul) and you do not want a next life of any form. So what 'we'
are saying is that this is an unfolding of karma (*udaya*), and you
are settling (doing *nikaal* of it), 'knowing', it.

To know that a mistake has occurred is called
*dharmadhyan*. And within that prevails *shukladhyan*. When
there are both *dharmadhyan* and *shukladhyan*, then one
becomes *ekavtari* (one more life before *moksha*). And when
only *shukladhyan* is there, one attains *moksha*.          (236)

Hence, when a mistake occurs, You should not touch it at
all; do not consider it as Yours. You have studied the old scriptures
and that is why you feel, 'What is this, how can it be, what is
going on?' 'We' (the Gnani Purush) have in the Gnan Vidhi
given the Knowledge that both the good habits and the bad
habits are part of the illusion of the non-Self. 'I am *Shuddhatma*
and I have become the Self.' From here on, whatever mistake
is there, I can 'see' it. These are now coming in my 'vision.'

You can now 'see' the mistakes. You will 'see' all minute
mistakes. You will 'see' more and more mistakes as this vision
of 'seeing' the mistakes blossoms.

Now, if *pratikraman* does not occur, I will tell you that
there is no problem. But keep 'seeing' those mistakes and

recognize that they are wrong. It is *dharmadhyan* the moment you know that. Therefore, externally there is *dharmadhyan* and internally there is *shukladhyan*; this is a completely different path. It is a natural path.

## Purusharth in Unfolding Karma

There is a knock at your door at eleven thirty at night. You call out to see who it is and the voice tells you that he is an acquaintance from your village and he has come with a group of ten to twelve people. What would you say to them this late in the night? Would you open the door or not?

**Questioner:** Yes, I would.

**Dadashri:** What would you tell them? Would you tell them to go away because it is so late?

**Questioner:** Of course not. How could I do that?

**Dadashri:** Well then, what would you say?

**Questioner:** I would invite them in.

**Dadashri:** You would invite them in. Because you have been brought up with good values, you would invite them into your home. You carry away your sleeping child to make room on the sofa for them. You do all this, but in your mind the thought arises, 'Why the heck do they have to come at such a time?'

When this happens, it is *raudradhyan*; it is not *artadhyan*. *Artadhyan* means that one only suffers from within. But in this case, you start *raudradhyan* and blame your guests for the problem. This is spoiling your internal intent (*bhaav*) towards your guests. You are blaming them for visiting you so late at night.

On the outside, however, you continue your appearance of being cordial. After they are seated, you ask them if they would like some tea. Your friend says that, instead of tea, they would prefer a simple, hot meal. You now think to yourself, 'Just wait until my wife hears this. She's going to go ballistic! What will happen in the kitchen?'

Now what are you supposed to do here? What is the Lord's Agna? What should the one who wants liberation do? The pressures of the current time cycle are such that they influence our *bhaav* negatively, so in such circumstances it is natural to have a *bhaav* like, 'Why are they here at this hour?' All prevailing circumstances, in such a time cycle, lead even the most noble of men to have such a *bhaav*. Even a *saiyami* (person in control of his *kashays*) will have such intent.

However, the one who is in control of his *kashay* will internally say, 'Why are you creating such a negative cause from within, when on the outside you are so gracious?'

Your welcoming them nicely is an effect of causes laid in the past life. Through your *bhaav* (your current inner intent), however, you are sowing new seeds, which will give their effect in the next life. With your negative *bhaav*, you are creating a new account.

When faced with such a situation, you should ask God (within) for forgiveness by saying, 'Dear Lord, I have made a mistake due to the pressures of circumstances. I 'said' these words, but it is not my desire to speak thus. Let them stay.' Thus, if you wipe it off, that is your *purusharth*.       (238)

These strange times will indeed pressure you to have such *bhaav*. Even the highly elevated beings who have 'control' over their *kashays* will be prone to such pressures which create negative *bhaav*. If you erase the negative *bhaav* with *pratikraman*, then you will attain its benefits. Even the wife will erase it from within, knowing full well that although they have come unannounced, they won't go without eating or drinking.

So why have negativity? Instead, let's just welcome them for a nice meal.

So you have to solve it this way. If you do not, they are already here uninvited and they are not likely to leave until their time is up.

**Questioner:** We do not feed anyone at night, because we practice no food intake after sunset (*chovihar*).

**Dadashri:** So what do you tell them? Do you tell them that they will not get anything to eat?

**Questioner:** We tell them, no.

**Dadashri:** What if they ask for tea?

**Questioner:** We will say no to that as well, even if they asked for it.

**Dadashri:** Is that so? Then what do people do? They take them out to eat.

**Questioner:** It is one and the same thing if you take them out to eat at night.

**Dadashri:** Then what else can you do? Should you send them to bed hungry? Our people of India will never do that. That is our cultural values (*sanskar*).

The guests have come, and that is an unfolding of their karma as well as your karma. And so, they are not likely to leave until that karma is over.

Now what does the wife tell 'Chandubhai'? 'When are your relatives going to leave?' So he will say, 'They are not my relatives. They could have come from anywhere!' Then she will not mention the relatives.

People today are 'developed,' are they not? So the wife will say 'Your relatives,' and when her relatives come, he will say, 'They are your relatives,' so it causes conflict and, therefore, the people 'let go' of it.

Nowadays people have become open minded in such matters and they feel they do not want to interfere in this way and that. Ultimately the guests are going to stay, so we might as well accept in our minds that, as long as the unfolding of karmas remains, let them be. Once our karma and their karma come to and end, they will leave on their own. If you say this, then you will not have *artadhyan* or *raudradhyan*.

Now when they are leaving after four days, even if you tell them, 'Stay for today,' they will break free from your grip and leave, because that is now the unfolding karma. He will not stay at all. He does not stay of his own free will; his karma keeps him here. And on the last day, even if you force him to stay, he will push you aside and leave.

Therefore, he is karma-dependent, so what you should do is not ruin your next life. Your next life is created through *bhaavkarma* (cause karma). So it will be enough if you take care of this much.

If you take care of *artadhyan* and *raudradhyan*, at least your next life will be good!                                            (240)

## Next Life Improves if the Bhaav Does Not Get Spoilt

**Questioner:** What advice would you give? We have a custom in our home that everyone does *chovihar* (not eating after dark). So what about the guest who comes late at night, should we feed him or not?

**Dadashri:** Tell him (Chandulal),' 'Feed this guest.' Even if the man of the house blames me for this, it is not a problem. And truly you are not at fault. I give you this Agna, so the liability is mine. But feed him. Feed him when he asks for some food.

**Questioner:** It is said, in religious texts, that in such circumstances it is really the celestials that come uninvited (*atithi devo bhav*). What is the truth in all this?

**Dadashri:** That is precisely why this is written in the scriptures. It has been said from the beginning, so that people do not spoil their intent (*bhaav*). What does *atithi* mean? It means without the letter of announcement, without a written time (*tithi*). It is only when you see them at your doorstep that you realize, 'Oh, ho ho! Chandu Sheth is here!'

The intent within (*bhaav*) should not be spoiled by, 'Why the heck did he have to come at this time of the night?' The next life will improve if the *bhaav* is not spoilt. And if the *bhaav* is spoilt, then do *pratikraman* immediately. It is not worth doing (*artadhyan-raudradhyan*) at all.

## Accept the Insults and Become Free

Everything is karma effect. Even when someone curses you, that is the unfolding of your own karma. A man comes along and swears at 'Chandulal' four times in the presence of a hundred people. Now, You should know that it is the unfolding of your karma. You have to know that it is the unfolding of your karma and he became a *nimit* in it. So what do you have to do in your mind? Do not spoil the intent towards him; bless him in your mind, 'He has freed me from that karma. He has freed me from this karma.'

You became free from this karma after accepting the four swear words he gave you; You become lighter. Now, in the process of becoming free, all You have to do is make sure you do not sow new negative seeds.

People sow negative seeds when they are being insulted. In return for the four curse words, they will curse the other person five times. Hey, you! You cannot deal with four curse words and you turn around and dish out five words! Why not credit the four in your karma account? If you cannot tolerate this insult, why are you dishing out a new one?

This is how man wanders around life after life. People take on needless liabilities. Do not spoil the *bhaav* for anyone, and if you do, then correct it immediately. But learn the art of how to get your work done from all this, if you want to go to *moksha*. The Gnani Purush will teach you that art. He will teach you how to come out of it.

## Pratikraman Erases Bad Intent

**Dadashri:** What does one say? 'Why the heck did he have to come this time of the night?' How does that help him?

**Questioner:** No, it does not help him at all. On the contrary, it will create problems.

**Dadashri:** On the contrary, it ruins his next life.

**Questioner:** But, Dada, what if one repents and does *pratikraman* at that time? When *mahatmas* do *pratikraman*, they change their intent, but still the newer *bhaavs* (intents) remain, do they not? When he changes his bad *bhaav* into a good *bhaav*, for him the *bhaavkarma* still remains, does it not?

**Dadashri:** Doing *pratikraman* does not produce good intent from a bad intent. *Pratikraman* just washes off the mistake: 'I do *pratikraman* for the *atikraman* I did and I will not do the same again.'                                                (242)

## Consequences of Effect (Prarabdha-karma) and Binding of Karma

Karma is bound with belief and intent of 'I am Chandulal.' For you, now that You have attained Self-realization, the remaining karmas are *prarabdha-karma*. You eat, you drink, you sleep; you can do everything.

**Questioner:** You have said that one will get burned if he touches hot charcoal. We have the knowledge that we can get burned by hot charcoal, and yet if we accidentally touch it, we will still get burned, will we not? Will it not give its 'effect'? It can be said that it gave its effect, can it not?

**Dadashri:** That is called effect (*prarabdha*). An *agnani* (not Self-realized) binds karma because of his belief, 'I am Chandulal.' When this belief breaks, he becomes free from karma bondage.

**Questioner:** So, Dada, it is correct by Gnan, but when he is doing something and he has bad thoughts, does he have to do *pratikraman*?

**Dadashri:** 'You' do not have to do *pratikraman*. 'You' have to make him ('Chandulal') do *pratikraman*. You have to erase the liability, do you not? When you do *pratikraman*, you are erasing the liability. You have to say, 'Chandubhai, why did you do *atikraman*? Now do *pratikraman*,' and thus You erase the liability.

**Questioner:** And if *pratikraman* is not done, is there danger of liability?

**Dadashri:** That is what remains. You will have to do *pratikraman*. Instead, is it not better to go ahead and do the *pratikraman*? 'Why did you do *atikraman*? So now do *pratikraman*.' Otherwise, after attaining this Gnan, all that remains is for one to suffer the effect of karma (*prarabdha*).

**Questioner:** *Atikraman* occurs while suffering the *prarabdha- karma*, but...

**Dadashri:** *Pratikraman* has to be done. 'You' have to make him ('Chandulal') do it and make him wash.

**Questioner:** What occurs if he does not wash it?

**Dadashri:** It will have to be washed again.

**Questioner:** 'Again' means how many more lifetimes will it take?

**Dadashri:** One or two more lifetimes. It is all your responsibility, no one else's. 'Chandubhai' did something wrong – and so You tell 'Chandubhai' that he did *atikraman* and so he has to do *pratikraman*. You have to make him do the 'washing.' 'You stained the cloth and so you do the washing.'

**Questioner:** Dada, this is a chore and a lot of work for 'Chandulal,' so he will avoid doing *pratikraman*. Therefore, *upayog* will not remain.

**Dadashri:** That (doing *pratikraman*) verily is applied awareness (*upayog*).

**Questioner:** Then awareness cannot be maintained if *atikraman* continues to occur the whole day.

**Dadashri:** That, itself, is the applied awareness (*upayog*).

**Questioner:** What applied awareness is that?

**Dadashri:** That is pure (*shuddha*) applied awareness (*upayog*).

**Questioner:** But what about the *atikraman* that occurred?

**Dadashri:** Yes, but making him do *pratikraman* is *shuddha upayog* (pure applied awareness).

**Questioner:** *Pratikraman* or the *atikraman*?

**Dadashri:** To make him do *pratikraman* for the *atikraman* he did, is *shuddha upayog* (pure, applied awareness). You have nothing to do with *atikraman*. You just have to know (*jaanyoo*) that *atikraman* occurred, and *pratikraman* is *shuddha upayog*.

**Questioner:** Generally, what if in an hour, five to twenty-five *atikramans* occurred?

**Dadashri:** Then do collective *pratikraman* for them.

**Questioner:** How do I do that? What should I say?

**Dadashri:** Confess that you have committed so many *atikramans* and that you are doing *pratikraman* for them all collectively. Specify your topic. For example, address your mistakes related to hurtful speech or anger, etc., and for each topic say that you are doing collective *pratikraman*. Everything will be resolved this way. If you cannot complete your *pratikraman*, you will be able to do so later. Just do not procrastinate, or else you will forgo doing them all together. You do not need to complicate the matter.

*****

## Release from Bondage of Inner Enemies

### Pratikraman Whenever Abhorrence Arises

This is all worldly misery. Whatever thoughts you have about him, do *pratikraman* for that repeatedly. For any thoughts that may occur on a given day, keep doing *pratikraman*, that is all. Erase them all immediately. With *pratikraman*, all your attacking thoughts will cease. Then the mind will not have any abhorrence. When the mind becomes irritated with someone, it will stop if you do *pratikraman* in his name. (245)

**Questioner:** Should *pratikraman* be done in the mind, by reading or by saying it?

**Dadashri:** No, just within the mind. You can do it in the mind, you can say it out loud, or in any other way, such as, 'I have made some mistake towards you and for that I am asking for Your forgiveness.' It will do even if you say it in your mind. Do *pratikraman* for the mental attack; that is all. People of a lower socio-economic class physically hit others, whereas we do it with words. Or else people hurt others with their minds. Do people hit others with words or not?

**Questioner:** Yes, they do.

**Dadashri:** The ladies will say, 'His words hurt me so badly that they are etched in my heart!' And even hurting others with the mind, it is all of the same family.

**Questioner:** 'With the mind' means without saying anything?

**Dadashri:** If he uses words, she will strike back. So then he will 'strike' her with his mind. Even the wife will strike her husband with her mind if he has a tendency to retaliate. She will say in her mind, 'I will take care of him when the time is right,' and then she waits for the right moment!

**Questioner:** In a situation if someone is saying negative things about me, I end up reacting angrily and saying things out loud in anger and attack. Which is worse, hurting others through spoken words or just through the mind?

**Dadashri:** Saying through words? Did you fight with him through words?

**Questioner:** Yes.

**Dadashri:** Quarrels created through words will give their effect here and now, and will dissipate right away, whereas quarrels through the mind will progress further. When you say things verbally, the other person will answer back and so you will face the consequences right away. But quarrels fought though the mind will sow seeds first, then, when that karma matures, it will give fruits. So now you are sowing the seeds – creating the cause. So you should do *pratikraman* so that this 'cause' is not created.

## Pratikraman for Attachment

**Questioner:** All the *pratikramans* we have done so far are for anger (*krodh*) or abhorrence (*dwesh*) that occurred. But do we have to do *pratikraman* for attachment (*raag*), or not?

**Dadashri:** You do not have to do *pratikraman* for attachment (*raag*). All you have to do is stop *raag*. That is all.

**Questioner:** How can we stop that?

**Dadashri:** 'I want to become *vitarag*, so I have to stop *raag*.' If you want to reach another station (*vitarag*) fast, then don't you have to get up from where you are right now (station of *raag*)? That is how you stop *raag*.

That is because after attaining Gnan, both attachment and abhorrence are in the form of discharge. Abhorrence will hurt the other person; it will have an effect on him. Therefore, you should do *pratikraman* and it will wash it off. Whereas *raag* is not going to do anything to the other person and, because it is a discharge, it will go away on its own. And, therefore, it is going to go away, whether you do *pratikraman* or not. Hence, nothing will happen even if you do not do *pratikraman* for *raag*.

As in your business, if someone owes you one million rupees and you owe some other person half a million rupees, the one whom you owe money will come to collect his money. Now, if he comes to collect at two o'clock in the morning, you have to pay him off because you want to go to *moksha*. And if you do not get your money owed to you from the other person, you can make a compromise or write it off. That is how it is with *raag* and *dwesh*.

**Questioner:** Does that mean that there is no problem with *raag*, and that *dwesh* is the problem? Does *raag* prevent spiritual progress towards full enlightenment?

**Dadashri:** Whatever *raag* is in your *karmic* stock is bound to arise and it is not going to increase, because it is a discharge. It does not hinder us. It is a *karmic* stock which is bound to come out, is it not? You are not doing any *raag*, it is just the *karmic* stock; it occurs. The only thing is that you speak sweetly with the ones you have *raag* for. That is all. It is all a discharge. You were supposed to obstruct it but now it has become a discharge.

So now, you should remain in the Agnas of the Gnani Purush, should you not? If you remain in the Agnas, then you are constantly the Self. No matter what you are doing, whether you are working or anything else, if you remain in the Agnas, then you are constantly the Self.

**Questioner:** How can one remain in the Agnas where there is *raag*?

**Dadashri:** What do you call *raag* and *dwesh*; what is the definition of *raag* and *dwesh*? Cause-*raag* (charge-*raag*) is considered as *raag*. Effect-*raag* (discharge-*raag*) is not considered *raag*. The *raag* that you have now is not a cause-*raag*. It is effect-*raag* because you have become a *Shuddhatma*. *Shuddhatma* does not have any *raag-dwesh* and the effect all belongs to 'Chandulal.'

If there is effect-*raag* or effect-*dwesh*, You have to tell 'Chandulal,' 'Why are you attacking when something wrong occurs? Therefore, do *pratikraman*.' And you do not have to do anything for *raag*, do you understand?                    (248)

If awareness of separation cannot be maintained during *raag*, if one cannot remain in the Agnas, then he has to do *pratikraman*.

## Self-Respect and Moksha

**Questioner:** Is there a way one can do *pratikraman* without losing his self-respect (*swamaan*)?

**Dadashri:** You can do *pratikraman*. Where does self-respect have any problem with *pratikraman*? How is self-respect lost in doing *pratikraman*? There is no such thing as self-respect in front of the Lord (the Lord within), is there? Self-respect is an issue with people. There is nothing wrong in showing helplessness in front of the Lord. You should not become helpless in front of people. Self-respect means you should not become helpless in front of others. And he that becomes free of self-respect, becomes entitled to *moksha*.

## The Effect of Pride with 'My-ness' Upon Others

**Questioner:** What should I do so that the pride or arrogance (*abhimaan*) does not cause any problem or hurt to others? How can I give happiness to others?

**Dadashri:** Just have this inner intent (*bhaav*), nothing else. Just maintain the *bhaav*, 'May no one be hurt because of my extra pride (*abhimaan*) and may people become happy.' And then, if someone does get hurt, do *pratikraman* and move on. What else can you do? Should you stay up the whole night for that? You do not have to do that. And it is not possible to stay up even if you want to. Then what will you do?

Nevertheless, you still have to be careful so that no one gets hurt because of your actions.

**Questioner:** In that sense, the entire worldly life is a result of the ego. The result of 'I am Chandulal' is the entire worldly life, is it not?

**Dadashri:** But now, after attaining Gnan, that ego is gone for You. If that ego was still there, then new consequences would continue to arise. New consequences do not arise after attaining this Gnan. And the old ones (effect in this life of causes created in the past life) keep going away. The old ones will go away. The ultimate solution (liberation) is at hand. That 'tank' (cycle of cause and effect of karma) is not being filled anew. Some people have a fifty-gallon tank and some have a two-hundred and fifty thousand gallon tank. The bigger the tank, the longer it will take to empty it. But it has started to drain for sure. For the one for whom it is emptying, what does it matter?

**Questioner:** But as it is emptying, like the force of the flood water, it will topple someone, and it may even collide with someone and kill him!

**Dadashri:** Yes, all that is its result. What does that have to do with You, the Self? But if someone gets hurt then you should do *pratikraman*.

## Anger and Its Reactions

**Questioner:** How should I do *pratikraman* for the anger

that arises within?

**Dadashri:** After this Gnan, anger never arises for You at all. The *taanto* (the prolonged feeling of grudge that continues linked with a conflict) that remains in the non-Self is what we consider as anger. There is no *taanto* (link of grudge) that remains after attaining the Gnan. Now there is only 'residual fieriness (*ugrata*),' and that is the attribute of the subatomic particles (*parmanus*).

After attaining this Gnan, anger, pride, deceit and greed all go away. If this man gets angry (*krodh*), someone else may say, 'He was just irritated (*gusso*).' I would tell him that there is a difference between *krodh* and *gusso*. *Gusso* is a *paudgalik* thing, meaning it is of the non-Self. *Krodh* (anger) is where there is a coming together of both the non-Self and the Self, where one becomes the non-Self. What is the difference between *gusso* and *krodh*? In *krodh* there is a violent intent (*himsak bhaav*) behind it. This man here does not have a violent intent. He may exhibit *gusso* (anger without violent intent) but he is doing *pratikraman* at the same time. Do you do that or not? He is constantly doing *pratikraman*.

He does not have *taanto* (link of grudge). What does *taanto* mean? It means that if you had a disagreement the night before, the next morning you will hear tea cups banging and doors of the cupboards in the kitchen slamming!          (250)

People of the world have live anger (*sajiv krodh*), whereas You (Self-realized) have dead anger (*nirjiv krodh*). But with whose *nimit* does this dead anger occur? The poor man does incur some damage, does he not?

## Difference between Krodh and Gusso

If there is a *taanto* (continued grudge linked with a certain disagreement) and violent intent (*himsak bhaav*), it is called *krodh*, it is called pride (*maan*), it is called greed (*lobh*). It is called *kashay*. That is what the *Tirthankar* Lord has said. Nevertheless, if *gusso* (anger without violent intent) still occurs, and you happen to say something that hurts someone, You have to tell 'Chandulal,' 'You are seventy-four years old now, why don't you behave yourself? Do *pratikraman* and repent and ask yourself why you had to do that.' Can you tell him this much or not?

**Questioner:** I can. I should say it.

**Dadashri:** No matter how important a government official he ('Chandubhai') is, do not be shy here in telling him off. Tell him, 'You need to smarten up now; you are seventy-four years old.' So apologize in this manner if you hurt someone. There is no problem with *kraman* (neutral actions) but the problem is with *atikraman*. Even the government considers *atikraman* breaking of law. Do you understand? There is nothing wrong in saying what all the others are saying, normal conversations. But he will say the strangest things. Even others listening will wonder, 'Oh no! Why should he say such things?' That is *atikraman*. If a person has dishonest intention or ulterior motives, it is *atikraman*.

When the *taanto* goes away, recognize that anger, pride, deceit and greed are no longer there. You have now become *shuddha* (pure); you are the Knower-Seer and in eternal bliss. 'You' have to continue 'Seeing' what 'Chandubhai' is doing. Who will run 'Chandubhai's life? The energy known as 'scientific circumstantial evidences' (*vyavasthit shakti*) will run his life and it will run it very well.

If *gusso* (anger without violent intent) occurs and it hurts the other person, even if it is not *krodh* (anger with violent intent), if it hurts the other person, You may now believe that you are *Shuddhatma* but You have to make the one who did *atikraman*, do *pratikraman*. Therefore, 'Chandulal,' the doer of *atikraman*, should be told to do *pratikraman*. 'You' do not

have to do it. There is no need for You to do *pratikraman* after
You become the Self. But make the one who did *atikraman*,
Your neighbor 'Chandulal,' do *pratikraman*.

Anger, pride, deceit and greed are not going to occur
now, but if you become very angry with your child, then ask
'Chandulal,' 'Why are you becoming so impatient with your
child? How bad will she feel? Ask for forgiveness from her from
within. You do not have to ask her in person, but ask for
forgiveness from within and say that you will not do it again.'
Otherwise, if you don't hurt her, then you don't have to ask for
forgiveness.

**Questioner:** *Pratikraman* does not occur when the links
of *kashay* continue.

**Dadashri:** *Pratikraman* occurs very late in intense
emotional upheaval with overt clash (*udvega*) and in a *taanto*,
it takes a little while. *Udvega* is tantamount to 'bombarding,'
whereas *taanto* is tantamount to 'tear gas.' It is like the
suffocation one experiences when tear gas is released. (252)

## To 'See' the Prakruti is Purusharth

**Questioner:** That is right. Whenever I get angry, from
within there is a *bhaav* of, 'This is wrong. You should not be
angry.'

**Dadashri:** That is correct. You have to tell 'Chandulal,'
'Do *pratikraman*. Why did you do *atikraman*?'

**Questioner:** When the anger arises, the awareness arises
at the same time, which says, 'Why is this 'Chandulal' doing
this? It is wrong.' But will this anger make me take a severe fall
some day in the future? What should I do?

**Dadashri:** No one will make you fall. They are corpses.
How can they make the living fall? Every *pudgal* (non-Self
complex) is a corpse. They cannot touch You. Just tell them, 'I

am Dada's. What are you doing here? Are you not ashamed?' All you have to do is take Dada's name.

**Questioner:** So I feel that such anger will send me back into the cycles of birth and death. It will create new *karmic* bondage.

**Dadashri:** How is it going to do that? That poor thing (anger) is neutral. What you say is applicable to those who are under the control of anger (those who do not have Self-realization). We are not under its control.

And if *pratikraman* is not being done, You can tell 'Chandulal,' 'Sir, do *pratikraman.*'

**Questioner:** Does anger arise first and then *pratikraman* starts?

**Dadashri:** They will start... both will occur simultaneously.

**Questioner:** Anger is continuing and *pratikraman* also occurs. They both occur simultaneously. Both fight each other. *Atikraman* against *pratikraman*.

**Dadashri:** Then nothing will remain. *Karmic* accounts (*hisaab*) are being cleared life after life. That is the *prakruti* (non-Self) and You are Purush (Self), *Shuddhatma*. Nothing touches *Shuddhatma*. The Self is the Knower-Seer (*Gnata-Drashta*). To continue 'seeing' the *prakruti* is *purusharth*.

Now you have become the Purush (the Self) and this is *prakruti* (the non-Self). 'You' (Purush) have to keep 'seeing' what this *prakruti* is doing. Whether it ('Chandulal,' *prakruti*) is doing the good or the bad, You have nothing to do with it. You (the 'Seer') are separate. It is just like watching a gigantic bonfire. Is the Seer not separate from the fire? Say your home is on fire, it is burning like a big bonfire, and You are 'seeing' it; you will not get burned. And the moment you say, 'My home is burning down,' you will get burned.

**Questioner:** The 'Seer' does not have 'my-ness' (*mamata*).

**Dadashri:** The 'Seer' does not have 'my-ness'; he is a spectator. You do not have 'my-ness'; 'we' removed it from you. You surrendered 'my-ness (*mamata*)' to 'Me' (Dada).

When You remain the 'Seer,' the *prakruti* will dissolve; that many karmas are gone.

## A Mistake of Discharge is a Lifeless Mistake

**Questioner:** Agitations caused by *atikraman* cool down with *pratikraman*?

**Dadashri:** Yes. One cools down. For 'sticky files,' in the excess of five thousand *pratikramans* need to be done before things cool down. Even if anger is not expressed externally, the irritation it creates will leave stains within if you do not do *pratikraman* for it. It will clear when you do *pratikraman*. Do *pratikraman* if you do *atikraman*.

**Questioner:** If I become angry with someone and then, at the same time, I realize that I have done something wrong and do *pratikraman*, what is that?

**Dadashri:** After attaining Gnan, when you ask for forgiveness for becoming angry with someone, then there is no problem; you are free. If you cannot apologize in person, then do so from within, and that is enough.

**Questioner:** In person, in front of everyone?      (254)

**Dadashri:** There is no problem if you do not do it in person, but do it from within; it is acceptable. This is because the mistake is not alive – it is a discharge. Discharge means that it is not living and it will not bring about that bad of a result.

## Instant Results with Sincere Pratikraman

**Questioner:** I became very angry with someone and I

lashed out, and we had a quarrel. And then, despite the silence, the inner turmoil continued. Can I do just one *pratikraman* to cover everything or do I have to do individual *pratikraman* for each fault?

**Dadashri:** Do *pratikraman* wholeheartedly two to three times and, if done in the exact method, everything will be resolved. Do it this way: Say, 'Dear Dada Bhagwan, a very grave mistake has occurred. Severe anger has taken place. How much hurt has it caused the other person? I am sincerely repenting for it and asking for his forgiveness with You as my witness. I am sincerely asking for forgiveness from his pure Soul.'

Who is asking for forgiveness? It is not to be asked by You. 'Chandulal' has to ask for forgiveness. The one who does *atikraman* has to do *pratikraman*. *Atikraman* is never done by You.

## Collective Pratikraman

**Questioner:** When prolonged arguments occur, the result is a greater rift within and aloofness from the other person. Sometimes I do a few *pratikramans*, and in other instances I have to do it five to six times. The question is, if I just do *pratikraman* once, will it suffice?

**Dadashri:** Do as many as you can individually. If it is not possible, do them collectively. If you come across too many at once, do them all together and state that you are doing them collectively, because you cannot do *pratikraman* for each and every one of your mistakes. Address your *pratikraman* to Dada Bhagwan and the message will reach him.

## Apology in Person

**Questioner:** Dada, many times it so happens that when I make a mistake, or become angry towards someone, from within I feel restless and uneasy. I know that I have done something wrong, but I do not have the courage to ask for forgiveness form him directly.

**Dadashri:** You should not even ask for forgiveness in that way. On the contrary, he will misuse the apology. He will say, 'Yes, now you have come to your senses.' That is how everything is. People are not noble these days. These people are not worthy of direct apologies. There may be ten in a thousand who will give in even before you ask them for forgiveness. Do you understand? Otherwise, he will say, 'See, I have been telling you for a long time. You did not believe me, did you? Now you have come to your senses, haven't you?' That is why you should ask for forgiveness, from his *Shuddhatma*, from within.

## That is Not Your Lookout (Concern)

**Questioner:** When I become very angry with someone, I do instant *pratikraman* for that mistake. Does the effect of the anger from my side, continue to linger within that person, or does it stop as soon as I do *pratikraman*?

**Dadashri:** You should not concern yourself with what is occurring within the other person. Just keep washing your 'clothes' and keep them clean. He came in front of you because of his and your past life account. Anger occurred even though you do not want it to. Anger arises against your wishes, does it not?

**Questioner:** Yes. Anger occurs.                          (256)

**Dadashri:** Then do not worry about that; continue doing *pratikraman*. Make 'Chandulal' do the *pratikraman* and he will handle the situation however it needs to be handled. If you become too concerned about it, you will ruin everything. Your job is to remain aware of the mistakes that occur.

## Dealing with Your Employees

**Questioner:** When we are very angry with someone, we begin to talk negatively about him in his absence.

**Dadashri:** That is called 'kashay.' When one comes under someone else's (the non-Self's) control, it is kashay. Then the anger-pride-deceit-greed take over. You know that it is wrong to speak negatively about someone in his absence, but you do it all the same. Sometimes you will become aware of it and sometimes it will pass, unnoticed. You will become aware of it sooner or later. This can only occur if you were the Knower of the mistake when it was occurring. The fact that you repent the event later means you were in fact aware as a Knower when the mistake was occurring.

**Questioner:** In my office, I have three to four secretaries. Despite multiple instructions on repeated occasions, they continue to make the same mistakes. This results in my getting angry and frustrated with them. What should I do?

**Dadashri:** You are now the pure Self, so how can You become angry? Anger comes to 'Chandulal,' so You should tell him, 'You have met Dada now. What reason is there for you to become so angry?'

**Questioner:** But those secretaries do not improve at all. Unless I say something to them, they will not change.

**Dadashri:** You can tell 'Chandulal' that he can scold his secretary with equanimity. He should scold her in a dramatic manner like, 'If you continue to be inefficient, your job will be at risk.'

**Questioner:** If I say that, she would feel hurt and you have said that we should not hurt anyone.

**Dadashri:** She would not feel hurt if you speak to her in a dramatic (natakiya) manner. In doing so, the ego does not arise in your words. This results in her becoming aware in her mind, and she will make a decision to improve. You are not hurting her in doing so. You can only hurt her if your intention is to hurt, like, 'I am going to straighten her out.' Then she will get hurt.

And then having told her, immediately tell 'Chandubhai', 'You made a mistake (*atikraman*) by speaking harsh words, so do *pratikraman*.' Then ask for forgiveness in your mind. But do speak with the secretary and then do the *pratikraman*. Do both together. You have to run your worldly life too, do you not?

## Discharge Abhorrence after Gnan

**Questioner:** Do I incur a *karmic* liability when I fire an employee who does not do his work? Or is it *vyavasthit* (scientific circumstantial evidences)?

**Dadashri:** That is not a mistake. When there is no attachment-abhorrence (*raag-dwesh*), it is just a play of the *pudgals* (non-Self complexes). One gets trapped where there is attachment-abhorrence. *Raag-dwesh* no longer remains after one attains Self-realization. If they did, then one would be liable. But now it is all in the form of discharge; it is discharge abhorrence (*dwesh*). There is no serious liability there.

Any action done is with either attachment (*raag*) or abhorrence (*dwesh*). After Gnan, attachment and abhorrence do not occur. Where there is no attachment-abhorrence, there are only the non-Self complexes (*pudgals*) clashing with each other. The one who 'sees' all that is the Self. If you become engrossed in it, then you will take a beating. When does one become engrossed in it? It is when there is a lot of entanglement (stickiness) with the discharge. But then You have to tell 'Chandubhai' to do *pratikraman* so that it will wash off.

If you remain the Knower and the Seer of the anger that occurs, it will leave. The subatomic particles (*parmanus*) of anger will become cleansed and they will dissipate. This much is Your obligation.                                           (258)

**Questioner:** Is the *pratikraman* I do after becoming angry called '*purusharth*' (spiritual effort) or '*parakram*' (extraordinary spiritual effort)?

**Dadashri:** That is called *purusharth*. It is not called *parakram*.

**Questioner:** Then what is *parakram*?

**Dadashri:** *Parakram* is higher than *purusharth*. This is certainly not *parakram*. How can you call this *parakram* when you are nursing a burn with a healing ointment? One 'knows' all this and one also 'knows' this 'Knower.' That is *parakram*. Doing *pratikraman* is *purusharth*. With continued *pratikraman*, everything, including verbal conflict, will decrease. Everything will decrease naturally. The ego is the first to go and then everything else will follow. Everything will fall into place and you will experience stillness from within. And there is peace within. Do you feel such peace?

**Questioner:** Absolutely, Dada.

**Dadashri:** Yes. Then that is all we need.

## The Spiritual Stages

**Questioner:** Please explain the fourteen spiritual stages (*gunasthanaks*)?

**Dadashri:** The first three *gunasthanaks* are of no use. They will not do for *moksha*. In those stages, one simply goes to temples; that is all. He just wanders around, life after life. When one attains right belief (*samkit*), he enters the fourth *gunasthanak*. Before that there is wandering around in the first three stages. There is enlightenment in the fourth *gunasthanak*. One progresses from there on. He then comes into the fifth. Then, as he does more and more *pratikraman*, he goes to the sixth. That is how one progresses by doing *pratikraman*.

## Four Levels of Intensity of Kashay

What have the writers of scripture written? Suppose this

man says something that breaks this woman's heart, such that it will not mend in her entire life. Her mind is permanently fractured. It cannot be mended. The scripture writers call this '*anantanubandhi krodh*' – anger that will make one bind karma for infinite lives.

Another kind of anger is one where she will not speak with him for a year or so. Her wounds will heal after a year and the anger will be gone. What is this kind of anger called? It is 'anger for which one did not do *pratikraman*' (*apratyakhyani krodh*). Because *pratikramans* were not done in the past life, the anger occurred.

**Questioner:** Is it the same anger that occurred in the past that is expressing now?

**Dadashri:** No. Not like that. If *pratikraman* is not done after anger occurs, then the anger will come out with the same intensity and force again. If one does not do *pratikraman* after anger, it will last for a year (*apratyakhyani krodh*). And if he does *pratikraman*, it will last for fifteen days. They will forget everything and become friends again within fifteen days. That is called *pratyakhyani krodh*.

The *anantanubandhi krodh* is anger that will ruin the entire life. It is like a big crack, of a foot or two, that forms between rock cliffs. No matter how much gets filled in it, the crack will still remain.

As compared to that, the one that lasts for a year or so is *apratyakhyani krodh*. That is comparable to the cracks that form in the earth in the farms and the fields. They will eventually fill up after a year.

Then there is the anger that lasts fifteen days or so. That is *pratyakhyani krodh*. It is like the markings in the sand. If you write in the sand on a beach, what will occur with that writing? How long will it be before it is erased?

**Questioner:** Immediately. If the wind blows, it will be erased immediately.

**Dadashri:** It will get smudged if the wind blows. It may take one hour or two hours. That is called *pratyakhyani krodh*.

(260)

And the fourth one is like a line one draws in the sand under water. It will get erased immediately. That is called 'a line in the water.' It is called *sanjvalan krodh*. Not all *mahatmas* have anger like 'a line in the water.' For most, it will mend after a fortnight or so. For some, it is like the line drawn in the sand in the water.

This is something that the intellect (*buddhi*) will accept, is it not?

**Questioner:** This is something that the self (*atma*) will accept.

**Dadashri:** Which *atma* are you talking about? The *vyavahar atma*, the *pratishthit atma* (the relative self)? It is all a play of the intellect (*buddhi*). And which kind of *atma* will be there? It is all *vyavahar atma* (the relative self). The main *Atma* (the Self) knows even all this; it 'knows' everything.

## Apratyakhyan Avaran Kashay

**Questioner:** Once the *anantanubandhi kashay* breaks, is overcome, it will go into the descending level and thus gradually decreases?

**Dadashri:** It can also increase. But when *apratyakhyan kashay* comes, it means that it is *kashay* for which one has never done *pratikraman* or *pratyakhyan* in the past life. That is why all the *kashays* that come, come because one has failed to do *pratyakhyan*. So once *pratikraman* and *pratyakhyan* start, and one continues to do them, then as a consequence of that he will move from the fifth into the sixth *gunasthanak*.

What occurs in the sixth *gunasthanak*? *Pratyakhyan avaran kashay* arises!

## Pratyakhyan Avaran Kashay

What does *pratyakhyan avaran* mean? It means *kashays* occur even when one does *pratikraman* and *pratyakhyan*. The ones that come have so many layers. Those with few layers are gone, but those with many layers are *pratyakhyan avaran*.

They will not go away even after hundreds of thousands of *pratikramans*.

**Questioner:** What kind of mistakes are they?

**Dadashri:** They are called *pratyakhyan avaran*. They do not go away even after one does *pratyakhyan*.

**Questioner:** What is the major reason behind it?

**Dadashri:** They are very deep and very thick. If an onion has five thousand layers, would it not look the same even if you peel off a layer at a time? This is like a layer of a kind, a veil of a kind (*avaran*). Everyone has one or two of these, not too many.

**Questioner:** They keep coming back, again and again.

**Dadashri:** Yes, they will keep coming back.

**Questioner:** But will they not leave, sooner or later?

**Dadashri:** They will begin to leave. As the *karmic* account (*hisaab*) matures, it will become less. There is no problem with them going. They will go away for sure, but what kind of problems do they create today? Despite doing *pratikraman* and *pratyakhyan*, they come back.

Hence, you created *pratyakhyan avaran* by doing *pratyakhyan* for *apratyakhyan avaran*. So now, what about the *pratyakhyan avaran* that is created?

**Questioner:** Does that become a layer too?

**Dadashri:** Yes, you remove the stain with the 'soap,' but what about the residual stains the soap leaves behind? So that is *pratyakhyan avaran*.

So when it becomes clean this way, it is *pratyakhyan avaran*. If mistakes occur, despite doing *pratyakhyan*, that is called *pratyakhyan avaran kashay*. That is because *pratikraman* was done in bulk.

## Sanjvalan Kashay

When there is constant *pratikraman-pratyakhyan*, it is called *pratyakhyan avaran*. That is the sixth *gunasthanak*; or *gunthanu* (spiritual stage). One is doing *pratyakhyan* of the past *apratyakhyan*. When can we say that the ascetic has reached the sixth *gunasthanak* of the real (*nischay*) and of relative (*vyavahar*)? It is when *pratikraman-pratyakhyan* occurs every moment. The *pratyakhyan* of the past life comes into unfolding today and, consequently, one is able to renounce naturally.                                               (262)

So what is the sixth *gunasthanak*? *Kashays* become effective. They become evident in their effect. They are not just concepts, but their effect is visible. They become effective despite *pratikraman*, therefore, despite *pacchkhani* (*pratyakhyani*) *pratikraman*, they still remain. Because it is a large *karmic* tuber, it is considered *pratyakhyani*. It is a *pratyakhyan avaran*. But if it comes into maturation from within, but does not become effective, expressed externally, then it is considered *sanjvalan*. It will not cause one to slap someone, or something like that. There is suffering within in the *pratyakhyan avaran*. But when one experiences *samadhi* (absolutely unaffected state) within, that is when one will understand what all this is about. So this is completely a different thing.

Anger, pride, deceit and greed are *pratyakhyani*, meaning

others will not know about them. Even a clever person will not be able to measure through his intellect (*buddhi*) whether or not a person has anger within him. Only the person who has it will be aware of it. That is *pratyakhyani*! So, what can you say about the one for whom the five major vows (*mahavrats*) are natural in his conduct? It would be more than enough if there was one such person in this current time cycle. Those *pratyakhyani kashays* are gone and, therefore, only the *sanjvalan kashays* remain.

## The Sixth to the Ninth Gunasthanaks

The *vyavahar* (worldly interaction) *gunasthanak* (stage of spiritual development) qualities of everyone will keep on changing. Some will come into the fourth, some -into the fifth and some into the sixth *gunasthanak*. Before, their *kashays* were *apratyakhyan*, *apratikraman* and now, because of *alochana*, *pratikraman* and *pratyakhyan*, even the *apratyakhyan avarans* have gone.

Those who have heavy 'files' in the worldly life are considered to be at the sixth *gunasthanak*.

What is the sixth *gunasthanak* in the worldly life interaction? It is not the one where one renounces a wife or a husband, but it is the one where there is no *apratyakhyan avaran*. You see the same thing again even after doing *pratyakhyan*; it is like seeing another layer of an onion. That is *pratyakhyan avaran*. If ever that *pratyakhyan avaran* goes away for an hour, then that is *apramat gunasthanak*, and that is the seventh *gunasthanak*. And rarely there comes the eighth *gunasthanak* where there is nothing but bliss! That is called *apurva gunasthanak*. But one cannot cross over to the ninth *gunasthanak* as long as there is sexuality (*stri parigraha*).

## Total Absence of Any Kashay

There should not be the slightest of anger in this body.

There should not be even a single *parmanu* (subatomic particle) of anger in this body. When there is not a single *parmanu* of greed, not a single *parmanu* of pride, not a single *parmanu* of deceit, then one is called a God.

**Questioner:** Should *kashay* end completely?

**Dadashri:** All the *kashays* are gone, but not even a *parmanu* of it should remain thereafter. Thereafter, it would not be there even in the form of an effect (discharge). Departure of *kashays* means there are no more causes of *kashays* being created. It means all effects of *kashays* are gone from the body; no trace of effect remains in the body. Right now, Your causes are gone but you still have *kashays* in the form of discharge (effect) stuck somewhere within.

**Questioner:** Even the discharge is gone completely?

**Dadashri:** Yes, I have seen such a state. That is when the absolute Self form (*mood swaroop*) arises. That is when total experience (*anubhav*) of the Self will arise, otherwise not. The Self cannot be seen. Where there is absence of *kashays* is verily where the Self is.                                              (264)

**Questioner:** And is that the state of complete absence of *kashays*?

**Dadashri:** That is impossible in this era of the current time cycle. And in *sushamkaal* (auspicious time cycle) there is no such thing as impossible.

**Questioner:** Therefore, it does not exist even in the origin of *kashay*. It does not exist even where it originates from.

**Dadashri:** Not even there.

## Religious Instructions with Kashays Lead to Hell

**Questioner:** Does that mean there is no *kashay* at all?

**Dadashri:** That is when this Gnan arises. So as far as this special seat is concerned, I tell all the gurus who come to me, 'Maharaj Sahib, I request you never to give discourses.' So they ask me, 'Why, what is wrong with us?' I tell them, 'If you want to go to hell, then carry on. This is the greatest sign for going to hell.' Now tell me, how would they realize this liability? How can a man full of mistakes find a mistake?

**Questioner:** One can never see his own mistakes.

**Dadashri:** They will not let go if they cannot see, will they? One can see the kind of mistakes that will take him to hell. Giving religious instructions (*prarupana*) in the presence of *kashay* is the sign of going to hell. Therefore, one should not give religious discourses if one has *kashays* within him. Now, which *kashays*? It is a rule that those who have *pratyakhyan avaran kashays* have a right to give discourses. It is those who have *anantanubandhi kashays*; those who have not attained *samkit* (the right vision) have *anantanubandhi* for sure. If you ask them if they have attained *samkit*, they will tell you, 'No, we have not.' They do not have the right belief (*samkit*). The one who gives spiritual instructions in the presence of *anantanubandhi kashay* is considered *mithyatvi* – one under illusion. What is it called?

**Questioner:** *Mithyatvi.*

**Dadashri:** And *mithyatvi* means poisonous. Therefore, the Lord has said that if a *mithyatvi* reads the speech of *Tirthankars*, it becomes poison. And if there is *mithyatvi* speech, *mithyatvi* books, or religious books, if ever an enlightened being (*samkit jiva*) were to read them, it becomes nectar (*amrut*). This is because, when milk is placed in a snake's mouth, it becomes poison.

Today, everywhere there are signs of people going to hell. If 'we' say this openly, it will incite violence and anger and so 'we' do not say anything. What is the fun of speaking words others do not understand? If someone were to ask me, I would tell them. One lady actually did stop giving sermons and came to take Gnan. That *mahasati* (a nun in Jainism) said, 'I am giving two discourses a day. I feel like giving religious instructions. This I know is going to land me in hell. If I take Gnan from you, will I be able to give religious instructions freely?' I said, 'Yes, you can.' Then she took Gnan. The outcome for those who are on such religious paths and have taken Gnan has been very good.

## Veils of Ignorance Can Only Be Destroyed with the Right Vision

**Questioner:** When the Knower, who is established in the Self, has to face unfolding of his karma, does he not become controlled by those circumstances?

**Dadashri:** No, he is the Knower of the unfolding circumstance (*udaya*). When he remains the Knower (*Gnata*) of the unfolding karma, he is considered to be the Knower (*Gnayak swabhav*). And when he is not the Knower of the karma effect, he is under the control of those circumstances (*udayavash*).

**Questioner:** Dada, when one becomes the Knower once, will he ever be controlled by the circumstances?

**Dadashri:** He will come under control of circumstances. When the unfolding karmas are very heavy and sticky, then he will become controlled by them. That is why we have these *pratyakhyan avaran kashays*. I used to think a lot about them, 'Oh, ho ho! What kind of *kashay* is this *pratyakhyan avaran kashay*?' I used to think a lot about them before I attained Gnan. Because what did people say? They said *avirat kashays* (never-ending *kashays*) means *anantanubandhi*, and then after that comes *apratyakhyani*. What are the *kashays*, for which no *pratikraman* and *pratyakhyan* has been done, called?

*'Apratyakhyani.'*

**Questioner:** Now, the process of going from *anantanubandhi* into *apratyakhyani*, and then into the *pratyakhyani*... is *samkit drashti* (right vision) behind that process?                                                                (266)

**Dadashri:** It verily is the *samkit* vision. One continues to proceed forward because of the right vision (*samkit drashti*).

## The Living Ego Departs and the Dying Ego is Left Behind

All of us in *Akram Vignan* do not have even a single one of these four *kashays*. We have become free from *kashays*. Man cannot become free from worries and there can never be a worry-free man in the *Kramic* path. Even a gnani of the *Kramic* path is not worry-free. He is blissful within but worried on the outside. He has worries and uncertainties in his worldly dealings about what the future holds. He is worried about the future. 'We' do not have *agrasocha* (worries about the future). 'We' leave everything to *vyavasthit*. How long can anxiety remain? As long as the one who has anxiety is living. And for You, he is no longer alive, is he? Who becomes anxious?

**Questioner:** 'Chandulal.'

**Dadashri:** Yes, that means the ego is alive. There are two kinds of ego. One is the 'doer' of karma and the other is the 'sufferer' of karma.

**Questioner:** Yes, and the ego as the 'doer' is gone.

**Dadashri:** As a 'doer', the ego is alive and as the 'sufferer', it is the dying ego. The dying ego cannot do anything else. And what can the living ego not do when pushed. Therefore, after Gnan Vidhi in *Akram Vignan*, the living one is gone and this dying one remains.

## In the Absence of the 'Doer,' Karmas Get Erased

So when anger arises, he says, 'Dear Dada Bhagwan! You have said 'no,' but this occurred and, therefore, I ask for your forgiveness.' And so that mistake gets erased.

**Questioner:** 'This should not be so.'

**Dadashri:** Yes.

**Questioner:** It should happen immediately?

**Dadashri:** Yes, that is why it gets erased. How are they erased? Through *pratikraman*. All the karmas get erased. Because the doer is no longer there, they get completely erased. When the doer is absent, only the effects of past karma are suffered. People who do not have the knowledge of the Self have to suffer the effect in the presence of the 'doer' (ego). Their karmas may weaken a little if they do *pratikraman*, but they are not erased completely. Their causes will not refrain from bringing about new karma effects, whereas for You, that karma is destroyed when you say, 'Dear Dada Bhagwan, this should not be so.'

## Sarvavirati Gunasthanak: The Sixth Gunasthanak

What more remains for the one who has 'shoot-on-sight' *pratikraman* in his hands? What is left when abhorrence (*dwesh*) goes away? Two of the four *kashays* have been eradicated. Eradicated, meaning what? Anger is gone but the subatomic particles (*parmanus*) of anger remain to discharge. Therefore, one will become angry but he will not like it at all and, therefore, *dwesh* is completely gone. But some fraction of deceit and greed still remain. One will become *vitarag* when they too go away completely. They will go away in the 'discharging conduct deluding karma' (*charitra mohaniya*). Everything will become separate when you divide it up.

What is *sarvavirati*? It is where You do not see any mistake in anyone. Even when someone is insulting you, You do not see mistakes in him. That is *sarvavirati*. There is no higher *sarvavirati* than this.                                         (268)

When you no longer see mistakes in anyone, know that you have attained the state of stillness, the state of the Self, even amidst the din of the worldly life. This state in *Akram Vignan* is very different. Even while enjoying life's pleasures, one sees the world as flawless.

*Akram Vignan's sarvavirati* state is that in which one does not see the slightest mistake in anyone. That is the state of *sarvavirati*; just know this much. Thereafter, I have no problems with whether or not one wears cologne and fragrances, as long as he sees no mistakes in others. Even if he gets bitten by a snake, he will not see any mistake of the snake. Such is our science.

**Questioner:** Thereafter, in that state in the path of *Akram*, there is no need for *pratikraman*, is there?

**Dadashri:** Then there is no need for *pratikraman*. But do not assume that you do not see any mistakes; instead do *pratikraman*. What are you going to lose by doing that? In trying to find something new like that, you may take it in the wrong direction.

The one who has become free from abhorrence (*vitadwesh*) will be liberated in one more lifetime (*ekavtari*). If elements of abhorrence remain, then it may take a person three or four more lives to attain *moksha*.

## No Kashay for the One Who 'Sees'

Mistakes will be erased if one does *pratikraman* given by the Gnani Purush. Otherwise, the mistakes will not leave. One binds merit karma (*punya*) for doing *pratikraman* and this is so for infinite lives. *Pratikraman* as done by the ascetics and the *acharyas* cannot destroy mistakes; it binds merit karma (*punya*). Whereas *pratikraman* as prescribed by the Gnani Purush is 'shoot-on-sight' *pratikraman*, it is done the moment the mistake occurs. All these *mahatmas* have so much awareness that they see their mistakes the moment they occur. They see thousands of their mistakes the moment they arise, because they have become free from *kashays* (anger-pride-deceit-greed).

Unawareness (*ajagruti*) is due to *kashays*.

**Questioner:** If one does no *atikraman* towards anyone and has no active, ongoing *kashay*, how can he remain a hundred percent in the Knower-Seer (*Gnata-Drashta*) state?

**Dadashri:** No, it is not like that. He may not have *atikraman* towards anyone even in his thought, but his mind is always in some kind of *kashay*. If it is not in *raag* (attachment), it is in *dwesh* (abhorrence). *Kashay* is always there when one is not in the Knower-Seer (*Gnata-Drashta*) state.

**Questioner:** Is there always some kind of *kashay* in a thought that is going on?

**Dadashri:** It is always there. It is always there for sure, but *kashay* is not there in the thoughts that one can 'see.'

**Questioner:** That entire ball of confusion comes and goes and only afterwards do I become aware of it.

**Dadashri:** No, You can 'see' (*joyee*) it, and then you know (*janavoo*) it. Still, until then it is considered a *kashay*.

**Questioner:** I 'see' it after fifteen or twenty minutes have passed.

**Dadashri:** *Kashay* stops our *jagruti* (awareness) and so it will not allow us to remain as the Knower-Seer. And if you have the worst of thoughts, and You keep 'seeing' them, then no part of *kashay* will touch you.

## Where There is No Anger, There is Forgiveness

People will say, 'Lord Mahavir had to suffer a lot. He had to suffer internally as well as tremendous bodily pain. He had to endure a lot in penance.' *Moksha* is not attained by enduring such physical suffering. What is such talk like? What people say is that the Lord has forgiveness for one, no matter how bad a deed he does. The Lord does 'have' forgiveness, so he can 'give' it to others; it may appear so to people. What does forgiveness (*kshama*) mean? There is no such thing as forgiveness. Absence of anger in itself is forgiveness. Hence one does not have to forgive. The Jain *sadhus* (ascetics), not having understood this, claim how wonderful the Lord's forgiveness is. There is no forgiveness. It is a different matter where, through the ego, one says, 'Go! I forgive you!' One can understand that forgiveness, but that is on a superficial and a gross level. The absence of anger is forgiveness in itself.                                          (270)

## Kashay is Not in Our Control but Pratikraman is

In *Akram Vignan*, true control (*saiyam*) is the cessation of anger, pride, deceit and greed. If any of these *kashays* occur, one has to do *pratikraman*, because that is *atikraman*. Sensual enjoyment (*vishay*) is not *atikraman*, but these *kashays* (anger, pride, deceit and greed) are *atikraman*. You have been taught to do *pratikraman* for the *atikraman*. The world has arisen because of *atikraman* and it will end with *pratikraman*. Worldly interaction with *kashays* have given rise to life-after-life world; not the worldly interaction in *vishay*. Worldly interaction with *kashays* has given rise to the worldly life, and that is the *atikraman* which can be washed off with *pratikraman*. Occurrence of *kashays* is not under Your control but doing *pratikraman* for it is under your control. Therefore, effort (*purusharth*) towards liberation is through *pratikraman*.

Has your ego (*ahamkar*) and pride (*maan*) gone away

or not; have they decreased or not?

**Questioner:** They are decreasing.

**Dadashri:** Yes. So all that filled *karmic* stock is beginning to go away; it will move away after twelve months. Once the stock decreases, You become the *Atma* (the Self).

**Questioner:** These anger, pride, deceit and greed are *karmic* discharge and so they are bound to arise, but then after 'seeing' them, how can I remain separate?

**Dadashri:** What does one have to do if the awareness (*jagruti*) decreases, when it becomes dim? You have to repeatedly try to remain in My Agnas only. But when you slip into the non-Self and do not stay in the Agnas, then it is the same old thing!

How much effort do you make in order to stay in the Agnas?

**Questioner:** A lot.

**Dadashri:** Are You, too, able to 'see' anger and pride?

**Questioner:** I see them after they have occurred.

**Dadashri:** There is no problem with that. You will 'see' them after they have occurred. They can be 'seen' while they are occurring as well as after they have happened.

**Questioner:** And sometimes it happens that they are 'seen' as the mistake is occurring, and yet this (non-Self) continues doing it.

**Dadashri:** No, You cannot stop them (*kashays*). It is wrong to stop them, because You have to 'see' the current film till it ends. The 'Seer' (Self) has no objection to whether one is fighting, or being non-violent, or being violent. The problem is if he interferes, starts crying, fights and says, 'Stop fighting! Stop fighting!' Hey, it is just a recorded film, and hence the 'Seer' has no problem with it.

**Questioner:** But when that is happening within, I 'know' it and I also scold him and tell him that what he is doing is not right. But even then, he will not listen and he will continue doing it.

**Dadashri:** There is no problem with it because the 'Seer' is pure (*shuddha*). He ('Chandulal') sees it as good or bad, but that is the relative view. There is no such thing as good-bad for the 'Seer'. They are both the same to the 'Seer'. Good and bad are for the worldly people and not so for the God (the Self). Society has the good and the bad. What the Lord says is that You are free once You 'see' them. The Self is separate and this is separate.

So settle the *karmic* debt (*hisaab*) that was bound in ignorance (*agnan*) and lack of understanding (*adarshan*) by 'seeing' (*joyeeney*). Then You are free and separate from it. The accounts bound without 'seeing' are settled by 'seeing'!

When this 'tank' (*karmic* stock called the non-Self complex) empties, and when it is just about to empty, your body will feel as light as a flower. You will feel free, here in this very life.

Now, why will the tank empty? This is because, as it is emptying (karmas are being discharged), nothing new is being filled in. What will remain in an emptying tank when nothing more is being put in it?

**Questioner:** Nothing will remain.

**Dadashri:** It will empty quicker.

*****

## [15]

## On The Path of Cause Ahimsa

### The Final Pratikraman

**Questioner:** On the path of liberation, before final enlightenment, if there is a pending account with someone, does repeated *pratikraman* clear off the account?

**Dadashri:** Yes. (273)

**Questioner:** Even with the living beings we do not know?

**Dadashri:** Only those whom we have met and have created accounts with; no one else.

**Questioner:** But what words do we say when doing *pratikraman*?

**Dadashri:** Say, 'Whatever living beings that I have hurt in any way, please forgive me.'

**Questioner:** Each and every living being?

**Dadashri:** Yes, to each and every living being.

**Questioner:** Does it include living beings like the ones present in air (*vayukaya*), water (*jalkaya*) and fire (*tejokaya*)?

**Dadashri:** It includes everything that you mentioned.

### Intent of Not Hurting Anyone

**Questioner:** What should I do if I hurt any living being (*jiva*) unknowingly?

**Dadashri:** When *himsa* (violence) occurs unknowingly

(*ajaanta*), you should feel repentance immediately, and that it should not be so. You should repent for it and do *pratyakhyan*. Keep the awareness that it does not occur again. This should be Your goal. The Lord had told us to be firm and resolute in our intent (*bhaav*) not to hurt any living thing. Every morning when you begin your day, you should repeat this five times: 'I do not wish to hurt any living being through this mind, speech and body.' Start your day by affirming this intent. This will decrease the liability. This is because the intent is under your control. The rest is not.

## Do Mistakes Made Unknowingly Bind Demerit Karma?

All the positive and negative inner intents that arise within is the result of seeds sown in the past. You do not desire to hurt any living being and yet if a bug gets crushed under your foot, realize that such was the seed sown in the past. Maintain awareness there and do *pratikraman*.

How do you know what kind of enmity the bug you crushed will bind? How great an enmity will the one that is unknowingly killed bind? It is because that bug has a wife and children, and relatives, does it not? They will think that you crushed it; you murdered it knowingly. You may feel that you did it unknowingly, but they think that their loved one was murdered. It, too, has a worldly life, does it not? It has a worldly life wherever it goes, does it not?

**Questioner:** Do we still commit a sin if we hurt someone unknowingly?

**Dadashri:** What will occur if you accidentally put your hand in a fire?

**Questioner:** My hand would get burned.

**Dadashri:** Would a child not get burned too?

**Questioner:** Yes, he would.

**Dadashri:** Even a child? So understand that you will not escape. Whether you do something knowingly or unknowingly, you cannot escape the consequences.

## That is Considered Lack of Awareness

**Questioner:** What occurs if a person who has received Gnan kills mosquitoes that bite him?

**Dadashri:** You can say that the intent got spoilt. That is not considered awareness of Gnan.

**Questioner:** Is that considered a violent intent (*himsak bhaav*)?

**Dadashri:** Not only that, but in doing so he has reverted to what he was. However, *pratikraman* would wash it off.

**Questioner:** What if he keeps killing the mosquitoes the next day?

**Dadashri:** Even if he were to do it a hundred times over, *pratikraman* washes it off.

## The Most Heavy Karma Becomes Light with Pratikraman

**Questioner:** We have to suffer the *nikachit* karma (heavy and 'sticky' karma that one has no choice but suffer its effect) from the past life, but what about the *nikachit* karma created in this life?

**Dadashri:** That has to be suffered in the next life. It will not give its fruit immediately, not before first maturing.

**Questioner:** It cannot be destroyed; it has to be suffered, is that right?

**Dadashri:** It can become lighter if you keep repenting repeatedly. Half of the bitter juice that had entered into it will be removed from it. *Nikachit* means that one has no choice but to suffer, but it can be made lighter, less bitter.

**Questioner:** Is there a change in the suffering?    (276)

**Dadashri:** Yes. If one person gets hurt in a certain part of his body, he will not be able to bear the pain; whereas another person will put bandages on his wound and move about freely.

**Questioner:** When the shepherd forced bamboo needles in Lord Mahavir's ears....

**Dadashri:** That was *nikachit* karma.

**Questioner:** He was a God, so it should have become lighter for him?

**Dadashri:** No, it did not become light.

**Questioner:** Then how can it become lighter for people like us?

**Dadashri:** It can still become lighter if you try. He was a special person and so he would not make it lighter. He was a King when he had ordered his servants to pour hot lead in his guard's ears and he did not do any *pratikraman* for it either.

**Questioner:** But he had done that knowingly, and I have pierced needles in bed bugs and killed them...

**Dadashri:** Do people poke needles into them? What kind of a person are you? Just because they do not have parents to defend them? Why don't you do that to people?

**Questioner:** Now give me a solution for that, please. I have done many such deeds; what should I do about that?

**Dadashri:** *Pratikraman*, do *pratikraman*! Take some bed bugs, put them in a cup, look at their bodies and do *pratikraman*, then feed them, let them bite you, and then let them go.

**Questioner:** I cry from within that I have done so many bad deeds. I think of that every day and I can see them.

**Dadashri:** Make it lighter by doing *pratikraman*. You should have asked someone before you did all that, should you not?

**Questioner:** But I did not find anyone then.

**Dadashri:** You should have asked someone at home or in your village.

**Questioner:** At home, our practice of killing them still continues.

**Dadashri:** Is that so? Both of you together?

**Questioner:** I killed them my way and she killed them her way.

**Dadashri:** Were you killing two hundred to five hundred a day?

**Questioner:** Yes. We would kill however many there were. But we have not killed since we met Dada.

**Dadashri:** You should not have a single thought about killing. If you cannot tolerate the insects, take them outside. The *Tirthankars* eliminated the word 'kill' from common usage, because it is laden with liability and risk. That is how non-violent (*ahimsak*) one should become. One should not have a single atom of violence. Thoughts about killing are laden with violent subatomic particles. Each and every atom of your body should be completely *ahimsak*.

**Questioner:** Otherwise, will change of becoming non-violent occur in the intent?

**Dadashri:** Yes. No one should be hurt in the slightest, because no one at all is at fault in this world.

## Causal and Effect Violence

**Questioner:** Are the consequences of 'violence in effect' (*dravya himsa*) and 'causal seed of violence' (*bhaav himsa*) the same?

**Dadashri:** Causal seed of *himsa* cannot be seen because it is subtle. Only effect *himsa* (*dravya*; violence) is visible; it can be experienced through mind, speech and body. In causal (*bhaav*) violence, there is subtle intent of violence present, whereas in the effect (*dravya*) violence, it is evident in front of you. When you say that, 'I want to save living beings,' it is called intent of non-violence (*bhaav ahimsa*). Thereafter, you are not responsible whether this occurs or not. If you say that life is worth preserving and, thereafter, if violence occurs, then you are not responsible for it. Nevertheless, you should repent and do *pratikraman*. Doing this eliminates the liability. (278)

## Special Pratikraman for the Farmers

**Questioner:** I have read in your book the prayer which says, 'Through this mind, speech and body, let me not hurt, even to the slightest degree, any living entity.' I am a farmer and I grow tobacco. While the plants are growing, I should constantly pinch off new tender leaves from the stalks. Would that not hurt the plant? Is that not a *paap* (sin, demerit karma)? We do this to thousands of our plants! How can we put an end to this wrongful act?

**Dadashri:** You should feel repentance for the act. You should repent and feel, 'Why has this painful task fallen upon me?' That is all. You can continue with your work then. Internally, you are repenting that it is not your wish to do this.

**Questioner:** Yes, but are we still committing a sin?

**Dadashri:** Yes, it is a sin. But you should not concern yourself with that. Do not look at the sinful act. Just commit to the decision that things should not be the way they are. Stand by your conviction that you would rather be doing something other than this. Before, when you were not aware of all this, you would not have been so reluctant to throw away the poor plants. Do you understand all that? If you follow My advice, the responsibility becomes Mine. I am taking on the responsibility for you. You can cast the plant aside but, at the same time, you should feel a deep repentance.

**Questioner:** I understand that now. These businessmen create greater demerit karma as compared to the farmer. And greater demerit karma than the businessmen cause, is caused by people sitting at home doing nothing. Demerit karma is caused through the mind and not the body.

**Dadashri:** You have to understand the facts. Others do not need to. You have to understand everything that is applicable to you. Whatever others understand is fine by their standards.

**Questioner:** What should I do about the pesticides used when spraying the crop? There is (himsa) violence in it, right?

**Dadashri:** When you have no choice, do whatever you have to but with a promise of doing pratikraman.

You do not know how to proceed with this worldly life. 'We' teach you all that, so that you do not bind new demerit karma (paap).

You are bound to bind demerit karma when you are farming but at the same time, 'we' give you the 'medicine' of what you should say so that the demerit karma decreases. 'We' give you the medicine to wash off the demerit karma. Does one not need the medicine? When you go to the farm and plough the fields, many insects die and you bind demerit karma. When you cut down sugarcane, is that not a demerit karma? Are they not living, embodied souls? But 'we' explain to you what you should do about that, so that you incur less karmic liability and enjoy your worldly comforts peacefully.

All farmers are liable for the death of so many living organisms in the fields. They should earnestly pray to God and ask to be forgiven for their mistakes, daily. I tell every farmer to take about five to ten minutes to repent in front of the Lord, for this violence. They should do *pratikraman* because the work they are engaged in involves so much violence. I show them how to do *pratikraman*.

## Pratikraman for Himsa

**Questioner:** While I was driving yesterday, I felt really bad when a pigeon came under my car.                    (280)

**Dadashri:** It was 'Chandubhai' who felt bad. So tell 'Chandubhai' to repent and do *pratikraman*.

**Questioner:** I did all that.

**Dadashri:** You did that, so that is good.

**Questioner:** But I do not know when and where it came from.

**Dadashri:** It is like this. That pigeon was going to die because of some mistake from its past life. It was looking for someone to kill it. It was looking for someone like 'Chandubhai' who had an inner intent (*bhaav*) of killing.

And to the one who has decided that he does not want to kill any living being, violence (*himsa*) will not touch him. 'I have no intent to kill, but what can I do if it comes underneath my car?' If someone says this, then he will encounter this. You just encountered a little of whatever intent you had. One being a Jain is rushing around and then if some bird gets in the way, he will say, 'What can I do?'!

The one who wants to save lives will come across circumstances that will allow him to do so. Whatever your *bhaav* (inner intent), such will be your *karmic* account (*hisaab*).

You have to have a strong policy, 'I do not want to hurt

even to the slightest extent, under any circumstance.'

'We' will make you do *pratikraman* which will wash off everything. This was a bird which you could see, but there are so many living things that you cannot see which also get crushed. Make 'Chandubhai' do *pratikraman* for that.

**Questioner:** In my mind, a thought had come that according to *vyavasthit* (scientific circumstantial evidences), that was the kind of *karmic* account (*hisaab*) that pigeon had, is that correct?

**Dadashri:** Of course, that was the account. It was its *hisaab* and you were the *nimit* (evidentiary doer; apparent doer). But our *mahatmas* do not become such *nimits*. While driving, they do not have any inner intent (*bhaav*) that they want to kill anything.

Whereas, if someone else is in a hurry and happens to run over some animal or bird, he will say, 'What could I do?'

**Questioner:** Now, how can the thoughts in the mind be changed?

**Dadashri:** He does not have to do anything. 'You' have to make 'Chandubhai' do *pratikraman* repeatedly.

But it has become clear, hasn't it?

**Questioner:** Yes, it has. Is it enough to just say the prayer you mentioned earlier that, 'Let no living being be hurt through the medium of the speech, thoughts, and acts,' in the morning?

**Dadashri:** It should be repeated five times a day, with the same intensity of applied awareness (*upayog*) as you would have when counting one hundred dollar bills. While counting money, there is one pointed state of the *antahkaran* (internal functioning mechanism in every human being composed of mind, intellect, *chit* and ego) and the *chit*. That is how it should be when reciting this intent.

*****

# [16]

## Revenge of Enmity is Unbearable

### Pratikraman for Enmity

**Questioner:** A man I know told me that his brother was looking to beat him up. At that time, I realized and thought to myself, 'Why should I create enmity (*veyr*) with him?' (282)

**Dadashri:** Yes, he will bind enmity. If he knows that you are having enmity towards him, then he will do the same with you and then sting you and kill you in your next life.

**Questioner:** He would not know who has enmity towards him, would he?

**Dadashri:** So he is not binding any enmity in this; you are doing that, unilaterally. It is considered enmity when it is from both the parties. And enmity means that he will avenge one day. Whereas this one, you create it on your own from within. What will you do now?

**Questioner:** After I had this thought, so much rigmarole came out from just that one thought.

**Dadashri:** But you just had a thought, there were no other wishes, were there? Did you do *pratikraman* after that?

**Questioner:** I am not able to do *pratikraman*.

**Dadashri:** You have to do that. How can you not do it? How is that acceptable?

**Questioner:** Is all the rigmarole that occurred, not a *pratikraman*?

*****

**Dadashri:** Would anyone think of hitting his own brother?

**Questioner:** But after all that, I thought very deeply about who binds enmity, why does he do so; so does that not all go into *pratikraman*?

**Dadashri:** That is nothing but rigmarole – long tedious talking back and forth.

Did you not feel that someone was binding it? That somebody was doing something?

**Questioner:** One does everything to his own self.

**Dadashri:** What else, then? Whether knowingly or unknowingly, when you say, 'Hey, you' (threaten) to someone's ego, then he will bind another karma (of enmity), and when the fruit of that enmity comes, it will bring on such a misery that you will forget the world. You can never harass or instill fear in anyone. If he is harassing you, then it is your own *karmic* account (*hisaab*) and so you should 'credit' it into your *karmic* account and stop creating a new one, if you want to be free. What have you decided?

**Questioner:** Whatever he gives me is my own *hisaab* (*karmic* account), due to me.

**Dadashri:** Yes. We have found a straightforward path. There are no external problems (*upadhi*), and the worries have gone; there is no other problem and so it is possible to do whatever you wish. And after you do *pratikraman*, no matter how much enmity there is, you can still be free in this very life. *Pratikraman* is the only solution.

## Retaliation towards Sticky Files

**Questioner:** I have three or four sticky files at the office. When these files harass me, I feel like retaliating with violence.

**Dadashri:** Is that so? You still have the old inner intent of striking back?

**Questioner:** So should the ego suppress such an inner intent (*bhaav*) or should it allow it to manifest in action? (284)

**Dadashri:** 'You' do not have to suppress them or let them manifest into action. Just keep 'seeing' what occurs. Do you understand that? You just have to 'see' what 'Chandulal' is doing; that is all. Your duty is to 'know' and 'see,' and on what basis is 'Chandulal' functioning? It is based on *vyavasthit*. Do you understand? All the files are to be settled with equanimity on the basis of scientific circumstantial evidences! There is no other problem; everything else is complete.

## This is How Enmity is Destroyed

**Questioner:** I am not able to break free from the links of enmity perpetuated through speech. These layers of enmity are so tightly bound that they are difficult to peel off. And remembering Dada when I try to do *pratikraman* for the *atikraman* I did, the *pratikraman* stops and instead leaves a link of grudge (*taanto*) behind. Then those links (*taanto*) come out even stronger. So I feel dejected as to why these links still remain. Why do they not go away?

**Dadashri:** That is because it has been made very compact, that is why. It is just like this bale of cotton. It will fill up the whole room if you cut off the ropes. That is how this *karmic* stock has been compacted together; therefore, you have to continue doing *pratikraman* to bring an end to it.

**Questioner:** No matter how much effort I put in, it stops me from doing *pratikraman*. Those links of enmity work against the *pratikraman* and so it exhausts any effort (*purusharth*) towards it.

**Dadashri:** No matter how hard it is, just go to sleep at night. The Lord has said to work during the day but to sleep at night. So when *atikraman* occurs while you are doing *pratikraman*, just stop it. You should not force it too much.

**Questioner:** What I mean by 'force' is that the link of grudge (*taanto*) and abhorrence stops all *pratikraman* even before it comes into my hands. So the *purusharth* stops.

**Dadashri:** But there is a reason that the *purusharth* comes to a stop. There you have to put an end to it. Take a little break and then start the *pratikraman* again. But you have to take a break. Do you understand that? This is because *atikraman* has occurred for infinite past lives. One has done nothing but *atikraman*. Nothing else occurs besides *atikraman*. One either loves someone or hates someone; they are both considered *atikraman*. And *pratikraman* has to be done wherever *atikraman* is done. There is no path to *moksha* where there is no *pratikraman*. *Pratikraman* should be 'shoot-on-sight' *pratikraman*; only then will *atikraman* be erased.

**Questioner:** I have to do a lot of *purusharth* there.

**Dadashri:** *Purusharth* is possible since you became a Purush (Self-realized).

**Questioner:** So what *purusharth* is needed to become free from this?

**Dadashri:** The *purusharth* is one of continuing to 'see' what the mind is doing, and what the *chit* is doing.

## The Enemy Has a Change of Heart with Pratikraman

**Questioner:** No matter how intense an enmity there is towards someone; no matter how strong malice exists in jealousy towards another human being; will *pratikraman* erase all that?

**Dadashri:** This world has arisen due to *atikraman*. All the bad attributes have occurred due to *atikraman*, and they will be erased with *pratikraman*. There are only these two.

**Questioner:** Does a change occur in the heart of the other person?

**Dadashri:** He will have change in his heart and he will come looking for you at your home. Do you understand? Everything will occur.                                              (286)

What does *pratikraman* mean? It means to 'see' your own mistakes. But if you see mistakes in others, then they will perpetuate. Therefore, do not look for mistakes in others. Only then will you be free of enmity (*veyr*).

## Enmity Continues Enmity, Life after Life

**Questioner:** So where is the need for doing *pratikraman* when he is never going to meet me again?

**Dadashri:** *Pratikraman* itself means that you are doing *pratikraman* for that which has 'already occurred' and not for what is 'going to occur.' When you do *pratikraman*, you are free from the inner intent (*bhaav*) of violence or *kashay*. You are the one letting go of it; he may or may not.

**Questioner:** Suppose I don't do any *pratikraman*. So will I have to go someplace in order to settle that score?

**Dadashri:** No, it does not have to be settled by meeting him again. You are the one who is bound; you have no concern with him at all. We have nothing to do with the other person.

**Questioner:** But am I not supposed to settle the account?

**Dadashri:** It means that you yourself are bound again and that is why you have to do *pratikraman*. Everything heals with *pratikraman*, which is why you have been given the weapon of *pratikraman*!

All *karmic* debts are paid off with *pratikraman* and *pratyakhyan*. Otherwise, enmity increases with revenge and opposition. It increases when you oppose someone, does it not?

**Questioner:** Yes, it does.

**Dadashri:** Have you experienced that? Therefore, because enmity increases with enmity, you should ask for forgiveness in whatever way you can and become free.

## Enmity Requires Many Pratikramans

**Questioner:** When I do *pratikraman*, I get over my enmity (*veyr*); but what about the other person? What if he still feels animosity towards me?

**Dadashri:** What did it matter to Lord Mahavir when those around him felt so much attachment towards him? Some even hated him. Nothing sticks to the *Vitarag*. A *Vitarag* goes around without putting 'oil on his body' (nothing will stick to them), whereas others go around with 'oil on their bodies' so all the dirt will stick to them. Do you want to remain in the Agnas? Then nothing in the world will stick to you. So remain in the Agnas, do you understand? Then it will not stick to you. If you rub 'oil' on, then it will stick, will it not?

When there is 'stickiness' (*raag-dwesh* of the body complex), it is called oil – and dirt will stick to it, but how can it stick if there is no stickiness? People do *raag-dwesh* (attachment-abhorrence) even with me. They also praise me. When someone does not agree with me, he may even curse me and say negative things. One can say that because he is independent and free to do so. And the responsibility of going to a lower life form is his own. He does as he pleases through his own responsibility. How can we say no? He will strike you too! What will he not do? What can ignorance not do? And the one with understanding will not take on any liability. Will an attorney not be scared of breaking the law?

**Questioner:** So the attachment-abhorrence (*raag-dwesh*) there are, are they associated with an individual?

**Dadashri:** They are one's own. He, himself has made

them sticky. What can we do when he makes them sticky by rubbing on oil?

Still, one thing is certain, that if it comes down to someone in the family, then You have to tell 'Chandulal' to keep doing *pratikraman* for him. This current friction is the result of the *karmic* account of the past life, but the reaction of the ego is not. 'This' gnan—knowledge (that clash is a result but egoism is not); is a result and, therefore, tell him to do *pratikraman*, because it is all from the past.

**Questioner:** There is animosity between myself and another person. There has been attachment and abhorrence between us. While I have managed to get rid of my enmity and abhorrence, the other person still continues to harbor deep enmity. Does this mean that in my next life, he will come to settle the account? After all, he is the one perpetuating enmity.    (288)

**Dadashri:** That is correct. He has been more hurt than you. You may forget his pain, but if he does not forget and he carries this on to the next life, you have to do *pratikraman* for it. The *pratikraman* is for the extra intensity of the *atikraman*, do you understand?

**Questioner:** If his enmity goes away, does that mean that my *pratikraman* has been effective?

**Dadashri:** Yes, with *pratikraman*, his animosity towards you will lessen. With each *pratikraman*, a layer of karma is shed. Karma comes in layers, like onions. You will have to do as many *pratikraman* as the number of layers you have caused. Do you understand?

**Questioner:** Yes. Many people used to do *raag-dwesh* towards Lord Mahavir but it did not touch Him.

**Dadashri:** They did endless *raag-dwesh*. They also used to hit Him. They used to hit Him and they also did *raag* towards

Him. Some even kidnapped Him.

**Questioner:** Yes, but none of that touched Him.

**Dadashri:** His applied awareness (*upayog*) was not in all that, was it? His *upayog* was not in his body at all. Let them do whatever they want to, to the body. Not only did he not have the ownership of that body, but he did not even have *upayog* (applied awareness) in the body.

If you hit this table and break it, it has reaction. You are responsible for it. In the same way, that is how separate the Lord was from his body.

Even if you do not want to remember something, if it comes into your memory it is a mistake that needs to be washed off with *pratikraman*.

## Stirring Up the Past with a Purpose

**Questioner:** Yesterday in *satsang*, it was said that one is not to think of the past and to remain in the present. Now, I feel that I do not want to think of the past, but suddenly it comes before the mind and the *chit*. The past brings back a lot of stinging memories and it fills up every pore in my body. So I feel at a loss as to how I can forget the past.

**Dadashri:** It is like this. This that is taking place within you is for the purpose of settling enmity. You can see the past and so you can start doing *pratikraman*. But without stirring up the past, you will not see those unsettled accounts, will you? Do you understand? Only a rare person will have this situation like yours. This is not how it is with others (*mahatmas*) and that is why 'we' tell others to 'live in the present.'

Even people with an intelligent approach to life, who do not have Gnan, never stir up the past. Why is that? How can you resolve that which has no solution? The past means something that has no solution. Therefore, we say that You have attained the Gnan, so do not stir up the past. Not even fools will stir up the past, whereas You have attained the Gnan and the future is left to *vyavasthit* (scientific circumstantial evidences). Therefore, remain in the present. You have faith in *vyavasthit*, don't you? Then nothing remains to be done for the future. And the past that You are 'stirring up' is to settle your past unsettled files with equanimity and, therefore, it is not considered as 'stirring up the past.'

**Questioner:** Yes, now that is correct.                        (290)

**Dadashri:** Some people unnecessarily stir up their past for no reason. In order to settle the past files, You have to stir up the files, because you want to get rid of the 'shop.' What do You have to do now? You have to sell off the old stock and not buy any new stock. But you have to maintain some discrimination. You cannot get rid of some stock, but if you have run out of sugar, then you have to buy some more; therefore, you have to exercise discrimination while getting rid of the shop.

**Questioner:** If we say not to stir up the past, then what is the need for doing *pratikraman*?

**Dadashri:** Those who do *pratikraman* have no problem with the past. With *pratikraman*, we are getting rid of *atikraman* and settling it. Not stirring the past means that if you had a quarrel with someone yesterday, you bury it in your mind (and not stir it up again). But there is nothing wrong if you recall it to do *pratikraman*. But do not keep it on your mind and think of it as a burden. You should not do that. Stirring up the past means when one remembers something about the past, he starts crying about it. If a person's son died two days ago, he remembers him today and cries. Is that not called stirring up the past?

One has to do *pratikraman*, does he not? And *pratikraman* is for what occurred in the past. For the future, there is *pratyakhyan*. Let *pratyakhyan* occur with the intent, 'I will never do it again.' But the future you are leaving under the control of *vyavasthit*. Then you have to remain in the present. This is all our science says: '*Vartman ma vartey sada so gnani jagmahi* – He who lives constantly in the present is verily the Gnani of the world.' Therefore, after attaining this Gnan, you should always remain in the present. Remain in the present, whenever and whatever the circumstance. Do not be out of the present even for a moment. 'We' are constantly in the present. 'We' remain the Self and this 'Patel' remains constantly in the present (*vartman*).

In order to do *pratikraman*, you have to recall the past. You have to recall all that you have forgotten and now if the *atikraman* has occurred again today, then you have to recall it specifically and do *pratikraman* for it. You have no choice. *Pratikraman* is the main thing on this path of ours. And after attaining this Gnan, after attaining the Self, there is no need for *pratikraman*, but this is the path of *Akram Vignan* and one has attained the Self without getting rid of one's karma.

## The Fireworks Will Always Go Off

**Questioner:** What should I do when, while doing *pratikraman*, *atikraman* occurs at that time?

**Dadashri:** Do your *pratikraman* later. When you attempt to extinguish a fire that was ignited by a firecracker, and in the process another firecracker is suddenly set off, you would have to jump aside and wait before making another attempt to put out the fire. These fireworks of life will keep exploding. Such is the worldly life.

## Atikraman While Doing Pratikraman

**Questioner:** Sometimes, what occurs is that while doing *pratikraman*, twice as many *atikraman* occur. I start to see mistakes in him with increased force. What kind of unfolding of karma is that?

**Dadashri:** When that occurs, stop everything and then 'see' it again. Stop everything and then start all over again.

For many, doing only a few *pratikraman* will clear up their account book. For others, they may have to do a lot of *pratikraman* because they may have made a lot of entries in their book.

**Questioner:** Does that mean that we have to keep on doing *pratikraman* again and again?                                    (292)

**Dadashri:** That is all; that is the *purusharth* you have to do.

**Questioner:** So when *atikraman* starts in this manner, while I am doing *pratikraman*, is anything wrong there?

**Dadashri:** No, you just stop doing *pratikraman* at that time. If you want to boil milk and it starts to overflow, you have to remove it from the heat for a while and then you have to put it back on again. And when it does not stop the second time round, You have to tell 'Chandulal,' 'He is very beneficial to you. Why are you creating more mess like this again? That person is very beneficial to you!'

**Questioner:** Everything settles down for a while when I say that 'he is of great benefit to me,' but then after a while, everything takes over again.

**Dadashri:** But even then, they (unfolding karma) will not become stickier. That too is a wonder, is it not? It is good that you have been able to sort this much of it out. This is a tremendous *kashay* and the account book is very big!

## Extended Pratikramans for One Individual

**Questioner:** My *pratikraman* for an individual continues for three days. It seems there is no end to it and so I get tired. I feel I do not want to do any more *pratikraman*. I wonder whether that is *pratikraman* or *atikraman*, but there is one thing for sure, I do feel at peace after that.

**Dadashri:** When you do *pratikraman*, tremendous peace (*shanti*) arises. There is so much peace, it is the kind that you have never experienced before.

**Questioner:** But what should I do when *pratikraman* goes on for three days regarding only one individual?

**Dadashri:** It is more complicated and entangled. It is because of bigger 'books.' People with such large books never turn around, but the fact that some, like you, have – is a wonder, is it not?

**Questioner:** That is all I wanted to know... that I am not on the wrong path, am I?

**Dadashri:** No, You are not on the wrong path. You are on the 'safe side' path.

**Questioner:** Give us just that much more energy.

**Dadashri:** Yes, 'we' keep giving you that energy, but it will increase when you come here.

I am convinced about that and that is why I have not paid any attention to him. I paid attention as long as there was no safe side for him (the questioner), but now he is on the safe side. He will get his work done in due time.

## Frequency of Pratikraman Depends on the Size of the Kashay

**Questioner:** If I have enmity with someone and I do *pratikraman* for it, why then do I have to do *pratikraman* again?

**Dadashri:** Yes, you have to do *pratikraman*. The mistake was big and with *pratikraman* you removed one layer, but hundreds of thousands more layers still remain. So you have to keep doing *pratikraman* until all the layers are shed. With some people, all the layers are shed, by doing *pratikraman* for a month to two, whereas with some others it will take a whole lifetime if the *karmic* tuber is large. When you peel off one layer of an onion, it still looks like an onion, does it not?

**Questioner:** Yes.                                          (294)

**Dadashri:** Similarly, this has such layers. When you do *pratikraman*, you shed that one layer for sure and you do not have to do any more *pratikraman* for that particular layer. Only one *pratikraman* per layer of mistake is necessary.

## One Has to Become Free from His Own Bondage

He was not likely to survive that accident but he did. One can survive those worldly accidents, but you survived the tremendous accidents that occur on the path of *kashays* and you became liberated from the path of *kashays*.

**Questioner:** And if I were to walk that path of *kashays*, then accidents would be inevitable; that much I understand now.

**Dadashri:** You know that it is bound to occur.

**Questioner:** So I keep doing *pratikraman*, then I will have the solution. Whatever negativity I feel about all these people, they feel the same about me too, and thus they will trap me. So if I keep doing *pratikraman*, then what about the negativity they have towards me? Will they put me in *karmic* bondage again?

**Dadashri:** No, you have to become free from your bondage and they have to free themselves from their own bondage. Otherwise, one will remain bound forever. This is the law of Lord Mahavir. Otherwise, Lord Mahavir would never have been free, would he? Some bondage would have remained and He would not have been free. You have to become free from wherever you are bound.

**Questioner:** So one has to become free from his own bondage, with *pratikraman*?

**Dadashri:** Yes, become free from all bondage.

## Compassion for the Weak One under Influence of Kashays

If someone were to insult 'us' or do wrong by 'us,' 'we' would still protect him. A man started to argue with me and became confrontational. So I told everyone around me that they should not have a single negative thought about him and if they did, they should do his *pratikraman*. He is a good man but he was under the control of *kashays* when it occurred. If he were under the realm of the Self, he would never speak the way he did. A person who succumbs to his internal enemies should be forgiven for whatever kind of mistake done, for he does not have any awareness-support of the Self. When someone exhibits *kashay*, at that time you should loosen the 'rope' of the ego, remain calm, or else he will ruin everything.

To be controlled by inner enemies (*kashays*) is to be swayed by the effects of the unfolding karma (*udayakarma*). He does according to the unfolding karma.

## Equanimity of Lord Parshvanath

**Questioner:** It came out in a discussion that someone had bound enmity against Lord Parshvanath (the twenty-third *Tirthankar*) and the Lord had no knowledge of this. And due to this enmity, the Lord encountered that person for ten lifetimes, and in each of those lives that person harmed the Lord in some way or the other. Is that possible? One is not even aware of it, and the other person continues to bind enmity which could last up to ten lifetimes.

**Dadashri:** It depends on how much damage you have caused. So do not cause any damage to anyone.

**Questioner:** But Lord Parshvanath was not even aware of it, was He?

**Dadashri:** How can everyone know about that? How can one know what the reason behind the current suffering is? It is certain that it is the fruit of one's own doing. Lord Parshvanath would at least know that people were giving Him back that which was his own. If the restlessness and anger get multiplied in this effect and unfolding, it will take longer to resolve and settle.

Lord Parshvanath did not react and, therefore, it was all over in ten lifetimes.

**Questioner:** Even then, it lasted for ten lifetimes; that is not a short time!

**Dadashri:** Do you know from how many lifetimes these ten lifetimes was the basis? Do you know that?

**Questioner:** I do not know anything about that.

**Dadashri:** It is the equivalent to one strand of hair! Ten lifetimes are not even one strand of hair!

**Questioner:** Oh! As compared to infinite lifetimes, it is nothing. That is why he maintained equanimity in the ten lifetimes.

**Dadashri:** That is why it came to an end. For the first two or three lives, it was not exact equanimity. There was some irritation and then it improved. It is not possible to suddenly maintain complete equanimity in this world. Even gnanis cannot do that. But this is the science of *Akram*, and so it is possible.

*****

# [17]

# Removing the Root Cause of Opinions

## Pratikraman for Prejudice

**Questioner:** You have told us to do *pratikraman*. If we were to do *pratikraman*, day and night, every moment of the day, then that *pratikraman* is for the mistakes of only one lifetime, is that not so? (297)

**Dadashri:** What does *pratikraman* mean? It means that you should not have an opinion. It means that you have changed your opinion. You have no opinion anymore. *Pratikraman* is to be done to get rid of the opinion, 'This is right,' in anything wrong that you do; the *pratikraman* that, 'I am repentant for it, and affirming that I will not repeat it.' So *pratikraman* is only to get rid of the opinion.

**Questioner:** But, since meeting You, the opinions have already changed.

**Dadashri:** That is fine, but you should still go ahead and do *pratikraman*.

**Questioner:** If there is any prejudice or a strong opinion, will it go away with repeated *pratikraman*?

**Dadashri:** Yes, it will.

**Questioner:** Should I do *pratikraman* for every time any strong opinion or prejudice arises?

**Dadashri:** If you keep doing *pratikraman*, it will wash off everything. What gives rise to prejudices? Repeated *atikraman* in the form of recurrent negative opinions about someone gives rise to prejudices. There are so many people out there, but why did he encounter only you?                    (298)

## Forgive the Thief but Do Not Keep His Company

**Dadashri:** If your anger hurts someone or causes him harm, then tell 'Chandulal,' 'Hey! Chandulal, do *pratikraman*; ask for forgiveness.' If someone is being awkward with you and you bow down to him, he will do further *atikraman*, 'See, you finally came to your senses!' Who is he to bring anyone to their senses? Decrease your association with people like that. But you have to forgive his wrongdoing. No matter what his intent when he comes to you, whether good or bad, you have to know how to deal with him. If his *prakruti* (the non-Self complex) is awkward and difficult, then you should not bother with him.

If you know that it is his nature to steal, and you have known him to steal for the last ten years, should you trust him just because he begs for your forgiveness? You cannot place trust in him. You can tell him that you do not have any bad feelings towards him and that he has your forgiveness, but that is as far as you can go with such a person. You cannot afford to place trust in him or become involved with him. On the other hand, if you were to become his friend, then it would be wrong not to trust him or become suspicious of him based on your previous opinions. It is best that you not associate with him, but if you do, you should not have any prejudice towards him. Just keep in mind that whatever occurs is correct.

## Unfailing Weapon of Pratikraman to Erase Opinions

**Questioner:** Still, what if I form a negative opinion about him?

**Dadashri:** Then you should ask for forgiveness. You should ask for forgiveness from whomever you have formed a negative opinion about.

**Questioner:** Is it okay to have positive opinions?

**Dadashri:** Do not give any opinions at all. If you do, you should erase them. You have the necessary, infallible weapons of *alochana*, *pratikraman* and *pratyakhyan* at your disposal.

**Questioner:** Where I have no attachment-abhorrence, or self interest, or no direct influence on any individual, if such a non-personal opinion arises, is there a need to do *pratikraman*?

**Dadashri:** There is no need at all to give out non-personal opinions. But if you do, then you have to do *pratikraman*. Whether it is personal or non-personal, you have no right to give an opinion. To do so is you becoming guided by your ego-intellect complex (*swachhand*) and so you should erase it.

**Questioner:** For example, I give an opinion that Hitler did great injustice to society and the world; did I say anything wrong there?

**Dadashri:** You should not stick your hand unnecessarily in that. You have nothing to do with Hitler. But if you end up saying anything, then it is *vyavasthit*. Then you have to wash it off. Words get spoken. Even 'we' end up saying things like, 'The *rotli* is good. The mango is good,' but then 'we' wash it off. Sometimes, for certain reasons, in order to help someone 'we' will say, 'You made good food,' but then 'we' wash it off. Whatever opinions 'we' give, 'we' immediately wash them off. You now have the tool to wash it off, do you not?

**Questioner:** What is the tool for that?

**Dadashri:** *Pratikraman*.

## Opinion is Reversed with Pratikraman

Whenever you see positive attributes in a person and you form an opinion that the person has good qualities, those qualities will arise in you. Opinions have to change. The moment you see mistake in others, that same mistake arises in you.

**Questioner:** If I see a mistake in someone by accident, I should immediately do *pratikraman*, and then there is no problem?                                                                        (300)

**Dadashri:** Yes, you should do *pratikraman*. There is no other solution other than that.

If you have a negative thought about 'Chandulal,' its effect will show on your face. 'Chandulal' will read those inner intents. So for that, you have to say, 'Chandulal is very beneficial to me.'

## This is How You Get Rid of Strong Opinions

**Questioner:** How can I get rid of my strong opinions?

**Dadashri:** They will begin to disappear the moment you decide you want to get rid of them. If they are stubborn, you should work on them several hours a day. They, too, will disappear. After you attain Self-realization, You come into *purusharth dharma* (religion of the Self effort). This *dharma* gives you extraordinary energy and power to overcome the most difficult of obstructions (*atkan*). However, You should first realize the cause behind the recurrent obstacle and then do *pratikraman* for it.

Do you give out opinions now?

**Questioner:** No, not at all anymore.

**Dadashri:** Then it is fine. The problem is solved.

## Be Very Aware Against Opinions

The most important thing is to 'see' that opinions do not form. This is where You need to be most cautious; nothing else matters. The awareness of the worldly life tends to form opinions, sometimes even before you see something, or someone. Therefore, opinion should be destroyed before it takes root. You should exercise extreme caution with regard to opinions. Nevertheless, you will still bind opinions, but they should be immediately destroyed. The *prakruti* (non-Self complex) creates opinions and *pragnya shakti* (the liberating energy of the Self) destroys them. The *prakruti* will continue to bind opinions for some time, but You should keep erasing them. Opinions are the underlying cause of this problem (*bhanjghad*).

If 'we' were to form an opinion about a person and if that person were to come here, he will see a change in 'our' mind and he will not see equanimity (*samata*) in 'us.' Before he even sees 'us,' he will understand that there is some kind of change in 'us.' So opinions have this kind of effect. But when You let go of the opinion, then there is nothing there. 'We' do not have any opinion about anyone and thus 'we' experience constant equanimity. Opinions are bound to be formed, because of the presence of the *prakruti*, and they will constantly be formed. You have to continue to let go of them.

**Questioner:** How do I get rid of opinions that have been formed?

**Dadashri:** To eliminate them, You should tell 'Chandulal,' 'You have formed such an opinion about this person and it is completely wrong. How can you bind such an opinion?' You will become free from it when You say this to 'Chandulal.'

## Divide, the Moment You Multiply

It is like this: whenever you multiply a number, with say seven, then you have to divide it by seven in order to return to the same number. You want to revert to the original 'number,' do you not? You know that it has been multiplied with a certain number and so you should divide it by the same number. If you realize that it has been multiplied by a very large number, then you have to divide it with that very large number. Hence multiplication will continue to occur, but we have the tool for dividing it. Having become a Purush (Self-realized), spiritual effort (*purusharth*) is our duty (*dharma*). When you see someone, you are bound to form an opinion. Thus, opinion gets formed and so You should immediately 'divide' it by telling 'Chandulal,' 'This is wrong, why should you do that?', and so You will be free. Otherwise, opinions will be formed and bound. Once they are bound, they will give their fruit for sure.                    (302)

**Questioner:** When you say 'it gives its fruits,' does that mean it makes one suffer?

**Dadashri:** What does 'give fruit' mean? It means that if you form an opinion about someone, it will continually have an affect on the other person, naturally. He, too, will immediately understand that you feel that way about him. But if you get rid of that opinion, then it will not affect your mind or his mind. If you 'divide by seven' as soon as the opinion is formed, then it will go away before it has any effect. Otherwise, nothing goes to waste and its effect cannot be stopped. Everyone's conduct is different towards 'us,' but 'we' do not have any opinion. 'We' realize that is just how it is. Do women not know what mother-in-laws are like in this *Kaliyug* (current time cycle era of lack of unity in thoughts, speech and acts)? So then why form any opinions? It is *Kaliyug*, so it is always like this.

It is like this: if you get things and circumstances to your liking, it is merit karma (*punya*); and facing things and circumstances that you do not like is demerit karma (*paap*). Hence, when the unfolding (*udaya*) is of demerit karma, you will encounter things or circumstances that you do not like. Whose *udaya* is it? It is of *paap* (demerit karma). Now it will give bitter fruit, which will not last long, but if you form an opinion about your mother-in-law during that time, then it will have an effect on her which will continue for a long time. Hence, never form an opinion about anyone because after all, he is an *Atma* (the Self), so how can you form an opinion about him? He is the Self. Do not see anything of the non-Self.

## You Have to Become Free From Opinions, Not from Things

**Questioner:** There is a lot in my understanding, but I am not able to put that into practice; so what about that?

**Dadashri:** There is no problem if it does not occur that way. All one needs is understanding (*samjan*). Understanding means that You are free from the moment You become separate from your opinion. If 'Chandulal' is doing anything negative and he says, 'I do not want this; I do not want to do this,' then he becomes free from his opinion. And if this opinion of his remains forever, then he is definitely separate from it.

So one has to be free from opinion, not from any thing. Whenever one becomes free from things (events and experiences through thoughts, speech and acts), it is fine. But it is more important to make it without any support (of the Self). Therefore, You have to be free from your opinions and not from the thing itself. That is why 'we' have given *pratikraman*. *Pratikraman* means that one has become free from opinion. If one does such firm and exact *pratikraman*, he will become free from the opinion.

Without *pratikraman*, your opinions will remain and you will stay bound to your mistakes. Your opinion is in whatever mistake occurs. Once you do this *pratikraman*, this opinion is erased.

The mind has arisen because of opinions. I never have any opinions about anyone. This is because after having 'seen' once, there is no second opinion. If a person steals due to circumstances, and I see it with my own eyes, even then I will not call him a thief. This is because it is his circumstances that lead him to steal. People would immediately label him a thief if they caught him stealing. Was it due to circumstances or not? Was he a thief forever? The world does not care about this. I would only call a person a thief if he were a thief forever (steals all the time), and not the one who steals only due to the bad circumstance. My opinion about a person does not change, once it is made. Until now I have not changed my opinion about anyone.

## Pratikraman is Disagreement with Old Opinion

**Questioner:** Now I have to continue doing *pratikraman* for the opinions that arise, do I not?

**Dadashri:** The opinions that arise are due to a past *karmic* account (*hisaab*). If you do *pratikraman* now, then you do not bind an opinion again. In doing so, You are saying, 'I am no longer of the same opinion, I am not in agreement in this matter,' and so You become free at that time. Opinion that was bound in the past was cleared this time around. Once You understand this much, there will be no problem. If a mistake is being protected (*rakshan*), then You should correct that. There is nothing else to it. If you make a mistake, if you do something that would harm someone, you will attain closure if you do *pratikraman*.

What does *pratikraman* mean? It means, 'I am not in agreement with the mistake being made.' *Pratikraman* itself proves that I do not agree with that. Before, I was of the opinion that it should be done a certain way, but now I do not agree with that. It is enough if the opinion changes. This world exists on opinions.

## You Need to Become Aware Right Away

For you, everything is proceeding in agreement, is it not? You are proceeding with what you agree with, do you not?

(304)

**Questioner:** Opinions I have today differ (from those of the past).

**Dadashri:** How does your opinion differ; were you not fighting with that man?

**Questioner:** Later, after everything was over, the opinion was different.

**Dadashri:** But after how long? Does unawareness (*ajagruti*) last for six to eight months? Your awareness should come within one or two hours! But so much bad *karmic* stock has been stored. What I am saying is that too much garbage (*karmic* stock) has been piling up. Do you not feel that way?

**Questioner:** That is correct.

**Dadashri:** Within how many hours should one become aware?

**Questioner:** Within two hours.

**Dadashri:** Two, four, or even twelve hours, but You should become aware that, 'This is wrong.' But here, even when 'we' tell you, You do not realize it. This still occurs in so many instances, but You are not aware of it. 'We' would know right away that you are doing something wrong. Would 'we' not know this?

**Questioner:** Yes, You will.

**Dadashri:** Despite that, 'we' allow it to continue. But 'we' also know that eventually, everything will work out fine.

## There Must Be No Intent of Violence

'We' are saying that this worldly life is worth knowing more and, at the same time, both the opinions remain separate. Both opinions run concurrently.

We should not have any violent intent (*himsak bhaav*) at all. Even if someone were to kill you, you should not feel that he is wrong for doing that.

**Questioner:** There should be no feeling that he is wrong at all.

**Dadashri:** Even when he is killing you, you cannot say, 'He is doing violence (*himsa*) against me.' My *udayakarma* (unfolding of karma) and his *udayakarma* are fighting with each other. I am the Knower; he too is the Knower. It does not matter whether he remains as the Knower; he may be drunk, but even then I don't have anything to do with it. But I am the Knower for sure.

## The Complaint of the Pudgal

The one who is very aware (*jagrut*) does not need to do *pratikraman*. But to the one who has less awareness, 'we' do tell him to do *pratikraman*.

**Questioner:** One has to do *pratikraman* if one has less awareness (*ajagruti*)?                                    (306)

**Dadashri:** Yes, *pratikraman* is to change the opinion that, 'This opinion is not mine. I am not part of this opinion. I was bound by the opinion, but I have let go of that opinion. I have a contrary opinion now. To swear at someone or hurt him is not my opinion. I became angry but that is not my opinion anymore.'

So, by doing *pratikraman*, the subatomic particles become pure (*shuddha*) and leave. When you purify the subatomic particles (*parmanus*), they become *vishrasa* (pure, subatomic particles in discharge process). There is no simultaneous new binding of *karmic* matter (*samvar*); bondage (*bandha*) does not occur and *vishrasa* occurs. Actually, *vishrasa* occurs for every living being (*jiva*), but it occurs along with a bondage. Whereas, here in *Akram*, discharge (*vishrasa*) occurs without bondage (*bandha*) occurring.

After You become Self-realized, it is your obligation to make 'Chandulal,' the relative self, pure (*shuddha*). If the non-

Self complex (*pudgal*) could express its feelings it would say:

'I was always pure! It is you who has contaminated me with your intent (*bhaav*). I had neither bones, nor blood, nor pus. I was absolutely pure. You have defiled me. Unless you make me as pure as You are, You will not attain final liberation.' Do you understand that?

**Questioner:** Yes, Dada.

**Dadashri:** So which Agna did 'we' put in place? The Agna to settle all accounts with equanimity. Yes, and to see only the pure Self in everyone. And if you do something that the other person does not like, the *atikraman* has occurred and so you have to make him, 'Chandulal,' do *pratikraman*. So what You are trying to say is that You are against his opinion. You changed the opinion. You do not hold the past opinion anymore. He becomes pure as the opinion changes. If the opinion had remained the same, then the main garbage would remain. This *pratikraman* is to change opinions.

## The Vision That is Beyond All Opinions

**Questioner:** So how can one be completely free of opinion?

**Dadashri:** You have been given the opinion free Gnan. By real view point, 'He' is *Shuddhatma* and by the relative view point he is 'Chandubhai.' And because the relative is karma-dependent, even 'Chandubhai' is faultless (*nirdosh*). If he were independent, then he would have been considered at fault (*doshit*). But he ('Chandulal') is like a 'top' (that spins dictated by his karma effect) and so he is *nirdosh* (faultless). 'He is a *Shuddhatma* and the external is *nirdosh*.' Now tell me, can you not remain opinion free all the time?

## Binding of Grave Karma

**Questioner:** A human being binds so many karmas, day

and night, that it will take infinite time to discharge karma (*nirjara*) of just one lifetime, so when can he ever be free?

**Dadashri:** Who told you that? This happens to others (non-Self-realized people), not to You (*mahatma*).

**Questioner:** I am talking about other people.

**Dadashri:** Those people bind so many karmas that if they run around on bikes or in airplanes from seven in the morning, they will not be done with their karma by eleven at night. (308)

**Questioner:** So, what kind of a predicament are they in? The karmas bound in one day are so many that even a year is not enough to discharge it.

**Dadashri:** Yes, so what will occur as he continues to bind karma? He will go from a human life with five senses to the one with four senses, then from four senses to the three senses, then from three to two and then he will become a one-sensed being. That is how grave the karmas are that they are binding.

**\*\*\*\*\***

## [18]

# He Who Conquers Sexuality is the Emperor of the World

## Now You Have to Be Free From the Atkan of Sexuality

Now everything within should become very clear. Having attained *Akram Gnan*, it is possible for one to remain in constant bliss if he so chooses. Such is the Gnan You have, so now your effort should be towards how you can break free from *atkan* (major blockade or impediment, within, for liberation). You have to do *alochana*, *pratikraman* and *pratyakhyan* and bring about a resolution. Before, when there was no bliss, it was natural for one to fall prey to *atkan*. But once eternal happiness arises, why should that be the case? Why does bliss not arise? It does not come because of this *atkan*.

## Be Warned About Only Sexuality

**Questioner:** Dada, I understand now that I am doing wrong, and yet it occurs.

**Dadashri:** Does *pratikraman* not occur afterwards?

**Questioner:** It does. But I cannot stop when 'Chandubhai' is doing wrong. Then I immediately do *pratikraman*. But within no time, he turns everything around and does the wrong thing.

**Dadashri:** There is nothing wrong with everything going wrong. But this sexuality is one thing that makes a person forget everything. So 'we' tell you to be vigilant when it comes to matters related to sexuality.

You are not able to see your mistakes as days go by. Eating heavy meals will cause sloth and dullness (*pramaad*); for the most part, your awareness will go down for several hours after you eat, then the intoxication will come down. But intoxication of sexuality remains for a whole twenty-four hours. This is the reason that one simply is not able to see his mistake. One will begin to see his mistake when he becomes free from sexuality. These mistakes are the serious mistakes, the subtle mistakes, and one does not see them because of his dependency on sexuality. So it is up to each individual to do *pratikraman*, depending on how much hurry he is in. As such, here there is no such rule that one should do this only in this way.    (310)

## Why Am I Attracted to a Specific Person?

**Questioner:** Having decided that I do not want to have bad thoughts about any young man, I do not get bad thoughts about him – but I keep seeing his face and the associated feelings, even after I do *pratikraman*. What should I do?

**Dadashri:** So what if you keep 'seeing' that? You have to keep 'seeing' it. Do you experience pain when you see a movie? You will see his face.

You will be able to 'see' more when the inside becomes cleansed; You will 'see' clearly. Do *pratikraman* and keep 'seeing' that which arises, that is all.

**Questioner:** She (the relative self) does *pratikraman* because she does not like the attraction that arises for him. Yet he appears within more and more.

**Dadashri:** It is fine if You 'see' that. But You must be able to 'see' all that (the attraction and associated feelings); it is useless if You cannot 'see' that. It cannot be considered *pratikraman* if You cannot 'see' that. *Pratikraman* can occur only if You can 'see.' Thereafter, with *pratikraman*, it (attraction; *raag*) will become less and less. If the *karmic* tuber is large, it will not decrease all of a sudden.

**Questioner:** If I keep seeing his face and have bad (sexual) thoughts about him, is that not wrong?

**Dadashri:** No, there is nothing wrong in that. You are strong so all You have to do is to 'see' that these sexual thoughts are still arising. If You are strong, then nothing will touch you. This is simply the *karmic* stock that was filled in the past life, that is coming out. If the stock was not there, then you would not be having any thoughts about anyone. There are so many young men; you don't have thoughts about all of them, do you? Whatever stock there is within is coming out. Would you not recognize that this is stored stock (*bharelo maal*)? There are so many young men but these thoughts do not arise for all of them, do they?

The thoughts arise about only those few whom you have seen and you get attracted when your eyes (*drashti*) fall on them.

## The Path as Suggested by the Gnani

If I ask if his mind still gets spoiled, he will say, 'Yes, it occurs even now.' Even at age seventy! Why don't you settle down? What kind of a man are you? Your 'shop' (body) is bankrupt and yet you are not settling down.

**Questioner:** If a person has such sexual thoughts, what should he do in that situation?

**Dadashri:** Let it come. When it comes, welcome it with flowers and tell the thought, 'I am glad that you came. I like that.' You will have at least this much pleasure, will you not? Instead of bringing thoughts of grief and sorrow, it is bringing these good thoughts!

You may get a sexual thought by looking at someone. Now, why did this thought arise? It is because there is *moha* (illusory attraction) inside, filled from the past life, and that is why this circumstance (*sainyog*) arose. When do such circumstances come together? It is not as if you went out to invite them! But they come together, all the same! When circumstances come together, your mind at that time is under the influence of *moha* and the subatomic particles of sexuality will show you all its phases. What should You do at that time? Who is the *nimit* for this wrong sexual thought? You should do *pratikraman* in the name of that *nimit*. Then do the *pratikraman* to the pure Soul of that lady by saying, 'Dear pure Soul, who is separate from the union of mind, speech and body, charge karma (*bhaavkarma*), subtle discharge karma (*dravyakarma*) and gross discharge karma (*nokarma*) of this lady (insert her name here)! I just had sexual thoughts about this lady. For that I am doing *alochana* (confession) in front of Dada Bhagwan.' To declare this is *alochana*. You do not need to call Me there for My physical presence. You can have Me there through this inner contemplation and then do the *pratikraman*: 'Dear pure Soul, grant me the power and energy not to have such thoughts about anybody. I am asking for Your forgiveness for such thoughts. Grant me the energy never to have such sexual thoughts about anybody.'

'It is my determination and desire never to harbor such thoughts in the future,' is called *pratyakhyan*.              (312)

Your wish is to never have such thoughts again, and yet they will come if they are in your *karmic* stock. But you will have to do *pratyakhyan* every time. However many times you do *pratyakhyan*, that many layers of the 'onion' are shed. Then the next layer will come. Which onions have more layers, small ones or big ones?

**Questioner:** Large ones have more.

**Dadashri:** Yes, so for the one who has a 'large onion,' for him more layers will be shed. But they are being shed.

Therefore, there is *moksha* with *alochana*, *pratikraman* and *pratyakhyan*. If there is one tool for *moksha* in this world, then this is the one. But *alochana*, *pratikraman* and *pratyakhyan* should be done as taught by the Gnani Purush. The *pratikraman* taught by others will not work.

Therefore, do *alochana*, *pratikraman* and *pratyakhyan* whenever you have sexual thoughts about anyone. You definitely have to do that.

**Questioner:** Dada, if one is attracted to the same place again and again, is that not because he has interest in it?

**Dadashri:** Of course, it has to do with interest. He would not be attracted if he was not interested, would he?

**Questioner:** Yes. But was the seed of karma sown (charged) because of his interest in it, or not?

**Dadashri:** Now you are talking crazy again. One will not be attracted if he is not interested, will he?

**Questioner:** There is interest within. I do *pratikraman* for the attraction, but when the night falls, I get attracted there again, the interest is there again, more *pratikraman* is done for it and that chapter is closed. Then, after five minutes or so, I am affected again and I feel, 'What nonsense is this?'

**Dadashri:** You should erase it again, that is all.

**Questioner:** Is that all? Should I not be concerned about anything else?

**Dadashri:** This is a *karmic* stock that you have accumulated and the responsibility is yours. Therefore, You have to keep 'seeing' it; you should not become lax in washing it off.

**Questioner:** What is considered, 'The cloth has been washed completely?'

**Dadashri:** You, yourself, will know that it has been washed off when you do *pratikraman*.

**Questioner:** Should some repentance remain within?

**Dadashri:** Of course repentance should remain! There should be repentance until it (sexuality) is completely resolved. 'You' just have to 'see' whether there is remorse (*khed*), or not. 'You' have to do Your job and he ('Chandulal') has to do his.

**Questioner:** Dada, it is very sticky. All this is very sticky, but it is changing gradually.                                    (314)

**Dadashri:** The kind of mistake (*dosh*) that was filled (as *karmic* stock in the past life) is the kind that comes out, but it will all empty in twelve, ten or five years. The whole 'tank' will be cleaned out. Then it will be clean! Then enjoy yourself!

**Questioner:** Once the seed (of sexuality) is planted, it is bound to sprout, is it not?

**Dadashri:** The seed will be sown without fail! It will manifest (come into effect in next life), but as long as it has not taken root, if you can decrease its energy, then by the time you die it will all become clean.

That is why I tell those who have made mistakes in matters of sexuality to fast on a Sunday and spend all day repenting about it and washing it off over and over again. If they were to do that in compliance with this Agna, it will all come to an end.

## When Pratikraman Fails, Confess to the Gnani

**Questioner:** Sometimes, when I look at someone sexually, then from within I feel, 'Why did I have to look at her in this way? I will have to do *pratikraman*.' I get really tired of doing this.

**Dadashri:** Yes, you will get tired. It is the inner vision, the sexual look that occurs; it occurs even though you do not wish it to. That is why you have to do *purusharth* and *pratikraman*.

**Questioner:** I get so angry about certain things that I feel, 'Why does it occur?' I can't understand it.

**Dadashri:** You did not do *pratikraman* last time. That is why this, your vision, spoilt again. Now if you do *pratikraman*, it will not be spoilt in the next life.

**Questioner:** Many times I feel tired of doing *pratikraman*. I have to do so many, all of a sudden.

**Dadashri:** Yes, this is the mistake which is the result of not doing *pratikraman* in the previous life. You did not do *pratikraman* at that time and that is why this occurs this time around. By doing *pratikraman* now, that mistake will not occur again, in the next life.

It should not become spoilt from within. Do *pratikraman* and wash it off if it gets ruined from within. Or come personally to Dada and tell Him that this is how much your mind was spoilt. Tell Dada that you do not want to hide anything from him. Then all will be erased. 'We' will give you the medicine for it right here. 'We' will wash off the mistake made elsewhere, but who will erase the mistake made directly in the presence of a Gnani Purush? That is why 'we' tell you not to spoil your mind here.

## Root Cause of Worldly Life from Birth to Birth

Sexuality is the only thing in this world that is the cause of bondage life after life. The world has arisen from this and it has given rise to everything else. Therefore, one should change his current opinion about sexuality right from the outset, so that no other opinion remains at all about it. Opinion should be changed every day through *samayik* and *pratikraman*.

**Questioner:** One should even change his opinion through *pratikraman*?

**Dadashri:** Yes.

There is an eight hundred page book on celibacy (*brahmacharya*) called *Samaj thi Prapt Brahmacharya* (Celibacy Attained through Understanding). Have you read it? People refer to it as 'the wonder of the world.' An invaluable weapon has been given for those who want to maintain celibacy.

(316)

## Substitute for Pratikraman

**Questioner:** You have said that every morning we should say five times, 'Let no living being be hurt, even to the slightest degree, through my mind, speech and body.' So if I do this much, will it work for that (sexuality)?

**Dadashri:** One can say it five times, but the way in which he says it should be with the same focused concentration and interest that he has when he is counting one hundred dollar bills.

**Questioner:** If I do *pratikraman* in matters of sex with the same intensity every morning five times (Sixth Kalam of Dadashri), is that acceptable? Otherwise, how many *pratikramans* does one have to do? The eyes get pulled (look sexually) so many times!

**Dadashri:** Yes, yes, it will do. But how should you say it? Just as you keep your *chit* (inner complex of knowledge and vision) focused when you are counting money. The way your *antahkaran* (the inner functioning components of the mind, intellect, *chit* and the ego) is when you are counting money; that is how it should be when you are doing this.

## For That, You Need to Do Thousands of Pratikraman a Day

For now, you should take care of your eyes as to where they wander. There was a time when people used to gouge out their eyes if they looked upon someone with lustful intentions.

That is sheer foolishness; you are not to do that. If it occurs for you, you should simply avert your eyes and if it occurs again, then do *pratikraman*. Do not forsake even a minute's worth of *pratikraman* in this matter. Mistakes associated with your eating and drinking habits are inconsequential, as compared to those of sexuality. Sexuality is the worst disease for the one who wants freedom from worldly life. Bondage to the worldly life exists because of sexuality.

You have to be wise and get your work done. If you buy goods from the black market, you will have to sell it on the black market, but you have to tell 'Chandubhai' to do *pratikraman* for it. Before, he did not do *pratikraman* and because of that, he has filled ponds and ponds of karma. Doing *pratikraman* means it is cleansed. When you do five hundred to a thousand *pratikraman* a day; that is when you will get your work done.

## You Can Never Take What is Not Rightfully Yours

If you take what is rightfully yours, you will be born as a human being, but if you violate this rule and take what is not rightfully yours, you will be born in the animal kingdom.

**Questioner:** I have taken something which has not been rightfully mine.

**Dadashri:** You should do *pratikraman* for that. The Lord (within) will still save you. You can still go into the Jain temple (*derasar*) and repent. As long as you are alive, you should continue to repent for taking things that were forbidden to you (illicit sex). Repent as long as you remain in this body.

**Questioner:** What occurs with just repenting?

**Dadashri:** If you have the understanding for it, then go ahead and do it. It is your choice whether to listen to what the Gnani Purush tells you or not. If you do not listen to Him, then there is no other solution.

Even now, if you repent, the *karmic* knots and tubers will loosen. When you made the mistake, you did it with your approval and pleasure and for that you have bound karma for a life in hell. It is one thing to take that which is forbidden, but if it is done with pleasure, one is bound for hell. But if he repents for it, it will take him to a life in the animal kingdom. One will have to suffer the horrors of hell. So take and enjoy as much as you want from people, that which is forbidden to you!

**Questioner:** What is the best solution to be free from all this?

**Dadashri:** Repent for anything that you have taken from others that was not yours by right. Repent all day. You cannot take what is not yours. It is only good if it is for you. You have your own wife, your own children, your own home, etc. So why should you take anything that belongs to others? Then you have no choice but become an animal; then you become worthy of a life in hell. You are trapped in grave misery. If you want to take heed, there is still time to do so. What this Gnani Purush is saying is that you have been given a weapon called repentance. Keep doing *pratikraman*.                                        (318)

'Dear Lord, I ask for forgiveness for the mistakes I have committed through misunderstanding and malicious intellect (*buddhi*), encouraged by *kashays*.'

You have done all this at the instigation of your *kashays*; You have not done them yourself. You are still free to continue doing them if you want to, and if you don't want to, then it is also up to you.

## Intense Greed Causes Grave Karmic Veils

One can become free if he sets aside all the things that tempt him, and does not think about them; and when he does think about them, he does *pratikraman* for them. However, scripture writers have not shown a solution for that. There is a solution for everything, but there is no solution for covetousness and intense greed (*lalach*). There is a solution for greed (*lobh*). When a greedy person incurs a loss, his greediness will go away very quickly.

**Questioner:** Will covetousness and intense greed (*lalach*) to enjoy that which is not rightful go away if one sits in the Gnan Vidhi again?

**Dadashri:** No, it will not. How can it go away by sitting in the Gnan Vidhi? It can be achieved if he decides that he wants to remain constantly in the Agnas and tries to abide by them, and does *pratikraman* if he does not.

## Even Now, Be Aware! Beware!! Beware!!!

**Questioner:** Dada, you have said that seventy percent of the human beings here will take birth in the animal kingdom in the next life. This bothers me. Is there any hope for us?

**Dadashri:** No, no, there is no hope, but if you become alert and aware...

**Questioner:** I am talking about those who have attained Self-realization (*mahatmas*).

**Dadashri:** Nothing in this world can touch a *mahatma* if he is following my Agnas.

**Questioner:** We will be firm and resolute from now on, but please do take care of us.

**Dadashri:** Yes, that is secured. 'We' will take good care of you.

In this peculiar time era, I am cautiously saying to follow seventy percent of the Agnas so that people will not feel bad. People will get scared, that is why. This percentage is even higher, because those with higher intellect (*buddhi*) have taken advantage of those with lesser intellect. The consequence of that is a life in hell. Not animal life form but a life in hell. Now tell me, what have people left alone? That is why I warn people and tell them to be very alert and aware and ask for forgiveness, because through *pratikraman*, there is still a way out.

If you were to write a letter to a relative of yours when you are in an angry mood, and you even curse him in the letter over and over again, your letter will offend him. But if, in the closing, you write a footnote with an apology and explain your angry frame of mind, because you had a quarrel with your wife, would he not be considerate and forgiving even though he has read the curses and insults from you? Likewise, all mistakes committed in life so far are erased, if *pratikraman* is done before leaving this body. You should ask for forgiveness from whomever you consider as your God. If not, you can come to me for forgiveness and I will help arrange for you to be free.

A very bleak and terrible time is yet to come, and still 'Chandulal' behaves recklessly. Your life carries a tremendous liability with it. I even hesitate when I say that seventy percent of the human race is doomed! This is the final assurance I give you in these terrible times. I am putting the weapon of *pratikraman* into your hands. With *pratikraman*, you stand a chance of being saved. And if you do it according to my Agnas, your salvation will come sooner. You will have to suffer the results of your mistakes, but not many.

Sooner or later, you will have to understand, won't you? You will have to understand it completely, will you not? You will have to turn towards *moksha*, will you not?          (320)

## How the Gnani Molds and Purifies the Prakruti

If someone tells you that you have no sense and insults you in public, and your spontaneous reaction is to want to bless him, you should know that You are separate form the world of the non-Self complex. At such a time of public insult, You are also aware that 'Chandulal' is being scolded and not You.

Normally, during *satsangs* I would invite 'Chandulal' to come and sit in the front. On some days, I would not even acknowledge his presence. What is My intention? I know that he will feel rejected for having to sit in the back. I would continue to give him praise at one time and deflate him at another. By doing this, he would progress further in Gnan. I employ different tactics with each person for their progress in this Gnan; it is different for each person. Getting rid of the *prakruti's* (the non-Self complex) weaknesses is very important, because how long can You go on keeping something that does not even belong to You?

**Questioner:** You are right; there is no escape as long as the weaknesses of the *prakruti* exist.

**Dadashri:** As for 'us,' it was this Gnan and Nature that helped 'us' get rid of 'our' *prakruti*. Yours will not go until 'we,' as your *nimit* (the one instrumental in a process), do it for you.

For You, a lot of the *prakruti* is gone, but because the mistake is still there you still have to do *pratikraman* at night. You will have to get rid of that mistake. You realize that afterwards, don't you?

**Questioner:** Yes, immediately.

**Dadashri:** You will realize it later. Your whole night will pass in doing *pratikraman*.

## As Mistakes Decrease, Awareness Increases

**Questioner:** It seems that for the last year or two, I am doing a lot less *pratikraman* than before.          (321)

**Dadashri:** Before, you were not even aware of the mistake.

**Questioner:** Yes.

**Dadashri:** You never did any *pratikraman* and believed that it was only the other person's fault.

**Questioner:** Then *pratikraman* continued for two or three years and for the past six months to a year and a half, they have become fewer. Do I still have to do *pratikraman* even when the sense of mistakes has gone down?

**Dadashri:** Yes, because mistakes are going to occur right until the end. This body verily is made up of mistakes.

**Questioner:** The level of mistakes is going down.

**Dadashri:** 'You' (the Self) have to 'see' and 'know'. Your awareness will increase as the mistakes decrease. You may end up doing *pratikraman* the whole night, but you do not blame the other person. You turn it around, which you never did before. You now have to see through Gnan that all his 'letters' (hurt) are coming to you, but now you know that he too can see his own mistakes. So he must be doing *pratikraman*. You have to understand that, 'This is fine with me, let the 'letters' come to me.' The one that writes letters is the *prakruti*, and the one that does *pratikraman* is the Self (awakened Self). Even now, he continues to write letters; that is all the *prakruti*, but he also does *pratikraman*. The *pratikraman* is the part of the Self.

## The Worst Form of Atikraman

**Questioner:** What is the extreme, the worst form of *atikraman*?

**Dadashri:** Only *Vasudevas* and *Prativasudevas* (*Salakha Purush* – human beings with extraordinary super human energies and accomplishments) have the extreme limit of *atikraman*. No one else can do *atikraman* beyond that. And also no one can suffer through hell, the worst level, the seventh hell, like them. The ultimate *atikraman* is when one kills and destroys everything. Common people do not have this.  (322)

In short, you should not spoil your inner intent (*bhaav*) towards your enemy. And if it does get spoilt, then improve it with *pratikraman*. The fact that it gets spoilt is due to your weakness (*kashay*) and, therefore, improve it with *pratikraman*. In this way, it will become *siddha* (ultimately attained to perfection).

**\*\*\*\*\***

# [19]
# The Problem of Compulsive Lying

## Karma: Cause and Effect

Do you now bind any new karma during the course of the day? What karma have you bound so far? You will have to suffer whatever karmas you have bound. It is your own responsibility. God is not responsible for any of them at all.

**Questioner:** Are we binding karma when we tell lies? (323)

**Dadashri:** Of course! But more than telling a lie, it is the intent (*bhaav*) to tell a lie that binds more karma. Telling lies is the effect of past life karma. The actual charging of karma occurs because of one's internal intent and determination to tell lies. Will this knowledge help you?

**Questioner:** One should stop telling lies.

**Dadashri:** No. You should let go of the very opinion (*abhipraay*) that it is acceptable to lie. If you lie, you must repent for it by saying, 'What should I do? I must not tell such lies.' You will not be able to stop lying but your opinion will change to, 'I am not going to lie from today onwards. Lying is a very big *karmic* offence (*sin*). Lying causes great pain and it creates karma bondage.' Once you form such an opinion, then your demerit karma of lying will cease. However, the effect of the prior wrong opinions, which were not corrected, will continue as the act of lying. That much account is left to come. That much lying will be mandatory for you and when it occurs, repent (*prashchyataap*) for it.

Now, even if you repent after telling lies, you will continue to tell lies because the effect of karma is inevitable. You have no choice but suffer it for sure. So when people leave your home, they will talk and make comments like, 'Why does an educated person like Chandulal have to lie? Does that suit him?' Hence you will have to suffer the fruit of that lying again, even if you repent. And if you stop that incoming 'water' in the 'tank' in the first place, if the causes are stopped in the first place, then the effect of the cause and its effect will not be there.

So what are 'we' saying? You may end up telling a lie, but are you opposed to that lie by having the opinion, 'I should not say things like that?' That shows that you do not like telling lies. When you do not have an opinion that you should tell lies, then Your responsibility ends.

**Questioner:** But what can one do if he has a habit of lying... become a compulsive liar?

**Dadashri:** He has to develop a simultaneous habit of doing *pratikraman*. And when he does *pratikraman*, then the responsibility is 'ours' (Dada's).'

So change your opinion! Lying is tantamount to killing one's self. To lie is the same as killing the self. That is what You have to decide. But at the same time, do not become obstinately attached to insisting on the truth.

## Lying in Worldly Life

What should the 'relative religion' (worldly interaction) be like? It should be that, 'If you have to lie, do so; but do *pratikraman*.'

**Questioner:** I say every day that, 'It is wrong to lie and I did not want to lie,' but it still occurs. Why does it occur even when I do not want it to?

**Dadashri:** You have brought with you that 'over-wiseness' (lying is beneficial) from the past life. That is why 'we' have never told you that you cannot tell a lie. Had 'we' done that, you would have taken heed. Have 'we' ever told you that you cannot lie?                                                                                    (324)

**Questioner:** Then, until I fall asleep, I keep doing *pratikraman*. Now, whenever I feel that I am doing something wrong, I have him, 'Chandubhai,' do *pratikraman*.

**Dadashri:** You have to do *pratikraman* if you do something wrong, don't you?

**Questioner:** But what if we do not do anything wrong in the first place, in that time...

**Dadashri:** But that will not work. You have to withdraw Your interest from it and maintain that, 'This that is occurring is wrong. It should not be this way.' As long as you like it, you will derive a taste from it. And if you get to the point where you don't like it, then there is no problem. You want to eat, and if it is something that you do not really like, then there is no problem if you eat it.

## After Entering Real Religion

**Questioner:** At the time of doing wrong, should the inner intent (*bhaav*) be, 'I should not be doing this,' or should I remain as the Knower-Seer (*Gnata-Drashta*)?

**Dadashri:** You have been told to remain the Knower-Seer and 'do (make 'Chandulal' do)' *pratikraman*, have you not?

**Questioner:** But such *bhaav* (to lie) should not occur, should it?

**Dadashri:** It is not that *bhaav* should not occur; you should give 'Chandulal' the awareness, 'Do *pratikraman*. Why did you do *atikraman*?' *Kraman* occurs the whole day; *atikraman* does not. *Atikraman* occurs once or twice a day, for which you have to do *pratikraman*.

You should be aware of all your weaknesses. 'You' are not weak; You have become the Self, but prior to Self-realization, you were the main creator of all these weaknesses, were you not? So now You, as a neighbor, should say, 'Chandulal, do *pratikraman*.'

Do a lot of *pratikraman*. Whatever fifty to a hundred, or so, persons you have mistreated and abused, do hours of *pratikramans* a day for each such individual at a time. You will have to wash off all that. Then the Gnan will manifest in you.

**Questioner:** But, Dada, I have abused only those who have abused me.

**Dadashri:** Those who have abused you will pay their own price. You are not responsible for that. They are not aware of their responsibility. He is eating *chapaati* (*rotli*; flat bread) in this life, but he does not have any problem with eating bales of hay in his next life!

## Merit and Demerit Karma in Operation

**Questioner:** There are some people who, even when they lie, people think they are telling the truth. And there are some people who, even when they tell the truth, people think they are lying. What is this puzzle?					(326)

**Dadashri:** That occurs on the basis of one's demerit karma (*paap*) and merit karma (*punya*). If one's unfolding of his demerit karma is in operation, then people will not believe him even when he is telling the truth; and if his merit karma is in operation, people will believe him even when he is telling lies.

**Questioner:** So is there no harm in it for him?

**Dadashri:** Of course, there is harm in it – but it is for the next life. Today, he is enjoying the fruit from his past life. But by telling lies today, he is sowing seeds, the fruit of which he will have to face in his next life. Today, he is sowing the seeds (creating causes); this world is not haphazard or slipshod such that one can do whatever one wants!

**Questioner:** Is it acceptable if a person deliberately does wrong and then says, 'I will do *pratikraman* for it'?

**Dadashri:** No. You should not do it deliberately. But you should do *pratikraman* when something wrong occurs.

If you tell someone, 'You are a liar,' there is so much science that stirs up instantly within that it gives rise to so many different phases, the consequence of which is there for two hours or so, it will be very hard to see anything attractive in him. That many phases can arise. Therefore, before saying a word…it is best if nothing is said. And if you end up saying something, then do *pratikraman*. 'We' cannot tell you that you cannot say anything, because it is *vyavasthit*; but do *pratikraman* if you do say something. That is the tool we have. Do you do *pratikraman*?

**Questioner:** Yes.

## You Have To Empty This Shop

**Questioner:** So then, how is one to live this life?

**Dadashri:** You have to 'see' how it is being lived.

**Questioner:** Then how is one to decide what is wrong and what is right?

**Dadashri:** 'You' have to keep 'seeing' what 'Chandulal' is doing.

**Questioner:** Is there no problem if 'Chandulal' does something wrong?

**Dadashri:** Whatever 'Chandulal' does is in the form of discharge. Nothing can be changed in that. Discharge (effect) can never be changed. Have you ever heard that? You can make changes when taking an examination, but can you change the result?

**Questioner:** No.

**Dadashri:** So, this all is a result.

**Questioner:** But if something wrong continues to be done, will I have problems in my next life?

**Dadashri:** You will not. All You have to do is to tell 'Chandulal' to do *pratikraman*. Even the good things one does in the non-Self-realized state comes back in the next life. 'We' (the enlightened ones in *Akram Vignan*) do not have anything to do with right or wrong. 'We' just have to let everything discharge (*nikaal*). 'We' have to get rid of the 'shop.' Whether the stock is good or bad, we just have to get rid of it all. Now, all this is an effect.

## A Firm Determination to Remain in the Agnas

**Questioner:** We have to live on the basis of the Agnas you have given us, is that not so?

**Dadashri:** You have to live by and follow the five Agnas. That protects the *Atma* and the Agnas protect the Gnan. It is not difficult, is it?                                      (328)

**Questioner:** No, they are difficult for sure. The equanimity you have told us to maintain means that we should not get angry with anyone, or we should not say anything to anyone.

**Dadashri:** No, you have to decide that, 'I want to settle with equanimity,' that is all. You do not have to 'see' anything else. You do not have to 'see' whether it occurred or not.

**Questioner:** In whatever manner it may occur, is that so?

**Dadashri:** 'You' do not have to enter into that complexity (*bhanjghad*) at all. Now, after Gnan, there is nothing as right or wrong. That which is right for the Hindus is wrong for the Muslims. And that which is right for the Muslims is wrong for the Hindus. As far as God is concerned, there is no such thing as right or wrong. They are just worldly arrangements. All He says is to do *pratikraman* if you hurt anyone. You should not hurt anyone. The belief that 'I am Chandulal' is true for the world, but in the realm of the Lord (the Self), there is no 'Chandulal'! This worldly truth is untruth there.

The worldly life will continue. It will not hinder you and Your work will get done; that is how things will work. You just have to follow my Agnas with devotion. Tell 'Chandulal' to do *pratikraman*. Telling a lie is an attribute of the relative self (*prakruti*) and, thus, it will not refrain from doing so. I do not object to telling a lie. I object to not doing *pratikraman* after telling a lie. When you tell a lie and, at that time, you have the inner intent (*bhaav*) of *pratikraman*, the meditation that is there is *dharmadhyan* (absence of adverse meditation). People are looking for *dharmadhyan*. When a lie is spoken, then request 'Dada' for forgiveness and ask for the energy not to do it again.

*****

## [20]

# Awareness When Words are Flowing in Speech...

## Speaking Causes Increased Bondage of Karma

The mind is not as much of a problem as the speech is, because the mind functions secretly, whereas words cause a deep wound in a person's heart and hurt him severely. You must ask for forgiveness from whomever you have hurt with your speech. You must recall each and every person and do *pratikraman* for that hurt.

**Questioner:** Can I expect to be forgiven with *pratikraman*, for all the hurt committed through speech? (330)

**Dadashri:** The faults will remain in the form of a burned rope. It looks like a rope, but it cannot bind like a rope. With *pratikraman* for these mistakes in this life, the residual effect will instantly disintegrate in the next life like the ashes of the burned rope. *Pratikraman* dissolves the binding nature of the mistakes.

Doership is the support on which karma is bound. Now that You are no longer the doer, no new karma will be bound. The remaining karmas from the past will bring forth their effects and then dissipate.

**Questioner:** But, Dada, what kind of an effect will this have on the other person?

**Dadashri:** That is not something You should be concerned

about. Once you do *pratikraman*, You do not have to worry about that. Just do more *pratikraman*.

**Questioner:** Suppose I happen to say it openly; then he will definitely be hurt by what I say, will he not?

**Dadashri:** Yes, but that pain and hurt arose against your wishes, did it not? Therefore, you should do *pratikraman*. Whatever account he had got settled.

**Questioner:** If I say something, he will feel badly from within, will he not?

**Dadashri:** Yes. He will feel bad. If the wrong has occurred, he will feel bad, will he not? The *karmic* account (*hisaab*) that has to be paid, you have no choice but pay it to be free.

**Questioner:** I cannot control it and that is why it comes out in words.

**Dadashri:** Yes. It will come out, but then you have to do *pratikraman* when that occurs; that is all. You have to repent and then decide not to do the same again.

Then, if you are sitting with some free time, keep doing *pratikraman* over and over again for it. In doing so, all those mistakes will become weak and then dissolve. Only the files that are sticky need to be tackled. They need to be made smooth and easy through *pratikraman*. Besides, there are only three or four such files, not many more.

## Worldly Interaction Cannot Be Remedied

**Questioner:** If a person speaks after becoming irritated, would that be considered *atikraman*?

**Dadashri:** Of course, it is *atikraman*.

**Questioner:** What occurs if speech that is hurtful comes out and hurts someone, and *pratikraman* is not done for it?

**Dadashri:** When such speech (*vani*) happens to come out, it wounds the other person; then suffering/pain (*dukh*) begins within him. How can you like that which hurts the other person?

**Questioner:** Does that bind karma?

**Dadashri:** Is it not against the law of nature to hurt anyone? And by doing so, have you not violated this law? When you follow my Agnas, you are practicing *dharma* (following my instruction), so then why not do *pratikraman*? What is wrong in doing it? Ask for forgiveness and make a firm resolution not to make the same mistake again. Is there even a need for you to look for justice? If a person understands that the relative life interaction (*vyavahar*) is exact as it is, then he would understand the natural justice. It is because of your own past accounts that your neighbor insults you. In the same token, it is because of the other person's past account that you speak harshly with him, but because you want liberation, you have to do *pratikraman*.

**Questioner:** But what about the 'bullet' that has already been fired?

**Dadashri:** That is dependant on the worldly interaction (*vyavahar*).

**Questioner:** Will this kind of approach not increase a revenge and vengeance cycle?

**Dadashri:** No, that is why we do *pratikraman*. *Pratikraman* is not just to take us to *moksha*, but it is also the direct phone call to God to block vengeance (*veyr*). Vengeance is created if one does not do *pratikraman*. Immediately do *pratikraman* when you realize that you have made a mistake; then you will not bind any vengeance, even when the other person wants to bind it, because *pratikraman* is the 'phone call' directly to his *Atma* (the Self). There is no remedy for the worldly life interaction. You do *pratikraman* if you want to go to *moksha*. Those who do not have the knowledge of the Self, if they want to keep the worldly life interaction (*vyavahar*) as the worldly life, then if someone says anything negative to them, they should look at it as being correct. But if one wants to go to *moksha*, then he has to do *pratikraman*, otherwise vengeance will be bound.

## Pratikraman in Hurtful Speech Effects

**Questioner:** Because of our Gnan, it does not affect me when people are rude or spiteful towards me. The problem is that sometimes I do end up speaking harshly during such times. At such times, if I take into account what you have said about speech being part of unfolding worldly interactions, is that not misusing the Gnan? Does this not support my own rude behavior towards others?

**Dadashri:** You must not use this as an excuse. Under such circumstances, you must do *pratikraman*. If you say something hurtful to someone, you must do *pratikraman*. (332)

No matter how rude the other person's speech may be, if You 'know' that it is of the non-Self and dependent on other factors, then you will not feel hurt at all.

Now, when you say something hurtful, then you should do *pratikraman* for it; that way you will not feel bad about what you said. Hence, this is how everything gets resolved. You are the Knower-Seer of what is being said, but for the hurt it causes others, You have to make the one ('Chandulal') who spoke the hurtful words do *pratikraman*.

## It Happens Even When You Do Not Wish It

**Questioner:** Even when I wish not to talk to someone, or I do not want to argue with him or fight with him, something happens and I end up saying things; I end up arguing and quarreling with him. What should I do to stop that?

**Dadashri:** That occurs on the final steps. When that path is close to ending, that is when things occur – even when you have no intention (desire) for it. What you should do at that time is repent and that will erase everything. That is the only solution when things go wrong; there is no other solution. It is only when things (karmas), are coming to an end that things occur against your wish and desire. This will happen when that specific task (karma) is coming to an end. Otherwise, if it is only halfway finished, things will occur and you will also have the inner intent (*bhaav*) for it to happen. You may have an inner intent of doing wrong and it will occur that way too. When you do not have the inner intent and things happen, then realize that the time has come for it to come to an end. From that you can know that the end is in sight. Therefore, 'Coming events cast their shadows before.'

## Cautionary Comment is Necessary

**Questioner:** You say that speech is dependent on the non-Self interaction (*paradhin*). So then I make a firm decision (*nischay*) that I do not want to talk badly with this person, no matter how sticky that file is. Will the 'code' (of speech) then become smaller?                                                  (334)

**Dadashri:** When you say something bad, tell him, 'Chandulal, do *pratikraman*,' and then tell 'Chandulal' not to speak badly again.

This way, it will gradually settle down. But You have to tell him that. If You do not make this cautionary comment (*takor*), it means that You are of the same opinion. Your opinion must be contrary to his.

**Questioner:** Many times it so happens that when I caution him, he improves again. Then such mistakes do not occur again. And sometimes, even when I caution him strongly and make a firm decision not to do it again, the mistake still occurs.

**Dadashri:** That occurs because of the mistake of past karma. It is your own weakness from the past, is it not? No one else is responsible for it. You will have to remove it yourself, will you not?

## A Lie for the Self is the Highest Truth

**Questioner:** If one tells a lie for the higher good (*parmartha*; for the Self), would he become liable for it?

**Dadashri:** Anything you do for the Self is not considered a mistake (*dosh*). And anything that is done for the body, is considered a mistake if it hurts others. It is a virtue if it helps others. When the intent is solely for the salvation of the Self, whatever deeds are done will not bind karma. However, if in the process someone is hurt, it is a mistake and calls for *pratikraman*.

## The Entire Worldly Life is Mandatory and it Occurs

**Questioner:** When I tell someone something without any negative intent in the mind but he feels, 'What he is saying is not right; it is wrong,' is that considered *atikraman*?

**Dadashri:** But because it hurts him, you should do *pratikraman*. What effort is that going to take? You can never be happy by hurting anyone.

**Questioner:** Many times, certain things have to be said in order to get work done in the worldly life. Otherwise, lethargy will take over and the other person will also become lethargic.

**Dadashri:** You may do that in the worldly life, but do *pratikraman* for it. You have to carry out the worldly interaction; you have no choice. It is mandatory (*farajiyat*). The whole world believes the worldly life to be voluntary (*marajiyat*). This *Akram Vignan* has disclosed that 'this worldly life is mandatory.' And only 'we' have declared that 'it occurs.'

**Questioner:** If I do not notice the effect of our *pratikraman* on the other person, does that mean that I am not doing it sincerely or is it because the other person has too many veils on his Self?

**Dadashri:** Do not concern yourself about the state of the other person. He may even be insane, who knows? You need to be sure that you are not instrumental in hurting him.

**Questioner:** Therefore, should I attempt to bring about a closure for any hurt I have caused him?

**Dadashri:** If you hurt the person, you will surely have to amend the situation. That is indeed your responsibility. This life of ours is not meant for hurting anyone.

From now on, you will not hurt others in the future. But you will have to resolve the mistakes that have already occurred, will you not?

**Questioner:** Even then, if the matter is not settled to his satisfaction, how much of it is my responsibility?

**Dadashri:** If you can meet the person face to face and apologize with humility, you should do so. However, if he taunts you instead, you should realize that you are dealing with an ignoble person. You must still resolve it, but it need not be done face to face. If, while asking for his forgiveness in person, he throws it back in your face, understand that you have made a mistake. But because he is what he is, you should no longer bow or belittle yourself in front of him.

## Golden Inner Intent but Wrong in the Eyes of the World

Do people suffer because of you?

**Questioner:** Yes, they do.                                   (336)

**Dadashri:** Do you realize that immediately?

**Questioner:** Immediately.

**Dadashri:** Is that so? What do you do then?

**Questioner:** I do *pratikraman*.

**Dadashri:** If you do *pratikraman* after you clash with them, what is wrong in that? Your intention is good, is it not? That is all that matters.

**Questioner:** Yes, the intention is good, so why do I need to do *pratikraman*?

**Dadashri:** You must do *pratikraman* because of the hurt caused to the other person. If people say, 'Oh, just look at how this woman is scolding her husband!' you have to do *pratikraman* for this. You must do *pratikraman* for everything that unfolds in front of you and is visible to the world. Your intentions may be as good as gold, but what good are they? Good intentions are not enough. Even though 'My' intentions are good, 'I' still have to do *pratikraman*. *Pratikraman* has to be done for any mistake that occurs. Everyone who has attained the Self has the intent for the salvation of the world, but that is simply not enough. *Pratikraman* must be done first and foremost. When you stain your clothes, do you not wash them? Likewise, these too, are considered 'stains.'

None of these people who are speaking in this world are really speaking! It is the 'tape record' that is speaking. Afterwards, he repents also, so that proves that he did not really do the talking, does it not? Now You react in a manner that will make him repent, but instead You say, 'Why did you say that?' so instead of repenting, he will strike back, 'What am I doing wrong?' Your approach should be conducive towards his repentance.

Whenever this 'tape recording' or 'ours (Dada's)' plays and there is a mistake in it, then 'we' immediately repent; it is not acceptable any other way.

## Say Cautionary Words Without the Hurt to Others

**Questioner:** If someone is doing something wrong in worldly interactions and I have to caution and warn him, what do I do if this speech hurts him?

**Dadashri:** You may be faced with the need to caution him, but because the ego becomes associated with it, you have to do *pratikraman*.

**Questioner:** If I do not caution and warn him, will he not get out of control?

**Dadashri:** You have to caution him, but you must know how to do so. If you do not know how to caution (*takor*), if you do not deal with that properly, then that caution becomes associated with the ego. Therefore, you must do *pratikraman*. When you caution him, he will indeed feel hurt, but if you keep doing *pratikraman*, within a few months your speech will begin to become pleasant to him. During current times, tested speech is needed. No one has the right to speak untested speech. If you do *pratikraman* in this way, it will all straighten out no matter what it is like.

**Questioner:** Many times we have to tell people for their own good, or stop them from doing harm. What about the hurt they feel at that time?

**Dadashri:** Yes, if it is something that is likely to hurt others, then You have to say, 'Chandulal, do *pratikraman*. Why did you do *atikraman*? Say you will not say that again and that you are repenting for what you said.' Do you understand? That is all the *pratikraman* you need.                (338)

You have a right to speak, but you should know how to say it. Generally, the moment one sees the other person, he pounces on him saying, 'You are like this and you are like that!'

That is considered *atikraman*, and so one has to do *pratikraman*.

## Saying Potentially Hurtful Words with Humility

**Questioner:** So it is not my look out (not my business) if the other person feels bad. I should go ahead and say it?

**Dadashri:** You should not say it; why should you say anything that will hurt anyone?

**Questioner:** Should I not say anything even when he is saying or doing something wrong?

**Dadashri:** You can say it. You can say, 'It is better if it does not occur that way, it is good if it occurs this way.' You should say it this way. But you talk to him as if you are his boss and that is why he feels hurt. Hurtful or negative words should be spoken with humility.

**Questioner:** Can humility be maintained while using hurtful words?

**Dadashri:** It can be maintained; that verily is called science (*vignan*)! That is because it is 'dramatic,' is it not? An actor named Lakshmichand plays the part of King Bhartruhari in the famous play. In the play he will say, 'I am King Bhartruhari. I am Queen Pingda's husband.' Then, in the play he cries out, 'Dear mother, please give me some food,' and tears are rolling from his eyes. Later, if you were to ask him, 'Hey! But you are Lakshmichand, are you not? Were you crying for real?' He will reply, 'Why should I cry? I have to act that way, otherwise they will cut my wages if I don't do a good job!' That is what you have to do – act after attaining Gnan. This worldly life is just a play!

**Questioner:** So do I not bind karma even when the other person feels hurt by me?

**Dadashri:** You should be careful that you do not become

instrumental (*nimit*) in hurting anyone. And if someone continues to hurt, that is his own karma. Make sure that you do not become the *nimit* for his pain.

**Questioner:** Still, what if in fury, or passion, I end up saying something hurtful?

**Dadashri:** Then do *pratikraman*.

## Pratikraman is Necessary Even if You Are Joking

When you raise your voice and someone gets hurt or, alas, even if you were joking with someone and that person is a little weak and puts up with your joking, then you have done *atikraman*. 'We' do joke with people but it is innocent fun and jokes. 'We' joke to remove their 'disease' and to make them stronger. 'We' have some fun and joy, and at the same time that person continues to make progress. But 'our' joke does not hurt him. Should there not be some joking and fun like that? He too will understand that 'we' are joking and that 'we' are not poking fun at him.

Now, whenever 'we' make fun of someone, 'we' have to do *pratikraman* for that also. 'We' are not exempt from that.

**Questioner:** Yes, but that's just simply having fun. Surely there is no problem with that.                              (340)

**Dadashri:** No, but even then 'we' have to do *pratikraman*. It is not so necessary for you, but it is imperative for 'us.' If 'we' do not do *pratikraman*, then the words from this taped record (speech of the Gnani) would not come out as clear.

**Questioner:** Your *pratikraman* must be occurring on the spot, a 'shoot-on-sight' *pratikraman*!

**Dadashri:** Yes. In that 'we' have no bad intent, yet it is considered a *kashay* (inner enemy) of laughter. Even though 'we' are not making fun of him, it is considered a *kashay* of laughing. 'That poor man is naïve, is that why you are poking fun at him?' But 'we' do *pratikraman*.

Even 'we' have a little fun in that. When 'we' 'poke fun' at them, there is a little enjoyment in it, but at the same time 'we' have a little fun with the knowledge that 'he is going to come out strong from this, so let things be. Everything will work out.'

**Questioner:** But the laughter you got at his expense: what kind of *pratikraman* does it call for?

**Dadashri:** Yes, it is *pratikraman* of compassion; it is for his progress. Other people will come and tell 'us,' 'Why don't you say something like that to me?' I tell them, "We' cannot tell you.' They do not need help to progress; they will do it on their own. They are capable of grasping everything through their wisdom. But 'we' have to do *pratikraman*. Is that not a wonder?

## There is Grave Danger in Making Fun of People

I too used to make fun of all sorts of people, from the ordinary to the very prominent and successful ones, from all walks of life. Egoistic intellect-laden people have a tendency to make fun of others. Is such an ego not futile? Is that not misuse of one's intellect? It is a sign of misguided intellect to make fun of others.

**Questioner:** Even now I feel like making fun of people.

**Dadashri:** There is grave danger in making fun at the expense of other people. One always has the capability of making fun through his intellect (*buddhi*), but it also carries a grave danger along with it. 'We' took on a grave liability 'our' entire life in this regard.

**Questioner:** What are the consequences of making fun of others?

**Dadashri:** It is better to slap someone than to make fun

of him. The liability involved in making fun of someone is infinitely greater than directly slapping him. You misuse your intelligence when you make fun of another person. You take advantage of your higher intellect to overcome his lesser intellect and thus make fun of him.

So then God within the other person will say, 'Are you taking advantage of him because of his lack of intellect?' Here, therefore, you make even God turn against you. Had you slapped the person on his face, he would have understood immediately and he would have taken matters into his own hands, but when you make fun of him, because he has lesser intellect, he is not able to respond. So God within him knows, 'Ah ha! You are cornering him because he is not intelligent enough? Very well then, come on to the battleground.' Then the Lord will sort us out!

**Questioner:** This is all I have ever done in my life.

**Dadashri:** But you can still do *pratikraman*, can't you? 'We' too have done the same thing, but it was wrong. That was the problem I had. Because the intellect before Gnan was being restricted, was without right direction; so what could one do? One will start bullying, won't he? So this is the advantage of having increased intellect (Dada being sarcastic), is it not? That is why the people who make fun of others have to suffer unnecessarily.

If you laugh at someone because of the way he walks, God will say, 'Here! Take this fruit!' Do not make fun of any kind at the expense of anyone in this world. All these hospitals have arisen because of such fun-making (*mashkari*). These broken legs and other limbs are a fruit of making fun of others (in the past life). Mine too (Dadashri had sustained hip fracture) was the fruit of making fun of others.

That is why 'we' say, 'It is very wrong to make fun of

people, because that is the same thing as making fun of God (within that person). It may be a donkey, but who is it in the real view? It is God.' Yes, ultimately it reaches the God within. Is God not present in every living being, in every creature? You cannot make fun of anyone. When you do that, the God within will know and say, 'Yes, come on; I will settle the score from this end!'                                                                    (342)

**Questioner:** Do I not have to do *pratikraman* as a solution to that?

**Dadashri:** Of course, you have to do that. You have no choice.

**Questioner:** What if I confess and repent the wrongful mistake with You as the witness and do *pratikraman* and ask for forgiveness?

**Dadashri:** It will be acceptable even when you just say, 'Dada! With You as the witness, I ask for forgiveness for whomever I have hurt with my speech,' and it will reach them.

## Silence is Golden

In this *dushamkaal* (current era of lack of unity in thoughts, speech and acts), karma is bound through speech. In *sushamkaal* (past era of time cycle where there was unity in thoughts, speech and acts), karma was bound through the mind. *Moksha* is natural and spontaneous, if it were not for the existence of these hurtful words. Therefore, you should not say a word about anyone. To say anything hurtful to anyone, to think negative of anyone, is tantamount to throwing dirt over one's own Self. Therefore, you have to do *pratikraman* so that you can be free. There is no problem with saying things as far as normal worldly interactions are concerned. But when you say anything negative about any living being, it all gets recorded (taped) within (both)! How long does it take to start 'recording a tape' within these worldly people? Even the slightest of provocations will incite a hostile inner intent and response, which will begin to be recorded.

You have such inner weakness that you will start talking (retaliating; reacting) even before you are provoked.

**Questioner:** Not only should one not say anything negative, but he should not even have a negative inner intent (*bhaav*), should he?

**Dadashri:** It is true that one should not have such an inner intent. Whatever is in the inner intent (*bhaav*) is bound to manifest in words. Hence the inner intent will stop if one stops saying anything. This inner intent is the echo behind the words. A hostile inner intent (*pratipakshi-bhaav*) cannot refrain from arising, can it? No hostile inner intent will arise in 'us (Dada).' You too have to come to this state, this level; that much of your weakness must go. The weakness of hostile inner intents arising must go. However, if it ever occurs, we have the weapon of *pratikraman* with which you can erase them. As long as the water has not turned to ice, there is no problem; but once it turns into ice, it is not under your control (as long as the karma has not been bound, you can do *pratikraman* and erase it).

When a man scolds his wife, he thinks, 'No one heard me say all that. Everything is fine as it is.' When husband and wife fight, they will say all kinds of things in front of their little children. They think the children are too young to know anything. Hey, you! What about the taping (recording) that is taking place within the child? It will all be expressed when he grows up!

## Wash Off the Mistakes of Speech in This Manner

**Questioner:** How can one prevent the tape from recording within?

**Dadashri:** Do not create any vibration (*spandan*) of any kind. Keep 'seeing' everything. However, it is not possible because even this is a machine (the relative self; the non-Self complex) and, furthermore, it is under the control of other factors. That is why 'we' are showing you an alternate way. If the taping occurs internally and you do *pratikraman* immediately, that taping is erased. *Pratikraman* is the tool used for erasing. With *pratikraman*, there will be a change in your speech within one or two lifetimes and then all such speech will stop altogether.

**Questioner:** After attaining the awareness (*laksha*) of the Self, *pratikramans* are occurring constantly.          (344)

**Dadashri:** Therefore, you are no longer accountable. If you do *pratikraman* for whatever you say, you will no longer be liable. If you have to speak sternly, do so but without any attachment or abhorrence, and do *pratikraman vidhi* immediately.

**Questioner:** What is the *pratikraman vidhi*?

**Dadashri:** For example, if you hurt 'Chandulal,' then you have to invoke the one who is separate from the thoughts, speech and actions, *bhaavkarma*, *dravyakarma*, and *nokarma* of 'Chandulal' (or the name of the person you hurt) and all illusions attached to that name. This One is the '*Shuddhatma Bhagwan*' (the pure Soul). Then say, 'Dear *Shuddhatma Bhagwan*, I have spoken in a harsh manner and that is a mistake of mine. I am repenting for this mistake. I am asking for Your forgiveness. I am resolving not to repeat this mistake. Please give me the energy and strength not to repeat the mistake again.'

When you do your *pratikraman*, you have to recall Dada Bhagwan (the fully enlightened Lord within the Gnani Purush) or the *Shuddhatma Bhagwan*. First do *alochana*, which is recall and confession of your mistake. Then do *pratikraman*, which is asking for forgiveness, and that will cleanse your mistakes; and lastly do *pratyakhyan*, which is your resolve never to repeat the mistake.

**Questioner:** Conflicts occur even when I do not wish

them to. What should I do about the negative and hurtful words that come out?

**Dadashri:** Anything that is coming to its end will continue to occur even when you do not wish it to. In these situations, you should do *pratikraman* after it occurs.

**Questioner:** Is it right to flatter someone? What about when you agree with something even though you don't?

**Dadashri:** That is not considered truth; it is not worth flattering anyone. It is a tactic one has discovered and he uses it to hide his own mistake.

You should speak in such a way that the other person will find it acceptable.

**Questioner:** How can I ever get anywhere if I worry about how the other person is going to take it?

**Dadashri:** You do not have to think about that. You have to just tell 'Chandulal' to do *pratikraman*. That is all.

This is *Akram Vignan* and that is why *pratikraman* had to be involved.

## Will Speech Improve in This Very Life?

**Questioner:** Will our speech become very good by doing *pratikraman*, and will that occur in this very lifetime?

**Dadashri:** It will indeed be something to 'see (experience)' after you do *pratikraman*. It is because of *pratikraman* that 'My' speech is of the highest quality. It is because of *pratikraman* that this speech is above any controversy or dispute, and is accepted by all. Elsewhere, all speech creates controversy. Purity in worldly interactions means there is no ego involved in any worldly interactions. Only such a person's speech is accepted by all (*syadvaad*).

\*\*\*\*\*

## [21]

## Faults of Prakruti Will Depart This Way...

## Obstacles in Current Life Are Results of Past Life Mistakes

**Questioner:** When I lose awareness as the Self (*laksha*), should I consider that as my mistake or *a karma* of obstruction (*antaray*)?

**Dadashri:** As far as mistakes are concerned, it is like this; the obstacles that arise are ones that you have created, and so the mistake is yours. Why did the obstacles arise? Now those obstacles will gradually go down. Hence there is no need to have remorse for mistakes.                                          (346)

**Questioner:** Are obstacles the result of my mistakes?

**Dadashri:** They are all the result of mistakes made in the past life. You have no choice but suffer them with those obstacles.

**Questioner:** So I don't need to have remorse for that afterwards?

**Dadashri:** No, no. Who will be having remorse? Having remorse is not the attribute of the Self, is it? You just have to maintain greater awareness. Whenever you say '*Shuddhatma....Shuddhatma....*,' the awareness will come.

**Questioner:** Is *pratikraman* needed instead of remorse?

**Dadashri:** The average man cannot do so many *pratikramans*. Not everyone has the capability. Whatever *pratikramans* they do in their worldly interactions are more than enough. One is not able to do as many *pratikramans*; one has all kinds of work to do the whole day long.

## Poison of Satsang is Preferable to Nectar of Kusang

**Questioner:** How can one take advantage from this constant suffering?

**Dadashri:** If you think deeper about this suffering, it will not feel like suffering. If you do exact *pratikraman*, then it will not feel as if you are suffering. It is without a thought that people have labeled it as suffering (*dukh*). Therefore, you should not oppose it. If you happen to oppose it, then do *pratikraman*. Even if you think about opposing it, you have to do *pratikraman*.

It is better to drink the poison of this *satsang* (company of those who promote the attainment of the Self) than to drink the nectar of the worldly life where there is no *satsang*. At least the poison of *satsang* has *pratikraman* in it. I have ingested all the goblets of poison and have become a 'Mahadev' – one who drinks the poison of the world without retaliation. You should do *pratikraman* for any difficulty or inconvenience you have caused others.

**Questioner:** If a person has unselfish deceit, will he bind karma after attaining Gnan?

**Dadashri:** Yes, but he should do *pratikraman*.

**Questioner:** Should I do *pratikraman* after having been deceived?

**Dadashri:** Yes, you should definitely do *pratikraman*. It is not the fault of the maharaj (religious teacher). He is sitting in his own place. It is your fault that you went to his 'shop.' You instigated him, so you should do *pratikraman*. You should not make any mistake.

**Questioner:** We do *pratikraman* but the other person

will bind karma, will he not?

**Dadashri:** You should do *pratikraman* in your mind. You should not concern yourself with the other person.

## Subtlety of Gnani's Pratikramans

**Questioner:** I think a lot about coming to you, but I am unable to do so.

**Dadashri:** Is anything in this world under your control? You should feel remorse when you are not able to come to this *satsang*. You have to tell 'Chandubhai', 'Chandubhai, do *pratikraman* so everything can be resolved quickly. Do *pratikraman* because you are not able to go to *satsang*. Do *pratyakhyan*.' Your mistake (in the past life) prevent you from coming here, so make sure that you do not make the same mistake again.                                    (348)

Why is your current intent to come to me growing stronger and yet your wishes are not being fulfilled? Coming events cast their shadows beforehand. This is an indication of things to come. Indeed, it is going to occur.

**Questioner:** How do I do *pratikraman* for all the worries that I have?

**Dadashri:** Do *pratikraman* in this way: 'It is because of my ego that I worry. I am not the doer. Dada Bhagwan, please forgive me.' You will have to do something, will you not?

**Questioner:** Do I have to do *pratikraman* when we make comments about the weather that it is too cold?

**Dadashri:** No, *pratikraman* is needed only where there is attachment or abhorrence (*raag* or *dwesh*). If the soup is very salty, you do not need to do *pratikraman*. But do *pratikraman* for the person who made the soup. *Pratikraman* causes internal changes in the other person.

While urinating, if an ant should get flushed away in the stream, 'we' do *pratikraman*. 'We' always maintain awareness. The fact that the ant drowns is a *karmic* effect, or discharge karma, but why did this mistake unfold for me? It is a mistake for which *pratikraman* was not done in the past life (*apratikraman dosh*). Why did the awareness become dim? Such mistake carries a *karmic* liability.

Whenever you read Dada's books, bow down to the book and say, 'Dada, give me the energy to read this as it is.' If you forget to do so, then bow down twice and tell Dada that it is not your intention to forget but because you did, you are asking for His forgiveness and you will not let it occur again.

If you forget to do your *vidhi* (Dadashri's prescribed daily instructions) at the right time, do *pratikraman* and then do the *vidhi*.

When 'we' separate two people, 'we' incur liability and, therefore, 'we' do *pratikraman*.

**Questioner:** Even when you do it without any doership?

**Dadashri:** Whatever the intent, you have to do *pratikraman* when you do anything that hurts others.

In *Akram Vignan*, we are doing *pratikraman* for the *atikramans* that are occurring during a *karmic* discharge. These *pratikramans* are for the discharge that hurts others. If you do something good for Dada or *mahatmas*, you do not have to do *pratikraman*. When you do something good for other people, you have to do *pratikraman* (as doership is involved); you are doing *pratikraman* for slipping from the awakened awareness (*upayog*).

## Phenomenal Value of Pratikraman

**Questioner:** When I do *pratikraman*, does it reach the other person?

**Dadashri:** Yes, it reaches him. He will start to soften from within, whether he is aware of it or not. His attitude towards you will improve. Our *pratikraman* is very effective. There is tremendous energy and power in *pratikraman*. If you do *pratikraman* for just one hour, you will see the changes in the other person. But that will only occur if the *pratikramans* are done exactly and sincerely. When you do *pratikraman* for the other person, not only will he not see your faults, but he will also begin to respect you.

**Questioner:** Do we not charge new karma by doing *pratikraman*?

**Dadashri:** If the Self becomes the doer, then karma will be charged. The Self does not do *pratikraman*; it is 'Chandubhai' who does it and You, the pure Self, are the 'Knower' and the 'Seer' of it all.                                    (350)

True *pratikraman* starts only after you become Self-realized. There has to be someone to do the *pratikraman* (i.e., 'Chandulal'), and someone to give the instructions that *pratikraman* be done (You, the pure Self).

What is our *pratikraman*? If you unwind a reel, whatever individual pieces come out of it, to patch them together and to clean them up is our *pratikraman*.

**Questioner:** Can one make mistakes in seeing *charitra moha* (seeing faults in discharge)? Can one make the same mistake after doing *pratikraman* every day, or not?

**Dadashri:** You should recognize the mistake that occurs every day. It will not go away even after you do *pratikraman*. One layer is being broken every time.

If you do *pratikraman* even for an hour, You will have the experience of the realm of the Self. If *pratikraman* is done instantly as 'shoot-on-sight,' then it is possible to enter into the state of God. There is beauty in each and every *pratikraman*, and lack of *pratikraman* (*apratikraman*) is a sign of ugliness.

## Living Pratikraman

**Questioner:** Should we do *pratikraman* collectively in a group?

**Dadashri:** That is not necessary. It is okay to do it on your own. You can do it in your mind or when you are trying to fall asleep.

What should the *pratikraman* be like? It should be alive.

This other (generally practiced *pratikraman*) is dead *pratikraman*. Not a single fault has gone away and, on the contrary, the faults have increased. The *pratikraman* have continued; people have been doing that other *pratikraman* for years and yet not a single fault has gone away.

## The One with Wrong Belief Now Becomes Pratikraman Soul

**Questioner:** *Pratikraman* starts from the moment I wake up.

**Dadashri:** The soul within you has now become a '*pratikraman*-soul'; the pure Soul (*Shuddhatma*) is there. Before, it used to be a '*pratishthit*-soul' – (the one with the wrong belief, 'I am Chandulal'). It has now become a '*pratikraman*-soul.' Other people have '*kashayi*-soul' (prone to attachment and abhorrence). No one is able to do even a single *pratikraman* in this world.

As instant *pratikraman* occurs, the purification begins. When you do instant *pratikraman* against any *atikraman*, your mind and speech begin to purify.

*Pratikraman* is the roasting of the seed, which would have otherwise grown into a plant.

Doing *alochana-pratikraman-pratyakhyan* is to review the entire day. The more mistakes you 'see,' that much is the profit. That many *pratikraman* need to be done.

## The Mistake of Prakruti Prevents Pratikraman

**Questioner:** Is it the fault of the *prakruti* that one is not able to do *pratikraman*, or is it due to some obstacle-causing karma (*antaray karma*)?

**Dadashri:** It is the *prakruti's* (non-Self's) fault. This is not prevalent in all situations. Sometimes this occurs and sometimes it does not. It does not matter if *pratikraman* is not done because of the mistake of *prakruti*, but the main thing is your inner intent (*bhaav*). All You have to do is to 'see' your intention and nothing else. Everything else is not to be 'seen.' Do you wish to do *pratikraman*?

**Questioner:** Yes, absolutely.

**Dadashri:** In spite of this *bhaav*, if you are not able to do *pratikraman*, then it is the fault of the *prakruti*. 'You' are not liable for such a fault. Sometimes the *prakruti* will speak the sentences of the *pratikraman vidhi* and sometimes it will not. It is like a gramophone; the record may or may not play. That is not considered the karma of obstruction.

## Profound Pratikramans for Heavy-Duty Karma

**Questioner:** Despite making the firm resolution to settle a dispute with equanimity, why does clash still continue?

**Dadashri:** In how many places does that occur, a hundred or so?

**Questioner:** No, in just one.                                    (352)

**Dadashri:** Then the karma is very solid and strong (*nikachit karma*). And it is *alochana, pratikraman* and *pratyakhyan* that will wash away this type of karma. They will lighten the karma and after that, You will be able to remain the 'Knower' and the 'Seer' of the effect. You must do continuous *pratikraman* for this type of karma.

With whatever force the karma became solid, a corresponding force of repentance will be needed for its *pratikraman*.

## The Burden of the Old Mistakes

**Questioner:** There is a lingering burden of what has occurred in the past.

**Dadashri:** You should throw the burden of the past aside. Why would You want to carry that burden? The burden will remain if it affects You.

**Questioner:** The burden of the old mistakes is felt.

**Dadashri:** How old a mistake?

**Questioner:** A month or two old.

**Dadashri:** What is so big about it? Just do *pratikraman*, what else can you do?

**Questioner:** I do *pratikraman* but I can see the mistake exactly.

**Dadashri:** It is the *prakruti* that you are seeing. The *prakruti* will not go away. What does *prakruti* mean? It is like layers of an onion; after you get rid of one mistake, a second one appears, then the third. It is the same mistake with many layers for which you have to do *pratikraman*.

**Questioner:** *Pratikraman* continues, but as long as I do not become free from the mistake, the weight of the burden remains.

**Dadashri:** You have no choice. There is no other way but doing *alochana*, *pratikraman* and *pratyakhyan*. *Atikraman* gave rise to it, and it will be destroyed with *pratikraman*; that is all.

**Questioner:** I make a firm resolution with absolute sincerity that I do not want to make the same mistake again. Despite this, the same mistake will occur, will it not? Is it in my hands?

**Dadashri:** Yes, it will occur again. For example, if I have a ball and I throw it, once I throw that ball, it will not stop bouncing even if I wish for it to stop. Throwing the ball was just a single action, but after throwing it, if I say that I do not wish to throw it, and I tell it to stop bouncing, will it stop?

**Questioner:** No, it will not.

**Dadashri:** Then what will occur?

**Questioner:** It will continue to bounce three or four times.

**Dadashri:** So it has gone out of my hands and into the hands of nature. Nature will make it still. That is how all this is. All our mistakes fall into nature's hands.

**Questioner:** Then what benefits are there in *pratikraman*, once it falls into the hands of nature?

**Dadashri:** Many benefits; tremendous benefits. *Pratikraman* has such an impact that if you do *pratikraman* for someone for one hour, it will bring about tremendous new changes within that person. But the person doing *pratikraman* must have this Gnan. He must be purified through Gnan. He has to have the experience of, 'I am a pure Soul (*Shuddhatma*).' *Pratikraman* will have a tremendous effect. *Pratikraman* is our biggest weapon.

## Can Prakruti Improve?

If a person does not have this Gnan, his *prakruti* will continue to go in the wrong direction throughout the day. But after Gnan, it will be on the right path. When you get upset and say something hurtful to someone, the inner one will say, 'No, no, this is wrong: you should not do that. Do *pratikraman* for having such a thought of getting upset and saying hurtful things.' Before Gnan, you would be supporting the abusive words by thinking of giving him some more.

The nature of human beings is such that they become their *prakruti*.

For us *mahatmas* in *Akram Vignan*, when the *prakruti* does not improve, we tell him within, 'Hey, you! Let go. Do not concern yourself with improving the *prakruti*. Why don't you at least improve your inner self?' Thereafter, You are not responsible for what occurs on the outside. This is all a Science. If you understand this much, everything will be resolved. Do you understand what I am saying?

**Questioner:** Yes, I do.                                 (354)

**Dadashri:** What did you understand?

**Questioner:** I just have to 'see' and not become one with it, not become engrossed (*tanmayakar*) in it.

**Dadashri:** Not like that. Even if you become one with it, You should say, 'It should not be like this. This is all wrong.' The *prakruti* will do anything because it is irresponsible. But You become free of that responsibility when you say this. Now, is there any problem with that?

**Questioner:** There is no problem but when we get angry, we lose awareness.

**Dadashri:** Our Gnan is such that it will keep You in awareness. You will do *pratikraman* and everything else. Are You able to maintain awareness?

**Questioner:** Yes, Dada.

# That is Called Pratyakhyan

**Questioner:** If one does *pratikraman* heartily for the mistake, what if the decision (*nischay*) not to repeat it is weak?

**Dadashri:** The firm resolution (*nischay*) is *pratyakhyan*. It is best if one does *nischay*. If one does not resolve to never repeat the mistake and only does *pratikraman*, the first mistake gets erased; then it will come again and he will erase it again. We need all three: *alochana*, *pratikraman* and *pratyakhyan*. *Pratyakhyan* means 'I will not do it again,' and that is the best thing.

*****

## [22]

## Solution for Sticky Files

### Settlement According to the Account

**Questioner:** His file number one is still embroiled in attachment (*raag*) and that attachment gives rise to all this. (356)

**Dadashri:** It is all the *karmic* stock from the past life, so that will occur and when he does *pratikraman*; that is called '*shuddha upayog* (applied awareness of the Self).' When one does *pratikraman*, it is called *shuddha upayog*. Is he doing *pratikraman* for the purpose of *shuddha upayog*? What is his intent? It is to attain pure awareness. Your file number two is tough and difficult too, is she not?

**Questioner:** I do not consider her tough and difficult; she is not so. But if I keep talking with feelings of attachment about my file, do I not become liable for karma?

**Dadashri:** Yes, you do! Why would you keep talking about your file? What do you have to do with her? This is a file and it is being settled according to the unfolding karma (*udayakarma*). Whatever connection of attachment and abhorrence (*roonanubandha*) there is from the past life, it will continue to be settled.

### Pratikraman of Sticky Karma

**Questioner:** *Atikraman* occurs even as I am settling old karma with equanimity.

**Dadashri:** Then for that you have been given the medicine of *pratikraman*. There is no problem if you are not able to do anything. I forgive you even if you do not do *alochana*. I realize that it may not quite 'fit' with people of today. What *alochana* are they going to do? Instead, why not let them do *pratikraman*?

**Questioner:** But *pratyakhyan* is also to be done in that, is it not?

**Dadashri:** It will be fine if he does not even do *pratyakhyan*. If he did *atikraman*, as long as he does *pratikraman*, he will be fine. People of today do not have the spiritual tenacity.

If one cannot do the whole *alochana*, *pratikraman* and *pratyakhyan*, it is fine if he just does *pratikraman*. Keep doing *pratikraman* for sticky files; do *pratikraman* for the mistakes. This way, its design will be intact but it will disintegrate at the mere touch; it will fall away. The stickiness of karma will no longer remain if you do *pratikraman* for it. *Pratikraman* removes the stickiness. Otherwise, no matter how much you scrub, it will not go away.

**Questioner:** So we have to do *pratikraman* to destroy sticky karma?

**Dadashri:** There is no other solution besides *alochana*, *pratikraman* and *pratyakhyan*. Therefore, invoke 'Dada' and say, 'I have made this mistake, I am very sorry for it,' and do *pratyakhyan*, 'I will not do it again.' This is the only solution. There is no other solution.

## Maintain the Intent of Settling with Equanimity

Many people come and tell 'Me,' 'Dada, I try to settle with equanimity, but it does not happen.' Then I reply, 'You do not have to enter the doership of trying to settle (*nikaal*) the file! You just have to have an inner intent (*bhaav*) to settle the file with equanimity. Whether it settles with equanimity (*sambhav*) or not, is not under Your control. Why don't You remain in My Agnas? That way most of Your work will be done and if it remains pending, it is in the control of nature.'

All 'we' look at is your decision of, 'I want to settle with equanimity.' Decide at least that much. Then 'we' are not concerned whether that occurs or not. How long can we sit here and watch the drama? When will it all come to an end? We have to move on. There may be times when it may not be settled with equanimity. If the bonfire does not light, we will light it later. Why sweat trying to light it? We tried everything and if it does not light, just move on. Otherwise, when will it all come to an end?                                                                (358)

This Gnan has been given to *sansaris* (married people; people living a worldly life). I have not asked them to renounce anything, but I have told them to settle their files with equanimity and to do *pratikraman*. I have shown them these two solutions. There is no one to mess with the state You are in when You 'do' these two. Without these two solutions, You would not be able to stand on the shore of the Self. There is danger on the shore.

## That Which is Within File One is Only To Be 'Seen'

**Questioner:** I may be able to settle all the other files with equanimity, but please explain in detail how to settle file number one with equanimity. I feel that all this meddling is of file number one.

**Dadashri:** The initial interference (*dakho*), 'I am Chandulal,' leaves only by 'seeing'. Whether it (file) is straightforward or awkward, You don't have much to do with it. All of it will go away by simply 'seeing' it. If another 'file' makes a claim against you, then you have to do *pratikraman*. Whereas, here with file number one, there is no one to file anything against you, is there? So, because there is no one to claim anything, it will go away by 'seeing' it. If you are having bad thoughts, even if they are crooked; if it spoils your intellect, You are to simply 'see' all that. Whatever 'work' the mind and the intellect are doing, there is a problem; You have to keep 'seeing' that.

This is the most straightforward path to *moksha*, the easiest *moksha*!

**Questioner:** Does 'continue seeing' mean that I should agree with what it shows?

**Dadashri:** The one who 'sees' is never in any kind of agreement with it. The 'Seer' who is continuously 'seeing' cannot be one with what is being 'seen'. Does a man get burned by watching a bonfire?

**Questioner:** No, he does not.

**Dadashri:** Even if there is a huge bonfire, the eyes 'see' …but what does it matter to the eyes?

**Questioner:** But, Dada, the interference (*dakho*) occurs and this hurts someone; do I not have to do *pratikraman* for it?

**Dadashri:** You have to do *pratikraman* for that. Why did you do *atikraman*? You should not do anything that hurts others.

**Questioner:** My daughter does *pratikraman* every day, and yet her internal state does not improve.

**Dadashri:** It is because of a huge *karmic* stock filled in the past life. *Pratikraman* is itself the real inner effort (*purusharth*).

**Questioner:** Dada, are we not taking protection by blaming the huge *karmic* stock?

**Dadashri:** No, no. There is no protection in this at all. The whole world does not do *pratikraman*. They push others around and then they say that they did the right thing by doing that.

## One Sees Only Other's Mistakes

**Questioner:** Many times, I feel that it is not my mistake. Sometimes I can see my own mistake and sometimes I (lady talking about her father) feel that it is not my mistake; I feel that 'he' is at fault.

**Dadashri:** Is that what you feel? Then what about while you are doing *pratikraman*?                                      (360)

**Questioner:** But when he experiences increasing mental torment and restlessness, then I feel that I should not become a *nimit* for that.

**Dadashri:** But you have to do *pratikraman* as if it is your mistake.

**Questioner:** But I do not feel that I am at fault. I feel that he is the one at fault.

**Dadashri:** Without a mistake, no one will get hurt. It is because of our mistake that another person feels hurt.

**Questioner:** I feel that it is because of his *prakruti* that he feels hurt.

**Dadashri:** You cannot consider the *prakruti* like that. All these people say that his *prakruti* is good, whereas you are the only one who says that his *prakruti* is bad. That, too, is a *roonanubandha* account (link of karma from the past life).

**Questioner:** I feel that he has a habit of nagging.

**Dadashri:** That is why it is your fault – it is your mistake. Why do you have to hurt your parents? That is why you have to do *pratikraman*. They should not get hurt. You should have in your mind that you have come to make them happy. You should be inquiring, 'What mistake did I make that keeps on making me hurt my parents?'

## That is When You Will Be Liberated

When You stop 'seeing' faults, then You will be liberated. If someone were to insult you, hurt you financially, or even physically, but despite all that You do not 'see' any faults in him, that is when You will be free from the entanglements of this worldly life.

Have You stopped 'seeing' faults in others?

**Questioner:** Yes, Dada. I do *pratikraman* when I 'see' faults in others.

## Satsang Destroys Mistakes

*Satsang* is of no use if it does not destroy your mistakes. *Satsang* itself means to destroy mistakes. No one should be hurt through your becoming the *nimit*. If someone does get hurt, then the mistake is yours and that mistake has to be destroyed. And if you cannot find the mistake, then it is the unfolding of your karma and so keep on asking for forgiveness. Ask for forgiveness directly from that person if he is a reasonable man. But if he is unreasonable, then keep asking for forgiveness internally.

**Questioner:** Sometimes in trying to settle all the files, I get so entangled that I do not even think about doing *pratikraman* and *samayik*. Is that being slack and lazy (*pol*)?

**Dadashri:** That is not considered being slack. Slack is when you have the desire but you do not do it.

**Questioner:** Sooner or later, one will have to do *pratikraman* for all one's mistakes, will he not?

**Dadashri:** Don't worry about that. To 'know' (*janavoo*) the mistakes is more than enough. *Pratikraman* has to be done when you hurt someone a lot.

Ours is the path of *Akram*, a path where karmas have not been dissipated, and thus weakness will not stop from occurring. Now, if just a mental weakness (*kashay*) arises, then one should do *pratikraman* for just that *kashay* in the mind. He does not have to do a lengthy *pratikraman*. And when *pratikraman* is done, it gets cleansed. But the *karmic* stock that has been stored is bound to come out, is it not? Weakness arises but he is not considered guilty if he does *pratikraman* through his mind, speech and body, because by doing *pratikraman*, he is within Dada's Agna. How is one to find that much energy? *Atikraman* does occur, but you should do *pratikraman* for it. Nevertheless, our Gnan is such that, no matter what the circumstances, one can be saved from them. That is called Gnan. In this *Vitarag* path of ours, *kraman* (neutral activities) occur as long as one is happy, but when things go to the contrary, we have to do *pratikraman* and wash it off.

## Missed Agnas? Do Pratikraman

The way to handle this is to firmly resolve, 'I want to stay in Dada's Agnas,' and then begin your day. Then do *pratikraman* for the times you have not been able to be in the Agnas. Keep everyone happy at home by settling all conflicts with them – with equanimity. In spite of doing this, if they are still unhappy with you, then understand that it is because of your past accounts and simply be a 'Seer' of everything. You have made this decision only today, so win them over with love. You will notice that everything will start to settle down. Still, you should only believe so when those at home certify that you are free from faults. Ultimately, they are all on your side.    (362)

## 'You' Are the Judge and 'Chandulal' is the Accused

Whatever *pudgal* (non-Self complex) is coming out, whether it is fighting with someone or hitting someone, if You continue to 'see' it, then You are not liable for it. Someone may ask you why you still fight after attaining Gnan. So what should you tell him? With whatever intensity of intent (*bhaav*) the *karmic* bondage occurred, it is with that same intent it will discharge. Continue to 'see' that discharge. But there should be one thing during the discharge and that is that no *atikraman* should occur in the process. Do *pratikraman* if *atikraman* occurs. *Pratikraman* is to be done by 'Chandulal' and not You. A judge does not have to do anything; he has to make the accused do it. The one who eats is the one who is guilty, and thus he has to go to the toilet. The judge simply gives judgments. He will never say, 'The crime of the accused is my crime.' What kind of mistake is it if our *mahatmas* say that? This is very subtle talk.

The *karmic* stock (likened to garbage) has been filled in the past life and it is precisely that which is discharging. One becomes lighter because no new stock is being filled. Day by day, his burden will feel lighter and then it will not be there anymore.

## When Will the 'Tank' Empty?

**Questioner:** Is *moksha* attained through *pratikraman*? Is it necessary to do *pratikraman* now to attain *moksha*?

**Dadashri:** *Pratikraman* is necessary only if you do *atikraman*. Otherwise, there is no need to do *pratikraman* If it is one's nature to do *atikraman*, then he should do *pratikraman*. Do you understand? And that too, how long does that nature remain? No matter how mischievous a person is, that 'tank' will empty in eleven to fourteen years. After that it is all empty. How long will a full tank last? A tank may be full now, but how long will it last when it is not being replenished? Nevertheless, it is better to do *pratikraman* when *atikraman* occurs.

## Is Interference Vyavasthit?

Interference (*dakho*) as 'I am Chandulal' occurs for you

rather frequently, does he not?

**Questioner:** It occurs sometimes.

**Dadashri:** What occurs if one dies 'sometimes'?

**Questioner:** Is *dakho* (interference; becoming 'Chandulal') under the control of *vyavasthit*?

**Dadashri:** Whatever 'has occurred' is under the control of *vyavasthit*, but not 'what is going to occur.' Do not worry about what has already happened. Do *pratikraman* for the wrongdoing and tell the one who did it, 'Do *pratikraman*.' If 'Chandulal' did it, then tell 'Chandulal' to do *pratikraman*.

**Questioner:** If I leave it to *vyavasthit*, then what *purusharth* (effort of the enlightened one) do I have to make?

**Dadashri:** The *purusharth* You have to 'do' is to continuously 'see' what 'Chandulal' is doing the whole day. That is your *purusharth*! (364)

As you continue to 'see' You can say, 'Chandulal, why are you being so strict with your son? Do *pratikraman* because you have done *atikraman*.' You can interject this way while You are 'seeing' what he does.

**Questioner:** *Pratikraman* occurs at this time.

**Dadashri:** That is what I am saying, that *pratikraman* occurs automatically at the same time. Therefore, You just have to 'see.' You have to continue 'seeing' that *pratikraman* is occurring.

## Keep 'Seeing' What 'Occurs'

We (Self-realized) do not have *bhaavkarma* (charging karma). We have become free of *bhaavkarma*. We are *Shuddhatma* (pure Soul) who is free of *bhaavkarma* (charging; causal karma), *dravyakarma* (subtle discharging karma) and *nokarma* (gross discharging karma). Therefore, You, the

*Shuddhatma* (the Self) and 'Chandulal' (the non-Self; *prakruti*) are separate. To keep 'seeing' *prakruti* is *purusharth* (real spiritual effort). When one does *purusharth* after becoming a Purush (the Self), it is considered *purusharth* towards *moksha*.

Whatever one has done, and no matter how horrible its effects, if he remains in the Gnan of *vyavasthit*, then he does not need to do *pratikraman*.

What is the other meaning of *vyavasthit*? It means to continue to 'see' what 'Chandulal' is doing. If 'Chandulal' does a million dollar damage to someone, continue 'seeing' that too. You should not become one in it (*tanmayakar*). 'Why did you do that? Do *pratikraman* for that.' Actually, not everyone understands this. *Vyavasthit* means that whatever it is, it is verily correct. But You are free if You continue to 'see' it.

## It Affects the Other Person the Moment You Do Pratikraman

**Questioner:** I become engrossed (*tanmayakar*; becoming 'Chandulal') in circumstances, so there is no opportunity for doing *pratikraman* there.

**Dadashri:** The opportunity of doing *pratikraman* arises when the other person gets hurt, You have to say, 'Chandulal, do *pratikraman*. He will bind vengeance. It seems that *atikraman* has occurred with him, his face becomes stern when he looks at you, so do *pratikraman*.' So he will ask, 'Should I do one *pratikraman*?' You should tell him, 'No, do twenty-five to fifty so that you see a smile on his face.' His face will be much better looking the next day, when you do *pratikraman* in this manner. Try it once. Have you experienced that before?

**Questioner:** Yes.

**Dadashri:** Is that so? So after tasting such experience, have you remained that way?

**Questioner:** Does the *pratikraman* that I do reach the other person?

**Dadashri:** He will not know that. He may or may not even know it, but it does have an effect on him. He will begin to become milder. His bad inner intent towards you will become milder.

And if you keep getting irritated with him from within, then his bad inner intent towards you gets stronger. He, too, will start wondering why his negative intents are getting stronger towards you.

**Questioner:** Those files will not get stuck to me in the next life, will they?

**Dadashri:** What for? Why be concerned with the next life? Do as many *pratikramans* as you can in this very life. Do *pratikraman* whenever you have free time.

## Pratikraman of the Files At Home

**Dadashri:** Are you able to do *pratikraman* now?

**Questioner:** Yes, I am.                                    (366)

**Dadashri:** Is that so?

**Questioner:** These files at home are the main ones, are they not, Dada?

**Dadashri:** How many files do you have at home?

**Questioner:** Just these two. Much of the *pratikraman* has to be done for these two.

**Dadashri:** You have only one son, do you?

**Questioner:** I do *pratikraman* mainly for him and for file number two. Most of the *pratikramans* are for them.

**Dadashri:** Is that so?

**Questioner:** Yes. I have done lots of *pratikramans*. That is why the son has become very quiet and gives me a lot of cooperation.

I also did *pratikramans* for my brother and that has brought about a change in all of them. I do *pratikraman* every day.

**Dadashri:** People have experienced that the inner state of the other person changes with *pratikraman*. That is why they will not let go of it, will they? 'This is the cash bank.' *Pratikraman* is considered a 'cash bank.' It gives instant results. Do you have to do a lot of *pratikramans*?

**Questioner:** Mainly for those at home.

**Dadashri:** How many *pratikramans* do you do?

**Questioner:** Fifty to a hundred. I do *pratikraman* for a few sticky files at home.

## The Effective Pratikraman

**Questioner:** If I do *pratikraman* with You as my witness, for the hurt I have caused to others by lying to them, it will get erased, will it not?

**Dadashri:** What do you consider as having done *pratikraman*? It is doing *pratikraman* or doing it silently, in your privacy. But when that *pratikraman* 'speaks' (when it brings about an effect in the other person), know that you have done *pratikraman*. Yes, 'we' too do *pratikraman* silently but after a few days, when that *pratikraman* 'speaks', 'we' will know that it has had an effect on the other person. You can do such a *pratikraman* in your mind and he will not even know, but even then he will be attracted towards you.

## The Science of Pratikraman

**Questioner:** The results I get from doing *pratikraman*

are based on what? Are they based on the ultimate, incontrovertible principle (*siddhant*) that by seeing the pure Self in the other person, my negative *bhaav* (attachment and abhorrence) towards him decrease? Is that correct?

**Dadashri:** Your negative *bhaavs* will be dissolved. All this is only for Your benefit; it has nothing to do with the other person. The only reason to see the pure Self in others is to remain as the Self and its awareness.

**Questioner:** So if someone has a negative *bhaav* towards me, will it become less by me seeing the Self in him?

**Dadashri:** No, that will not occur. It will only lessen if you do *pratikraman*. That does not happen simply by seeing the Self in him, but it does occur if you do *pratikraman*.

**Questioner:** Does the *pratikraman* have an effect on him?

**Dadashri:** Yes, it does have an effect. (368)

'Seeing' will also give the benefit. Although the benefits may not be so apparent in the beginning, they will gradually increase. This is because You have never seen the other person as the pure Soul before. You have only seen him as either a good person or a bad person, but never as the pure Soul.

## Even a Tiger Will Forget Its Violent Intent

**Questioner:** It is written in the Aptasutra, 'If you do *pratikraman* for a tiger, then it too will forget its violent intent.' What does that mean?

**Dadashri:** Yes, when the tiger forgets its violent intent, then you will lose your fear.

**Questioner:** Our fear will go away. That is fine, but does that have any effect on its soul?

**Dadashri:** Nothing occurs. When your fear goes away,

the connection (with the tiger) becomes free.

**Questioner:** But did you not say that its violent intent goes away.

**Dadashri:** Its violent intent goes away.

**Questioner:** How does that occur?

**Dadashri:** When your fear goes away, its violent intent goes away.

**Questioner:** So does that mean that it had an effect on its soul?

**Dadashri:** There is a direct effect on the soul. It does reach its soul.

Even a tiger will do whatever you command it, if you were to do its *pratikraman*. There is no difference between a tiger and a human. The difference is in the vibrations you emit. It is your vibrations that will affect the tiger. As long as you believe in your mind that a tiger is a violent animal, the tiger will remain violent. If you are aware that the tiger is the Soul, then it will have no violence with you. Everything is possible.

## Pratikraman is Addressed to the Pure Soul

You must understand how effective your intent (*bhaav*) can be in causing an effect that can be destructive. If a monkey destroys all the mangos on your mango tree, then, in a moment of frustration you say it would be better to just chop down the mango tree altogether. Beware of the inner intent behind what you say. Words spoken in the presence of the Self do not go to waste. If you are careful not to cause a negative effect, then everything will be fine.

Everything around you is the effect of what you yourself have created. From this moment onwards, stop any vibrations or thoughts towards others. If a thought arises, wash it off by doing *pratikraman*. That way the entire day will pass without any vibrations towards anyone. If you can get through the whole day this way, it is enough. That by itself is a great achievement towards liberation.

When we talk about the other person's soul, which soul are we talking about? You are aware of the *pratikraman* you do, are you not? You are not doing *pratikraman* to their *pratishthit atma* (the self that has wrong beliefs; the person in an ignorant state); you are doing it to his main/absolute Soul – the *Shuddhatma*. You are doing *pratikraman* for what occurred in the presence of his *Shuddhatma*. That is why you are asking for forgiveness from the *Shuddhatma*. Then you have nothing to do with his *pratishthit atma*.

## Purification of Impure Phases

After this Gnan, new phases that arise will not become impure. The old phases, however, will have to be made pure by 'seeing' them or dealing with them with equanimity. Equanimity (*samata*) means *vitaragata* (the state without *raag*/attachment and *dwesh*/abhorrence). New phases that arise will remain pure. If the old phases are becoming impure, they will need to be purified. Remaining in 'our' Agnas and maintaining equanimity will accomplish that.

**Questioner:** How are those phases (karmas), which were bound to arise (give effect) in this life, because of causes created before receiving Gnan, to be purified or dissolved?       (370)

**Dadashri:** As long as you are living, you can wash them away by *pratikraman*. But a few will still remain and those that remain will become very weak. So, in your next life, by merely touching them, they will fall away like a burned rope.

**Questioner:** Before Gnan, if one had bound karma for going to hell, will he still go to hell after Gnan?

**Dadashri:** This Gnan has the ability to completely burn and disintegrate all sinful karma. Even people who are headed for a life in hell can wash away the effect of their karma, as long as they do *pratikraman* in this life. If you put a disclaimer on your letter, before you mail it, stating that your mind was unstable when you wrote the letter, then the contents will have no value.

**Questioner:** Does intense repentance destroy causal seeds of bondage of karma?

**Dadashri:** Yes, they will be destroyed. Our *pratikraman* has tremendous energy and power. Only certain very strong karma effects are such; however, they are weakened through repentance. If you keep 'Dada' as your witness, it will be very effective.

**Questioner:** From birth to death, the mind, body and speech are in the mode of discharge, but during their discharge, if I create new inner intent (*bhaav*), is that *atikraman*?

**Dadashri:** Yes, purify that inner intent.

## This is Great Justice

There may be another life on account of karma. You may have one or two more lives to go to finish off your past karma, but after that, you have no choice but to go to Simandhar Swami, the current living *Tirthankar*. Sticky accounts of this life, created in past lives, will be washed away. This is a Science of absolute, accurate and pure justice. It is as precise and accurate as the weighing scales of an honest goldsmith. There is no room for imprecision here.

**Questioner:** Does the force of karma become weak by doing *pratikraman*?

**Dadashri:** Yes, of course! Not only that, but you will be able to accomplish everything quicker.

## Pratikraman for the Deceased

**Questioner:** How do I ask for forgiveness from someone

who is no longer living?

**Dadashri:** Although he is no longer living, you still have the memory of his face and you may have his photographs, so you can do his *pratikraman*. Even if you cannot remember his face, but you remember his name, you can still do *pratikraman* using the name. It reaches him.

If you had any problems or entanglements with someone who is now dead, you should recall him and 'wash' away those problems with *pratikraman* so that it is resolved. The entanglements should be resolved with *alochana*, *pratikraman* and *pratyakhyan*, because the memory of the dead, as well as the living, comes to mind. Do *pratikraman* of whoever comes in your memory, because you know that 'the Self' is eternally alive; the Self never dies. In doing this, it will benefit his Soul and also you can become free from the entanglements.

It is like having expensive china. They will remain 'alive' (intact) as long as you have some connection with them. Then, as the *karmic* account (*hisaab*) comes to an end, they will break. It is *vyavasthit* when they break. You do not have to think about them afterwards. People, too, are like china, are they not? They seem to be dead, but they do not really die. They come back right here. That is why, when you do *pratikraman* for the deceased, it reaches them, wherever they may be.

**Questioner:** How do we do that?                          (372)

**Dadashri:** Invoke the pure Soul (*Shuddhatma*) that is separate from the person's mind-body-speech, the charge karma (*bhaavkarma*), subtle effect-discharge karma (*dravyakarma*), gross discharge karma (*nokarma*), his name and all illusory attachment connected with his name. Then recall your mistakes: 'I made this mistake' (*alochana*). I regret making such a mistake and so forgive me for it (*pratikraman*). I make a firm decision not to repeat such a mistake (*pratyakhyan*).' 'You' should remain the Knower-Seer of 'Chandulal,' and know how many *pratikramans* 'Chandulal' did. You should know how well and how many he did.

## For the Mahatma, All These Are Discharge Karma

**Questioner:** Dada, after attaining Gnan, what should one do when sometimes bad inner intents (*bhaav*) arise? Why does that occur, Dada?

**Dadashri:** That, too, is the doing of the karma. 'You' are not the doer of that. You are needlessly getting perplexed by saying that you are doing them.

**Questioner:** So then do I have to just continue 'seeing' when such bad *bhaav* arises?

**Dadashri:** When you say they are 'bad,' that in itself is a danger. There is no such thing as 'bad.' If someone gets hurt, tell 'Chandulal,' 'Why did you hurt him, 'Chandulal'? Now do *pratikraman* for that.' There is no such thing as good and bad as far as God is concerned; all that is applicable in the society and the worldly life.

*Mahatmas* have *bhaav-abhaav* (good-bad inner intents) but they are settling karma (*nikaali*); discharging karma. They do not represent *bhaavkarma* (charge karma). Anger-pride-deceit-greed-attachment-abhorrence and good and bad intents are all discharging (*nikaali*), settling karma. They need to be settled with equanimity. These karmas settle with *pratikraman*. They will not settle on their own.

*****

## [23]

# When the Mind Becomes Turbulent

## The Stain in the Mind Needs To Be Cleansed

**Questioner:** Sometimes when I feel insulted, I may not say anything but my mind will revolt and retaliate and continues to do so.

**Dadashri:** 'You' should not be concerned with what occurs during that time. Even if you get into a physical fight, the interactions that take place are dependent upon one's strength and capacity. It all depends on how strong You have grown in this Gnan. If You have complete energy and power (*shakti*) of this Gnan, then even the mind will not revolt. What are 'we' saying? Whenever you revolt through the mind, speech or even the body, you must do *pratikraman* for all three, because there exist three types of weakness.                          (373)

**Questioner:** Do I have to do *pratikraman* for thoughts?

**Dadashri:** The thoughts are to be 'seen.' There is no *pratikraman* for thoughts. However, if you have bad thoughts about someone, then *pratikraman* is necessary. Only for those that are harmful to anyone. Thoughts about cows and buffaloes and anything else just disappear in the presence of Gnan. If you 'see' them with awareness, they will just pass. They only need to be 'seen.' There is no need for *pratikraman* for these.

Suppose, when you come to *satsang* and you see everyone standing around, you may become irritated and think, 'Why are they all standing around?' For such a negative thought, you should do *pratikraman* right away.

**Questioner:** Should one do that even when the inner intent becomes spoilt that way?

**Dadashri:** Yes. If *abhaav* (dislike, aversion) or something like that has occurred; even if the slightest contempt has occurred in the mind, you have to do *pratikraman*. What is considered a spoilt mind? It is not just the mind that goes bad. When the whole 'parliament' (mind, intellect, *chit* and ego) agrees, then only will *abhaav* (opposition; counter-attacking intent) occur. You feel, 'I will do this to him, I will do that to him;' this is not just caused by the mind. The mind is a *gneya* (that which is to be 'known'). The mind by nature is *vitarag* – free from attachment or abhorrence. Just do *pratikraman* if the mind gets spoilt. Agreement and final decision of the parliamentary *antahkaran* (mind, intellect, *chit* and ego complex) and spoiling of the mind are two separate things. If you do *pratikraman*, the mind will get cleaned and cooled. So You should keep making 'Chandulal' do *pratikraman*.

**Questioner:** I made him do *pratikraman* this afternoon.

**Dadashri:** Even then, make him do it again and again. The more You make him do *pratikraman*, the stronger it will become from within. A stain will be caused if the mind becomes spoilt, therefore, do not let a single thought become spoilt, especially in *satsang*. That is what You have to understand. Everything spoilt when the mind gets spoilt. A mere thought of, 'I will fall' will make you fall. Therefore, do *pratikraman* immediately upon having a stained thought. Be the Self. Do *pratikraman* if anything irritates the mind. You do not have to do *pratikraman* for putting a garland around my neck. This is a 'credit' (merit karma). It is a very big 'credit.'

## When the Inner Intent Spoilt

If you come here when it is very crowded, and when

someone comes and the thought arises, 'Why did he have to come back now?' Such a thought will come to the mind, but then what kind of speech comes out? 'Welcome, welcome, come on,' you will say. The negative inner intent (*bhaav*) is *atikraman* and that requires *pratikraman*.

Your inner intent should not get spoilt. Whatever they may be externally, they may be.

**Questioner:** What if both the inner and the external are excellent?

**Dadashri:** There is nothing better than that! However, do *pratikraman* when the inner intent gets spoilt.

## Subtle Pratikraman for the Spoilt Thoughts

**Questioner:** Should we do *pratikraman* for the effects of karma or for the subtle things that occur within?

**Dadashri:** *Pratikraman* is for that subtle thing that occurs within.

**Questioner:** Is it for the thoughts or for the intent?

**Dadashri:** For the intent (*bhaav*). Behind every thought there is always an intent. If there has been *atikraman*, then *pratikraman* should be done. *Atikraman* is when bad thoughts arise in the mind.

If a bad thought arises for this lady sitting here, it should be turned around by saying, 'Have good thoughts about her.' Your mind may show that this person sitting here is useless. Why do such thoughts arise? You have no right to assess anyone's worth. If you must say anything at all, then say that 'everyone is good.' By saying this, you will not be liable for the karma, but if you say or hold in your mind that this person is worthless, then that is *atikraman*. For this, you must do *pratikraman*.

So if another thought like that arises again, it is the inner content of *karmic* stock filled in the last life and so the thoughts will come. Whatever is in the stock is what will continue to come out. A person may not have a lot of understanding, and in his mind he thinks he is very wise and smart. That is what was stocked within. That does not cause the other person any harm and so there is no need for him to do *pratikraman*.

Thoughts will come without fail, but you should make them weak and ineffective (*nirmalya*). Do *pratikraman* for them. Thoughts are non-living (*nirjiv*).                    (376)

How does it reach the pure Soul of the other person? It reaches it when you say, 'Dear *Shuddhatma* of Chandubhai, thou art separate from the body of (*dehadhari*) 'Chandubhai,' all illusory attachment (*maya*) to the name of 'Chandubhai,' the union (*yoga*) of mind, body and speech of 'Chandubhai,' charge karma (*bhaavkarma*), subtle discharge karma (*dravyakarma*) and gross discharge karma (*nokarma*). I wish to send You this message. I do *pratikraman* and ask for forgiveness for having these thoughts about you. I will not do this again.'

Thoughts will not come without there being a knot of karma within. You should definitely do *pratikraman* of any negative thought you have. Do collective *pratikraman*. Whatever thoughts you have had in the last ten minutes, do a collective *pratikraman* for them.

## That is Considered Settling with Equanimity

**Questioner:** There are some faults, which are such that if a certain person comes in front of me, the moment I see him, I feel that this man is useless and unworthy. So should I do *pratikraman* right there? What if I miss doing *pratikraman* for it?

**Dadashri:** There is no problem if you miss doing *pratikraman*. There is no problem with doing collective *pratikraman* once a year for all those that you missed. Do their *pratikraman* in three or six months. That is still acceptable, but do not misuse this by thinking if I can do it once a year, I might as well put them all together and do yearly *pratikraman* for them. If you forget to do *pratikraman*, then you can do a collective *pratikraman* later.

When you meet a man who is dumb and irritating, the moment you see him at a distance you should know, 'This is a file and it is coming!' Here you need to settle with equanimity. Do You caution from within or do you forget? Are you cautioned right away? Do you get cautioned too? Therefore, the greatest duty (*dharma*) is to settle with equanimity (*sambhave nikaal*) and do *alochana*, *pratikraman* and *pratyakhyan*. Despite this, if any negative intent of the non-Self complex (*paudgalik bhaav*) arises for someone, then tell him (file number 1) to do *pratikraman*. Wash off any stain that may have occurred. Not letting any new stain occur is considered 'settling with equanimity' (*sambhave nikaal*).

## When the Other Person's Inner Intent is Spoilt

**Questioner:** Suppose my intent does not get spoilt but when talking to another person, the look on his face changes, his inner intent (*bhaav*) towards me becomes spoilt; what kind of *pratikraman* do I have to do for that?

**Dadashri:** You have to do *pratikraman* because you have to investigate, 'What fault still remains within me that spoils his inner intent (*bhaav*) towards me?' His inner intent should not be spoiled. Only purity of intent (*bhaav shuddhi*) should remain.

**Questioner:** Suppose you and I are talking and all of a sudden a third person comes along; she does not do or say anything but just stands there, but your *bhaav* gets spoilt and there is a changed look on your face. Upon seeing that I feel, 'Why is he spoiling his intent in this way?' How should I do *pratikraman* for that?

**Dadashri:** It is a fault to question and analyze another person's change of intent. So you have to do *pratikraman* for it. If you see a frown on the other person's face, then it is due to your mistake. If you invoke and recall the *Shuddhatma* within him and keep asking for forgiveness from him, then you will become free from the account of karma connection (*roonanubandha*).

## Suffering Without Blaming Cleans the Mind

When you suffer through something that you dislike, with a clean mind, you will become *vitarag*.

**Questioner:** What is a clean mind?

**Dadashri:** A clean mind is one where one does not have any negative thoughts for his opponent. What does that mean? That means that one does not 'bite' (attack) his *nimit* (evidentiary instrument or person). If bad thoughts arise against the *nimit*, then these are immediately washed off by doing *pratikraman*.

**Questioner:** A clean mind is there in the final stage, is it not? Will I have to continue doing *pratikraman* until it becomes clean?                                                        (378)

**Dadashri:** Yes, that is right. The mind has become clean in certain matters but not in other matters. These are all different steps. Where the mind is dirty and spoilt, *pratikraman* is required.

## Knots in the Mind Sprout with External Evidences

Thoughts sprout from the tubers of karma that lie within. A thought sprouts when evidences come together. One may appear to be a celibate (*brahmachari*), but he starts to have sexual thoughts when he comes across the circumstances.

**Questioner:** Do thoughts not arise due to the environment? Is it not due to the circumstantial evidences that one's nature, one's friends, etc., come together?

**Dadashri:** Yes, one has to have external evidences and, based on that, the tuber of thought sprouts; otherwise, it will not.

**Questioner:** Who guides one to latch on to those certain thoughts?

**Dadashri:** It is all verily natural. But at the same time, You have to understand that this intellect (*buddhi*) is wrong, and tubers are destroyed from there on. Gnan is the only light in this world. If a person attains such a Gnan that helps him assess what is beneficial for him and what is harmful, then he can destroy the tubers.

You have to keep the account book of the pure Self clean. So at night before you go to bed, tell 'Chandulal' to do *pratikraman* for whoever he saw at fault during the day. He must keep his books clean. Any negative intent (*bhaav*) will be purified through *pratikraman*. There is no other solution. Even if an income tax officer were to come and harass you, you should not see faults in him. Tell 'Chandulal' that he has to see the whole world as faultless before he goes to bed.

## It Reaches Him Even If It is Done in Your Mind

It is *atikraman* when you quarrel with someone and, therefore, you have to do *pratikraman* for that. That repenting will settle that account.

**Questioner:** Should *pratikraman* be done in the presence of the other person?

**Dadashri:** There is no problem if the *pratikraman* is done later on.

**Questioner:** If I have slandered you or hurt you, should I come to you personally and do *pratikraman*?

**Dadashri:** If you can do it personally, that would be good; and if that is not feasible, then the *pratikraman* you do later on brings about the same results.

**Questioner:** But how does it reach the other person?

**Dadashri:** 'We' know how it reaches him. It is not possible for you to understand through your intellect (*buddhi*). The Gnani Purush is able to know all that. So you should do what 'we' tell you. Do not involve yourself in unnecessary discussion or intellect. Nevertheless, what should you do if you do not meet him? Should you just sit around doing nothing? What should you do if you do not meet him again? What 'we' are telling you is the process.

## In This Era, There Are More People Who Are Negative

What 'we' are saying is that if you have a negative thought about Dada, you should continue doing *pratikraman*. People are not to be blamed for their hostile, critical and negative nature (*viradhak swabhav*). People of this current time cycle have hostility in them. It is a characteristic of this time cycle for all living beings to be hostile. All those who are not hostile have left the world and moved on. However, there are still many elevated Souls who can improve.

## Negativity Towards Tirthankars and Gnanis

If you have negative thoughts about 'us,' you should do *pratikraman* immediately. The human mind is capable of seeing faults even in a Gnani Purush and of trying to uproot/negate him completely. What will the mind not do? The mind that has been burned will burn others. An unhappy mind will burn even Lord Mahavir.                                                         (380)

**Questioner:** Those who have departed cannot do anything for others. So if you say anything negative about Lord Mahavir, does it reach him?

**Dadashri:** Yes, it reaches him, but he does not accept it and it is returned to you with double the repercussions. So you have to ask for forgiveness for yourself. Keep asking for forgiveness until you forget the words you had uttered. If you have said anything negative about Mahavir, you have to keep asking for forgiveness and it will be immediately erased. The 'arrow' you fired does reach Him, but He does not accept it.

## That is the Result of Defilement

**Questioner:** There are forty Jain temples (*derasars*) in our town, but what kind of irreverence (*ashatna*) or other such reasons would have occurred that, to this day, there is no *abhyudaya* (prosperity or uplifting in the worldly life) in our town?

**Dadashri:** It will occur. Prosperity will come. Now the time has come for prosperity.

**Questioner:** Did some kind of sacrilege occur?

**Dadashri:** Nothing like this will occur without sacrilege. Nothing but sacrilege and defilement has occurred; what else is there?

**Questioner:** What can we do to prevent that from occurring? What can we do to remove it?

**Dadashri:** It can be removed if you repent; if you do real *pratikraman*, it can be removed. There is no other way it can be removed. Keep repenting for the fact that sacrilege did occur; some changes will take place then. But only when everyone repents will the change take place. How much can you accomplish if you alone were to do it?

*****

# [24]
# Gnan Rescues Those Drowning in the River of Worldly Life after Life

## That Which Comes in Memory Calls for Pratikraman

**Questioner:** Is it possible to 'see' past faults by trying to
remember them?

**Dadashri:** Past faults can only be 'seen' by applied,
focused awareness of the Self (*upayog*) and not by recalling
them through the memory. You have to work hard to try and
recall, do you not? They need recalling when a veil comes over
them. If you had some problems with 'Chandulal' and you did
his *pratikraman*, 'Chandulal's' presence will be there. You need
to apply this awareness. In this path of *Akram* there is nothing
to remember or recall. Recollection of events is dependent upon
memory. Whatever events spontaneously arise in the mind come
in order to become cleansed by *pratikraman*. They come so
that they may be cleansed. (382)

This memory itself tells you, 'Get rid of me; wash everything
off.' If it did not come into the memory, there would be all kinds
of problems. What would you 'wash' off if it did not come?
How would You know where the attachment-abhorrence (*raag-
dwesh*) lies? The memory comes on its own to be settled. It
comes so that the 'stickiness' can be removed. So wash off
whatever comes into the memory, clear it all, so that it will be
erased from the memory. The reason it comes in the memory is
because of your 'sticking point.' Erase it, repent for it and make

a firm decision that it will not occur again. This will erase it and remove it from the memory. You have to do *pratikraman* one time for that which comes once in the memory, but as a whole, you have to do *pratikraman* as many times as it comes in the memory.

Have you not already made the decision that you do not want any worldly things when you say your prayers, 'I do not want any temporary thing of this life except for the experience of the absolute Self'? Despite saying this, why does it come in your memory? For that, you should do *pratikraman*. Understand that despite doing *pratikraman*, if anyone or anything comes in the memory, it means that there is a pending complaint and that calls for more *pratikraman*.

**Questioner:** Dada, the *pratikraman* continues as long as it continues to come in the memory. I do not need to recall it.

**Dadashri:** Yes, you do not have to recall it. Once you have decided to do *pratikraman*, it will occur on its own.

## That Which Arises As Desire Calls for Pratyakhyan

Remembering, or memory, is based on attachment and abhorrence. If they did not come to mind, you would forget the mistakes you have made. Why do you not remember people you met in passing, but you remember the loved ones who are now dead? It is because you still have some pending attachment and abhorrence. Doing *pratikraman* will dissolve this.

Desires (*ichchha*) come because *pratyakhyan* has not been done, and events and people come into the memory (*smruti*) because *pratikramans* have not been done.

**Questioner:** Is *pratikraman* associated with intent or desire of ownership (*maliki bhaav*)?

**Dadashri:** For desire or intent of ownership, *pratyakhyan* is needed. For the faults there is *pratikraman*.

## And Yet Atikraman Continues

**Questioner:** The intensity of mistakes made in the past is going down and there are many things that I don't remember as much. So when I do *pratikraman*, how much of that which has been forgotten will come into my memory? You had once said that one has to do a hundred or even more *pratikramans* daily. Now all those faults have been forgotten but they are already bound, how can they be brought into the memory?

**Dadashri:** There is no need to do all that. Most of them are burned immediately when 'we' give you the Gnan. And that is why Gnan is present when you need it. If a grave mistake has occurred, and it comes into your memory, then do *pratikraman*. Otherwise, you do not have to do anything. You do not have to do *pratikraman* for mistakes you do not remember. You don't have to do anything if nothing comes into your memory. (384)

**Questioner:** Even after doing *pratikraman*, if that mistake recurs in my memory, does it mean that I am not free from that mistake?

**Dadashri:** The faults are like layers of an onion. As you peel off the outer layer of an onion, there is yet another layer beneath. These faults have many layers. With each *pratikraman* you do, one layer is shed. In this way, when you do a hundred or more *pratikramans*, the fault will eventually go away. Some faults will go away after five *pratikramans* and some may require more. A fault requires as many *pratikraman* as the number of layers it has. The longer it takes to do *pratikraman*, the bigger and heavier the fault.

**Questioner:** Many times I know that a mistake has occurred. I also do *pratikraman* for it, and yet the same mistake continues to occur.

**Dadashri:** When that happens again and again, keep doing

*pratikraman*, because they are in layers and so each layer goes away with *pratikraman*. It is not the fault of the mistake or the one making it. It occurs because there are many layers to that mistake.

**Questioner:** Does that occur because of one's nature or is it because there is lack of awareness?

**Dadashri:** No, no, no. If one has done the same thing over and over for a thousand lifetimes, then there are that many layers. If it was done for just five lifetimes, then there would be a corresponding amount of layers. And they will still occur again. Say if you take one layer away from an onion, does the onion disappear? You will get another layer, a third layer and so on. Similarly, there are mistakes with so many layers. A mistake with ten layers will be resolved with ten *pratikramans* and mistakes with fifty layers will require fifty *pratikramans* to be resolved. There will be a result for the *pratikraman* for sure. Everything definitely becomes clean.

There should be *pratikraman* for any *atikraman*. You have not done any *atikraman* after coming here and so you do not need to do *pratikraman*. *Pratikraman* is necessary only when you do *atikraman*.

## Memory? Pratikraman. Desire? Pratyakhyan.

**Questioner:** Please explain what You mean when You say, 'That which arises in the memory needs *pratikraman*, and that which arises as desire requires *pratyakhyan*.'

**Dadashri:** When it comes into the memory, know that there is stickiness present and repeated *pratikraman* will make it loose and free you from it.

**Questioner:** Should we do *pratikraman* as many times as it comes to memory?

**Dadashri:** Yes, that many times. You should keep the

intent of *pratikraman*. It is like this: for them to come to mind, time is required; then they will come. Do they not come to you at night?

**Questioner:** They come depending upon the circumstances.

**Dadashri:** Yes, because of the circumstances.

**Questioner:** And what about when desire arises?

**Dadashri:** Desire means the subtle inner tendencies become evident externally. The intent (*bhaav*) that you had previously made is now surfacing again and so here you need to do *pratyakhyan*.

**Questioner:** Dada, during such times You tell us to say, 'This should not be there anymore.' Do we say this every time?

**Dadashri:** You have to do *pratyakhyan* in the following manner, 'This is not mine. I am surrendering everything. I had invited all these in ignorance. But today, they are not mine, so I am surrendering them through the mind, speech and body. Now I do not want anything. I had invited this pleasure (*sukh*) in my ignorant state. Today, this pleasure is not mine and, therefore, I am surrendering it. I surrender it through the mind-body-speech; I do not need anything anymore.' You had invited that which you believed gave you pleasure, but your vision (*drashti*) has changed and, therefore, that so-called 'pleasure' now appears as illusory, transient pleasure to you. Not only was it not real pleasure, but it was not even false illusory pleasure.

(386)

## Short Pratikraman

The whole goal behind *Akram Vignan* is 'shoot-on-sight' *pratikraman*. This is the foundation upon which *Akram Vignan* stands. No one is making mistakes. If you become instrumental in hurting someone, invoke that person's pure Soul, who is completely separate from that person's *dravyakarma*, *nokarma* and *bhaavkarma*, and do *pratikraman*.

**Questioner:** Do I have to say all this long sentence when I do *pratikraman*?

**Dadashri:** No, it is not necessary. Make it short. Make a phone call to the pure Soul of the opponent and say, 'I have made this mistake, please forgive me.'

**Questioner:** Even when doing 'shoot-on-sight' *pratikraman*, is there any need for one to sit still?

**Dadashri:** It is acceptable even if one does not sit still but does *pratikraman*; but it should be 'shoot-on-sight.' It should be done immediately after the mistake occurs. Otherwise, you may forget to do *pratikraman*.

## Then It Will Not Stick To You in Your Next Life

**Questioner:** How many *pratikramans* should one do in a day?

**Dadashri:** As many as the number of mistakes that are made, not more. They should be 'shoot-on-sight' *pratikramans*. The moment any fault occurs, shoot it down. It will be shot down. *Pratikraman* can be done while you are drinking your tea or while taking a bath. Where there are bodily actions (*deha-dharma*), functioning of the mind (*mano-dharma*) or functioning of the intellect (*buddhi-dharma*), the location also has to be considered. Ours is religion of the Self (*Atma-dharma*) and so it is not necessary to look into the relative; we can do *pratikraman* anywhere.

However many mistakes you destroy with *pratikraman*, that is how much closer you come towards *moksha*.

**Questioner:** Will those files not stick to us in our next life?

**Dadashri:** For what? Why worry about the next life? You should do all the *pratikramans* in this very life. Keep doing *pratikraman* every free moment you get.

So you have to keep making him ('Chandulal') do *pratikraman*. In the worldly life, tell him to do *pratikraman* whenever possible.

## Pratikraman for the Family and Close Relatives

Moreover, *pratikraman* should be done for all the people in the home. Each day, do *pratikraman* for your father, mother, brother and sister, and even for your extended family members, because these are the people with whom you have very sticky accounts.

So if you do *pratikraman* for your family for one hour, starting from everyone close to you to the extended family and going back two to three generations, recall all of them and do *pratikraman*; thus you will destroy the most grave and serious faults. Their minds will be cleansed towards you. You should do this for all your close relatives. If you cannot sleep at night, you should do *pratikraman* in this manner. When you start doing *pratikraman* in this way, it will start a film. When that occurs, much bliss will arise – so much so, that it will overflow.

**Questioner:** Yes, that is true.                                  (388)

**Dadashri:** During the time of *pratikraman*, the Self is in complete, pure, focused awareness (*shuddha upayog*). There is no interference from anything.

Who does the *pratikraman*? 'Chandulal' does the *pratikraman*. And for whom does he do *pratikraman*? He does *pratikraman* for his whole family. He recalls all his extended family, to do *pratikraman*. The Self is the 'Seer' (*jonaaro*) of this process; the Self does nothing. There is no other interference and, therefore, much pure, focused awareness (*shuddha upayog*) remains.

Tonight, do *pratikraman* for everyone in your family. If you run out of time, then do it tomorrow night. If you still run out of time, then do it the night after that. And when you are done with that, stop and then remember everyone that you know in your town and do their *pratikraman*. Anyone you have bumped into and have become irritated with, will you not have to cleanse all that? You will have to clear all the 'paperwork.'

**Questioner:** What if something occurred many years ago, which I do not even remember?

**Dadashri:** Something that you do not remember? That will remain just as it is. You will then have to do *samayik* (to Be the Self and 'see' the self) and it will come to you.

**Questioner:** Will I be able to recall it in the *samayik*?

**Dadashri:** Yes, some people can recall all the way back to when they were five years of age.

## The Tuber-Free State, after Tubers are Destroyed

**Questioner:** I have made mistakes during my childhood, during my adult years and even later in life. I can 'see' all that – everything, one after the other.

**Dadashri:** Now that you have the time, do *samayik* for an hour every day. You may not find time every day, so do at least one *samayik* every two days. 'See' faults related to sexuality (*vishay*). One day, see faults related to violence (*himsa*) in the *samayik*. You should arrange to do *samayik* for all these mistakes. With the grace of this 'Dada,' you will 'see' all the faults in *samayik*. You will see all the mistakes back to your young age. Those mistakes will wash away as You 'see' them. Even when they are washed away, grab hold of the largest tuber of mistake and keep bringing it back in the *samayik* every day. So keep doing *samayik* in this way.

**Questioner:** How would I know whether a tuber is large?

**Dadashri:** When there are recurrent thoughts about something, that tuber is large. If there is a pile of some lemons here, some oranges over there and some onions over there, you will smell all of them. But 'know' that the pile that smells the most is the largest. Therefore, You will 'know' from within. If you have thought after thought about something, then realize that that stock is large. Make a note of it being number one, another as number two; check to see how many such tubers there are within. Then take each of them in *upayog* (focused awareness of the Self). Once You 'see', 'know' and do *pratikraman*, one layer is removed. Some have more than five hundred such layers, some have a hundred layers, some have two hundred layers; but all of them will empty eventually. You have to become *nirgranth* (free from tubers of *kashay* and *vishay*) to attain *moksha*. *Nirgranth* means that the inner *karmic* tubers are gone, only the external tubers remain. And those external tubers belong to 'Chandulal' (the non-Self).

**Questioner:** Dada, should we arrange for a session of doing *pratikraman* in Your presence before You go to America?

**Dadashri:** Yes, we will do it this very evening. We will do it in 'My' presence. I will sit there. We will make everyone do it in 'My' presence. Many years ago, I made some people do *pratikraman* in My presence for mistakes related to sexuality (*vishay*). They all went into it so deeply that they could not stop. Their *pratikraman* continued even when they went home. Even during sleep and while eating, their *pratikraman* continued. This continued to take place day and night. Then I had to stop it for them. Even when they wanted to stop the *pratikraman*, it would not stop. Once this machinery of *pratikraman* is set in motion, it will continue on its own.                                              (390)

**Questioner:** In *pratikraman*, Dada says that past mistakes will overflow and no matter how hard you try, they will not be contained; they will overflow.

**Dadashri:** Yes, they will continue to overflow.

## Pratikraman of Mistakes from the Past Life

**Questioner:** How can we do *alochana* of the mistakes committed in the past life in the *pratikraman vidhi*?

**Dadashri:** *Pratikraman vidhi* means that *alochana* has to be done when the effect of the mistakes of the past life arise in this life. The effect in this life is of mistakes that were committed in the past life. Mistakes took place in the previous life; they are in the form of a plan and then they come into effect in this life. When they do, you can 'see' that these are the mistakes that were done in the past life. That is what You 'see' and 'experience.'

**Questioner:** Are there not certain mistakes that bypass this life and go straight into the next life? Or can they come early?

**Dadashri:** No, there are no such mistakes. Are there any mango trees that will give you the fruit before the blossom?

**Questioner:** No.

**Dadashri:** Similarly, you get the 'flowers' first for this; everything is orderly, not disorderly. It is not a falsehood. Therefore, in the past life you got the 'flower' and in this life the mangos get ready to grow. Thereafter it gives bitter or sweet fruit.

**Questioner:** The fruit comes after one life and not later?

**Dadashri:** No, it is not like that.

**Questioner:** Will all the fruits come in this very life?

**Dadashri:** They all have to come in this life because, how can one rely upon the next life? He will have human karmas, but he may be a donkey in his next life! As a donkey, how can he discharge the karma created before his past human life? Therefore, all the fruits come in the current human life.

## Set Aside an Hour Daily for Pratikraman

**Dadashri:** Have you ever done *pratikraman* for your older brother?

**Questioner:** I have not done any such *pratikraman*.

**Dadashri:** You have to do all those *pratikramans*. That is when you will become free from all the karma that you have accumulated. The bliss (*anand*) that You experience when you do *pratikraman* is true bliss. First, you should do *pratikraman* for all the people in your family, then for your relatives, then compare the residual *kashays* with reference to each one of them, daily. When you are resting in the afternoon, do *pratikramans* then. Do it for each and every person. First do it for your children, sons and their wives, and see the bliss that arises. Do *pratikraman* in this way at home. Keep a practice of this for an hour and see the bliss you get from that by recalling everything! You will be able to 'see' even a small child.

Just look at our Gnan, it is so effective! You may not remember ordinarily but as you sit down to do *pratikraman*; you will 'see' the children and everything else.          (392)

**Questioner:** Dada, if You had cautioned me to do *pratikraman* every day about a certain thing. Then, when I am not able to do it for one day, or if I do fewer *pratikramans* during the time I set aside for them, it bothers me. Before, I used to feel that it is no big deal if I cannot do them.

**Dadashri:** If that bothers you, then recognize that you have come over on this side. Your 'vote' is for this side now (pro-*pratikraman*).

**Questioner:** Dada, this *pratikraman* is a very good thing for us.

**Dadashri:** *Pratikraman* will get your work done.

Tonight, starting with all those who are close to you – first your father, then your sister, all the way to the youngest child, your uncles and aunts – do *pratikraman* for all of them. Then tomorrow, expand that circle to include other family members. In this way, extend it every day. Then do *pratikraman* for all those you know; this would also include your teachers. Then do *pratikraman* for all those you know at college. You have to -clear accounts with everyone. Relationships you have created in your mind, too, have to be cleared. We will worry later about karmas that have already been bound that will express later.

Do you ever do *pratikraman* for anyone? You have to do *pratikraman* for all the bosses you know, bosses you have met, and for anyone you became instrumental (*nimit*) in hurting.

Will you not have to do *pratikraman* for all the attachment-abhorrence (*raag-dwesh*) you have done in the past? And no bliss will come close to the bliss that is experienced while clearing this with *pratikraman*. Whatever occurred in the past occurred in ignorance, but if you do not wash it off now that You have the Gnan, will it not be like keeping soiled clothes in a suitcase? What will happen?

You have kept a lot in the suitcases, haven't you? Look inside; there may be some clothes with stains on them.

Then take all your friends and all the rest. There is a lot work to be-done. Plan it this way and check to see where you still have accounts remaining; and continue doing their *pratikraman*. Yes, otherwise, what work should you give to the mind? Let it do this *pratikraman*. This is not for any worldly benefits. For worldly benefits, the businessmen make the mind work by making plans like, 'Next year we will do this; we will build a warehouse over there, then we will do this or that.' In this way, they will take up several hours.

## This is How 'We' Attained Closure with the Universe

'You' can see all the mistakes that 'Chandulal' has. What good is this Gnan if you cannot see the mistakes? That is why Krupadudev said,

'I am a vessel of infinite mistakes, oh compassionate One! Without 'seeing' these mistakes of the self, how will I attain salvation?'

One has to 'see' his mistakes. There is nothing wrong with having mistakes. Some may have twenty-five mistakes and some may have a hundred. 'We' may have two. That is of no significance. You simply have to maintain Your *upayog* (focused awakened awareness as the Self) and You will continue to 'see' the mistakes. You don't have to do anything else.

You have to tell 'Chandulal' to continue doing *pratikraman* for the entire family and all the people he has hurt. 'Chandulal' must do *pratikraman* for his countless previous lives in which he had committed mistakes related to attachment (*raag*), abhorrence (*dwesh*) and sexuality (*vishay*). Taking one person at a time, the *pratikraman* must be done in the way I have shown you. After that, with the same focused awareness (*upayog*), *pratikraman* must be done for the neighbors too. After doing this, your burden will lessen. Your burden will not lessen any other way.

This is how 'we' removed all our mistakes with the entire world, and it is how 'we' became free. As long as you see mistakes in 'us,' I do not have peace. So whenever 'we' do *pratikraman* in this manner, everything over there gets erased. You do not have to do *alochana* in my presence; You are *Shuddhatma* (pure Soul) and at that time, 'Chandulal' does *alochana* in the presence of the *Shuddhatma*. Tell 'Chandulal' to do *alochana* and then make him do *pratikraman* and *pratyakhyan*. Make him do this for an hour at a time. Make him do this for all the members of the family, whomever he has relations with.                                                   (394)

## Stickiness Where There is Intense Prior Life Account

You can reduce the 'stickiness' of *raag-dwesh* (attachment-abhorrence) by constantly doing *pratikraman*. It is your mistake that the other person is being difficult; you have not washed it off, and if you have washed it off, then the *purusharth* has not been adequate. Whenever you have a free moment, keep doing *pratikraman* and wash off all the mistakes with the past life karma accounts (*roonanubandhi*) with whom there is a 'sticky' relationship. Usually there are not many such people – there may be five or ten individuals with whom you have a sticky relation from the past life. Those are the ones you have to do *pratikraman* for and thus wash away the stickiness. You have to find out who they are. You will immediately know the new ones when they arise, but you have to find the old ones. There is greater stickiness with the ones who have a closer relationship with you. What will start sprouting? Only that which is sticky!

Your speech will come out better if everything is cleared, otherwise it will not. Everything should be cleared up, wherever you have acquaintances. Then do *pratikraman* of people in specific areas of the county, state and then by profession, for example, lawyers, judges, accountants, etc.

You have to do a lot of other kind of *pratikramans*. If you meet someone when you are going somewhere and you start talking to him, and he may feel hurt in the conversation, do *pratikraman* in his name. If you are walking along and trip on the road, why did you trip? Investigate why you tripped; you encountered a problem that made you fall on a specific course of action. Clean it through *pratikraman* without delving too much into it.

You must do lots of *pratikraman* for all the people you have harassed and hurt. Whenever you have free time, take an hour or so recalling each person and do his *pratikraman*. Whomever you have hurt, will you not have to wash that off? Thereafter, the Gnan will come into experience.

## Helping or Hurting – Both Bind Karma

**Questioner:** When I was young, I stole ten rupees from one girl and then put it in the compass box of another girl who was in need of the money. I did *pratikraman* of that.

**Dadashri:** What is that like? You earned merit karma (*punya*) for giving the money and demerit karma (*paap*) for stealing. For the *punya* you earned, say, one hundred points, you lost three hundred points for stealing. This is how the world is. There is harm in also doing such interference.

So take everyone that you know and do their *pratikraman*. Then take all the clients, all the attorneys, all the judges and do their *pratikraman*. Then do *pratikraman* for those who are acquainted with you. Try and do *pratikraman* in the afternoon while you are resting. This way, you will not fall asleep; *pratikraman* will be done and at the same time you will get the rest. This is what 'we' do, but for 'us' everything is finished.

## Pratikraman of Religious People

After this, with Dada Bhagwan as your witness, take all the religions and their religious heads, monks, nuns, and ascetics, and do *pratikraman* for any negative comments or criticisms you have made, instigated others to make, in this life, the past life, past calculable lives, and past infinite lives. Ask for the strength not to repeat any such transgression against such people, in the slightest degree.

## Do Pratikraman This Way

Before Gnan, I had a very strong ego. I used to criticize people and was very disrespectful and scornful to them, but at the same time, I used to be full of praise for some people. I would scorn one and praise another. After 1958, when Gnan manifested, I told A. M. Patel, 'Wash away all the contempt you had towards others. Put soap of *pratikraman* on it and wash it off!' After that, I recalled each and every person I had treated with contempt, including neighbors, uncles, aunts and in-laws. I had treated many people with contempt so I washed it off.

**Questioner:** Did you do *pratikraman* in your mind or did you personally ask for their forgiveness?        (396)

**Dadashri:** I told Ambalal that, 'I can see all the wrong you have done. Now wash off all of those wrongdoings.' So what did he start to do? How would he wash them off? Then I gave him the understanding that, 'Remember and recall that you have hurt the other person and have abused him verbally and scorned him.' I would show him the whole thing. I would tell him to first describe the mistake in this manner, in detail (*alochana*), and then say,

'Dear *Shuddhatma Bhagwan*! You are completely separate from the union (*yoga*) of mind, speech and body of 'Chandubhai' and his *bhaavkarma*, *dravyakarma* and *nokarma*. Dear *Shuddhatma Bhagwan*, I am asking for Your forgiveness for all these errors committed towards 'Chandubhai' (insert name of the person hurt). I am asking this in the presence of Dada Bhagwan. I will never repeat such mistakes again.'

Do *pratikraman* in this manner and you will notice a change on the other person's face. You do the *pratikraman* here and the changes will be taking place over there within him.

**Questioner:** Can *pratikraman* be done directly by being in front of the other person?

**Dadashri:** It can be done, but only if the other person is noble and reasonable. Otherwise, he will say, 'Now she has become wise! She did not believe me when I told her, and now she has shaped up.' The fool! He took it the wrong way! Then he will scold the poor woman. So do not do that. These people (nowadays) lack understanding; they are unwise and immature. There are only a few that are noble and who will calm down, but others will make comments like, 'So, you realize it now? I have been telling you for a long time but you would not listen!' I even know what he will say and I also know how you will feel. This life is all a drama! A play! So this is how we do *pratikraman*.

## The World of Intellect and Interference

'We' did so much cleaning and only then did the 'book' (of the *karmic* account) become clean. 'We' have been cleaning in this way from countless past lives and that is why 'we' became free from the account book of karma. I have shown you the way so you can free yourself quickly. 'We' had to do the washing over many lifetimes.

You should do *pratikraman* so that you can become free from the liability of these mistakes. In the beginning after Gnan, people used to attack me and question my integrity, but later, they got tired of doing this because I never retaliated. If we become belligerent and attack, then they will never get tired of counterattacking. This world, with the interfering intellect, will not let anyone attain liberation. So you should be careful and conduct yourself with awareness, avoiding all conflicts. The one who becomes aware and moves carefully by withdrawing, thus avoiding all conflicts, will attain liberation.

At least try doing *pratikraman*, and then see the changes in the people in your household. There will be magical changes and effects.

It is better to remain stuck here in this *satsang*, even if you have to take a beating, as compared to being stuck over there in the worldly life with no *satsang*. Don't you have to check into whether the place where you are is good or bad?

**Questioner:** The *pratikraman* you gave me when I had a problem with my leg brought about a magical change within two days.

**Dadashri:** 'We' had sent 'our' blessings.

**Questioner:** It brought about a magical effect within two days.

**Dadashri:** This is a magical effect of 'ours', this doing of *pratikraman* according to the Agna. It does what even God cannot do.                                                      (398)

## Now You Can No Longer Afford to be Tempted

**Questioner:** I had a good experience in that.

**Dadashri:** Yes, because from the exact perspective, this is such an easy path. It is straightforward. It is one of equanimity and impartiality. There is no difficulty in it. And yet what does the One who shows you this path and impart His grace on you say? He tells you that He is just instrumental in the process (a *nimit*). He does not take credit for it. Otherwise, a person will take at least some credit for it. Then there will be a burden of that credit and fame. So, everything has become so very straightforward that You need to get Your work done; that is what I am saying. Another straightforward (*sarad*) path will not come again; it will not be so straightforward again. You will never get the same chance again.

Therefore, this is the greatest chance you will get, so why don't you curb all that 'tickles your fancy,' all that tempts you. There is no joy in these things that entice you. You will find many people who will tempt you and allure you away but there is no benefit to You in that. So let go of your fondness for all that 'tickles your fancy' and tempts you, just for one life; besides, now only half the life remains. It is not even one full lifetime anymore, is it?

## Bow Down to His Shuddhatma and Then...

**Questioner:** When you told us to do *pratikraman* for our friends and relatives, do we just have to 'see' it all or do we have to say something?

**Dadashri:** You have to say it in your mind.

**Questioner:** Having attachment (*raag*) for anyone is a mistake and having abhorrence (*dwesh*) against anyone is also a mistake, so do I have to do *pratikraman* for that?

**Dadashri:** Not just *raag-dwesh*. You have to say a lot of other things. You have to say that you are doing *alochana*, *pratikraman* and *pratyakhyan* for whatever mistakes you have made in this life, and countless previous lives, due to ignorance.

**Questioner:** Is that for the *raag-dwesh* of this life and of countless past lives?

**Dadashri:** *Raag-dwesh*, all the mistakes made in ignorance, any accusations, for hurting someone's ego; you have to mention all that and when you say all that, your one file is cleared. Then you have to take the next file, clear it and dismiss it just like the doctor dismisses his patients.

'We' also cleared out all the accounts with people in 'our' village – people who lived on 'our' street – 'we' searched for all of them. Only mistakes done in ignorance are bound. Have you bound mistakes like those at all?

**Questioner:** Many.

## Do As Dadashri Has Instructed; Do Not Add Anything Else

**Questioner:** I have read in a book that if one does

*pratikraman* for numerous and innumerous past lives, then everything will become clean for sure, is that true?

**Dadashri:** There is no estimate of what has occurred in the past. One simply comes (is born) with claims; he will bring forward some kind of a claim or a 'letter', therefore, you have to recognize that it is an account from the past. It appears that it is not a claim of the present life, but of the past.

**Questioner:** Yes, but what if I want to do all the *pratikraman* in advance so that everything becomes so pure that no claim comes calling? What if I do *pratikraman* in advance for claims that I have not even brought? Is it possible to do this kind of *pratikraman* if I say it in this manner?

**Dadashri:** It will only occur if one brings forth a claim. If there is no claim, then he has nothing to do with it. You can only do *pratikraman* for the claim that exists and arises.

**Questioner:** So one cannot be free until the claim for each and every mistake is settled, is that so? Is there not a general *pratikraman* that you have talked about for the purpose of erasing mistakes of numerous and innumerous past lives?

**Dadashri:** Yes.                                                    (400)

**Questioner:** I am asking for forgiveness for that. I am doing *pratikraman* for that. How should I do *pratikraman* for that?

**Dadashri:** That is all you need to say, nothing else. Do not make it your agenda to inquire into details. Do it only the way it is written. Another thing is, do *pratikraman* only for all the 'attacks,' claims that you have brought with you that will arise as conflicts and *kashays* and nothing more. Do general *pratikraman* as you have been told in Gnan.

**Questioner:** But, Dada, the 'attack,' the effect of clash seems to be the same again and again, and I do 'shoot-on-sight' *pratikraman.* But...

**Dadashri:** You have to do only as much as 'we' have told you and nothing more.

**Questioner:** No, but when I have that surplus time, if I continue to say the same thing over and over again for hours on end, will that work?

**Dadashri:** You have to do as 'we' have told you. When you have the surplus time, you cannot put in your own wisdom by saying, 'Everything done in this lifetime, numerous or innumerous lifetimes, everything...' You cannot add your own 'ingredients' into it. You will poison half of it. And finish all the claims that you have brought with you and nothing new. Do not say anything new. Do you understand? Continue doing everything the way it is supposed to be done. The intellect will paint something negative. It will kill you. 'What's wrong with doing it this way?' That is what it will show you.

When does attachment (*raag*) arise? It arises from abhorrence (*dwesh*). And then *raag* gives rise to *dwesh* again. Therefore, they are all mistakes. There is *raag-dwesh* wherever there is a mistake. That is considered a 'sticky' file.

## Lord Mahavir's Principle is Based On This

Whoever's *pratikraman* we do, he may not have any bad feelings towards us, but respect for us will arise within him because the *pratikramans* have been done. No matter how much enmity there may be, it will go away in this very life. This is the only solution. The whole principle of Lord Mahavir is based verily on *pratikraman*. It is *alochana*, *pratikraman* and *pratyakhyan*! There is no religion (*dharma*) where there is no *alochana*, *pratikraman* and *pratyakhyan*. The people of the world will not remember this *alochana*, *pratikraman* and *pratyakhyan*, whereas You have become a *Shuddhatma* and, therefore, You will remember them immediately.

## Pratikraman for What Bothers You

You will not have peace as long as you see others' mistakes. When you do *pratikraman*, this mistake will be erased. You should do *pratikraman* for every sticky file of *raag-dwesh* by focused awareness (*upayog*) and thereby it gets cleaned. It is important to do *pratikraman* for files due to attachment (*raag*).

If you are sleeping on a nice comfortable mattress but there are pebbles underneath in it, would it not bother you until you shake it out? In the same manner, *pratikraman* is called for when things bother you. *Pratikraman* needs to be done only where there is an internal signal of discomfort and pain. And whatever bothers the other person, he, too, will do the same! Everyone has different kinds of *pratikraman*.

There are instances where a man will oblige everyone else but in his home he behaves badly, so here he has to do *pratikraman*. *Pratikraman* has to be done wherever things bother you, but everyone's *pratikraman* is different. When anything bothers you, you will realize that you are the one at mistake. Won't it bother you until you do *pratikraman* for it?

**Questioner:** It used to bother me a lot.

**Dadashri:** It bothers you because of past mistakes. We are bound by our mistakes. Whether the bondage is of *raag* (attachment) or *dwesh* (abhorrence), you have to do *pratikraman* for it. If the other person is gentle and straightforward, then you can ask him directly for his forgiveness; even that will clear your account.

## When Both the Parties Do Pratikraman

If you have done *atikraman* towards someone, then all day you should do *pratikraman* in his name. When both the parties do *pratikraman*, they can become free of mistakes much quicker. If you both do five thousand *pratikramans* or more, then things can be resolved faster. However, if the other person does not do *pratikraman*, you will have to do ten thousand in order to be free.                                                    (402)

**Questioner:** It bothers me if something like this remains pending.

**Dadashri:** Do not carry around such a burden. Instead, sit down for an hour one day and do collective *pratikraman* for all your mistakes towards anyone you did *atikraman* with. Do not go around carrying the burden of an unfinished task.

**Questioner:** When I sit down to do *samayik* in the morning, half an hour to three quarters of an hour goes into doing *pratikraman*.

**Dadashri:** You should not have such burden at that time. Whenever you do *pratikraman*, whether it is after fifteen days, a month or a year, then do them all together.

## Atikraman of Atikramans

In order to take care of one *atikraman*, a person does greater *atikraman* and even greater *atikraman* to take care of that *atikraman*.

**Questioner:** So the entanglements keep increasing.

**Dadashri:** The entanglement increases in such a way that there will never be a resolution. Day and night it torments the owner. That is why human beings cannot become free from their entanglements. And that is why they go into a four-legged life – for the very purpose of becoming free from the entanglements.

**Questioner:** Meaning, first the *atikraman* stops. Then while it is halted, one goes into animal life and suffers the effects of the mistakes of karma.

**Dadashri:** No. To suffer means to repay. Through suffering it gets washed off. He does *pratikraman* for all the *atikraman* he did.

**Questioner:** So he does not do any *atikraman* in a 'four-legged' life. He goes there to suffer.

**Dadashri:** There is no other problem. He suffers it for the sake of suffering; that is all. He returns to human life after suffering it all. It is not that he will remain stuck there; he will not be able to remain stuck there even if he says he wants to. He will be asked to leave as soon as he has paid off his *karmic* debt (*hisaab*).

**Questioner:** Will one go to the animal life if he has done a lot of *atikraman*?

**Dadashri:** The fruit of many *atikraman* is a life in the animal form. And the consequence of even worse *atikraman* is a life in hell.

**Questioner:** Many people take better care of pets than they do of humans.

**Dadashri:** That is because there are some fortunate ones (*punyashadi* – one with merit karma) too; even those who do *atikraman* have merit karma (*punya*) and these pets are treated royally.

**Questioner:** So they have done hurtful karma (*atikraman*) as well as merit karma (helpful karma); both karmas together.

**Dadashri:** They do *atikraman* for the good of others.

(404)

**Questioner:** But you said that *atikraman* done for the good of others is not considered a mistake.

**Dadashri:** It gives merit karma (*punya*). He would even come as an ox belonging to royalty.

## Suffering According to the Account of Karma

All this corruption and adulteration is equivalent to bestiality (*paashavata*). This will lead to a life in the animal form. One will have to go there and suffer it, won't he?

**Questioner:** Whatever it is, good or bad; one has to pay off the *karmic* account and then leave, does he not?

**Dadashri:** Yes, all the accounts, credit or debit, will have to be paid off. After attaining this Gnan, we have a way not to create any new accounts. You do not bind any karma as long as You remain as the *Shuddhatma*, and if you slip from the *Shuddhatma* state and do *atikraman*, then by doing *pratikraman* you will wash it off – provided that You remain in awareness! Otherwise, some of the karmas that were bound prior to attaining this Gnan have been dissolved and are gone, and those karmas that have jelled solid will have to be suffered. But that will not be for too long.

**Questioner:** What should I do about all kinds of mistakes that I made before meeting You, Dada?

**Dadashri:** You have to do collective (*jathu*) *pratikraman* for that. Collective means together. Do it for half an hour a day. Do *pratikraman* even for throwing a stone at some boy when you were young. The *pudgal* (the non-Self complex of mind, speech and body) will become pure (*shuddha*) when you do *pratikraman*.

**Questioner:** Can *pratikraman* destroy demerit karma (*paap*), regardless of how grave it is?

**Dadashri:** No matter how grave a sin (*paap*) one has committed, it will be destroyed if one does *pratikraman*.

**Questioner:** Even if one has murdered someone?

**Dadashri:** Yes, not just one or two murders, but even for burning down an entire village.

**Questioner:** But that should be a *pratikraman*?

**Dadashri:** It should be good *pratikraman* (done with deep remorse and sincerity). The intensity of *pratikraman* must equal the intensity of the *atikraman*.

## Target Specific Individual Pratikramans Are Best

*Pratikraman* will occur as You 'see' all the mistakes. That is when You will become free. However many *pratikraman* you do, you are free from that many mistakes. However many are left, you will have to continue doing *pratikraman* for them.

**Questioner:** When we ask for forgiveness from all the living beings of the world, then *pratikraman* is considered done, is it not?

**Dadashri:** When can you consider *pratikraman* as being done? When it is done individually, one by one.

**Questioner:** I am trying to get the balance sheet of all the karmas done before attaining Gnan. When will all that come to light?

**Dadashri:** Do *pratikraman* when they come into your memory. Do *pratikraman* for whatever comes in your memory; otherwise, sit in *samayik* that 'we' hold here for everyone. Sit on that day and 'do' it exactly, and some of it will be washed off that day. In this way, everything will be washed off.

## Software of Pratikraman

Such knowledge about *pratikraman* has never before been disclosed to the world. The world has never read or heard of such knowledge before.

What occurs when I make people sit and do *pratikraman*?

People are made to recall the mistakes from their childhood onwards, and wash them off with *pratikraman* by seeing the pure Self of the person against whom the errors were committed. In doing such *pratikraman*, which takes about two hours, a large portion of one's major mistakes are erased.          (406)

One has to continue doing *pratikraman* in this manner. In repeating this process, the smaller mistakes will begin to come to mind and they will be washed off. Subsequently, even smaller mistakes will become visible and be washed off. Thus, practically all mistakes are wiped off.

In the two-hour session of *pratikraman*, you should wash off all past mistakes of this life that have adhered to you. Then when you make a firm decision not to repeat such mistakes again, that is considered *pratyakhyan*.

When you sit down to do *pratikraman*, you will experience the 'nectar' from within and you will feel very light.

Are you doing *pratikraman*? Do you feel light (a sense of freedom) when you do *pratikraman*? Are you doing *pratikraman* intensely? Recall everyone and do their *pratikraman*. Start digging and looking for your mistakes and do *pratikraman*. As you start, you will recollect your mistakes and you will begin to see everything clearly. If you kicked someone eight years ago, you will see that incident too. How do these events come into your recollection when otherwise they do not come even if you try to recall them? The moment you begin your *pratikraman*, a link is established. Have you tried even once to do *pratikraman* for your whole life?

**Questioner:** Yes, once I did.

**Dadashri:** Has anyone told you not to do it again?

**Questioner:** No, I was doing it recently. One day, all of us sat down to do it.

**Dadashri:** This you can even do at home if you want to.

**Questioner:** This is the first time I was able to sit down to do *samayik*. I felt very blissful.

**Dadashri:** So do *pratikraman* for everyone; do *pratikraman* every day for people at home, then do it for your close relatives. First do *pratikraman* for all those who have been hurt. Do you remember them or not?

**Questioner:** Yes, I do. Every day I do that in a *samayik*.

**Dadashri:** By doing this *pratikraman*, did you get convinced that it is a good experience?

**Questioner:** Dada, before, whenever I did *pratikraman*, I used to feel that, 'why do I have to do *pratikraman* unnecessarily, when it is not even my fault?'

**Dadashri:** No, but what about now?

**Questioner:** Now I understand.

**Dadashri:** Did you feel bliss (*anand*) today?

**Questioner:** Yes, I understand where I was wrong. That was not the case before. For some time now I understand it.

**Dadashri:** Still, when you come to see the roots of your major mistake, you will experience a lot of bliss. If you do not feel bliss when you do *pratikraman*, it means that you have not learned to do it properly. If a person does *atikraman* and does not feel a sense of remorse, then that person is not human.

**Questioner:** Dada, which is the main mistake?   (408)

**Dadashri:** Before, you could not see any mistakes at all, could you? The mistakes you see now are your tangible/gross (*sthool*) mistakes. You will see even beyond this level.

**Questioner:** Are we talking about the subtle (*sookshma*), subtler (*sookshmatar*)…?

**Dadashri:** You will continue to see your mistakes. Right now there is a density of veils. You can see the external body but how can you know what he is like from within? These two ladies are very fair on the outside but how can you know what they are like from the inside? So when You 'see' what is within, then You will understand the main mistake. Do you understand?

**Questioner:** Yes, Dada.

## The Sign of a Living Pratikraman

Here when you do *pratikraman* for two, three hours, you see nothing but your mistakes during that time. That is called live *pratikraman*. When you sit down to do this *pratikraman*, You become a pure Soul (*Shuddhatma*). When you sit down to do *pratikraman*, does *pratikraman* continue to occur? Does it occur even when you don't want it to?

**Questioner:** Yes, it does.

**Dadashri:** What if I said, 'Now stop doing it'?

**Questioner:** Then the pulley just keeps running.

**Dadashri:** Who makes it run? The answer is, 'Now that you have attained the state of *Shuddhatma*, all these actions are of the *pragnya shakti* – the energy of the awakened Self after Self-realization. Prior to attaining Gnan, they were actions of *agnya shakti* (energy of ignorance mediated through the ego-intellect complex). For people who use the word '*Shuddhatma*' but do not have Self-realization, their actions of power, or energy, of ignorance (*agnya shakti*) continues; for them, the actions of *pragnya* have not yet arisen. What has occurred with us? For us, the activities of ignorance (*agnya*) have stopped and activities of *pragnya* have started. What does *agnya* do? It continues to bind one to the worldly life (*sansar*). It will keep giving rise to new worldly life every day.

## Hardware of Pratikraman

When you do *pratikraman* for your entire life, you are neither in the state of liberation nor in this worldly life. When you do *pratikraman*, you are actually watching a 'documentary' of your past. As such, you are exposing everything of the past during *pratikraman*. During that time, there are no interruptions from your mind, intellect, *chit* or ego. The entire internal mechanism of the mind, intellect, *chit* and ego (*antahkaran*) is silent. During that time, only *pragnya* (direct energy of the Self) is working. The pure Self is not doing anything.

Once a mistake occurs, it gets hidden. Then another layer will come on top of that; then another layer and so forth; this way the mistakes build up in layers. These layers continue to grow and at the time of death, in the final hour, a summary of all these mistakes takes place.

When mistakes of the past are 'seen' in the present, it is due to the Light of awakened awareness (*Gnan prakash*). It has nothing to do with memory (*smruti*).

**Questioner:** Does *pratikraman* have any effect on the Soul (the Self)?

**Dadashri:** No effect whatsoever can touch the Self. There is no effect on the Self. There is absolutely no doubt that the Self exists. It reigns beyond the boundaries of memory and that is why You are able to go beyond the memory. The Self is infinite energy. This energy is called *pragnya shakti* and it can break through all the layers from the core of the earth. By doing *pratikraman*, You become filled with a sense of freedom and that freedom is freedom from all attachment and abhorrence. All animosity is naturally broken. And it does not matter if the other person is not there for your *pratikraman*. Your *pratikraman* does not require his signature. When you committed the mistakes, no witness was present. You commit most of the mistakes against people in their absence anyway. In essence, although their very presence has precipitated these mistakes, they have not put their live signatures on them. The signatures came from your internal attachment and abhorrence.

Some day, if you are sitting alone and you start to do *pratikraman*, the experience of the Self will begin to solidify from within. The taste will arise. This is the experience of the Self.                                                                      (410)

## The Moment You Accept Your Mistake, It is Gone

Eventually, you will not see anyone's mistakes. You will first 'see' them and then you will do *pratikraman*. Then you will not 'see' anyone's mistake at all. If you can maintain that the whole night and your book of seeing mistakes is closed, then your work for that day is done. Then you don't have to worry about your liability for that day in the coming life. This Gnan is such that it will bring a satisfactory solution for everything for You. Nothing will be left out. It will clear everything if you do *pratikraman* for any mistake which hurts anyone. *Pratikraman* means to return what you had taken before. Your *karmic* account is cleared when you do *pratikraman*. So accept your mistake and, when you do that, you are no longer held responsible for that mistake. This is considered a science. It gives you instant results. Cash in hand. That will occur gradually. What 'we' have said does not occur all of a sudden. Accept your mistakes and they will be washed off. Do *pratikraman* and they will wash away.

## That is When Real Pratikraman Will Occur

When you begin to see everyone in your family as faultless, then you will know that your *pratikraman* is true. People definitely are faultless; the whole world is flawless. You are bound by your own mistakes, not by theirs. When You understand this, you will be able to resolve everything.

## See the Fault, Do Not See Him As At Fault

Seeing mistakes of the others gives rise to worldly life (*sansar*) and 'seeing' your own mistakes gives you *moksha*.

**Questioner:** It is natural to see the relative at fault, is it not?

**Dadashri:** When is a person considered at fault (*doshit*)? He is at fault if his *Shuddhatma* (the Self) makes the mistake. But the Self is the non-doer. The Self cannot do anything. Everything that is occurring is a discharge; it is the unfolding effects of the past life's karma and you consider him to be at fault (*doshit*). You should do *pratikraman* for seeing him at fault. As long as you see any living being at fault, understand that purification has not occurred completely; until then, the knowledge is relative and sense-oriented (*indriya gnan*).

## By Conviction Faultless, By Conduct at Fault

A person may appear at fault based on the discharging *karmic* stock. But your mind should not hold this impression. You should see him as faultless (*nirdosh*).

**Questioner:** It is absolutely resolved in my unflinching determination (*nischay*) that the whole world is flawless.

**Dadashri:** That is called your 'conviction' (*pratiti*). It has come into Your conviction that the world is flawless, but how much of that is your experience (*anubhav*)? It is not that easy. You can say that it has come into your experience when mosquitoes, bedbugs and snakes surround you and attack you, and You 'see' them as flawless. Nevertheless, at least it should remain in your conviction that they are faultless. When you see a mistake in anyone, it is your own mistake; you verily are at fault and for that you must do *pratikraman*. In 'our' conviction and experience, the world is flawless and the same is evident in 'our' conduct (*vartan, charitra*). You, however, do not have the same experience. You still see mistakes in the world. You have to do *pratikraman* when someone does something wrong to you because you see him as being at fault, do you not?

**Questioner:** If I do *pratikraman* afterwards, is that not considered a conviction (*pratiti*)?

**Dadashri:** But in the beginning, he is looked upon as the one at fault (*doshit*), and that is why you have to do the *pratikraman*, do you not?

**Questioner:** Yes, I have to do *pratikraman* afterwards.

**Dadashri:** But that is because you see him at fault, is it not? That means flawless vision (*nirdosh*) has not become fully established within, has it?

**Questioner:** But *pratikraman* can only be done if the conviction of flawlessness (*nirdosh*) has become established, is that not so?                                                              (412)

**Dadashri:** But keep 'seeing' the one who sees the fault.

## Atikraman Decreases As Awakened Awareness Increases

**Questioner:** As the awakened awareness (*jagruti*) becomes more continuous, *pratikraman* decreases by that much.

**Dadashri:** *Pratikraman* is to be done only when a mistake occurs within, only if *atikraman* has occurred. It is not a rule that there is increased *atikraman* the day the awareness is greater.

**Questioner:** Does *atikraman* occur if one remains in the awareness of the pure Self (*shuddha upayog*)?

**Dadashri:** Yes, *atikraman* as well as *pratikraman* can occur in *shuddha upayog*.

## Pratikraman for Missing Applied Focused Awareness

Who would let go of such a wonderful science once he has attained it? Before, one could not maintain focused, awakened awareness of the Self (*upayog*) even for five minutes. One had great difficulty in doing a forty-eight minute *samayik*, whereas here, no matter where you go, it is possible for You to maintain *upayog*. That is what has occurred.

**Questioner:** I understand that, Dada.

**Dadashri:** Now, obstruct the mistakes a little by doing *pratikraman*. Before you leave home, make a decision that, 'Today I want to remain in pure awareness (*shuddha upayog*).' If you don't make that decision, You will miss the *upayog*. Our science is very good; there is no other problem.

If You feel that You did not stay in the pure awareness and went off on the wrong path and became one with 'Chandulal,' then you should do *pratikraman* for losing the awareness as the Self. Taking the wrong path means a waste of time and energy, but there is no loss from this, because it does not hurt anyone and so *pratikraman* is not necessary. You still have one more life to go, so you need not worry about this for the time being. But those who absolutely want to remain in awakened awareness should do *pratikraman*. *Pratikraman* means to turn back. One has never before turned back, has one?

**Questioner:** Does doing *pratikraman* send a clean reflection in the future?

**Dadashri:** Of course, everything will become clear. The vision (*darshan*) becomes clean and it will increase. No one has ever attained *moksha* without doing *pratikraman*. When one does *pratikraman*, his mistakes decrease and gradually come to an end.

## Amazing Yearly Pratikraman in Aurangabad

'We' do not generally use this *vidhi* (special inner-energizing message and prayers of the Gnani Purush to higher powers) anywhere else. In Aurangabad, 'we' did a *vidhi* to wash away mistakes of countless past lives of *mahatmas*. It was an hour of *pratikraman* after the *vidhi* in which everyone's ego was dissolved. 'We' used to do this *pratikraman vidhi* once a year. There were about three hundred or more people there and they wept intensely after the *vidhi*. All their internal weakness of *kashay* dissipated. Even the husbands prostrated at the feet of their wives and asked for forgiveness. Bondages of so many lives were washed away.

In Aurangabad, a major *vidhi* had to be performed each year to clean the minds of *mahatmas* and their worldly interacting selves. 'We' would perform a major *vidhi* and let it flow and then everyone's minds became clear. During that time, everyone's minds became very clean; they were not even aware of what they were writing in their confession letter to 'us,' but they wrote down everything. The moment they confessed everything to 'us,' they surrendered themselves and became one with 'us' (*abheda bhaav*). Their inner energy grew.

After you confess, 'I' would come to know your mistakes and I would continue to do the *vidhi* for those mistakes. In the present time cycle, is there any shortage of mistakes? In this time cycle, you are the one at mistake if you look at another person's mistakes. You should be looking at the positive qualities of the other person and not at his mistakes. You should 'know' and 'see' his virtues. In this age, there will be no *sillak* (useful inner energy which helps the self and others; the state free of *kashays*). Those who have any *sillak* are these *mahatmas*.

## Enmity with Spiritual Colleagues

*Pratikraman* done with the Gnani Purush's Agna will

destroy demerit karma-sins (*paap*) of infinite past lives. What kind of *pratikraman* is this? All enmity (*veyr*) comes to an end. The highest enmity is bound with fellow students on the same path (*sahadhyayi*; fellow spiritual colleagues). Here, for *mahatmas*, it is the spiritual path and, therefore, the highest enmity is bound with a fellow *mahatma*. There is no enmity with the rest of the world at any given day, whereas the *sahadhyayi* is on your mind the whole day.                    (414)

**Questioner:** Was enmity bound with fellow students even in *Satyug* (time cycle of unity in mind, speech and body actions)?

**Dadashri:** No, enmity was not bound at that time. People's understanding was very elevated then. Their love was very sticky.

**Questioner:** What is the reason for enmity towards fellow students on the same path of study (liberation)?

**Dadashri:** Wrong understanding. There was no such thing during the *Satyug*. A thief was a thief; a cunning person was cunning and a noble person was noble. The world has never been without thieves, but there are fewer thieves in *Satyug*.

All those who are close to us now, and those in our proximity, have been with us in past lives and are together with us even now. Many of them may be considered our spiritual colleagues. It is with these very people that we have bound vengeance over past lives. If both the sides did *pratikraman*, their accounts would clear very quickly. Do not forget anyone. Vengeance is bound more strongly especially with spiritual colleagues (*sahadhyayi*), and if you do face-to-face *pratikraman* with them, your mistakes will be washed away. This is the kind of *pratikraman* we did in Aurangabad. Such *pratikraman* has never been done before, anywhere else in the world.

## There is No Place to Cry Like the Feet of the Gnani Purush

**Questioner:** Everyone, including all the prominent famous people, were crying, Dada.

**Dadashri:** Yes. What occurred in Aurangabad was amazing. They all wept intensely. Even just one such *pratikraman* done throughout an entire lifetime would be enough.

**Questioner:** Where else can a prominent person find the place to cry? This (with the Gnani) is a very rare place.

**Dadashri:** You are right, they cried a lot.

**Questioner:** That was the first time I witnessed such famous people cry so openly.

**Dadashri:** They cried openly and fell at the feet of their wives. You must have been there; did you see all that?

**Questioner:** Yes, I have never seen anything quite like it before.

**Dadashri:** It could never be anywhere else. Nowhere else is there such an *Akram Vignan*, such *pratikraman*. There's nothing like this!

**Questioner:** And nowhere else is there such a 'Dada'!

**Dadashri:** Yes, nowhere else is there such a 'Dada'!

## The Greatest Wonder of the World in Aurangabad

Once a year, 'we' make everyone do *pratikraman* in a special group in Aurangabad; is that not a wonder? This *pratikraman* of ours is the greatest wonder in the world.

Tremendous energy grows within with this. It is nothing but an energy factory. During that time, 'we' do such a *vidhi* that tremendous energies arise within everyone. Otherwise, is this attorney some ordinary man? He will tell you that he would rather die than bow down to anyone. But once, such energy did arise within him when he did *pratikraman* in Aurangabad. At that time, he realized that there was great benefit in that for him. Tremendous energy arises within. All weaknesses go away. (416)

## Confess Only to an Apta Purush

**Questioner:** There are people who come to you to do *alochana* of their past mistakes. Do you help them become free?

**Dadashri:** When one does *alochana* to Me, it means he becomes 'one' with Me (*abheda*). I have to free him. There is no other place to do *alochana*. If he goes to tell his wife, his wife will get angry with him and she will take advantage of him; if he goes to his friend, the friend will take advantage of him; if he goes to tell himself, the self will take advantage of him. So he tells no one and consequently he cannot get rid of his load.

That is why 'we' have kept the system of direct *alochana*.

**Questioner:** Can we ask for forgiveness in the live presence of a Gnani Purush for all the mistakes done in this life?

**Dadashri:** Yes. Those mistakes then become insipid and weak if he can do so in front of the Gnani Purush; it is best if he does it in person, saying it out verbally. If he cannot say it in person, then the next best thing is to write it on paper and give it to the Gnani. The third standard is to do it in the mind. So sit in whichever standard you want to sit in. It is your choice whether you want to sit in the first or the second standard.

**Questioner:** So is it possible?

**Dadashri:** Yes, it is the greatest possibility. Of all the questions here, this is the biggest question.

When one comes and confesses in person in the presence of others, that is 'orchestra class'; then if you say that you will tell me in privacy, that is first class; and not telling me in person but confessing it on paper is second class. And if you tell me that you will not do it even on paper, but you will do it in your mind at home, that is the third class. You are free to sit in whichever class you want to. There is no exchange of money here.

**Questioner:** I was just asking to see if it was possible.

**Dadashri:** It is one hundred percent possible.

## Direct Alochana in the Presence of a Living Gnani

Why does one not tell a personal secret to anyone? It is because the other person will intimidate and take advantage of him; because he has the upper hand now, does he not? Will the other person intimidate him or not? And 'we' do not do this to intimidate him. 'We' are doing it to free him from all his mistakes. This 'Dada Bhagwan' has manifested! This is the greatest sentence in this world. The main thing to understand is that karmas are destroyed when one does *alochana* in 'our' presence. The *Kramic* path (the traditional path of penance and austerities) is different, whereas this path is one of oneness (*abheda-dharma*). There is no separation here at all between 'Me-the Self' and you at all!

One day, I told all these people to do *pratikraman*. For the *alochana* portion, I asked them to write it down on paper and bring it to Me. Normally they do *pratikraman* every day. But I told them to do *alochana* in My presence that day. So what kind of *alochana* did they do? The kind of *alochana* they had never done before. They confessed the worst of their mistakes, but on paper. It was not a verbal confession. So even when it is done on paper, it is more than enough. They wrote it on paper and they also signed their names at the bottom. Even the ladies did the same and gave their confessions to Me. They could 'see' all their mistakes. So everyone wrote down all their mistakes; they did not leave any out.

Now, do you know when that can occur? That can happen when there is oneness (*abhedta*). When can one find such courage? Only when there is *abhedta*. Even the women confessed, 'This is what occurred in this place and this is what occurred at some other place.' They confessed everything and they even disclosed their names at the bottom. No matter what the mistake, there is nothing wrong in it. I am ready to destroy hundreds and thousands of your mistakes within an hour, but You have to be ready for that. How can any mistake touch the *nirdosh* (the flawless, the Self)?

There must be some ten thousand people who have disclosed their weaknesses to me. It is for removing those weaknesses that you have come to me. I can never divulge those weaknesses to others… not even to your brother or your wife. You can disclose to Me all your weaknesses that you are not able to tell anyone; you should not disclose them to anyone else. You can confess all your weaknesses from the smallest to the largest. That is called *alochana*; it washes them all off. But we know that this is how the world is. What can it be like in the era of *Kaliyug*?

**Questioner:** That is how it is.

**Dadashri:** We know that this is how it is and compassion flows from us, 'Oh no! What state is this?' We wash it off for them and do 'we' ever say that we had no mistakes at all? 'We' too were born in the *Kaliyug*, were we not? There have to be some kind of mistakes, right? Some have more and some have less.

## Alochana in Complete Privacy

If someone else were to read that letter, and if the writer came to know about it, he would commit suicide; hence 'we' do a special ceremony (*vidhi*) for that letter. 'We' destroy his mistake and return that letter to him, because if 'we' tell others of your mistake; you would commit suicide. These are mistakes that cannot be disclosed to others. They are not the kind you read of in newspapers. These are mistakes one has never heard or thought of before. These are very private mistakes being confessed.

**Questioner:** But having come to the feet of the Gnani, why would he commit suicide?

**Dadashri:** It is fine as long as the Gnani knows of his mistakes, but if others were to know of them, it will cause problems in his worldly life interactions (*vyavahar*). So we do not do that. We do not divulge any of them to anyone else. How candidly and openly they disclose them, with an open heart! Why do I give their letters back to them? I tell them to keep it private and read it and repent for it over and over again for a month, shed some tears over it and then burn it.

Read it and keep repenting for a month. I have removed the root of all that. All you have to do is to cleanse the rest that is evident externally.

## Unity Lies Where There is Purity in Heart

When you attain the unity/oneness (*ekata*), it is considered purity of the heart. I attain unity with everyone because there is purity of heart, is it not? I feel oneness (*abhedta*) with everyone. And when a person writes an 'affidavit' (a confession letter), he does not leave out a single mistake. All the mistakes, from the age of fifteen to age forty, they do not leave out a single mistake when disclosing them to Me. All these boys and girls disclose all their mistakes to Me. Why is that?

**Questioner:** That is the purity.                                      (420)

**Dadashri:** That is purity. When he discloses everything, I look at it, do a *vidhi* and give his letter back to him.

What did the *Tirthankars* say? *Alochana, pratikraman* and *pratyakhyan*. When one does *alochana* with 'us,' then that is all. Thereafter, there is no other superior above to accept it. This is the final acceptance. After it has been accepted, you do the *pratikraman* on your own and maintain an inner intent that you do not want to repeat the mistake.

## Different Types of Alochana

So the girls ask for forgiveness by recalling all of their mistakes. 'I made this mistake fifteen years ago, I made this mistake twenty years ago; these are the mistakes I made.' They will recall all of them and say, 'I am asking for forgiveness, so please forgive me.'

Then, do you know what remains after that? If one has tied a 'double running knot (that which cannot be undone, disentangled, opened),' then in the next life, the ongoing effect will be very difficult for the girls to suffer. But if you burn them now, a burned and cindered, double running knot will remain intact but it will disintegrate with just a mere touch. So in the next life, one has to do just that; that is all. Do you understand?

So is this an easy path or is it wrong? 'We' help wash off everything. One lady tells me, 'Dada, I have bound enmity with that lady.' I asked her, 'Why have you bound enmity with her? What kind of enmity is it?' She told me, 'I vowed that I will come as a snake in my next life and bite her. That is the kind of enmity I have bound.' I told to her, 'Do not bind any enmity.' She said, 'But I have already bound it, so what should I do?' So then I washed it off for her. But what revenge (*veyr*) did she bind for the next life?

**Questioner:** That she will become a snake and then bite her.

**Dadashri:** I asked her, 'Sister, why have you taken on such a grave liability?' and she told me, 'She and my husband were friends when I married my husband. She does not leave him alone, so that day I had decided that I will not leave her alone in her next life, I will bite her as snake in her next life.' So

I asked her, 'Do you still have this enmity towards her?' She replied, 'No Dada, I want to be free from that enmity.' So I told her that I would help her free herself. I did not call for her husband. I explained everything to her in his absence. On the contrary, if we call the husbands, we create even more problems.

A person can become unconscious if he is hit in the head. Hey! One will become unconscious even if he drinks a couple of bottles of alcohol. Becoming unconscious is not a crime. So do not worry if that occurs to you. But if a mistake occurs, do *alochana* in Dada's presence and ask for forgiveness. That is when 'we' do a *vidhi* for him and we 'roast the seeds' of whatever mistakes he committed so they will not have the potential to germinate and grow. They will not produce any fruit. They become ineffective.

## Conduct Worthy of Alochana

This awakened awareness is the awareness (*jagruti*) 'we' have given you, none other. That awareness would be at a very high level if there were no veils over it. When 'we' give you Gnan, the awareness is very high that day. That is real awareness.

**Questioner:** All of us do not confess to Dadashri. We do not tell Him everything; we come here and sit down without saying a word. We do not say anything about our mistakes...

(422)

**Dadashri:** It is fine if you do not talk about your mistakes here, but you do open up in detail to the 'Dada' within, don't you?

**Questioner:** Yes, I do that but should the awareness not increase? Or should I keep showing the mistakes to Dada to increase the awareness?

**Dadashri:** You do not have to tell Me all your mistakes. If you did, when would it all end?

Those who want to get rid of their mistakes should do *alochana* to Me. If someone has made a big mistake and he wants to remove it, then the moment he does *alochana* to Me, that mistake is tied up (it will not be free to occur again). His mind becomes tied up (surrendered) to Me. So how can he untie it then? Then 'we' shower him with the Lord's grace; but his mind must become bound with 'us.' Why would I bother with all this on my own? So when he comes on his own to Me and requests Me to help him, then I will give him the cure. Why would I go to everyone's home and ask?

Whatever the benefit, at least one gains that much. Otherwise, there is no end to this. And the one who has a lot of awareness and has a desire to cleanse, he will come to Me. If he comes and tells me in privacy and confidence that he has made such and such a mistake, then that mistake is bound and arrested. A mistake always gets arrested when you do the *alochana*. And once it is arrested, it can no longer stick to you.

Confess to Me only the mistakes the world accepts when confessed in the presence of others. All other mistakes, tell Me only in private. Many people talk to Me about their mistakes in private. They are personal. If the mistakes are openly declared, people will misuse the information. Only the Gnani will not misuse it. Other people will misuse the information the moment they learn of it.

When people sit in a group to eat, one will eat a lot of vegetables and sweets, but at least he eats in a group, does he not? That is not considered as hiding your mistakes; hiding or covering up mistakes is where people go behind closed doors. Things they do in secret behind closed doors. It is where people look for darkness. You do not go around looking for such darkness, do you? Those are called secret deeds. Now if you were to disclose those kinds of clandestine mistakes here, you will experience aversion from people. You cannot talk about things that create contempt. All other things such as, 'I happened to steal something the other day,' or, 'I ended up lying to him,' or 'I cheated him' can be discussed here openly. But some things require to be said to me in private. Do you not recognize a secret? You were aware of all the secrets before you attained Gnan, were you not? Similarly, after attaining Gnan, would you not know what a secret is? There is no problem if there are no secrets.

**Questioner:** So, Dada, those mistakes have come into my vision.

**Dadashri:** Having come into vision means that you have known your mistakes but they still remain hidden, do they not? You have deposited them, have you not?

If a person likes vegetables and he eats too much, people will complain that he eats too much. Then he will say, 'I want to eat. Who are you to tell me otherwise?' So what does it mean to be keeping a secret in this world? It means that when something is disclosed, people will start to complain and criticize, 'You did that!? Is this what you've resorted to?' These are all the things that people of the world disapprove of and criticize (loknindya). Will anyone scold you for shaving in the middle of the street in the daytime? If you say you want to shave in the daylight, on the street, you can say it, couldn't you? Someone may say that he wants to shave sitting on the toilet. You have to tell him to go ahead and do whatever he wants. People are free to do things like that. Those are not activities that one has to hide from.                                                                     (424)

## True Alochana

No one has done true *alochana*. That is the very obstacle that prevents one from going to *moksha*. There is no problem with the mistakes. And if one is able to do true *alochana*, there is no problem. And *alochana* has to be done to a Gnani Purush who is almighty. Have you ever confessed your mistakes in this way? Who could you confess to? Without doing *alochana*, there is no liberation. Without *alochana*, who will forgive you? The Gnani Purush can do anything, because he is not the doer. If he were the doer, then he too would bind karma. But because he is not a doer, he can do whatever he chooses.

## 'Dada Bhagwan' The Final Guru

You should do *alochana* to your guru. Your final guru is your 'Dada Bhagwan' (The Self that has awakened within you after Gnan Vidhi); I merely show you the way. Now that I have shown you your final guru, He will continue to answer your questions and that is why He is 'Dada Bhagwan' (the Lord within). However, until He takes over being your living, internal Lord, you may consider this 'Dada' (the Gnani Purush) and the Lord as Your pure Self. When He becomes established within You, the answers will come from within. Ultimately, He will be fully enlightened.

## If You Hide a Mistake from 'Us,' it is Very Grave

If you hide things from the Gnani Purush, it will hinder you severely. People do *pratikraman* in order to bring things out into the open. That man brought so much baggage with him and he came here to confess everything. What occurs when you try to hide things? Your mistakes will remain hidden and they will double.

## It is Just Like an Affidavit

Men and women come to me to give their 'affidavit,' just as they do to the priest in the Catholic Church. There they go inside the confession stand and it is dark in there. They don't show their faces because the offender cannot bear to show his face. People do not have enough courage to confess their mistakes face-to-face with the other person.

Whereas here, many men and women give me the entire mirror image of their lives from age sixteen until the present. There has never been such a large 'affidavit.' It is called *alochana*. They show the whole mirror to me and so I look at it. I give them My blessing and so all their misdeeds are removed. The essence and grip hold of those mistakes within go away. Just as you burn a rope full of knots, the knots will remain intact, but will they cause any harm? No. Similarly, I burn the rope. Then you will still have the knots, but you will have to shake them with *pratikraman* so that everything will fall off.

## Extreme Faults in Sexuality

People bring their letter of *alochana* to 'us.' They write down their every mistake on paper. Not just one person but thousands have done that. What do I do about all those mistakes? I read their letters; I do a *vidhi* on it and give the letters back to their owners. If 'we' were to ever tell others that such and such a person committed such and such a mistake; if ever a little bit of the information were to leak out and made public, then… one does not disclose his mistakes openly and that is why the poor man keeps protecting them and keeps them hidden.

Do people protect their mistakes or not? Why do they not make them public? It is because they will lose their reputation. Does he give it to me in writing so that he can ruin his reputation? He tells me, 'Sir, these are the mistakes I have committed. Please wash them off for me. Please forgive me.' How much trust he must have in me! People write of mistakes which have never occurred in the world before! You would be flabbergasted just reading them.

Thousands of people have written down such mistakes for me. Women have completely disclosed all their mistakes to me. If one has had seven lovers, she will give the names of all seven in her confession. Now tell me, what should 'we' do? She would commit suicide even if a word of it was to get out, and that would place a grave liability on us. The liability is ours. So what do 'we' do? If 'we' let it get out, then all seven of her mistakes would be exposed, and is that why she confided in 'us'? Therefore, 'we' have taken on a great responsibility. A man who has a young daughter will come and tell me, 'Dada, I am worthy of being killed.' I ask him, 'Hey, you! Why is that?' He would tell me he molested his daughter.

**Questioner:** What kind of karma does he bind because of this?

**Dadashri:** It is not just one man; so many such men have come to 'us.' He told his wife, 'Now that she is ten, eleven years old, why don't you let me enjoy her!' The father would touch her and molest her and so her view changes and then she starts looking at other men. The girl then becomes tainted with abnormal sexuality. A father has to maintain strict discipline. He should not look at any other woman than his wife. Men are not aware of such things! That man was beaten up. His wife and everyone got together and beat him up; how dare he make a suggestion like that? So you now know about conduct in the *dushamkaal* – current time cycle where pain and misery is dominant.                                                      (426)

**Questioner:** Yes.

**Dadashri:** Some boys had come to *satsang*, came to the pilgrimage (*jatra*) with married people. One twenty-five year old boy wrote confessing that his intentions towards a thirty-five year old married woman were sexual. He said he was doing *pratikraman* for it.

'You fool! Is that what you did? Hey, you! You did not have any shame or respect for the fifteen people around in the *satsang*?' All these kinds of things are to be repented and they need to be forgiven. This is the effect of this time cycle! How can they have such thoughts about fellow *mahatmas*, men and women? What kind of nonsense is this? Things go on which have never been heard of before; things that would bring pain to the eyes and ears! People have gone astray and out of control! Enough, be aware, even now be warned!

## Each and Every Mistake with Innumerable Layers

Repentance and forgiveness (*maafi*) is the greatest weapon in this world. God does not forgive you. He does not have the right to forgive. The Gnani Purush will forgive everyone's mistakes. He is the agent of God. God in reality does not have a body; only those who have a body can forgive. So, even now, if you have made any mistakes, come and ask for forgiveness.

**Dadashri:** How many mistakes of yours are You able to see every day?

**Questioner:** I can 'see' two hundred to three hundred.

**Dadashri:** For seven years, You have been 'seeing' two hundred to three hundred, so those will go away. Then You will 'see' new ones.

Or there may be many petals of that mistake. It may also be a new mistake; all these mistakes contain endless layers.

**Questioner:** If we continue making mistakes every day and we continue repenting in this way, when will they come to an end?

**Dadashri:** It will end for certain. All the mistakes will come to an end if you do it this way. I am showing you the path that I myself have traveled.

## Love Pratikraman Just Like You Love Your Wife

You ought to have the same familiarity with *pratikraman* as you do with your wife. Just as you cannot forget the wife, in the same manner you cannot forget to do *pratikraman*. All day long, you should keep asking for forgiveness. You should make it a habit to ask for forgiveness. But instead, you make it a habit to see mistakes in others.

**Questioner:** How many *pratikraman* do I have to do?

(428)

**Dadashri:** You eat, drink and breathe all day. That is how you have to do *pratikraman* the whole day.

## Caravans of Pratikraman

The more *pratikraman* you do; the more mistakes You will be able to 'see.' There are some who can see up to two hundred mistakes at a time. One man once asked me, 'How can I cope with it when I see five hundred to thousands of mistakes every day and that too is not enough. My mind gets exhausted.' That is because that is the kind of stock he has filled. This poor man, on the other hand, does not have any stock. He has stocked only a small shop, whereas the other man has stocked big warehouses. A lot has been emptied.

**Questioner:** *Mahatmas* immediately have the inner intent of doing *pratikraman* when anything occurs.

**Dadashri:** Immediately. It occurs automatically. It occurs naturally and spontaneously. How many *pratikramans* do you have to do?

**Niruben:** Over five hundred every day.

**Dadashri:** This lady here does up to five hundred *pratikramans* every day. Some do fifty and some do hundred. As the awareness increases, the more *pratikraman* one does. This is the path of constant *pratikraman*.

This is a 'shoot-on-sight' *pratikraman*. 'Shoot-on-sight' means the mistake is removed with *pratikraman* the moment it occurs. That is how much awareness one maintains. One will have so much awareness that he will not fail to do 'shoot-on-sight' *pratikraman*. He does not miss seeing a single mistake. That is why all the mistakes go away and one constantly remains *kashay*-free (*saiyam*). I have told everyone to eat whatever they enjoy; eat all they wish – and yet they remain in *saiyam*. Such is this path of the *Vitarags*.

**Questioner:** You said that people do up to five hundred *pratikramans* a day. So which is better, more *pratikramans* occurring or less?

**Dadashri:** The more the better. This is nothing but warehouses of mistakes. Krupadudev Shrimad Rajchandra has said, 'I am a vessel of infinite mistakes, oh compassionate One! If I cannot 'see' these mistakes, how will I attain liberation?' How can one overcome these warehouses of mistakes when he cannot even see five mistakes? It is nothing but a warehouse full of mistakes. Therefore, if one does up to five hundred *pratikraman* daily, then his warehouse of mistakes will empty quicker. For some, fifty mistakes will come out and for others, a hundred mistakes will come out; but they have started to come out.

**Questioner:** But as one rises higher in awareness (*urdhavikaran*), the mistakes will begin to decrease, will they not?

**Dadashri:** There is no need for one to rise higher (*urdhavikaran*). A mistake will be spotted immediately if there is awareness. And once the mistake is spotted, one does *pratikraman* right then and there. He will do *alochana*, *pratikraman* and *pratyakhyan* immediately, in the moment. A 'shoot-on-sight' *pratikraman*!

**Questioner:** After doing so many *pratikramans*, there will come a time when they will decrease in number, will they not? How can they continue to increase?

**Dadashri:** It takes a long time for them to go down because this is the *karmic* stock accumulated over infinite past lives.

## He Will End Up Becoming and Being a God

Niruben has been doing more than five hundred *pratikramans* daily for years and today most of the mistakes have come to an end. There is nothing else to be done. All one has to do is get in the Agna and do the 'shoot-on-sight' *pratikraman*. If someone comes here and inside you feel, 'Why did he have to come when it is so crowded here?' With this, you just did disrespect (*viradhana*) and, therefore, his Self within knows that. Do you understand that? So you should immediately say, 'Chandubhai, why did you have such an intent (*bhaavna*)? You did *atikraman* and so do *pratikraman*.' Do you understand this?

This is the path of *pratikraman*. It is the path of *alochana*, *pratikraman* and *pratyakhyan*, a path of 'shoot-on-sight' *pratikraman*. You will be able to see three hundred to four hundred mistakes daily. The one who can see only one of his own mistakes, can become a God. And if there were no mistakes in man, then there would be Gods everywhere. Any man who becomes flawless is a God.

Your work is done. Still, as the energy of the awareness increases, You will be able to 'see' more mistakes. For now, You 'see' gross (*sthool*) mistakes. Then You will be able to see subtle (*sookshma*) mistakes. Whatever mistakes You 'see,' they are gone. The rule is that whatever mistakes lie within, the moment You 'see' them, they leave. Like the analogy of a robber entering your home while you are sleeping. What occurs when you wake up? The robber will run away the moment you wake up. Similarly, these mistakes will get ready to leave the moment you wake up!

(430)

## The Shortest and Methodical Pratikraman

**Questioner:** Dada, please explain the process of

*pratikraman*. Some people say that they did two hundred *pratikramans*. How do they do them?

**Dadashri:** It is like this: as one goes deeper, he is able to 'see' more mistakes.

**Questioner:** I can only 'see' my own mistakes.

**Dadashri:** That is because You have now been given the Gnan; otherwise, you could not 'see' your mistakes before, could you? You can 'see' them now, can't you? You can 'see' them now and so you have to ask for forgiveness for the ones You 'see'. You begin to 'see' the mistakes as you do *pratikraman*. Some can 'see' twenty-five mistakes daily, some can 'see' fifty mistakes and some can 'see' a hundred mistakes. It is possible for one to 'see' up to five hundred mistakes a day; such is the vision that can open up. The *darshan* (vision as the Self) will continue to open up.

If he is talking to you, he may use harsh words. But at the same time he can 'see' his mistake that he did something wrong. And can you see mistakes, or not?

**Questioner:** Yes, I can see my mistakes.

**Dadashri:** Then You are blessed, are you not?

What kind of *pratikraman* do our *mahatmas* do? They do instant, 'shoot-on-sight' *pratikraman*. Then the mistake does not arise, does it?

**Questioner:** Do I have to recite the full long special ceremony (*vidhi*) of *pratikraman* or can I shorten it and do it with positive inner intent?

**Dadashri:** Do it in short with the inner intent (*bhaav*). We write '*dravyakarma* (effect karma), *bhaavkarma* (cause karma) and *nokarma* (neutral karma; gross discharging karma)' and all that in the *pratikraman vidhi*, however, you can shorten it and that is acceptable.

**Questioner:** So, Dada, how should I do short *pratikraman*?

**Dadashri:** You should feel that what occurred is not good.

**Questioner:** Yes, but what is the way to do the shortest *pratikraman*?

**Dadashri:** Say, 'In the presence of Dada Bhagwan, I am asking for forgiveness for this mistake which just occurred and I will not do it again.' That is all. That is considered the shortest *pratikraman*. There is no need to say '...separate from his mind-speech-body, *bhaavkarma, dravyakarma* and *nokarma*...'; all that is to teach the newcomers.

Now, when a person has enmity (*veyr*) towards someone, he has to say this methodically so that it reaches the other person, and then he can be freed from the enmity. When he keeps saying it methodically in details, then enmity in all will continue to go down. And, at the same time, the other person will know that his mind is getting better towards you. There is a tremendous energy in *pratikraman*.

**Questioner:** With reference to the mistakes, can I say that I am doing *pratikraman* for 'this life, countless past lives, mistakes of speech from countless past lives, all mistakes related to attachment and abhorrence' – can I say all that?

**Dadashri:** Yes, you should say all that. For mistakes with certain people, you can also do it another way. Ask for forgiveness. If you repent for the mistakes, that will be acceptable.

(432)

## That is Our Subtlest Discovery

You should start the 'sacrificial fire' (*yagna*) of intense *pratikraman* with whomever you have had excessive *atikraman*. You have done so many *atikramans* and all these problems that you have are because you have not done *pratikraman*.

This *pratikraman* is 'our' most subtle discovery. If you can understand this discovery of *pratikraman*, then you will not have any problems with anyone at all.

## One Can Even See His Past Life in Deep Pratikraman

The one who dwells deep into *pratikraman* can also 'see' right through to his past life. Some can also 'see' their past life; not everyone can do that. For some, that occurs naturally – they can 'see' clearly through it. Now what will you do by 'seeing' your past life? We want *moksha*, do we not?

## Collective Pratikraman

**Questioner:** In the *pratikraman* I do, I recall all the mistakes and ask for forgiveness for them. If there are many mistakes and I have forgotten them, why should I invite misery by revisiting them again?

**Dadashri:** It is not to invite misery. However much of your book of accounts of karma you clear, that much becomes clear. You will eventually clear the book, will you not? What is wrong in using an hour of your free time for that?

**Questioner:** My list of mistakes is very long.

**Dadashri:** If it is long, then for a hundred different kinds of mistakes with just one person, you should do collective *pratikraman* – 'I am asking for forgiveness from you for all these mistakes that I have committed.'

**Questioner:** The collective (*jathu*) *pratikraman* we do, is that the same as '*samuhik*' (collective) *pratikraman*?

**Dadashri:** Yes, that is the *samuhik pratikraman*.

## Individualized Target, Specific Pratikraman

For whom do you have to do individualized *pratikraman*? It is specifically for the one with whom you do *atikraman*.

Collective (*samuhik*) *pratikraman* is done for karma of the past life, all other karma of those who are not related to you, or incidents you are not aware of where you may have hurt someone. For all that, you have to do collective *pratikraman*. And if I know that I have hurt you with my leg, then I have to do individual *pratikraman* for that. That has to be done immediately.

## Powerful Circumstances Obstruct Pratikraman

**Questioner:** Dada, many times when I make a mistake, I remember You and all I say is, 'Dear Dada, I am asking for forgiveness for the mistake I made.' I do not do a lengthy *pratikraman*.

**Dadashri:** There is nothing wrong in asking for forgiveness, but make sure you do the *pratikraman*. Ask for forgiveness if you are not able to do *pratikraman*.

**Questioner:** Sometimes the circumstances are so strong that they prevent me from doing *pratikraman*.          (434)

**Dadashri:** Ask for forgiveness for that.

## Bombardment of Atikraman

**Questioner:** Five to twenty-five *atikraman* occur within an hour.

**Dadashri:** Then you can combine them and do *pratikraman* for them together. If they occur together, then say that you are doing collective *pratikraman* for them.

**Questioner:** How do we do collective *pratikraman*?

**Dadashri:** Say, 'All these *atikramans* have occurred for which I am doing collective *pratikraman*.' If *atikraman* has occurred on a certain topic, then say that, '*Atikraman* occurred on this subject, on this subject and on this subject; so I am doing a collective *pratikraman* for *atikraman* done on all these subjects.' And so they will all be resolved. And if some still remain, then I will wash them off for you. But do not sit around because of that. Everything will remain stagnant within if you sit idle. There is no need to get entangled in all this.

One man tells me, 'I have to do up to two thousand *pratikramans* a day. I get tired of it. What should I do?' So 'we' told him to do collective *pratikraman*. How can a man do two thousand *pratikramans* at a time? How can one say and do it two thousand times over? Now whatever mistakes You 'see', they go away and then others come. Whatever mistakes You 'see', they fall off, whereas someone else would say, 'I see the same mistake again and again.' So 'we' tell him that the same mistake cannot come back. An onion has many layers. As you remove one layer, another layer comes forth. Similarly, these mistakes have layers. When one layer is removed, it is replaced by the next one. So it is not the same layer; the previous layer is gone. If there were thirty layers, twenty-nine will remain. Then when you remove another layer from that, twenty-eight layers will remain.

This is a receptacle of infinite mistakes. You may 'see' up to three thousand mistakes a day. That man got tired so 'we' lowered the level for him. One cannot do so much. He could 'see' many mistakes because his awareness has increased a lot. Now he would find it very difficult to do that many *pratikramans* as he is a working man, would he not? Therefore, 'we' dimmed his awareness and told him to do collective (*jathu*) *pratikraman*. *Jathu* means to do *pratikraman* of everything together. However, what should our *pratikraman* be like? It should be 'shoot-on-sight' *pratikraman*. It should be 'cash.'

*Pratikraman* is done the moment the mistake occurs. There are some who go as far as to tell me, 'Dada, I cannot bear it. I cannot do *pratikraman* at all. I have to do so many *pratikramans* that in doing them one by one, there is no end to them. I can see that many mistakes.' So 'we' tell them to do collective *pratikraman*. What can you do when so many mistakes occur? It is a warehouse full of mistakes. And, in his mind, he thinks, 'I am something special...I am something special.' You will know exactly what you are when someone insults you!

## Solution for the Residual Mistakes

**Questioner:** If, by mistake, we forget to do *pratikraman*, will they go away with collective (*samuhik*) *pratikraman*?

**Dadashri:** Yes, collective *pratikraman* will remove a lot of mistakes. That is the greatest way to quickly remove the balance of *pratikraman* of many days. On the contrary, that is a better way.

## Mistakes Before Gnan

**Questioner:** How can one do 'shoot-on-sight' *pratikraman* for all the mistakes that occurred prior to attaining Gnan?

**Dadashri:** Those mistakes are 'thick' and, therefore, they will keep showing up in the non-Self (*prakruti*). So you will recognize that they are from the past. You have to do more *pratikraman* for them.

**Questioner:** They can be recognized more by a *samayik*, can they not?

**Dadashri:** Yes, you can recognize a lot more in *samayik*. But when this mistake comes before you, it is of the *prakruti*, so these mistakes were there before. Therefore, you have to do more *pratikraman* for them. And you don't have to do anything for mistakes you don't have.                                    (436)

## You Can Become Free from Karma through Gnan

**Questioner:** Can karmas be bound after attaining Gnan?

**Dadashri:** If you say anything negative, you will not bind any new karma, but you will not be free from the karma either. When can you become free from karma? It is when you clear them according to Gnan. Therefore, it can be resolved with understanding and Gnan. They were bound through *agnan* (ignorance of the Self) hence we can be free of them if they are resolved through Gnan. Even if you do not like them now, you have to resolve them through Gnan. Come into Your state as 'I am *Shuddhatma*' and keep 'seeing' what occurs; that is how You are to resolve everything.

## Energies Arise At the Feet of the Gnani Purush

**Questioner:** What if I do *pratikraman*? Will that not bring about a quicker resolution?

**Dadashri:** When?

**Questioner:** When I do Charan Vidhi at Your feet.

**Dadashri:** No, at that time You are filling energy within. *Pratikraman* has to be done later on its own.

## Pratikraman Even at the Time of Marriage

**Questioner:** I keep on washing and yet there are so many sticky karmas.

**Dadashri:** Worldly life (*sansar*) means *atikraman*. It has to be washed off with *pratikraman*. Do you not eat regularly, drink and breathe air all day? Similarly, *pratikraman* has to be done regularly every day.

Did you not feel embarrassed wearing a tassel headgear on the head when you were getting married? Did everyone not get married wearing a tassel that way? Did you not think at that time that you will have to do *pratikraman* for all that? Now when you have to do collective *pratikraman*, you find it difficult.

# The Mistake is There and The 'Seer' is Also There

**Questioner:** Dada, do something so that the mistakes cease to be 'seen.'

**Dadashri:** No, mistakes will be 'seen.' The mistakes are 'seen' because the 'Seer,' the Self, is there and the mistakes are '*gneya*' – that which is to be known.

**Questioner:** But can something be done so that one does not see them?

**Dadashri:** No, if they can no longer be 'seen,' then the Self will leave. It is because the Self is there that You can see the mistakes. But now they are not mistakes anymore. They are now '*gneya*' and You are the Knower (the *Gnata*).

## Be Tired of Atikraman Now

**Questioner:** I still have many files and, therefore, I 'see' so many mistakes all day long that I am completely tired and frustrated.

**Dadashri:** That will occur.

**Questioner:** Every moment of the day I can see so many mistakes.

**Dadashri:** Those mistakes are being 'seen' and, therefore, they are going away. The mistakes will be 'seen' for sure. If you can 'see' your mistakes, then You have become the Self – the *Atma*. You can only 'see' them when you become '*shuddha* (pure),' will you not?                              (438)

**Questioner:** But the whole day, every moment of the day?

**Dadashri:** Yes, on the contrary, it is good that you can 'see' them. You are told to do penance (*tapa*) so that You can 'see' the mistakes. That is awareness. The awareness is verily the one that shows you the mistakes.

## The Repenting is Done by Chandulal

**Questioner:** When I make a mistake and then do *pratikraman* for it afterwards, why do I not become pure despite doing *pratikraman*? Why does the mind continue to feel unhappiness? Why does that state still remain stuck with me for a day or so?

**Dadashri:** What is wrong with that? A mistake will not be repeated if your repenting is more. Awareness will prevail so there is no harm. Let the mistake latch on to you; the mistake will not be repeated.

**Questioner:** When I repent, my focus (*dhyan*) shifts from other things to repenting. Is that true?

**Dadashri:** It is better if you repent. You (the Self) are not to repent, 'Chandulal' has to repent. You (the Self) have not made the mistake.

## Can a Movie be Stopped in the Middle?

**Questioner:** It will be better if this drama of life comes to an end quickly.

**Dadashri:** Why did you say such a thing? Then who will wear these bangles?

**Questioner:** I do not want to wear them any more.

**Dadashri:** No, wear them, go out, enjoy. You cannot ask to end it quicker. There is still a lot of work for You to do. You have to take care of this body. Why are you saying such things?

**Questioner:** You were in this city for twenty days and I was not able to attend even one of your *satsangs*.

**Dadashri:** Do you have to bring an end to your life

because of that?

**Questioner:** But how weak it all is.

**Dadashri:** You have come to know 'Dada Bhagwan' through your body, so You should be indebted to it. You must take care of it. You have to take whatever medicine is necessary to care for it. It is through this body that you have met Dada. You have lost countless bodies; all of them were wasted away. This body has become a second friend because you met Dada through it, so look after it. Tonight do *pratikraman* for having spoken this way. Do you do *pratikraman* for what you say?

**Questioner:** Yes, Dada.

**Dadashri:** If you are sitting in a cinema, what should you do if the movie stops in the middle?

*****

**[25]**

# Understanding the Principles of Pratikraman

## To Become One with the Non-Self

**Questioner:** You have suggested that we do *pratikraman* immediately for any *atikraman* that occurs in our worldly interactions, but what should we do if we get drawn from the Self into the non-Self, or when we become one with the non-Self (*tanmayakar*)? Is this an *atikraman* against pure Soul?

(440)

**Dadashri:** You should do *pratikraman*. Now, the one who remains in 'our' Agnas can never go into the non-Self. He cannot go there even if he wants to. Therefore, start applying the Agnas so that You will not at all go into the non-Self. You will never be drawn into the state of the non-Self (*par-dravya*). So do not worry. Even if you become engrossed (*tanmayakar*), you are not into being the non-Self (*par-bhaav*) or in the non-Self state (*par-dravya*). If you practice the Agnas, then you cannot be in that state, and if that state were not to be, then you could not practice the Agnas. That is how scientific this all is.

**Questioner:** When I become *tanmayakar* (one with the non-Self), the awareness becomes veiled and consequently the karmas are not discharged completely. The realization comes later on, so is there a way to do *pratikraman* for this so that karma gets discharged properly?

**Dadashri:** When you do *pratikraman*, the karmas will become lighter. When they come again, they will be even lighter. But if you do not do *pratikraman*, then the same burden will return with the same weight. All these are discharge karma and through repeated *pratikramans*, they will become progressively lighter and then end.

**Questioner:** You say that *atikraman* is 'neutral' (does not create new karma for *mahatmas*) so why is there a need to do *pratikraman*?

**Dadashri:** *Atikraman* is indeed 'neutral,' but a seed is planted (for the one who is not separated as the Self) when one becomes one with it (*tanmayakar*). If he does not become *tanmayakar* during *atikraman*, then a new cause is not created. *Atikraman* in itself does not do anything. And *pratikraman* is occurring even when You do not become one with it. You are the Knower of, "Chandubhai – the ego' has become one with the non-Self, and also when he is not.' You (the Self) never become *tanmayakar*. It is the mind, the intellect, the *chit* and the ego that become engrossed and You are the Knower and the Seer of these.

**Questioner:** If 'Chandubhai' becomes *tanmayakar*, then I have to tell 'Chandubhai' to do *pratikraman*, right?

**Dadashri:** Yes, 'Chandubhai' has to do *pratikraman*

## Pratikraman and Dreams

**Questioner:** Is it possible to do *pratikraman* in a dream?

**Dadashri:** Yes, very good *pratikraman* can occur in a dream. The *pratikraman* that occurs in a dream is better than the one that occurs in the awakened state. Right now you 'do' them quickly, but whatever work gets done during the state of dreaming is very methodical. It is also very good when You 'see' Dada in your dream. You can 'see' Dada better in a dream than you can in your wakeful state. This is because a dream is a natural and spontaneous state (*sahaj*) and here, this awake state is unnatural (*asahaj*).

**Questioner:** If I have committed a sin, a hurtful act, in a dream, can I do *pratikraman* for it upon awakening?

**Dadashri:** Of course you can. Whenever it arises in your awareness (*laksha*), you can do *pratikraman* for it because you were the one in the dream.

**Questioner:** Does it then become cleansed?          (442)

**Dadashri:** Yes, the guilty one may confess at any time. The laws in the worldly courts are different, but here you can confess anytime.

**Questioner:** Karma occurs in a dream. When should I do *pratikraman* for that? Am I to do them after awakening?

**Dadashri:** Yes. If you remember when you wake up, then do it. In the dream, if you hit someone, there is a violent intent (*himsak bhaav*) behind it; that is for certain, isn't it? And whether it hurt the other person or not, is a different matter. So you have to do *pratikraman*. You can get irritated even in your dream. You see your uncle and you get irritated.

**Questioner:** Many a times, *pratikraman* for a mistake made in a dream occurs in the same dream.

**Dadashri:** Yes, that can occur.

**Questioner:** But, Dada, sometimes *pratikraman* does not occur in the dream, and then I realize that I did not do *pratikraman* for it when I woke up in the morning. So should I go ahead and do the *pratikraman* in the morning?

**Dadashri:** Yes, do that. You can do *pratikraman* anytime. When you fight with your husband and then you ask for forgiveness with pure Soul (*Shuddhatma*) as a witness, then that is acceptable too. When you get upset with him, it is acceptable to just say, 'I am asking for forgiveness in the presence of *Shuddhatma*.' These are technical words, but simple words will do also. The 'cloth' has to be washed, one way or another.

## Dream is Always a Discharge Karma

**Questioner:** When I have sexual dreams, it leaves its effect on me.

**Dadashri:** You can do *pratikraman* for that, can you not?

**Questioner:** That can be done.

**Dadashri:** On the contrary, that is even better. It is beneficial if *pratikraman* occurs. There is no problem with that. And *pratikraman* must be done. If You let go, then it will remain unresolved and pending. By doing *pratikraman*, you remove it from its roots. And that is good. When that occurs, you say that 'this is wrong,' don't you? If you feel it was wrong, that is good.

What is a dream? It is a discharge (*galan*), not charge (*puran*). That which has no new charging (*puran*) at all is called a dream. And in the awakened state, both charge and discharge occur due to the presence of the ego, whereas in a dream there is only discharge. Discharge means *galan* and no one has to worry about discharge. Stop worrying about something that has already occurred.

## What Can One Do Where There is No Solution?

**Questioner:** After attaining this 'Gnan,' you have called the worldly life interaction (*vyavahar*) a discharge (*nikaali*) and that is fine. But there are some interactions that are such that they cannot be avoided and there is no cure for it. Where is the danger point for charging there?

**Dadashri:** There are no danger points, situations, at all where charging (of karma) occurs. But charging may occur where there are doubts and suspicion. Whenever suspicion arises, recognize that there is danger there for charging. What kind of suspicion? The kind of suspicion that will not let one sleep at all;

not little suspicion which goes away (the kind that is easily forgotten). There is no significance to suspicions.

**Questioner:** So then should one remain carefree and nonchalant?

**Dadashri:** No. You will suffer if you are carefree. Why do people not stick their hands in a fire? (444)

**Questioner:** Then what kind of appropriate action should one take?

**Dadashri:** What other action will You take? The only action needed there is repenting and *pratikraman*.

## Do Mahatmas Charge Karma?

**Questioner:** The most important thing I wanted to know is, can *mahatmas* bind karma?

**Dadashri:** You do not charge karma. But it is better to do *pratikraman*. Doing *pratikraman* means You are following 'our' Agna. Do *pratikraman* when *atikraman* occurs. You (the Self) never do *atikraman*. You (the Self) do not even like to do *atikraman* and nor do You have a desire to do so, do You?

**Questioner:** No, no desire at all.

For *mahatmas*, when every karma is a discharge, then is there a need to do *pratikraman*?

**Dadashri:** Because it is a discharge, there is no need to do *pratikraman*. *Pratikraman* is to be done when *atikraman* occurs. *Pratikraman* is not to be done for eating or drinking. Do I keep asking you, 'Have you eaten a mango or not? Why did you eat fritters? Why did you go to a hotel?' Do 'we' ask you all that? No, because 'we' know that all of that is discharge.

If you accuse or hurt someone as part of discharge intent (*discharge bhaav*), then do *pratikraman*.

**Questioner:** Should the one who is blamed also do *pratikraman*?

**Dadashri:** Yes, he too should do *pratikraman* by saying, 'What mistake did I commit that caused him to accuse me?' Nevertheless, the accuser is more at fault.

**Questioner:** Are new *bhaavs* (inner intents) not caused by becoming *tanmayakar* (one with the discharge)?

**Dadashri:** Yes, everything carries a danger. Everything gets washed off when you do *pratikraman*. Doing *pratikraman* if one is not Self-realized binds merit karma (*punya*). The one binding the karma is not the Self. Binding of merit (*punya*) or demerit (*paap*) karma is all of the non-Self. When you deal with them with equanimity (*sambhav*), it will decrease by that much.

## After Gnan, You have to Continue 'Seeing'

**Questioner:** After Gnan, if I insult someone and then I feel I want to do it again, and I also do it, then I 'see' that 'Chandubhai' was the one who felt like doing it and that he did it again, and I 'see' 'Chandubhai' doing it again. What is that called? Is that considered 'charging' of karma?

**Dadashri:** Did You keep 'seeing' all that occurred?

**Questioner:** Yes.

**Dadashri:** Then that is gone. You, the Self, have nothing to do with it.

**Questioner:** When someone insults me, 'I' (the Self) feel that 'I' should not insult him back. But 'Chandubhai' says no, and that I should insult him and then he goes ahead and does it. But even then, from within, 'I' feel it was wrong. 'I' continue to 'see' all that but 'I' (the Self) am not able to stop 'Chandubhai.'

**Dadashri:** There is no problem with that. That is not Your responsibility, but it is the responsibility of 'Chandubhai.'

That other man will scold 'Chandubhai' and tell him, 'You are worthless. Why do you keep talking in this manner?' Or he may even slap you - 'Chandubhai'; the guilty one has to take the beating.                                                                     (446)

**Questioner:** So does that mean that he 'charged' that karma?

**Dadashri:** No. That is why *pratikraman* has to be done. But You do not have to do the *pratikraman*, 'Chandubhai' has to do it. You (the Self) have to tell 'Chandubhai', 'Why did you do *atikraman*? Do *pratikraman* for it.'

**Questioner:** But suppose that 'Chandubhai' does not do *pratikraman*, then what?

**Dadashri:** Then it can be acceptable.

**Questioner:** So it got 'charged,' did it not?

**Dadashri:** No. It does not get 'charged.'

**Questioner:** *Pratikraman* should be done.

**Dadashri:** All the files will be cleared if you do it. They got cleared with Gnan and got put away. Whatever clothes you wash, put them away. They will go for ironing automatically.

## When Does Karma Get Charged?

**Questioner:** Does charging of karma take place after Gnan?

**Dadashri:** How can charging take place? When does charging occur? Are you convinced that *vyavasthit* (scientific circumstantial evidences) is the doer?

**Questioner:** Yes.

**Dadashri:** And that 'Chandubhai' is not the doer - are you convinced of that?

**Questioner:** Yes.

**Dadashri:** If 'Chandubhai' were the doer, then the charging would take place. So that question no longer applies. Do you understand? Did you get a clarification to your question?

**Questioner:** If I do *pratikraman*, will I not charge a new karma?

**Dadashri:** If the Self becomes the doer, only then will karma be charged.

## No New Credit or Debit after Gnan

**Questioner:** Is there a charging of the good karma, just as there is charging of the bad karma?

**Dadashri:** No. Even bad deeds do not get charged after Gnan. We do *pratikraman* when *atikraman* occurs during discharge of past karma. *Atikramans* that were done in the past are such that they hurt others now.

**Questioner:** Do I have to do *pratikraman* for the attachment-abhorrence (*raag-dwesh*) that occurs during discharge?

**Dadashri:** You have to do *pratikraman* for the discharge, and there is no charging, so that is out of the question. So, for 'us,' there is no new credit or debit of karma.

If credit takes place, one will get a life in the celestial world. If there is debit, one will spend a life in the animal world, but that does not occur anymore for you *mahatmas*. But we are talking about this current credit-debit, which is discharge; when there is *atikraman* during that then you have to do *pratikraman*.

## Correct Understanding of Doership

**Questioner:** Some individuals say that we have been given a state of *Shuddhatma* – the pure Self. The Self does not do anything and, therefore, nothing obstructs us. There is no need to do anything. There is no need to do *pratikraman*.

**Dadashri:** That is all wrong.

**Questioner:** Now that is one viewpoint. Others say that one needs to do *pratikraman* when certain karmas come into effect.

**Dadashri:** If there is no need to do anything then ask him, 'Why do you eat? Especially when you are saying 'nothing needs to be done'?' If he stops eating, then there is nothing to be done. But has he stopped eating?                                    (448)

**Questioner:** No, that still continues.

**Dadashri:** Does, 'nothing needs to be done' mean that You should not have any sense of 'doership'? One becomes a spinning top (binding karma life after life) through doership.

## Pratikraman is Discharge Too

**Questioner:** If nothing affects me, *raag-dwesh* no longer occurs; then is there a need to do *pratikraman*?

**Dadashri:** *Raag-dwesh* do not occur to You, therefore, You do not have to do *pratikraman*. But if *raag-dwesh* do occur to 'Chandubhai,' then he has to do *pratikraman*, does he not?

**Questioner:** Many times my conduct occurs as 'I am Chandubhai.' I realize this after a long time. Sometimes I do not even become aware of that, so should I do *pratikraman* for that?

**Dadashri:** Do *pratikraman* for whatever is in Your awareness.

**Questioner:** Why do I have to do it?

**Dadashri:** You (the Self) are not doing *pratikraman*, are

You? It is 'Chandubhai' that has to do it.

**Questioner:** Why does 'Chandubhai' have to do it?

**Dadashri:** Why?

**Questioner:** When everything is in the form of discharge?

**Dadashri:** No. *Pratikraman* has to be done if your conduct hurts anyone. If your action causes someone pain, then you have to do *pratikraman*, otherwise you do not have do anything.

**Questioner:** But this 'Chandubhai' is a discharge, is he not? Then what is the need for *pratikraman*? I still do not understand that.

**Dadashri:** Even *pratikraman* is a discharge. Saying, 'What is the need for *pratikraman*?' is also discharge.

**Questioner:** So when one thinks, 'Why should I do so many *pratikramans*?' is that also a discharge?

**Dadashri:** That, too, is a discharge. Do not object to *pratikraman*. If you say or do something that hurts someone, do *pratikraman*. You should tell 'Chandubhai', 'Do *pratikraman*, and don't behave in a way that hurts people.'

**Questioner:** If 'Chandubhai' becomes obstinate and says, 'I do not want to do *pratikraman*'?

**Dadashri:** No problem. He will settle down in time, and then make him do *pratikraman*. Make him do a big *pratikraman* in the evening. If he becomes obstinate, then tell him to go to sleep.

## Why Do Pratikraman?

**Questioner:** Here in America, people immediately say, 'Sorry,' even when a mistake has been made unknowingly. Is that saying 'sorry' something like *pratikraman*?

**Dadashri:** That 'sorry' is not *pratikraman*, but it is a good thing. It is good because, in that way the other person will not have an 'attacking' intent in his mind. It will stop the attacking intent. So it is very good that he has learned to say 'sorry' to others. But there is nothing comparable to *pratikraman*.

**Questioner:** If the Self is the non-doer, then whether one does *atikraman* or *pratikraman*, what does it matter to 'me'? Do I not have to just keep 'seeing' all that?                    (450)

**Dadashri:** You (the Self) continue to 'see' who does the *atikraman* and tell him, 'Why did you do *atikraman*? Now do *pratikraman* for it. I would not have asked you to do *pratikraman* had you not done *atikraman*.' That is what You say to him.

**Questioner:** Do we do *pratikraman* so that the next life will be easy?

**Dadashri:** It is to cleanse everything. You are removing the stain immediately after it occurs, otherwise you will have to come back to wash it off. Wash off the stain. A stain occurs when you do *atikraman*. Whatever the 'color' of the stain, wash it off and then you can relax. If 'Chandubhai' is being obstinate at that time, then wash the whole thing off at night. If five or seven or ten *atikramans* have occurred, then do collective *pratikraman* and cleanse them.

**Questioner:** Is doing *pratikraman* part of the fourth Agna (Dadashri's five directives prescribed after Self-realization) of 'settling with equanimity'?

**Dadashri:** Settling with equanimity and *pratikraman* have nothing to with each other. Settling of files is a different thing.

## Pratikraman in the Akram Path

**Questioner:** One person had so much aversion to *pratikraman* that he told me that when you do *pratikraman*, you are not the *Atma* (the Self) and that in doing *pratikraman;* you are losing your Self.

**Dadashri:** The *Kramic* path is such that, once you attain the Self, there is no *pratikraman*. He loses the Self if he does *pratikraman*.

**Questioner:** But, Dada, the *pratikraman* we do is done according to your Agna (special directive), 'by remaining separate.'

**Dadashri:** Yes, 'Chandubhai', the one who made the mistake, the one who did *atikraman*, he does the *pratikraman*.

In the *Kramic* path, there is no need for *pratikraman* after attaining the Self. *Pratikraman* is considered poison in that. 'We' too do not have to do *pratikraman* (in the *Akram* path). 'We' make 'Chandubhai' do it, because this is *Akram* and all the *karmic* stock is still present within. There is all kind of stock within. How can one cope with all of that? And people keep wondering what this is all about. They think, 'These people are crazy; so how can they do *satsang* about *moksha*?' Therefore, the world says that crazy people have no right to *moksha* or to do *satsang* about *moksha*; they have a right to do *satsang* on good and bad (*shubhashubh*). So then I have to tell them that the Gnan that I have discovered is a discovery of a very high level.

## Pratikraman in the Kramic Path

**Questioner:** Is there *pratikraman* in the *Kramic* path?

**Dadashri:** There is *pratikraman* in the *Kramic* path, but it is not of this type. In the *Kramic* path, doing *pratikraman* after attaining the Self is like poison, because one would never do *atikraman* in the *Kramic* path. A person who has attained the Self in the *Kramic* path will never do *atikraman*. So then why does he have to do *pratikraman*? They do *kraman* (natural and neutral activities), and their *atikraman* is only about two-five percent. And for that he will have to suffer the consequences. Otherwise, they would never do *atikraman*.

Whereas here (in the *Akram* path), we have attained Gnan out of the blue and, therefore, will have to do *pratikraman* for whatever kind of stock we have filled, whenever it comes out.

In the *Kramic* path, there is no need to do *pratikraman* after Self-realization. But because ours is the *Akram* path, we still have a large stock of baggage of karma and, despite this, we became the pure Soul (*Shuddhatma*), so doing *pratikraman* will wash away the stock! But 'we – the Self' do not have to do *pratikraman*. 'We' have become the pure Self and so 'we' have to tell 'Chandubhai', 'Dear man, you had spoilt this and so now improve it.'

This *pratikraman* stops all enmity between people. If you have any problems with this man, if he were to say something unpleasant, then you would feel very hurt and consequently you will think badly of him. You will have a negative meditation about him, so you should do *pratikraman* directly to his *Shuddhatma* and become free from that mistake. You have to do *pratyakhyan* that you will not do it again and so that mistake will be washed away.                                                            (452)

## The Self is Never the Doer of Pratikraman

It is not acceptable if I don't tell you to do *pratikraman*.

What you are saying is completely true, that *pratikraman* is considered poisonous. If one were to do *pratikraman* after attaining the Self and the natural meditation as the Self (*shukladhyan*), then it can never be a *shukladhyan*. But this *pratikraman* is not to be done by the Self. Who do you ask to do *pratikraman*?

**Questioner:** I make 'Chandubhai' do *pratikraman*, but

who is the one that tells 'Chandubhai' to do *pratikraman*?

**Dadashri:** The *pragnya shakti* (the awakened energy of the Self) that is within is the energy that does all the work.

**Questioner:** That which is leaving naturally, it is being halted and being given a home.

**Dadashri:** If you go deeper than that, you will find mud. This is all circumstantial evidence. Everyone will say that one does not need a blanket in the summer. Everyone will say that but 'circumstantial evidences' will make one use a blanket. What if you are running a fever in the summer? So that is evidence. Evidence cannot be measured by saying, 'Why are you asking for a blanket when you said that you will not need it for the summer?' Hey, you! It is because I have a fever, so just give me the blanket. You do not have the understanding. Besides, the Self does not have to do *pratikraman*. You have to make 'Chandubhai' do *pratikraman*. When the Self is not the doer of *atikraman*, why should the Self do *pratikraman*?

## 'He' Does Not Have To Do Pratikraman

When 'we' give you Gnan, You say, 'I am *Shuddhatma*'; is that not exact? Yes, then what is left? Your *vyavasthit*! What does *vyavasthit* mean? Just keep on 'seeing' what 'Chandubhai' is doing; that is *vyavasthit*. If 'Chandubhai' causes someone a damage of two hundred thousand, You have to keep 'seeing' that. But when you don't understand, then 'we' tell you to do *pratikraman*. *Vyavasthit* means to 'see' it exactly as it is; whatever it may be; so then You are free.

You have to do *pratikraman* because you are facing the circumstances due to your interference-related effects (*viparinam*). *Pratikraman* will erase that. The exact scientist does not need to do *pratikraman*. But people make the mistake of becoming 'Chandulal'; that is why they need *pratikraman*. A real scientist will never 'stick his finger, interfere (*dakho*)' in it.

The world is the science.

## Not a Slightest Contradiction in This

**Questioner:** Your speech is dependent on the *nimit* and, therefore, sometimes 'Dada' says to do *pratikraman* and sometimes he says not to. So what is that?

**Dadashri:** 'We' will never tell you that there is no need to do *pratikraman*. And if 'we' have ever said that, it is for the circumstances that were of no significance. 'Our' speech is circumstance-dependent.

**Questioner:** That is why this puzzle has arisen.   (454)

**Dadashri:** No, there is no need to give rise to that puzzle.

And our statements are never one-sided and they are dependent upon circumstances. They depend on the circumstances of the other person.

**Questioner:** That is correct.

**Dadashri:** If a person is likely to get tired, 'we' would go a little further and help him progress. If a person is tired, then what will happen if 'we'' put the extra burden of *pratikraman* on him? 'We' would tell him he does not need to do *pratikraman* and that he may do something else. In this way, 'we' would help him move forward. So 'we' speak according to circumstances. But 'our' main opinion is that 'one has to do *pratikraman*.'

**Questioner:** It is because the other person's enthusiasm does not die...

**Dadashri:** If he is doing just this much, he will not be able to tolerate it if you give him the burden of *pratikraman*; then he will drop everything. So 'we' have to say different things to different individuals.

Therefore, if 'we' have said one thing once, and then

another thing at another time, understand that 'our' speech is dependent upon circumstances. That is why people do not misunderstand. But those who want to get hold of the wrong thing, they will find a way to do so.

And there is nothing wrong with that either; if he takes it the wrong way, he will get rid of it himself. This science is such that if he gets hold of the wrong thing, then that in itself will trouble him. Therefore, do not worry about that.

So what 'we' are saying is that you have to do *pratikraman*, if you do *atikraman*, and when *pratikraman* is going on, You keep 'seeing' what is going on.

## What Forgiveness You Ask for As The Self?

**Questioner:** The one that asks for forgiveness, it is the relative self (the *pratishthit atma*) that is asking for it, right?

**Dadashri:** Yes. Why would the Self have to ask for it? The one who makes a mistake has to ask for it. *Pratishthit atma* (the one who believes I am 'Chandulal') makes the mistake and *pratishthit atma* asks for forgiveness.

It is not just *atikraman*, but 'Chandubhai' does everything else too. The Self does not do anything in it; it simply gives the light.

## Lord Mahavir Continuously 'Saw' Only One Pudgal

**Dadashri:** Now what kind of fear do you expect to arise?

**Questioner:** What do I have to fear? Now that I have surrendered everything to You, why would I want anything?

**Dadashri:** But do you not have any fear that still remains? If you have surrendered your all, then you should not have the slightest fear. Not even a palpitation of your heart remains; that is how wonderful this is.

Whatever you surrender is good. Having surrendered, sit down and have a nice meal in comfort. Then there is no one out there to scold you. There is no one superior to boss you around. Your mistakes (I-ness) and your blunder (my-ness) were your superiors before. Dada has destroyed your blunder and you will have to wash off your mistakes. Do you ever see some five or ten of your mistakes?

**Questioner:** I am beginning to see them. Five or ten mistakes at a time – I ask for forgiveness for them.

**Dadashri:** No. You will have to learn to do *pratikraman* because this is the *Akram* path. The *Acharya* (spiritual master in Jain faith) may ask you why you are doing *pratikraman*, having attained Self-realization. Do you understand? But this is the *Akram* path so what do You (the Self) have to do? You (the Self) do not have to do anything. You (the Self) have to tell 'Chandubhai' that, since he has done *atikraman*, he has to do *pratikraman*. This is because You are free, but You cannot be freed completely until 'Chandubhai' also becomes free. You will have to cleanse all these subatomic *karmic* particles (*parmanus*) within before you let them go. They had been spoilt through you as the *nimit*.

**Questioner:** The bungling mess of 'Chandubhai' is still there and it needs to be cleansed.                                    (456)

**Dadashri:** Yes, it is not the Self that does the *vidhi* (special ceremony) of Dada. 'You' have to tell 'Chandubhai' to do Dada's *vidhi*. You still have to purify things. So You as the Self have to continue to 'know' as to how 'Chandubhai' did Dada's *vidhi* today? Did he do it well?

Continuously 'knowing' is 'our' job and constantly 'doing' is 'Chandubhai's' job. 'Chandubhai' is the servant and You (the Self) are the boss!

**Questioner:** I am glad I became the boss. I like this.

**Dadashri:** Yes, and since 'Chandubhai' is the servant, You have to maintain your royalty and aura. You (the Self) have to tell 'Chandubhai,' 'Sit at the table and eat well. I am with you now.' He will say, 'But, *Maharaj*, subatomic *karmic* particles within said not to.' So you can tell him, 'The *Maharaj* may say no, but you just eat with splendor. You have now met Dada!'

Make the one who did the *atikraman* do all the *pratikraman*. You (the Self) do not have to do it. You (the Self) are the Knower of what 'Chandubhai' does. Is there any problem then? Lord Mahavir did the same. He constantly saw just one body complex (*pudgal*). He would not see any other *pudgal*, just His.

## Pratikraman by Force

**Questioner:** Dada, even when I feel 'this is not mine,' I still get trapped there.

**Dadashri:** There is no problem with that. Who gets caught?

**Questioner:** I know that certain things are wrong and that I should not do them, but even then I end up doing them.

**Dadashri:** But 'Chandubhai' does it, does he not? You are not doing it, are You?

**Questioner:** That is when I feel that there is so much worthlessness in 'Chandubhai.'

**Dadashri:** No, no, 'Chandubhai' will be caught because he has done it. Therefore, tell him to do *pratikraman* even if he is reluctant to do so. Make him do *pratikraman* 'by force.' Tell him, 'Why did you do *atikraman*? So now do *pratikraman*.' 'Chandubhai' is the one who gets caught; You do not get caught, do You?

As a neighbor, You have to tell 'Chandubhai,' 'How are

you going to become free if you make such mistakes? You will have to become free from 'Me' (Self) and you have to become clean. So do *pratikraman*.' That is all You have to tell him. That is all You have to say. *Pratikraman* has to be done whenever *atikraman* occurs. You do not have to get it done it for good things.

## You Begin To Be Free with That

**Questioner:** With some of the insistence (*pakkad*) that I tend to get into, I know that it is wrong and yet that insistence occurs even when I do not wish. Then I repent and do *pratikraman*. But why does the insistence not go away?

**Dadashri:** You (the Self) are letting go of it and it leaves You. You are becoming free from it, if you do *pratikraman*. They go further away from you as you do *pratikraman*. However many *pratikramans* you do, that much further (not return in memory) they go.

**Questioner:** Then I go in front of Dada's picture and cry.
(458)

**Dadashri:** Yes, but as many *pratikramans* as you do, You become free and separate by that much. You do one *pratikraman* and it is pushed away. Then you do *pratikraman* again, and it is pushed away even more. Then, as it goes farther, it becomes separate and less.

This lady causes problems at home only once in three months now. She used to do it two to four times every day, so for every ninety days she would do it three hundred and sixty times! But now, she clashes only once. That will occur for you too. There was another lady just like her who would fight every day at home. She would say only negative things. Only through *pratikraman* was she able to get rid of it. She does *pratikraman* every day.

**Questioner:** I have made a firm decision (*nischay*) that

I do not want to enjoy (suffer) a single worldly thing, but when certain desires arise within, I end up behaving accordingly. So what should I do?

**Dadashri:** Then do *pratikraman* for it. Ask for forgiveness that, 'Despite having no new desires, I made this mistake. I ask for forgiveness, so please forgive me so that I do not do that again.'

## Pratikraman is the Purusharth of Awareness

**Questioner:** *Pratikraman* is considered of the non-Self (*paudgalik*), so then is it not under the control/influence of *vyavasthit*?

**Dadashri:** No. *Pratikraman* is not the Self. It is of and by the non-Self (*paudgalik*). But it is a spiritual, inner effort (*purusharth*); it is dependent on awareness (*jagruti*). Awareness is verily *purusharth*. Once awareness prevails, you will not have to do it; it will occur on its own.

**Questioner:** When I do *pratikraman*, I do it for all the infinite phases created of the non-Self and all the obstacles created in countless past lives.

**Dadashri:** Here we do *pratikraman* for all the mistakes; the phases of the non-Self (*pudgal paryaya*) are automatically included in that.

## Pudgal (the relative-self or the non-Self) Runs the World

**Questioner:** How does the *pudgal* (the non-Self) do *atikraman*?

**Dadashri:** The *pudgal* doesn't do just *atikraman*; this whole world is being run only by the *pudgal*. All the fighting is carried out by the *pudgal*. All this is run by the *pudgal*. How is anyone else to comprehend the language of the Gnanis? The

Gnanis tell you everything, having 'seen' it all, whereas others have to bring it into their conviction (*pratiti*). All this is nothing but *pudgal*.

**Questioner:** Everything that occurs with and to the *pudgal* is being dictated by *vyavasthit*, but how does it do *atikraman*?

**Dadashri:** It can do *kraman* and it can also do *atikraman*.

**Questioner:** It can only occur when the energy of the Self (*chetana*) enters into the body (*pudgal*), is that not so?

**Dadashri:** That verily is called *pudgal*. These *pudgal parmanus* (the smallest part of matter), 'we' call it '*pudgal*,' that is all. The Lord has called that *pudgal* as '*mishrachetan*.' What is *pudgal parmanu*? *Mishrachetan* is that which is charged with 'the life energy of the Self (*chetan bhaav*)' and is called '*puran*' (to fill) and which will empty (*galan*) in the next life. Then it charges again. It gets charged (*puran*; filling or coming together) and discharges (*galan*; emptying or dissipating).

*Atikraman* is considered *galan* (discharge of past karma). But if *atikraman* occurs after Gnan, and if it has occurred through the self (*mishrachetan*), then it is considered *puran*. (This does not occur after Gnan because the Self is not the doer; the *mishrachetan* is the doer).

**Questioner:** If 'Chandubhai' does it, he does not have any attachment-abhorrence (*raag-dwesh*), so for him there is no such thing as *atikraman* or *pratikraman*!

**Dadashri:** *Raag-dwesh* all belongs only to 'Chandubhai' (the one with the wrong belief).

## Who is Asking for Forgiveness and from Whom?

Our *pratikraman* is one that follows *atikraman*; it is not for *kraman* (that which is occurring without *kashay*). When you make a 'phone call' to the pure Soul of the other person, it reaches Him immediately, and his pure Soul also passes your 'phone message' on to his *pudgal* non-Self complex. *Pratikraman* has to be done with living beings, not with the *jada* (inanimate, non-living).

**Questioner:** 'You are the Self (*Shuddhatma*)', so the Self does not have to do *pratikraman*. When one does *atikraman*, it is not directed towards the pure Soul (*Shuddhatma*); it is directed towards the other person's *pudgal*. So when I ask for forgiveness in *pratikraman*, do I have to ask for it from the other person's *Shuddhatma* or his *pudgal*? (460)

**Dadashri:** The forgiveness has to be asked from the *Shuddhatma*. But who is asking for forgiveness? The *pudgal*. And you have to ask for forgiveness from the *Shuddhatma* of the other person: 'Dear *Shuddhatma Bhagwan*, with you as a witness, I am asking for forgiveness.'

## Pratikraman Even of the Pudgal

**Questioner:** The *pratikraman* we do – is it of the *pudgal* or of something else?

**Dadashri:** It is only of the *pudgal*, the non-Self complex, who else?

**Questioner:** It is of the *pudgal*! So can similar *pratikraman* be done for my own *pudgal* too?

**Dadashri:** It has to be done for verily your own *pudgal*. You do *pratikraman* of the other person if you have hurt the other person's *pudgal*. Otherwise, you have to do *pratikraman* of your own *pudgal*, do you not?

**Questioner:** Who does the *pratikraman* of our *pudgal*?

**Dadashri:** All that is done by 'our' *pragnya shakti* (the energy that takes the awakened one in *Akram Vignan* to final liberation); *pragnya shakti* makes 'Chandubhai' do it.

## Who Tells Us To Do Pratikraman?

**Questioner:** But, Dada, in the *pratikraman vidhi* we say, 'Dear *Shuddhatma Bhagwan*, who is completely separate from the mind, body and speech…,' do we not? So then how can we say it is of the *pudgal*?

**Dadashri:** You are asking for forgiveness from the *Shuddhatma* for the mistake you made.

**Questioner:** But we have to ask for forgiveness (*maafi*) from the *Shuddhatma* and do *pratikraman* of the *pudgal*?

**Dadashri:** No. *Pratikraman* and forgiveness are the same thing. You have to ask for forgiveness from his *Shuddhatma* saying, 'I have made a mistake with your *pratishthit atma* (the relative self, the one wrong belief); for that I am asking for forgiveness.'

**Questioner:** The one who has not received the Self in *Akram Vignan*, the one who has not taken Gnan, does he have to do *pratikraman* the same way?

**Dadashri:** He cannot do that. It will not work. The one who has not taken Gnan has to apologize in a simple, standard way.

**Questioner:** What if I have taken Gnan and the other person has not, what then?

**Dadashri:** No problem with that. There is no problem if the other person has not taken Gnan. You can still do the *pratikraman*.

**Questioner:** Who tells 'Chandubhai,' from within, that you have made a mistake so do *pratikraman*? Who is the one saying that?

**Dadashri:** It is our energy (*shakti*), known as *pragnya*, that is alerting and calling for the need to do *pratikraman*.

**Questioner:** When we do our own *pratikraman*, then is it the *pudgal* doing *pratikraman* of the *Shuddhatma*?

**Dadashri:** He is doing it to the *Shuddhatma*. Therefore, the Self (*shuddha chetan*) and *pragnya shakti* (energy of the Self), are working in *pratikraman*.

**Questioner:** *Atikraman* can occur towards one's own self and not just towards others, right?                (462)

**Dadashri:** You have to do *pratikraman* with your *Shuddhatma* for your own self. You have to say, 'Dear 'Chandubhai', do *pratikraman*; why do you make such mistakes?'

## The Mistake and the Knower of the Mistake are Separate

**Questioner:** When 'I' 'know' (*janavoo*) the mistake, then how can it be considered a mistake?

**Dadashri:** You are the Knower. Then it is not the mistake of the Knower. But You know what 'Chandubhai' is doing. There is no problem with *kraman* (neutral activities). But when he is scolding someone, You tell 'Chandubhai' that it is his mistake. This is the path of *Akram* and in this path, if the discharging stock is 'seen' (by the non-Self) as good (*shubha*), then there is no problem.

**Questioner:** If one is the Knower (*gnayak*), then what is wrong with even the bad (*ashubha*)?

**Dadashri:** But one does not have such awareness (*jagruti*), does one? That is why 'we' tell you to do *pratikraman*.

This 'packing' (the body complex, the relative-self) should

become just like the image of the Self. It, too, has to be made Godlike. That is why you have to do *pratikraman*, do you not? In the *Kramic* path, everything is good, auspicious (*shubha*). That is why they do not have to do *pratikraman*. *Pratikraman* is considered a mistake in the *Kramic* path. There, there is only *kraman* (neutral activities) and *shubha* (good).

## There is No Pratikraman For The 'Seer'

**Questioner:** Do I have to do *pratikraman* when a bad thought arises about someone?

**Dadashri:** Yes, that thought reaches him immediately and then his mind is spoilt. If you do *pratikraman*, then even if his mind is spoiled, it will get better. You should never have bad thoughts about anyone.

**Questioner:** A bad thought that arises about anyone, I only 'see' that thought.

**Dadashri:** There is nothing wrong if there is the 'Seer.' But if You fail to 'see,' then do *pratikraman*. It will automatically go away if You 'see.' Through Gnan, if you are able to 'see' it 'correctly,' then there is no problem.

**Questioner:** If one is able to remain separate and 'see,' then no such thoughts will come at all?

**Dadashri:** They will come. They will come even if You remain completely separate. It is a stock of karma that was within, is it not? Effect of karma will come without fail.

## The Mistake Vanishes Where the Knower is

**Questioner:** What if the mistake has occurred only from my side?

**Dadashri:** Those are to be 'seen.' When you see others mistakes you should dissolve them with *pratikraman*.

**Questioner:** If I remain the Knower-Seer of the mistakes, will they go away or do I have to do *pratikraman*?

**Dadashri:** Then the mistakes do not remain, do they? However, one is not aware and does not 'know' at the time of the mistake. He does not remain the Knower-Seer (*Gnata-Drashta*).

## There is Nothing to be Done When One is the Knower-Seer

One is the Knower-Seer (*Gnata-Drashta*) only if he has awakened awareness (*jagruti*) – and *pratikraman* occurs only with such awareness. Now You do not have to do the *pratikraman*. The one who is the Knower-Seer does not 'do' anything. The one who 'does' anything, he cannot be the Knower-Seer. Hence, 'Chandubhai' has to do the *pratikraman*. The one who does the *atikraman* has to be told to do *pratikraman*.

Tell the one who has the attacking nature to do *pratikraman*. When You tell 'Chandubhai' to do *pratikraman*, it can occur only if You are a *Shuddhatma*.

## Ego in Atikraman and Pratikraman

**Questioner:** Who does the *pratikraman*?          (464)

**Dadashri:** The one who does the *atikraman*.

**Questioner:** But who does the *atikraman*?

**Dadashri:** The ego does *atikraman*.

**Questioner:** If the ego does *atikraman*, then does the ego have to do *pratikraman*?

**Dadashri:** Yes, even the *pratikraman* has to be done by the ego. But who does the cautioning? It is *pragnya shakti* (the liberating energy of the Self). *Pragnya* says, 'Why did you do *atikraman*? So do *pratikraman*.'

**Questioner:** So does *pragnya* come from the real or

from the relative?

**Dadashri:** It comes from the real. It is the energy arising from the real. There are two kinds of energies. One arising from the real is *pragnya*. And that arising from the relative is called *agnya*. *Agnya* will not allow one to get out of the worldly life (*sansar*) and *pragnya* will not let You go until You attain *moksha*. During the time when the body is discarded and one's *moksha* is ready, at that time *pragnya shakti* becomes one with the Self. It is not a separate energy.

**Questioner:** So then the ego comes under the relative, does it not?

**Dadashri:** Everything goes only into the relative.

**Questioner:** Then, Dada, the real and the relative are separate so why did we have to be in the middle? What is the need for us to do *pratikraman*? Why do we have to interfere with the relative?

**Dadashri:** There is no need to interfere with the relative. But when someone gets hurt, You have to tell 'Chandubhai' (the relative self), 'Why did you hurt him? Now do *pratikraman* for that.' That is it; wash it off. Wash off the stain that occurs. You also have to keep the 'relative' cloth clean.

**Questioner:** Dada, the one causing the pain, is it the real that does it?

**Dadashri:** The 'Real' does not do anything. Everything is in the 'relative plane.' Even the pain is experienced by the relative; it does not touch the real at all.

## Who Experiences the Pain?

**Questioner:** When the other person gets hurt, is it his ego that experiences the pain and hurt?

**Dadashri:** Yes. It is the ego that experiences the pain (*dukh*).

**Questioner:** Then what is the need for *pratikraman*? Why is the need there to enter the relative again?

**Dadashri:** But the 'stain' of pain caused to that person remains on our relative, does it not? You are not to keep the relative stained. You will have to remove the stain eventually. You have to make this 'cloth' (non-Self complex) clean, do you understand? You will have to leave this cloth (non-Self complex) in a clean state (before Your liberation).

There is nothing wrong with *kraman. Kraman* is that which occurs without *kashay*. There is nothing wrong; when it gets dirty on its own, there is no problem. If it suddenly gets stained due to *atikraman*, then you have to wash off the stain immediately.

**Questioner:** So it is imperative to keep the relative clean, is that so?

**Dadashri:** Not like that. The relative will get old. There is nothing wrong with the cloth getting old with *kraman*. But if it stains suddenly, then it goes against you. So you must remove that stain. Hence, do *pratikraman* if such *atikraman* occurs. And that occurs only sometimes, not every day. And if *pratikraman* does not occur, then it is not a big mistake. But, it is better to do *pratikraman*.

**Questioner:** If *atikraman* is not under our control, then how is it that we have control over *pratikraman*?          (466)

**Dadashri:** *Atikraman* is not under your control. *Pratikraman*, it is the cautionary warning that comes from *pragnya shakti* of the Self (*chetan*) that resides within. It is that energy that cautions.

## The Science of Akram in Operation

**Questioner:** Then who does the *pratikraman*?

**Dadashri:** The one doing *atikraman* is made to do

*pratikraman.*

**Questioner:** Tell me the most obvious thing here; is it the body that does *pratikraman*? If I go and tell 'Chandubhai,' 'Forgive me for hurting you yesterday,' that *pratikraman* is carried out by the body. So that is at the gross level; so what is the subtle (*sookshma*) part in that?

**Dadashri:** Why? The inner intent (*bhaav*) that occurred within, that is the subtle part. And all that which occurred externally, that is all gross. It is fine even if the gross does not occur, but it is more than enough if you do the subtle. And the one who did *atikraman*, make him do the *pratikraman*. Tell him, 'You did *atikraman*, so now do *pratikraman* and become pure.' So the one who did the *atikraman*, he has to nullify it. Tell him, 'Sir, why are you doing all this now?' There is no other solution, other than *pratikraman*.

If Gnan remains 'scientifically' (*vignan in operation*), then there is no problem even if You remain silent (*maun*). There is no internal conversation either. But it does not remain 'scientifically' for our people (*mahatmas*), so you have to say something like this, because the one doing the saying is not the pure Soul (*Shuddhatma*); it is the energy known as *pragnya shakti* that is saying so. Do you understand? So the *Shuddhatma* has no need to say anything, does it? The energy known as *pragnya* says, 'Why are you doing this? This should not be so!' That is all it says and that is enough. Do you understand? Or if your conduct is such that it has hurt someone, *pragnya* will say, 'Do *pratikraman* and *pratyakhyan*.' That is all. Is there anything difficult in this?

## Pratikraman Again and Again

**Questioner:** One does *pratikraman* once, but what if he does the same *atikraman* again?

**Dadashri:** If that occurs again, then do *pratikraman*

again. If *pratikraman* is done again, eventually it will all end.

**Questioner:** If a person hangs on to these talks about *pratikraman*, not through words but through experience, then he will readily have awareness. It does give results.

**Dadashri:** Our *mahatmas* have already experienced that, but for people elsewhere to experience that will take time. Whatever the distance you have traveled in the wrong direction as *atikraman*, if you do a corresponding amount of *pratikraman*, you will come back to the starting point, so then have you lost anything?

**Questioner:** Then no more loss remains.

## Got On the Right Path

**Dadashri:** After Gnan, everything within runs on the right track. Before, the entire day used to pass with the inner state in turmoil and wrong direction. This Gnan 'does' everything right. Even if you slap someone, it will tell you from within, 'No, no, you cannot do that; do *pratikraman*,' whereas before Gnan, it would say, 'He deserves more! This is the way he needs to be treated!' So now everything that is going on within is the energy of the Self-realized (*samkit bud*). It is a tremendous energy. It works day and night. It works constantly.

**Questioner:** Is *pragnya* doing all that?        (468)

**Dadashri:** Yes, *pragnya* is doing it all in order to take You to *moksha*. It will take you to *moksha*, dragging along your bedding and luggage!

## Absolute Conviction of Akram Vignan

Our *mahatmas'* conviction (*pratiti*), 'I am pure Soul,' does not leave even when they are clashing with someone. They may slip from their awareness (*laksha*) but they will never lose their *pratiti*, because it is absolute (*kshayak*) conviction (*pratiti*). It will not leave them even for a moment.

If they are fighting with someone, 'we – Dadashri' will not rebuke them. Even if two gnanis (*mahatmas*) are quarrelling, 'we' will not rebuke them. 'We' recognize that they are settling their files. Then they immediately turn around and do *pratikraman*. 'We' do not have to say anything; they will do *pratikraman* on their own. This is how *pratikraman* is in this path.

The Self is a *Shuddhatma* and the one within that carries out the internal actions is called *pragnya bhaav*. And it is this *pragnya bhaav* that says, 'Do *pratikraman*.' That is how, in a different way, the dialogue is carried out within. 'It,' *pragnya shakti*, tells 'Chandubhai', 'You did *atikraman*, so do *pratikraman*.' *Atikraman* means if you were coming here and his *bhaav* (inner intent) changes even a little (it becomes negative), you would not be aware of it, nor would anyone else. But he would know that his inner intent became spoilt. So then *pragnya shakti* will immediately tell him, 'Do *pratikraman* for that person.' So he will do *pratikraman* in your name; he will do a 'shoot-on-sight' *pratikraman* in your name. Not a single *pratikraman* will remain to be done.

## Make the Neighbor Do Pratikraman

**Questioner:** When I keep awareness of the Self, the Self does not bind karma, so then why do I have to do *pratikraman*?

**Dadashri:** This is all a neighborly duty. You are taking Your closest neighbor, Your first neighbor ('Chandubhai'), and explaining to him that he has done *atikraman*, so he should do *pratikraman*. Otherwise he will have to face the liability. *Pratikraman* has to be done for *atikraman*. This is the path of *Akram* and so nothing will burn out (mistakes will not be destroyed) on its own. Without *alochana*, *pratikraman* and *pratyakhyan*, not a single thing in this world will burn out and one will not attain *moksha*.

## Bails and Bails of Mistakes

**Questioner:** *Pratikraman* should be done only if a mistake has occurred, is that not so?

**Dadashri:** There is nothing but mistakes. One is full of mistakes (*aparadha*). He is indeed covered with mistakes. Even those at the fourth *gunasthanak* (spiritual level) are considered to be with mistakes. One has not become without mistakes (*niraparadhi*) at all, not even for a moment.

One becomes *niraparadhi* only when he attains the Self. When one becomes *niraparadhi*, it means that the ego (*ahamkar*) and my-ness (*mamata*) is gone. But the neighbor ('Chandulal,' non-Self complex) is *aparadhi*. So then here 'we' have separated everything into two parts, the *prakruti* (the non-Self) and the Purush (the Self). Having become the Purush (the Self), You are letting the *prakruti* know that, 'You are my neighbor. That is why I advise you to do *pratikraman* for the *atikraman* you do.'

So all this occurs naturally, does it not? This Gnan is such. And then we have the Agnas. So the Agnas will take it up and get things done. The Self does not have to do anything. With our Agnas, everything can be done. Therefore, this 'file' (file number one) will not see the other file at fault (*doshit*). No man appears as *doshit* (at fault) to 'us' whatsoever. Whether he offers flowers or throws stones, he is flawless. This *Akram* Science is available very rarely, once in a million years.

## Mistakes Are Washed Through Repenting

Insistence (*aagraha*) is the greatest poison. Insistence in any matter is poisonous. 'We' do not have any insistence (*niragrahi*). Whatever part of you becomes free from insistence (*niragrahi*), that much has been corrected.

Not a single living being is at fault in this world; that is the vision of a Gnani. If one appears at fault (*doshit*), that is a mistake of our own vision (*drashti*); it is our own *raag-dwesh*. (470)

If anyone appears at fault, it is all egoism; it is all *raag-dwesh* (attachment-abhorrence). If someone were to slap us, to 'us' he would appear flawless (*nirdosh*).

**Questioner:** I regret a lot after seeing someone at fault. But it still happens again.

**Dadashri:** Repenting begins to wash off whatever mistakes are created against him. Whatever mistake you created, it will wash off.

The world cannot see others as *nirdosh* (faultless). To the world, the court system is the only place to resolve faults. Otherwise, everyone appears as *doshit*, at fault; whether it is his father or his mother, regardless of who it is, they all appear at fault.

You haven't seen anyone at fault, have you?

**Questioner:** Fundamentally, everyone is *nirdosh*; I understand that much but the 'seeing mistakes' starts again sometimes. But at the same time, *pratikraman* starts instantly.

**Dadashri:** So then they get washed off. Whatever mistake occurs, it gets washed off. When a mistake occurs and You can 'see' it and you wash it off, that itself is the process of 'seeing' the world as *nirdosh* (faultless). You have to do that. Even for 'us', 'we' have to do this *pratikraman*.

**Questioner:** When we do *pratikraman*, does that mean we are adjusting again?

**Dadashri:** It occurs automatically. There are some people who do a hundred to six hundred *pratikramans* a day. They do *pratikraman* for the *atikramans* they do.

## We Have To Do Pratikraman for This

When I go to Aurangabad, all the ministers, members of parliament and M.L.A. (member of legislative assembly), they all came to visit me. Now, when they come, I have to do everything. One will say, 'I am a M.L.A.; I want to increase my fame in this way, so please do a *vidhi* for me!' Now the man may have no substance whatsoever; there is nothing within! He is not even worthy of being given a job!

**Questioner:** In plain language, they have the intellect of a bull.

**Dadashri:** What can 'we' do? But, if 'we' say something like this, then 'we' have to do *pratikraman*; 'we' have no choice! There is no way out. 'We' would never say such a thing but 'we' do *pratikraman* afterwards. What else can 'we' do? Even this *karmic* stock has been stored and that is why it comes out, does it not? Would it come out otherwise? In return 'we' have to do *pratikraman* for it; 'we' have no choice! It is not acceptable for 'us' not to. Such irresponsible conduct is not acceptable from anyone.

## The Cause, The Effect And The Effect of Effect

The consequences of actions (*kriya*) are not to be received in the future. The consequence of the inner intent (*bhaav*) will be received in the future. The consequences of action are received here and now.

'We' also have to do *pratikraman* but it is on a very rare occasion. 'Our' subtle discharging karma (*dravya*) is also completely clean. Not a single *kriya* (action) of 'ours' can be criticized. They are all actions that win over people's minds (*manohar*).

**Questioner:** None will warrant criticism or censure.

**Dadashri:** They will not warrant criticism and they will

win your mind over. That speech, conduct and humility will win over minds. It wins the minds of others. And only then is it possible for this world to become free. Otherwise, if they read books, scriptures and do other *kriyas* (rituals), those actions will give results. Many *kriyas* are such that they will give effects. God's law is that whatever *kriya* (action) you do; you will have to suffer the consequences, pleasant or painful, of that action... without fail. So if you have the desire to enjoy the fruits of your actions, then continue doing the actions which, in turn, will sow new seeds of causes. Hence this problem of cause and effect will continue!

## Dadashri Talks About His Pratikraman

**Questioner:** I liked one thing you had said. You said that your *pratikraman* occurs even before the mistake occurs. (472)

**Dadashri:** Yes. These *pratikramans* that occur are the 'shoot-on-sight' kind. They start even before the mistake has occurred. We could not even know where it came from. That is because it is the fruit of awakened awareness (*jagruti*). And absolute awareness is called *Keval Gnan* (absolute knowledge). What else? Awakened awareness is the main thing.

Just now 'we' did *atikraman* towards the *sanghapati* (the head of the association), and *pratikraman* for that is already done. Our *pratikraman* occurs simultaneously. 'We' talk and 'we' even do *pratikraman*. If 'we' do not speak, things will not occur.

**Questioner:** Dada, the same thing happens to us too sometimes. We could be saying something hurtful and *pratikraman* is also occurring simultaneously. But the way You are doing it and the way we are doing it; we see the difference between the two.

**Dadashri:** 'Ours' is different. How can we compare this difference? It is like the difference in the smoothness between black hair and white hair.

**Questioner:** Tell us how you do *pratikraman*, please.

**Dadashri:** Alas, you cannot find its method. After attaining Gnan, and until the intellect (*buddhi*) goes away, do not try to look for the method. You should continue to climb on your own; whatever progress you make, that much is good.

**Questioner:** We do not want to look for the method; we just want to know, Dada.

**Dadashri:** No, but that method can never be found. When everything has become 'clean,' where everything is 'clear,' what else remains to be done there? On the one hand a mistake is being made, and on the other hand it is being washed off. Here there is no other interference. Elsewhere, everything is 'unclear' – there are piles and piles of dirt and rocks lying around; that is not acceptable. Nevertheless, now that You are beginning to 'see' the dirt on the road, understand that you will reach your destination. What is the problem now that You are able to 'see'?

**Questioner:** No, I simply asked because I wanted to know.

**Dadashri:** As long as You can 'see' your mistake, realize that your work is done.

When a person from Bhadran comes, I may even say to him, 'Your uncle was like this.'

**Questioner:** It is different for You.

**Dadashri:** No. No matter how different it is for 'us,' 'we' still have to do *pratikraman* for the other person, for that mistake. 'We' cannot let even one word slip by because he is God. What do you think? Should a person stop backbiting and criticize negatively (*ninda*)?

**Questioner:** A person would not do *ninda* (backbiting)

if he had awareness.

**Dadashri:** One has the awareness. On the one hand there is awareness and on the other hand he is also talking that way; he even realizes that what he is saying is wrong; he has knowledge of that also.

**Questioner:** That is applicable to the Gnani Purush.

**Dadashri:** No, the same is the case with You too!

**Questioner:** What occurs is that the awareness is there and, at the same time, *ninda* is occurring; both are occurring at the same time. And at that time *pratikraman* occurs.

## Our Mistakes Are Subtler and Subtlest

Our *prakruti* is free from mistakes. No one can find any mistakes in 'us' because 'we – the Gnani' are without mistakes. What kind of mistakes do 'we' have? 'We' do not have any gross (*sthool*) mistake. 'We' do not have any subtle mistake. Your gross mistakes are gone, but the subtle ones still remain, whereas 'we' have neither gross nor subtle mistakes. 'We' have subtler (*sookshmatar*) and subtlest (*sookshmatam*) mistakes, which cause no harm to anyone. These mistakes of the level of *sookshmatar* and *sookshmatam* do not hurt anyone.    (474)

There is no superior over a person who is able to 'see' his own mistakes. As long as You cannot 'see' your own mistakes, there is a superior above you. There is no one above you when You 'see' your own mistakes. This is the law of nature.

Whatever mistakes I 'see' occurring by 'Me – the Gnani Purush,' if I were to disclose it to the world, the world would be full of praise and awe (*aafrin*). Is this considered a mistake? 'We' no longer have these kinds of mistakes (gross and subtle). That is all garbage. My mistakes that I can see, if I were to declare them to everyone, people would be awed and question as to how it can be regarded as a mistake. So imagine what the Lord is like! What absoluteness (*keivalya*), what Godly qualities (*aishwarya*); full *aishwarya*! Everywhere in the world. That is why 'we' tell you to remain close to me even if you do not understand.

**Questioner:** Dada, give one example of one such mistake that you said would amaze people.

**Dadashri:** When the time is right, I will give you the example and you will be delighted.

'We' will not miss 'seeing' that mistake and, if you were to look at that, you would question how it can even be considered a mistake. 'We' can see the mistake when eating; 'we' can 'see' all the mistakes. The mistakes are of the *pudgal*, the non-Self complex, nevertheless who is the owner? Ultimately, 'we' are responsible, are 'we' not? The 'title' belonged to 'us' before, did it not? Right now 'we' have relinquished the 'title,' but are the 'attorneys' likely to let 'us' off? They will hold 'us' to the law, will they not?

**Questioner:** You are saying that the 'ownership' has been relinquished, so how can they be Your mistakes? What do You have to do with the mistakes of the *pudgal*?

**Dadashri:** They are not considered 'yours,' but you are responsible for sure.

**Questioner:** No, I am talking about You.

**Dadashri:** 'We' can see that mistake; 'we' understand that. O, ho, ho! How much energy has arisen in God – the Self that He can still see mistakes within me – the Gnani Purush? And I accept them as such. We understand where I am and where 'He' is. What other problem is there? They are not worldly mistakes.

**Questioner:** Are those mistakes very subtle (*sookshma*)?

**Dadashri:** Subtler than very subtle. That which 'we' call *sookshmatam* – the subtlest. Therefore, I can understand, 'O, ho, ho! Where this Gnani is and where the Lord (Dada Bhagwan) is!' Would I not understand that?

**Questioner:** Yes.

**Dadashri:** That is why I do this (Dadashri folds his hands towards his heart) and say, *'Dada Bhagwan na aseem jai jaikar ho!'*

I got hold of the real God! I showed Him to you. And I will continue to show the world this real God in this world! People have no faith in whether there is God or Soul. Even the ones who did not have faith have now seen Him. People are convinced that there is a Soul (*Atma*).

We show you the mistakes. The mistakes that You are not able to 'see' in you, will remain as your superior even in the future. You need someone to show them to you, do you not? That is why I have had to become your 'superior'; otherwise, I should not have to become your 'superior.' I am free after giving you Gnan. But I have to remain your superior because you need someone to show you your mistakes. It is because you are not able to see your mistakes. Whatever few that You are able to 'see' are because of the vision that I have given You. Are You now able to 'see' more and more, or not?     (476)

**Questioner:** Yes, I am.

**Dadashri:** Nevertheless, you have still not reached the subtle (*sookshma*) level. All this is still at the gross (*sthool*) level.

## The Gnani's Vision towards His Followers

The subtlest of mistakes (within the Gnani Purush) do not escape 'my' vision. 'We' immediately become aware of the subtlest mistake the moment it occurs. None amongst you can tell that these mistakes are occurring because they are not gross (*sthool*).

**Questioner:** Can you see our mistakes too?

**Dadashri:** 'We' can see; 'we' can see all of them but 'our' vision is not directed towards the mistakes. 'We' will immediately know about the mistakes of all of you, but 'our' vision is directed exclusively towards your pure Soul (*Shuddhatma*). It is never focused on the unfolding effects of your karma (*udayakarma*). 'We' are aware of everyone's mistakes but they have no effect on 'us.' And that is why Kavi has written:

'*A mother never sees mistakes; Dada too does not see mistakes in anyone.*'

'We' know that such weaknesses will be there for sure. And that is why 'we' have *sahaj kshama* – natural and instantaneous forgiveness. And that is why we never have to scold anyone. If 'we' feel that someone is making a grave mistake, then 'we' will call for him and say a few words to him. 'We' will only do so if 'we' feel that he is going to go astray from the *satsang* or slip from the *satsang*. 'We' know that if he does not wake up today, he will tomorrow because this is the path of awareness (*jagruti*). There is constant alertness in this path.

## No Laziness in the Path of Akram

**Questioner:** Who gives support to laziness (*pramaad*)?

**Dadashri:** That is talk of the *Kramic* path. There is no *pramaad* (spiritual sloth or laziness) in the path of *Akram*. *Pramaad* (idleness) means that if there is ego, then there is *mada* (pride); there will be *pramaad* (spiritual laziness). There is no such thing as that in the *Akram* path. This path is a completely different path. This path is such that not even a day will go by without one cleaning his books of *karmic* accounts.

One will do *pratikraman* at night and will clear out his books without fail. And no one will be seen at fault (*doshit*) in this world. They will all be seen as faultless (*nirdosh*).

All the mistakes are one's own. Hence the whole world is *nirdosh* – flawless. No one is at fault. One's mistakes are the cause of everything in this world. Therefore, wash off all the mistakes. What are 'we' saying? 'We' are telling you to do *pratikraman*. This world has arisen from seeing mistakes of others; and by 'seeing' your own mistakes, You will attain *moksha*. No one can 'see' his own mistakes in this world, not even the monks and the religious masters (the *acharyas and sadhus*). It is because of the power of this Gnan, the power of the *Akram Vignan*, that one can 'see' his own mistakes. Otherwise, one would not be able to 'see' even one mistake, and having done *atikraman*, one would not be able to do *pratikraman*. How wonderful a science this is! It gives constant *samadhi* (inner blissful state of being the Self) even while fighting. Fighting, when it occurs, is the effect of a cause from the past life. Yes, it is due to the stock of karma from the past life, but this science gives constant *samadhi*!

## Spontaneous and Natural Forgiveness of the Gnani

Whether one does something positive or negative, it is dependant upon *vyavasthit*.

**Questioner:** But what if one has a habit of seeing the negative from time immemorial?                                    (478)

**Dadashri:** Yes, but You have to maintain *upayog* (focused, awakened awareness) and clear it off with *pratikraman*.

**Questioner:** If one is hurt from an insult, how can it be improved - how can he do *pratikraman*?

**Dadashri:** *Pratikraman* for someone insulting you and

you feeling hurt?

**Questioner:** Yes, how should I do *pratikraman* for that?

**Dadashri:** You do not have to do *pratikraman* for that. He has to do it.

**Questioner:** With what inner intent (*bhaav*) can he be improved?

**Dadashri:** He has to improve himself. You do not have to improve him. You have to forgive him.

**Questioner:** So, on my part, I have to grant forgiveness, do I not?

**Dadashri:** Whatever occurs, you have to say it in worldly language, otherwise it is not the forgiveness of a *vir purush* – an enlightened One in whom there is spontaneous forgiveness.

**Questioner:** It is mandatory for me to forgive?

**Dadashri:** No, it is only *vyavasthit*. In doing that, what did you do for the other person? What new thing did you do in that?

'Ours' is a spontaneous and natural forgiveness (a *sahaj kshama*). When the other person makes a mistake, he regrets it from within. I tell him, 'Don't feel bad, it is fine.' Therefore, there is always natural and spontaneous forgiveness from 'us' without fail.

Forgiveness should be natural and spontaneous (*sahaj*).

**Questioner:** When I make a mistake in Dadashri's presence, within a second I experience the feeling of tremendous grace from Dada.

**Dadashri:** Yes, that is *sahaj kshama*.

The other forgiveness (*kshama*), which is not spontaneous

and natural, is the attribute neither of the Self, nor of the non-Self. Forgiveness is such a thing. People use that word in the worldly life and they 'give' 'forgiveness'; they do it through the ego. It still is good. It is good to use it as a language to communicate. Still it is a good, 'ornamental' word. A greater man forgives the lesser. One will say, 'Sir, please forgive him.' He will say, 'Yes, I forgive you.' That is good – ornamentally. However, forgiveness should be natural and spontaneous (*sahaj*). Forgiveness is an attribute; it is something that is naturally there.

I have met many such people, but still 'we' remain *vitarag* (absolutely without attachment and abhorrence). He may become obstinate and awkward but 'we' will remain *vitarag*. If 'we' punish him, he may suffer the punishment but it will leave a stain on 'us,' will it not? Even those who deserve punishment for their karma have our forgiveness and that forgiveness is spontaneous and natural. They do not have to ask for forgiveness from 'us'.

Wherever there is natural and spontaneous forgiveness, there people become cleansed.

Wherever one has to say, 'Sir, please forgive me,' that is the very place they become stained and dirty. Where one can get *sahaj kshama* (spontaneous and natural forgiveness), there, one can become very much cleansed.

**Questioner:** If one gets *sahaj kshama* from me, then he does not need to do *pratikraman*, does he?

**Dadashri:** He has to do *pratikraman*. He will be hurt if he does not. But 'we' ask for him to be forgiven. The Gnani Purush asks Ambalal to forgive the offender. *Sahaj kshama* can only be found with 'us'; no one else can give it, can they? If you do *pratikraman* for 'me,' then your obstructions on the path of liberation will break. There is never a reason for anyone to do *pratikraman* for 'us.' No one has to do *pratikraman* for 'us.' There is not a single mistake in 'us' such that the other person has to do 'our' *pratikraman*. If you have erred and you do *pratikraman* for it, you will benefit by that much. Otherwise, spontaneous forgiveness is always there through 'us.'

**Questioner:** Why should we make the effort to do *pratikraman* if there is natural and spontaneous forgiveness from You?                                                     (480)

**Dadashri:** Yes, but whatever you ruined for yourself still remains unwashed, does it not? 'We' forgive you but what will become of that which is spoilt on your part? Forgiveness means that you will not be punished from this end.

## Pratikraman for Loss of Spontaneity and Naturalness

**Questioner:** Our awareness should be such that we should not make Dada do many *pratikramans*.

**Dadashri:** It is very good if a person has this kind of understanding. Without any purpose, if a person discusses something he may have heard elsewhere, then he comes and tells 'Me'. At that time from within, the mind will not like it. His intention may not be that way, but he has brought such a *prakruti* and he is not at fault. The mistake is 'ours' so 'we' have to do the *pratikraman*. The mistake is of the one whose time is wasted. The 'band' will play the music. It is the nature of the band to play music.

As long as there is naturalness (*sahajikata*) within 'us,' no *pratikraman* is required. This would also apply to you if you were to become natural as well. The moment one loses the natural state, he must do *pratikraman*. Whenever you see 'Me,' you will see naturalness. 'We' always remain in 'our' natural state, the pure Self. There is never a change in 'our' natural state.

## Pratikraman in the Famous Pilgrimage with Dada

Tremendous energies will blossom by doing *pratikraman*, but only if it is done as per 'our' Agna.

**Questioner:** When and how should it be done?

**Dadashri:** If a person does it after taking 'our' Agna, then his work will be accomplished. Especially in this pilgrimage (*jatra*). Even in circumstances as these, one should do it according to 'our' Agna.

In 1973, 'we' had gone on a thirty-eight day *jatra* (pilgrimage). There too 'we' had the 'law' of 'no-laws.' That meant that there was no law that people were forbidden to quarrel or fight with each other. That did not mean that they were given the freedom to fight and clash, nor were they forbidden. In fact, they were free to fight with anyone they chose. If they fought, then 'we' would just 'see' them fighting. But at night, they would wash off their mistakes by doing *pratikraman* in 'our' presence. They would 'stain' themselves and then they would wash it off. This is a pure *vitarag* path and, therefore, one has to do 'cash' (instant) *pratikraman*. Here there is no fortnightly or yearly *pratikraman*. *Pratikraman* is done the instant a mistake occurs.

**Questioner:** There is this awareness that 'I am *Shuddhatma*' yet all that stuff from before...

**Dadashri:** Any garbage (of karma effect) that does not come out will remain within. So it is better if it gets out. In the *jatra*, some of them were Patels and some were Vaniks; they would fight amongst themselves. They would fight so much that others would come and tell me, 'Dada, please separate them! They are using bad words and they are fighting very intensely.' My reply was if they fought in My presence, then their problem would be resolved quickly and the poor people would not bind any karma. So even if they were physically attacking each other, I would let them fight. I would tell them, 'Go ahead hit to your hearts' content!' That is what I used to say, 'Hit properly!' They would hit only if they had the baggage within. How were they going to hit if they did not have the baggage within?

Therefore, these problems would continue the whole day long in the bus, so the bus driver tells me, 'Dada, you are like God... how did you come to have love for such people?' I told him, 'These people are of the highest quality. They will improve one day!'

Then, in the evening, they would all get together in the bus and do offering prayer with sacred light (do *arati*) of Dada Bhagwan. They would fight and hit each other, but they would all do the *arati*. Then they would do *pratikraman*. All those who fought would go over to each other, bow down and ask for forgiveness and do *pratikraman* together.

So then the driver would say, 'I have never seen anything like this before in this world.' They would do *pratikraman* right away. Every day they would do *pratikraman* at least once a day. They were to do *pratikraman* only for the fighting they did and that, too, by bowing down at each other's feet. Now is there any problem?

'We' give you thoughts in the form of *pratikraman*. If you do *pratikraman* as per Agna, then you will be blessed in no time. You will have to suffer the demerit karma – sins, but not so many.                                                    (482)

## Pratikraman for Not Being in the Agnas

After 'I' give you this Gnan, 'I' also give you the Five Agnas for your protection, so that You remain as the Self. And if you remain within these Agnas, you will attain liberation. And what was given as the sixth instruction? Whenever *atikraman* occurs, you should do *pratikraman*. If you forget to remain in the Agnas, do *pratikraman*. To forget is human, but do *pratikraman* nevertheless. Do *pratikraman* in this way: 'Dada, I forgot to remain in Your Agnas for the last two hours. I want to follow Your Agnas without fail. Please forgive me.' Then everything of the past will be forgiven. You will get full 100 out of 100. Therefore, no liability remains. The one who does not have the desire to repeat his mistakes is forgiven. 'We' have a license to grant forgiveness.

Your work will be done if You remain within 'our' Agnas. But what will occur if you churn things over and over again and make them 'sticky'?

You have to do *pratikraman* if you are not able to remain within the Agnas. Leave home every day with the decision that you want to remain within the Agnas and then immediately do *pratikraman* if you cannot. Everything will be settled within six to twelve months. Then it will be settled forever.

Everyone sitting in a train or a bus is free, is he not? What do they care? They will look here and there and here, and have all kinds of thoughts. One must not miss being in pure awakened awareness as the Self (in *shuddha upayog*) in such situations. Why do you not miss your awareness (*upayog*) when you are counting money? You do not even take your eyes away from it. If you were counting thousand rupee notes, you would not take your eyes off them, whereas this Self that you have attained is priceless! People keep counting even ten cent coins! And that too without making a single mistake!

You (the Self) do not have to do anything. All You have to 'do' is decide that you want to remain in Dada's Agnas. Then do not worry if you cannot. For your mother-in-law, who scolds you, you have to simply make a firm decision (*nischay*), before you even see her that you want to remain in Dada's Agnas and deal with her with equanimity, without fail! Then You are not responsible if you are not able to do so.

Your domain and energy is to remain in the Agnas. You are the holder of Your determination (*nischay*), but have no claim over its result. You should hold the *nischay* that You want to remain in the Agnas. Thereafter, you do not have to have remorse for not being able to remain in them. But you should do *pratikraman* as I show you. Do *pratikraman* for the *atikraman* that occurs. This path is so simple, straightforward and attainable; all You have to do is understand it.

## Pratikraman Pump

You should increasingly remain in the five Agnas. Nothing else is worth attaining. Decide in the morning that You want to remain in the five Agnas and if you cannot remain in them, then do *pratikraman* at night. So, the next day You will be able to remain in them. Then the force will increase later on. There is no other 'pump' for it; just this one.

**Questioner:** Yes, a pump for *pratikraman*.

**Dadashri:** *Pratikraman* pump! So the rule 'I' made was that you follow as many Agnas as you can. If you cannot, then ask for forgiveness from Dada, 'Dada I am trying to follow your Agnas as much as I can, but what can I do about the ones I could not follow? So I am asking for Your forgiveness.' By doing this, it is considered that you have followed all Agnas. But don't use this approach to avoid and bypass Your effort (*purusharth*).

**Questioner:** Yes, that is correct.          (484)

**Dadashri:** If you cannot follow it 'heartily,' with sincere effort, then do it this way. Then I will accept it as if You have followed all the Agnas.

This is because, how much can a person do? He will do as much as he can. And ask for forgiveness for the rest. And for all that I will ask God – Dada Bhagwan within, 'What is wrong with that? He is following Your Agnas for sure. What can he do if he cannot follow Your Agnas?'

So all our rules are very wonderful! You have to do *pratikraman*. And that *pratikraman* will take You higher; all the way to the top. With *pratikraman*, You will be able to reach the top.

'We' have the ways and the path and you have to remain on this path. There is no need to have any tension or worries. You do not lose anything here. All you need to do is to hold on tenaciously to this path and to this Gnan.

## Parmatma As Long As You Remain in the Agnas

You are a *Parmatma* (absolute Self) as long as You remain within the Agnas, but if you go out of the Agnas, that is the end of it. There is no problem if you can follow it less, but You must have a desire to be more in it. Have the inner intent to be in the Agnas. However, if you follow them less, then you should do *pratikraman* every day. If one does *swachhand* (to be guided by one's own whim and intellect) in Gnani's Agnas, he qualifies for a life in hell. He did *swachhand* where one is absolutely not supposed to! He was deceitful there. This is a major betrayal.

## No Obstacles in Pratikraman

**Questioner:** When obstacles or laziness arises in doing *pratikraman*, what should I do?

**Dadashri:** No obstacles ever come in *pratikraman*.

**Questioner:** Dada, *pratikraman* does not occur properly.

**Dadashri:** You even have to do *pratikraman* for not being able to do the *pratikraman*. You also have to do *pratikraman* for not being able to remain in the Agnas, so that there is no liability in the future.

What is the meaning of *shuddha vyavahar* (pure worldly interaction) in the path of *Akram*? It is to remain in the five *Agnas*. Remain in them as much as You can and do *pratikraman* for the rest.

## Shuddha Upayog

The Self is nothing but knowledge-vision (*gnan-darshan*). To be in *shuddha upayog* means to be the Knower-Seer (*Gnata-Drashta*). What is pure knowledge-vision (*shuddha gnan-darshan*)? That which is without attachment-abhorrence (*raag-dwesh*) is *shuddha gnan-darshan*. The worldly *gnan-darshan* has attachment-abhorrence in it. It is impure (*ashuddha*) 'knowing-seeing'. What is it?

**Questioner:** *Ashuddha* (impure).

**Dadashri:** It is with attachment-abhorrence… and that which is without attachment-abhorrence is considered pure (*shuddha*) Gnan. Any kind of pure awakened awareness (*shuddha upayog*) can be attained with pure Gnan. If not, then if you just sit and 'see' everything by simply being in *shuddha upayog* (by being in the awareness as the Self); that is fine too. It will work even when you are walking on the street. If nothing else, then keep doing *pratikraman* while at home. This all has come together from the connection of so many past lives, has it not? So even if you spend half an hour a day to do *pratikraman*, so much of it (*karmic* baggage) will come out. Take the name of each person at home and keep doing his *pratikraman*. Each and every mistake of this and countless past lives will remain in the *upayog* (focused, awakened awareness) and will be cleared. You have many such things that need to be done – that is considered *shuddha upayog*. Why have all these people become your relatives? It is because of all the entanglements that have been woven with them in the past life. You can become free from them if you do *pratikraman*. It is one's choice whether he wants to be free or not. We have become free.

There is no one to bind the one who wants to be free.

Even Lord Mahavir was loved by many, but that did not bind Him. But if the Lord showed any attachment then he would have become bound.

So people ask me, 'What will happen to me if the other person hurts me?' Hey! The other person can do whatever he wants to. Why should you care? If people believe a man to be a woman, can you tell them not to believe so? Then if one were to file a complaint in the court, would you do the same? One can do as he pleases; one is independent; one can do whatever he wants to, can he not?

**Questioner:** Yes, he can.                                        (486)

**Dadashri:** Why should we be concerned with that? You take care of your own self. So you have to put many such things in *upayog* (focused, awakened awareness). There is *upayog* even when you are just 'seeing.' Your work does not end when you become a *Shuddhatma*. Who is *Shuddhatma*? If someone insults you and it affects you, then you are not a *Shuddhatma*. You should be able to 'see' the *Shuddhatma* of the person insulting you at that time. When he insults you, it is the unfolding of your own karma (*udayakarma*). It is an 'instrument' that is playing; it is a 'taped record' that is playing, nevertheless the unfolding of karma is your own, is it not? To 'see' the Self as being pure (*shuddha*) is called *shuddha upayog*. To 'see' every living being as *shuddha* is called *shuddha upayog*.

## Knowledge of Separation through Akram

**Questioner:** The superiority of this *Akram Vignan* is that the separation between the Self and the non-Self has occurred through a *bheda-vignani* – a scientist who separates. That is the divinity of *Akram*, whereas in the *Kramic* path, the mixture of the Self and the non-Self continues right until the end (*moksha*).

**Dadashri:** The ego is present until the end, but it does decrease.

**Questioner:** In the *Kramic* path, the ego decreases gradually. Here it has become separate from day one, and the state one experiences due to that is the superiority (*visheshata*) of *Akram Vignan*.

**Dadashri:** That is why one has to do *pratikraman* in *Akram*. One has attained Gnan at an untimely state (one's spiritual state is not ready).

## The Greatest Tool to Attain Moksha

**Questioner:** If one wants to go to the terrace, the stairs are the only tool to get there. Similarly, if one wants to go to *moksha*, after attaining this Gnan, *pratikraman* is the only tool to do so. That is what I believe.

**Dadashri:** No, not like that. *Pratikraman* is one of many other tools available. Knowledge of the Self (*swaroop gnan*) is the only vehicle or tool for attaining *moksha*; there is no other.

**Questioner:** Yes, you have given us that Gnan but after that, is *pratikraman* not the main tool?

**Dadashri:** Some people do not have to do any *pratikraman*.

**Questioner:** If one does not make mistakes, then he does not have to do *pratikraman*.

**Dadashri:** For that reason, many people do not have to do *pratikraman*. Hence that tool is used by those who find it necessary to do so. The main thing is the Gnan. You can attain *moksha* if you have Gnan. But if you do not have Gnan, then no matter how many *pratikramans* you do, you will still remain in the worldly life.

**Questioner:** But how can one do *pratikraman* without attaining Gnan?

**Dadashri:** People do that! They do *pratikraman* with the ego by saying, 'I will not do it again.' People are doing it anyway! And their life goes on too. Just as they do *atikraman* through the ego, they also do *pratikraman* through the ego. It is all a doing of the non-Self (*pudgal*); it is all a creation of the non-Self, there is no Self in it.

## Moksha Only through Pratikraman of the Akram Path

**Questioner:** But, Dada, this is one weapon with which one is going to attain *moksha*.                                    (488)

**Dadashri:** That is one way. And this is *Akram*, so liberation (*moksha*) is its nature.

**Questioner:** That is true, but we will have to continue doing *pratikraman* and *pratyakhyan*, will we not?

**Dadashri:** You will have to do it. But even then, only those who can do it will do it. What about those who cannot? If a person cannot walk, I have to carry him on my back. So when they do it on their own, then the energy will arise within them and they will do *pratikraman* again. They are not so shameless that they will not do it at all. Those who have met Dada do have shame.

**Questioner:** Dada, please explain that in detail.

**Dadashri:** For what I have to explain to you, I will tell you to do *alochana*, *pratikraman* and *pratyakhyan*; and you are to do all three. This is because you all have become free from such pain. For these other people (those who do not have Self-realization), they can never be free from pain. How is one to become free from pain in this era, *Kaliyug*?

## This is a Scientific Discovery

**Questioner:** If I have done something wrong and I know about it, and do *pratikraman* for it, then how does *pratikraman* make me free? Do I become free from the liability of that mistake?

**Dadashri:** The mistake that occurs is an effect of past karma. It is a result. So what was the cause (*bhaav*) behind it? Those causes were bad, and that is why you do *pratikraman* for the causes and not for the result-effect. The result in this life can be anything. So this is how You get rid of all the mistakes.

**Questioner:** So *pratikraman* is for the causes?

**Dadashri:** Yes, *pratikraman* destroys the causes, not the results (effect). Did you understand that?

We hurt someone, then we do *pratikraman*. Hurting him is an effect. It is a result. The intention (*bhaav, irado*) to hurt him was the cause (in the past life). So by doing *pratikraman*, that intention is destroyed – and that is why *pratikraman* destroys the causes. Otherwise, whatever occurs is a result and, by doing *pratikraman*, it is cleared. This is a 'scientific discovery!'

**Questioner:** How does *pratikraman* that cleanses our mistakes and brings us in our pure form work? Does that *pratikraman* reach the other person's *Shuddhatma* and wipe everything clean? What is it?

**Dadashri:** It is like this; if you press the button, the light will come on and if you press the button again, the light will go off. Similarly, if you have made a mistake and you do *pratikraman*, the mistake stops.

## Unique Atikraman of Dadashri

**Questioner:** Does *atikraman* ever give anyone happiness?

**Dadashri:** Yes, one will laugh even when 'we' tell him,

'Hey, you! You have no sense.'

**Questioner:** We, too, feel joy when You scold us.

**Dadashri:** That way, some people's *atikraman* will give happiness to others.

## The Beauty and Exactness of Akram Vignan

**Questioner:** Many times, a lot of churning occurs in the mind.

**Dadashri:** You have to keep 'seeing' it.                    (490)

**Questioner:** Then I do *pratikraman* and the problem starts all over again.

**Dadashri:** Keep 'seeing' also the one who is doing the *pratikraman.*

As much of the continuous state of knowledge-vision (*gnan-darshan*) that accumulates, that much conduct (*charitra*) of the Self will arise.

Now, where will that experience (*anubhav*) arise? By 'seeing' discharging illusory effect (*charitra moha*), the experience of the Self (*anubhav*) occurs. So the experience 'sees' everything that 'Chandubhai' is doing.

**Questioner:** What about a bad thought that arises when I am 'seeing' the *charitra moha* (discharge) of 'Chandubhai'?

**Dadashri:** A bad thought that arises is also *charitra moha.*

**Questioner:** Does it go away merely by 'seeing' it continuously, or do I have to do *pratikraman* for it?

**Dadashri:** *Pratikraman* is not to be done. *Pratikraman* is for when after everything is over, and You feel that *atikraman* has occurred, then You tell 'Chandubhai', 'Do *pratikraman.*' You (the Self) do not have to do it; the one who did the *atikraman* has to do *pratikraman*.

**Questioner:** So, does the entire *charitra moha* (discharging illusory effect) dissipate by simply 'seeing' it?

**Dadashri:** They (non-Self subatomic particles) become pure because they are 'seen.' Your vision as the Self (*atmadrashti*) verily falls on it.

**Questioner:** 'Chandubhai' is constantly doing *atikraman*, is he not?

**Dadashri:** The one doing the *atikraman* has to do *pratikraman*.

**Questioner:** In doing so, are we asking for the energy (*shakti*) from the other person's *Shuddhatma*?

**Dadashri:** That is simply the *vyavahar* (interaction of the non-Self complex; worldly interaction). There is no *vyavahar-nischay* (relative-real) in *pratikraman*. (*Pratikraman* is done entirely by the non-Self complex; the Self is never involved in it). For the sake of humility (*vinaya*), You have to ask for the energy (*shakti*).

**Questioner:** All the desires that occur are *charitra moha*, is it not? But what about the desire which is not fulfilled, and that for which proper *pratikraman* has not occurred?

**Dadashri:** What I am saying is that One who continuously 'sees,' does not even need to do *pratikraman*. He does not have to 'do' anything.

## Purification of Subatomic Particles by 'Knowing-Seeing'

**Questioner:** Dada, in order to purify each and every *parmanu* (smallest particle of matter) of this body, do they become pure (*shuddha*) if I keep 'seeing' whatever occurs by remaining the Knower-Seer (*Gnata-Drashta*) or by doing *pratikraman*?

**Dadashri:** They become pure by remaining as the Knower-Seer.

**Questioner:** So then what occurs with *pratikraman*?

**Dadashri:** What occurs in *pratikraman* is that if a major mistake has been made which hurt the other person, then You have to tell 'Chandubhai', 'Please do not do that, and since *atikraman* has been done, *pratikraman* is required.' There is no need to do *pratikraman* if *atikraman* has not occurred.

**Questioner:** But do *parmanus* not become pure with *pratikraman*?

**Dadashri:** No, *pratikraman* is done in order to become free. The *parmanus* do not become pure by doing *pratikraman*. They remain as they are. 'We' have to 'see' the 'Self' in all. 'We' become free the moment 'we' 'see' them.

The non-Self complex (the *pudgal*) will make a claim, 'You have become a *Shuddhatma*, but I will not attain *moksha*.' 'We' say, 'Why? What is the problem? I have become pure. I have realized the Self.' So then the *pudgal* will say, 'You will not go to *moksha*. How are you going to go until I let go of you?' So then we ask, 'Sir, what is your objection?' The *pudgal* will say, 'You have spoilt us. We were in our nature. You have become pure, now you have to make us pure. So you make us the way we were to begin with so that we, too, become free!'

So that is why You have to 'see' the pure, the *shuddha*. The world sees the impure (*ashuddha*), because they do it with the inner intent (*bhaav*) of 'I am the doer.' Now the inner intent is, 'I am not the doer,' so they (*pudgal parmanus*) become free.

**Questioner:** What occurs with *pratikraman*? What is the effect of *pratikraman*? You said that the subatomic particles (*parmanus*) do not become pure, so what occurs with *pratikraman*?                                        (492)

**Dadashri:** The *parmanus* only become pure through 'seeing' them. The effect of the hurt caused will remain, and so when you do *pratikraman*, it will be washed away. As much as possible, one should not be the cause (*nimit*) of that hurt.

**Questioner:** Can it be said that it becomes pure with *pratikraman*?

**Dadashri:** You may in general gross terms.

## Pratikraman Has Been Inserted in Akram Vignan

**Questioner:** One life is to be spent by constantly 'seeing.' Is the 'seeing' to be done while doing *pratikraman*?

**Dadashri:** You should be constantly aware that 'I am not doing anything at all.' If this remains continuously, then there is no need for you to do *pratikraman*. 'We' have the constant, continuous awareness. 'We' tell you what 'we' experience. After attaining the Gnan, 'we' constantly experience that.

Nevertheless, *pratikraman* is not at all necessary in this Gnan. This Gnan is the ultimate kind where *pratikraman* does not exist at all. But here, 'we' graduate even the one who is at the level of the fourth grade. So then what happens to all those skipped middle grades? So 'we' have added *pratikraman* and taken on the responsibility. Otherwise, there is no *pratikraman* in this Gnan; nevertheless, it has been put in the middle at 'our' own liability.

Except for the *Shuddhatma*, everything else is garbage. In that, one is *kraman* and the other is *atikraman*. Everything other than the *Shuddhatma* are mistakes and *pratikraman* has to be done for them.

## Just Look at the Beauty of the Akram Vignan

**Questioner:** We are satisfied having heard the clarification from You, personally.

**Dadashri:** So in all this, You are separate for sure. *Pratikraman* occurs simultaneously. So then tell me who is going to bother you?

**Questioner:** With this body, *pratikraman* continues every moment, day and night. Due to this, before the *pratikraman* even starts, *atikraman* simply vanishes.

**Dadashri:** This is a science that works instantly. This is the *Akram* science. It is a whole *siddhant* (established, incontrovertible principle which attains the ultimate) that will produce results. Just as when you remove one layer of an onion, all the qualities of the onion express (water in the eyes); in the same manner if you were to cut a slice of this Gnan, it will give you nothing but the reward of the *siddhant* of Gnan itself. In the same token if you were to take a slice of ignorance (*agnan*), you will get the fruit of ignorance. Even just a single slice will show the attributes, will it not?

This is *Akram Vignan*. '*Vignan*' means that it is a science and, therefore, it gives immediate results. Where there is no need to do anything, it is called *vignan*, and wherever one has to 'do' something, that is called *gnan* (relative knowledge).

Would a thinking person not wonder how, without doing anything, all this is? That is the wonder of *Akram Vignan*.

*****

# PART 2

# UNDERSTANDING SAMAYIK

## Definition of Samayik

**Questioner:** What is a *samayik*?

**Dadashri:** There are two kinds of *samayik*. One is prevalent in the world, where the doer of the *samayik* does not allow the mind to move away from a certain circle defined prior to the process. Thus, he attempts to keep the mind confined within a circle, a boundary. Where the mind remains still in what is occurring outside is called *vyavahar samayik*. (495)

And the other kind of *samayik* is the exact *samayik* that Lord Mahavir had spoken of; the kind that we all do in this path of *Akram*. (The *samayik* of *Akram Vignan* is where for forty-eight minutes (*gunthanu*), one remains as the Self and 'sees' file number one).

**Questioner:** Please explain the *samayik* of our *Akram* path.

**Dadashri:** In our *samayik*, one becomes the Self (*atmaswaroop*), and 'sees' (*jovoo*) what is going on within 'Chandubhai' (file number one). There You 'see' what kind of thoughts 'Chandubhai' is having. We have to 'see' all of them, and You are the Seer.

Thoughts are *drashya* – that which is to be seen. And You are *drashta* – the Seer. Those thoughts we are able to understand are called *gneya* (that which is known) and You are *Gnata* – the Knower.

Then You have to 'know' what 'Chandubhai's' intellect (*buddhi*) is doing, what his *chit* is doing, that he has pain in his leg and whether 'Chandubhai' is paying attention to it or not. You have to 'know' all that. If he has hunger pangs in his stomach, You have to 'know' that too.

When the thoughts of someone outside come, 'see' him as pure (*shuddha*). That is our *samayik*. It is to remain pure (*shuddha*) and to 'see' the pure (*shuddha*).

If he has quarreled all night with someone, then later when sitting in *samayik*, 'see' the *shuddha*, the Self, and say, 'Chandubhai, come, ask for forgiveness.'

**Questioner:** Dada, how can I do that *samayik* properly and precisely?

**Dadashri:** Everyone here does such *samayik*. They take a certain topic, and they do a *samayik* on that specific topic, so that particular topic will begin to dissolve and will eventually come to an end. Whatever you want to dissolve, you can do so by doing this *samayik*. If you have a dislike for a certain taste in food, then take that very subject in the *samayik*, and continue 'seeing' what 'this'– *pragnya shakti* 'shows' You. Merely by 'seeing', all tubers (*granthi*) dissolve. The tubers of *kashay* will dissolve by simply 'seeing' them in *samayik*. The worst and the largest of tubers that trouble you can be dissolved in the *samayik*. Do the kind of *samayik* that are being done here.          (496)

## Definition of Samayik-Pratikraman

**Questioner:** What is the connection between our *samayik* (of *Akram Vignan*) and *pratikraman*?

**Dadashri:** *Pratikraman* is for any *atikraman* that occurs. Your day-to-day activities is *kraman* (neutral activities that do not hurt anyone), then if you say something that hurts someone; that is called *atikraman*. Then you have to tell 'Chandubhai',

'Why did you do *atikraman*? So do *pratikraman* now.' If you do *atikraman*, you should do *pratikraman* for it.

*Samayik* means the awareness of, 'I am *Shuddhatma*.' *Samayik* prevails continuously in the five Agnas. To settle with equanimity is the first *samayik*. To remain in a state of naturalness as the Self constantly, is a *samayik* like 'ours' (the Gnani Purush and the Lord within). To a lesser degree, this state can prevail for You too.

When You 'do' *samayik*, at that time the *prakruti* (the non-Self complex) is considered completely natural (*sahaj*). After a series of *samayiks*, You will learn to catch onto the present (*vartman kaal*). You cannot attain this directly. When you sit in a *samayik* for an hour, you are only in the present.

## Samayik of the Kramic Path and That of the Akram Path

The *samayik* that people do in this world is different from the *samayik* that we do here. This *samayik* that we do is incredibly magnificent and supreme. Such a *samayik* cannot be found anywhere, can it?

Elsewhere, when people sit to do *samayik*, they create a little boundary and then, if they get a thought, they will push it out of this boundary. If they think about their shop, they will push that thought away, and then they will push out another thought. So they just keep pushing away their thoughts and when they pass one *gunthanu* (48 minutes) doing this, they call it a *samayik*.

And our *samayik* is of a completely different nature. What is this *samayik* for? It is for dissolving the tubers of anger-pride-deceit-greed (*kashays*) in the non-Self complex, the external. It can be done only after one has become the Self.

We say, 'I know the habits and the nature of the habits

of the mind, speech and body and I also know the nature of 'my' own Self.' Therefore, You have to dissolve the nature of the mind, speech and body. When someone asks me how it can be dissolved, I tell him, 'By 'seeing' what the nature of the mind, body and speech is. By 'seeing' how intense and dense it is.' Can you not know the density of it?

**Questioner:** Yes, I can.

**Dadashri:** So You have to take the nature (*swabhav*) of that habit and make it the focus of Your *samayik*. In doing so, that much of 'the nature' will be dissolved. Then you take another 'nature' of another habit. So the *samayik* is for the purpose of dissolving these tubers of *kashays*. Our path is *Akram* and is without any specific steps. So in order to dissolve the nature of different habits, you have to 'do' the *samayik*. If it was not for these *kashays*, this Gnan is such that one will be verily in *samayik* the whole day long.

Absence of *kashays* (anger-pride-deceit-greed) is called *samayik*. That is true *samayik*. But how are people to be free from *kashays*?                                        (498)

For us here, there is *samayik* the whole day long, but why do we have to do this particular *samayik*? It is to get rid of all the *karmic* baggage from the past life that still remains within. There is a lot of baggage within. There are so many 'spices' within; you have even brought them from many other markets. Hey, you! Why don't you just buy from the Indian market? But he will say, 'No this looks like potatoes!' In this way, so many different kinds of things have been filled within. It is shameful even to discuss this!

## Worldly Samayik

In the *vyavahar samayik*, worldly *samayik*, one tries to still the mind just like a cow that will be kept confined within a certain area. If the mind wanders outside its limit, one will keep confining it. If one has a thought about her mother-in-law, she will push away that thought. She will push that thought outside her designated 'circle'; she will not let it enter the circle. Any thoughts that come along, one will keep pushing them away. But even then, the mind has become weak and prone to temptations (*lapatu*). It is bound to stray, isn't it? By *lapatu* 'we' mean that when a bottle topples over and loses its cork, its contents slowly spill. So this method of trying to pull the mind back within a boundary and keeping it there, this is the kind of *samayik* people do elsewhere.

During that time, no one bothers him. He is able to sit peacefully. He keeps an hourglass in one place. The sand will fall into the section below. When the top section becomes empty, he turns it over again. It takes forty-eight minutes for the sand from the top section to fall into the bottom one. So when there is a heap of sand in the bottom one, he will claim, 'My *samayik* is done.' That is why he keeps an hourglass. But what does he do? He will decide from the day before, 'Tomorrow I don't want to think about my shop when I do *samayik*.' So the moment he closes his eyes in the *samayik*, the very first thing that will raid his thoughts is his shop! That, which he does not want to remember is the first thing that will come to him.

So the poor fellow gets tired and the next day he will tell me, 'This is what occurred.' So I tell him, 'Why do you remember it by saying, 'Tomorrow I don't want to think about the shop'?' You created an action and that is why the reaction came. Why must you create an action in the first place? But what is he to do in the *samayik*? He has not become a *Shuddhatma*, so whatever thoughts he gets, he pushes them away. Thoughts that do not belong within his circle, he will push away. And so the time for the *samayik* ends. During the forty-eight minutes, he goes on looking at the hourglass; still, there is some time left. Even though the Lord said not to, he keeps looking at the hourglass!

So be it; people say that at least he is sitting quietly in one place instead of running around. Otherwise, outside the fishermen are killing fish and this guy is killing fish (jumping thoughts) within. This cannot be called a *samayik* at all! It is a kind of stillness (*sthirata*). Nevertheless, from the overall perspective such *samayik* is not wrong. At least he is able to remain still for that amount of time. We cannot call it wrong at all.

Even in his shop, if a man is not able to sit still for three hours, he would not be able to do business. His income is based on how long he is able to sit there. He should stay put for three hours in one place. Many people are so hyper that they cannot sit for even five minutes.

## Swadhyaya Samayik

**Seeker:** When we do *samayik* of two *ghadis* (forty-eight minutes; one g*hadi* is twenty-four minutes), what action (*kriya*) can be carried out in that?

**Dadashri:** It is like this; this *samayik* is the *samayik* of the mind. When a person has thoughts about his shops, or the kitchen, he will keep pushing them away.

**Seeker:** I do not get such thoughts.                          (500)

**Dadashri:** Then what do you get?

**Seeker:** Whatever occurs but I do not get thoughts. I read books.

**Dadashri:** So *samayik* will occur by reading books. What does *samayik* mean? It means that during the time of forty-eight minutes, instead of being in other things, your meditation (*dhyan*) remained in this; it remained in s*wadhyaya* (here scripture study). That is called (*swadhyaya samayik*). The relative awareness (*upayog*) is in something else. However, the true *samayik* is one which, if you were to do it just once, there would be no end to Your bliss; all Your demerit karma – sins will be destroyed.

**Seeker:** So is there no discharge (*nirjara*) of karma in this?

**Dadashri:** There is *nirjara* (discharge of karma) but very little. There cannot be significant *nirjara*. Everyone can do *samayik* by reading a book. Reading books feels good. Instead of reading fiction novels, one reads the scriptures. Even the scriptures can be interesting. You can get a lot of joy from it. But one will not gain anything from it. You will only gain if you do the real *samayik* of the Self. Anything You 'do' as the Self (*Atma*), after becoming the Self, will bring You salvation. But you have to become the Self first (one must have Self-realization). When You feel that you have become the Self, then you will be able to say so. If you become the Self for only a minute, it is more than enough.

So with this worldly *samayik*, it is acceptable for one to sit in it reading scriptures, but that is all considered *samayik* of the mind. *Samayik* of the mind means the Self has nothing to do with it. That *samayik* will still the mind, it strengthens the mind. The other benefit is that while he reads the scriptures, he will not have any other thoughts.

## Samayik through One's Own Understanding

**Seeker:** What is the benefit of doing *samayik* every day?

**Dadashri:** Yes, but you are talking about doing a *samayik* through your own understanding, are you not? It is not the *samayik* the Lord had prescribed, is it? It is a *samayik* of your own understanding.

**Seeker:** We are doing it just the way the Lord had prescribed.

**Dadashri:** Is that where one keeps looking at the hourglass to see whether all the sand has fallen through or not?

**Seeker:** One needs to look to see if the time is over or not.

**Dadashri:** You do not have to keep looking at that. When you look and see that the sand has fallen through, you will know that the *samayik* is over. *Samayik* is to increase the strength of the mind (*manobud*) and it increases your faith in the Self.

**Seeker:** One will bind merit karma (*punya*) with it, right?

**Dadashri:** Yes, the *punya* increases. If you are able to keep the mind confined within the circle, you will increase your merit karma for sure.

**Seeker:** But the mind does not remain confined within the circle. It wanders everywhere.

**Dadashri:** Then that *samayik* is not considered complete. For however long the mind remains in the circle, that much of it is *samayik*. That is worldly (*vyavahar*) *samayik* and the real *samayik* is one which takes place everywhere you go.

## Such a Samayik is Useless

**Seeker:** I do *samayik*, *pratikraman* and all other rituals but I cannot maintain my attention in what I do.

**Dadashri:** Then what good is that? What good is it if your *dhyan* (natural meditation and attention) is not in it? It is only good if there is *dhyan* in it. Where does your attention (*dhyan*) lie?

**Seeker:** It goes into the worldly life (*sansar*).

**Dadashri:** But what do you like about the *sansar*? When it (the *chit*) leaves from here, it will go and sit somewhere else, will it not? So where does your mind (*mun*) sit?        (502)

**Seeker:** It goes into whatever work I may be involved with at that time. If there is any work at home that I am doing, it will go there.

**Dadashri:** So then you should do that work. Do the work where your *dhyan* goes. What will you gain by doing things where it does not remain? All your efforts will be wasted and you will not gain anything.

## Living a Good Worldly Life is Itself a Samayik

**Seeker:** I have made a firm decision that I want to do certain *kriyas* (rituals) every day, so what will occur about that?

**Dadashri:** It will go to waste. All your efforts will be in vain. Spend less effort but make the effort meaningful. And live well in the worldly life (*sansar*).

Do *samayik* in it; there is *samayik* in the worldly life. Raising your children without scolding them, not getting angry with them; that in itself is a *samayik*. What is the point of doing this *samayik*? Do *samayik* with your children, with your husband, with your mother-in-law, with your sister-in-law. Do all those *samayiks*. It is worth doing if your mind is in it. What good is a *samayik* in which your mind is not engaged?

**Seeker:** But these are daily rituals and routines, so I keep doing them.

**Dadashri:** Yes, but what is the point in doing it if your mind is not in it? Your *chit* should be in it, should it not?

**Seeker:** The *chit* does not remain in it.

**Dadashri:** Then what will you do?

**Seeker:** That is what we have come to ask from you.

**Dadashri:** Yes. So this is not dear to you. You do not like this. You like your children and other things. The *chit* will always go to things you like. Remove the value of your children, devalue them and increase the value of this (*samayik*), then you will benefit from it; how can it be otherwise?

If you want to do *samayik*, then do the *samayik* of

repentance. Repentance for what? Repent for taking money from others wrongfully; repent for any sexual desire that is not right.

**Seeker:** So should I not consider the *samayik* of the Navkar Mantra as *samayik*?

**Dadashri:** Alas, it is because you have considered it as a *samayik* that you find yourself in this predicament. You have not recited the Navkar Mantra correctly even once. Don't you have to take into consideration the person that is prescribing these rituals?

## These Are All Gross Samayiks

Wherever there is *artadhyan* (adverse internal meditation that hurts the self) and *raudradhyan* (adverse internal meditation that hurts the self and others), there is no Jain religion.

**Seeker:** Is doing *samayik* not the Jain religion?

**Dadashri:** What do you consider as *samayik*? Do you call *samayik* a *samayik* or *asamayik* (that which is not *samayik*) a *samayik*?

**Seeker:** Please explain what *samayik* and *asamayik* are?

**Dadashri:** What kind of *samayik* do these people do? The monks and religious teachers do gross (*sthool*) *samayik*. Gross *samayik* means to bring a restless mind into concentration on a target.

Some people take a book and read for hours. Some do deep thinking, some are doing *mantras*, whatever it may be in, but they remain in that *samayik*. But even then they do not remain still. How can even God give them any credit for all that? One does not remain still for even forty-eight minutes. What can anyone do?

Even the laborers have such gross (*sthool*) *samayik*. All the businessmen, whose minds have become restless, are not able to do *samayik*. The laborers are able to do gross (*sthool*) *samayik*, but it is of no use to them. It is only helpful if it makes the restless mind still.                                                  (504)

## The Essence of Jain Religion

The cessation of *artadhyan* (adverse internal meditation that hurts the self) and *raudradhyan* (adverse internal meditation that hurts the self and others) is the essence of the Jain religion.

**Seeker:** In *pratikraman*, we say, 'May *artadhyan* and *raudradhyan* go away, and may *dharmadhyan* (absence of adverse internal meditation) and *shukladhyan* (meditation as the Self) occur.' Then we ask for forgiveness (*michhami dukkadam*) for that.

**Dadashri:** Yes, but you gain nothing from that. Is that all possible by just saying so? The consequences of *artadhyan* are a life in an animal form, and of *raudradhyan* are a life in hell. So what can one do? One may go into an animal life despite being born a Jain! What a waste of this life!

## Rituals of Other Religions

**Seeker:** Do other religions also have the rituals like those in the Jain religion?

**Dadashri:** It is there everywhere. They too have rituals to bring about a state of stillness. There they do *bhakti* (devotional singing) and here they do *samayik*. All this stills the mind for a while.

## To Block Or Obstruct the Mind in Samayik

What *samayik* are you talking about?

**Seeker:** When we do *samayik* for an hour, what are we to do in it?

**Dadashri:** In order to still the mind, you have to keep

pushing away all external thoughts. That kind of worldly *samayik* is done in the worldly life.

**Seeker:** Is it what the ascetics and the monks do in a Jain meditation hall (*apasara, upashraya*)?

**Dadashri:** All that involves the mind. It is all worldly in nature. It is all aimed at making the mind still. The mind will not remain still, will it? It is great if they can still the mind for an hour. Then the energy of the mind will increase. And one gains that much space. So for that duration of time, he stops binding karma and that will improve his coming life. They obstruct the mind; they make it still. This binds merit karma (*punya*).

**Seeker:** There may be a rare person whose mind can remain confined within the circle. When they go to the Jain monastery (the *upashraya*) where discourses are going on, people will sit in *samayik*, but their minds are always wandering outside; they never remain still.

**Dadashri:** The mind is not in the discourse; it is the *chit* that remains in the discourse and that, too, if he likes the discourse. If one likes the discourse of the guru, then his *chit* will remain there for a little while; it will not wander off outside. And the mind simply does the thinking on one side. Only when the mind can be brought under control can one make any progress. That is when *samayik* occurs properly.

**Seeker:** If someone has been told to recite the Navkar Mantra a hundred times in the *samayik*, his attention will be on when he will finish the hundredth *mantra*.

**Dadashri:** Yes, there they are always in a rush. Even during the *samayik*, they will keep looking at the hourglass. Then he says *paushadha*, but what good does that do sitting in the monastery? People of other castes say, 'When we take a bull to drink water, we say *posho… posho…*- that is how the bull is prompted to drink water.' *Paushadha-vrat* means to nurture the Soul. So that is why they leave home and live a life of a monk in the monastery. That is when they nurture (*poshey*) a spiritual life, leaving aside their worldly life.

## Samrambha, Samaarambha and Arambha

People use the word *arambha* but do they understand what it means? They will use the word *samaarambha*, but what is *samaarambha*? They do not understand even that. Even the great scholars do not understand it. They do not know up to what degree it is considered a state of *samaarambha*, and then up to what degree it is *arambha*. They do not know the degrees. They just use the words. These words are in the scriptures.

(506)

**Questioner:** *Samrambha* causes karma bondage, does it not?

**Dadashri:** *Samrambha* itself is karma. That is the first karma; it is considered a mental karma. *Samaarambha* is a karma of both the mind and the speech. And *arambha* is a karma of all three – the mind, speech and the body. And after attaining this Gnan, if you curse someone, if you do such an *arambha*, it will still not touch You. That is how this science is. The only thing You have to do is to tell 'Chandubhai' to do *pratikraman* for the *atikraman* he did in the process. That is all You have to do. It is never our intent to hurt anyone. It is not possible to hurt anyone and attain *moksha*, no matter what kind of a science we have.

**Questioner:** Is the binding of karma through *samrambha* less or is it more when all the three come together?

**Dadashri:** *Samrambha* is considered less. *Samrambha* means 'only through the mind.' It is a much larger karma when all the three come together. That is why the Lord has called it *arambha*.

**Questioner:** If I do karma only through the mind, and then I stop, then will that not cause much bondage?

**Dadashri:** It will not remain for long. You will just think about it and then you will become free; you will become free by simply thinking about it.

**Questioner:** In the scriptures, one is told to put a limit to *arambha-parigraha* (to move out of the confines of that which is good and beneficial). So what is the difference between one placing a limit or not placing it? Does it make a difference if one does or does not place a limit?

**Dadashri:** If he puts a limit, then the consequences of karma will be less. If he does that in this life, then the karma effect will be less in the next life. In doing this, one will gradually climb higher spiritually.

**Questioner:** Is it like that *samayik*?

**Dadashri:** *Samayik* means without any *arambha*, without any involvement of mind, speech or body. To become free from *arambha-parigraha* (being 'Chandulal'), i.e., to be the Self for an hour, is *samayik*.

## Who Does Such A Samayik?

**Seeker:** When a person is doing a *samayik*, then even if there is an earthquake, he should not leave his *samayik*, should he?

**Dadashri:** Who does such a *samayik*? No one would do such a *samayik*, would he?

So *samayik* in this sense is a process to make the body still. If one remains still, then there will be a worldly benefit; he will get more material wealth. How can wealth come to the one who cannot sit still for even a minute? So that *samayik* is not true *samayik*.

## Samayik That is Not Given By an Enlightened One

That which people have believed to be the soul (*atma*) is

the mechanical *atma* – mechanical soul. It can never be the real Self. That mechanical self is what they try to make still. Hey, you! It is mechanical; it can never be made still!

**Seeker:** I did not understand that. (508)

**Dadashri:** This '*vyavahar atma*' (the relative self; the non-Self complex) is a mechanical self. It is not to be stilled. You (the Self) are to simply study whether the mind can remain still or not. That is all You have to 'see.' This *samayik* is done to still the mind so that this body will remain still for a while. The mind will remain still for awhile. This is meant to hold the mind steady for a little while. Just as when a tired person sits down to rest, that does not mean he is going to remain seated forever, does he?

**Seeker:** No.

**Dadashri:** That is how this is.

This *samayik* is like sitting down when you are tired.

Here in *Akram Vignan*, this machinery runs day and night and the Self remains constantly in the *samayik*. It is not outside of *samayik* even for a moment. It constantly remains in *samayik* even while moving about in the worldly life, or when at home with wife and children.

And the Self is verily *samayik*. Elsewhere, the *samayik* they do is *vyavahar samayik*. The *vyavahar samayik* is to be done for the purpose of attaining the real *samayik*.

This worldly *samayik* should be given – prescribed by a true Purush (the Gnani Purush)

**Seeker:** What is the definition of true Purush?

**Dadashri:** True Purush means, for example, say the collector of the Thana district has written an order for you that this much land has been given to you. Now what would occur if he is really not a collector, and had just written the order, and stamped it as if signed by the collector? That order would not be valid, would it? It would not have any legal backing. Similarly, all these 'collectors' – worldly spiritual teachers that prescribe *samayiks*, are not true Purush.

## Useless Samayik

I was sitting at a table drinking tea and a seventy-five year old businessman (*sheth*) was doing *samayik*, when some glasses fell in the adjacent room and broke. I am hard of hearing so I did not hear them break, but the businessman had good hearing and heard them. So then he calls out, 'What broke?' I said to him, 'Your *atma* broke! What else was going to break?' Otherwise, if a woman were to fall, would she make such a noise? Nothing else will break, only the glasses broke! It was just the noise of the breaking glass. So while doing the *samayik*, the man is asking, 'What broke?' How can you consider that a *samayik*? When one does not leave the *samayik* even if his wife is dying, that is called a *samayik*. How can you call this a *samayik*? Why should you cry over broken glasses and cups? Is it still like this everywhere?

**Questioner:** Yes.

**Dadashri:** Is that so? So then would the cups and glasses come alive again because you left the *samayik*?

## Gross Karma and Subtle Karma

When *Acharya Maharaj* (religious head or teacher) does *pratikraman*, *samayik*, gives a discourse or a lecture; that is his vocation and external conduct; that is his gross (*sthool*) karma, but his inner state is important. What is being charged within him is what is going to be of benefit to him in his next life. His conduct of today is a discharge. The entire external conduct is in the form of discharge. And yet people claim, 'I did a *samayik*. I did auspicious (*dhyan*) meditation, I donated money.' For that, he will get the reward in this very life. What does all that have to do with the next life? The Lord is not so naïve that he will allow such hollowness.

One may be doing *samayik* on the outside, but God knows what is going on within him! One businessman (*sheth*) was sitting in *samayik* when someone knocked on his door. His wife opened the door. The man outside asked her, 'Where is the *sheth*?' The wife replied, 'In the dumping yard.' The *sheth* heard that and when he checked within, he realized that that was exactly where he was. There were negative thoughts going on within him while externally he was doing the *samayik*. The Lord does not allow such hollowness – insincerity. It is acceptable if there is a *samayik* going on within, whereas it may not be on the outside. This external pomp and showcasing is not acceptable over there.

## Lord Mahavir's Samayik

What does the Lord consider as *samayik*? He has said that the one who does not have *artadhyan* (adverse internal meditation that hurts the self) and *raudradhyan* (adverse internal meditation that hurts the self and others) is in *samayik* the whole day. How wise is Lord Mahavir! He does not leave any effort for You to make.                                                      (510)

The Lord would not accept any *samayik* these people practice today. *Artadhyan* and *raudradhyan* should stop for one *gunthanu* (forty-eight minutes), should they not?

One sits down to do *samayik* with the ego of, 'I am Chandulal.' This *samayik* is like the Neem tree growing back even after it has been cut down, and it will still remain bitter in taste, will it not? If you put sugar on the trunk after it has been cut down, will it not grow back bitter?

**Seeker:** Yes, because bitterness is in its roots, Dada.

**Dadashri:** That bitterness is its main nature (*swabhav*).

So when 'Chandubhai' sits in a *samayik*, having stopped all the attachment-abhorrence (*raag-dwesh*), then what will he do the *samayik* on? He has not known the Self, nor does he understand *mithyatva* (to believe the illusion as real, the belief, 'I am Chandulal'). The one who understands *mithyatva* is bound to attain *samkit* or *samyakatva* (established in the right vision, 'I am the Self'). So when the *sheth* sits down in the *samayik*, he does not know how to do anything else. So what does he do? He sets himself a circle (boundary) and then, if he has any thoughts about his shop, money, sex, etc., he will push them out of that circle. Just as cows and dogs get entry into a closed yard, he will drive out his thoughts and will not allow them back in. They call that a *samayik*. Nevertheless, they are able to do that *samayik* because there is no *artadhyan* or *raudradhyan* while doing it.

**Seeker:** If there is no *artadhyan* or *raudradhyan*, then that is considered equanimity (*samata*), is it not?

**Dadashri:** But *artadhyan* and *raudradhyan* do not go away. They are always there. In order for them to go away, you have to establish some discipline before doing *samayik*. You have to say, 'Dear Dada Bhagwan, I surrender this 'Chandulal,' my name, my body, my wrong beliefs, all to You. Please give me *vitarag bhaav* (intent free of attachment and abhorrence) while I am doing the *samayik*.' It will work if you do it with such a *vidhi*.

## True Samayik Gives Moksha

**Seeker:** Can one attain *moksha* by doing the *dharmadhyan* via *samayik* and *pratikraman*?

**Dadashri:** Yes, one can, but not with the *samayik* and *pratikraman* that people do today. These 'products' are not authentic. If the *samayik* was real, then doing just one *samayik* will give you *moksha*. Right now, no one is to be blamed. It is the nature of the current time cycle.

**Seeker:** How can we know that the *samayik* we are doing is wrong? We do it with the assurance and hope that we are doing the right thing.

**Dadashri:** You can do the right *samayik* after knowing the Self, not until then. Until then, it is a good tool to still the mind and the body.

They are all worldly (*laukik*) *samayiks*, whereas this is beyond the worldly, of the Self (*alaukik*). It is to still the '*vyavahar atma*' (relative self, non-Self complex). After attaining Gnan, You can still the relative self, can You not? How is it possible to do so without knowing the Self? The Gnan that is attained will keep making the relative self still. There is great awareness (*jagruti*) here, whereas over there, there is no awareness at all.

## Who is the Doer of Samayik?

If a person does *samayik*, he will tell people, 'I do four *samayiks* every day. That man does only one.' So you will understand that he has the egoism of doing *samayik*, and that is why he sees the mistake of the other person by saying, 'He does only one *samayik*, whereas I do four.' Then, if you were to visit him after a few days and ask him, 'Why are you not doing *samayik* today?' He will tell you, 'My legs are hurting.' So 'we' ask him, 'Do your legs do the *samayik*, or do you? If your legs do the *samayik*, then you were lying before when you told me that you did the *samayik*.' Therefore, one needs his legs to be healthy, his mind to be healthy, and his intellect and ego must be accommodating in order to do *samayik*. All the circumstances have to be right for a *samayik* to occur.

(512)

Even the ego has to be straight at that time; otherwise, the *samayik* will not occur. Therefore, when all these circumstances come together, then the work gets done. So in all this, why do you take the credit for doing it? What is your contribution in what external circumstances accomplish? Do people not take credit for doing such things? It is just the egoism people have of doing something. Scientific circumstantial evidences do everything and yet a person claims, 'I am doing it.' That is all to taste 'the sweet juice of doership' (garvaras). And as long as one has the habit of tasting this sweet juice (ras) one gives rise to the worldly life (sansar). You will have to understand the facts, won't you? Will such falsehood work?

That is why we have the expression of a 'noose around the neck.' When a person takes credit for doing samayik, pratikraman; it is the same as having a noose around the neck, because they enjoyed the taste of doership.

## Samayik of Puniyaa Shravak

**Questioner:** What was the samayik of Puniyaa Shravak like?

**Dadashri:** It was just like the one we do here in Akram Vignan. He took it to that level in the Kramic path.

When King Shrenik was doomed to spend a life in hell, he asked Lord Mahavir to show him ways to prevent this. He said to the Lord, 'Lord, I have just met you and I have to go to hell?' the Lord said, 'What can anyone do now? No one can do anything about it. Once the karma for the next life is bound, it is bound, and nothing can be done about it.' But even then, he pleaded with the Lord to give him a solution, so the Lord showed him a way. The Lord told him to accomplish one of four tasks and, if he were successful, he would avoid a life in hell. Three of the solutions failed. That left the samayik of Puniyaa Shravak. So the King said he would go to Puniyaa Shravak and get the samayik from him.

King Shrenik goes to Puniyaa Shravak and tells him, 'Give

me the *samayik*. You live in my kingdom. I will give you whatever you ask for it. Give me the fruit of your forty-eight minute *samayik*; give it to me. Just say to me, 'I give it to you; I surrender it to you.' That is all!' So Puniyaa Shravak replies, 'Sir, I cannot give you that. It is not something that I can give to you.' So the King asks, 'Why not? You will have to give it to me. I do not want to hear the word 'no.'' Shravak says, 'I cannot give it to you until the Lord says so.'

The King tells him, 'The Lord has told me to get the *samayik* from you, so name your price.' So then Shravak gives in and agrees to give it to him, since the Lord had said so. The King thought it would be a promise that would exchange hands and so he asked Puniyaa Shravak for his asking price. Since he was the King, naturally he would not do anything that would bring an obligation on him. So the King asks Puniyaa Shravak again, 'Tell me your price,' to which Puniyaa Shravak replies, 'I will charge you whatever the Lord says to.'

The King thought, since Puniyaa Shravak has agreed to give it to me, Lord will not have any problems. So he comes to the Lord and says, 'I had a good fortune today.' The Lord asked him, 'What was that good fortune?' And the king replied, 'Shravak has agreed to give me the *samayik*. He has happily agreed to do so. So now I will not have to go to hell, will I?' The Lord asked, 'How did he give it to you?' The King thought the Lord would make him pay Shravak five or ten hundred thousand rupees; what else would he do? All that for forty-eight minutes!

He thought, now I will not have to go to hell. The Lord replied, 'Then you will not have to. But who told you this? How did he give you the *samayik*?' The King replied, 'He has left it up to You, my Lord. You just tell me the price and I will pay him.' The Lord questioned, 'He left it up to me? Of course, I would know its worth, wouldn't I? And I cannot say anything wrong, can I?' So then the King said, 'Tell me the price so that

I can pay him right now.'

So the Lord replied, 'Let me explain to you. Do you realize the value of that *samayik*? Your entire kingdom will go into paying only the commission for it. The commission alone, which is three percent of your entire kingdom! The rest will still remain to be paid. How are you going to pay that?' So the King says, 'My entire kingdom will go into commission? So then where will I get the rest? So that means that my life in hell cannot be avoided, can it?'

The Lord said, 'This *samayik* is worth so much that you can never pay for it.' So the King agreed and accepted that he could not afford it and so he stopped trying, and went to hell. He will come back as the first *Tirthankar* by the name of Lord Padmanabha in the next *chovisi* (a time cycle of twenty-four *Tirthankars*). That is the kind of *samayik* 'we' have you do every day, but people do not realize or appreciate its value. They 'chew' *paan* (betel nut in leaves) and then they spit it out. They have no appreciation for its value.                    (514)

**Questioner:** If you give a diamond to a primitive man, will he not see it as a piece of glass?

**Dadashri:** Yes, that is the way it is. It is like giving a diamond to a child; that is what has occurred. Still, someday it will start working. The child will grow up. Once or twice someone will take it away from him, but then he will come to 'Dada' and get it again and then he will never give it up. He will not be deceived again when he has been punished once. He will not give it up again, will he?

And at that time, there is great bliss (*anand*). When such a *samayik* is done, like the one of Puniyaa Shravak, there will be great bliss. It does not matter if, at that time, the body is emitting vibrations; it may continue emitting vibrations. The bliss that one feels during the *samayik* is because there are no vibrations of *kashays*.

## With Kayotsarg

What kind of *samayik* has the Lord said to do? It should be done with the meditation, 'This body and all in it, is not mine.'

*Samayik* should be with renunciation of the body complex (*kayotsarg*). Those who have attained this Gnan, their *samayik* is inclusive of *kayotsarg*. That is very valuable.

Now, how was *kayotsarg* done? The *ganadhars* (enlightened masters who managed the masses who came to the Lord) and other prominent disciples used to do *kayotsarg*. They would stand like this, like a pole, and then they first decided, 'I am not the leg; I am not the stomach, not the chest, not the head,' and so on; they did such inner renunciation (*utsarg*). And then they meditated from within, 'I am *Shuddhatma* (pure Soul).' If you were to ask them, '*Atma* of what kind?' They would say, 'One with infinite knowledge (*anant gnan*), infinite vision (*anant darshan*), infinite energy (*anant shakti*).' They would know five or six such attributes of the Self and they would tell you of them. Based on these scriptural words, they would keep churning these sentences over and over again. First they renounce (do *utsarg*). The Lord has considered *kayotsarg* as the ultimate solution (*upachaar*).

The meditation, the awareness that, 'I am not this mind-body-speech; I am a *Shuddhatma*,' is *kaoosagga* or *kayotsarg*. Now, people do not understand this *kaoosagga*. This *kaoosagga* or *kayotsarg* occurred just now when 'we' made you speak the sentences of the Gnan Vidhi.

When 'we' made you say, 'I am the manifest *Shuddhatma* who is absolutely separate from mind-speech-body'; all that was *kayotsarg*.

## The Gnan Vidhi is the Samayik of the Self

The one hour Gnan Vidhi that was conducted for you by

Me, is a *samayik* in itself. *Samayik* means to remain in one meditation state in the spiritual realm. Human beings of this era cannot complete that *samayik* properly on their own. For that, one needs a Gnani Purush to wash away the demerit karma (sins). Until then, nothing can be attained.

What do 'we' say when 'we' give Gnan again? We tell you to sit in it, Gnan Vidhi, again. Such a *samayik* will not occur again. Therefore, if you do not have anything to do, sit in the Gnan Vidhi again. If you do not have free time, then finish what you have to do and then come here.                        (516)

## Constant Samayik in Akram Vignan

**Questioner:** What is the special significance of *samayik* in our *Akram* path?

**Dadashri:** 'We' are constantly in *samayik* all day long. For us all, the state is more than a *samayik*. 'We' have the awareness (*laksha*) of 'I am *Shuddhatma*.' That itself is considered a *samayik*. And furthermore, it is true *samayik*. It stays with 'us' the whole day.

'I am *Shuddhatma*,' when it remains for one hour, that itself is *samayik*. To 'do' *sambhave nikaal* (settling with equanimity) is *samayik*. To 'see' the relative and the real is *samayik*. Our five sentences (Agnas) are in the form of *samayik*.

**Questioner:** Is Puniyaa Shravak's *samayik*, the highest *samayik* in the *Kramic* path?

**Dadashri:** Yes, it is the same as the *samayik* you are 'doing.' When you leave home in the morning and you see a cow through your physical eyes, and with your inner vision (Gnan) You 'see' the pure Soul in it, that is the *samayik* of Puniyaa Shravak. That is why I tell you that I have given you Puniyaa Shravak's *samayik* – pure *samayik*. Now, if you know how to enjoy this, then do so.

Such a *samayik* is possible in the current era. Is it not a mistake if you do not take advantage of it?

If you keep the *upayog* (focused, awakened awareness) of seeing the relative and the real as separate for one hour, the Lord has called this *upayog, shuddha upayog* – pure awakened awareness. If that pure *upayog* can be maintained for forty-eight minutes (one *gunthanu*), then it is possible to attain Puniyaa Shravak's *samayik*. So take advantage of that if you can.

No matter what the mind instigates from within, tell it, 'Stay out right now and come back in an hour if you want to. Whatever is to come, come later.' Inside, there are all kinds of things that will come to complain and make noise. Tell them all to be quiet for an hour. Tell them to come back in an hour because your *samayik* is going on. No one has a right to enter the 'home department.' Tell them, 'Shut up and stay in the relative department. I will deal with you when I come out of my home department after an hour.' If you say this, they will stop automatically. They will behave the way you order them to, because all those things are non-living (*nischetan*), but they have been powered with the energy of the animate (*sachetan*), so they have become alive – *sachetan*. So do Puniyaa Shravak's *samayik* for an hour and everything will be shed and vanish!

## That Which Makes You Forget the World is Samayik

What does *samayik* mean? It is that which makes you forget the world. Even if there is 'interesting' discussion about fugitives and outlaws, it makes you forget them. When you go home and the dinner is not ready, you get upset and irritated. So then you start reading a book. After awhile, your wife calls out saying that dinner is ready, but you don't get up to eat. Hey, you! How come? You say you became engrossed reading the book. That is because habits (*sanskars*) that make men fall (attributes that impact negatively, against spirituality), will make a man become focused faster in them; his concentration will be very strong. He is so strongly focused, that he will not get up.

Now at that time, he forgets the world (too), but that will take him to a lower life form. It will cash in your own 'wealth' (spiritual), give you a beating and make you suffer. Whereas the *samayik* that takes you spiritually higher takes longer time. It will take longer time for you to forget the world there.

## Dada On Your Mind Makes You Forget the World

Does everyone (*mahatmas*) have Dada on his or her mind the whole day? And what occurs when Dada remains on your mind the whole day? One forgets the world. You can have only one thing on your mind. Either you have the world on your mind or you have Dada on your mind. And when you have Dada on your mind, you will forget the world. Karma will seem less when you forget the world. Krupadudev Shrimad Rajchandra used to speak about forgetting the world. He has put a tremendous value for that state, where one is able to forget the world (*vismrut*) for just one hour.

What can one do if the mind is that way (remains absorbed in worldly things)? That may well be on the mind, but it is separate from the Self. Even the *sheth* (businessman) that sits down to do the *samayik* will know that his mind is wandering around in dirt. Now, who is the 'Knower' that 'knows' this? The mind gets pleasure from it, so it runs there again. Because he gets pleasure from it, he starts a collection of things there. He starts a collection!                                                      (518)

Right now, in my presence, have you forgotten everything or not? That is called a *samayik*. Here there is no talk at all about the worldly life. Here there is only talk of two things; the *Atma* (pure Soul) and the *Parmatma* (Supreme Soul). You forgot everything didn't you; that is the greatest *samayik*. If you do not know how to do anything else, come and sit here, even for an hour, and then you can leave. You will see that so many of your demerit karmas will be washed away. They will be destroyed. In this *samayik*; demerit karma gets destroyed. That is the wonder of the Gnani Purush!

## Settling with Equanimity is Samayik

What is the *samayik* of the Jains? It nurtures the intent of equanimity (*samata-bhaav*).

Now, when you practice the Agna of settling with equanimity (*sambhave nikaal*, to be without *kashays*), that verily is *samayik*. And to remain in *visham-bhaav* (to be in *kashay*) is worldly life (*sansar*). And what is this worldly (*vyavahar*) *samayik*? It is to not come into any other thoughts for forty-eight minutes; it is to remain in one thought. That is that *samayik*.

When only the thoughts of the Self are there, and there are no other worldly thoughts, that is considered *shuddha samayik* (pure *samayik*). This is possible for forty-eight minutes, not any longer. No one can do it longer than that.

## The Exact Definition of Samayik

**Questioner:** Can you please explain the meaning of the word (*bhaavarth*) *samayik*?

**Dadashri:** *Samayik* does not mean *ekagrata* (concentration on one topic). It exists when you hear ten pieces of your precious china break in the next room, and equanimity remains within you. The scale of equanimity does not tip on either side, neither towards *raag*, nor towards *dwesh*; that is called a *samayik*. *Samayik* means that the needle of the scale is exactly in the center.

The other *samayik* means that whatever (thoughts) is coming in, he keeps pushing it away. So then who remains? He does (is the doer of) this *samayik*. He can never do the other *samayik* of equanimity. Equanimity can never be maintained, can it?

Before sitting down to do the *samayik*, if he decides that he does not want to think about his shop, the moment he closes his eyes, his shop is the first thing that will raid his thoughts. Whereas here (in the *Akram* Path) we say, 'Shop or whatever else that wants to, come; let them do so. You can all come and create your mischief in *samayik*.' And all of them will run away. They will wonder what you have done and that maybe you must have some medicine with you. If they light the fireworks, what should we do? Why do you feed the flame by saying, 'I don't want to think about the shop.' You have to challenge it, 'Come, I am sitting here.' But here he says, 'Dear Lord, do not let thoughts of my shop come in my *samayik*.' Hey, you! What kind of foolishness is this? If you don't get thoughts about your shop, you will have thoughts about your wife, but the thoughts will come for sure. She too is a 'shop,' is she not? Is the wife not a shop?

**Questioner:** A big shop!

**Dadashri:** Just look! This man is saying that the wife is a big shop!

The real meaning of *samayik* is to not allow (*visham-bhaav*) attachment-aversion (*raag-dwesh*) to occur under any circumstances. *Equanimity* (*sam*) may not prevail, but do not let *visham-bhaav* occur, meaning equanimity may not prevail, but do not react with attachment-abhorrence. That is considered a *samayik*.

A son may be insulting his mother and the father happens to overhear, but the father will not allow *visham-bhaav* (*kashay bhaav*) to occur. He may get a little agitated from within, but he will bring everything into balance. Just as when one is weighing on a weighing scale. If the scale tips to the left, he will add weight on the right side to balance it, and vice versa. The scales would not work like that if one used a frog as a weight!

## That Which Does Not Allow Kashay to Occur

When you go to buy vegetables in the morning, 'seeing' *Shuddhatma* (pure Soul) in everyone, is anyone likely to get upset with you? Is that so? Will the donkey complain, 'Why are you looking at the *Shuddhatma* in me?' Will it say that? Therefore, that is equanimity (*samata*) and not *vishamta* (*imbalance; uneven*). It becomes a problem when you try to balance using 'frogs' as weights! You will not find equanimity there.   (520)

It is like this: say you have a five-pound weight on a scale and you want to increase it to ten pounds, then you have to put five pounds weight on the scale. So having used the five pounds, you have to add another five pounds; then you will be able to weigh ten pounds. What does one do to add another five pounds of weight if one does not have anything to increase the weight with? So what did one man do? He put frogs on the scale! But by the time he went to add two more frogs, the other three would jump off. So as he tried to catch them and put them back on, the others would jump off. So he would never be able to keep the scale steady. That is what occurs with these people's *samayik*.

So their scales would keep tipping back and forth. In this manner, one can never do a *samayik* using 'frog weights.' If we were to compare it with 'frog weights,' people would start quarrelling. 'Hey, you! You are calling our *samayik* 'frog weights'?' Very well, we will not call it that. We will just say that the scales keep tipping back and forth. But otherwise, it is like the 'frog weights,' is it not? By the time you get two of them on, three would jump off. Can you have a stable scale?

**Questioner:** No.

**Dadashri:** So the exact meaning of *samayik* has been revealed today. That which was in the hearts of the *Tirthankars*, is not what is being practiced today. For two thousand years, no one has known that real *samayik* means to not allow *visham-bhaav* (*kashay*) to occur. To begin with, one does not have Gnan (knowledge of the Self) and then not to allow *visham-bhaav* to occur – my goodness that is a great wonder! Mind you, that is not the meaning of *samayik* that prevails currently, but that is the true definition of *samayik*.

A man cannot bear it when his son is cursing his wife. But if he is sitting in the *samayik*, he is certain that he does not want to do any *vishamta – raag-dwesh*. If he were to do such a *samayik*, then his work is verily done. Our *mahatmas* have such equanimity (*samata*) of the *samayik*. There is no question about it.

## In Samayik, the Married One Becomes a Monk

**Questioner:** In doing *samayik*, even a seeker – listener (*shravak*) becomes like a monk (*sadhu*).

**Dadashri:** What is the definition of a monk (*shraman*)? It is one who has greater equanimity (*samata*). Those who have attained equanimity are called *shraman*. So such a seeker becomes like a *sadhu*, does he not?

**Questioner:** My understanding of a *shravak* is someone who leads a worldly life, someone who is a householder (*grahasthi*).

**Dadashri:** Yes, but a married person (*grahasthi*) cannot have equanimity (be *shraman*). But when he does *samayik* for an hour, he becomes like a *shraman* for that day. If the real meaning of *samayik* did not come out as it just did, then saying that one becomes like a *shraman* (monk), would cause problems.

This is because concentration (*ekagrata*) is done even by the *bavas* (*bavas* - those who renounce their worldly life and live through begging; the ascetics) and all others including married people who practice different *yogas*.

## Nothing Can Compare to the Samayik that Exists Continuously

**Questioner:** It is said that one should do all kinds of *samayiks*. What are the different forms of *samayik*?    (522)

**Dadashri:** Yes, by various forms, it means that the one we do for forty-eight minutes is considered *samayik*, but when you go out on a street and happen to get into a clash with someone, take that incident into a *samayik*. You should come back into equanimity. Wherever you find yourself in such situations, You should come into the balanced state (equanimity). And that is our path; the path of equanimity. Our whole path is that of *samayik*. This path of ours is the ultimate path of *alochana*, *pratikraman*, *pratyakhyan* and *samayik*.

Is there anything else you want to know?

**Questioner:** Why should we come into *samayik* for just forty-eight minutes? Do we not only have to remain in equanimity, all twenty-four hours?

**Dadashri:** There is nothing better than that, is there? That is completely unique. You know, you cannot put a value on the *pratikraman* that we do here. People forget the world for two to three hours, and they continue to see their own mistakes!

Whatever mistakes You 'see' will go away. That is considered live *pratikraman*. The other is non-living (*nirjiv*) *pratikraman*, but one binds merit karma with that. It will not go unrewarded.

## How Critical is Padmaasan in Samayik?

One man asked me if he should sit in a crossed-leg sitting posture (*padmaasan*) when he does *samayik*. I told him, 'In this time cycle, do not do *padmaasan*, otherwise you will have to go for therapy for your knees. But do sit still during *samayik* and if you cannot do that, then you can do it lying down. Close your eyes when you do. Only a Gnani Purush can do *samayik* with the eyes open. Others do not have the capacity to do so.

## You Have To Continue To 'See' In The Samayik

**Questioner:** It is fine, I remain the Knower-Seer during a *samayik*, but what is the state of the mind, the intellect, the *chit* and the ego during that time? What should I pay specific attention to during the *samayik*?

**Dadashri:** You have to 'see' what the mind, the intellect, the *chit* and the ego are doing. Just like a supervisor. What does a supervisor do when his boss tells him to supervise a task?

**Questioner:** He has to keep an eye on everyone and see what each one is doing.

**Dadashri:** He only has to supervise everything and not go and slap or interfere with anyone. In the same way, You have to 'see' what the mind, intellect, *chit* and ego are doing, and only keep 'seeing'.

In *samayik*, you have to keep separating the Self and keep 'seeing' the rest within (the *chit*, the mind, the intellect, the ego and what they are doing). To 'see' and 'know' are the two functions of the Self, that is all. The Self does not get involved in anything else. It continues to 'see' 'what happened, what the mind is doing (*dharma* of the mind), what the intellect is doing (*dharma* of the intellect). Just like when you are watching a movie and in the movie people are fighting, you do not become part of the movie, do you? You do not become emotional, do you? Similarly, just as you watch a movie, You have to watch the 'cinema' inside. That is *samayik*. It is very beneficial if you do it for forty-eight minutes.

**Questioner:** So then, is there no need to remember the past in this?

**Dadashri:** You are not to recall the past; you are to do the *samayik*. *Samayik* means the Self continues to simply 'see' that which jumps around within. During that time, the Self is completely the Knower and the Seer (*Gnata-Drashta*).

## Samayik is For Shuddha Upayog

**Questioner:** Is there a need for *samayik* in the path of *Akram*?

**Dadashri:** If you have the awareness of 'Dada' (the Self), if other awareness prevails, if You have learned to remain within the Five Agnas, then it is fine if you do not do *samayik*. (524)

However, you all have to do *samayik* for wherever you have entered into the mistakes of sexuality (*abrahmacharya*) or other similar mistakes.

**Questioner:** The interest to do *samayik* has not arisen yet.

**Dadashri:** It is not mandatory that you do *samayik*. There is no problem if you can maintain '*shuddha upayog* (pure awareness as the Self)'. *Samayik* is to be done in order to maintain '*shuddha upayog*' and not the other way around, meaning you don't have to maintain *shuddha upayog* in order to do *samayik*.

## Tuber of Sexuality Dissolves with Samayik

**Questioner:** I am young so, my tuber of sexuality (*vishay granthi*) is large. So that tuber will only dissolve if my *upayog*, focus of awakened awareness, is in *samayik*, am I right?

**Dadashri:** Yes, it will dissolve just by 'seeing' it.

**Questioner:** Yes, so I have to dissolve it by constantly 'seeing' it. That is why it is good if I sit in the *samayik*, is it not? But I do not feel that I want to sit in the *samayik*.

**Dadashri:** If you cannot sit in the *samayik*, then whenever the tuber within sprouts and sexual thoughts arise, cleansing them with Gnan is called awareness (*jagruti*). Ultimately, if nothing else, then even if You say, 'This thought is not mine,' You become free from it. Whenever the thought arises and the 'vision' is spoilt, and it becomes sexual, saying, 'This is not mine,' will stop it.

**Questioner:** So in doing that, it is not necessary to do an hour long *samayik*.

**Dadashri:** It is good if you can do this *samayik*. But if you cannot, then as the mistakes arise within, you have to keep getting rid of them in this manner.

**Questioner:** My desire is to do *samayik* and yet why is it that I am not able to sit and do it?

**Dadashri:** You will be able to do so when you sit down to do it as a group. You will not find it easy to do it by yourself. There is strength in numbers. A special environment arises when people sit in a group. So you should all sit down again as a group for *samayik*.

**Questioner:** How can we arrange it such that we reap the most benefit?

**Dadashri:** The more people that get together, the greater the benefit. There is an effect of the *satsang*. When you sit down to do *samayik*, if there are ten-twelve people, then the *samayik* will go well. It will not have the same effect if you were to do it alone. The effect arises from the group.

## There is No Doership in This

**Questioner:** This is about our science; that is why. You have said that we should do *samayik* for forty-eight minutes to dissolve our tubers of *kashay*?

**Dadashri:** Ours is *Akram Vignan*. Therefore, this *samayik* is to sit still and dissolve the tubers. *Samayik* is not the ideal word for this in *Akram Vignan*. 'We' have to give it another unique name but because 'we' cannot find another name, 'we' are making do with this one.

And *samayik* does not mean anything but to remain the Knower-Seer (*Gnata-Drashta*) of whatever sprouts from the mind (*gneya*).

**Questioner:** Are *samayik* and *pratikraman* considered a *kriya* (ritual)?

**Dadashri:** No, *samayik* and *pratikraman* are not *kriyas*. They are *gnan-kriya*. That which is carried out in ignorance is *agnan-kriya* and that which is 'done' – occurs through Gnan (the Self) – is *gnan-kriya*. *Gnan-kriya* liberates, whereas this *agnan-kriya* brings worldly happiness.

**Questioner:** My personal experience is that awareness (*jagruti*) increases a lot with *samayik*. (526)

**Dadashri:** *Jagruti* will increase a lot. There is nothing better than a *samayik* for awareness.

**Questioner:** But I understood it to be a *kriya* (ritual).

**Dadashri:** No. It is a *gnan-kriya*. *Gnan-kriya* is not considered a *kriya* action. As far as worldly interaction (*vyavahar*) is concerned, you have to say that you are 'doing' *samayik*.

'We' just use the word 'doing,' that is all. You (the Self) have to 'remain' in *samayik*, not 'do' the *samayik*. It is an old habit of speaking and using such words and that is why we speak that way. The language has developed such that we say, 'We have to 'do' the *samayik*,' but otherwise, *samayik* is what You have be 'in.' In our path of *Akram*, there is no 'doership,' is there? The language has simply become so and that is why we have to speak that way. We in the *Akram* path do not have to 'do' anything, do we?

## Inner Purity through Samayik

**Questioner:** When I am sitting in *samayik* and a bad thought arises, should I do *pratikraman* right away at that time?

**Dadashri:** Yes, You should do everything at that time. You, the Self are not to 'do' it; You are the Knower (*Gnata*) of that thought, and 'Chandubhai' does not have the awareness and he is the doer (*karta*). Therefore, You have to tell the doer, 'Why did you do that? Do *pratikraman* for it.' You are the Knower and he is the 'doer.'

When you come here next time, 'we' will show you (the *vidhi* of) *dhyan-sadhana* (the way to meditate as the Self). There is one such a *samayik* by which You will be able to 'see' within, all the mistakes of your entire life. You (the Self) will be able to 'see' all those mistakes and by simply 'seeing' them, they will decrease. 'We' will show you such a *samayik* when you come here next time. But until then, why don't you try and remain in the Five Agnas.

## Samayik Dissolves All Tubers

**Questioner:** My mind is weak and that is why I am not able to sit in our *samayik*.

**Dadashri:** You will be able to do it when you sit down to do *samayik* in a group; in doing so, there is a mutual effect of others around. You do not have to place any particular tuber (to 'see' a specific tuber) in the *samayik*. You just have to 'see' what the mind is doing. You just have to spend the entire *samayik* 'seeing' within. Keep 'seeing' what the weakness of the mind is doing. Sooner or later, You will have to dissolve these tubers, will You not? Whatever You dissolve, that much will be the benefit in this very life. The energy of the free state (*saiyam*-control of *kashay*) will increase greatly.

This path, this opportunity, will never come again and again, so get Your work done. No matter what kind of tuber (problematic karma effect which recurs, usually of pride, greed or sexuality) there is, it will be dissolved with this *samayik*. This path of ours is one of constant *samadhi* (the state of the Self which is free from any effects of mental, physical or externally induced pain). However much You remain in 'our' Agna; that much You will be in *samadhi*. The more You remain in 'our' Agnas, the more You will reap the benefit of *samadhi*.

## The Science of the Samayik of Akram Vignan

There is no need for *samayik* after Self-realization (*Atmagnan*). *Shuddhatma*, the Self, is verily *samayik*. We do not have to do the *samayik* that the world does no longer. Nevertheless, why do we do the *samayik* that is done here? In the *Akram* path, we have gone high (spiritual level of the Self) in the 'lift' (elevator), without having taken care of (settling with equanimity) the discharging karma. The *karmic* tubers are still intact and so the *samayik* is done to dissolve these tubers. Large tubers are 'placed' as *gneya* (that which is to be known) and You 'see' them, as the Knower (*Gnata*), for forty-eight minutes. Thereby, that tuber will dissolve by that much. If the tuber is large, it will need many hours of *samayik*. If one takes one hour daily, then such a tuber will be dissolved completely. In this very life, everything will come to dissolution.

What does one do in *samayik*? Our Gnan is, 'I 'know' the habits of the mind, speech and body and their nature (*swabhav*) and 'I' (the Self) also 'know' My *swabhav* (nature).' But what occurs with the nature (*swabhav*) of those habits? Some habits have a strong nature and some have a mild nature. Now, in the *samayik*, if You 'place' that nature in it, it will dissolve. If You become the Knower-Seer (*Gnata-Drashta*) of that nature, then it will begin to dissolve.

What is 'our' *samayik* like? It is a *samayik* of the *Gnata-*

*Drashta* (Knower-Seer); it is inclusive of internal renunciation of the mind, speech and body complex (*kayotsarg*). No one does this *samayik*, do they? This is a completely different type of *samayik*.                                                                                           (528)

Whatever needs to be dissolved, that *swabhav* (nature) has to be placed in the *samayik* and it will dissolve as You 'know' it. And the other benefit is that You experience the bliss of the Self. The Self is still, and so You will experience the bliss if You 'make' the non-Self still. If the external becomes still, then You will taste the blissful sweetness of it. That is why other people do *samayik*, they do *kayotsarg* (internal renunciation of mind, speech and body complex) and experience the sweetness of it within. They thus come to believe that happiness does not lie in the senses (*indriyas*); it lies within. Whereas we know that it lies within, so now we have to do *samayik* to experience this bliss, to enjoy the 'juice, the essence' of the Self (*atmaras*). And others have to do it to become aware that this bliss is there within.

## The Nature of the Mistake and the Intensity of Interest

'The Self (*Shuddha chetan*) knows the nature (*swabhav*) of the mind, body and speech and also knows its own nature – because it illuminates the Self as well as the non-Self (it is '*swapar prakashak*').'

The nature of the Self is to move towards liberation; it is the Knower-Seer. And after attaining the knowledge of the Self, You know Your own nature and You also know the habits of the mind, body and speech. Would You not 'know' (*jaano*) that the mind is like this, this is the habit of speech, it is not pleasant to others, it is bad language, etc.? You 'know' this and you 'know' the 'other-the non-Self' as well, because You illuminate the Self and the non-Self; whereas an *agnani* (without the knowledge of the Self) can only illuminate the non-Self but not the Self. He does know that the mind is very bad, but where can he go from there? Whereas, the one who has the knowledge of the Self (*Atmagnan*) remains separate from the mind.

**Questioner:** I did not understand the term, 'habits and their nature.'

**Dadashri:** Not only the habits of the mind, body, and speech but also their nature have been mentioned along with them. Nature (*swabhav*) means that some habits are very strong and some are very weak; the latter can be dissolved with just a few *pratikramans*. Those that are very strong need a lot of *pratikraman*. You will have to constantly keep scrubbing away before they dissolve completely.

The habits of the mind, body and speech will not go away until one dies, but You need to erase their nature (*swabhav*). Those habits that were bound by light interest (*ras*) can be removed with two to five *pratikramans*, whereas those that were bound by very deep interest will require up to five hundred *pratikramans* a day. And there are some tubers, such as tubers of greed (*lobh*), which are so large that even if you do two to three hours of *pratikraman* a day for them, they will not be gone even after six years! While others have such a tuber of greed that they can get rid of them within a day or even a few hours. That is how there are all intensity of interest inherent in the nature of the habits of the mind, speech and body.

The *samayik* of our *Akram Vignan* is different altogether. We take all tubers of mistakes within and place them in the *samayik*. Tubers of greed, anger, pride, etc., are placed in the *samayik*. These 'tubers' are all '*gneya*' (that which is to be known) and You, the Self, are the '*Gnata*.' This is how You do *samayik* for forty-eight minutes. The tubers can dissolve through the 'Knower-known' (*Gnata-gneya*) relationship. The *samayik* that they do elsewhere is a *samayik* for concentration (*ekagrata*), whereas our *samayik* is for the purpose of dissolving the *kashay* tubers within. The tuber that harasses you the most, the greater the number of thoughts about a certain topic, the bigger that tuber is within you.

During this *pratikraman*, the mind is absent; nothing else. There is a relationship of *Gnata-gneya* with thoughts. No thoughts will come during *pratikraman*; they will stop. However, if you do have thoughts then if you 'see and know' those thoughts, then the thoughts are '*gneya*'; and You are the *Gnata*.

## Samayik Related to Sexuality

Once 'we' made *mahatmas* do *samayik* for mistakes related to sexuality. They were to 'see' deep within, going back from their current age of forty years and 'see' what occurred. Then they were to go back to when they were thirty-nine years old and they were to 'see' what occurred then. They were to keep going back in this manner. Some even reached the age of ten! It is a different matter that they went so far back but afterwards, they continued to 'see' those mistakes for up to eight days. They could not stop. They continued at home even while eating and drinking. It kept gnawing and scratching them from within; they got very tired of this. So then they came and told 'us' they were exhausted from it and wanted 'us' to stop it, and so 'we' had to have it stopped. It remained 'turned on' from within and kept finding mistakes within, non-stop. They could 'see' all the phases like what they did at the age of twenty-five and so forth. To 'see' the phases of that which was established in the past is our *samayik*.                                   (530)

Mistakes can be washed off in this *samayik*. This is a *samayik* to 'see' all the mistakes that occurred prior to attaining Gnan. What mistakes do you want to 'see'? By 'seeing' the mistakes which occurred prior to attaining Gnan, in the *samayik* they can be washed off. They will get washed off even if You were to 'see' them now. But if you try to recall them in your memory, you will not remember any. It is through this Gnan that

You are able to 'see' them all. In the presence of the Self, everything can be 'seen.' You can 'see' it all the way back; You can see your entire life and all the mistakes related to sexual matters...

**Questioner:** I did *samayik* on sexuality related mistakes.

**Dadashri:** Yes, You will be able to 'see' all sexual mistakes that took place all the way back. As You keep 'seeing,' You will 'see' them all the way back to when you were twelve years old. You will see all the way back to when they started. Whatever You 'see,' from the beginning until the end, will all go away.

## Keep Tearing Away All the Paintings That You Had Painted

And what is a *samayik*? Whatever habit you have, for example, like that man who said that he has a habit of reading; so to break the habit of reading, imagine a pile of books in front of you, then remain the Knower-Seer and keep ripping those books. Do that for an hour. You just 'see' and tell 'Chandubhai' to rip all those books. Thus the tuber of reading will dissolve. If you have a tuber of greed, then place the tuber of greed in your *samayik*. *Samayik* is an instrument to dissolve tubers. You have all these tubers within you and so you will have to become tuber-free (*nirgranth*) one day. You have no choice but become tuber-less.

## Begin Samayik in This Manner

**Questioner:** How many *atikramans* must I have done in my past life? What kind of *atikraman*? What did I do in the past life? I have no knowledge of that. How can I know about them?

**Dadashri:** What do you have to do with the past life? You have to wash off the *atikramans* you have done in this life.

**Questioner:** I do not even know all the *atikramans* I have done in this life.

**Dadashri:** You will be able to 'see' in detail all the *atikramans* you have done in this life, if You make it a point that you want to track it all down in a *samayik*. Then you will be able to find it very precisely.

Today, do one *samayik*.

**Questioner:** Yes, how should I do the *samayik*?

**Dadashri:** Yes. From the time you were young up until now, whomever you have made mistakes with, made mistakes of violence (*himsa*) with any living being, whomever you have hurt, whomever you have spoken harshly to and hurt; these are all mistakes related to *himsa* (violence).

Then 'see' mistakes about lying, cheating, mistakes of sexual nature, attachment to things and acquisitiveness (*parigraha*). Whatever mistakes of this nature you have committed, recall all these mistakes, bow to Simandhar Swami or Dada Bhagwan, and ask for forgiveness. Do this much; can you do that much?

**Questioner:** I can. However many I am able to remember, I will.

**Dadashri:** Do them for as long as you can recall these mistakes; continue doing *pratikraman* for them. The one who has the desire to see his own mistakes will not refrain from 'seeing' them. In the Lord's path, straightforwardness is the easy path to liberation. It is the highest path. If a person does not become straightforward, then he is not in the Lord's path.
(532)

If you have hurt any animals in your childhood; if you have thrown a stone at a monkey, You will be able to 'see' all that within. You will be able to 'see' all the different phases, if you do many *samayiks*. You may not be able to see all of a sudden in the first few *samayiks*. However, after you do more *samayiks*, You will be able to 'see' in great detail.

First, hold Dada in your meditation (*dhyan*), recall Him, read one or two *pads* (Dada's spiritual hymns), recite the Trimantra and repeat several times, 'I am pure Soul,' and come into the stillness of the Self. Then whatever You 'see,' starting from today going back to your younger years, whatever mistakes committed with reference to violence (*himsa*), lying, fraud, deceit, sexual mistakes, etc.; start doing *pratikraman* for whatever You 'see.' Go back in time starting from today. Recall all that You can from your childhood, or else recall with whomever you did *atikraman* yesterday and the day before, and so on; they will naturally come to you. If they do not come to You naturally, do not worry.

Once you begin, there will be a very heavy 'rainfall'; it will 'rain' even in the desert! Then, if you have hurt anyone through any wrongdoing, through speech, deceit, greed, pride; if you insulted or talked negatively about any religion; do *pratikraman* for all that and move forward. Then, if you have made mistakes regarding sexuality, adultery, or even had thoughts about them, recall them, too, and do *pratikraman*. Where anything occurs that the world looks down on, are the acts which bring on a future life in a lower life form; and so do *pratikraman* for all that.

This speech (of the Gnani Purush) is filled with life (*chetan*), thus this speech will verily do the work, take you to liberation. Start doing *pratikraman* with purity. There are five *Mahavrats* (five cardinal vows of non-possession, non-violence, not stealing, not lying and celibacy) and you have to do *pratikraman* for wherever you have violated these *mahavrats*; you do not have to do anything else. You don't have to do *pratikraman* if you have gone out, eaten a *paan*, smoked a cigarette, etc. Human beings have to do *pratikraman* for *atikraman* done against each other; meaning do *pratikraman* for mistakes against *mishrachetan* (the one who believes 'I am Chandulal'). So I am telling you to do *pratikraman* for mistakes committed against other people (*mishrachetan*).

This is now being given to You as Dada's Agna and follow it as such. As it is, you do *pratikraman* every day. If you have had any sexual thoughts about another living being, or any other such mistakes, recall them, going back to your childhood and do *pratikraman* for them. Because this *pratikraman* is through the Agna of the Gnani Purush, everything will be erased. What are human beings not capable of doing? But if you follow My Agna, everything will clear up.

**Questioner:** What falls in the category of *mishrachetan*?

**Dadashri:** *Mishrachetan* means, if you have kicked a dog, this means you have bound vengeance with it. If you have pushed at or shoved someone in the way, that too is a mistake against *mishrachetan*. Recall all such mistakes committed against every *mishrachetan* (mixture of the Self and the non-Self); do *alochana*, *pratikraman* and *pratyakhyan*. You can 'operate' on all your mistakes by remaining in the Agnas of the Gnani Purush. This is a 'lift (elevator; a quick shortcut)' path. You happen to come across it in passing (it is not something you have worked to earn), so by remaining in the Agnas, You will clear everything. In so doing, You will be able to go to *moksha*.

**Questioner:** What if I am not able to remember my mistakes?                                                                 (534)

**Dadashri:** Then recall Dada and tell him, 'Oh, Dada Bhagwan, I can't remember anymore,' and it will come to You. As many mistakes You are able to 'see,' that many will be destroyed. Now, Your experience of your inner bliss has begun but whatever mistakes you have committed with other *mishrachetan* will come for collection. So instead of shaping up after taking a beating, if you start asking for forgiveness for mistakes committed with all *mishrachetan*, your load of liability will begin to lighten. Do *pratikraman* for your children, your wife, your father and your mother; these are all *mishrachetan*. Do *pratikraman* for all of them. The energy and power of the Gnani's speech is behind His Agnas, and so Your work will be accomplished.

Now keep on 'seeing' and go all the way back and 'see' into your life when you were very young. Go from the age of one year to the next and You will be able to 'see' everything – all the way to when you were young.

You can start 'seeing' either from your young age to now, or start from now and go all the way back to when you were young; whatever it may be. But do one of the two studies. 'See' it through the Self; continue 'seeing' even if you get stuck. So You will be able to 'see' further and further ahead. Many times there are no obstacles, but if one has obstacles, then he will get stuck. If a person has no obstacles, then he will be able to 'see' all the way to his childhood. You will 'see' everything that you did when you were young.

## The Vidhi of Samayik

### For Those Who Have Attained the Self through Gnan Vidhi

**Niruben:** Dear Dada Bhagwan, Dear Simandhar Swami, give me the energy to do *samayik – pratikraman*, with pure awakened awareness, of all the mistakes of sexuality done in my life.

**Dadashri:** Energy to 'see' the mistakes.

**Niruben:** Give me energy to 'see' the sexually related mistakes.

I surrender my mind-body-speech, all the illusory attachments associated with my name, *bhaavkarma* (charge karma), *dravyakarma* (subtle discharge karma), *nokarma* (gross discharge karma), at Your lotus feet, Oh manifest absolute Self.

**Dadashri:** I am pure Soul (*Shuddhatma*).(5 times)

I am absolutely pure Soul (*Vishuddhatma*).

I am the light of Absolute Knowledge.

I am pure Soul that is completely separate from mind, speech and body.

I am pure Soul free from *bhaavkarma*.

I am pure Soul free from *dravyakarma*.

I am pure Soul free from *nokarma*.

I am full of infinite knowledge. (5 times)

I am full of infinite vision. (5 times)

I am full of infinite energy. (5 times)

I am the abode of infinite bliss. (5 times)

I am pure Soul.(*Hoo Shuddhatma chhu.*)(5 times)

Now go deep within.

(After the forty-eight minutes *samayik*...)

**Questioner:** *Samayik* does wonders.

**Dadashri:** When you do it alone, it does not work as well as You would like it too. When 'I' (Dada) make you say the *vidhi*, everything separates within.

**Questioner:** This is the first time I did a *samayik*. I liked it.                                                                 (536)

**Dadashri:** It will work out. In our *samayik*, that non-Self complex 'thing' (tuber) is made to come in front of the Self. This is considered the *samayik* of the Self. The non-Self complex (*pudgal*) has nothing to do with it. There is no exchange between the *pudgal* and the Self. This *samayik* is such that it works by being the *Gnata* (Knower) of the *pudgal*.

'You' have not 'seen' anything like that before, have You?

**Questioner:** No.

**Dadashri:** It is absolutely new. It may not work properly for someone in the beginning, but this is the best solution. How far could You 'see'?

**Questioner:** From the time when I was young, until now.

**Dadashri:** Everything can be 'seen' just like seeing photographs. You will even 'see' where you pinched someone or bit someone.

**Dadashri addressing a seeker:** You should not worry too much if you did not see anything. You will not see anything yet because 'I' have not given you that vision (*drashti*) yet. You will see all that after 'I' give you such a vision. Where will you sit when everyone is doing *samayik*? Where could you have gone when they were all doing *samayik*?

**Seeker:** I can try to see.

**Dadashri:** Yes, for sure, otherwise you will feel, 'Why has Dada put me in this jungle?'

## Different Kinds of Experiences in Samayik

**Dadashri:** Is this your first *samayik*?

**Questioner:** Yes.

**Dadashri:** Now, no one else (non-*mahatma*), no saint, monk or ascetic can do such a *samayik*.

**Questioner:** This *samayik* that was done today is the

most powerful technique.

**Dadashri:** This is not a *samayik*; this is 'our' discovery. *Samayik* means to be in equanimity. It is to not allow attachment-abhorrence (*raag-dwesh*) to occur. You experience that all day anyway, do You not? You are in *samayik* the whole day. You do not experience any attachment-abhorrence and, therefore, your whole day, your days and days that unfold, are in *samayik*.

And when You went deep within to 'see,' at that time what did the Self become! How much energy it has! During that time, You were not 'Chandubhai,' You were not anyone's husband, You were nothing to anyone; that is why You could 'see' all that. Otherwise, what is the one who has become a husband, the 'blind' (ignorant) one, going to see? That will require the full light of the Self.

You will not think of a single such phase if you try to recall it from the memory, and yet look at all the phases You 'saw'! Otherwise, memory cannot work that fast. This *samayik* will continue to show You everything that occurred when you were young, when you were growing; it will continue to showing You everything.

Now that which is 'seen' is different for everyone. Some can 'see' it very clearly, some 'see' it through a veil; there is a difference in what everyone 'sees' and with what clarity it is 'seen.'

**Questioner:** The 'film' came to an end within fifteen to twenty minutes into the *samayik*.

**Dadashri:** Yes, it will end.

**Questioner:** What should I do then?

**Dadashri:** Then remain still as You are; there is nothing wrong with that. Or else You may switch the *upayog* on to something else.

**Questioner:** But, I saw that film twice.              (538)

**Dadashri:** Good, nothing wrong with that. Whatever You can 'see,' you have that much time to wash it off. This is a pure (*shuddha*) Self (*Atma*).

Otherwise, if you want to remember all your mistakes, you will not be able to. But if you sit in a *samayik*, You will 'see' them effortlessly. So the Seer that saw that 'film' is the Self who is the Knower-Seer. The Self 'sees' what you are doing.

Does anyone else want to talk about his experience of the *samayik*?

**Questioner:** I absolutely feel at peace; I was able to see lots of my mistakes.

**Dadashri:** Whatever mistakes You saw are gone. Now the remaining small ones, if there are any, will go away when you do a *samayik* like this again.

Did anything else come to you?

**Questioner:** Yes, I 'saw' all the mistakes from the young age up until now. And now I have a special prayer and request, Dada, please do something so that I will not repeat any mistakes in sexuality.

**Dadashri:** Yes, 'I' will do that for you. But up to what age did you see them?

**Questioner:** From a very young age.

**Dadashri:** Did You 'see' all the mistakes, beginning from a very young age up until now? That is very good.

The Seer is the Self (*Gnata-Drashta*); you 'saw' the Self (experienced the Self)! Otherwise, if you try to recall the mistakes, you will not be able to do that at all, whereas here You 'saw' all this. That is a lot. Still, whatever You saw, it is all gone. Those mistakes will not come again.

## The Mind is Not Involved In Samayik

**Questioner:** When I am 'seeing' my 'film' and the mind gets involved in it, it likes it, gets stuck in places, yet in all that there is no feeling (*bhaav*) of 'I have done something bad or wrong'; how does that appear?

**Dadashri:** The mind is not present at all during *samayik*. There is no existence of the mind at that time. You were only to 'see'. You are not to see whether anything was good or bad.

**Questioner:** After 'seeing,' do I not have to say that I am asking for forgiveness?

**Dadashri:** *Pratikraman* is a different thing. But you cannot say things like, 'It was like this and like that, that it got stuck'; there is nothing there to get stuck. It is not the activity of the mind; it is the 'activity' of the Self. You (the Self) can 'see' all that because it is the activity of the Self; and that is why the mind has nothing to do with it.

## You Can See the Conduct of the Atma

**Questioner:** If I do *pratikraman* once, will they (mistakes) come back again?

**Dadashri:** If it is with very thick and heavy veils (of karma effect), then it will keep coming back. If it is long in duration, that karma will stay with you right until the end. And that is why You have to 'see' it again, and keep 'seeing' it until it comes to an end. And all this time, You got to 'see' – experience the conduct (*charitra*) as the Self, in the *samayik*. This is called *charitra* (conduct); it is pure conduct (*shuddha charitra*).

Anyone here that was able to 'see' properly, raise your hand please. You too could see! Even one from a *patidar* (Patel community) could 'see'?

**Questioner:** I 'saw' very clearly.

**Dadashri:** They will not let even a snake go by without killing it first. Such are the *patidars*. If such *patidars* can 'see' too, then what kind of an *Atma* they must have attained?

This is considered the wonder of the world! To attain one hour of Puniyaa Shravak's *samayik*, it would take King Shrenik's entire kingdom just to cover the commission for it, so imagine the total value of this one hour! Do you now understand what Dada has given to you?

## Then It Will Automatically Keep Searching for Mistakes Within

**Dadashri:** Have you lost anything by sitting the whole day with 'me'?

**Questioner:** I have not lost anything.                    (540)

**Dadashri:** So then why do you not run around with 'me'? What is wrong with running around with 'me' instead of running around the world?

**Questioner:** That is major running around; this with You, Dada, cannot be called running around.

**Dadashri:** You have been given the reign of the whole universe. I have given you something that no *sadhu* or *acharya* will ever attain.

I have helped You launch Your kite with, 'I am *Shuddhatma*.' A while ago, I had people do *samayik* on violence (*himsa*), so when they went home, they kept seeing their mistakes of violence even when they went to the bathroom. It would not stop. It continued like that for three days. It kept bothering them because it kept going deeper and deeper, seeking mistakes of violence. I had to put a stop to it by doing a *vidhi*.

## Why Only for Forty-Eight Minutes?

**Questioner:** Whose Agna should I take for *samayik* in your absence?

**Dadashri:** 'We' (the supreme Self; Dada) are never absent; 'our' presence is always there. And as far as You are concerned, there is never an absence of 'us' for you; you are very particular and shrewd!

**Questioner:** What is the minimum time one should do a *samayik* for?

**Dadashri:** The minimum is eight minutes and the maximum is forty-eight minutes.

**Questioner:** When I do *samayik* in the morning, then after forty-eight minutes, bliss overflows.

**Dadashri:** Of course, there will be! Because what I have given to you is the Self; and it is unshakable Self and You are in *samayik* as the Self. Hence you will have tremendous bliss (*anand*). The more still you become; the more bliss you will experience.

**Questioner:** Why is the *samayik* kept for forty-eight minutes?

**Dadashri:** Not forty-seven minutes, it is for forty-eight minutes. Do you know that if you can do a forty-eight minute *samayik* for even one day, that is more than enough. It is the glorious Self! It is the tested experience!

If one's mind-speech-body stops for eight minutes, the Lord has called it the beginning of a *samayik*, and if it stays like that from eight minutes to forty-eight minutes, He calls it a *samayik*. No one can maintain more than forty-eight minutes. *Samayik* means to remain as the Self.

## Samayik in the Akram Path

**Questioner:** In the *samayik*, thoughts come and at the

same time, '*Dada Bhagwan na aseem jai jaikar ho*' continues within. What is that?

**Dadashri:** If there is an oil mill in your neighborhood and you hear the churning of the wheels in the mill, and you are sitting here spinning a spinning wheel, what would you do? It is the same with the mind; the mind keeps spinning round and round. You just have to keep 'seeing' it. Whether it is a good thought or a bad thought, You just have to keep 'seeing' it.

Now how can you stop your neighbor from speaking? Say we are doing *satsang* here, in your study room, what is it to you if there is a riot going on outside? The mind is a *gneya* (that which is to be known) and You are a Knower (*Gnata*); and this is how the mind is under Your control. 'We' too have a mind until 'we' attain final *moksha*. But what is 'our' mind like? It continues to move forward like the second hand on the clock; it does not stop anywhere. 'Our' mind has come to an end. The mind comes to an end if You remain its 'Knower-Seer.'

**Questioner:** What is the difference between *vyavahar samayik* (worldly *samayik*) and *nischay samayik* (*samayik* of the Self)? Which is more beneficial?

**Dadashri:** *Nischay samayik*! *Vyavahar samayik* (worldly *samayik*) occurs through the mind and *nischay samayik* occurs through the Self. *Vyavahar samayik* is to focus the mind and not allow it to wander around on the outside.

**Questioner:** What is the fruit of the *vyavahar samayik*?

(542)

**Dadashri:** *Punyanubandhi punya* (merit karma which binds more merit karma).

*Nischay samayik* makes You further established as the Self- *Shuddhatma*. Then It (the Self) starts to 'see' sexual mistakes from one's current age, say age 35 to 34 to 33, and all the way back. Then It (the Self) 'sees' violence (*himsa*) related mistakes, and *kashay* mistakes (mistakes of anger-pride-deceit-greed). There is only the Self in all this. The mind, the intellect (*buddhi*), etc., remain idle.

To keep 'seeing' is considered *samayik*, whereas this worldly *samayik* is considered *pratikraman*.

**Questioner:** Can karma be washed off just with *samayik* or do I have to do *pratikraman* for it?

**Dadashri:** One has to do *pratikraman*. This is called *samayik-pratikraman*. *Samayik* means that external interactions stop and *pratikraman* means that it continues within.

**Questioner:** We get together and do *samayik*. What should we all do in that?

**Dadashri:** Do more *samayik* on the topic of sexuality (*vishay*). First take the *pratikraman* for mistakes of sexuality and go back all the way to your childhood. Then do *pratikraman* for the *roonanubandha*. *Roonanubandha* means all those you have met (interaction with others due to *karmic* connection from the past) and do their *pratikraman*. Then by seeing *himsa* (violence) related mistakes, the subatomic particles (*parmanus*) of *himsa* will go away. By doing *samayik* on sexuality, the subatomic particles (*parmanus*) of sexuality will go away.

One can recognize that there are tubers of *kashay* or *vishay*, but it is not possible to understand them through external, worldly interaction. And that is why 'we' tell You to 'see' those tubers in *samayik*. When You try to dissolve one tuber in the *samayik*, another tuber will sprout within, then you will 'see' the thoughts. This will not allow You to have *upayog* (focused, awakened awareness) on the tuber. During such a time, 'see' whatever arises in front of You.

**Questioner:** If one 'sees' mistakes in the *'samayik-pratikraman'* process and does *pratikraman*, then one still has to suffer the effect of those mistakes, does one not?

**Dadashri:** No, they are washed off. Some sticky ones may remain. But what are they like? They will stick to the wall, but the minute you touch them, they will fall away.

**Questioner:** How should I do *pratikraman* of the mistakes that I 'see' in the *samayik*?

**Dadashri:** There is no need for *pratikraman* of all that You 'see' in the *samayik*. That which You 'see' is all gone. *Pratikraman* has to be done for those that are not 'seen' ('seeing' was not done through the Self, or when the person gets hurt). What You 'saw' is cleared. It became clean the moment You 'saw' it.

**Questioner:** But it will be 'seen' again, will it not?

**Dadashri:** You 'see' different phases, layers again. By 'seeing,' it is like peeling away of one layer of an onion at a time. It will still look like an onion.

**Questioner:** But I can 'see' the same scene (*drashya*), that which is to be 'seen' again, can I not?

**Dadashri:** You (the Self) cannot 'see' the same *drashya* (scene) again; You cannot 'see' it twice.

**Questioner:** If I do *pratikraman* for an enmity (*veyr*) towards someone, do I have to do *pratikraman* for the same person again?

**Dadashri:** Yes, when you do *pratikraman* for a major mistake that exists, you peel off one layer, but hundreds of thousands of other layers still remain intact. Those layers are deeper. So you will have to keep on doing *pratikraman* until those layers are finished. With some people, your account of karma will be paid off in a month or two of *pratikraman*. And with some, it continues for the whole life. That tuber (*granthi*) is very large. When you peel off one layer of this onion, will you not see the onion again? Similarly, mistakes have layers. So by doing *pratikraman* once, you definitely peel one layer off. So you do not have to do *pratikraman* for that layer again. One layer requires only one *pratikraman*.                                        (544)

## Effect of Dada's Presence or Absence

**Questioner:** The experience we have when we do this *pratikraman* and *samayik* in Dadashri's presence, does it also occur in Dadashri's absence?

**Dadashri:** No, the experience is much better if Dada's presence is there. There will be no external effect and the atmosphere is of a very high level. And when I also say, 'I am *Shuddhatma*' five or six times, that works a lot for You too. 'Our' words have a lot of effect.

**Questioner:** But the effect is still there, even in Dadashri's absence, is it not?

**Dadashri:** You can do it, you can do it; it is just that things will go back and forth, that is all. Even then, it is more than enough even if it occurs for two minutes. Some people have an immediate experience. The *samayik* that 'we' have You do here is a great *purusharth* (spiritual effort as the Self). It is a vitamin for the Self. In the worldly dealings, you have to take vitamins for the body. This is the vitamin that you have to take for the Self. For You, the whole day and the whole life is a *samayik*. Does it not remain even when you are driving the car? That is how it should be. *Atma* (the Self) itself is *samayik*. There is infinite energy within, it is just that it has not manifested fully yet.

## Samayik of Separation

'We' are showing you the *samayik* to separate the Self

and the non-Self today. This is the greatest method of separating 'Chandubhai' (non-Self) and *Shuddhatma* (the Self). In this *samayik*, you have to keep saying this:

1. 'Dear *Shuddhatma Bhagwan*! You are separate and 'Chandubhai' is separate.'

2. 'Dear *Shuddhatma Bhagwan*! You are real and 'Chandubhai' is relative.'

3. 'Dear *Shuddhatma Bhagwan*! You are permanent and 'Chandubhai' is temporary.'

Do this for forty-eight minutes. 'I' (the Self) and 'Chandubhai' are absolutely separate; give me such energy to remain so. Give me energy to remain separate like You and let 'Chandubhai' remain separate. Dear Dada Bhagwan! Shower me with Your grace. 'My' only 'work' is to 'know' and 'see,' what 'Chandubhai' is doing.

You can ask *Shuddhatma Bhagwan* for whatever energy you feel you are lacking, when you are doing *samayik*. This will definitely result in complete separation. Whenever you think about it during the day, if you say these three sentences five or twenty-five times, even then everything will separate and become clear within.

## Samayik in Front of the Mirror

In the mirror you will see 'Chandubhai' in front of you. In that, one is the Self (*Atma*) and the one standing across is 'Chandubhai'. You (the Self) can tell him, 'Chandubhai, how long are you going to keep making these mistakes? You need to be scolded a little.' You can even say that.

Do you ever look into the mirror and scold 'Chandubhai'? Seat 'Chandubhai' in front of the mirror, look at him in the mirror and say, 'You have helped in printing Dada's books with your donations. You have done good work. But then why do you go and make mistakes like this?' Should you not be telling the self – 'Chandulal' this? Should only Dada keep saying it? But instead, 'Chandubhai' will listen more if You, too, were to say something to him. He will listen to You more. If I were to tell you that, how would you feel? You would feel, 'Why does Dada not say anything to the one who is next to me, and why is he telling me?' So You should reprimand him yourself. (546)

One is generally very good at pointing out others' mistakes but he cannot see even one of his own mistakes. But You do not have to look for mistakes; You just have to scold 'Chandubhai' a little. You know 'Chandubhai's' mistakes, so now 'You' have to scold 'Chandubhai.' But then 'Chandubhai' is full of pride (*maani*). So you can achieve everything when you cajole him.

Now when will You practice scolding him? You can employ one or two people to do that, but they will not truly scold him, will they? Only when you have someone who truly scolds will you get results. Artificial scolding will not produce results. You should take advantage of the situation when someone scolds you. But you do not know how to arrange for it, do you?

**Questioner:** I would not like it if there was someone to scold me regularly.

**Dadashri:** You do not like that, but if you find someone to scold you every day, then would you not know how to settle it because you would accept that it is an everyday thing, so when is it likely to end? Instead, why not just go back deep within the Self?

**Questioner:** You have told me that I am not mortal (*jiva*) and I am immortal (*Shiva*), but that separation does not occur.

**Dadashri:** It – the non-Self complex (*prakruti*) will not let go of its nature (*bhaav*), will it? He will not let go of his claim, will he? Therefore, You have to slowly coax him into getting your work done, because he is naïve (*bhodo*). What is the nature of the non-Self complex (*pudgal*)? It is naïve. So You can catch him with this technique. *Jiva* and *Shiva* are both separate, are they not? When he comes into *jiva bhaav*, he will eat potato fritters and everything, and when he comes into *shiva bhaav*, he will do *darshan*.

**Questioner:** But is the mind of a *jiva* (that which lives and dies), independent?

**Dadashri:** Absolutely independent. Have you or have you not seen the mind confront and oppose you? Hey, you! How can it confront or oppose you if it were 'your' mind? You will realize whether it is independent or not when it confronts you.

**Questioner:** Because I do not have control over my speech and that is why I have no control over the mind.

**Dadashri:** You do not have control over anything that confronts or opposes you. Before, you believed that 'I am *jiva*' (I am living). Now that belief has been destroyed and You have the realization of 'I am Shiva' (I am eternal), but the *jiva* part will not let go of his *bhaav*, he will not let go of his claim or his rights. But he will let go if you coax him gently. Just as when bad company (*kusang*) touches him, he becomes a *kusangi* (tainted by bad habits of the company); when *satsang* touches him, he becomes a *satsangi*; and when you explain things to him, he will listen and leave the bad habits; he is good in that way.

Now what you have to do is to sit down with 'Chandubhai' and talk to him, 'You have been coming to *satsang* every day even at the age of sixty-seven years; you are doing a good job of making sure of that.' But, at the same time, you have to make him understand and give him advice, 'Why are you taking so much care of this body? If this occurs to the body, let it occur. Why don't you come and sit here at the table with 'me.' There lies infinite bliss with 'me.' That is what you should tell

'Chandubhai.' If you were to sit 'Chandubhai' in front of You, can You or can You not 'see' him exactly?

**Questioner:** My talks with him go on for hours. (548)

**Dadashri:** But there are others within him who also accept the 'phone call (conversation)'; that is why You have to make him sit in front of You and talk to him, loudly and directly. That way some one else will not take the phone.

**Questioner:** How should I make him sit across from me?

**Dadashri:** 'Chandubhai' will become very wise if You seat him across from You and keep scolding him. You should scold him personally. Say to him, 'Chandubhai, should you be doing this? What nonsense is this? Why don't you become straightforward?' What is wrong in speaking to him this way? Does it look good if someone else has to correct you? That is why 'we' tell You to scold 'Chandubhai,' otherwise he will continue walking in complete darkness. What the *pudgal* is saying now is, 'You have become a *Shuddhatma*, but what about me?' He will put in a claim; he has a right too. He too has a desire that he wants something. He is naïve so you can coax him. Naïve, because in the company of fools, he becomes a fool and in the company of wise, he becomes wise. In a company of thieves, he becomes a thief. *Jevo sang evo rang!* One becomes like the company that he keeps.

You have to seat him in front of the mirror, and then start this process. You can see his whole face in the mirror. Then You tell 'Chandubhai', 'Why did you do that? You are not to do that. Why do you have separation due to difference in opinion (*matbhed*) with your wife? Is this why you got married to her? Why are you doing this after getting married?' You have to tell him such things. When you scold him like this, in front of the mirror for one hour, then tremendous energy will manifest. This is considered the highest of all *samayik*. 'You' 'know' of all

'Chandubhai's' mistakes, do You not? Whatever mistakes You 'see', when You seat 'Chandubhai' in front of You in the mirror for an hour and tell him about them, that is the highest *samayik*.

**Questioner:** If I do not do it in front of the mirror, but instead I talk to the mind within, will it work?

**Dadashri:** No, that is not possible. 'You' should be able to 'see' 'Chandubhai' in the mirror. You will not know how to do it if You do it alone within. Only the Gnani Purush can do that. But You have to be taught at kindergarten level. It is good that mirrors exist abundantly; otherwise you would have to buy a mirror worth hundreds of thousands of rupees. Mirrors nowadays are inexpensive. Only Emperor Bharat had built a palace of mirrors in the time of Lord Rushabhdev (first *Tirthankar*). And today, one sees large mirrors everywhere.

All this is the science of smallest indivisible parts of matter (*parmanus*). But if You seat him in front of You in a mirror and do the scolding, then it is possible to achieve a lot. But no one does that, does he? He does it once or twice, when 'we' instruct him; then he forgets.

Lord Rushabhdev gave the knowledge of *Akram Gnan* to Emperor Bharat and ultimately, when the Emperor Bharat took the help of the mirrors in his palace, that is when the Gnan expressed precisely. When he looked in the mirror, he noticed that one of his fingers looked different from his other fingers. Then he realized that the ring on that finger had fallen off. That is when he started thinking, 'The finger looks different. Was it the ring that made the finger look beautiful? It looked beautiful because of the ring and not me?' In this way, he went on thinking and questioning deeply within. Then by process of elimination, 'This is not mine, this is not mine…' he attained *Keval Gnan* – absolute enlightenment. So you should take advantage of the mirrors in the home. Ours is the science of *Akram*. Whoever takes advantage of this will get his work done. But no one can know about this, can he? It does not matter if he is not Self-realized; even then, the mirror *samayik* can give great benefits.

## Samayik of Scolding

You should go to your room and say to 'Chandubhai', 'Chandubhai, who do you think you are? Take your left hand and slap your right cheek!' A young man could not get rid of his anger, so I told him, 'Scold him!' The poor man would do *pratikraman* all day, but still he would not listen to the *pratikraman*. He would go back to the way he was. So I told him to go up to the terrace and scold him. So He scolded his file number one, 'Who do you think you are?' He scolded him so hard that he burst out crying. 'He' did the scolding and he began to cry and the Self became separate. The Self separates when You do such scolding.                                    (550)

So you should go into your room and scold 'Chandubhai.' You are to do this scolding *samayik* only after taking 'our' Agna (after taking Dada's permission). Only then will *pragnya* (energy of the Self that arises in Gnan Vidhi) remain, otherwise something else will latch on and cause problems.

**Questioner:** The process of doing *samayik* in the mirror and talking to the *prakruti* seems good when You show us; and it lasts for two to three days but then it becomes weak.

**Dadashri:** When weakness arises, then you should start that process all over again. Once it becomes old, all kinds of weakness will come. The nature of the *pudgal* is that once it gets old, it loses interest and energy. You have to start by making it new.

**Questioner:** So I am not able to accomplish the work through this process as I ought to, and the process ends midway.

**Dadashri:** That is how it will be accomplished gradually; it cannot occur all of a sudden.

**Questioner:** One process remains unfinished and I start a new one. I leave that unfinished and start a third one, so they all remain unfinished.

**Dadashri:** You should take them up again, and complete those processes gradually. It is not yet over, is it?

## Samayik is Occurring

**Questioner:** I can never do the *samayik*.

**Dadashri:** Then You should do a *samayik* for, 'Can't do it, can't do it.'

The only thing the Lord asks is whether You were attentive (in *dhyan*) or inattentive (*bedhyan*). Yes, there was no inattentiveness (*bedhyan*). One was aware of 'I can't do it,' and the other person had the awareness (*dhyan*) of 'I can do it.' There are no other issues. It is one and the same thing, whether You look at it this way or that way. If you were to turn and face this way, this would be your back; and if you were to turn around and face the other way, this would be your back.

So 'we' acknowledge this negative—wrong of 'I cannot do it.' But 'I, as the Seer' do not have to give in to it, be moved by it. So all the obstacles or anything else would all go away. The obstacles will say, 'We cannot conquer him. He is doing the contrary.' If one direction or way is not working out for 'us,' 'we' simply turn the other way. Then if 'we' go forward in that direction, it will be contrary to this side, so then 'we' turn the other way. Direction will keep on changing, but it is all the same. But there, one should not become unaware (*bedhyan*). If the *dhyan* is on 'I can't do it...I can't do it...' that should be the only thing that prevails, then you should not be thinking of your home or anything else. Here Dadashri's hair looks all grey. For some people in their *dhyan* they look all black. There is no problem with that.

What is of significance to us all? It is whether there was

unchanging meditation (*ekagra dhyan*) or not? When can it be said that *dhyan* has occurred? It is when there is only one thing in the *dhyan* (*ekagra*). Elsewhere, when people recite the Lord's name 'Ram... Ram,' that is not *dhyan*.

And this *dhyan* is called '*Dadayi*' *dhyan* (meditation as awakened by Dadashri, the Gnani Purush, meditation as the Self). That is considered a wonder!

The one doing the meditating (*dhyan*) is 'Chandubhai,' the one experiencing the *dhyan* is 'Chandubhai,' and the Knower (*jaannaar*) is the Self. So You know that the meditation is not occurring properly when you say 'I can't do it, I can't do it.' The Self of the other person knows that, 'it is occurring, it is occurring.'

So all the paths are open. When Gnan is there, then all the paths are open; and when Gnan is not there, then only one path is open. Any other path will lead to confusion.

## You 'Saw' the Seer in Samayik

You saw the Seer in the *samayik*. All the mistakes are washed off in the *samayik*! At the time of *samayik*, You are the absolute Self, and You are also seeing the Seer (*jonaaro; awakened one, gnani bavo*) within. Otherwise, a human being does not have the capacity to remember so much, does he? Here the Seer 'sees' every layer.

Did You 'see' some of it within? Is that so? What are you saying! And what about you, what is it like for You within? Did you find some solution? You got the benefit of this *samayik* because this is the *samayik* of the Self. And what is *vyavahar samayik*? It is the *samayik* they do out there (in the *Kramic* path); it is a *samayik* to still the mind. Even that is very good... if the mind does become still. And here, in *Akram Vignan*, there is no mention of the mind, is there? These are all *samayiks* of Puniyaa Shravak!

**Questioner:** I did not quite understand what You just said about, 'seeing' the Seer in the *samayik*?

**Dadashri:** Besides the Self, even the intellect (*buddhi*) has its own energy (*shakti*) and that is why it is able to see everything on the outside; it can see all worldly things. And 'it' (*pragnya*) 'sees' all these mistakes. And so this 'knowing' (*janavani*) energy is of the Self.

The Self is *swa-par prakashak* (that which illuminates the Self and the ñon-Self). So it can 'see' both.

**Questioner:** But you said that 'it' 'sees' the Seer.

**Dadashri:** Yes, there, it is actually the absolute Self that is 'involved.' That is why 'we' made the distinction. It is verily the *swa-par prakashak* (the awakened Self, the *gnani bavo*, the one who attained the Gnan) who is working there. And that is why You have the assurance that there is the *swa-par prakashak* (awakened one within), and that is the entity doing the work; this You have 'seen.' Hence You have 'seen' the Seer (*the swa-par prakashak*). There is no other study for the Seer other than to 'see.' Now here 'we' are convinced about who did the 'seeing.' The answer is the Seer. That is why 'we' say, 'I' 'saw' the Seer.

**Questioner:** You are in *samayik* twenty-four hours, are You not?

**Dadashri:** Yes, the *samayik* is always there. *Samayik* is a natural attribute, is it not? That is because the Self is *sam*, and it verily is *samayik*. When the self comes into the Self (*swabhav*), it is a state of *samayik*. But the Gnani Purush is beyond *samayik*. He has many other attributes that are manifest. He has many natural attributes.

## The Self is Samayik

You are not the doer of the *samayik*; You are not the

doer of *pratikraman*. It is the unfolding karma effect (*udayakarma*) that makes you do them, and yet these *sadhus* claim out of ignorance, 'I did *samayik*. I am doing it.' It is all ignorance (*agnan*) that has taken hold.

**Questioner:** Equanimity (*sambhav*) means *samayik*, so does one have to do *samayik* if he can maintain equanimity?

**Dadashri:** The Self verily is *samayik*. You have attained this Gnan and if You remain in my Agnas, that is considered *samayik* all day long.

And you do not have to do that other *samayik*. This is just to wash off past mistakes. This is a kind of very elevated *pratikraman*. It washes off past mistakes. People call it a *samayik*. However, the Self is itself *samayik* and having attained the Self, one can remain in *samayik* the whole day.

## Jai Sat Chit Anand

# Glossary

| | |
|---|---|
| Aadayee | Obstinacy |
| Aagraha | Insistence |
| Aakraman | Attacking nature |
| Aantarik tapa | Inner penance |
| Abhaav | Dislike; aversion |
| Abheda-dharma | Path one of oneness |
| Abhedta | Oneness |
| Abhimaan | Pride or arrogance |
| Abhipraay | Opinion |
| Abhyudaya | Prosperity or uplifting in the worldly life |
| Abrahmacharya | Non-celibacy |
| Acharyas | Self-realized masters |
| Achaurya | Non-stealing |
| Adeetha tapa | Internal penance; invisible penance |
| Adharma | Wrong karma through thought, speech and actions |
| Adhyatma vani | Spiritual language |
| Agna | Special directive |
| Agnya shakti | Energy of ignorance mediated through ego-intellect complex |
| Agnan | Ignorance of the Self |
| Agnani | One who is not Self-realized |
| Agrasocha | Worries about the future |
| Ahamkar | Ego |
| Aishwarya | Godly qualities |
| Ajaanta | Unknowingly |
| Ajagrut | Unaware |
| Akram | Step-less |
| Alaukik | Beyond worldly; of the Self |
| Alochana | Recall and confession of mistakes |
| Amrut | Nectar |
| Anand | Bliss |
| Anant darshan | Infinite vision |
| Anant gnan | Infinite knowledge |
| Anant shakti | Infinite energy and power |
| Anantanubandhi krodh | Anger that will make one bind karma for infinite lives |

| | |
|---|---|
| Anekant | All-inclusive, impartial and acceptance of all viewpoints |
| Antahkaran | Inner working components of the mind, intellect, chit and the ego |
| Antaray | Obstruction |
| Antaray karma | Obstacle causing karma |
| Antaratma | Awakened pure Self; Shuddhatma |
| Anubhav | Experiential |
| Aparigraha | Non-acquisitiveness |
| Apratikraman dosh | Mistake for which pratikraman was never done in the past life |
| Apratyakhyani krodh | Anger for which one did not do pratikraman |
| Aropit bhaav | False assertion |
| Arati | Devotional singing accompanied with burning oil wicks |
| Aropit | False assertion |
| Artadhyan | Adverse internal meditation that hurts the self |
| Asahaj | Unnatural state |
| Asaiyam parinam | Presence of kashay reaction |
| Ashata-vedaniya karma | Karma which brings pain |
| Ashatna | Irreverence |
| Ashrit | Dependant |
| Ashubha | Bad |
| Ashuddha | Impure |
| Atichar | Transgression of code of conduct; doing something in excess |
| Atikraman | Aggression towards other living beings through thoughts, speech and action |
| Atikraman | Hurtful karma |
| Atkan | Major blockade or impediment in the path of liberation |
| Atma-dharma | Religion of the Self |
| Atmadrashti | Vision as the Self |
| Atmaghat | Violence against the self; killing of the self |
| Atmagnan | Knowledge of the Self |
| Avarnavaad | To not say as it is |

| | |
|---|---|
| Avirat kashays | Never-ending kashays |
| Bandha | Bondage |
| Bavas | Those who renounce their worldly life and live through begging; the ascetics |
| Bedhyan | Unaware |
| Beyavtari | Two lives before attaining moksha |
| Bhaav | Intent |
| Bhaavna | Inner intent |
| Bhaav shuddhi | Purity of intent |
| Bhaav-abhaav | Good-bad inner intents |
| Bhaavkarma | Charging karma |
| Bhaav-parinam | The cause |
| Bhaav-pratikraman | Pratikraman of inner intent, at the causal level |
| Bhakti | Worshipping |
| Bhanjghad | Problem |
| Bhaavna | Desire |
| Bhaya | Fear |
| Bhaya sangnya | Self preservation instinct |
| Bheda | Separation |
| Bheda-vignani | Scientist who separates the Self and the non-Self |
| Bhoda and jada | Naïve and unaware |
| Bhranti | Wrong belief; illusion |
| Bhrant-purusharth | Relative spiritual effort; illusory spiritual effort |
| Brahmachari | Celibate |
| Brahmacharya | Celibacy |
| Buddhi | Intellect; knowledge through the medium of the ego |
| Buddhi-dharma | Functioning of the intellect |
| Charitra mohaniya | Conduct deluding karma; Discharging illusory conduct |
| Chaturgati | Four worlds of existence within which the Soul migrates |
| Chetana | Energy of the Self |
| Chintavan | Envisioned |
| Chovihar | Practice of no food intake after sunset |

| | |
|---|---|
| Chovisi | Succession of twenty-four Tirthankars in the third and fourth era of each of the Time-cycles |
| Dada Bhagwan | Fully enlightened Lord within the Gnani Purush |
| Dakho | Interference |
| Darshan | Enlightened vision |
| Darshan mohaniya | Right belief deluding karma or ignorance of the Self; Karma of illusory attachment which is there due to 'I am Chandulal' |
| Darshan-avaran | Vision-covering karma |
| Deha-dharma | Functions of the body |
| Dehadhyas | Belief that, 'I am this body' |
| Dehadhari | Embodied |
| Deshna | Speech of the Omniscient One |
| Devlokas | Celestial beings |
| Devshi | Late evening pratikraman |
| Dharma | Religion; rightful action; duty |
| Dharmadhyan | Absence of artadhyan-raudradhyan; absence of adverse internal meditation |
| Dhyan | Meditation |
| Dosh | Mistake |
| Doshit | One who has faults |
| Dosho | Wrongdoing; mistakes |
| Drashta | Seer |
| Drashya | That which is to be seen |
| Dravya | Effect of past life karma |
| Dravyakarma | Discharging karma |
| Dravya-pratikraman | Pratikraman done in discharging effect |
| Dravya-parinam | The effect; result |
| Dukh | Suffering; pain |
| Dushamkaal | Current era where there is lack of unity of mind-body-speech |
| Dushkrut | Wrong actions; bad deeds |
| Dwesh | Abhorrence |
| Ekagra dhyan | Unchanging meditation |

| | |
|---|---|
| Ekavtari Gnan | One more life remains before attaining moksha |
| Farajiyat | Mandatory |
| Five Agnas | Special directives given by Dadashri after Self-realization in Gnan Vidhi |
| Gaanth | Tuber |
| Ghadi | One ghadi is twenty-four minutes |
| Galan | Discharge |
| Ganadhars | Enlightened masters who managed the masses who came to the Lord |
| Garbhit | Internally |
| Garvaras | To taste the sweet juice of doership |
| Gnan | Knowledge |
| Gnan-avaran karma | Knowledge-covering karma |
| Gnanis | Self-realized |
| Gnan prakash | Light of awakened awareness |
| Gnata | Knower |
| Gnayak | Knower |
| Gneya | That which is to be 'known' |
| Gooncha | Inner conflict |
| Gunthanu | Spiritual stage; period of 48 minutes |
| Grahan | Acquisitiveness |
| Grahasthi | Householder |
| Guna | Qualities |
| Gunasthanaks | Spiritual stages |
| Gusso | Anger without violent intent |
| Hisaab | Karmic account |
| Himsa | Violence |
| Himsak bhaav | Violent intent |
| Ichchha | Desires |
| Indriya gnan | Relative and sense oriented knowledge |
| Indriyas | Senses |
| Iriyapathiki kriya | Walking with extreme caution so as not to hurt any living being |
| Jad | Water |
| Jada | Inanimate |
| Jagruti | Awareness |

| | |
|---|---|
| Jalkaya | Living beings present in water |
| Janavoo | Know |
| Japas | Chanting |
| Jathu | Collective |
| Jathu pratikraman | Pratikraman of everything together |
| Jatra | Pilgrimage |
| Jiva | Living being |
| Jivatma | Embodied self |
| Kaliyug | Period of difficulties due to lack of unity in thoughts, speech and acts |
| Kalpana | Imagination |
| Kapat | Deceit |
| Karela | Bitter gourds |
| Kashays | Internal anger, pride, deceit, greed, attachment and abhorrence |
| Kayotsarg | Renunciation of the body complex |
| Keval Gnan | Absolute Knowledge; absolute Enlightenment |
| Keval Darshan | Absolute vision |
| Keivalya | Absoluteness |
| Keyf | Intoxication |
| Khed | 'Burning' from within |
| Khed | Remorse |
| Khuda | Muslim word for God; divine |
| Kirtan-bhakti | Chanting worship |
| Kram | Step by step |
| Kraman | Neutral actions; actions that do not have any good or bad implications; Worldly interactions one carries |
| Kramic path | Traditional path of penance and austerities |
| Kriya | Action |
| Kriyakand | Rituals |
| Krodh | Anger with violent intent |
| Kshama | Forgiveness |
| Kshayak-samkit | Permanent conviction of the right belief, 'I am pure Soul' |
| Kusang | Bad company |
| Kusangi | Tainted by bad habits of the company |

| | |
|---|---|
| Laksha | Awareness as the Self |
| Lalach | Covetousness and intense greed |
| Laukik | Worldly |
| Lobh | Greed |
| Loknindya | That which is worthy of worldly disapproval and criticism |
| Maafi | Forgiveness |
| Mada | Pride |
| Maagdhi language | Language spoken during the time of Lord Mahavir 2500 years ago |
| Mahasati | A nun in Jainism |
| Mahatmas | Self-realized ones in Akram Vignan |
| Mahavrats | Five supreme vows; . ahimsa–non-violence; satya–truth; achaurya–non-theft; aparigraha–non-acquisitiveness and brahmacharya–celibacy. |
| Maliki bhaav | Intent or desire of ownership |
| Mamata | My-ness |
| Manan | Contemplates |
| Manobud | Power of the mind |
| Mano-dharma | Functioning of the mind |
| Manohar | Win over people's minds |
| Marajiyat | Free will |
| Mashkari | Poking fun |
| Matagraha | Obstinacy of viewpoint |
| Matignan | Intellect-based knowledge |
| Maun | Silent |
| Mishrachetan | Mixture of the Self and the non-Self |
| Mithyatva | To believe the illusion as real, the belief, 'I am Chandulal' |
| Mithyatvi | One under illusion |
| Moha | Illusion or ignorance of the Self; Illusory attractions |
| Mohaniya karma | Karma of illusory attraction |
| Moksha | Liberation |
| Mokshamarg | Path of moksha |
| Moodhatma | Not awakened to the Self |
| Mood swaroop | Absolute Self form |
| Natakiya | Dramatic |

| | |
|---|---|
| Nigod | Lowest form of life |
| Nikachit karma | Heavy and 'sticky' karma that one has no choice but suffer its effect |
| Nikaali | Discharging |
| Nimit | Someone instrumental in the process |
| Ninda | Backbiting; criticize negatively |
| Niragrahi | Non-insisting |
| Niraparadhi | Without mistakes |
| Nirdosh | Without any fault |
| Nirgranth | Free from tubers of kashay and vishay |
| Nirjara | Discharge of karma |
| Nirjiv | Non-living |
| Nirmalya | Weak and ineffective |
| Nischay | Firm resolution |
| Nischay-gnan | Knowledge of the Self |
| Nischetan | Non-living |
| Nischetan kriya | Non-living actions |
| Nihshank | Suspicion-free |
| Nivedo | Settles the mistake for once and all |
| Niyam | Rules; discipline |
| Nokarma | Gross discharging karma |
| Ugrata | Residual fieriness |
| Paap | Demerit karma; sin; wrongdoing |
| Paashavata | Bestiality |
| Padakmanu | Jain ritual of doing pratikraman |
| Pakkad | Insistence |
| Pakshik pratikraman | Fortnightly pratikraman |
| Paradhin | Dependent on the non-Self interaction |
| Parakram | Extraordinary spiritual effort |
| Param vinayata | State of humility |
| Paramhansa | One who separates the Self from the non-Self |
| Par-bhaav | Being the non-Self |
| Par-dravya | In the state of the non-Self |
| Parigraha | Attachment to things and acquisitiveness |
| Parmanus | Subatomic particles |
| Parmartha | Higher good; Ultimate aim |

| | |
|---|---|
| Parmatma | Absolute Self |
| Paroksha bhakti | Indirect worship |
| Paryushan | Most important Jain religious observance of the year. This is a time of intensive study, reflection and purification |
| Pragnya shakti | Energy of the awakened Self after Self-realization |
| Prakruti | Mind-speech-body complex; the relative self, the non-Self |
| Pramaad | Sloth and dullness |
| Pramaad | Spiritual sloth or laziness |
| Prarabdha | Karma effect |
| Prashchyataap | Repentance |
| Pratikraman | Asking for forgiveness; three step process of reversal from aggression through thought, speech and action. |
| Pratipakshi-bhaav | A hostile inner intent |
| Pratishthit atma | Relative self; The self that has wrong beliefs, the person in ignorant state |
| Pratiti | Conviction |
| Pratyakhyan | Resolve never to repeat the mistake and asking for the energies for this |
| Pudgal | Non-Self complex |
| Pudgal parmanus | Smallest part of matter |
| Pudgal paryaya | Phases of the non-Self |
| Punya | Merit karma |
| Punyanubandhi punya | Merit karma which binds more merit karma |
| Punyashadi | One with merit karma; fortunate one |
| Puran | Charge |
| Purush | Those who are spiritually enlightened; Self |
| Purusharth dharma | Religion of the Self effort |
| Purusharth | Real spiritual effort |
| Raag | Attachment |
| Rayshi | Early morning pratikraman |
| Rakshan | Protection |

| | |
|---|---|
| Rasa | Interest and degree of intensity |
| Raudradhyan | Adverse internal meditation that hurts the self and others |
| Roonanubandha | Bondage created due to attachment-abhorrence in previous life |
| Rotli | Chapaati; flat bread |
| Sachetan | Animate |
| Sadhana | Efforts of activity necessary to achieve or accomplish a goal |
| Sadhus | Those who live and strive for only the state of the Self; Ascetics |
| Sadhvijis | Jain nuns |
| Sadvivek | Right discretion |
| Sahadhyayi | Fellow spiritual colleagues |
| Sahaj | Natural and spontaneous |
| Sahaj kshama | Natural and spontaneous forgiveness |
| Sahajikata | Naturalness |
| Saiyam | Kashay free |
| Saiyami | Person in control of his kashays |
| Sajiv | Live |
| Sakshi bhaav | Being a witness |
| Samadhan | Mutually satisfactory solution |
| Samadhi | State of the Self which is free from any effects of mental, physical or externally induced pain |
| Samata | Equanimity |
| Samaya | Smallest indivisible time unit |
| Samayik | To be the Self and to 'see' the self |
| Sambhave nikaal | Settle with equanimity |
| Samkit | Enlightened; right belief |
| Samkit bud | Energy of the Self-realized |
| Samkit jiva | An enlightened being |
| Samuhik pratikraman | Collective pratikraman |
| Samvar | Binding of karmic matter |
| Samvatsari | Annual holy day when Jains repent for all their wrongdoings through the year |
| Samvatsari pratikraman | Once a year pratikraman |
| Sanghapati | Head of the association |
| Sansar | Worldly life |

| | |
|---|---|
| Sansaris | Married people; people living worldly life |
| Sanskar | Effects of karma caused in past life; cultural values |
| Saiyam parinam | Absence of kashay reaction |
| Sanyasis | Monks |
| Sarad | Straightforward |
| Saraswati | Goddess of speech |
| Satsang | Company of those who promote the attainment of the Self |
| Satta | Power |
| Satya | Truth |
| Satyug | Time cycle of unity in mind, speech and body actions |
| Shakti | Energy and power |
| Shanka | Suspicion |
| Shrutgnan | Scriptural or literate knowledge received through hearing |
| Shubha | Good |
| Shubhashubh | Good and bad |
| Shuddha | Pure |
| Shuddha chetan | The Self |
| Shuddha upayog | Pure applied awareness of the Self |
| Shuddhata | Purity |
| Shuddhatma | Pure Soul |
| Shukladhyan | 'I am Shuddhatma-pure Soul'; the state of the Self |
| Siddhant | Principle |
| Smruti | Memory |
| Sukh | Pleasure |
| Sookshmatar | Subtler |
| Sookshma | Subtle |
| Sookshmatam | Subtlest |
| Spandan | Vibration |
| Sthool | Gross; tangible-gross |
| Sushamkaal | Past era of time cycle where there was unity in thoughts, speech and acts |

| Sutras | Concise statement that usually requires a commentary for understanding |
|---|---|
| Swabhav | Nature |
| Swachhand | Guided by one's own whim and intellect |
| Swamaan | Self-respect |
| Swa-par prakashak | Illuminates the Self as well as the non-Self |
| Swaroop gnan | Knowledge of the Self |
| Syadvaad | That which is accepting of, and acceptable to all |
| Taanto | Prolonged feeling of grudge that continues to be linked with that conflict |
| Takor | Cautionary comment |
| Tanmayakar | Become the body and the mind |
| Tapa | Penance |
| Tejokaya | Living beings present in fire |
| Tiraskar | Scorn |
| Tiryanch | Lower life forms |
| Tranavtari | Three lives before moksha |
| Tyaag | Renunciation |
| Udayakarma | Karma effect; unfolding of karma |
| Udayavash | Under the control of circumstances |
| Udvega | Intense emotional upheaval with overt clash |
| Upadhi | External problems |
| Upadhyayas | Those who have attained Self-realization and help others do the same |
| Upashraya | Jain monastery |
| Upaya | Solution |
| Updeshaks | Religious teachers |
| Urdhavikaran | To rise higher |
| Utsarg | Inner renunciation |
| Vaanka and jada | Obstinate and unaware |
| Vaav | Step-well |
| Vartan, charitra | Conduct |
| Vartman | Present |

| | |
|---|---|
| Vayukaya | Living beings present in air |
| Vedaniya | Suffering |
| Vedaniya karma | Karma that brings physical suffering |
| Veyr | Enmity |
| Vichakshan | Alert thinkers |
| Vignan | Science |
| Vikalp | Ego, 'I am Chandulal' |
| Vimukta | Absolutely free |
| Viparinam | Circumstances due to your interference related effects |
| Viradhak swabhav | Negative nature |
| Viradhana | Disrespect |
| Vishay | Sexuality |
| Visheshata | Superiority |
| Vishrasa | Pure subatomic particles in discharge process |
| Vitadwesh | Free from abhorrence |
| Vitarag dharma | Religion as prescribed by the Omniscients |
| Vitarag Lords | Supreme enlightened beings |
| Vitarag speech | Speech that will be accepted by the speaker and the listener |
| Vitaragata | Total absence of attachment and abhorrence |
| Vivek | Discretion |
| Vrat | Vow |
| Vyavahar | Worldly interactions |
| Vyavahar atma | The relative self; the non-Self complex |
| Yagna | Sacrificial fire |
| Yathartha | As it should be |
| Yoga | Union |

# Pratikraman Key Points

❀ What does the world exist on? It exists on the mistakes of *atikraman*. There is no problem with *kraman*, but *pratikraman* has to be done if *atikraman* occurs.

❀ Occurring of *atikraman* is natural; doing *pratikraman* needs your *purusharth* (spiritual effort).

❀ The one who repents after his action will one day attain *moksha*; that is certain.

❀ When *pratikraman* is done after a conflict, that conflict gets washed off. Newly attained energy goes away by entering into conflict again.

❀ It is natural for a human being to enter into a mistake. But what is the way to be free from the mistake? Only a Gnani Purush can show this, the *pratikraman* that liberates.

❀ Generally, when people ask for forgiveness, there is no *pratikraman* in it. It is comparable to the common practice of saying 'sorry' and 'thank you.' It has no significant value. The importance is in doing *alochana-pratikraman-pratyakhyan*.

❀ It is possible to attain the state of Godhood if one does instant *pratikraman*.

❀ That which you do not want to remember, but still comes into your memory, is a mistake that needs *pratikraman*.

❀ True *pratikraman* occurs when you see others in the family as faultless/flawless (*nirdosh*) and when you only can see your own mistakes.

❀ We end up saying things we do not want to. It is the *prakruti* that 'dances' (does everything) and creates problems. After many *pratikramans*, that *prakruti* will come to an end.

❀ What occurs when you do *pratikraman*? When the reactions of your past mistakes come into fruition, you will not feel like interfering in them again.

❀ The one whose *alochana-pratikraman-pratyakhyan* are real is sure to attain the Self.

# Books of Akram Vignan of Dada Bhagwan

1. Adjust Everywhere
2. Ahimsa : Non-Violence
3. Anger
4. Aptavani 1
5. Aptavani 2
6. Aptavani 6
7. Aptavani 9
8. Autobiography of Gnani Purush A.M.Patel
9. Avoid Clashes
10. Brahmacharya : Celibacy Attained With Understanding
11. Death : Before, During & After...
12. Flawless Vision
13. Generation Gap
14. Harmony In Marriage
15. Life Without Conflict
16. Money
17. Noble Use of Money
18. Pratikraman : The master key that resolves all conflicts
19. Pure Love
20. Right Understanding to Help Others
21. Science of Karma
22. Science of Speech
23. Shree Simandhar Swami : The Living God
24. The Essence Of All Religion
25. The Fault Is Of the Sufferer
26. The Guru and The Disciple
27. Tri Mantra : The mantra that removes all worldly obstacles
28. Whatever Happened is Justice
29. Who Am I ?
30. Worries
31. Pratikraman (Big Volume) - NEW

'Dadavani' Magazine is published Every month

## Persons to Contact

### Dada Bhagwan Parivar

Adalaj : **Trimandir**, Simandhar City,
Ahmedabad-Kalol Highway, Adalaj,
Dist.: Gandhinagar - 382421, Gujarat, India.
**Tel :** (079) 39830100, **Email :** info@dadabhagwan.org

Ahmedabad : **"Dada Darshan"**, 5, Mamtapark Society, B/h. Navgujarat
College, Usmanpura, Ahmedabad- 380 014.
Tel. : (079) 27540408, 27543979

Rajkot : **Trimandir**, Ahmedabad-Rajkot Highway, Nr. Targhadiya
Chokdi, Maliyasan Village, Rajkot. Tel.: 9274111393

Bhuj : **Trimandir,** Behind Hill Garden, Near Sahyognagar,
Airport Road, Bhuj (Kutchh), Gujarat. **Tel. :** 02832 236666

---

**Other than Gujarat :**

Chennai : Tel : (044) 52146652
Mumbai : Tel. : (022) 24137616
Pune : Mobile : 9822037740
Kolkata : Mobile : 9330133885
Bangalore : Mobile : 9341948509

---

U.S.A. : **Dada Bhagwan Vignan Institute** : Dr. Bachu Amin,
100, SW Redbud Lane, Topeka, Kansas 66606
**Tel :** +1 785 271 0869, **Email :** bamin@cox.net
Dr. Shirish Patel, 2659, Raven Circle, Corona, CA 92882
**Tel.:**+1 951 734 4715, **Email:**shirishpatel@sbcglobal.net

U.K. : **Dada Centre**, 236, Kingsbury Road, (Above Kingsbury
Printers), Kingsbury, London, NW9 0BH
Tel. : +44 07954 676 253
Email : dadabhagwan_uk@yahoo.com

Canada : **Dinesh Patel**, 4, Halesia Drive, Etobicock,
Toronto, M9W 6B7. Tel. : 416 675 3543
E-mail: ashadinsha@yahoo.ca

**Australia** : 0423211778; **Dubai** : 506754832; **Singapore** : 81129229

---

**Website : www.dadabhagwan.org & www.dadashri.org**

## What Is the Gnan Vidhi?

It is a scientific spiritual process of gracing people with the experience of Self-realization. It is the gracing of real Knowledge that separates the Self from the non-Self or the worldly self. This session is different from the regular *satsangs* in the form of questions-answers sessions.

The Knowledge that manifested within Pujya Dadashri, also known as Dada Bhagwan in 1958, is the very same Knowledge that is graced upon all seekers through the medium of *Atmagnani* Param Pujya Deepakbhai, with the grace of Dada Bhagwan and the blessings of Pujya Niruma.

### Why Should You Take Gnan – Knowledge of the Self?

1. To awaken and experience the Soul; your real Self.

2. Inner peace due to destruction of all wrong beliefs and the attainment of the right belief of 'I, the real Self am pure Soul'.

3. To attain liberation from the cycle of birth and death.

4. Demerit *karma* of infinite past lives are destroyed.

5. To experience eternal peace, happiness and harmony with all living beings.

6. To get solutions to carry out your worldly life through right understanding.

7. You finish paying off all past *karma* and you do not bind any new ones.

# Is It Necessary for One to be Physically Present for the Gnan Vidhi?

1. *Gnan Vidhi* is the result of the *Gnani's* grace and blessings. It is necessary to attend this *Gnan Vidhi* in the direct presence of an *Atmagnani*.

2. Spiritual information acquired through watching *satsang* programs of Pujya Niruma and Pujya Deepakbhai on TV or VCD, books etc. can help you to prepare the background for attaining *Gnan* but they cannot give you Self-realization.

3. Any instrument used for attaining *Gnan* can help you to attain peace but for awakening of the Soul, only the *Gnan* taken in the direct presence of an *Atmagnani* will give you the experience. For example if you want to light your candle, you need a real burning candle, a picture of a burning candle will not do.

- **You do not have to change your religion or your guru to attain this *Gnan*.**

- **You do not have to pay anything to attain this *Gnan*.**

**Jai Sat Chit Anand**